P9-DYY-791

INSTRUCTORS...

Would you like your **students** to show up for class **more prepared**?
(Let's face it, class is much more fun if everyone is engaged and prepared...)

Want an **easy way to assign** homework online and track student **progress**?
(Less time grading means more time teaching...)

Want an **instant view** of student or class performance? *(No more wondering if students understand...)*

Need to **collect data and generate reports** required for administration or accreditation? *(Say goodbye to manually tracking student learning outcomes...)*

Want to **record and post your lectures** for students to view online?

With **McGraw-Hill's** *Connect® Plus Economics,*

INSTRUCTORS GET:

- Simple **assignment management,** allowing you to spend more time teaching.
- **Auto-graded** assignments, quizzes, and tests.
- **Detailed Visual Reporting** where student and section results can be viewed and analyzed.
- Sophisticated **online testing** capability.
- A **filtering and reporting** function that allows you to easily assign and report on materials that are correlated to accreditation standards, learning outcomes, and Bloom's taxonomy.
- An easy-to-use **lecture capture** tool.
- The option to **upload course documents** for student access.

Want an online, **searchable version** of your textbook?

Wish your textbook could be **available online** while you're doing your assignments?

Connect® Plus Economics eBook

If you choose to use *Connect® Plus Economics*, you have an affordable and searchable online version of your book integrated with your other online tools.

Connect® Plus Economics eBook offers features like:

- Topic search
- Direct links from assignments
- Adjustable text size
- Jump to page number
- Print by section

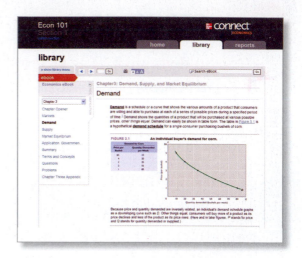

Want to get more **value** from your textbook purchase?

Think learning economics should be a bit more **interesting**?

Check out the STUDENT RESOURCES section under the *Connect®* Library tab.

Here you'll find a wealth of resources designed to help you achieve your goals in the course. Every student has different needs, so explore the STUDENT RESOURCES to find the materials best suited to you.

Microeconomics
BRIEF EDITION

Second Edition

Microeconomics
BRIEF EDITION

Campbell R. McConnell
University of Nebraska

Sean M. Flynn
Scripps College

Stanley L. Brue
Pacific Lutheran University

With the special assistance of
Randy R. Grant
Linfield College

The McGraw-Hill Economics Series

The Six Versions of McConnell, Brue, Flynn

Chapter	Economics	Economics: Brief Edition	Microeconomics	Microeconomics: Brief Edition	Macroeconomics	Macroeconomics: Brief Edition	Essentials of Economics
1. Limits, Alternatives, and Choices	X	X	X	X	X	X	X
2. The Market System and the Circular Flow	X	X	X	X	X	X	X
3. Demand, Supply, and Market Equilibrium	X	X	X	X	X	X	X
4. Elasticity	X	X	X	X	X		X
5. Market Failures: Public Goods and Externalities	X	X	X	X	X	X	X
6. Consumer Behavior	X		X				
7. Businesses and the Costs of Production	X	X	X	X			X
8. Pure Competition in the Short Run	X	X	X	X			X
9. Pure Competition in the Long Run	X	X	X	X			X
10. Pure Monopoly	X	X	X	X			X
11. Monopolistic Competition and Oligopoly	X	X	X	X			X
11W. Technology, R&D, and Efficiency (Web Chapter)	X		X				
12. The Demand for Resources	X		X				
13. Wage Determination	X	X	X	X			X
14. Rent, Interest, and Profit	X		X				
15. Natural Resource and Energy Economics	X		X				
16. Public Finance: Expenditures and Taxes	X	X	X	X			
17. Asymmetric Information, Voting, and Public Choice	X		X				
18. Antitrust Policy and Regulation	X		X				
19. Agriculture: Economics and Policy	X		X				
20. Income Inequality, Poverty, and Discrimination	X	X	X	X			X
21. Health Care	X		X				
22. Immigration	X		X				
23. An Introduction to Macroeconomics	X				X		
24. Measuring Domestic Output and National Income	X	X			X	X	X
25. Economic Growth	X	X			X	X	X
26. Business Cycles, Unemployment, and Inflation	X	X			X	X	X
27. Basic Macroeconomic Relationships	X				X		
28. The Aggregate Expenditures Model	X				X		
29. Aggregate Demand and Aggregate Supply	X	X			X	X	X
30. Fiscal Policy, Deficits, and Debt	X	X			X	X	X
31. Money, Banking, and Financial Institutions	X	X			X	X	X
32. Money Creation	X				X		
33. Interest Rates and Monetary Policy	X	X			X	X	X
34. Financial Economics	X				X		
35. Extending the Analysis of Aggregate Supply	X	X			X	X	
36. Current Issues in Macro Theory and Policy	X				X		
37. International Trade	X	X	X	X	X	X	X
38. The Balance of Payments, Exchange Rates, and Trade Deficits	X	X	X	X	X	X	X
39W. The Economics of Developing Countries (Web Chapter)	X				X		

*Chapter numbers refer to *Economics: Principles, Problems, and Policies*.

*A Red "X" indicates chapters that combine or consolidate content from two or more *Economics* chapters.

McGraw-Hill
Irwin

MICROECONOMICS: BRIEF EDITION

Published by McGraw-Hill/Irwin, a business unit of The McGraw-Hill Companies, Inc., 1221 Avenue of the Americas, New York, NY, 10020. Copyright © 2013, 2010 by The McGraw-Hill Companies, Inc. All rights reserved. No part of this publication may be reproduced or distributed in any form or by any means, or stored in a database or retrieval system, without the prior written consent of The McGraw-Hill Companies, Inc., including, but not limited to, in any network or other electronic storage or transmission, or broadcast for distance learning.

Some ancillaries, including electronic and print components, may not be available to customers outside the United States.

This book is printed on acid-free paper.

1 2 3 4 5 6 7 8 9 0 RJE/RJE 1 0 9 8 7 6 5 4 3 2

ISBN   978-0-07-741620-1
MHID   0-07-741620-1

Vice president and editor-in-chief: *Brent Gordon*
Publisher: *Douglas Reiner*
Executive director of development: *Ann Torbert*
Director of digital content: *Douglas Ruby*
Sponsoring Editor: *Scott Smith*
Development editor: *Noelle Bathurst*
Senior marketing manager: *Melissa Larmon*
Senior marketing manager: *Katie White*
Senior project manager: *Harvey Yep*
Lead production supervisor: *Michael R. McCormick*
Interior designer: *Mary Kazak Sander*
Photo researcher: *Keri Johnson*
Senior media project manager: *Kerry Bowler*
Cover design: *Mary Kazak Sander*
Cover image: *Peter Gridley*
Typeface: *10/12 Janson Text 55 Roman*
Compositor: *Aptara®, Inc.*
Printer: *R. R. Donnelley*

Library of Congress Control Number: 2012930343

www.mhhe.com

To **Mem**, to **Terri** and **Craig**, and to **past instructors**

About the Authors

CAMPBELL R. MCCONNELL earned his Ph.D. from the University of Iowa after receiving degrees from Cornell College and the University of Illinois. He taught at the University of Nebraska–Lincoln from 1953 until his retirement in 1990. He is coauthor of *Economics*, nineteenth edition (McGraw-Hill/Irwin); *Contemporary Labor Economics*, ninth edition (McGraw-Hill/Irwin); and *Essentials of Economics*, second edition (McGraw-Hill/Irwin) and has edited readers for the principles and labor economics courses. He is a recipient of both the University of Nebraska Distinguished Teaching Award and the James A. Lake Academic Freedom Award and is past president of the Midwest Economics Association. Professor McConnell was awarded an honorary Doctor of Laws degree from Cornell College in 1973 and received its Distinguished Achievement Award in 1994. His primary areas of interest are labor economics and economic education. He has an extensive collection of jazz recordings and enjoys reading jazz history.

STANLEY L. BRUE did his undergraduate work at Augustana College (SD) and received its Distinguished Achievement Award in 1991. He received his Ph.D. from the University of Nebraska–Lincoln. He is a professor at Pacific Lutheran University, where he has been honored as a recipient of the Burlington Northern Faculty Achievement Award. Professor Brue has also received the national Leavey Award for excellence in economic education. He has served as national president and chair of the Board of Trustees of Omicron Delta Epsilon International Economics Honorary. He is coauthor of *Economics*, nineteenth edition (McGraw-Hill/Irwin); *Economic Scenes*, fifth edition (Prentice-Hall); *Contemporary Labor Economics*, ninth edition (McGraw-Hill/Irwin); *Essentials of Economics*, second edition (McGraw-Hill/Irwin); and *The Evolution of Economic Thought*, seventh edition (South-Western). For relaxation, he enjoys international travel, attending sporting events, and skiing with family and friends.

SEAN M. FLYNN did his undergraduate work at the University of Southern California before completing his Ph.D. at U.C. Berkeley, where he served as the Head Graduate Student Instructor for the Department of Economics after receiving the Outstanding Graduate Student Instructor Award. He teaches at Scripps College in Claremont, California and is the author of *Economics for Dummies*, second edition (Wiley) and coauthor of *Economics*, nineteenth edition (McGraw-Hill/Irwin) and *Essentials of Economics*, second edition (McGraw-Hill/Irwin). His research interests include finance and behavioral economics. An accomplished martial artist, he has represented the United States in international aikido tournaments and is the author of *Understanding Shodokan Aikido* (Shodokan Press). Other hobbies include running, traveling, and enjoying ethnic food

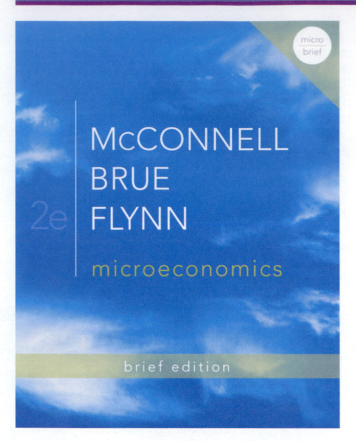

Welcome to *Microeconomics: Brief Edition*, second edition, the trimmed and edited version of *Economics*, nineteenth edition, the nation's best-selling economics textbook.

Fundamental Objectives

We have three main goals for *Microeconomics: Brief Edition*:

- Help the beginning student master the principles essential for understanding the economizing problem, specific economic issues, and the policy alternatives.
- Help the student understand and apply the economic perspective and reason accurately and objectively about economic matters.
- Promote a lasting student interest in economics and the economy.

Integrated, Distinct Book

Although *Microeconomics: Brief Edition* is a spin-off of *Economics*, nineteenth edition, it is not a cut-and-paste book that simply eliminates several chapters of *Economics* and reorders and renumbers the retained content. We can pre-

pare such books via custom publication. Instead, the *Brief Edition* is a very concise, highly integrated economics textbook that is distinct in purpose, style, and coverage from *Economics* and its Micro and Macro splits.

What's New and Improved?

One of the benefits of writing a successful text is the opportunity to revise—to delete the outdated and install the new, to rewrite misleading or ambiguous statements, to introduce more relevant illustrations, to improve the organizational structure, and to enhance the learning aids.

We trust that you will agree that we have used this opportunity wisely and fully. Some of the more significant changes include the following:

New Public Finance Chapter

This traditional public finance chapter adds considerable new content to existing material that previously appeared in Chapter 5: Market Failures: Public Goods and Externalities. The chapter includes a circular flow diagram with government; an overview of federal, state, and local tax revenues and expenditures; explanations of marginal and average tax rates; discussions of the benefits-received and ability-to-pay principles of taxation; an explanation of progressive, regressive, and proportional taxes; tax incidence and efficiency losses due to taxation; and the redistributive incidence of the overall tax-spending system in the United States.

New and Updated "Illustrating the Idea," "Applying the Analysis," and "Photo Op" Pieces

These examples, applications, and illustrations help drive home central economic ideas in a student-oriented, real-world manner. New content includes a discussion of beekeepers to explain the Coase Theorem, analysis of the effects of rising gas prices on companies like FedEx and Symantec, and an illustration of federal versus state and local spending.

Reworked End-of-Chapter Questions and Problems

We have extensively reworked the end-of-chapter questions, and we have added new problems to each chapter. The questions are analytic and often ask for free responses, whereas the problems are mainly quantitative. We have aligned the questions and problems with the learning objectives presented at the beginning of the chapters. All of the questions and problems are assignable through McGraw Hill's *Connect Economics*, and many contain additional algorithmic variations and can be automatically graded within the system.

Chapter-by-Chapter Changes

In addition to the changes and new features listed above, chapter-specific revisions include:

Chapter 1: Limits, Alternatives, and Choices features updated discussion of the 2007–2009 recession and streamlined coverage of the main concepts.

Chapter 2: The Market System and the Circular Flow includes an improved discussion of the circular flow model, additional coverage of property rights, and updated global data.

Chapter 3: Demand, Supply, and Market Equilibrium begins with a revised introduction to supply and demand and contains additional clarifications of key concepts.

Chapter 4: Elasticity of Demand and Supply provides an updated discussion of elasticity.

Chapter 5: Market Failures: Public Goods and Externalities features improved coverage of market failures and the distinction between demand-side and supply-side market failures, new topics including consumer and producer surplus and efficiency (deadweight) loss, enhanced discussion of public versus private goods, a new "Illustrating the Idea" piece on the Coase Theorem, and a more complete discussion of correcting for externalities. The coverage of financing public goods and taxation has been moved to Chapter 12 on public finance.

Chapter 6: Businesses and Their Costs includes an improved discussion of costs and a new "Applying the Analysis" piece that discusses rising gas prices.

Chapter 7: Pure Competition features revised discussions of pure competition in the long run and efficiency in pure competition, plus an expanded figure illustrating a competitive firm and market in long-run equilibrium.

Chapter 8: Pure Monopoly contains an updated figure showing the inefficiency of pure monopoly relative to a purely competitive industry and a revised discussion of efficiency.

Chapter 9: Monopolistic Competition and Oligopoly includes a revised introduction, an updated figure illustrating the inefficiency of monopolistic competition, and an improved discussion of cartels and collusion.

Chapter 10: Wage Determination features improved discussions to clarify the main concepts.

Chapter 11: Income Inequality and Poverty contains extensive updates to the data on the distribution of income, poverty, and family wealth, plus revised coverage of income-maintenance programs.

Chapter 12: Public Finance: Expenditures and Taxes is a new chapter that incorporates the taxation content from the first-edition chapter "Public Goods and Externalities," plus an expanded circular flow model; content on government purchases and transfer payments; material on federal, state, and local tax sources; efficiency losses from taxes; and additional discussion of tax incidence.

Chapter 13: International Trade and Exchange Rates includes updated material on recent U.S. trade deficits and a revised discussion related to changes in the relative value of the U.S. dollar.

Distinguishing Features

Microeconomics: Brief Edition includes several features that encourage students to read and retain the content.

Design and Pedagogy

The *Brief Edition* incorporates a single-column design with a host of pedagogical aids, including a strategically placed "To the Student" statement, chapter opening objectives, definitions in the margins, combined tables and graphs, complete chapter summaries, lists of key terms, carefully constructed questions and problems, connections to our website, an appendix on graphs and a web appendix on additional examples of demand and supply, and an extensive glossary.

Focus on Core Models

Microeconomics: Brief Edition shortens and simplifies explanations where appropriate but stresses the importance of the economic perspective, including explaining and applying core economic models. Our strategy is to develop a limited set of essential models, illustrate them with analogies or anecdotes, explain them thoroughly, and apply them to real-world situations. Eliminating unnecessary graphs and elaborations makes perfect sense in a brief edition, but cutting explanations of the truly fundamental graphs does not. In dealing with the basics, brevity at the expense of clarity is false economy.

We created a student-oriented textbook that draws on the methodological strengths of the discipline and helps students improve their analytical reasoning skills. Regardless of students' eventual occupations, they will discover that such skills are highly valuable in their workplaces.

Illustrating the Idea

Numerous analogies, examples, and anecdotes are included throughout the book to help drive home central economic ideas in a lively, colorful, and easy-to-remember way. For instance, elastic versus inelastic demand is illustrated by comparing the stretch of an Ace bandage and that of a tight rubber tie-down. A piece on Bill Gates, Oprah Winfrey, and Alex Rodriguez illustrates the importance of opportunity costs in decision making. Art in the public square brings clarity to public goods and the free-rider problem. These brief vignettes flow directly from the preceding content and segue to the content that follows, rather than being "boxed off" away from the flow and therefore easily overlooked.

Applying the Analysis

A glance though this book's pages will demonstrate that this is an application-oriented textbook. *Applying the Analysis* pieces immediately follow the development of economic analysis and are part of the flow of the chapters, rather than segregated from the main body discussion in a traditional boxed format. For example, the basics of the economic perspective are applied to why customers choose the shortest checkout lines. Differences in elasticity of supply are contrasted by the changing prices of antiques versus reproductions. The book describes the principal–agent problem via the problems of corporate accounting and financial fraud. The concept of price discrimination is illustrated by the difference in adult and child pricing for ballgame tickets compared to the pricing at the concession stands. These and many other applications clearly demonstrate the relevance and usefulness of mastering the basic economic principles and models to beginning students.

Photo Ops

Photo sets under the title *Photo Op* are included throughout the book to add visual interest, break up the density, and highlight important distinctions. Just a couple of the many examples are sets of photos on traffic congestion and holiday lighting to contrast negative and positive externalities, and Social Security checks and food stamps to highlight the differences between social insurance and public assistance. Other photo sets illustrate normal versus inferior goods, complements versus substitutes in consumption, homogeneous versus differentiated prod-

ucts, substitute resources versus complementary resources, and more.

Web Buttons

The in-text web buttons (or indicators) merit special mention. Three differing colors of rectangular indicators appear throughout the book, informing readers that complementary content on a subject can be found at our website, **www.mcconnellbrief2e.com.** Scattered throughout the text you'll see:

Worked Problems   Written by Norris Peterson of Pacific Lutheran University, these pieces consist of side-by-side computational questions and procedures used to derive the answers. From a student perspective, they provide "cookbook" help for problem solving.

> **WORKED PROBLEMS**
> **W 1.1**
> Budget Lines

Interactive Graphs   These pieces (developed under the supervision of Norris Peterson) depict major graphs and instruct students to shift the curves, observe the outcomes, and derive relevant generalizations. This hands-on graph work will greatly reinforce the main graphs and their meaning.

> **INTERACTIVE GRAPHS**
> **G 3.1**
> Supply and Demand

Origin of the Ideas   These brief histories, written by Randy Grant of Linfield College (OR), examine the origins of major ideas identified in the book. Students will find it interesting to learn about the economists who first developed such ideas as opportunity costs, equilibrium price, elasticity, creative destruction, and comparative advantage.

> **ORIGIN OF THE IDEA**
> **O 2.2**
> Specialization/division of labor

Global Snapshots

Global Snapshot pieces include bar charts and line graphs that compare data for a particular year or other time period among selected nations. Examples of these lists and comparisons include income per capita, the world's 10 largest corporations, the world's top brand names, the index of economic freedom, the differing economic status of North Korea and South Korea, and so forth. These *Global Snapshots* join other significant international content to help convey that the United States operates in a global economy.

Digital Solutions

McGraw-Hill's *Connect™ Economics*

Less Managing. More Teaching. Greater Learning.
McGraw-Hill's *Connect™ Economics* is a

web-based assignment and assessment platform that connects students with the tools and resources they'll need to achieve success. *Connect™ Economics* helps prepare students for their future by enabling faster learning, more efficient studying, and higher retention of knowledge. *Connect™ Economics* offers a number of powerful tools and features to make managing assignments easier, so faculty can spend more time teaching. With *Connect™ Economics*, students can engage with their coursework anytime and anywhere, making the learning process more accessible and efficient. *Connect™ Economics* offers the features as described here.

Simple Assignment Management
With *Connect™ Economics*, creating assignments is easier than ever, so you can spend more time teaching and less time managing. The assignment management function enables you to

- Create and deliver assignments easily with selectable end-of-chapter questions and test bank items.
- Streamline lesson planning, student progress reporting, and assignment grading to make classroom management more efficient than ever.
- Go paperless with the e-book and online submission and grading of student assignments.

Smart Grading
When it comes to studying, time is precious. *Connect™ Economics* helps students learn more efficiently by providing feedback and practice material when they need it, where they need it. When it comes to teaching, your time also is precious. The grading function enables you to

- Score assignments automatically, giving students immediate feedback on their work and side-by-side comparisons with correct answers.
- Access and review each response; manually change grades or leave comments for students to review.
- Reinforce classroom concepts with practice tests and instant quizzes.

Instructor Library
The *Connect™ Economics* Instructor Library is your repository for additional resources to improve student engagement in and out of class. You can select and use any asset that enhances your lecture.

Student Study Center
The *Connect™ Economics* Student Study Center is the place for students to access additional resources. The Student Study Center

- Offers students quick access to lectures, practice materials, e-book, and more.
- Provides instant practice material and study questions, easily accessible on the go.
- Gives students access to the Self-Quiz and Study described below.

LearnSmart: Diagnostic and Adaptive Learning of Concepts
Students want to make the best use of their study time. The LearnSmart adaptive self-study technology within *Connect™ Economics* provides students

with a seamless combination of practice, assessment, and remediation for every concept in the textbook. LearnSmart's intelligent software adapts to every student response and automatically delivers concepts that advance the student's understanding while reducing time devoted to the concepts already mastered. The result for every student is the fastest path to mastery of the chapter concepts. LearnSmart

- Applies an intelligent concept engine to identify the relationships between concepts and to serve new concepts to each student only when he or she is ready.
- Adapts automatically to each student, so students spend less time on the topics they understand and practice more those they have yet to master.
- Provides continual reinforcement and remediation, but gives only as much guidance as students need.
- Integrates diagnostics as part of the learning experience.
- Enables you to assess which concepts students have efficiently learned on their own, thus freeing class time for more applications and discussion.

Self-Quiz and Study
The Self-Quiz and Study (SQS) connects each student to the learning resources needed for success in the course. For each chapter, students

- Take a practice test to initiate the Self-Quiz and Study.
- Immediately upon completing the practice test, see how their performance compares to chapter Learning Objectives to be achieved within each section of the chapter.
- Receive a Study Plan that recommends specific readings from the text, supplemental study material, and practice work that will improve their understanding and mastery of each learning objective.

Student Progress Tracking Connect™ Economics keeps instructors informed about how each student, section, and class are performing, allowing for more productive use of lecture and office hours. The progress-tracking function enables you to

- View scored work immediately and track individual or group performance with assignment and grade reports.
- Access an instant view of student or class performance relative to learning objectives.
- Collect data and generate reports required by many accreditation organizations, such as AACSB.

Lecture Capture Increase the attention paid to lecture discussion by decreasing the attention paid to note taking. For an additional charge, Lecture Capture offers new ways for students to focus on the in-class discussion, knowing they can revisit important topics later. Lecture Capture enables you to

- Record and distribute your lecture with a click of a button.
- Record and index PowerPoint presentations and anything shown on your computer so it is easily searchable, frame by frame.
- Offer access to lectures anytime and anywhere by computer, iPod, or mobile device.
- Increase intent listening and class participation by easing students' concerns about note-taking.

Lecture Capture will make it more likely you will see students' faces, not the tops of their heads.

- To learn more about Tegrity, watch a 2-minute Flash demo at **http://tegritycampus.mhhe.com.**

McGraw-Hill's Connect™ Plus Economics

McGraw-Hill reinvents the textbook learning experience for the modern student with *Connect™ Plus Economics*. A seamless integration of an e-book and *Connect™ Economics*, *Connect™ Plus Economics* provides all of the features mentioned above plus the following:

- An integrated e-book, allowing for anytime, anywhere access to the textbook.
- Dynamic links between the problems or questions you assign to your students and the location in the e-book where that problem or question is covered.
- A powerful search function to pinpoint and connect key concepts in a snap.

In short, *Connect™ Economics* offers you and your students powerful tools and features that optimize your time and energies, enabling you to focus on course content, teaching, and student learning.

For more information about Connect, please visit **www.mcgrawhillconnect.com,** or contact your local McGraw-Hill sales representative.

McGraw-Hill Customer Care Contact Information

At McGraw-Hill, we understand that getting the most from new technology can be challenging. That's why our services don't stop after you purchase our products. You can e-mail our Product Specialists 24 hours a day to get product-training online. Or you can search our knowledge bank of frequently asked questions on our support website. For customer support, call **800-331-5094,** e-mail hmsupport@mcgraw-hill.com, or visit **www.mhhe.com/support.** One of our technical support analysts will be able to assist you in a timely fashion.

CourseSmart

CourseSmart is a new way for faculty to find and review e-textbooks. It's also a great option for students who are interested in accessing their course materials digitally. CourseSmart offers thousands of the most commonly adopted textbooks across hundreds of courses from a wide variety of higher education publishers. It is the only place for faculty to review and compare the full text of a textbook online. At CourseSmart, students can save up to 50 percent off the cost of a print book, reduce their impact on the environment, and gain access to powerful web tools for learning including full text search, notes and highlighting, and e-mail tools for sharing notes between classmates. Your e-book also includes tech support in case you ever need help. Finding your e-book is easy. Visit **www.CourseSmart.com** and search by title, author, or ISBN.

Online Learning Center

At **www.mcconnellbrief2e.com,** students have access to several learning aids. Along with the Interactive Graphs, Worked Problems, and Origin of the Idea pieces, the student portion of the website includes web-based study questions, self-grading quizzes, and PowerPoint presentations. For math-minded students, there is a "See the Math" section, written by Norris Peterson, where the mathematical details of the concepts in the text can be explored.

The password-protected instructor's side of the Online Learning Center holds all of the supplementary instructor resource materials.

Premium Content

The Premium Content, available at the Online Learning Center, enables students to study and self-test on their computer or on the go.

- One of the world's leading experts on economic education—William Walstad of the University of Nebraska at Lincoln—has prepared the *Study Guide.* Each chapter contains an introductory statement, a checklist of behavioral objectives, an outline, a list of important terms, fill-in questions, problems and projects, objective questions, and discussion questions. Many students will find this "digital tutor" indispensable.
- The Solman Videos, a set of more than 250 minutes of video created by Paul Solman of *The News Hour with Jim Lehrer*, cover core economic concepts such as elasticity, deregulation, and perfect competition.

Study Econ Mobile App

 McGraw-Hill is proud to offer a new mobile study app for students learning economics from McConnell, Brue, and Flynn's *Brief Edition.* The features of the Study Econ app include: flashcards for all key terms, a basic math review, customizable self quizzes, common mistakes, and games. For additional information please refer to the back inside cover of this book. Visit your mobile app store and download a trial version of the McConnell: Brief Edition Study Econ app today!

Supplements for Instructors

Instructor's Manual

Amy Stapp of Cuesta College prepared the Instructor's Manual. It includes chapter learning objectives, outlines, and summaries; numerous teaching suggestions; discussions of "student stumbling blocks;" listings of data and visual aid sources with suggestions for classroom use; and sample chapter quizzes. Available in MS Word on the instructor's side of the website, the manual enables instructors to print portions of the contents, complete with their own additions and alterations, for use as student handouts or in whatever ways they wish.

Test Bank

The *Microeconomics: Brief Edition* Test Bank, originally written by William Walstad and newly compiled and updated by Mark Wilson of West Virginia University and Jeffrey Phillips of Colby-Sawyer College, contains multiple choice and true-false questions. Each question is tied to a learning objective, topic, and AACSB Assurance of Learning and Bloom's Taxonomy guidelines. While crafting tests in EZ Test Online, instructors can use the whole chapter, scramble questions, and narrow the group by selecting the criteria. The Test Bank is also available in MS Word on the instructor's side of the website.

PowerPoint Presentations

Amy Chataginer of Mississippi Gulf Coast Community College created these in-depth slides to accompany lectures. The slides highlight all the main points of each chapter and include all of the figures and key tables from the text, as well as additional discussion notes. Each slide is tied to a learning objective.

Digital Image Library

Every graph and table in the text is available on the website. These figures allow instructors to create their own PowerPoint presentations and lecture materials.

Computerized Test Bank Online

A comprehensive bank of test questions is provided within McGraw-Hill's flexible electronic testing program EZ Test Online, www.eztestonline.com. EZ Test Online allows instructors to simply and quickly create tests or quizzes for their students. Instructors can select questions from multiple McGraw-Hill test banks or author their own, and then either print the finalized test or quiz for paper distribution or publish it online for access via the Internet.

This user-friendly program allows instructors to sort questions by format; select questions by learning objectives or Bloom's taxonomy tags; edit existing questions or add new ones; and scramble questions for multiple versions of the same test. Instructors can export their tests for use in WebCT, Blackboard, and PageOut, making it easy to share assessment materials with colleagues, adjuncts, and TAs. Instant scoring and feedback are provided, and EZ Test Online's record book is designed to easily export to instructor gradebooks.

Assurance of Learning Ready

Many educational institutions today are focused on the notion of *assurance of learning*, an important element of many accreditation standards. *Microeconomics: Brief Edition*, 2nd edition is designed specifically to support your assurance of learning initiatives with a simple, yet powerful, solution.

Each chapter in the book begins with a list of numbered learning objectives, which appear throughout the chapter as well as in the end-of-chapter content. Every Test Bank question for the *Brief Edition* maps to a specific chapter learning objective in the textbook. Each Test Bank question also identifies topic area, level of difficulty, Bloom's Taxonomy level, and AACSB skill area. You can use our Test Bank software, *EZ Test* and *EZ Test Online*, or *Connect Economics* to easily search for learning objectives that directly relate to the learning objectives for your course. You can then use the reporting features of *EZ Test* to aggregate student results in similar fashion, making the collection and presentation of Assurance of Learning data simple and easy.

AACSB Statement

McGraw-Hill/Irwin is a proud corporate member of AACSB International. Understanding the importance and value of AACSB accreditation, *Microeconomics: Brief Edition* recognizes the curriculum guidelines detailed in the AACSB standards for business accreditation by connecting selected questions in the text and the Test Bank to the general knowledge and skill guidelines in the AACSB standards.

The statements contained in *Microeconomics: Brief Edition* are provided only as a guide for the users of this textbook. The AACSB leaves content coverage and assessment within the purview of individual schools, the mission of the school, and the faculty. While *Microeconomics: Brief Edition* and the teaching package make no claim of any specific AACSB qualification or evaluation, we have, within the *Brief Edition*, labeled selected questions according to the six general knowledge and skills areas.

Acknowledgments

We give special thanks to Randy R. Grant of Linfield College, who not only wrote the Origin of the Idea pieces on our website but also served as the content coordinator for the *Brief Edition*. Professor Grant modified and seamlessly incorporated appropriate new content and revisions that the authors made in the nineteenth edition of *Economics* into this second edition of the *Brief Edition*. He also updated the tables and other information in *Microeconomics: Brief Edition* and made various improvements that he deemed helpful or were suggested to him by the authors, reviewers, and publisher.

We also want to acknowledge Norris Peterson of Pacific Lutheran University, who created the See the Math pieces and the Worked Problem pieces on our website. Professor Peterson also oversaw the development of the Interactive Graph pieces that are on the site. Finally, we wish to acknowledge William Walstad and Tom Barbiero (the coauthor of the Canadian edition of *Economics*) for their ongoing ideas and insights.

We are greatly indebted to an all-star group of professionals at McGraw-Hill—in particular Douglas Reiner, Noelle Bathurst, Harvey Yep, Melissa Larmon, Katie White, and Brent Gordon for their publishing and marketing expertise. We thank Keri Johnson and Michelle Buhr for their selection of Photo Op images. Mary Kazak Sander provided the vibrant interior design and cover.

The second edition has benefited from a number of perceptive formal reviews. The reviewers, listed at the end of the preface, were a rich source of suggestions for this revision. To each of you, and others we may have inadvertently overlooked, thank you for your considerable help in improving *Microeconomics: Brief Edition*.

Stanley L. Brue
Sean M. Flynn
Campbell R. McConnell

Contributors

Brief Contents

Contents

PART FOUR
Resource Markets and Government

INTRODUCTION

To the Student

This book and its ancillaries contain several features designed to help you learn economics:

- *Icons in the margins*   A glance through the book reveals many pages with web buttons in the margins. Three differing colored rectangular indicators appear throughout the book, alerting you when complementary content on a subject can be found at our Online Learning Center, **www.mcconnellbrief2e.com.** The **Worked Problems** serve as your "cookbook" for problem solving. Numeric problems are presented and then solved, side-by-side, step-by-step. Seeing how the problems are worked will help you solve similar problems on quizzes and exams. Practice hands-on graph work with the **Interactive Graphs** exercises. Manipulate the graphs by clicking on a specific curve and dragging it to a new location. This interaction will enhance your understanding of the underlying concepts. The **Origin of the Idea** pieces trace a particular idea to the person or persons who first developed it.

WORKED PROBLEMS	INTERACTIVE GRAPHS	ORIGIN OF THE IDEA
W 1.1	**G 3.1**	**O 2.2**
Budget lines	Supply and demand	Specialization/division of labor

- *Other Internet aids*   Our Internet site contains many other aids. In the student section at the Online Learning Center, you will find self-testing multiple-choice quizzes, PowerPoint slides, and much more.
- *Appendix on graphs*   To understand the content in this book, you will need to be comfortable with basic graphical analysis and a few quantitative concepts. The appendix (pages 25–30) at the end of Chapter 1 reviews graphing and slopes of curves. Be sure not to skip it.
- *Key terms*   Key terms are set in boldface type within the chapters, defined in the margins, listed at the end of each chapter, and again defined in the Glossary toward the end of the book.
- *"Illustrating the Idea" and "Applying the Analysis"*   These sections flow logically and smoothly from the content that precedes them. They are part and parcel of the development of the ideas and cannot be skipped. Each "Illustrating the Idea" and "Applying the Analysis" section is followed by a question.
- *Questions and Problems*   The end of each chapter features separate sections of Questions and Problems. The Questions are analytic and often ask for free responses, while the Problems are more computational. Each is keyed to a particular learning objective (LO) in the list of LOs at the beginning of the chapter. At the Online Learning Center, there are multiple-choice quizzes and one or more web-based questions for each chapter.
- *Study Guide*   We enthusiastically recommend the *Study Guide* accompanying this text. This "portable tutor" contains not only a broad sampling of various kinds of questions but a host of useful learning aids.

Our two main goals are to help you understand and apply economics and help you improve your analytical skills. An understanding of economics will enable you to comprehend a whole range of economic, social, and political problems that otherwise would seem puzzling and perplexing. Also, your study will enhance reasoning skills that are highly prized in the workplace.

Good luck with your study. We think it will be well worth your time and effort.

After reading this chapter, you should be able to:

1 Define economics and the features of the economic perspective.

2 Describe the role of economic theory in economics.

3 Distinguish microeconomics from macroeconomics.

4 List the categories of scarce resources and delineate the nature of the economizing problem.

5 Apply production possibilities analysis, increasing opportunity costs, and economic growth.

6 (Appendix) Understand graphs, curves, and slopes as they relate to economics.

Limits, Alternatives, and Choices

(An appendix on understanding graphs follows this chapter. If you need a quick review of this mathematical tool, you might benefit by reading the appendix first.)

Economics is about wants and means. Biologically, people need only air, water, food, clothing, and shelter. But in modern society people also desire goods and services that provide a more comfortable or affluent standard of living. We want bottled water, soft drinks, and fruit juices, not just water from the creek. We want salads, burgers, and pizzas, not just berries and nuts. We want jeans, suits, and coats, not just woven reeds. We want apartments, condominiums, or houses, not just mud huts. And, as the saying goes, "That's not the half of it." We also want flat-panel TVs, Internet service, education, homeland security, cell phones, and much more.

Fortunately, society possesses productive resources such as labor and managerial talent, tools and machinery, and land and mineral deposits. These resources, employed in the economic system (or simply the economy), help us produce goods and services that satisfy many of our economic wants. But the blunt reality is that our economic wants far exceed the productive capacity of our scarce (limited) resources. We are forced to make choices. This unyielding truth underlies the definition of **economics,** which is the social science concerned with how individuals, institutions, and society make choices under conditions of scarcity.

The Economic Perspective

economics
The study of how people, institutions, and society make economic choices under conditions of scarcity.

economic perspective
A viewpoint that envisions individuals and institutions making rational decisions by comparing the marginal benefits and marginal costs of their actions.

opportunity cost
The value of the good, service, or time forgone to obtain something else.

Economists view things through a particular perspective. This **economic perspective,** or economic way of thinking, has several critical and closely interrelated features.

Scarcity and Choice

From our definition of economics, it is easy to see why economists view the world through the lens of scarcity. Scarce economic resources mean limited goods and services. Scarcity restricts options and demands choices. Because we "can't have it all," we must decide what we will have and what we must forgo.

At the core of economics is the idea that "there is no free lunch." You may be treated to lunch, making it "free" to you, but someone bears a cost. Because all resources are either privately or collectively owned by members of society, ultimately, scarce inputs of land, equipment, farm labor, the labor of cooks and waiters, and managerial talent are required. Because these resources could have been used to produce something else, society sacrifices those other goods and services in making the lunch available. Economists call such sacrifices **opportunity costs:** To obtain more of one thing, society forgoes the opportunity of getting the next best thing. That sacrifice is the opportunity cost of the choice.

ILLUSTRATING THE IDEA

Did Gates, Winfrey, and Rodriguez Make Bad Choices?

The importance of opportunity costs in decision making is illustrated by different choices people make with respect to college. College graduates usually earn about 50 percent more during their lifetimes than persons with just high school diplomas. For most capable students, "Go to college, stay in college, and earn a degree" is very sound advice.

Yet Microsoft cofounder Bill Gates and talk-show host Oprah Winfrey* both dropped out of college, and baseball star Alex Rodriguez ("A-Rod") never even bothered to enroll. What were they thinking? Unlike most students, Gates faced enormous opportunity costs for staying in college. He had a vision for his company, and his starting work young helped ensure Microsoft's success. Similarly, Winfrey landed a spot in local television news when she was a teenager, eventually producing and starring in the *Oprah Winfrey Show* when she was 32 years old. Getting a degree in her twenties might have interrupted the string of successes that made her famous talk show possible. And Rodriguez knew that professional athletes have short careers. Therefore, going to college directly after high school would have taken away 4 years of his peak earning potential.

So Gates, Winfrey, and Rodriguez understood opportunity costs and made their choices accordingly. The size of opportunity costs greatly matters in making individual decisions.

QUESTION: Professional athletes sometimes return to college after they retire from professional sports. How does that college decision relate to opportunity costs?

* Winfrey eventually went back to school and earned a degree from Tennessee State University when she was in her thirties.

i) ✱ Purposeful Behavior

Economics assumes that human behavior reflects "rational self-interest." Individuals look for and pursue opportunities to increase their **utility:** pleasure, happiness, or satisfaction. They allocate their time, energy, and money to maximize their satisfaction. Because they weigh costs and benefits, their decisions are "purposeful" or "rational," not "random" or "chaotic."

Consumers are purposeful in deciding what goods and services to buy. Business firms are purposeful in deciding what products to produce and how to produce them. Government entities are purposeful in deciding what public services to provide and how to finance them.

"Purposeful behavior" does not assume that people and institutions are immune from faulty logic and therefore are perfect decision makers. They sometimes make mistakes. Nor does it mean that people's decisions are unaffected by emotion or the decisions of those around them. People sometimes are impulsive or emulative. "Purposeful behavior" simply means that people make decisions with some desired outcome in mind.

Nor is rational self-interest the same as selfishness. We will find that increasing one's own wage, rent, interest, or profit normally requires identifying and satisfying somebody else's want. Also, many people make personal sacrifices to others without expecting any monetary reward. They contribute time and money to charities because they derive pleasure from doing so. Parents help pay for their children's education for the same reason. These self-interested, but unselfish, acts help maximize the givers' satisfaction as much as any personal purchase of goods or services. Self-interested behavior is simply behavior designed to increase personal satisfaction, however it may be derived.

utility
The satisfaction obtained from consuming a good or service.

ORIGIN OF THE IDEA
O 1.2
Utility

Greatest Pleasure

i) ✱ Marginalism: Comparing Benefits and Costs

The economic perspective focuses largely on **marginal analysis**—comparisons of marginal benefits and marginal costs. To economists, "marginal" means "extra," "additional," or "a change in." Most choices or decisions involve changes in the status quo, meaning the existing state of affairs.

Should you attend school for another year? Should you study an extra hour for an exam? Should you supersize your fries? Similarly, should a business expand or reduce its output? Should government increase or decrease its funding for a missile defense system?

Each option involves marginal benefits and, because of scarce resources, marginal costs. In making choices rationally, the decision maker must compare those two amounts. Example: You and your fiancée are shopping for an engagement ring. Should you buy a $\frac{1}{2}$-carat diamond, a $\frac{5}{8}$-carat diamond, a $\frac{3}{4}$-carat diamond, a 1-carat

marginal analysis ✱
The comparison of marginal ("extra" or "additional") benefits and marginal costs, usually for decision making.

MB= MC
↑

MB< MC = not happy

ORIGIN OF THE IDEA

O 1.3

Marginal analysis

diamond, or something even larger? The marginal cost of a larger-size diamond is the added expense beyond the cost of the smaller-size diamond. The marginal benefit is the perceived greater lifetime pleasure (utility) from the larger-size stone. If the marginal benefit of the larger diamond exceeds its marginal cost (and you can afford it), buy the larger stone. But if the marginal cost is more than the marginal benefit, you should buy the smaller diamond instead—even if you can afford the larger stone!

In a world of scarcity, the decision to obtain the marginal benefit associated with some specific option always includes the marginal cost of forgoing something else. The money spent on the larger-size diamond means forgoing some other product. An opportunity cost, the value of the next best thing forgone, is always present whenever a choice is made.

APPLYING THE ANALYSIS

Economic Perspective
- utility = rational decisions
- MB = MC
marginal benefit
marginal cost

Fast-Food Lines

The economic perspective is useful in analyzing all sorts of behaviors. Consider an everyday example: the behavior of fast-food customers. When customers enter the restaurant, they go to the shortest line, believing that line will minimize their time cost of obtaining food. They are acting purposefully; time is limited, and people prefer using it in some way other than standing in a long line.

If one fast-food line is temporarily shorter than other lines, some people will move to that line. These movers apparently view the time saving from the shorter line (marginal benefit) as exceeding the cost of moving from their present line (marginal cost). The line switching tends to equalize line lengths. No further movement of customers between lines occurs once all lines are about equal.

Fast-food customers face another cost-benefit decision when a clerk opens a new station at the counter. Should they move to the new station or stay put? Those who shift to the new line decide that the time saving from the move exceeds the extra cost of physically moving. In so deciding, customers must also consider just how quickly they can get to the new station compared with others who may be contemplating the same move. (Those who hesitate in this situation are lost!)

Customers at the fast-food establishment do not have perfect information when they select lines. Thus, not all decisions turn out as expected. For example, you might enter a short line and find someone in front of you is ordering hamburgers and fries for 40 people in the Greyhound bus parked out back (and the employee is a trainee)! Nevertheless, at the time you made your decision, you thought it was optimal.

Finally, customers must decide what food to order when they arrive at the counter. In making their choices, they again compare marginal costs and marginal benefits in attempting to obtain the greatest personal satisfaction for their expenditure.

Economists believe that what is true for the behavior of customers at fast-food restaurants is true for economic behavior in general. Faced with an array of choices, consumers, workers, and businesses rationally compare marginal costs and marginal benefits in making decisions.

QUESTION: Have you ever gone to a fast-food restaurant only to observe long lines and then leave? Use the economic perspective to explain your behavior.

Theories, Principles, and Models

Like the physical and life sciences, as well as other social sciences, economics relies on the **scientific method.** That procedure consists of several elements:

- Observing real-world behavior and outcomes.
- Based on those observations, formulating a possible explanation of cause and effect (hypothesis).
- Testing this explanation by comparing the outcomes of specific events to the outcome predicted by the hypothesis.
- Accepting, rejecting, or modifying the hypothesis, based on these comparisons.
- Continuing to test the hypothesis against the facts. As favorable results accumulate, the hypothesis evolves into a *theory*. A very well-tested and widely accepted theory is referred to as a *law* or *principle*. Combinations of such laws or principles are incorporated into *models*, which are simplified representations of how something works, such as a market or segment of the economy.

Economists develop theories of the behavior of individuals (consumers, workers) and institutions (businesses, governments) engaged in the production, exchange, and consumption of goods and services. Economic theories and **principles** are statements about economic behavior or the economy that enable prediction of the probable effects of certain actions. They are "purposeful simplifications." The full scope of economic reality itself is too complex and bewildering to be understood as a whole. In developing theories and principles, economists remove the clutter and simplify.

Economic principles and models are highly useful in analyzing economic behavior and understanding how the economy operates. They are the tools for ascertaining cause and effect (or action and outcome) within the economic system. Good theories do a good job of explaining and predicting. They are supported by facts concerning how individuals and institutions actually behave in producing, exchanging, and consuming goods and services.

There are some other things you should know about economic principles:

- *Generalizations*   Economic principles are *generalizations* relating to economic behavior or to the economy itself. Economic principles are expressed as the tendencies of typical or average consumers, workers, or business firms. For example, economists say that consumers buy more of a particular product when its price falls. Economists recognize that some consumers may increase their purchases by a large amount, others by a small amount, and a few not at all. This "price-quantity" principle, however, holds for the typical consumer and for consumers as a group.

- *Other-things-equal assumption*   Like other scientists, economists use the *ceteris paribus* or **other-things-equal assumption** to construct their theories. They assume that all variables except those under immediate consideration are held constant for a particular analysis. For example, consider the relationship between the price of Pepsi and the amount of it purchased. It helps to assume that, of all the factors that might influence the amount of Pepsi purchased (for example, the price of Pepsi, the price of Coca-Cola, and consumer incomes and preferences), only the price of Pepsi varies. The economist can then focus on the relationship between the price of Pepsi and purchases of Pepsi in isolation without being confused by changes in other variables.

- *Graphical expression*   Many economic models are expressed graphically. Be sure to read the special appendix at the end of this chapter as a review of graphs.

scientific method
The systematic pursuit of knowledge by observing facts and formulating and testing hypotheses to obtain theories, principles, and laws.

principles
Statements about economic behavior that enable prediction of the probable effects of certain actions.

other-things-equal assumption
The assumption that factors other than those being considered do not change.

ORIGIN OF THE IDEA

O 1.4

Ceteris paribus

Microeconomics and Macroeconomics

Economists develop economic principles and models at two levels.

Microeconomics   *individual units*

microeconomics
The part of economics concerned with individual decision-making units, such as a consumer, a worker, or a business firm.

Microeconomics is the part of economics concerned with decision making by individual consumers, households, and business firms. At this level of analysis, we observe the details of their behavior under a figurative microscope. We measure the price of a specific product, the number of workers employed by a single firm, the revenue or income of a particular firm or household, or the expenditures of a specific firm, government entity, or family.

Macroeconomics   *sums / total / whole*

macroeconomics
The part of economics concerned with the economy as a whole or major components of the economy.

Macroeconomics examines either the economy as a whole or its basic subdivisions or aggregates, such as the government, household, and business sectors. An **aggregate** is a collection of specific economic units treated as if they were one unit. Therefore, we might lump together the millions of consumers in the U.S. economy and treat them as if they were one huge unit called "consumers."

aggregate
A collection of specific economic units treated as if they were one unit.

In using aggregates, macroeconomics seeks to obtain an overview, or general outline, of the structure of the economy and the relationships of its major aggregates. Macroeconomics speaks of such economic measures as total output, total employment, total income, aggregate expenditures, and the general level of prices in analyzing various economic problems. Very little attention is given to specific units making up the various aggregates.

Micro

© Robert Holmes/CORBIS

Macro

PHOTO OP   Micro versus Macro

Figuratively, microeconomics examines the sand, rock, and shells, not the beach; in contrast, macroeconomics examines the beach, not the sand, rocks, and shells.

Individual's Economic Problem

economic problem
The need for individuals and society to make choices because wants exceed means.

It is clear from our previous discussion that both individuals and society face an **economic problem:** They need to make choices because economic wants are unlimited, but the means (income, time, resources) for satisfying those wants are limited.

Unlimited wants with limited Resources!

Let's first look at the economic problem faced by individuals. To explain the idea, we will construct a very simple microeconomic model.

Limited Income

We all have a finite amount of income, even the wealthiest among us. Sure Bill Gates earns a bit more than the rest of us, but he still has to decide how to spend his money! And the majority of us have much more limited means. Our income comes to us in the form of wages, interest, rent, and profit, although we may also receive money from government programs or family members. As Global Snapshot 1.1 shows, the average income of Americans in 2009 was $46,360. In the poorest nations, it was less than $500.

Unlimited Wants

For better or worse, most people have virtually unlimited wants. We desire various goods and services that provide utility. Our wants extend over a wide range of products, from *necessities* (food, shelter, clothing) to *luxuries* (perfumes, yachts, sports cars). Some wants such as basic food, clothing, and shelter have biological roots. Other wants, for example, specific kinds of food, clothing, and shelter, arise from the conventions and customs of society.

Over time, economic wants tend to change and multiply, fueled by new and improved products. Only recently have people wanted iPods, Internet service, digital cameras, or camera phones because those products did not exist a few decades ago. Also, the satisfaction of certain wants may trigger others: The acquisition of a Ford Focus or a Honda Civic has been known to whet the appetite for a Lexus or a Mercedes.

GLOBAL SNAPSHOT 1.1

Average Income, Selected Nations

Average income (total income/population) and therefore typical budget constraints vary greatly among nations.

Country	Per Capita Income, 2009*
Switzerland	$65,430
United States	46,360
France	42,620
Japan	38,080
South Korea	19,830
Mexico	8,960
Brazil	8,070
China	3,650
Nigeria	1,190
Pakistan	1,000
Rwanda	490
Liberia	160

*U.S. dollars.
Source: World Bank, **www.worldbank.org**.

© Bill Aron/PhotoEdit

© F. Schussler/PhotoLink/Getty Images

PHOTO OP Necessities versus Luxuries

Economic wants include both necessities and luxuries. Each type of item provides utility to the buyer.

Services, as well as goods, satisfy our wants. Car repair work, the removal of an inflamed appendix, legal and accounting advice, and haircuts all satisfy human wants. Actually, we buy many goods, such as automobiles and washing machines, for the services they render. The differences between goods and services are often smaller than they appear to be.

For most people, the desires for goods and services cannot be fully satisfied. Bill Gates may have all that he wants for himself, but his massive charitable giving suggests that he keenly wants better health care for the world's poor. Our desires for a *particular* good or service can be satisfied; over a short period of time we can surely obtain enough toothpaste or pasta. And one appendectomy is plenty. But our broader desire for more goods and services and higher-quality goods and services seems to be another story.

Because we have only limited income but seemingly insatiable wants, it is in our self-interest to economize: to pick and choose goods and services that maximize our satisfaction, given the limitations we face.

A Budget Line

budget line
A line that shows various combinations of two products a consumer can purchase with a specific money income, given the products' prices.

The economic problem facing individuals can be depicted as a **budget line** (or, more technically, *budget constraint*). It is a schedule or curve that shows various combinations of two products a consumer can purchase with a specific money income.

To understand this idea, suppose that you received a Barnes & Noble gift card as a birthday present. The $120 card is soon to expire. You take the card to the store and confine your purchase decisions to two alternatives: DVDs and paperback books.

FIGURE 1.1 A consumer's budget line. The budget line (or budget constraint) shows all the combinations of any two products that can be purchased, given the prices of the products and the consumer's money income.

The Budget Line: Whole-Unit Combinations of DVDs and Paperback Books Attainable with an Income of $120		
Units of DVDs (Price = $20)	Units of Books (Price = $10)	Total Expenditure
6	0	$120 = ($120 + $0)
5	2	$120 = ($100 + $20)
4	4	$120 = ($80 + $40)
3	6	$120 = ($60 + $60)
2	8	$120 = ($40 + $80)
1	10	$120 = ($20 + $100)
0	12	$120 = ($0 + $120)

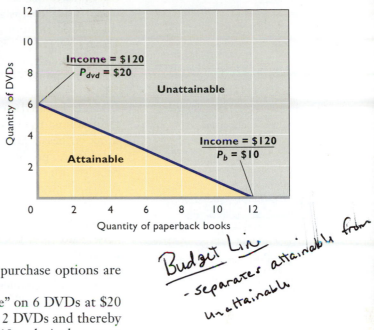

Budget Line
– separates attainable from unattainable

DVDs are $20 each, and paperback books are $10 each. Your purchase options are shown in the table in Figure 1.1.

At one extreme, you might spend all of your $120 "income" on 6 DVDs at $20 each and have nothing left to spend on books. Or, by giving up 2 DVDs and thereby gaining $40, you can have 4 DVDs at $20 each and 4 books at $10 each. And so on to the other extreme, at which you could buy 12 books at $10 each, spending your entire gift card on books with nothing left to spend on DVDs.

The graph in Figure 1.1 shows the budget line. As elsewhere in this book, we represent discrete (separate element) numbers in tables as points on continuous-data smooth curves. Therefore, note that the line (curve) in the graph is not restricted to whole units of DVDs and books as is the table. Every point on the line represents a possible combination of DVDs and books, including fractional quantities. The slope of the graphed budget line measures the ratio of the price of books (P_b) to the price of DVDs (P_{dvd}); more precisely, the slope is $P_b/P_{dvd} = \$-10/\$+20 = -\frac{1}{2}$ or $-.5$. So you must forgo 1 DVD (measured on the vertical axis) to buy 2 books (measured on the horizontal axis). This yields a slope of $-\frac{1}{2}$ or $-.5$.

The budget line illustrates several ideas.

Attainable and Unattainable Combinations All the combinations of DVDs and books on or inside the budget line are *attainable* from the $120 of money income. You can afford to buy, for example, 3 DVDs at $20 each and 6 books at $10 each. You also can obviously afford to buy 2 DVDs and 5 books, thereby using up only $90 of the $120 available on your gift card. But to achieve maximum utility, you will want to spend the full $120. The budget line shows all combinations that cost exactly the full $120.

In contrast, all combinations beyond the budget line are *unattainable*. The $120 limit simply does not allow you to purchase, for example, 5 DVDs at $20 each and 5 books at $10 each. That $150 expenditure would clearly exceed the $120 limit. In Figure 1.1, the attainable combinations are on and within the budget line; the unattainable combinations are beyond the budget line.

Trade-offs and Opportunity Costs The budget line in Figure 1.1 illustrates the idea of trade-offs arising from limited income. To obtain more DVDs, you have to

ORIGIN OF THE IDEA

O 1.5

Opportunity cost

give up some books. For example, to acquire the first DVD, you trade off 2 books. So the opportunity cost of the first DVD is 2 books. To obtain the second DVD, the opportunity cost is also 2 books. The straight-line budget constraint, with its constant slope, indicates **constant opportunity cost.** That is, the opportunity cost of 1 extra DVD remains the same (= 2 books) as more DVDs are purchased. And, in reverse, the opportunity cost of 1 extra book does not change (= $\frac{1}{2}$ DVD) as more books are bought.

constant opportunity cost
An opportunity cost that remains the same as consumers shift purchases from one product to another along a straight-line budget line.

Choice Limited income forces people to choose what to buy and what to forgo to fulfill wants. You will select the combination of DVDs and paperback books that you think is "best." That is, you will evaluate your marginal benefits and your marginal costs (here, product price) to make choices that maximize your satisfaction. Other people, with the same $120 gift card, would undoubtedly make different choices.

WORKED PROBLEMS

W 1.1
Budget lines

Income Changes The location of the budget line varies with money income. An increase in money income shifts the budget line to the right; a decrease in money income shifts it to the left. To verify this, recalculate the table in Figure 1.1, assuming the card value (income) is (a) $240 and (b) $60, and plot the new budget lines in the graph. No wonder people like to have more income: That shifts their budget lines outward and enables them to buy more goods and services. But even with more income, people will still face spending trade-offs, choices, and opportunity costs.

Society's Economic Problem

Society must also make choices under conditions of scarcity. It, too, faces an economic problem. Should it devote more of its limited resources to the criminal justice system (police, courts, and prisons) or to education (teachers, books, and schools)? If it decides to devote more resources to both, what other goods and services does it forgo? Health care? Homeland security? Energy development?

Scarce Resources

economic resources
The land, labor, capital, and entrepreneurial ability used in the production of goods and services.

Society's economic resources are limited or scarce. By **economic resources** we mean all natural, human, and manufactured resources that go into the production of goods and services. That includes the entire set of factory and farm buildings and all the equipment, tools, and machinery used to produce manufactured goods and agricultural products; all transportation and communication facilities; all types of labor; and land and mineral resources.

Resource Categories

Economists classify economic resources into four general categories.

land
Natural resources ("gifts of nature") used to produce goods and services.

Land Land means much more to the economist than it does to most people. To the economist **land** includes all natural resources ("gifts of nature") used in the production process. These include mineral and oil deposits, arable land, forests, and water resources.

labor
The physical and mental talents and efforts of people used to produce goods and services.

Labor The resource **labor** consists of the physical actions and mental activities that people contribute to the production of goods and services. The work-related activities of a logger, retail clerk, machinist, teacher, professional football player, and nuclear physicist all fall under the general heading "labor."

Capital For economists, **capital** (or *capital goods*) includes all manufactured aids used in producing consumer goods and services. Included are all factory, storage, transportation, and distribution facilities, as well as all tools and machinery. Economists use the term **investment** to describe spending that pays for the production and accumulation of capital goods.

Capital goods differ from consumer goods because consumer goods satisfy wants directly, while capital goods do so indirectly by aiding the production of consumer goods. For example, large commercial baking ovens (capital goods) help make loaves of bread (consumer goods). Note that the term "capital" as used by economists refers not to money but to tools, machinery, and other productive equipment. Because money produces nothing, economists do not include it as an economic resource. Money (or money capital or financial capital) is simply a means for purchasing goods and services, including capital goods.

Entrepreneurial Ability Finally, there is the special human resource, distinct from labor, called **entrepreneurial ability.** The entrepreneur performs several socially useful functions:

- The entrepreneur takes the initiative in combining the resources of land, labor, and capital to produce a good or a service. Both a spark plug and a catalyst, the entrepreneur is the driving force behind production and the agent who combines the other resources in what is hoped will be a successful business venture.
- The entrepreneur makes the strategic business decisions that set the course of an enterprise.
- The entrepreneur innovates. He or she commercializes new products, new production techniques, or even new forms of business organization.
- The entrepreneur bears risk. Innovation is risky, as nearly all new products and ideas are subject to the possibility of failure as well as success. Progress would cease without entrepreneurs who are willing to take on risk by devoting their time, effort, and ability—as well as their own money and the money of others—to commercializing new products and ideas that may enhance society's standard of living.

capital
Human-made resources (buildings, machinery, and equipment) used to produce goods and services.

investment
The purchase of capital resources.

entrepreneurial ability
The human talent that combines the other resources to produce a product, make strategic decisions, and bear risks.

factors of production
Economic resources: land, labor, capital, and entrepreneurial ability.

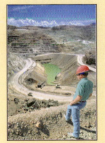
© Lester Lefkowitz/CORBIS

© Lance Nelson/Stock Photos/zefa/CORBIS

© Creatas/PunchStock

© Neville Elder/Corbis

PHOTO OP Economic Resources

Land, labor, capital, and entrepreneurial ability all contribute to producing goods and services.

Because land, labor, capital, and entrepreneurial ability are combined to produce goods and services, they are called the **factors of production** or simply inputs.

Production Possibilities Model

Assumptions on factors of production

Society uses its scarce resources to produce goods and services. The alternatives and choices it faces can best be understood through a macroeconomic model of production possibilities. To keep things simple, we assume:

- *Full employment*   The economy is employing all of its available resources.
- *Fixed resources*   The quantity and quality of the factors of production are fixed.
- *Fixed technology*   The state of technology (the methods used to produce output) is constant.
- *Two goods*   The economy is producing only two goods: food products and manufacturing equipment. Food products symbolize **consumer goods**, products that satisfy our wants directly; manufacturing equipment symbolizes **capital goods**, products that satisfy our wants indirectly by making possible more efficient production of consumer goods.

consumer goods
Products and services that directly satisfy consumer wants.

capital goods
Items that are used to produce other goods and therefore do not directly satisfy consumer wants.

Production Possibilities Table

A production possibilities table lists the different combinations of two products that can be produced with a specific set of resources, assuming full employment. Figure 1.2 contains such a table for a simple economy that is producing food products and manufacturing equipment; the data are, of course, hypothetical. At alternative A, this economy would be devoting all its available resources to the production of manufacturing equipment (capital goods); at alternative E, all resources would go to food-product production (consumer goods). Those alternatives are unrealistic extremes; an economy typically produces both capital goods and consumer goods, as in B, C, and D. As we move from alternative A to E, we increase the production of food products at the expense of the production of manufacturing equipment.

Because consumer goods satisfy our wants directly, any movement toward E looks tempting. In producing more food products, society increases the satisfaction of its current wants. But there is a cost: More food products mean less manufacturing equipment.

FIGURE 1.2 **The production possibilities curve.** Each point on the production possibilities curve represents some maximum combination of two products that can be produced if resources are fully and efficiently employed. When an economy is operating on the curve, more manufacturing equipment means less food products, and vice versa. Limited resources and a fixed technology make any combination of manufacturing equipment and food products lying outside the curve (such as at *W*) unattainable. Points inside the curve are attainable, but they indicate that full employment is not being realized.

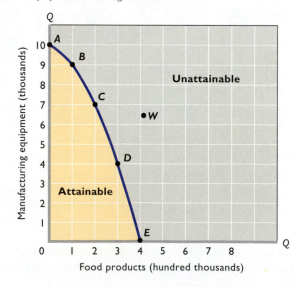

Type of Product	Production Alternatives				
	A	**B**	**C**	**D**	**E**
Food products (hundred thousands)	0	1	2	3	4
Manufacturing equipment (thousands)	10	9	7	4	0

Opportunity Cost

MB=MC

Society Decides

This shift of resources to consumer goods catches up with society over time because the stock of capital goods expands more slowly, thereby reducing potential future production. By moving toward alternative E, society chooses "more now" at the expense of "much more later."

By moving toward A, society chooses to forgo current consumption, thereby freeing up resources that can be used to increase the production of capital goods. By building up its stock of capital this way, society will have greater future production and, therefore, greater future consumption. By moving toward A, society is choosing "more later" at the cost of "less now."

Generalization: At any point in time, a fully employed economy must sacrifice some of one good to obtain more of another good. Scarce resources prohibit such an economy from having more of both goods. Society must choose among alternatives. There is no such thing as a free bag of groceries or a free manufacturing machine. Having more of one thing means having less of something else.

Production Possibilities Curve

The data presented in a production possibilities table can also be shown graphically. We arbitrarily represent the economy's output of capital goods (here, manufacturing equipment) on the vertical axis and the output of consumer goods (here, food products) on the horizontal axis, as shown in Figure 1.2.

Each point on the **production possibilities curve** represents some maximum output of the two products. The curve is a "constraint" because it shows the limit of attainable outputs. Points on the curve are attainable as long as the economy uses all its available resources. Points lying inside the curve are also attainable, but they reflect less total output and therefore are not as desirable as points on the curve. Points inside the curve imply that the economy could have more of both manufacturing equipment and food products if it achieved full employment. Points lying beyond the production possibilities curve, like *W*, would represent a greater output than the output at any point on the curve. Such points, however, are unattainable with the current availability of resources and technology.

Law of Increasing Opportunity Costs

Figure 1.2 clearly shows that more food products mean less manufacturing equipment. The number of units of manufacturing equipment that must be given up to obtain another unit of food products, of course, is the opportunity cost of that unit of food products.

In moving from alternative A to alternative B in the table in Figure 1.2, the cost of 1 additional unit of food products is 1 less unit of manufacturing equipment. But when additional units are considered—B to C, C to D, and D to E—an important economic principle is revealed: The opportunity cost of each additional unit of food products is greater than the opportunity cost of the preceding one. When we move from A to B, just 1 unit of manufacturing equipment is sacrificed for 1 more unit of food products; but in going from B to C, we sacrifice 2 additional units of manufacturing equipment for 1 more unit of food products; then 3 more of manufacturing equipment for 1 more of food products; and finally 4 for 1. Conversely, confirm that as we move from E to A, the cost of an additional unit of manufacturing equipment (on average) is $\frac{1}{4}$, $\frac{1}{3}$, $\frac{1}{2}$, and 1 unit of food products, respectively, for the four successive moves.

Our example illustrates the **law of increasing opportunity costs:** The more of a product that society produces, the greater is the opportunity cost of obtaining an extra unit.

INTERACTIVE GRAPHS

G 1.1

Production possibilities curve

production possibilities curve
A curve showing the different combinations of goods and services that can be produced in a fully employed economy, assuming the available supplies of resources and technology are fixed.

Production of goods increase, opportunity cost of producing an additional unit rises.

law of increasing opportunity costs
The principle that as the production of a good increases, the opportunity cost of producing an additional unit rises.

Shape of the Curve The law of increasing opportunity costs is reflected in the shape of the production possibilities curve: The curve is bowed out from the origin of the graph. Figure 1.2 shows that when the economy moves from *A* to *E*, it must give up successively larger amounts of manufacturing equipment (1, 2, 3, and 4) to acquire equal increments of food products (1, 1, 1, and 1). This is shown in the slope of the production possibilities curve, which becomes steeper as we move from *A* to *E*.

Economic Rationale The law of increasing opportunity costs is driven by the fact that economic resources are not completely adaptable to alternative uses. Many resources are better at producing one type of good than at producing others. Consider land. Some land is highly suited to growing the ingredients necessary for pizza production. But as pizza production expands, society has to start using land that is less bountiful for farming. Other land is rich in mineral deposits and therefore well-suited to producing the materials needed to make manufacturing equipment. That land will be the first land devoted to the production of manufacturing equipment. But as society steps up the production of manufacturing equipment, it must push resources that are less and less suited to making that equipment into its production.

If we start at *A* and move to *B* in Figure 1.2, we can shift resources whose productivity is relatively high in food production and low in manufacturing equipment. But as we move from *B* to *C*, *C* to *D*, and so on, resources highly productive of food products become increasingly scarce. To get more food products, resources whose productivity in manufacturing equipment is relatively great will be needed. It will take increasingly more of such resources, and hence greater sacrifices of manufacturing equipment, to achieve each 1-unit increase in food products. This lack of perfect flexibility, or interchangeability, on the part of resources is the cause of increasing opportunity costs for society.

Optimal Allocation

Of all the attainable combinations of food products and manufacturing equipment on the curve in Figure 1.2, which is optimal (best)? That is, what specific quantities of resources should be allocated to food products and what specific quantities to manufacturing equipment in order to maximize satisfaction?

Recall that economic decisions center on comparisons of marginal benefits (MB) and marginal costs (MC). Any economic activity should be expanded as long as marginal benefit exceeds marginal cost and should be reduced if marginal cost exceeds marginal benefit. The optimal amount of the activity occurs where MB = MC. Society needs to make a similar assessment about its production decision.

Consider food products. We already know from the law of increasing opportunity costs that the marginal cost of additional units of food products will rise as more units are produced. At the same time, we need to recognize that the extra or marginal benefits that come from producing and consuming food products decline with each successive unit of food products. Consequently, each successive unit of food products brings with it both increasing marginal costs and decreasing marginal benefits.

The optimal quantity of food production is indicated by the intersection of the MB and MC curves: 200,000 units in Figure 1.3. Why is this amount the optimal quantity? If only 100,000 units of food products were produced, the marginal benefit of an extra unit of them would exceed its marginal cost. In money terms, MB is $15, while MC is only $5. When society gains something worth $15 at a marginal cost of only $5, it is better off. In Figure 1.3, net gains of decreasing amounts can be realized until food-product production has been increased to 200,000.

In contrast, the production of 300,000 units of food products is excessive. There the MC of an added unit is $15 and its MB is only $5. This means that 1 unit of food

---

WORKED PROBLEMS

W 1.2

Production possibilities

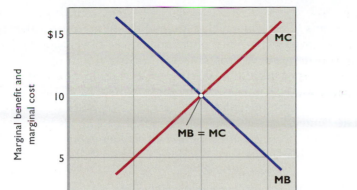

FIGURE 1.3 **Optimal output:
MB = MC.** Achieving the optimal output
requires the expansion of a good's output
until its marginal benefit (MB) and marginal
cost (MC) are equal. No resources beyond
that point should be allocated to the
product. Here, optimal output occurs
when 200,000 units of food products
are produced.

products is worth only $5 to society but costs it $15 to obtain. This is a losing proposition for society!

So resources are being efficiently allocated to any product when the marginal benefit and marginal cost of its output are equal (MB = MC). Suppose that by applying the above analysis to manufacturing equipment, we find its optimal (MB = MC) quantity is 7000. This would mean that alternative *C* (200,000 units of food products and 7000 units of manufacturing equipment) on the production possibilities curve in Figure 1.2 would be optimal for this economy.

APPLYING THE ANALYSIS

The Economics of War

Production possibilities analysis is helpful in assessing the costs and benefits of waging the war on terrorism, including the wars in Afghanistan and Iraq. At the end of 2010, the estimated cost of these efforts exceeded $1.05 trillion.

If we categorize all of U.S. production as either "defense goods" or "civilian goods," we can measure them on the axes of a production possibilities diagram such as that shown in Figure 1.2. The opportunity cost of using more resources for defense goods is the civilian goods sacrificed. In a fully employed economy, more defense goods are achieved at the opportunity cost of fewer civilian goods—health care, education, pollution control, personal computers, houses, and so on. The cost of waging war is the other goods forgone. The benefits of these activities are numerous and diverse but clearly include the gains from protecting against future loss of American lives, assets, income, and well-being.

Society must assess the marginal benefit (MB) and marginal cost (MC) of additional defense goods to determine their optimal amounts—where to locate on the defense goods–civilian goods production possibilities curve. Although estimating marginal benefits and marginal costs is an imprecise art, the MB-MC framework is a useful way of approaching choices. Allocative efficiency requires that society expand production of defense goods until MB = MC.

The events of September 11, 2001, and the future threats they posed increased the perceived marginal benefits of defense goods. If we label the horizontal axis in Figure 1.3 "defense goods," and draw in a rightward shift of the MB curve, you will see that the optimal quantity of defense goods rises. In view of the concerns relating to September 11, the United States allocated more of its resources to defense. But the MB-MC analysis also reminds us we can spend too much on defense, as well as too little. The United States should not expand defense goods beyond the point where MB = MC. If it does, it will be sacrificing civilian goods of greater value than the defense goods obtained.

QUESTION: Would society's costs of war be lower if it drafted soldiers at low pay rather than attracted them voluntarily to the military through market pay?

Unemployment, Growth, and the Future

In the depths of the Great Depression of the 1930s, one-quarter of U.S. workers were unemployed and one-third of U.S. production capacity was idle. Subsequent downturns have been much less severe. During the deep 2007–2009 recession, for instance, production fell by a comparably smaller 5.1 percent, and 1 in 10 workers was without a job.

Almost all nations have experienced widespread unemployment and unused production capacity from business downturns at one time or another. Since 2000, for example, several nations—including Argentina, Japan, Mexico, Germany, and South Korea—have had economic downturns and unemployment.

How do these realities relate to the production possibilities model? Our analysis and conclusions change if we relax the assumption that all available resources are fully employed. The five alternatives in the table of Figure 1.2 represent maximum outputs; they illustrate the combinations of food products and manufacturing equipment that can be produced when the economy is operating at full employment. With unemployment, this economy would produce less than each alternative shown in the table.

Graphically, we represent situations of unemployment by points inside the original production possibilities curve (reproduced in Figure 1.4). Point *U* is one such point. Here the economy is falling short of the various maximum combinations of food products and manufacturing equipment represented by the points on the production possibilities curve. The arrows in Figure 1.4 indicate three possible paths back to full employment. A move toward full employment would yield a greater output of one or both products.

A Growing Economy

When we drop the assumptions that the quantity and quality of resources and technology are fixed, the production possibilities curve shifts positions, and the potential maximum output of the economy changes.

 Increases in Resource Supplies Although resource supplies are fixed at any specific moment, they change over time. For example, a nation's growing population brings about increases in the supplies of labor and entrepreneurial ability. Also, labor

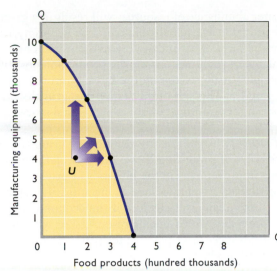

*Labor — maxed out
Land
Capital
Entrepreneurial ability*

FIGURE 1.4 **Unemployment and the production possibilities curve.** Any point inside the production possibilities curve, such as *U*, represents unemployment or a failure to achieve full employment. The arrows indicate that, by realizing full employment, the economy could operate on the curve. This means it could produce more of one or both products than it is producing at point *U*.

any shift in curve is a result in change of Scarce Resource.

quality usually improves over time. Historically, the economy's stock of capital has increased at a significant, though unsteady, rate. And although some of our energy and mineral resources are being depleted, new sources are also being discovered. The development of irrigation systems, for example, adds to the supply of arable land.

The net result of these increased supplies of the factors of production is the ability to produce more of both consumer goods and capital goods. Thus, 20 years from now, the production possibilities in Figure 1.5 may supersede those shown in

FIGURE 1.5 **Economic growth and the production possibilities curve.** The increase in supplies of resources, the improvements in resource quality, and the technological advances that occur in a dynamic economy move the production possibilities curve outward and to the right, allowing the economy to have larger quantities of both types of goods.

Type of Product	Production Alternatives				
	A′	**B′**	**C′**	**D′**	**E′**
Food products (hundred thousands)	0	2	4	6	8
Manufacturing equipment (thousands)	14	12	9	5	0

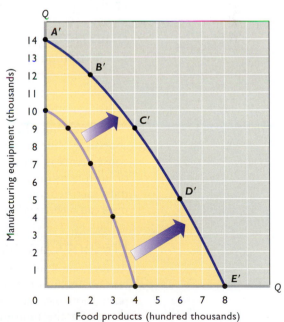

Figure 1.2. The greater abundance of resources will result in a greater potential output of one or both products at each alternative. The economy will have achieved economic growth in the form of expanded potential output. Thus, when an increase in the quantity or quality of resources occurs, the production possibilities curve shifts outward and to the right, as illustrated by the move from the inner curve to curve *A′ B′ C′ D′ E′* in Figure 1.5. This sort of shift represents growth of economic capacity, which, when used, means **economic growth**: a larger total output.

economic growth
An outward shift of the production possibilities curve that results from an increase in resource supplies or quality or an improvement in technology.

*Improved Quality of Resources

Advances in Technology An advancing technology brings both new and better goods and improved ways of producing them. For now, let's think of technological advance as being only improvements in the methods of production, for example, the introduction of computerized systems to manage inventories and schedule production. These advances alter our previous discussion of the economic problem by allowing society to produce more goods with available resources. As with increases in resource supplies, technological advances make possible the production of more manufacturing equipment *and* more food products.

APPLYING THE ANALYSIS

Information Technology and Biotechnology

A real-world example of improved technology is the recent surge of new technologies relating to computers, communications, and biotechnology. Technological advances have dropped the prices of computers and greatly increased their speed. Improved software has greatly increased the everyday usefulness of computers. Cellular phones and the Internet have increased communications capacity, enhancing production and improving the efficiency of markets. Advances in biotechnology have resulted in important agricultural and medical discoveries. These and other new and improved technologies have contributed to U.S. economic growth (outward shifts of the nation's production possibilities curve).

QUESTION: How have technological advances in medicine helped expand production possibilities in the United States?

Conclusion: Economic growth is the result of (1) increases in supplies of resources, (2) improvements in resource quality, and (3) technological advances. The consequence of growth is that a full-employment economy can enjoy a greater output of both consumption goods and capital goods. While static, no-growth economies must sacrifice some of one good to obtain more of another, dynamic, growing economies can have larger quantities of both goods.

Present Choices and Future Possibilities

An economy's current choice of positions on its production possibilities curve helps determine the future location of that curve. Let's designate the two axes of the production possibilities curve as "goods for the future" and "goods for the present," as in Figure 1.6. Goods for the future are such things as capital goods, research and education, and

FIGURE 1.6 **Present choices and future locations of production possibilities curves.** A nation's current choice favoring "present goods," as made by Presentville in (a), will cause a modest outward shift of the production possibilities curve in the future. A nation's current choice favoring "future goods," as made by Futureville in (b), will result in a greater outward shift of the curve in the future.

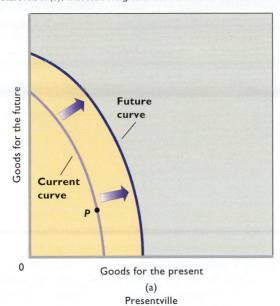

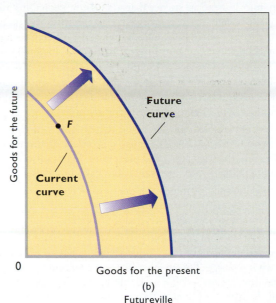

(a)
Presentville

(b)
Futureville

preventive medicine. They increase the quantity and quality of property resources, enlarge the stock of technological information, and improve the quality of human resources. As we have already seen, goods for the future, such as capital goods, are the ingredients of economic growth. Goods for the present are consumer goods such as food, clothing, and entertainment.

Now suppose there are two hypothetical economies, Presentville and Futureville, which are initially identical in every respect except one: Presentville's current choice of positions on its production possibilities curve strongly favors present goods over future goods. Point *P* in Figure 1.6a indicates that choice. It is located quite far down the curve to the right, indicating a high priority for goods for the present, at the expense of less goods for the future. Futureville, in contrast, makes a current choice that stresses larger amounts of future goods and smaller amounts of present goods, as shown by point *F* in Figure 1.6b.

Now, other things equal, we can expect Futureville's future production possibilities curve to be farther to the right than Presentville's future production possibilities curve. By currently choosing an output more favorable to technological advances and to increases in the quantity and quality of resources, Futureville will achieve greater economic growth than Presentville. In terms of capital goods, Futureville is choosing to make larger current additions to its "national factory" by devoting more of its current output to capital than Presentville. The payoff from this choice for Futureville is greater future production capacity and economic growth. The opportunity cost is fewer consumer goods in the present for Futureville to enjoy.

Is Futureville's choice thus necessarily "better" than Presentville's? That, we cannot say. The different outcomes simply reflect different preferences and priorities in the two countries. But each country will have to live with the consequences of its choice.

INTERACTIVE GRAPHS

G 1.2

Present choices and future possibilities

Summary

1. Economics is the social science that studies how people, institutions, and society make choices under conditions of scarcity. Central to economics is the idea of opportunity cost: the value of the good, service, or time forgone to obtain something else.

2. The economic perspective includes three elements: scarcity and choice, purposeful behavior, and marginalism. It sees individuals and institutions making rational decisions based on comparisons of marginal costs and marginal benefits.

3. Economists employ the scientific method, in which they form and test hypotheses of cause-and-effect relationships to generate theories, laws, and principles. Economists often combine theories into representations called models.

4. Microeconomics examines the decision making of specific economic units or institutions. Macroeconomics looks at the economy as a whole or its major aggregates.

5. Individuals face an economic problem. Because their wants exceed their incomes, they must decide what to purchase and what to forgo. Society also faces an economic problem. Societal wants exceed the available resources necessary to fulfill them. Society therefore must decide what to produce and what to forgo.

6. Graphically, a budget line (or budget constraint) illustrates the economic problem for individuals. The line shows the various combinations of two products that a consumer can purchase with a specific money income, given the prices of the two products.

7. Economic resources are inputs into the production process and can be classified as land, labor, capital, and entrepreneurial ability. Economic resources are also known as factors of production or inputs.

8. Society's economic problem can be illustrated through production possibilities analysis. Production possibilities tables and curves show the different combinations of goods and services that can be produced in a fully employed economy, assuming that resource quantity, resource quality, and technology are fixed.

9. An economy that is fully employed and thus operating on its production possibilities curve must sacrifice the output of some types of goods and services to increase the production of others. The gain of one type of good or service is always accompanied by an opportunity cost in the form of the loss of some of the other type.

10. Because resources are not equally productive in all possible uses, shifting resources from one use to another results in increasing opportunity costs. The production of additional units of one product requires the sacrifice of increasing amounts of the other product.

11. The optimal point on the production possibilities curve represents the most desirable mix of goods and is determined by expanding the production of each good until its marginal benefit (MB) equals its marginal cost (MC).

12. Over time, technological advances and increases in the quantity and quality of resources enable the economy to produce more of all goods and services, that is, to experience economic growth. Society's choice as to the mix of consumer goods and capital goods in current output is a major determinant of the future location of the production possibilities curve and thus of the extent of economic growth.

Terms and Concepts

economics	macroeconomics	investment
economic perspective	aggregate	entrepreneurial ability
opportunity cost	economic problem	factors of production
utility	budget line	consumer goods
marginal analysis	constant opportunity cost	capital goods
scientific method	economic resources	production possibilities curve
principles	land	law of increasing opportunity costs
other-things-equal assumption	labor	economic growth
microeconomics	capital	

Questions

1. Ralph Waldo Emerson once wrote: "Want is a growing giant whom the coat of have was never large enough to cover." How does this statement relate to the definition of economics? **LO1**

2. "Buy 2, get 1 free." Explain why the "1 free" is free to the buyer but not to society. **LO1**

3. Which of the following decisions would entail the greater opportunity cost: allocating a square block in the heart of

New York City for a surface parking lot or allocating a square block at the edge of a typical suburb for such a lot? Explain. **LO1**

4. What is meant by the term "utility," and how does it relate to purposeful behavior? **LO1**

 5. Cite three examples of recent decisions that you made in which you, at least implicitly, weighed marginal cost and marginal benefit. **LO1**

6. What are the key elements of the scientific method, and how does this method relate to economic principles and laws? **LO2**

7. Indicate whether each of the following statements applies to microeconomics or macroeconomics: **LO3**
   a. The unemployment rate in the United States was 9.0% in April 2011.
   b. A U.S. software firm discharged 15 workers last month and transferred the work to India.
   c. An unexpected freeze in central Florida reduced the citrus crop and caused the price of oranges to rise.
   d. U.S. output, adjusted for inflation, grew by 2.9% in 2010.
   e. Last week Wells Fargo Bank lowered its interest rate on business loans by one-half of 1 percentage point.
   f. The consumer price index rose by 1.6% in 2010.

8. What are economic resources? What categories do economists use to classify them? Why are resources also called factors of production? Why are they called inputs? **LO4**

9. Why isn't money considered a capital resource in economics? Why is entrepreneurial ability considered a category of economic resource, distinct from labor? What are the major functions of the entrepreneur? **LO4**

10. Specify and explain the typical shapes of marginal-benefit and marginal-cost curves. How are these curves used to determine the optimal allocation of resources to a particular product? If current output is such that marginal cost exceeds marginal benefit, should more or fewer resources be allocated to this product? Explain. **LO5**

11. Explain how (if at all) each of the following events affects the location of a country's production possibilities curve: **LO5**
   a. The quality of education increases.
   b. The number of unemployed workers increases.
   c. A new technique improves the efficiency of extracting copper from ore.
   d. A devastating earthquake destroys numerous production facilities.

12. Suppose that, on the basis of a nation's production possibilities curve, an economy must sacrifice 10,000 pizzas domestically to get the 1 additional industrial robot it desires but that it can get the robot from another country in exchange for 9000 pizzas. Relate this information to the following statement: "Through international specialization and trade, a nation can reduce its opportunity cost of obtaining goods and thus 'move outside its production possibilities curve.'" **LO5**

Problems

1. Potatoes cost Janice $1 per pound, and she has $5.00 that she could possibly spend on potatoes or other items. If she feels that the first pound of potatoes is worth $1.50, the second pound is worth $1.14, the third pound is worth $1.05, and all subsequent pounds are worth $0.30, how many pounds of potatoes will she purchase? What if she only had $2 to spend? **LO1**

2. Pham can work as many or as few hours as she wants at the college bookstore for $9 per hour. But due to her hectic schedule, she has just 15 hours per week that she can spend working at either the bookstore or at other potential jobs. One potential job, at a café, will pay her $12 per hour for up to 6 hours per week. She has another job offer at a garage that will pay her $10 an hour for up to 5 hours per week. And she has a potential job at a day care center that will pay her $8.50 per hour for as many hours as she can work. If her goal is to maximize the amount of money she can make each week, how many hours will she work at the bookstore? **LO1**

3. Suppose you won $15 on a lotto ticket at the local 7-Eleven and decided to spend all the winnings on candy bars and bags of peanuts. The price of candy bars is $.75 and the price of peanuts is $1.50. **LO4**
   a. Construct a table showing the alternative combinations of the two products that are available.
   b. Plot the data in your table as a budget line in a graph. What is the slope of the budget line? What is the opportunity cost of one more candy bar? Of one more bag of peanuts? Do these opportunity costs rise, fall, or remain constant as each additional unit of the product is purchased?
   c. How, in general, would you decide which of the available combinations of candy bars and bags of peanuts to buy?
   d. Suppose that you had won $30 on your ticket, not $15. Show the $30 budget line in your diagram. Why would this budget line be preferable to the old one?

4. Suppose that you are on a desert island and possess exactly 20 coconuts. Your neighbor, Friday, is a fisherman, and he is willing to trade 2 fish for every 1 coconut that you are willing to give him. Another neighbor, Kwame, is also a fisherman, and he is willing to trade 3 fish for every 1 coconut. **LO4**
   a. On a single figure, draw budget lines for trading with Friday and for trading with Kwame. (Put coconuts on the vertical axis.)
   b. What is the slope of the budget line from trading with Friday?
   c. What is the slope of the budget line from trading with Kwame?

d. Which budget line features a larger set of attainable combinations of coconuts and fish?

e. If you are going to trade coconuts for fish, would you rather trade with Friday or Kwame?

5. Below is a production possibilities table for consumer goods (automobiles) and capital goods (forklifts): **LO5**

Type of Production	Production Alternatives				
	A	B	C	D	E
Automobiles	0	2	4	6	8
Forklifts	30	27	21	12	0

a. Show these data graphically. Upon what specific assumptions is this production possibilities curve based?

b. If the economy is at point *C*, what is the cost of two more automobiles? Of six more forklifts? Explain how the production possibilities curve reflects the law of increasing opportunity costs.

c. If the economy characterized by this production possibilities table and curve were producing 3 automobiles and 20 forklifts, what could you conclude about its use of its available resources?

d. What would production at a point outside the production possibilities curve indicate? What must occur before the economy can attain such a level of production?

6. Referring to the table in problem 5, suppose improvement occurs in the technology of producing forklifts but not in the technology of producing automobiles. Draw the new production possibilities curve. Now assume that a technological advance occurs in producing automobiles but not in producing forklifts. Draw the new production possibilities curve. Now draw a production possibilities curve that reflects technological improvement in the production of both goods. **LO5**

7. On average, households in China save 40 percent of their annual income each year, whereas households in the United States save less than 5 percent. Production possibilities are growing at roughly 9 percent annually in China and 3.5 percent in the United States. Use graphical analysis of "present goods" versus "future goods" to explain the differences in growth rates. **LO5**

Chapter One Appendix

Graphs and Their Meaning

If you glance quickly through this text, you will find many graphs. These graphs are included to help you visualize and understand economic relationships. Most of our principles or models explain relationships between just two sets of economic data, which can be conveniently represented with two-dimensional graphs.

Construction of a Graph

A graph is a visual representation of the relationship between two variables. The table in Figure 1 is a hypothetical illustration showing the relationship between income and consumption for the economy as a whole. Because people tend to buy more goods and services when their incomes go up, it is not surprising to find in the table that total consumption in the economy increases as total income increases.

The information in the table is also expressed graphically in Figure 1. Here is how it is done: We want to show visually or graphically how consumption changes as income changes. Since income is the determining factor, we follow mathematical custom and represent it on the horizontal axis of the graph. And because consumption depends on income, it is represented on the vertical axis of the graph.

The vertical and horizontal scales of the graph reflect the ranges of values of consumption and income, marked in convenient increments. As you can see, the values on the scales cover all the values in the table.

Because the graph has two dimensions, each point within it represents an income value and its associated consumption value. To find a point that represents one of the five income-consumption combinations in the table, we draw lines from the appropriate values on the vertical and horizontal axes. For example, to plot point *c* (the $200 income–$150 consumption point), lines are drawn up from the horizontal (income) axis at $200 and across from the vertical (consumption) axis at $150. These lines intersect at point *c*, which represents this particular income-consumption combination. You should verify that the other income-consumption combinations shown in the table in Figure 1 are properly located in the graph that is there.

Finally, by assuming that the same general relationship between income and consumption prevails for all other incomes, we draw a line or smooth curve to connect these points. That line or curve represents the income-consumption relationship.

If the graph is a straight line, as in Figure 1, the relationship is said to be *linear*.

Direct and Inverse Relationships

The line in Figure 1 slopes upward to the right, so it depicts a **direct relationship** between income and consumption. A direct relationship, or positive relationship, means that two variables (here, consumption and income) change in the same direction. An increase in consumption is associated with an increase in income; a decrease in consumption accompanies a decrease in income. When two sets of data are positively or directly related, they always graph as an upsloping line, as in Figure 1.

direct relationship The (positive) relationship between two variables that change in the same direction.

FIGURE 1 **Graphing the direct relationship between consumption and income.** Two sets of data that are positively or directly related, such as consumption and income, graph as an upsloping line.

Income per Week	Consumption per Week	Point
$ 0	$ 50	a
100	100	b
200	150	c
300	200	d
400	250	e

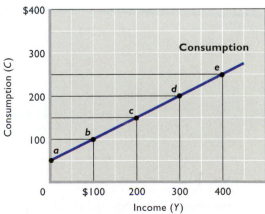

FIGURE 2 **Graphing the inverse relationship between ticket prices and game attendance.** Two sets of data that are negatively or inversely related, such as ticket price and the attendance at basketball games, graph as a downsloping line.

Ticket Price	Attendance, Thousands	Point
$50	0	a
40	4	b
30	8	c
20	12	d
10	16	e
0	20	f

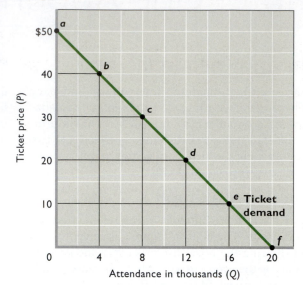

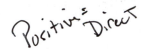
Positive
Direct

In contrast, two sets of data may be inversely related. Consider the table in Figure 2, which shows the relationship between the price of basketball tickets and game attendance for Big Time University (BTU). Here there is an **inverse relationship,** or negative relationship, because the two variables change in opposite directions. When ticket prices for the games decrease, attendance increases. When ticket prices increase, attendance decreases. The six data points in the table are plotted in the graph in Figure 2. This inverse relationship graphs as a downsloping line.

inverse relationship The (negative) relationship between two variables that change in opposite directions.

Dependent and Independent Variables

Economists seek to determine which variable is the "cause" and which the "effect." Or, more formally, they seek the independent variable and the dependent variable. The **independent variable** is the cause or source; it is the variable that changes first. The **dependent variable** is the effect or outcome; it is the variable that changes because of the change in the independent variable. As in our income-consumption example, income generally is the independent variable and consumption the dependent variable. Income causes consumption to be what it is rather than the other way around. Similarly, ticket prices (set in

independent variable The variable causing a change in some other (dependent) variable; the "causal variable."

dependent variable The variable that changes as a result of a change in some other (independent) variable; the "outcome variable."

advance of the season and printed on the ticket) determine attendance at BTU basketball games; attendance at games does not determine the printed ticket prices for those games. Ticket price is the independent variable, and the quantity of tickets purchased is the dependent variable.

Mathematicians always put the independent variable (cause) on the horizontal axis and the dependent variable (effect) on the vertical axis. Economists are less tidy; their graphing of independent and dependent variables is more arbitrary. Their conventional graphing of the income-consumption relationship is consistent with mathematical convention, but economists historically put price and cost data on the vertical axis of their graphs. Contemporary economists have followed the tradition. So economists' graphing of BTU's ticket price–attendance data differs from normal mathematical procedure. This does not present a problem, but we want you to be aware of this fact to avoid any possible confusion.

Other Things Equal

Our simple two-variable graphs purposely ignore many other factors that might affect the amount of consumption occurring at each income level or the number of people who attend BTU basketball games at each possible ticket price. When economists plot the relationship between any two variables, they employ the *ceteris paribus* (other-things-equal) assumption. Thus, in Figure 1 all factors other than income that might affect the amount of consumption are presumed to be constant or unchanged. Similarly, in Figure 2 all factors other than ticket price that might influence attendance at BTU basketball games are assumed constant. In reality, "other things" are not equal; they often change, and when they do, the relationship represented in our two tables and graphs will change. Specifically, the lines we have plotted would *shift* to new locations.

Consider a stock market "crash." The dramatic drop in the value of stocks might cause people to feel less wealthy and therefore less willing to consume at each level of income. The result might be a downward shift of the consumption line. To see this, you should plot a new consumption line in Figure 1, assuming that consumption is, say, $20 less at each income level. Note that the relationship remains direct; the line merely shifts downward to reflect less consumption spending at each income level.

Similarly, factors other than ticket prices might affect BTU game attendance. If BTU loses most of its games, attendance at BTU games might be less at each ticket price. To see this, redraw Figure 2, assuming that 2000 fewer fans attend BTU games at each ticket price.

Slope of a Line

Lines can be described in terms of their slopes. The **slope of a straight line** is the ratio of the vertical change (the rise or drop) to the horizontal change (the run) between any two points of the line.

slope (of a straight line) The ratio of the vertical change (the rise or fall) to the horizontal change (the run) between any two points on a line.

Positive Slope Between point *b* and point *c* in the graph in Figure 1, the rise or vertical change (the change in consumption) is +$50 and the run or horizontal change (the change in income) is +$100. Therefore:

$$\text{Slope} = \frac{\text{vertical change}}{\text{horizontal change}} = \frac{+50}{+100} = \frac{1}{2} = .5$$

Note that our slope of $\frac{1}{2}$ or .5 is positive because consumption and income change in the same direction; that is, consumption and income are directly or positively related.

Negative Slope Between any two of the identified points in the graph of Figure 2, say, point *c* and point *d*, the vertical change is −10 (the drop) and the horizontal change is +4 (the run). Therefore:

$$\text{Slope} = \frac{\text{vertical change}}{\text{horizontal change}} = \frac{-10}{+4} = -2\frac{1}{2} = -2.5$$

This slope is negative because ticket price and attendance have an inverse relationship.

Slopes and Marginal Analysis Economists are largely concerned with changes in values. The concept of slope is important in economics because it reflects marginal changes—those involving 1 more (or 1 fewer) unit. For example, in Figure 1 the .5 slope shows that $.50 of extra or marginal consumption is associated with each $1 change in income. In this example, people collectively will consume $.50 of any $1 increase in their incomes and reduce their consumption by $.50 for each $1 decline in income. Careful inspection of Figure 2 reveals that every $1 increase in ticket price for BTU games will decrease game attendance by 400 people and every $1 decrease in ticket price will increase game attendance by 400 people.

Infinite and Zero Slopes Many variables are unrelated or independent of one another. For example, the quantity of wristwatches purchased is not related to the price of bananas. In Figure 3a the price of bananas is measured on the vertical axis and the quantity of watches demanded on the horizontal axis. The graph of their relationship is the line parallel to the vertical axis, indicating that the same quantity of watches is

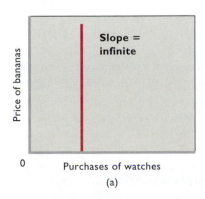

(a)

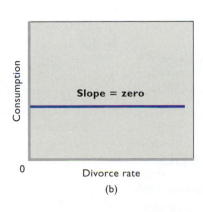

(b)

FIGURE 3 Infinite and zero slopes. (a) A line parallel to the vertical axis has an infinite slope. Here, purchases of watches remain the same no matter what happens to the price of bananas. (b) A line parallel to the horizontal axis has a slope of zero. In this case, total consumption remains the same no matter what happens to the divorce rate. In both (a) and (b), the two variables are totally unrelated to one another.

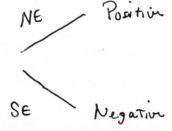

purchased no matter what the price of bananas. The slope of such a line is infinite.

Similarly, aggregate consumption is completely unrelated to the nation's divorce rate. In Figure 3b we put consumption on the vertical axis and the divorce rate on the horizontal axis. The line parallel to the horizontal axis represents this lack of relatedness. This line has a slope of zero.

Slope of a Nonlinear Curve We now move from the simple world of linear relationships (straight lines) to the somewhat more complex world of nonlinear relationships. The slope of a straight line is the same at all its points. The slope of a line representing a nonlinear relationship changes from one point to another. Such lines are always referred to as *curves*.

Consider the downsloping curve in Figure 4. Its slope is negative throughout, but the curve flattens as we move down along it. Thus, its slope constantly changes; the curve has a different slope at each point.

To measure the slope at a specific point, we draw a straight line tangent to the curve at that point. A line is tangent at a point if it touches, but does not intersect, the curve at that point. So line *aa* is tangent to the curve in Figure 4 at point *A*. The slope of the curve at that point is equal to the slope of the tangent line. Specifically, the total vertical change (drop) in the tangent line *aa* is −20 and the total horizontal change (run) is +5. Because the slope of the tangent line *aa* is −20/+5, or −4, the slope of the curve at point *A* is also −4.

FIGURE 4   Determining the slopes of curves. The slope of a nonlinear curve changes from point to point on the curve. The slope at any point (say, B) can be determined by drawing a straight line that is tangent to that point (line bb) and calculating the slope of that line.

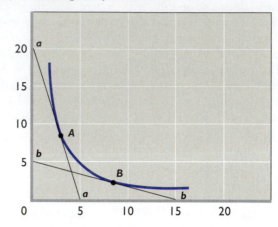

Line *bb* in Figure 4 is tangent to the curve at point *B*. Using the same procedure, we find the slope at *B* to be −5/+15, or −$\frac{1}{3}$. Thus, in this flatter part of the curve, the slope is less negative.

Several of the Appendix questions are of a "workbook" variety, and we urge you to go through them carefully to check your understanding of graphs and slopes.

Appendix Summary

1. Graphs are a convenient and revealing way to represent economic relationships.

2. Two variables are positively or directly related when their values change in the same direction. The line (curve) representing two directly related variables slopes upward.

3. Two variables are negatively or inversely related when their values change in opposite directions. The curve representing two inversely related variables slopes downward.

4. The value of the dependent variable (the "effect") is determined by the value of the independent variable (the "cause").

5. When the "other factors" that might affect a two-variable relationship are allowed to change, the graph of the relationship will likely shift to a new location.

6. The slope of a straight line is the ratio of the vertical change to the horizontal change between any two points. The slope of an upsloping line is positive; the slope of a downsloping line is negative.

7. The slope of a line or curve is especially relevant for economics because it measures marginal changes.

8. The slope of a horizontal line is zero; the slope of a vertical line is infinite.

9. The slope of a curve at any point is determined by calculating the slope of a straight line tangent to the curve at that point.

Appendix Terms and Concepts

direct relationship

inverse relationship

independent variable

dependent variable

slope of a straight line

Appendix Questions

1. Briefly explain the use of graphs as a way to represent economic relationships. What is an inverse relationship? How does it graph? What is a direct relationship? How does it graph? **LO6**
2. Describe the graphical relationship between ticket prices and the number of people choosing to visit amusement parks. Is that relationship consistent with the fact that, historically, park attendance and ticket prices have both risen? Explain. **LO6**
3. Look back at Figure 2, which shows the inverse relationship between ticket prices and game attendance at Big Time University. (a) Interpret the meaning of the slope. (b) If the slope of the line were steeper, what would that say about the amount by which ticket sales respond to increases in ticket prices? **LO6**

Appendix Problems

1. Graph and label as either direct or indirect the relationships you would expect to find between (a) the number of inches of rainfall per month and the sale of umbrellas, (b) the amount of tuition and the level of enrollment at a university, and (c) the popularity of an entertainer and the price of her concert tickets. **LO6**
2. Indicate how each of the following might affect the data shown in the table and graph in Figure 2 of this appendix: **LO6**
   a. BTU's athletic director hires away the coach from a perennial champion.
   b. An NBA team locates in the city where BTU plays.
   c. BTU contracts to have all its home games televised.
3. The following table contains data on the relationship between saving and income. Rearrange these data into a meaningful order and graph them on the accompanying grid. What is the slope of the line? What would you predict saving to be at the $12,500 level of income? **LO6**

Income per Year	Saving per Year
$15,000	$1,000
0	−500
10,000	500
5,000	0
20,000	1,500

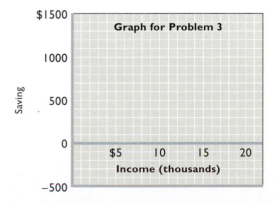

4. Construct a table from the data shown on the graph below. Which is the dependent variable and which the independent variable? **LO6**

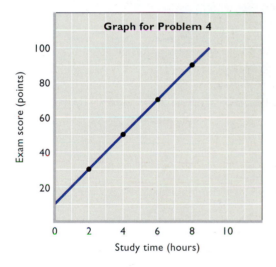

5. Suppose that when the price of gold is $100 an ounce, gold producers find it unprofitable to sell gold. However, when the price is $200 an ounce, 5000 ounces of output (production) is profitable. At $300, a total of 10,000 ounces of output is profitable. Similarly, total production increases by 5000 ounces for each successive $100 increase in the price of gold. Describe the relevant relationship between the price of gold and the production of gold in a table and on a graph. Put the price of gold on the vertical axis and the output of gold on the horizontal axis. **LO6**

6. The accompanying graph shows curve *XX′* and tangents to the curve at points *A*, *B*, and *C*. Calculate the slope of the curve at each of these three points. **LO6**

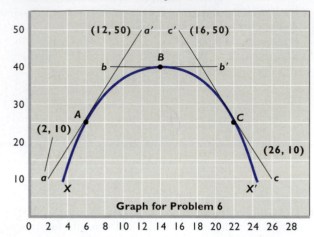

Graph for Problem 6

7. In the accompanying graph, is the slope of curve *AA′* positive or negative? Does the slope increase or decrease as we move along the curve from *A* to *A′*? Answer the same two questions for curve *BB′*. **LO6**

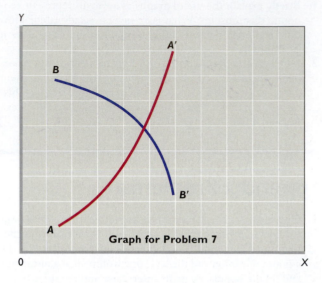

Graph for Problem 7

After reading this chapter, you should be able to:

1 Differentiate between a command system and a market system.

2 List the main characteristics of the market system.

3 Explain how the market system answers the four fundamental questions.

4 Discuss how the market system adjusts to change and promotes progress.

5 Describe the mechanics of the circular flow model.

The Market System and the Circular Flow

You are at the mall. Suppose you were assigned to compile a list of all the individual goods and services there, including the different brands and variations of each type of product. That task would be daunting and the list would be long! And even though a single shopping mall contains a remarkable quantity and variety of goods, it is only a tiny part of the national economy.

Who decided that the particular goods and services available at the mall and in the broader economy should be produced? How did the producers determine which technology and types of resources to use in producing these particular goods? Who will obtain these products? What accounts for the new and improved products among these goods? This chapter will answer these questions.

Societies Decide

Economic Systems

Every society needs to develop an **economic system**—a particular set of institutional arrangements and a coordinating mechanism—to respond to the economic problem. The economic system has to determine what goods are produced, how they are produced, who gets them, and how to promote technological progress.

Economic systems differ as to (1) who owns the factors of production and (2) the method used to motivate, coordinate, and direct economic activity. There are two general types of economic systems: the command system and the market system.

The Command System — Communists

The **command system** is also known as *socialism* or *communism*. In a command system, government owns most property resources and economic decision making occurs through a central economic plan. A central planning board appointed by the government makes nearly all the major decisions concerning the use of resources, the composition and distribution of output, and the organization of production. The government owns most of the business firms, which produce according to government directives. The central planning board determines production goals for each enterprise and specifies the amount of resources to be allocated to each enterprise so that it can reach its production goals. The division of output between capital and consumer goods is centrally decided, and capital goods are allocated among industries on the basis of the central planning board's long-term priorities.

A pure command economy would rely exclusively on a central plan to allocate the government-owned property resources. But, in reality, even the preeminent command economy—the Soviet Union—tolerated some private ownership and incorporated some markets before its collapse in 1992. Recent reforms in Russia and most of the eastern European nations have to one degree or another transformed their command economies to capitalistic, market-oriented systems. China's reforms have not gone as far, but they have greatly reduced the reliance on central planning. Although there is still extensive government ownership of resources and capital in China, the nation has increasingly relied on free markets to organize and coordinate its economy. North Korea and Cuba are the last remaining examples of largely centrally planned economies. Global Snapshot 2.1 reveals how North Korea's centrally planned economy compares to the market economy of its neighbor, South Korea. Later in this chapter, we will explore the main reasons for the general demise of the command systems.

The Market System — US

The polar alternative to the command system is the **market system,** or *capitalism*. The system is characterized by the private ownership of resources and the use of markets and prices to coordinate and direct economic activity. Participants act in their own self-interest. Individuals and businesses seek to achieve their economic goals through their own decisions regarding work, consumption, or production. The system allows for the private ownership of capital, communicates through prices, and coordinates economic activity through *markets*—places where buyers and sellers come together to buy and sell goods, services, and resources. Goods and services are produced and resources are supplied by whoever is willing and able to do so. The result is competition among independently acting buyers and sellers of each product and resource. Thus, economic decision making is widely dispersed. Also, the high potential monetary rewards create powerful incentives for existing firms to innovate and entrepreneurs to pioneer new products and processes.

GLOBAL SNAPSHOT 2.1

The Two Koreas

North Korea is one of the few command economies still standing. After the Second World War, Korea was divided into North Korea and South Korea. North Korea, under the influence of the Soviet Union, established a command economy that emphasized government ownership and central government planning. South Korea, protected by the United States, established a market economy based upon private ownership and the profit motive. Today, the differences in the economic outcomes of the two systems are striking:

	North Korea	South Korea
GDP	$40 billion*	$1.3 trillion*
GDP per capita	$1800*	$27,700*
Exports	$2.0 billion	$355 billion
Imports	$3.5 billion	$313 billion
Agriculture as % of GDP	23 percent	3 percent

*Based on purchasing power equivalencies to the U.S. dollar.
Source: CIA World Fact Book, 2010, **www.cia.gov**.

In *pure* capitalism—or *laissez-faire* capitalism—government's role would be limited to protecting private property and establishing an environment appropriate to the operation of the market system. The term "laissez-faire" means "let it be," that is, keep government from interfering with the economy. The idea is that such interference will disturb the efficient working of the market system.

But in the capitalism practiced in the United States and most other countries, government plays a substantial role in the economy. It not only provides the rules for economic activity but also promotes economic stability and growth, provides certain goods and services that would otherwise be underproduced or not produced at all, and modifies the distribution of income. The government, however, is not the dominant economic force in deciding what to produce, how to produce it, and who will get it. That force is the market.

Characteristics of the Market System

It will be very instructive to examine some of the key features of the market system in more detail.

Private Property

In a market system, private individuals and firms, not the government, own most of the property resources (land and capital). It is this extensive private ownership of capital that gives capitalism its name. This right of **private property,** coupled with the freedom to negotiate binding legal contracts, enables individuals and businesses to obtain, use, and dispose of property resources as they see fit. The right of property owners to designate who will receive their property when they die sustains the institution of private property.

The most important consequence of property rights is that they encourage people to cooperate by helping to ensure that only *mutually agreeable* economic transactions

private property
The right of persons and firms to obtain, own, control, employ, dispose of, and bequeath land, capital, and other property.

take place. In a world without legally enforceable property rights, the strong could simply take whatever they wanted from the weak without giving them any compensation. But in a world of legally enforceable property rights, any person wanting something from you has to get you to agree to give it to them. And you can say no. The result is that if that person really wants what you have, she must offer you something that you value more highly in return. That is, she must offer you a mutually agreeable economic transaction—one that benefits you as well as her.

Property rights also encourage investment, innovation, exchange, maintenance of property, and economic growth. Why would anyone stock a store, build a factory, or clear land for farming if someone else, or the government itself, could take that property for his or her own benefit?

Property rights also extend to intellectual property through patents, copyrights, and trademarks. Such long-term protection encourages people to write books, music, and computer programs and to invent new products and production processes without fear that others will steal them and the rewards they may bring.

Moreover, property rights facilitate exchange. The title to an automobile or the deed to a cattle ranch assures the buyer that the seller is the legitimate owner. Also, property rights encourage owners to maintain or improve their property so as to preserve or increase its value. Finally, property rights enable people to use their time and resources to produce more goods and services, rather than using them to protect and retain the property they have already produced or acquired.

Freedom of Enterprise and Choice

Closely related to private ownership of property is freedom of enterprise and choice. The market system requires that various economic units make certain choices, which are expressed and implemented in the economy's markets:

freedom of enterprise
The freedom of firms to obtain economic resources, to use those resources to produce products of the firms' own choosing, and to sell their products in markets of their choice.

- **Freedom of enterprise** ensures that entrepreneurs and private businesses are free to obtain and use economic resources to produce their choice of goods and services and to sell them in their chosen markets.
- **Freedom of choice** enables owners to employ or dispose of their property and money as they see fit. It also allows workers to enter any line of work for which they are qualified. Finally, it ensures that consumers are free to buy the goods and services that best satisfy their wants.

freedom of choice
The freedom of owners of resources to employ or dispose of their resources as they see fit, and the freedom of consumers to spend their incomes in a manner they think is appropriate.

These choices are free only within broad legal limitations, of course. Illegal choices such as selling human organs or buying illicit drugs are punished through fines and imprisonment. (Global Snapshot 2.2 reveals that the degree of economic freedom varies greatly from nation to nation.)

Self-Interest — most advantageous outcome viewed by each firm.

self-interest
The most-advantageous outcome as viewed by each firm, property owner, worker, or consumer.

In the market system, **self-interest** is the motivating force of the various economic units as they express their free choices. Self-interest simply means that each economic unit tries to achieve its own particular goal, which usually requires delivering something of value to others. Entrepreneurs try to maximize profit or minimize loss. Property owners try to get the highest price for the sale or rent of their resources. Workers try to maximize their utility (satisfaction) by finding jobs that offer the best combination of wages, hours, fringe benefits, and working conditions. Consumers try to obtain the products they want at the lowest possible price and apportion their expenditures to maximize their utility. The motive of self-interest gives direction and consistency to what might otherwise be a chaotic economy.

GLOBAL SNAPSHOT 2.2

Index of Economic Freedom, Selected Economies

The Index of Economic Freedom measures economic freedom using 10 broad categories such as trade policy, property rights, and government intervention, with each category containing more than 50 specific criteria. The index then ranks 183 economies according to their degree of economic freedom. A few selected rankings for 2011 are listed below.

FREE

| 1 Hong Kong |
| 3 Australia |
| 5 Switzerland |

MOSTLY FREE

| 9 United States |
| 20 Japan |
| 28 Czech Republic |

MOSTLY UNFREE

| 111 Nigeria |
| 139 Vietnam |
| 143 Russia |

REPRESSED

| 171 Iran |
| 174 Burma |
| 179 North Korea |

Source: The Heritage Foundation, **www.heritage.org**.

Competition

The market system depends on **competition** among economic units. The basis of this competition is freedom of choice exercised in pursuit of a monetary return. Very broadly defined, competition requires:

- Independently acting sellers and buyers operating in a particular product or resource market.
- Freedom of sellers and buyers to enter or leave markets, on the basis of their economic self-interest.

Competition diffuses economic power within the businesses and households that make up the economy. When there are independently acting sellers and buyers in a market, no one buyer or seller is able to dictate the price of the product or resource because others can undercut that price.

Competition also implies that producers can enter or leave an industry; there are no insurmountable barriers to an industry's expanding or contracting. This freedom of an industry to expand or contract provides the economy with the flexibility needed to remain efficient over time. Freedom of entry and exit enables the economy to adjust to changes in consumer tastes, technology, and resource availability.

competition
The presence in a market of independent buyers and sellers vying with one another, and the freedom of buyers and sellers to enter and leave the market.

ORIGIN OF THE IDEA

O 2.2
Self-interest

The diffusion of economic power inherent in competition limits the potential abuse of that power. A producer that charges more than the competitive market price will lose sales to other producers. An employer who pays less than the competitive market wage rate will lose workers to other employers. A firm that fails to exploit new technology will lose profits to firms that do. And a firm that produces shoddy products will be punished as customers switch to higher-quality items made by rival firms. Competition is the basic regulatory force in the market system.

Markets and Prices

market
An institution or mechanism that brings buyers and sellers together.

Markets and prices are key components of the market system. They give the system its ability to coordinate millions of daily economic decisions. A **market** is an institution or mechanism that brings buyers ("demanders") and sellers ("suppliers") into contact. A market system conveys the decisions made by buyers and sellers of products and resources. The decisions made on each side of the market determine a set of product and resource prices that guide resource owners, entrepreneurs, and consumers as they make and revise their choices and pursue their self-interest.

Just as competition is the regulatory mechanism of the market system, the market system itself is the organizing mechanism. It is an elaborate communication network through which innumerable individual free choices are recorded, summarized, and balanced. Those who respond to market signals and heed market dictates are rewarded with greater profit and income; those who do not respond to those signals and choose to ignore market dictates are penalized. Through this mechanism society decides what the economy should produce, how production can be organized efficiently, and how the fruits of production are to be distributed among the various units that make up the economy.

Technology and Capital Goods

In the market system, competition, freedom of choice, self-interest, and personal reward provide the opportunity and motivation for technological advance. The monetary rewards for new products or production techniques accrue directly to the innovator. The market system therefore encourages extensive use and rapid development of complex capital goods: tools, machinery, large-scale factories, and facilities for storage, communication, transportation, and marketing.

Advanced technology and capital goods are important because the most direct methods of production are often the least efficient. The only way to avoid that inefficiency is to rely on capital goods. It would be ridiculous for a farmer to go at production with bare hands. There are huge benefits to be derived from creating and using such capital equipment as plows, tractors, storage bins, and so on. The more efficient production means much more abundant outputs.

Specialization

specialization
The use of resources of an individual, region, or nation to produce one or a few goods and services rather than the entire range of goods and services.

The extent to which market economies rely on **specialization** is extraordinary. Specialization is using the resources of an individual, region, or nation to produce one or a few goods or services rather than the entire range of goods and services. Those goods and services are then exchanged for a full range of desired products. The majority of consumers produce virtually none of the goods and services they consume, and they consume little or nothing of the items they produce. The person working nine to five installing windows in commercial aircraft may rarely fly. Many farmers sell their milk to the local dairy and then buy margarine at the local grocery store. Society learned long ago that self-sufficiency breeds inefficiency. The jack-of-all-trades may be a very colorful individual but is certainly not an efficient producer.

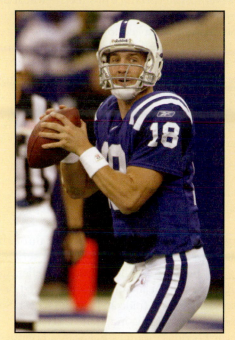

© Brent Smith/Reuters/Corbis © PRNewsFoto/Diamond information Center

PHOTO OP Peyton Manning and Beyoncé Knowles

It makes economic sense for Peyton Manning and Beyoncé Knowles to specialize in what they do best.

Division of Labor Human specialization—called the **division of labor**—contributes to a society's output in several ways:

- *Specialization makes use of differences in ability* Specialization enables individuals to take advantage of existing differences in their abilities and skills. If Peyton is strong, athletic, and good at throwing a football and Beyoncé is beautiful, agile, and can sing, their distribution of talents can be most efficiently used if Peyton plays professional football and Beyoncé records songs and gives concerts.
- *Specialization fosters learning by doing* Even if the abilities of two people are identical, specialization may still be advantageous. By devoting time to a single task rather than working at a number of different tasks, a person is more likely to develop the skills required and to improve techniques. You learn to be a good lawyer by studying and practicing law.
- *Specialization saves time* By devoting time to a single task, a person avoids the loss of time incurred in shifting from one job to another.

For all these reasons, specialization increases the total output society derives from limited resources.

Geographic Specialization Specialization also works on a regional and international basis. It is conceivable that oranges could be grown in Nebraska, but because of the unsuitability of the land, rainfall, and temperature, the costs would be very high. And it is conceivable that wheat could be grown in Florida, but such production would

division of labor
The separation of the work required to produce a product into a number of different tasks that are performed by different workers.

ORIGIN OF THE IDEA

O 2.3
Specialization: Division of labor

be costly for similar geographical reasons. So Nebraskans produce products—wheat in particular—for which their resources are best suited, and Floridians do the same, producing oranges and other citrus fruits. By specializing, both economies produce more than is needed locally. Then, very sensibly, Nebraskans and Floridians swap some of their surpluses—wheat for oranges, oranges for wheat.

Similarly, on an international scale, the United States specializes in producing such items as commercial aircraft and computers, which it sells abroad in exchange for video recorders from Japan, bananas from Honduras, and woven baskets from Thailand. Both human specialization and geographic specialization are needed to achieve efficiency in the use of limited resources.

Use of Money

A rather obvious characteristic of any economic system is the extensive use of money. Money performs several functions, but first and foremost it is a **medium of exchange**. It makes trade easier.

Specialization requires exchange. Exchange can, and sometimes does, occur through **barter**—swapping goods for goods, say, wheat for oranges. But barter poses serious problems because it requires a *coincidence of wants* between the buyer and the seller. In our example, we assumed that Nebraskans had excess wheat to trade and wanted oranges. And we assumed that Floridians had excess oranges to trade and wanted wheat. So an exchange occurred. But if such a coincidence of wants is missing, trade is stymied.

Suppose that Nebraska has no interest in Florida's oranges but wants potatoes from Idaho. And suppose that Idaho wants Florida's oranges but not Nebraska's wheat. And, to complicate matters, suppose that Florida wants some of Nebraska's wheat but none of Idaho's potatoes. We summarize the situation in Figure 2.1.

In none of the cases shown in the figure is there a coincidence of wants. Trade by barter clearly would be difficult. Instead, people in each state use **money**, which is simply a convenient social invention to facilitate exchanges of goods and services. Historically, people have used cattle, cigarettes, shells, stones, pieces of metal, and many other commodities, with varying degrees of success, as money. To serve as money, an item needs to pass only one test: It must be generally acceptable to sellers in exchange for their goods and services. Money is socially defined; whatever society accepts as a medium of exchange *is* money.

medium of exchange
Any item sellers generally accept and buyers generally use to pay for goods and services.

barter
The exchange of one good or service for another good or service.

money
Any item that is generally acceptable to sellers in exchange for goods and services.

FIGURE 2.1   Money facilitates trade when wants do not coincide. The use of money as a medium of exchange permits trade to be accomplished despite a noncoincidence of wants. (1) Nebraska trades the wheat that Florida wants for money from Floridians; (2) Nebraska trades the money it receives from Florida for the potatoes it wants from Idaho; (3) Idaho trades the money it receives from Nebraska for the oranges it wants from Florida.

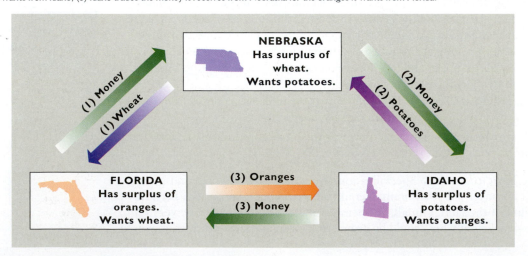

Today, most economies use pieces of paper as money. The use of paper dollars (currency) as a medium of exchange is what enables Nebraska, Florida, and Idaho to overcome their trade stalemate, as demonstrated in Figure 2.1.

On a global basis, specialization and exchange are complicated by the fact that different nations have different currencies. But markets in which currencies are bought and sold make it possible for people living in different countries to exchange goods and services without resorting to barter.

Active, but Limited, Government

An active, but limited, government is the final characteristic of market systems in real-life advanced industrial economies. Although a market system promotes a high degree of efficiency in the use of its resources, it has certain inherent shortcomings. We will discover in Chapter 5 that government can increase the overall effectiveness of the economic system in several ways.

Four Fundamental Questions

The key features of the market system help explain how market economies respond to four fundamental questions:

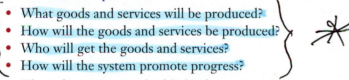

- What goods and services will be produced?
- How will the goods and services be produced?
- Who will get the goods and services?
- How will the system promote progress?

These four questions highlight the economic choices underlying the production possibilities curve discussed in Chapter 1. They reflect the reality of scarce resources in a world of unlimited wants. All economies, whether market or command, must address these four questions.

What Will Be Produced? Continuing Profit

How will a market system decide on the specific types and quantities of goods to be produced? The simple answer is this: The goods and services that can be produced at a continuing profit will be produced, while those whose production generates a continuing loss will be discontinued. Profits and losses are the difference between the total revenue (TR) a firm receives from the sale of its products and the total cost (TC) of producing those products. (For economists, total costs include not only wage and salary payments to labor, and interest and rental payments for capital and land, but also payments to the entrepreneur for organizing and combining the other resources to produce a product.)

Continuing economic profit (TR > TC) in an industry results in expanded production and the movement of resources toward that industry. The industry expands. Continuing losses (TC > TR) in an industry leads to reduced production and the exit of resources from that industry. The industry contracts.

In the market system, consumers are sovereign (in command). **Consumer sovereignty** is crucial in determining the types and quantities of goods produced. Consumers spend their income on the goods they are most willing and able to buy. Through these **"dollar votes"** they register their wants in the market. If the dollar votes for a certain product are great enough to create a profit, businesses will produce that product and offer it for sale. In contrast, if the dollar votes do not create sufficient revenues to cover costs, businesses will not produce the product. So the consumers are sovereign. They collectively direct resources to industries that are meeting consumer wants and away from industries that are not meeting consumer wants.

consumer sovereignty
Determination by consumers of the types and quantities of goods and services that will be produced with the economy's scarce resources.

dollar votes
The "votes" that consumers and entrepreneurs cast for the production of consumer and capital goods when they purchase them in product and resource markets.

McHits and McMisses

McDonald's has introduced several new menu items over the decades. Some have been profitable "hits," while others have been "misses." Ultimately, consumers decide whether a menu item is profitable and therefore whether it stays on the McDonald's menu.

- Hulaburger (1962)—McMiss
- Filet-O-Fish (1963)—McHit
- Strawberry shortcake (1966)—McMiss
- Big Mac (1968)—McHit
- Hot apple pie (1968)—McHit
- Egg McMuffin (1975)—McHit
- Drive-thru (1975)—McHit
- Chicken McNuggets (1983)—McHit
- Extra Value Meal (1991)—McHit
- McLean Deluxe (1991)—McMiss
- Arch Deluxe (1996)—McMiss
- 55-cent special (1997)—McMiss
- Big Xtra (1999)—McHit
- McSalad Shaker (2000)—McMiss
- McGriddle (2003)—McHit
- Snack Wrap (2006)—McHit

QUESTION: Do you think McDonald's premium salads will be a lasting McHit, or do you think they eventually will become a McMiss?

Source: Dyan Machan, "Polishing the Golden Arches," *Forbes,* June 15, 1998, pp. 42–43, updated. Used with permission of Forbes Media LLC © 2011.

The dollar votes of consumers determine not only which industries will continue to exist but also which products will survive or fail. Only profitable industries, firms, and products survive.

How Will the Goods and Services Be Produced?

What combinations of resources and technologies will be used to produce goods and services? How will the production be organized? The answer: In combinations and ways that minimize the cost per unit of output. This is true because inefficiency drives up costs and lowers profits. As a result, any firm wishing to maximize its profits will make great efforts to minimize production costs. These efforts will include using the right mix of labor and capital, given the prices and productivity of those resources. They also mean locating production facilities optimally to hold down production and transportation expenses. Finally, it means using the most appropriate technology in producing and distributing output.

Those efforts will be intensified if the firm faces competition, as consumers strongly prefer low prices and will shift their purchases over to the firms that can produce a quality product at the lowest possible price. Any firm foolish enough to use higher-cost production methods will go bankrupt as it is undersold by its more efficient competitors who can still make a profit when selling at a lower price. Simply stated: Competition eliminates high-cost producers.

Prices of goods & services

Who Will Get the Output?

The market system enters the picture in two ways when determining the distribution of total output. Generally, any product will be distributed to consumers on the basis of their ability and willingness to pay its existing market price. If the price of some product, say, a small sailboat, is $3000, then buyers who are willing and able to pay that price will "sail, sail away." Consumers who are unwilling or unable to pay the price will "sit on the dock of the bay."

The ability to pay the prices for sailboats and other products depends on the amount of income that consumers have, along with the prices of, and preferences for, various goods. If consumers have sufficient income and want to spend their money on a particular good, they can have it. And the amount of income they have depends on (1) the quantities of the property and human resources they supply and (2) the prices those resources command in the resource market. Resource prices (wages, interest, rent, profit) are key in determining the size of each household's income and therefore each household's ability to buy part of the economy's output.

If you can afford it, buy it.

How Will the System Promote Progress?

Society desires economic growth (greater output) and higher standards of living (greater output *per person*). How does the market system promote technological improvements and capital accumulation, both of which contribute to a higher standard of living for society?

Technological Advance   The market system provides a strong incentive for technological advance and enables better products and processes to supplant inferior ones. An entrepreneur or firm that introduces a popular new product will gain revenue and economic profit at the expense of rivals. Firms that are highly profitable one year may find they are in financial trouble just a few years later.

Technological advance also includes new and improved methods that reduce production or distribution costs. By passing part of its cost reduction on to the consumer through a lower product price, the firm can increase sales and obtain economic profit at the expense of rival firms.

Moreover, the market system promotes the *rapid spread* of technological advance throughout an industry. Rival firms must follow the lead of the most innovative firm or else suffer immediate losses and eventual failure. In some cases, the result is **creative destruction:** The creation of new products and production methods completely destroys the market positions of firms that are wedded to existing products and older ways of doing business. Example: The advent of compact discs largely demolished long-play vinyl records, and iPods and other digital technologies are now supplanting CDs.

creative destruction
The idea that the creation of new products and production methods may simultaneously destroy the market power of existing firms.

Capital Accumulation   Most technological advances require additional capital goods. The market system provides the resources necessary to produce additional capital through increased dollar votes for those goods. That is, the market system acknowledges dollar voting for capital goods as well as for consumer goods.

But who counts the dollar votes for capital goods? Answer: Entrepreneurs and business owners. As receivers of profit income, they often use part of that income to purchase capital goods. Doing so yields even greater profit income in the future if the technological innovation that required the additional capital goods is successful. Also, by paying interest or selling ownership shares, the entrepreneur and firm can attract some of the income of households to cast dollar votes for the production of more capital goods.

"invisible hand"
The tendency of firms and resource suppliers that are seeking to further their own self-interest in competitive markets to also promote the interest of society as a whole.

The "Invisible Hand"

In his 1776 book *The Wealth of Nations*, Adam Smith first noted that the operation of a market system creates a curious unity between private interests and social interests. Firms and resource suppliers, seeking to further their own self-interest and operating within the framework of a highly competitive market system, will simultaneously, as though guided by an **"invisible hand,"** promote the public or social interest. For example, we have seen that in a competitive environment, businesses seek to build new and improved products to increase profits. Those enhanced products increase society's well-being. Businesses also use the least costly combination of resources to produce a specific output because it is in their self-interest to do so. To act otherwise would be to forgo profit or even to risk business failure. But, at the same time, to use scarce resources in the least costly way is clearly in the social interest as well. It "frees up" resources to produce something else that society desires.

Self-interest, awakened and guided by the competitive market system, is what induces responses appropriate to the changes in society's wants. Businesses seeking to make higher profits and to avoid losses, and resource suppliers pursuing greater monetary rewards, negotiate changes in the allocation of resources and end up with the output that society wants. Competition controls or guides self-interest such that self-interest automatically and quite unintentionally furthers the best interest of society. The invisible hand ensures that when firms maximize their profits and resource suppliers maximize their incomes, these groups also help maximize society's output and income.

QUESTION: Are "doing good for others" and "doing well for oneself" conflicting ideas, according to Adam Smith?

The Demise of the Command Systems

Now that you know how the market system answers the four fundamental questions, you can easily understand why command systems of the Soviet Union, eastern Europe, and prereform China failed. Those systems encountered two insurmountable problems.

The first difficulty was the *coordination problem*. The central planners had to coordinate the millions of individual decisions by consumers, resource suppliers, and businesses. Consider the setting up of a factory to produce tractors. The central planners had to establish a realistic annual production target, for example, 1000 tractors. They then had to make available all the necessary inputs—labor, machinery, electric power, steel, tires, glass, paint, transportation—for the production and delivery of those 1000 tractors.

Because the outputs of many industries serve as inputs to other industries, the failure of any single industry to achieve its output target caused a chain reaction of repercussions. For example, if iron mines, for want of machinery or labor or transportation, did not supply the steel industry with the required inputs of iron ore, the steel mills were unable to fulfill the input needs of the many industries that depended on steel. Those steel-using industries (such as tractor, automobile, and transportation) were unable to fulfill their planned production goals. Eventually the chain reaction spread to all firms that used steel as an input and from there to other input buyers or final consumers.

The coordination problem became more difficult as the economies expanded. Products and production processes grew more sophisticated, and the number of industries requiring planning increased. Planning techniques that worked for the simpler economy proved highly inadequate and inefficient for the larger economy. Bottlenecks and production stoppages became the norm, not the exception.

A lack of a reliable success indicator added to the coordination problem in the Soviet Union and prereform China. We have seen that market economies rely on profit as a success indicator. Profit depends on consumer demand, production efficiency, and product quality. In contrast, the major success indicator for the command economies usually was a quantitative production target that the central planners assigned. Production costs, product quality, and product mix were secondary considerations. Managers and workers often sacrificed product quality because they were being awarded bonuses for meeting quantitative, not qualitative, targets. If meeting production goals meant sloppy assembly work, so be it.

It was difficult at best for planners to assign quantitative production targets without unintentionally producing distortions in output. If the production target for an enterprise manufacturing nails was specified in terms of *weight* (tons of nails), the producer made only large nails. But if its target was specified as a *quantity* (thousands of nails), the producer made all small nails, and lots of them!

The command economies also faced an *incentive problem*. Central planners determined the output mix. When they misjudged how many automobiles, shoes, shirts, and chickens were wanted at the government-determined prices, persistent shortages and surpluses of those products arose. But as long as the managers who oversaw the production of those goods were rewarded for meeting their assigned production goals, they had no incentive to adjust production in response to the shortages and surpluses. And there were no fluctuations in prices and profitability to signal that more or less of certain products was desired. Thus, many products were unavailable or in short supply, while other products were overproduced and sat for months or years in warehouses.

The command systems of the Soviet Union and prereform China also lacked entrepreneurship. Central planning did not trigger the profit motive, nor did it reward innovation and enterprise. The route for getting ahead was through participation in the political hierarchy of the Communist Party. Moving up the hierarchy meant better housing, better access to health care, and the right to shop in special stores. Meeting production targets and maneuvering through the minefields of party politics were measures of success in "business." But a definition of business success based solely on political savvy is not conducive to technological advance, which is often disruptive to existing products, production methods, and organizational structures.

QUESTION: In market economies, firms rarely worry about the availability of inputs to produce their products, whereas in command economies input availability was a constant concern. Why the difference?

FIGURE 2.2 **The circular flow diagram.** Products flow from businesses to households through the product market, and resources flow from households to businesses through the resource market. Opposite those real flows are monetary flows. Households receive income from businesses (their costs) through the resource market, and businesses receive revenue from households (their expenditures) through the product market.

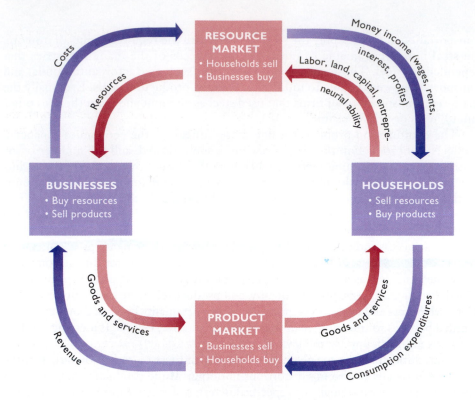

The Circular Flow Model

The dynamic market economy creates continuous, repetitive flows of goods and services, resources, and money. The **circular flow diagram,** shown in Figure 2.2, illustrates those flows for a simplified economy in which there is no government. Observe that in the diagram we group this economy's decision makers into *businesses* and *households*. Additionally, we divide this economy's markets into the *resource market* and the *product market*.

Households

circular flow diagram
The flow of resources from households to firms and of products from firms to households.

The blue rectangle on the right side of the circular flow diagram in Figure 2.2 represents **households,** which are defined as one or more persons occupying a housing unit. There are currently about 116 million households in the U.S. economy. Households buy the goods and services that businesses make available in the product market. Households obtain the income needed to buy those products by selling resources in the resource market.

households
One or more persons occupying a housing unit that provide resources to the economy and use income received to purchase goods and services that satisfy economic wants.

All the resources in our no-government economy are ultimately owned or provided by households. For instance, the members of one household or another directly provide all of the labor and entrepreneurial ability in the economy. Households also own all of the land and all of the capital in the economy either directly, as personal property, or indirectly, as a consequence of owning all of the businesses in the economy (and thereby controlling all of the land and capital owned by businesses). Thus, all of the income in the economy—all wages, rents, interest, and profits—flows to households because they provide the economy's labor, land, capital, and entrepreneurial ability.

Businesses

businesses
Firms that purchase resources and provide goods and services to the economy.

The blue rectangle on the left side of the circular flow diagram represents **businesses,** which are commercial establishments that attempt to earn profits for their owners by offering goods and services for sale. Businesses sell goods and services in the product market in order to obtain revenue, and they incur costs in the resource markets when they purchase the labor, land, capital, and entrepreneurial ability that they need to produce their respective goods and services.

Product Market

The red rectangle at the bottom of the diagram represents the **product market,** the place where goods and services produced by businesses are bought and sold. Households use the income they receive from the sale of resources to buy goods and services. The money that consumers spend on goods and services flows to businesses as revenue. Businesses compare those revenues to their costs in determining profitability and whether or not a particular good or service should continue to be produced.

Resource Market

Finally, the red rectangle at the top of the circular flow diagram represents the **resource market** in which households sell resources to businesses. The households sell resources to generate income, and the businesses buy resources to produce goods and services. The funds that businesses pay for resources are costs to businesses but are flows of wage, rent, interest, and profit income to the household. Productive resources therefore flow from households to businesses, and money flows from businesses to households.

The circular flow model depicts a complex, interrelated web of decision making and economic activity involving businesses and households. For the economy, it is the circle of life. Businesses and households are both buyers and sellers. Businesses buy resources and sell products. Households buy products and sell resources. As shown in Figure 2.2, there is a counterclockwise *real flow* of economic resources and finished goods and services and a clockwise *money flow* of income and consumption expenditures.

product market
A market in which goods and services (products) are sold by firms and bought by households.

resource market
A market in which households sell and firms buy economic resources.

ORIGIN OF THE IDEA

O 2.4

Circular flow diagram

©T. O'Keefe/PhotoLink/Getty Images

© Royalty Free/CORBIS

PHOTO OP   Resource Markets and Product Markets

The sale of a grove of orange trees would be a transaction in the resource market; the sale of oranges to final consumers would be a transaction in the product market.

Some Facts about U.S. Businesses

Businesses constitute one part of the private sector. The business population is extremely diverse, ranging from giant corporations such as Walmart, with 2010 sales of $405 billion and 2.1 million employees, to neighborhood specialty shops with one or two employees and sales of only $200 to $300 per day. There are three major legal forms of businesses: sole proprietorships, partnerships, and corporations.

A *sole proprietorship* is a business owned and operated by one person. Usually, the proprietor (the owner) personally supervises its operation. In a *partnership*, two or more individuals (the partners) agree to own and operate a business together.

A *corporation* is a legal creation that can acquire resources, own assets, produce and sell products, incur debts, extend credit, sue and be sued, and perform the functions of any other type of enterprise. A corporation sells stocks (ownership shares) to raise funds but is legally distinct and separate from the individual stockholders. The stockholders' legal and financial liability is limited to the loss of the value of their shares. Hired executives and managers operate corporations on a day-to-day basis.

Figure 2.3a shows how the business population is distributed among the three major legal forms. About 72% of firms are sole proprietorships, whereas only 18% are corporations. But as Figure 2.3b indicates, corporations account for 82% of total sales revenue (and therefore total output) in the United States. Virtually all the nation's largest business enterprises are corporations. Global Snapshot 2.3 lists the world's largest corporations.

QUESTION: Why do you think sole proprietorships and partnerships typically incorporate (become corporations) when they experience rapid and sizable increases in their production, sales, and profits?

FIGURE 2.3 **The business population and shares of total revenue.** (a) Sole proprietorships dominate the business population numerically, but (b) corporations dominate total sales revenue (total output). *Source:* U.S. Census Bureau, **www.census.gov**.

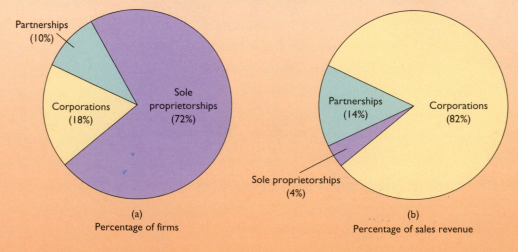

GLOBAL SNAPSHOT 2.3

The World's 10 Largest Corporations

Two of the world's ten largest corporations, based on dollar revenue in 2010, were headquartered in the United States. For the first time, China was home to the most, with three of the top ten.

Corporation	Revenue
Walmart (USA)	$408 billion
Royal Dutch Shell (Netherlands)	$285 billion
ExxonMobil (USA)	$285 billion
BP (Britain)	$246 billion
Toyota Motor (Japan)	$204 billion
Japan Post Holdings (Japan)	$202 billion
Sinopec (China)	$188 billion
State Grid (China)	$184 billion
AXA (France)	$175 billion
China National Petroleum (China)	$165 billion

Source: "Global 500," Fortune Magazine, July 26, 2010. © Time Inc., used under license.

Some Facts about U.S. Households

Households constitute the second part of the private sector. The U.S. economy currently has about 114 million households. These households consist of one or more persons occupying a housing unit and are both the ultimate suppliers of all economic resources *and* the major spenders in the economy.

The nation's earned income is apportioned among wages, rents, interest, and profits. *Wages* are paid to labor; *rents* and *interest* are paid to owners of property resources; and *profits* are paid to the owners of corporations and unincorporated businesses.

Figure 2.4a shows the categories of U.S. income earned in 2010. The largest source of income for households is the wages and salaries paid to workers. Notice that the bulk of total U.S. income goes to labor, not to capital. Proprietors' income—the income of doctors, lawyers, small-business owners, farmers, and owners of other unincorporated enterprises—also has a "wage" element. Some of this income is payment for one's own labor, and some of it is profit from one's own business.

The other three types of income are self-evident: Some households own corporate stock and receive dividend incomes as their share of corporate profits. Many households also own bonds and savings accounts that yield interest income. And some households receive rental income by providing buildings and natural resources (including land) to businesses and other individuals.

U.S. households use their income to buy (spend), save, and pay taxes. Figure 2.4b shows how households divide their spending among three broad categories of goods and services: *consumer durables* (goods such as cars, refrigerators, and personal computers that have expected lives of 3 years or longer), *nondurables* (goods such as food, clothing, and gasoline that have lives of less than 3 years), and *services* (the work done by people such as lawyers, physicians, and recreational workers). Observe that approximately 65% of consumer spending is on services. For this reason, the United States is known as a *service-oriented economy.*

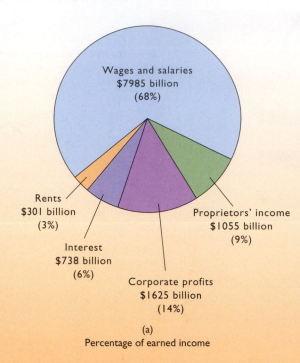

Wages and salaries
$7985 billion
(68%)

Rents
$301 billion
(3%)

Interest
$738 billion
(6%)

Corporate profits
$1625 billion
(14%)

Proprietors' income
$1055 billion
(9%)

(a)
Percentage of earned income

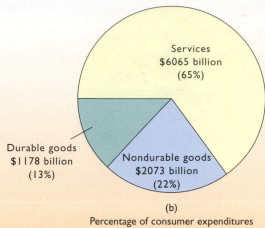

Services
$6065 billion
(65%)

Durable goods
$1178 billion
(13%)

Nondurable goods
$2073 billion
(22%)

(b)
Percentage of consumer expenditures

FIGURE 2.4 **Sources of U.S. income and the composition of spending.** (a) Sixty-eight percent of U.S. income is received as wages and salaries. Income to property owners—corporate profit, interest, and rents—accounts for about 23% of total income. (b) Consumers divide their spending among durable goods, nondurable goods, and services. Roughly 65% of consumer spending is for services; the rest is for goods. *Source:* Bureau of Economic Analysis, **www.bea.gov.**

Question: Over the past several decades, the service share of spending in the United States has increased relative to the goods share. Why do you think that trend has occurred?

© PRNewsFoto/Whirlpool Corporation

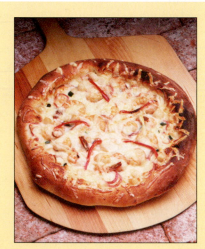

© Ed Carey/Cole Group/Getty Images

© Royalty-Free/CORBIS

PHOTO OP Durable Goods, Nondurable Goods, and Services

Consumers collectively spend their income on durable goods (such as the washer-dryer combo), nondurable goods (such as the pizza), and services (such as hair care).

Summary

1. The market system and the command system are the two broad types of economic systems used to address the economic problem. In the market system (or capitalism), private individuals own most resources, and markets coordinate most economic activity. In the command system (or socialism or communism), government owns most resources, and central planners coordinate most economic activity.

2. The market system is characterized by the private ownership of resources, including capital, and the freedom of individuals to engage in economic activities of their choice to advance their material well-being. Self-interest is the driving force of such an economy, and competition functions as a regulatory or control mechanism.

3. In the market system, markets, prices, and profits organize and make effective the many millions of individual economic decisions that occur daily.

4. Specialization, use of advanced technology, and the extensive use of capital goods are common features of market systems. Functioning as a medium of exchange, money eliminates the problems of bartering and permits easy trade and greater specialization, both domestically and internationally.

5. Every economy faces four fundamental questions: (a) What goods and services will be produced? (b) How will the goods and services be produced? (c) Who will get the goods and services? (d) How will the system promote progress?

6. The market system produces products whose production and sale yield total revenue sufficient to cover total cost. It does not produce products for which total revenue continuously falls short of total cost. Competition forces firms to use the lowest-cost production techniques.

7. Economic profit (total revenue minus total cost) indicates that an industry is prosperous and promotes its expansion. Losses signify that an industry is not prosperous and hasten its contraction.

8. Consumer sovereignty means that both businesses and resource suppliers are subject to the wants of consumers. Through their dollar votes, consumers decide on the composition of output.

9. The prices that a household receives for the resources it supplies to the economy determine that household's income. This income determines the household's claim on the economy's output. Those who have income to spend get the products produced in the market system.

10. The market system encourages technological advance and capital accumulation, both of which raise a nation's standard of living.

11. Competition, the primary mechanism of control in the market economy, promotes a unity of self-interest and social interests. As if directed by an invisible hand, competition harnesses the self-interested motives of businesses and resource suppliers to further the social interest.

12. The circular flow model illustrates the flows of resources and products from households to businesses and from businesses to households, along with the corresponding monetary flows. Businesses are on the buying side of the resource market and the selling side of the product market. Households are on the selling side of the resource market and the buying side of the product market.

Terms and Concepts

economic system	self-interest	barter	circular flow diagram
command system	competition	money	households
market system	market	consumer sovereignty	businesses
private property	specialization	dollar votes	product market
freedom of enterprise	division of labor	creative destruction	resource market
freedom of choice	medium of exchange	"invisible hand"	

Questions

1. Contrast how a market system and a command economy try to cope with economic scarcity. LO1

2. How does self-interest help achieve society's economic goals? Why is there such a wide variety of desired goods and services in a market system? In what way are entrepreneurs and businesses at the helm of the economy but commanded by consumers? LO2

3. Why is private property, and the protection of property rights, so critical to the success of the market system? How do property rights encourage cooperation? LO2

4. What are the advantages of using capital in the production process? What is meant by the term "division of labor"? What are the advantages of specialization in the use of human and material resources? Explain why exchange is the necessary consequence of specialization. LO2

5. What problem does barter entail? Indicate the economic significance of money as a medium of exchange. What is meant by the statement "We want money only to part with it"? LO2

6. Evaluate and explain the following statements: LO2
   a. The market system is a profit-and-loss system.

b. Competition is the disciplinarian of the market economy.

7. In the 1990s thousands of "dot-com" companies emerged with great fanfare to take advantage of the Internet and new information technologies. A few, like Google, eBay, and Amazon, have generally thrived and prospered, but many others struggled and eventually failed. Explain these varied outcomes in terms of how the market system answers the question "What goods and services will be produced?" **LO3**

8. Some large hardware stores such as Home Depot boast of carrying as many as 20,000 different products in each store. What motivated the producers of those individual products to make them and offer them for sale? How did the producers decide on the best combinations of resources to use? Who made those resources available, and why? Who decides whether these particular hardware products should continue to be produced and offered for sale? **LO3**

9. What is meant by the term "creative destruction"? How does the emergence of MP3 (or iPod) technology relate to this idea? **LO3**

10. In a sentence, describe the meaning of the phrase "invisible hand." **LO4**

11. Distinguish between the resource market and the product market in the circular flow model. In what way are businesses and households both sellers and buyers in this model? What are the flows in the circular flow model? **LO5**

12. What are the three major legal forms of business enterprises? Which form is the most prevalent in terms of numbers? Which form is dominant in terms of total sales revenues? **LO5**

13. What are the major forms of household income? Contrast the wage and salary share to the profit share in terms of relative size. Distinguish between a durable consumer good and a nondurable consumer good. How does the combined spending on both types of consumer goods compare to the spending on services? **LO5**

Problems

1. Suppose Natasha currently makes $50,000 per year working as a manager at a cable TV company. She then develops two possible entrepreneurial business opportunities. In one, she will quit her job to start an organic soap company. In the other, she will try to develop an Internet-based competitor to the local cable company. For the soap-making opportunity, she anticipates annual revenue of $465,000 and costs for the necessary land, labor, and capital of $395,000 per year. For the Internet opportunity, she anticipates costs for land, labor, and capital of $3,250,000 per year as compared to revenues of $3,275,000 per year. (a) Should she quit her current job to become an entrepreneur? (b) If she does quit her current job, which opportunity would she pursue? **LO3**

2. With current technology, suppose a firm is producing 400 loaves of banana bread daily. Also assume that the least-cost combination of resources in producing those loaves is 5 units of labor, 7 units of land, 2 units of capital, and 1 unit of entrepreneurial ability, selling at prices of $40, $60, $60, and $20, respectively. If the firm can sell these 400 loaves at $2 per unit, what is its total revenue? Its total cost? Its profit or loss? Will it continue to produce banana bread? If this firm's situation is typical for the other makers of banana bread, will resources flow toward or away from this bakery good? **LO3**

3. Let's put dollar amounts on the flows in the circular flow diagram of Figure 2.2. **LO5**

   a. Suppose that businesses buy a total of $100 billion of the four resources (labor, land, capital, and entrepreneurial ability) from households. If households receive $60 billion in wages, $10 billion in rent, and $20 billion in interest, how much are households paid for providing entrepreneurial ability?

   b. If households spend $55 billion on goods and $45 billion on services, how much in revenues do businesses receive in the product market?

FURTHER TEST YOUR KNOWLEDGE AT
www.mcconnellbrief2e.com

At the text's Online Learning Center, **www.mcconnellbrief2e.com**, you will find one or more web-based questions that require information from the Internet to answer. We urge you to check them out, since they will familiarize you with websites that may be helpful in other courses and perhaps even in your career. The OLC also features multiple-choice quizzes that give instant feedback and provides other helpful ways to further test your knowledge of the chapter.

Visit your mobile app store and download the McConnell Brief Edition: Study Econ app *today*!

PRICE, QUANTITY, AND EFFICIENCY

3

After reading this chapter, you should be able to:

1 Describe *demand* and explain how it can change.

2 Describe *supply* and explain how it can change.

3 Relate how supply and demand interact to determine market equilibrium.

4 Explain how changes in supply and demand affect equilibrium prices and quantities.

5 Identify what government-set prices are and how they can cause product surpluses and shortages.

Demand, Supply, and Market Equilibrium

The model of supply and demand is the economics profession's greatest contribution to human understanding because it explains the operation of the markets on which we depend for nearly everything that we eat, drink, or consume. The model is so powerful and so widely used that to many people it *is* economics.

Markets bring together buyers ("demanders") and sellers ("suppliers") and exist in many forms. The corner gas station, an e-commerce site, the local music store, a farmer's roadside stand—all are familiar markets. The New York Stock Exchange and the Chicago Board of Trade are markets where buyers and sellers of stocks and bonds and farm commodities from all over the world communicate with one another to buy and sell. Auctioneers bring together potential buyers and sellers of art, livestock, used farm equipment, and, sometimes, real estate.

Some markets are local, while others are national or international. Some are highly personal, involving face-to-face contact between demander and supplier; others are faceless, with buyer and seller never seeing or knowing each other. But all competitive markets involve demand and supply, and this chapter discusses how the model works to explain both the *quantities* that are bought and sold in markets as well as the *prices* at which they trade.

ORIGIN OF THE IDEA

O 3.1

Demand and supply

Demand

Demand is a schedule or a curve that shows the various amounts of a product that consumers will purchase at each of several possible prices during a specified period of time.[1] The table in Figure 3.1 is a hypothetical demand schedule for a *single consumer* purchasing a particular product, in this case, lattes. (For simplicity, we will categorize all espresso drinks as "lattes" and assume a highly competitive market.)

The table reveals that, if the price of lattes were $5 each, Joe Java would buy 10 lattes per month; if it were $4, he would buy 20 lattes per month; and so forth.

The table does not tell us which of the five possible prices will actually exist in the market. That depends on the interaction between demand and supply. Demand is simply a statement of a buyer's plans, or intentions, with respect to the purchase of a product.

To be meaningful, the quantities demanded at each price must relate to a specific period—a day, a week, a month. Here that period is 1 month.

demand
A schedule or curve that shows the various amounts of a product that consumers will buy at each of a series of possible prices during a specific period.

Law of Demand

A fundamental characteristic of demand is this: Other things equal, as price falls, the quantity demanded rises, and as price rises, the quantity demanded falls. In short, there

ORIGIN OF THE IDEA

O 3.2

Law of demand

---

[1]This definition obviously is worded to apply to product markets. To adjust it to apply to resource markets, substitute the word "resource" for "product" and the word "businesses" for "consumers."

FIGURE 3.1 Joe Java's demand for lattes. Because price and quantity demanded are inversely related, an individual's demand schedule graphs as a downsloping curve such as *D*. Other things equal, consumers will buy more of a product as its price declines and less of the product as its price rises. (Here and in later figures, *P* stands for price and *Q* stands for quantity demanded or supplied.)

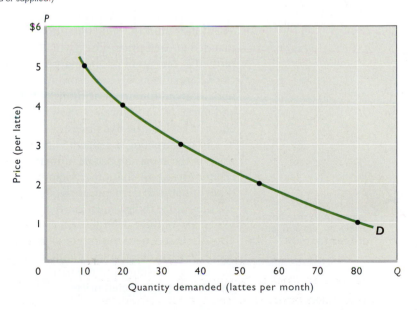

Joe Java's Demand for Lattes	
Price per Latte	**Quantity Demanded per Month**
$5	10
4	20
3	35
2	55
1	80

law of demand
The principle that, other things equal, as price falls, the quantity demanded rises, and as price rises, the quantity demanded falls.

is an *inverse* relationship between price and quantity demanded. Economists call this inverse relationship the **law of demand.**

The other-things-equal assumption is critical here. Many factors other than the price of the product being considered affect the amount purchased. The quantity of lattes purchased will depend not only on the price of lattes but also on the prices of such substitutes as tea, soda, fruit juice, and bottled water. The law of demand in this case says that fewer lattes will be purchased if the price of lattes rises while the prices of tea, soda, fruit juice, and bottled water all remain constant.

The law of demand is consistent with both common sense and observation. People ordinarily *do* buy more of a product at a low price than at a high price. Price is an obstacle that deters consumers from buying. The higher that obstacle, the less of a product they will buy; the lower the obstacle, the more they will buy. The fact that businesses reduce prices to clear out unsold goods is evidence of their belief in the law of demand.

The Demand Curve

The inverse relationship between price and quantity demanded for any product can be represented on a simple graph, in which, by convention, we measure *quantity demanded* on the horizontal axis and *price* on the vertical axis. In Figure 3.1 we have plotted the five price-quantity data points listed in the table and connected the points with a smooth curve, labeled *D*. This is a **demand curve.** Its downward slope reflects the law of demand: People buy more of a product, service, or resource as its price falls. They buy less as its price rises. There is an inverse relationship between price and quantity demanded.

demand curve
A curve illustrating the inverse relationship between the price of a product and the quantity of it demanded, other things equal.

The table and graph in Figure 3.1 contain exactly the same data and reflect the same inverse relationship between price and quantity demanded.

Market Demand

So far, we have concentrated on just one consumer, Joe Java. But competition requires that more than one buyer be present in each market. By adding the quantities demanded by all consumers at each of the various possible prices, we can get from *individual* demand to *market* demand. If there are just three buyers in the market (Joe Java, Sarah Coffee, and Mike Cappuccino), as represented by the table and graph in Figure 3.2, it is relatively easy to determine the total quantity demanded at each price. We simply sum the individual quantities demanded to obtain the total quantity demanded at each price. The particular price and the total quantity demanded are then plotted as one point on the market demand curve in Figure 3.2.

Competition, of course, ordinarily entails many more than three buyers of a product. To avoid hundreds or thousands of additions, let's simply suppose that the table and curve D_1 in Figure 3.3 show the amounts all the buyers in this market will purchase at each of the five prices.

In constructing a demand curve such as D_1 in Figure 3.3, economists assume that price is the most important influence on the amount of any product purchased. But economists know that other factors can and do affect purchases. These factors, called **determinants of demand,** are held constant when a demand curve like D_1 is drawn. They are the "other things equal" in the relationship between price and quantity demanded. When any of these determinants changes, the demand curve will shift to the right or left. For this reason, determinants of demand are sometimes referred to as *demand shifters*.

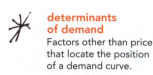

determinants of demand
Factors other than price that locate the position of a demand curve.

The basic determinants of demand are (1) consumers' tastes (preferences), (2) the number of consumers in the market, (3) consumers' incomes, (4) the prices of related goods, and (5) expected prices.

FIGURE 3.2 Market demand for lattes, three buyers. We establish the market demand curve D by adding horizontally the individual demand curves (D_1, D_2, and D_3) of all the consumers in the market. At the price of $3, for example, the three individual curves yield a total quantity demanded of 100 lattes.

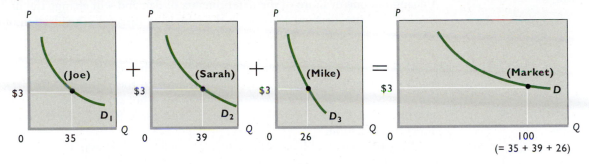

Market Demand for Lattes, Three Buyers

Price per Latte	Joe Java		Sarah Coffee		Mike Cappuccino		Total Quantity Demanded per Month
$5	10	+	12	+	8	=	30
4	20	+	23	+	17	=	60
3	35	+	39	+	26	=	100
2	55	+	60	+	39	=	154
1	80	+	87	+	54	=	221

FIGURE 3.3 Changes in the demand for lattes. A change in one or more of the determinants of demand causes a change in demand. An increase in demand is shown as a shift of the demand curve to the right, as from D_1 to D_2. A decrease in demand is shown as a shift of the demand curve to the left, as from D_1 to D_3. These changes in demand are to be distinguished from a change in *quantity demanded*, which is caused by a change in the price of the product, as shown by a movement from, say, point a to point b on fixed demand curve D_1.

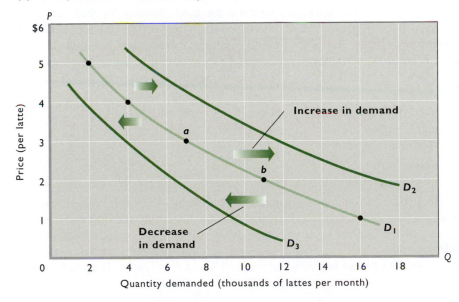

Market Demand for Lattes (D)	
(1)	**(2)**
Price per Latte	Total Quantity Demanded per Month
$5	2,000
4	4,000
3	7,000
2	11,000
1	16,000

Changes in Demand

A change in one or more of the determinants of demand will change the underlying demand data (the demand schedule in the table) and therefore the location of the demand curve in Figure 3.3. A change in the demand schedule or, graphically, a shift in the demand curve is called a *change in demand.*

If consumers desire to buy more lattes at each possible price, that *increase in demand* is shown as a shift of the demand curve to the right, say, from D_1 to D_2. Conversely, a *decrease in demand* occurs when consumers buy fewer lattes at each possible price. The leftward shift of the demand curve from D_1 to D_3 in Figure 3.3 shows that situation.

Now let's see how changes in each determinant affect demand.

Tastes   A favorable change in consumer tastes (preferences) for a product means more of it will be demanded at each price. Demand will increase; the demand curve will shift rightward. For example, greater concern about the environment has increased the demand for hybrid cars and other "green" technologies. An unfavorable change in consumer preferences will decrease demand, shifting the demand curve to the left. For example, the recent popularity of low-carbohydrate diets has reduced the demand for bread and pasta.

Number of Buyers   An increase in the number of buyers in a market increases product demand. For example, the rising number of older persons in the United States in recent years has increased the demand for motor homes and retirement communities. In contrast, the migration of people away from many small rural communities has reduced the demand for housing, home appliances, and auto repair in those towns.

Income   The effect of changes in income on demand is more complex. For most products, a rise in income increases demand. Consumers collectively buy more airplane tickets, projection TVs, and gas grills as their incomes rise. Products whose demand increases or decreases *directly* with changes in income are called *superior goods*, or **normal goods.**

Although most products are normal goods, there are a few exceptions. As incomes increase beyond some point, the demand for used clothing, retread tires, and soy-enhanced hamburger may decline. Higher incomes enable consumers to buy new clothing, new tires, and higher-quality meats. Goods whose demand increases or decreases *inversely* with money income are called **inferior goods.** (This is an economic term; we are not making personal judgments on specific products.)

Prices of Related Goods   A change in the price of a related good may either increase or decrease the demand for a product, depending on whether the related good is a substitute or a complement:

- A **substitute good** is one that can be used in place of another good.
- A **complementary good** is one that is used together with another good.

Beef and chicken are substitute goods or, simply, *substitutes*. When two products are substitutes, an increase in the price of one will increase the demand for the other. For example, when the price of beef rises, consumers will buy less beef and increase their demand for chicken. So it is with other product pairs such as Nikes and Reeboks, Budweiser and Miller beer, or Colgate and Crest toothpaste. They are *substitutes in consumption.*

normal good
A good (or service) whose consumption rises when income increases and falls when income decreases.

inferior good
A good (or service) whose consumption declines when income rises and rises when income decreases.

substitute good
A good (or service) that can be used in place of some other good (or service).

complementary good
A good (or service) that is used in conjunction with some other good (or service).

© Bambu Producoes/Getty Images © Doug Menuez/Getty Images

PHOTO OP   Normal versus Inferior Goods

New television sets are normal goods. People buy more of them as their incomes rise. Hand-pushed lawn mowers are inferior goods. As incomes rise, people purchase gas-powered mowers instead.

Complementary goods (or, simply, *complements*) are products that are used together and thus are typically demanded jointly. Examples include computers and software, cell phones and cellular service, and snowboards and lift tickets. If the price of a complement (for example, lettuce) goes up, the demand for the related good (salad dressing) will decline. Conversely, if the price of a complement (for example, tuition) falls, the demand for a related good (textbooks) will increase.

The vast majority of goods that are unrelated to one another are called *independent goods*. There is virtually no demand relationship between bacon and golf balls or pickles and ice cream. A change in the price of one will have virtually no effect on the demand for the other.

Expected Prices   Changes in expected prices may shift demand. A newly formed expectation of a higher price in the future may cause consumers to buy now in order to "beat" the anticipated price rise, thus increasing current demand. For example, when freezing weather destroys much of Brazil's coffee crop, buyers may conclude that the price of coffee beans will rise. They may purchase large quantities now to stock up on beans. In contrast, a newly formed expectation of falling prices may decrease current demand for products.

© Michael Newman/PhotoEdit

© John A. Rizzo/Getty Images

PHOTO OP Substitutes versus Complements

Different brands of soft drinks are substitute goods; goods consumed jointly such as hot dogs and mustard are complementary goods.

Changes in Quantity Demanded

change in demand
A change in the quantity demanded of a product at every price; a shift of the demand curve to the left or right.

Be sure not to confuse a *change in demand* with a *change in quantity demanded*. A **change in demand** is a shift of the demand curve to the right (an increase in demand) or to the left (a decrease in demand). It occurs because the consumer's state of mind about purchasing the product has been altered in response to a change in one or more of the determinants of demand. Recall that "demand" is a schedule or a curve; therefore, a "change in demand" means a change in the schedule and a shift of the curve.

change in quantity demanded
A movement from one point to another on a fixed demand curve.

In contrast, a **change in quantity demanded** is a movement from one point to another point—from one price-quantity combination to another—on a fixed demand curve. The cause of such a change is an increase or decrease in the price of the product under consideration. In the table in Figure 3.3, for example, a decline in the price of lattes from $5 to $4 will increase the quantity of lattes demanded from 2000 to 4000.

In the graph in Figure 3.3, the shift of the demand curve D_1 to either D_2 or D_3 is a change in demand. But the movement from point a to point b on curve D_1 represents a change in quantity demanded: Demand has not changed; it is the entire curve, and it remains fixed in place.

Supply

supply
A schedule or curve that shows the amounts of a product that producers are willing to make available for sale at each of a series of possible prices during a specific period.

Supply is a schedule or curve showing the amounts of a product that producers will make available for sale at each of a series of possible prices during a specific period.[2] The table in Figure 3.4 is a hypothetical supply schedule for Star Buck, a single supplier of lattes. Curve S incorporates the data in the table and is called a *supply curve*. The

---

[2]This definition is worded to apply to product markets. To adjust it to apply to resource markets, substitute "resource" for "product" and "owners" for "producers."

FIGURE 3.4 **Star Buck's supply of lattes.** Because price and quantity supplied are directly related, the supply curve for an individual producer graphs as an upsloping curve. Other things equal, producers will offer more of a product for sale as its price rises and less of the product for sale as its price falls.

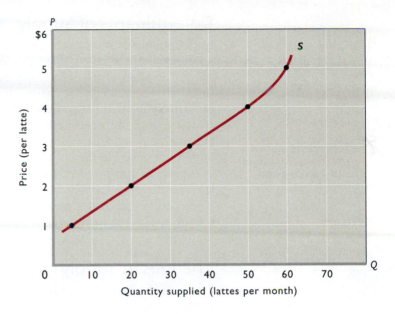

Star Buck's Supply of Lattes	
Price per Latte	Quantity Supplied per Month
$5	60
4	50
3	35
2	20
1	5

schedule and curve show the quantities of lattes that will be supplied at various prices, other things equal.

Law of Supply

Figure 3.4 shows a positive or direct relationship that prevails between price and quantity supplied. As price rises, the quantity supplied rises; as price falls, the quantity supplied falls. This relationship is called the **law of supply.** A supply schedule or curve reveals that, other things equal, firms will offer for sale more of their product at a high price than at a low price. This, again, is basically common sense.

Price is an obstacle from the standpoint of the consumer (for example, Joe Java), who is on the paying end. The higher the price, the less the consumer will buy. But the supplier (for example, Star Buck) is on the receiving end of the product's price. To a supplier, price represents *revenue*, which is needed to cover costs and earn a profit. Higher prices therefore create a profit incentive to produce and sell more of a product. The higher the price, the greater this incentive and the greater the quantity supplied.

Market Supply

Market supply is derived from individual supply in exactly the same way that market demand is derived from individual demand (Figure 3.2). We sum (not shown) the quantities supplied by each producer at each price. That is, we obtain the market **supply curve** by "horizontally adding" (also not shown) the supply curves of the individual producers. The price and quantity-supplied data in the table in Figure 3.5 are for an assumed 200 identical producers in the market, each willing to supply lattes according to the supply schedule shown in Figure 3.4. Curve S_1 is a graph of the market supply data. Note that the axes in Figure 3.5 are the same as those used in our

law of supply
The principle that, other things equal, as price rises, the quantity supplied rises, and as price falls, the quantity supplied falls.

supply curve
A curve illustrating the direct relationship between the price of a product and the quantity of it supplied, other things equal.

graph of market demand (Figure 3.3). The only difference is that we change the label on the horizontal axis from "quantity demanded" to "quantity supplied."

Determinants of Supply

determinants of supply
Factors other than price that locate the position of the supply curve.

In constructing a supply curve, we assume that price is the most significant influence on the quantity supplied of any product. But other factors (the "other things equal") can and do affect supply. The supply curve is drawn on the assumption that these other things are fixed and do not change. If one of them does change, a *change in supply* will occur, meaning that the entire supply curve will shift.

The basic **determinants of supply** are (1) resource prices, (2) technology, (3) taxes and subsidies, (4) prices of other goods, (5) expected price, and (6) the number of sellers in the market. A change in any one or more of these determinants of supply, or *supply shifters*, will move the supply curve for a product either right or left. A shift to the *right*, as from S_1 to S_2 in Figure 3.5, signifies an *increase* in supply: Producers supply larger quantities of the product at each possible price. A shift to the *left*, as from S_1 to S_3, indicates a *decrease* in supply: Producers offer less output at each price.

Changes in Supply

Let's consider how changes in each of the determinants affect supply. The key idea is that costs are a major factor underlying supply curves; anything that affects costs (other than changes in output itself) usually shifts the supply curve.

Resource Prices   The prices of the resources used in the production process help determine the costs of production incurred by firms. Higher *resource* prices raise production costs and, assuming a particular *product* price, squeeze profits. That reduction

FIGURE 3.5   Changes in the supply of lattes. A change in one or more of the determinants of supply causes a change in supply. An increase in supply is shown as a rightward shift of the supply curve, as from S_1 to S_2. A decrease in supply is depicted as a leftward shift of the curve, as from S_1 to S_3. In contrast, a change in the *quantity supplied* is caused by a change in the product's price and is shown by a movement from one point to another, as from *a* to *b* on fixed supply curve S_1.

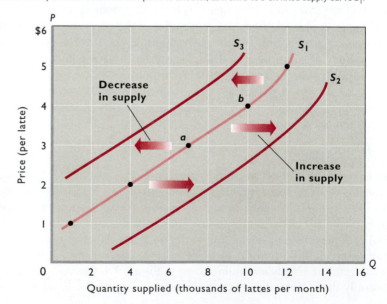

Market Supply of Lattes (S_1)	
(1) Price per Latte	(2) Total Quantity Supplied per Month
$5	12,000
4	10,000
3	7000
2	4000
1	1000

in profits reduces the incentive for firms to supply output at each product price. For example, an increase in the prices of coffee beans and milk will increase the cost of making lattes and therefore reduce their supply.

In contrast, lower *resource* prices reduce production costs and increase profits. So when resource prices fall, firms supply greater output at each product price. For example, a decrease in the prices of sand, gravel, and limestone will increase the supply of concrete.

Technology   Improvements in technology (techniques of production) enable firms to produce units of output with fewer resources. Because resources are costly, using fewer of them lowers production costs and increases supply. Example: Technological advances in producing flat-panel computer monitors have greatly reduced their cost. Thus, manufacturers will now offer more such monitors than previously at the various prices; the supply of flat-panel monitors has increased.

Taxes and Subsidies   Businesses treat sales and property taxes as costs. Increases in those taxes will increase production costs and reduce supply. In contrast, subsidies are "taxes in reverse." If the government subsidizes the production of a good, it in effect lowers the producers' costs and increases supply.

Prices of Other Goods   Firms that produce a particular product, say, soccer balls, can usually use their plant and equipment to produce alternative goods, say, basketballs and volleyballs. The higher prices of these "other goods" may entice soccer ball producers to switch production to those other goods in order to increase profits. This *substitution in production* results in a decline in the supply of soccer balls. Alternatively, when basketballs and volleyballs decline in price relative to the price of soccer balls, firms will produce fewer of those products and more soccer balls, increasing the supply of soccer balls.

Expected Prices   Changes in expectations about the future price of a product may affect the producer's current willingness to supply that product. It is difficult, however, to generalize about how a new expectation of higher prices affects the present supply of a product. Farmers anticipating a higher wheat price in the future might withhold some of their current wheat harvest from the market, thereby causing a decrease in the current supply of wheat. In contrast, in many types of manufacturing industries, newly formed expectations that price will increase may induce firms to add another shift of workers or to expand their production facilities, causing current supply to increase.

Number of Sellers   Other things equal, the larger the number of suppliers, the greater the market supply. As more firms enter an industry, the supply curve shifts to the right. Conversely, the smaller the number of firms in the industry, the less the market supply. This means that as firms leave an industry, the supply curve shifts to the left. Example: The United States and Canada have imposed restrictions on haddock fishing to replenish dwindling stocks. As part of that policy, the federal government has bought the boats of some of the haddock fishers as a way of putting them out of business and decreasing the catch. The result has been a decline in the market supply of haddock.

Changes in Quantity Supplied

The distinction between a *change in supply* and a *change in quantity supplied* parallels the distinction between a change in demand and a change in quantity demanded. Because

change in supply
A change in the quantity supplied of a product at every price; a shift of the supply curve to the left or right.

change in quantity supplied
A movement from one point to another on a fixed supply curve.

supply is a schedule or curve, a **change in supply** means a change in the schedule and a shift of the curve. An increase in supply shifts the curve to the right; a decrease in supply shifts it to the left. The cause of a change in supply is a change in one or more of the determinants of supply.

In contrast, a **change in quantity supplied** is a movement from one point to another on a fixed supply curve. The cause of such a movement is a change in the price of the specific product being considered. In Figure 3.5, a decline in the price of lattes from $4 to $3 decreases the quantity of lattes supplied per month from 10,000 to 7000. This movement from point *b* to point *a* along S_1 is a change in quantity supplied, not a change in supply. Supply is the full schedule of prices and quantities shown, and this schedule does not change when the price of lattes changes.

Market Equilibrium

With our understanding of demand and supply, we can now show how the decisions of Joe Java and other buyers of lattes interact with the decisions of Star Buck and other sellers to determine the price and quantity of lattes. In the table in Figure 3.6, columns 1 and 2 repeat the market supply of lattes (from Figure 3.5), and columns 2 and 3 repeat the market demand for lattes (from Figure 3.3). We assume this is a competitive market, so neither buyers nor sellers can set the price.

Equilibrium Price and Quantity

equilibrium price
The price in a competitive market at which the quantity demanded and quantity supplied of a product are equal.

equilibrium quantity
The quantity demanded and quantity supplied that occur at the equilibrium price in a competitive market.

We are looking for the equilibrium price and equilibrium quantity. The **equilibrium price** (or *market-clearing* price) is the price at which the intentions of buyers and sellers match. It is the price at which quantity demanded equals quantity supplied. The table in Figure 3.6 reveals that at $3, *and only at that price*, the number of lattes that sellers wish to sell (7000) is identical to the number that consumers want to buy (also 7000). At $3 and 7000 lattes, there is neither a shortage nor a surplus of lattes. So 7000 lattes is the **equilibrium quantity:** the quantity at which the intentions of buyers and sellers match so that the quantity demanded and the quantity supplied are equal.

Graphically, the equilibrium price is indicated by the intersection of the supply curve and the demand curve in Figure 3.6. (The horizontal axis now measures both quantity demanded and quantity supplied.) With neither a shortage nor a surplus at $3, the market is *in equilibrium*, meaning "in balance" or "at rest."

To better understand the uniqueness of the equilibrium price, let's consider other prices. At any above-equilibrium price, quantity supplied exceeds quantity demanded. For example, at the $4 price, sellers will offer 10,000 lattes, but buyers will purchase only 4000. The $4 price encourages sellers to offer lots of lattes but discourages many consumers from buying them. The result is a **surplus** or *excess supply* of 6000 lattes. If latte sellers made them all, they would find themselves with 6000 unsold lattes.

surplus
The amount by which the quantity supplied of a product exceeds the quantity demanded at a specific (above-equilibrium) price.

Surpluses drive prices down. Even if the $4 price existed temporarily, it could not persist. The large surplus would prompt competing sellers to lower the price to encourage buyers to stop in and take the surplus off their hands. As the price fell, the incentive to produce lattes would decline and the incentive for consumers to buy lattes would increase. As shown in Figure 3.6, the market would move to its equilibrium at $3.

Any price below the $3 equilibrium price would create a shortage; quantity demanded would exceed quantity supplied. Consider a $2 price, for example. We see in column 4 of the table in Figure 3.6 that quantity demanded exceeds quantity

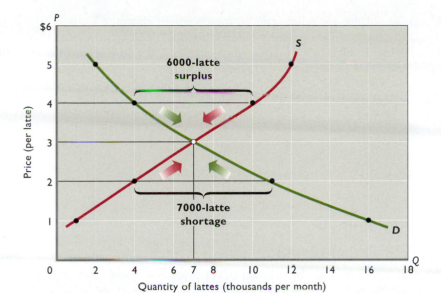

FIGURE 3.6 **Equilibrium price and quantity.** The intersection of the downsloping demand curve D and the upsloping supply curve S indicates the equilibrium price and quantity, here $3 and 7000 lattes. The shortages of lattes at below-equilibrium prices (for example, 7000 at $2) drive up price. The higher prices increase the quantity supplied and reduce the quantity demanded until equilibrium is achieved. The surpluses caused by above-equilibrium prices (for example, 6000 lattes at $4) push price down. As price drops, the quantity demanded rises and the quantity supplied falls until equilibrium is established. At the equilibrium price and quantity, there are neither shortages nor surpluses of lattes.

Market Supply of and Demand for Lattes			
(1) Total Quantity Supplied per Month	(2) Price per Latte	(3) Total Quantity Demanded per Month	(4) Surplus (+) or Shortage (−)*
12,000	$5	2000	+10,000 ↓
10,000	4	4000	+6000 ↓
7000	3	7000	0
4000	2	11,000	−7000 ↑
1000	1	16,000	−15,000 ↑

*Arrows indicate the effect on price.

supplied at that price. The result is a **shortage** or *excess demand* of 7000 lattes. The $2 price discourages sellers from devoting resources to lattes and encourages consumers to desire more lattes than are available. The $2 price cannot persist as the equilibrium price. Many consumers who want to buy lattes at this price will not obtain them. They will express a willingness to pay more than $2 to get them. Competition among these buyers will drive up the price, eventually to the $3 equilibrium level. Unless disrupted by supply or demand changes, this $3 price of lattes will continue.

shortage
The amount by which the quantity demanded of a product exceeds the quantity supplied at a specific (below-equilibrium) price.

Rationing Function of Prices
The ability of the competitive forces of supply and demand to establish a price at which selling and buying decisions are consistent is called the *rationing function of prices*. In our case, the equilibrium price of $3 clears the market, leaving no

INTERACTIVE GRAPHS

G 3.1

Supply and demand

burdensome surplus for sellers and no inconvenient shortage for potential buyers. And it is the combination of freely made individual decisions that sets this market-clearing price. In effect, the market outcome says that all buyers who are willing and able to pay $3 for a latte will obtain one; all buyers who cannot or will not pay $3 will go without one. Similarly, all producers who are willing and able to offer a latte for sale at $3 will sell it; all producers who cannot or will not sell for $3 will not sell their product.

APPLYING THE ANALYSIS

Ticket Scalping

Ticket prices for athletic events and musical concerts are usually set far in advance of the events. Sometimes the original ticket price is too low to be the equilibrium price. Lines form at the ticket window, and a severe shortage of tickets occurs at the printed price. What happens next? Buyers who are willing to pay more than the original price bid up the equilibrium price in resale ticket markets. The price rockets upward.

Tickets sometimes get resold for much greater amounts than the original price—market transactions known as "scalping." For example, an original buyer may resell a $75 ticket to a concert for $200. The media sometimes denounce scalpers for "ripping off" buyers by charging "exorbitant" prices.

But is scalping really a rip-off? We must first recognize that such ticket resales are voluntary transactions. If both buyer and seller did not expect to gain from the exchange, it would not occur! The seller must value the $200 more than seeing the event, and the buyer must value seeing the event at $200 or more. So there are no losers or victims here: Both buyer and seller benefit from the transaction. The "scalping" market simply redistributes assets (game or concert tickets) from those who would rather have the money (other things) to those who would rather have the tickets.

Does scalping impose losses or injury on the sponsors of the event? If the sponsors are injured, it is because they initially priced tickets below the equilibrium level. Perhaps they did this to create a long waiting line and the attendant media publicity. Alternatively, they may have had a genuine desire to keep tickets affordable for lower-income, ardent fans. In either case, the event sponsors suffer an opportunity cost in the form of less ticket revenue than they might have otherwise received. But such losses are self-inflicted and quite separate and distinct from the fact that some tickets are later resold at a higher price.

So is ticket scalping undesirable? Not on economic grounds! It is an entirely voluntary activity that benefits both sellers and buyers.

QUESTION: Why do you suppose some professional sports teams are setting up legal "ticket exchanges" (at buyer- and seller-determined prices) at their Internet sites? (*Hint:* For the service, the teams charge a percentage of the transaction price of each resold ticket.)

Changes in Demand, Supply, and Equilibrium

We know that prices can and do change in markets. For example, demand might change because of fluctuations in consumer tastes or incomes, changes in expected price, or variations in the prices of related goods. Supply might change in response to changes in resource prices, technology, or taxes. How will such changes in demand and supply affect equilibrium price and quantity?

Changes in Demand

Suppose that the supply of some good (for example, health care) is constant and the demand for the good increases, as shown in Figure 3.7a. As a result, the new intersection of the supply and demand curves is at higher values on both the price and the quantity axes. Clearly, an increase in demand raises both equilibrium price and equilibrium quantity. Conversely, a decrease in demand, such as that shown in Figure 3.7b, reduces both equilibrium price and equilibrium quantity.

Changes in Supply

What happens if the demand for some good (for example, cell phones) is constant but the supply increases, as in Figure 3.7c? The new intersection of supply and demand is located at a lower equilibrium price but at a higher equilibrium quantity. An increase in supply reduces equilibrium price but increases equilibrium quantity. In contrast, if supply decreases, as in Figure 3.7d, equilibrium price rises while equilibrium quantity declines.

Complex Cases

When both supply and demand change, the effect is a combination of the individual effects.

Supply Increase; Demand Decrease   What effect will a supply increase for some good (for example, apples) and a demand decrease have on equilibrium price? Both changes decrease price, so the net result is a price drop greater than that resulting from either change alone.

What about equilibrium quantity? Here the effects of the changes in supply and demand are opposed: The increase in supply increases equilibrium quantity, but the decrease in demand reduces it. The direction of the change in equilibrium quantity depends on the relative sizes of the changes in supply and demand. If the increase in supply is larger than the decrease in demand, the equilibrium quantity will increase. But if the decrease in demand is greater than the increase in supply, the equilibrium quantity will decrease.

Supply Decrease; Demand Increase   A decrease in supply and an increase in demand for some good (for example, gasoline) both increase price. Their combined effect is an increase in equilibrium price greater than that caused by either change separately. But their effect on the equilibrium quantity is again indeterminate, depending on the relative sizes of the changes in supply and demand. If the decrease in supply is larger than the increase in demand, the equilibrium quantity will decrease. In contrast, if the increase in demand is greater than the decrease in supply, the equilibrium quantity will increase.

FIGURE 3.7 **Changes in demand and supply and the effects on price and quantity.** The increase in demand from D_1 to D_2 in (a) increases both equilibrium price and equilibrium quantity. The decrease in demand from D_3 to D_4 in (b) decreases both equilibrium price and equilibrium quantity. The increase in supply from S_1 to S_2 in (c) decreases equilibrium price and increases equilibrium quantity. The decrease in supply from S_3 to S_4 in (d) increases equilibrium price and decreases equilibrium quantity. The boxes in the top right summarize the respective changes and outcomes. The upward arrows in the boxes signify increases in equilibrium price (P) and equilibrium quantity (Q); the downward arrows signify decreases in these items.

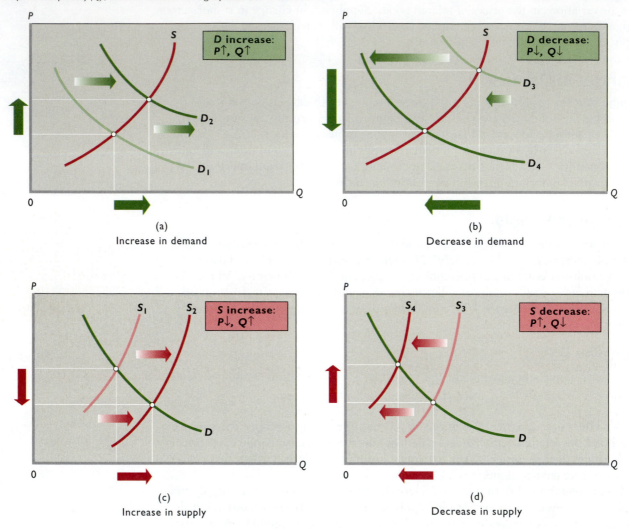

(a)
Increase in demand

(b)
Decrease in demand

(c)
Increase in supply

(d)
Decrease in supply

Supply Increase; Demand Increase What if supply and demand both increase for some good (for example, sushi)? A supply increase drops equilibrium price, while a demand increase boosts it. If the increase in supply is greater than the increase in demand, the equilibrium price will fall. If the opposite holds, the equilibrium price will rise. If the two changes are equal and cancel out, price will not change.

The effect on equilibrium quantity is certain: The increases in supply and in demand both raise the equilibrium quantity. Therefore, the equilibrium quantity will increase by an amount greater than that caused by either change alone.

Supply Decrease; Demand Decrease What about decreases in both supply and demand for some good (for example, new homes)? If the decrease in supply is greater than the decrease in demand, equilibrium price will rise. If the reverse is true, equilibrium price will fall. If the two changes are of the same size and cancel out, price will not change. Because the decreases in supply and demand both reduce equilibrium quantity, we can be sure that equilibrium quantity will fall.

Government-Set Prices

In most markets, prices are free to rise or fall with changes in supply or demand, no matter how high or low those prices might be. However, government occasionally concludes that changes in supply and demand have created prices that are unfairly high to buyers or unfairly low to sellers. Government may then place legal limits on how high or low a price or prices may go. Our previous analysis of shortages and surpluses helps us evaluate the wisdom of government-set prices.

Price Ceilings on Gasoline

A **price ceiling** sets the maximum legal price a seller may charge for a product or service. A price at or below the ceiling is legal; a price above it is not. The rationale for establishing price ceilings (or ceiling prices) on specific products is that they purportedly enable consumers to obtain some "essential" good or service that they could not afford at the equilibrium price.

Figure 3.8 shows the effects of price ceilings graphically. Let's look at a hypothetical situation. Suppose that rapidly rising world income boosts the purchase of automobiles and increases the demand for gasoline so that the equilibrium or market price reaches $3.50 per gallon. The rapidly rising price of gasoline greatly burdens low- and moderate-income households, which pressure government to "do something." To keep gasoline prices down, the government imposes a ceiling price of $3 per gallon. To impact the market, a price ceiling must be below the equilibrium price. A ceiling price of $4, for example, would have no effect on the price of gasoline in the current situation.

What are the effects of this $3 ceiling price? The rationing ability of the free market is rendered ineffective. Because the $3 ceiling price is below the $3.50 market-clearing price, there is a lasting shortage of gasoline. The quantity of gasoline demanded at $3 is Q_d, and the quantity supplied is only Q_s; a persistent excess demand or shortage of amount $Q_d - Q_s$ occurs.

The $3 price ceiling prevents the usual market adjustment in which competition among buyers bids up the price, inducing more production and rationing some buyers out of the market. That process would normally continue until the shortage disappeared at the equilibrium price and quantity, $3.50 and Q_0.

How will sellers apportion the available supply Q_s among buyers, who want the greater amount Q_d? Should they distribute gasoline on a first-come, first-served basis, that is, to those willing and able to get in line the soonest or stay in line the longest? Or should gas stations distribute it on the basis of favoritism? Since an unregulated shortage does not lead to an equitable distribution of gasoline, the government must establish some formal system for rationing it to consumers. One option is to issue ration coupons, which authorize bearers to purchase a fixed amount of gasoline per

price ceiling
A legally established maximum (below-equilibrium) price for a product.

FIGURE 3.8 A price ceiling.
A price ceiling is a maximum legal price, such as $3, that is below the equilibrium price. It results in a persistent product shortage, here shown by the distance between Q_d and Q_s.

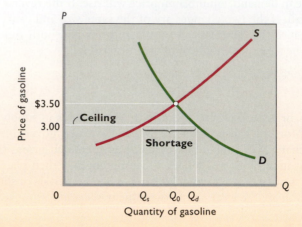

month. The rationing system might entail first the printing of coupons for Q_s gallons of gasoline and then the equal distribution of the coupons among consumers so that the wealthy family of four and the poor family of four both receive the same number of coupons.

But ration coupons would not prevent a second problem from arising. The demand curve in Figure 3.8 reveals that many buyers are willing to pay more than the $3 ceiling price. And, of course, it is more profitable for gasoline stations to sell at prices above the ceiling. Thus, despite a sizable enforcement bureaucracy that would have to accompany the price controls, *black markets* in which gasoline is illegally bought and sold at prices above the legal limits will flourish. Counterfeiting of ration coupons will also be a problem. And since the price of gasoline is now "set by government," there might be political pressure on government to set the price even lower.

QUESTION: Why is it typically difficult to end price ceilings once they have been in place for a long time?

APPLYING THE ANALYSIS

Rent Controls

About 200 cities in the United States, including New York City, Boston, and San Francisco, have at one time or another enacted price ceilings in the form of rent controls—maximum rents established by law—or, more recently, have set maximum rent increases for existing tenants. Such laws are well intended. Their goals are to protect low-income families from escalating rents caused by demand increases that outstrip supply increases. Rent controls are designed to alleviate perceived housing shortages and make housing more affordable.

What have been the actual economic effects? On the demand side, the below-equilibrium rents attract a larger number of renters. Some are locals seeking to move into their own places after sharing housing with friends or family. Others are outsiders attracted into the area by the artificially lower rents. But a large problem occurs on the supply side. Price controls make it less attractive for landlords to offer housing on the rental market. In the short run, owners may sell their rental units or convert them to condominiums. In the long run, low rents make it unprofitable for owners to repair or renovate their rental units. (Rent controls are one cause of the many abandoned apartment buildings found in some larger cities.) Also, insurance companies, pension funds, and other potential new investors in housing will find it more profitable to invest in office buildings, shopping malls, or motels, where rents are not controlled.

In brief, rent controls distort market signals, and thus resources are misallocated: Too few resources are allocated to rental housing, and too many to alternative uses. Ironically, although rent controls are often legislated to lessen the effects of perceived shortages, controls in fact are a primary cause of such shortages. For that reason, most American cities either have abandoned rent controls or are gradually phasing them out.

QUESTION: Why does maintenance tend to diminish in rent-controlled apartment buildings relative to maintenance in buildings where owners can charge market-determined rents?

APPLYING THE ANALYSIS

Price Floors on Wheat

A **price floor** is a minimum price fixed by the government. A price at or above the price floor is legal; a price below it is not. Price floors above equilibrium prices are usually invoked when society feels that the free functioning of the market system has not provided a sufficient income for certain groups of resource suppliers or producers. Supported prices for agricultural products and current minimum wages are two examples of price (or wage) floors. Let's look at the former.

Suppose that many farmers have extremely low incomes when the price of wheat is at its equilibrium value of $2 per bushel. The government decides to help out by establishing a legal price floor (or "price support") of $3 per bushel.

What will be the effects? At any price above the equilibrium price, quantity supplied will exceed quantity demanded—that is, there will be a persistent surplus of the product. Farmers will be willing to produce and offer for sale more wheat than private buyers are willing to buy at the $3 price floor. As we saw with a price ceiling, an imposed legal price disrupts the rationing ability of the free market.

Figure 3.9 illustrates the effect of a price floor graphically. Suppose that S and D are the supply and demand curves for wheat. Equilibrium price and quantity are $2 and Q_0, respectively. If the government imposes a price floor of $3, farmers will produce Q_s but private buyers will purchase only Q_d. The surplus is the excess of Q_s over Q_d.

price floor
A legally established minimum (above-equilibrium) price for a product.

FIGURE 3.9 **A price floor.** A price floor is a minimum legal price, such as $3, that results in a persistent product surplus, here shown by the distance between Q_s and Q_d.

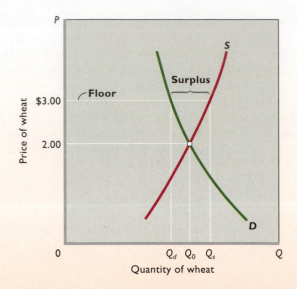

The government may cope with the surplus resulting from a price floor in two ways:

- It can restrict supply (for example, by instituting acreage allotments by which farmers agree to take a certain amount of land out of production) or increase demand (for example, by researching new uses for the product involved). These actions may reduce the difference between the equilibrium price and the price floor and that way reduce the size of the resulting surplus.
- If these efforts are not wholly successful, then the government must purchase the surplus output at the $3 price (thereby subsidizing farmers) and store or otherwise dispose of it.

Price floors such as $3 in Figure 3.9 not only disrupt the rationing ability of prices but also distort resource allocation. Without the price floor, the $2 equilibrium price of wheat would cause financial losses and force high-cost wheat producers to plant other crops or abandon farming altogether. But the $3 price floor allows them to continue to grow wheat and remain farmers. So society devotes too many scarce resources to wheat production and too few to producing other, more valuable, goods and services. It fails to achieve an optimal allocation of resources.

That's not all. Consumers of wheat-based products pay higher prices because of the price floor. Taxpayers pay higher taxes to finance the government's purchase of the surplus. Also, the price floor causes potential environmental damage by encouraging wheat farmers to bring hilly, erosion-prone "marginal land" into production. The higher price also prompts imports of wheat. But, since such imports would increase the quantity of wheat supplied and thus undermine the price floor, the government needs to erect tariffs (taxes on imports) to keep the foreign wheat out. Such tariffs usually prompt other countries to retaliate with their own tariffs against U.S. agricultural or manufacturing exports.

QUESTION: To maintain price floors on milk, the U.S. government has at times bought out and destroyed entire dairy herds from dairy farmers. What's the economic logic of these actions?

It is easy to see why economists "sound the alarm" when politicians advocate imposing price ceilings or price floors such as price controls, rent controls, interest-rate lids, or agricultural price supports. In all these cases, good intentions lead to bad economic outcomes. Government-controlled prices lead to shortages or surpluses, distort resource allocations, and cause negative side effects.

For additional examples of demand and supply, view the Chapter 3 Web appendix at www.mcconnellbrief2e.com. There, you will find examples relating to such diverse products as lettuce, corn, salmon, gasoline, sushi, and Olympic tickets. Several of the examples depict simultaneous shifts in demand and supply curves—circumstances that often show up in exam questions!

INTERACTIVE GRAPHS

G 3.2

Price floors and ceilings

Summary

1. Demand is a schedule or curve representing the willingness of buyers in a specific period to purchase a particular product at each of various prices. The law of demand implies that consumers will buy more of a product at a low price than at a high price. So, other things equal, the relationship between price and quantity demanded is inverse and is graphed as a downsloping curve.

2. Market demand curves are found by adding horizontally the demand curves of the many individual consumers in the market.

3. Changes in one or more of the determinants of demand (consumer tastes, the number of buyers in the market, the money incomes of consumers, the prices of related goods, and expected prices) shift the market demand curve. A shift to the right is an increase in demand; a shift to the left is a decrease in demand. A change in demand is different from a change in the quantity demanded, the latter being a movement from one point to another point on a fixed demand curve because of a change in the product's price.

4. Supply is a schedule or curve showing the amounts of a product that producers are willing to offer in the market at each possible price during a specific period. The law of supply states that, other things equal, producers will offer more of a product at a high price than at a low price. Thus, the relationship between price and quantity supplied is positive or direct, and supply is graphed as an upsloping curve.

5. The market supply curve is the horizontal summation of the supply curves of the individual producers of the product.

6. Changes in one or more of the determinants of supply (resource prices, production techniques, taxes or subsidies, the prices of other goods, expected prices, or the number of suppliers in the market) shift the supply curve of a product. A shift to the right is an increase in supply; a shift to the left is a decrease in supply. In contrast, a change in the price of the product being considered causes a change in the quantity supplied, which is shown as a movement from one point to another point on a fixed supply curve.

7. The equilibrium price and quantity are established at the intersection of the supply and demand curves. The interaction of market demand and market supply adjusts the price to the point at which the quantities demanded and supplied are equal. This is the equilibrium price. The corresponding quantity is the equilibrium quantity.

8. A change in either demand or supply changes the equilibrium price and quantity. Increases in demand raise both equilibrium price and equilibrium quantity; decreases in demand lower both equilibrium price and equilibrium quantity. Increases in supply lower equilibrium price and raise equilibrium quantity; decreases in supply raise equilibrium price and lower equilibrium quantity.

9. Simultaneous changes in demand and supply affect equilibrium price and quantity in various ways, depending on their direction and relative magnitudes.

10. A price ceiling is a maximum price set by government and is designed to help consumers. Effective price ceilings produce persistent product shortages, and if an equitable distribution of the product is sought, government must ration the product to consumers.

11. A price floor is a minimum price set by government and is designed to aid producers. Price floors lead to persistent product surpluses; the government must either purchase the product or eliminate the surplus by imposing restrictions on production or increasing private demand.

12. Legally fixed prices stifle the rationing function of prices and distort the allocation of resources.

Terms and Concepts

demand	change in demand	change in quantity supplied
law of demand	change in quantity demanded	equilibrium price
demand curve	supply	equilibrium quantity
determinants of demand	law of supply	surplus
normal good	supply curve	shortage
inferior good	determinants of supply	price ceiling
substitute good	change in supply	price floor
complementary good		

Questions

1. Explain the law of demand. Why does a demand curve slope downward? How is a market demand curve derived from individual demand curves? **LO1**

2. What are the determinants of demand? What happens to the demand curve when any of these determinants changes? Distinguish between a change in demand and a change in the quantity demanded, noting the cause(s) of each. **LO1**

3. What effect will each of the following have on the demand for small automobiles such as the Mini Cooper and Smart car? **LO1**
   a. Small automobiles become more fashionable.
   b. The price of large automobiles rises (with the price of small autos remaining the same).
   c. Income declines and small autos are an inferior good.
   d. Consumers anticipate that the price of small autos will greatly come down in the near future.
   e. The price of gasoline substantially drops.

4. Explain the law of supply. Why does the supply curve slope upward? How is the market supply curve derived from the supply curves of individual producers? **LO2**

5. What are the determinants of supply? What happens to the supply curve when any of these determinants changes? Distinguish between a change in supply and a change in the quantity supplied, noting the cause(s) of each. **LO2**

6. What effect will each of the following have on the supply of auto tires? **LO2**
   a. A technological advance in the methods of producing tires.
   b. A decline in the number of firms in the tire industry.
   c. An increase in the price of rubber used in the production of tires.
   d. The expectation that the equilibrium price of auto tires will be lower in the future than currently.
   e. A decline in the price of the large tires used for semi trucks and earth-hauling rigs (with no change in the price of auto tires).
   f. The levying of a per-unit tax on each auto tire sold.
   g. The granting of a 50-cent-per-unit subsidy for each auto tire produced.

7. "In the latte market, demand often exceeds supply and supply sometimes exceeds demand." "The price of a latte rises and falls in response to changes in supply and demand." In which of these two statements are the concepts of supply and demand used correctly? Explain. **LO4**

8. In 2001 an outbreak of hoof-and-mouth disease in Europe led to the burning of millions of cattle carcasses. What impact do you think this had on the supply of cattle hides, hide prices, the supply of leather goods, and the price of leather goods? **LO4**

9. Critically evaluate: "In comparing the two equilibrium positions in Figure 3.7a, I note that a larger amount is actually demanded at a higher price. This refutes the law of demand." **LO4**

10. For each stock in the stock market, the number of shares sold daily equals the number of shares purchased. That is, the quantity of each firm's shares demanded equals the quantity supplied. So, if this equality always occurs, why do the prices of stock shares ever change? **LO4**

11. Suppose the total demand for wheat and the total supply of wheat per month in the Kansas City grain market are as shown in the table below. Suppose that the government establishes a price ceiling of $3.70 for wheat. What might prompt the government to establish this price ceiling? Explain carefully the main effects. Demonstrate your answer graphically. Next, suppose that the government establishes a price floor of $4.60 for wheat. What will be the main effects of this price floor? Demonstrate your answer graphically. **LO5**

Thousands of Bushels Demanded	Price per Bushel	Thousands of Bushels Supplied
85	$3.40	72
80	3.70	73
75	4.00	75
70	4.30	77
65	4.60	79
60	4.90	81

12. What do economists mean when they say "price floors and ceilings stifle the rationing function of prices and distort resource allocation"? **LO5**

Problems

1. Suppose there are three buyers of candy in a market: Tex, Dex, and Rex. The market demand and the individual demands of Tex, Dex, and Rex are shown below. **LO1**
   a. Fill in the table for the missing values.
   b. Which buyer demands the least at a price of $5? The most at a price of $7?
   c. Which buyer's quantity demanded increases the most when the price is lowered from $7 to $6?
   d. Which direction would the market demand curve shift if Tex withdrew from the market? What if Dex doubled his purchases at each possible price?
   e. Suppose that at a price of $6, the total quantity demanded increases from 19 to 38. Is this a "change in the quantity demanded" or a "change in demand"?

Price per Candy	Individual Quantities Demanded						Total Quantity Demanded
	Tex		Dex		Rex		
$8	3	+	1	+	0	=	___
7	8	+	2	+	___	=	12
6	___	+	3	+	4	=	19
5	17	+	___	+	6	=	27
4	23	+	5	+	8	=	___

2. The figure below shows the supply curve for tennis balls, S_1, for Drop Volley Tennis, a producer of tennis equipment. Use the figure and the table below to give your answers to the following questions. **LO2**

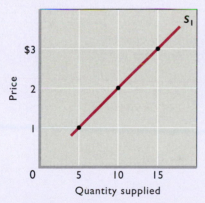

a. Use the figure to fill in the quantity supplied on supply curve S_1 for each price in the table below.

Price	S_1 Quantity Supplied	S_2 Quantity Supplied	Change in Quantity Supplied
$3	___	4	___
2	___	2	___
1	___	0	___

b. If production costs were to increase, the quantities supplied at each price would be as shown by the third column of the table ("S_2 Quantity Supplied"). Use that data to draw supply curve S_2 on the same graph as supply curve S_1.
c. In the fourth column of the table, enter the amount by which the quantity supplied at each price changes due to the increase in product costs. (Use positive numbers for increases and negative numbers for decreases.)
d. Did the increase in production costs cause a "decrease in supply" or a "decrease in quantity supplied"?

3. Refer to the expanded table below from question 11. **LO3**
   a. What is the equilibrium price? At what price is there neither a shortage nor a surplus? Fill in the surplus-shortage column and use it to confirm your answers.
   b. Graph the demand for wheat and the supply of wheat. Be sure to label the axes of your graph correctly. Label equilibrium price P and equilibrium quantity Q.
   c. How big is the surplus or shortage at $3.40? At $4.90? How big a surplus or shortage results if the price is 60 cents higher than the equilibrium price? 30 cents lower than the equilibrium price?

Thousands of Bushels Demanded	Price per Bushel	Thousands of Bushels Supplied	Surplus (+) or Shortage (−)
85	$3.40	72	___
80	3.70	73	___
75	4.00	75	___
70	4.30	77	___
65	4.60	79	___
60	4.90	81	___

4. How will each of the following changes in demand and/or supply affect equilibrium price and equilibrium quantity in a competitive market; that is, do price and quantity rise, fall, or remain unchanged, or are the answers indeterminate because they depend on the magnitudes of the shifts? Use supply and demand to verify your answers. **LO4**
   a. Supply decreases and demand is constant.
   b. Demand decreases and supply is constant.
   c. Supply increases and demand is constant.
   d. Demand increases and supply increases.
   e. Demand increases and supply is constant.
   f. Supply increases and demand decreases.
   g. Demand increases and supply decreases.
   h. Demand decreases and supply decreases.

5. Use two market diagrams to explain how an increase in state subsidies to public colleges might affect tuition and enrollments in both public and private colleges. **LO4**

6. **ADVANCED ANALYSIS** Assume that demand for a commodity is represented by the equation $P = 10 - .2Q_d$ and supply by the equation $P = 2 + .2Q_s$, where Q_d and Q_s are quantity demanded and quantity supplied, respectively, and P is price. Using the equilibrium condition $Q_s = Q_d$, solve the equations to determine equilibrium price. Now determine equilibrium quantity. **LO4**

7. Suppose that the demand and supply schedules for rental apartments in the city of Gotham are as given in the table below. **LO5**

Monthly Rent	Apartments Demanded	Apartments Supplied
$2500	10,000	15,000
2000	12,500	12,500
1500	15,000	10,000
1000	17,500	7500
500	20,000	5000

a. What is the market equilibrium rental price per month and the market equilibrium number of apartments demanded and supplied?

b. If the local government can enforce a rent-control law that sets the maximum monthly rent at $1500, will there be a surplus or a shortage? Of how many units? And how many units will actually be rented each month?

c. Suppose that a new government is elected that wants to keep out the poor. It declares that the minimum rent that can be charged is $2500 per month. If the government can enforce that price floor, will there be a surplus or a shortage? Of how many units? And how many units will actually be rented each month?

d. Suppose that the government wishes to decrease the market equilibrium monthly rent by increasing the supply of housing. Assuming that demand remains unchanged, by how many units of housing would the government have to increase the supply of housing in order to get the market equilibrium rental price to fall to $1500 per month? To $1000 per month? To $500 per month?

4

After reading this chapter, you should be able to:

1 Discuss price elasticity of demand and how it can be measured.

2 Explain how price elasticity of demand affects total revenue.

3 Describe price elasticity of supply and how it can be measured.

4 Apply price elasticity of demand and supply to real-world situations.

5 Explain income elasticity of demand and cross-elasticity of demand and how they can be applied.

Elasticity of Demand and Supply

Why do buyers of some products respond to price increases by substantially reducing their purchases while buyers of other products respond by only slightly cutting back their purchases? Why do price hikes for some goods cause producers to greatly increase their output while price hikes on other products barely cause any output increase? Why does the demand for some products rise a great deal when household incomes increase while the demand for other products rises just a little? How can we tell whether a given pair of goods are complements, substitutes, or unrelated to each other?

Elasticity extends our understanding of markets by letting us know the degree to which changes in prices and incomes affect supply and demand. Sometimes the responses are substantial, other times minimal or even nonexistent. But by knowing what to expect, businesses and the government can do a much better job in deciding what to produce, how much to charge, and, surprisingly, what items to tax.

Price Elasticity of Demand

ORIGIN OF THE IDEA

O 4.1

Price elasticity of demand

price elasticity of demand
A measure of the responsiveness of the quantity of a product demanded by consumers when the product price changes.

The law of demand tells us that, other things equal, consumers will buy more of a product when its price declines and less of it when its price increases. But how much more or less will they buy? The amount varies from product to product and over different price ranges for the same product. And such variations matter. For example, a firm contemplating a price hike will want to know how consumers will respond. If they remain highly loyal and continue to buy, the firm's revenue will rise. But if consumers defect en masse to other sellers or other products, its revenue will tumble.

The responsiveness of the quantity of a product demanded by consumers when the product price changes is measured by a product's **price elasticity of demand**. For some products (for example, restaurant meals), consumers are highly responsive to price changes. Modest price changes cause very large changes in the quantity purchased. Economists say that the demand for such products is *relatively elastic* or simply *elastic*.

For other products (for example, medical care), consumers pay much less attention to price changes. Substantial price changes cause only small changes in the amount purchased. The demand for such products is *relatively inelastic* or simply *inelastic*.

The Price-Elasticity Coefficient and Formula

Economists measure the degree of price elasticity or inelasticity of demand with the coefficient E_d, defined as

$$E_d = \frac{\text{percentage change in quantity demanded of X}}{\text{percentage change in price of X}}$$

The percentage changes in the equation are calculated by dividing the *change* in quantity demanded by the original quantity demanded and by dividing the *change* in price by the original price. So we can restate the formula as

$$E_d = \frac{\text{change in quantity demanded of X}}{\text{original quantity demanded of X}} \div \frac{\text{change in price of X}}{\text{original price of X}}$$

WORKED PROBLEMS

W 4.1

Elasticity of demand

Using Averages Unfortunately, an annoying problem arises in computing the price-elasticity coefficient. A price change from, say, $4 to $5 along a demand curve is a 25 percent (=$1/$4) increase, but the opposite price change from $5 to $4 along the same curve is a 20 percent (=$1/$5) decrease. Which percentage change in price should we use in the denominator to compute the price-elasticity coefficient? And when quantity changes, for example, from 10 to 20, it is a 100 percent (=10/10) increase. But when quantity falls from 20 to 10 along the identical demand curve, it is a 50 percent (=10/20) decrease. Should we use 100 percent or 50 percent in the numerator of the elasticity formula? Elasticity should be the same whether price rises or falls!

The simplest solution to the problem is to use the averages of the two prices and the two quantities as the reference points for computing the percentages. That is

$$E_d = \frac{\text{change in quantity}}{\text{sum of quantities}/2} \div \frac{\text{change in price}}{\text{sum of prices}/2}$$

For the same $5–$4 price range, the price reference is $4.50 [= ($5 + $4)/2], and for the same 10–20 quantity range, the quantity reference is 15 units [= (10 + 20)/2]. The percentage change in price is now $1/$4.50, or about 22 percent, and the percentage change in quantity is 10/15, or about 67 percent. So E_d is about 3. This solution eliminates the "up versus down" problem. All the elasticity coefficients that follow are calculated using averages, also known as the *midpoints approach.*

Elimination of Minus Sign   Because demand curves slope downward, the price-elasticity coefficient of demand E_d will always be a negative number. As an example, if price declines, quantity demanded will increase. This means that the numerator in our formula will be positive and the denominator negative, yielding a negative E_d. For an increase in price, the numerator will be negative but the denominator positive, again producing a negative E_d.

Economists usually ignore the minus sign and simply present the absolute value of the elasticity coefficient to avoid an ambiguity that might otherwise arise. It can be confusing to say that an E_d of −4 is greater than one of −2. This possible confusion is avoided when we say an E_d of 4 reveals greater elasticity than an E_d of 2. In what follows, we ignore the minus sign in the coefficient of price elasticity of demand and show only the absolute value.

Interpretations of E_d

We can interpret the coefficient of price elasticity of demand as follows.

Elastic Demand   Demand is **elastic** if a specific percentage change in price results in a larger percentage change in quantity demanded. In such cases, E_d will be greater than 1. Example: Suppose that a 2 percent decline in the price of cut flowers results in a 4 percent increase in quantity demanded. Then demand for cut flowers is elastic and

elastic demand
Product demand for which price changes cause relatively larger changes in quantity demanded.

$$E_d = \frac{.04}{.02} = 2$$

Inelastic Demand   If a specific percentage change in price produces a smaller percentage change in quantity demanded, demand is **inelastic.** In such cases, E_d will be less than 1. Example: Suppose that a 2 percent decline in the price of tea leads to only a 1 percent increase in quantity demanded. Then demand is inelastic and

inelastic demand
Product demand for which price changes cause relatively smaller changes in quantity demanded.

$$E_d = \frac{.01}{.02} = .5$$

Unit Elasticity   The case separating elastic and inelastic demands occurs where a percentage change in price and the resulting percentage change in quantity demanded are the same. Example: Suppose that a 2 percent drop in the price of chocolate causes a 2 percent increase in quantity demanded. This special case is termed **unit elasticity** because E_d is exactly 1, or unity. In this example,

unit elasticity
Product demand for which relative price changes and changes in quantity demanded are equal.

$$E_d = \frac{.02}{.02} = 1$$

Extreme Cases   When we say demand is "inelastic," we do not mean that consumers are completely unresponsive to a price change. In that extreme situation, where a price change results in no change whatsoever in the quantity demanded,

perfectly inelastic demand
Product demand for which quantity demanded does not respond to a change in price.

economists say that demand is **perfectly inelastic.** The price-elasticity coefficient is zero because there is no response to a change in price. Approximate examples include an acute diabetic's demand for insulin or an addict's demand for heroin. A line parallel to the vertical axis, such as D_1 in Figure 4.1a, shows perfectly inelastic demand graphically.

© Royalty-Free/CORBIS

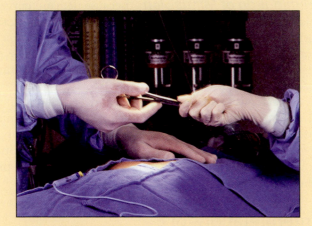

© PhotoLink/Getty Images

PHOTO OP Elastic versus Inelastic Demand

The demand for expensive leisure activities such as cruise vacations is elastic; the demand for surgery or other nonelective medical care is inelastic.

perfectly elastic demand
Product demand for which quantity demanded can be any amount at a particular price.

Conversely, when we say demand is "elastic," we do not mean that consumers are completely responsive to a price change. In that extreme situation, where a small price reduction causes buyers to increase their purchases from zero to all they can obtain, the elasticity coefficient is infinite (∞) and economists say demand is **perfectly elastic.** A line parallel to the horizontal axis, such as D_2 in Figure 4.1b, shows perfectly elastic demand. Such a demand curve, for example, faces wheat growers who can sell all or none of their wheat at the equilibrium market price.

FIGURE 4.1 Perfectly inelastic and elastic demands. Demand curve D_1 in (a) represents perfectly inelastic demand ($E_d = 0$). A price increase will result in no change in quantity demanded. Demand curve D_2 in (b) represents perfectly elastic demand. A price increase will cause quantity demanded to decline from an infinite amount to zero ($E_d = \infty$).

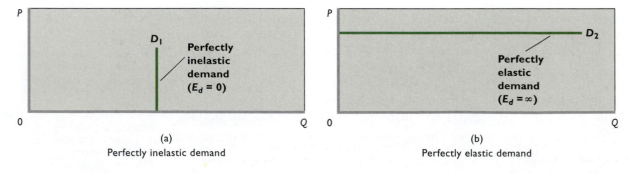

(a)
Perfectly inelastic demand

(b)
Perfectly elastic demand

A Bit of a Stretch

The following analogy might help you remember the distinction between "elastic" and "inelastic." Imagine two objects: (1) an Ace elastic bandage used to wrap injured joints and (2) a relatively firm rubber tie-down used for securing items for transport. The Ace bandage stretches a great deal when pulled with a particular force; the rubber tie-down stretches some, but not a lot.

Similar differences occur for the quantity demanded of various products when their prices change. For some products, a price change causes a substantial "stretch" of quantity demanded. When this stretch in percentage terms exceeds the percentage change in price, demand is elastic. For other products, quantity demanded stretches very little in response to the price change. When this stretch in percentage terms is less than the percentage change in price, demand is inelastic.

In summary:

- Elastic demand displays considerable "quantity stretch" (as with the Ace bandage).
- Inelastic demand displays relatively little "quantity stretch" (as with the rubber tie-down).

And through extension:

- Perfectly elastic demand has infinite quantity stretch.
- Perfectly inelastic demand has zero quantity stretch.

QUESTION: Which do you think has the most quantity stretch, given an equal percentage increase in price—toothpaste or townhouses?

The Total-Revenue Test

The importance of elasticity for firms relates to the effect of price changes on total revenue and thus on profits (total revenue minus total costs).

Total revenue (TR) is the total amount the seller receives from the sale of a product in a particular time period; it is calculated by multiplying the product price (P) by the quantity demanded and sold (Q). In equation form:

$$TR = P \times Q$$

Graphically, total revenue is represented by the $P \times Q$ rectangle lying below a point on a demand curve. At point a in Figure 4.2a, for example, price is \$2 and quantity demanded is 10 units. So total revenue is \$20 (= \$2 × 10), shown by the rectangle composed of the yellow and green areas under the demand curve. We know from basic geometry that the area of a rectangle is found by multiplying one side by the other. Here, one side is "price" (\$2) and the other is "quantity demanded" (10 units).

Total revenue and the price elasticity of demand are related. In fact, the easiest way to infer whether demand is elastic or inelastic is to employ the **total-revenue test**.

total revenue (TR)
The total number of dollars received by a firm from the sale of a product in a particular period.

total-revenue test
A test that determines elasticity by examining what happens to total revenue when price changes.

FIGURE 4.2 **The total-revenue test for price elasticity.** (a) Price declines from $2 to $1, and total revenue increases from $20 to $40. So demand is elastic. The gain in revenue (blue area) exceeds the loss of revenue (yellow area). (b) Price declines from $4 to $1, and total revenue falls from $40 to $20. So demand is inelastic. The gain in revenue (blue area) is less than the loss of revenue (yellow area). (c) Price declines from $3 to $1, and total revenue does not change. Demand is unit-elastic. The gain in revenue (blue area) equals the loss of revenue (yellow area).

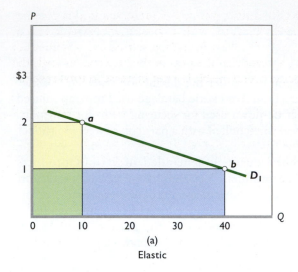

(a)
Elastic

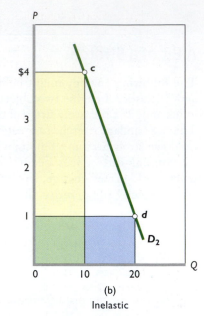

(b)
Inelastic

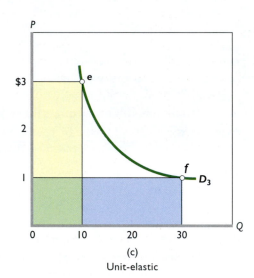

(c)
Unit-elastic

Here is the test: Note what happens to total revenue when price changes. If total revenue changes in the opposite direction from price, demand is elastic. If total revenue changes in the same direction as price, demand is inelastic. If total revenue does not change when price changes, demand is unit-elastic.

Elastic Demand If demand is elastic, a decrease in price will increase total revenue. Even though a lesser price is received per unit, enough additional units are sold to more than make up for the lower price. For an example, look at demand curve D_1 in Figure 4.2a. We have already established that at point *a*, total revenue is $20 (= $2 × 10), shown as the yellow plus green area.

If the price declines from $2 to $1 (point *b*), the quantity demanded becomes 40 units and total revenue is $40 (= $1 × 40). As a result of the price decline, total

WORKED PROBLEMS

W 4.2

Total-revenue test

revenue has increased from $20 to $40. Total revenue has increased in this case because the $1 decline in price applies to 10 units, with a consequent revenue loss of $10 (the yellow area). But 30 more units are sold at $1 each, resulting in a revenue gain of $30 (the blue area). Visually, it is apparent that the gain of the blue area exceeds the loss of the yellow area. As indicated, the overall result is a net increase in total revenue of $20 (= $30 − $10).

The analysis is reversible: If demand is elastic, a price increase will reduce total revenue. The revenue gained on the higher-priced units will be more than offset by the revenue lost from the lower quantity sold. Bottom line: Other things equal, when price and total revenue move in opposite directions, demand is elastic. E_d is greater than 1, meaning the percentage change in quantity demanded is greater than the percentage change in price.

Inelastic Demand   If demand is inelastic, a price decrease will reduce total revenue. The increase in sales will not fully offset the decline in revenue per unit, and total revenue will decline. To see this, look at demand curve D_2 in Figure 4.2b. At point c on the curve, price is $4 and quantity demanded is 10. So total revenue is $40, shown by the combined yellow and green rectangle. If the price drops to $1 (point d), total revenue declines to $20, which obviously is less than $40. Total revenue has declined because the loss of revenue (the yellow area) from the lower unit price is larger than the gain in revenue (the blue area) from the accompanying increase in sales. Price has fallen, and total revenue has also declined.

Our analysis is again reversible: If demand is inelastic, a price increase will increase total revenue. So, other things equal, when price and total revenue move in the same direction, demand is inelastic. E_d is less than 1, meaning the percentage change in quantity demanded is less than the percentage change in price.

Unit Elasticity   In the special case of unit elasticity, an increase or a decrease in price leaves total revenue unchanged. The loss in revenue from a lower unit price is exactly offset by the gain in revenue from the accompanying increase in sales. Conversely, the gain in revenue from a higher unit price is exactly offset by the revenue loss associated with the accompanying decline in the amount demanded.

In Figure 4.2c (demand curve D_3), we find that at the $3 price, 10 units will be sold, yielding total revenue of $30. At the lower $1 price, a total of 30 units will be sold, again resulting in $30 of total revenue. The $2 price reduction causes the loss of revenue shown by the yellow area, but this is exactly offset by the revenue gain shown by the blue area. Total revenue does not change. In fact, that would be true for all price changes along this particular curve.

Other things equal, when price changes and total revenue remains constant, demand is unit-elastic (or unitary). E_d is 1, meaning the percentage change in quantity equals the percentage change in price.

Price Elasticity along a Linear Demand Curve

Now a major confession! Although the demand curves depicted in Figure 4.2 nicely illustrate the total-revenue test for elasticity, two of the graphs involve specific movements along linear (straight-line) demand curves. That presents no problem for explaining the total-revenue test. However, you need to know that elasticity typically varies over different price ranges of the same demand curve. (The exception is the curve in Figure 4.2c. Elasticity is 1 along the entire curve.)

FIGURE 4.3 Price elasticity of demand along a linear demand curve as measured by the elasticity coefficient and the total-revenue test. Demand curve D is based on columns (1) and (2) of the table and is labeled to show that the hypothetical weekly demand for movie tickets is elastic at higher price ranges and inelastic at lower price ranges. That fact is confirmed by the elasticity coefficients (column 3) as well as the total-revenue test (columns 4 and 5) in the table.

(1) Total Quantity of Tickets Demanded per Week, Thousands	(2) Price per Ticket	(3) Elasticity Coefficient (E_d)	(4) Total Revenue, (1) × (2)	(5) Total-Revenue Test
1	$8		$ 8,000	
		5.00		Elastic
2	7		14,000	
		2.60		Elastic
3	6		18,000	
		1.57		Elastic
4	5		20,000	
		1.00		Unit elastic
5	4		20,000	
		0.64		Inelastic
6	3		18,000	
		0.38		Inelastic
7	2		14,000	
		0.20		Inelastic
8	1		8,000	

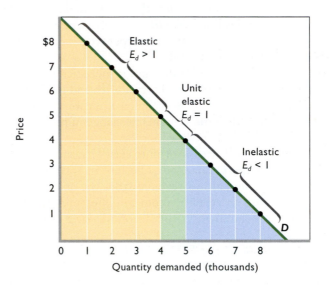

INTERACTIVE GRAPHS

G 4.1

Elasticity and revenue

Consider columns 1 and 2 of the table in Figure 4.3, which shows hypothetical data for movie tickets. We plot these data as demand curve D in the accompanying graph. The notation above the curve correctly suggests that demand is more price-elastic toward the upper left (here, the $5–$8 price range of D) than toward the lower right (here, the $4–$1 price range of D). This fact is confirmed by the elasticity coefficients in column (3) of the table: The coefficients decline as price falls. Also, note from column (4) that total revenue first rises as price falls and then eventually declines as price falls further. Column (5) employs the total-revenue test to show that elasticity declines as price falls along a linear demand curve.

The demand curve in Figure 4.3 illustrates that the slope of a demand curve (its flatness or steepness) is an unreliable basis for judging elasticity. The slope of the curve is computed from *absolute* changes in price and quantity, while elasticity involves *relative* or *percentage* changes in price and quantity. The demand curve in Figure 4.3 is linear, which means its slope is constant throughout. But this linear curve is elastic in its high-price ($8–$5) range and inelastic in its low-price ($4–$1) range.

Determinants of Price Elasticity of Demand

We cannot say what will determine the price elasticity of demand in each individual situation, but the following generalizations are often helpful.

Substitutability Generally, the larger the number of substitute goods that are available, the greater is the price elasticity of demand. Mercedes, BMWs, and Lincolns are effective substitutes for Cadillacs, making the demand for Cadillacs elastic. At the other extreme, we saw earlier that the diabetic's demand for insulin is highly inelastic because there simply are no close substitutes.

The elasticity of demand for a product depends on how narrowly the product is defined. Demand for Reebok sneakers is more elastic than is the overall demand for shoes. Many other brands are readily substitutable for Reebok sneakers, but there are few, if any, good substitutes for shoes.

Proportion of Income Other things equal, the higher the price of a product relative to one's income, the greater the price elasticity of demand for it. A 10 percent increase in the price of low-priced pencils or chewing gum amounts to a very small portion of most people's incomes, and quantity demanded will probably decline only slightly. Thus, price elasticity for such low-priced items tends to be low. But a 10 percent increase in the price of relatively high-priced automobiles or houses means additional expenditures of perhaps $3000 or $20,000. That price increase is a significant fraction of the incomes and budgets of most families, and the number of units demanded will likely diminish significantly. The price elasticities for such items tend to be high.

Luxuries versus Necessities In general, the more that a good is considered to be a "luxury" rather than a "necessity," the greater is the price elasticity of demand. Electricity is generally regarded as a necessity; it is difficult to get along without it. A price increase will not significantly reduce the amount of lighting and power used in a household. (Note the very low price-elasticity coefficient of these goods in Table 4.1.) An extreme case: A person does not decline emergency heart bypass surgery because the physician's fee has just gone up by 10 percent.

On the other hand, vacation travel and jewelry are luxuries that can easily be forgone. If the prices of vacation travel and jewelry rise, a consumer need not buy them and will suffer no great hardship without them.

What about the demand for a common product like salt? It is highly inelastic on three counts: There are few good substitutes available; salt is a negligible item in the family budget; and it is a "necessity" rather than a luxury.

Time Generally, product demand is more elastic the longer the time period under consideration. Consumers often need time to adjust to changes in prices. For example, consumers may not immediately reduce their purchases very much when the price of beef rises by 10 percent, but in time they may shift to chicken, pork, or fish.

Another consideration is product durability. Studies show that "short-run" demand for gasoline is more inelastic ($E_d = .2$) than is "long-run" demand ($E_d = .7$).

TABLE 4.1 Selected Price Elasticities of Demand

Product or Service	Coefficient of Price Elasticity of Demand (E_d)	Product or Service	Coefficient of Price Elasticity of Demand (E_d)
Newspapers	.10	Milk	.63
Electricity (household)	.13	Household appliances	.63
Bread	.15	Liquor	.70
Major-league baseball tickets	.23	Movies	.87
Cigarettes	.25	Beer	.90
Telephone service	.26	Shoes	.91
Sugar	.30	Motor vehicles	1.14
Medical care	.31	Beef	1.27
Eggs	.32	China, glassware, tableware	1.54
Legal services	.37	Residential land	1.60
Automobile repair	.40	Restaurant meals	2.27
Clothing	.49	Lamb and mutton	2.65
Gasoline	.60	Fresh peas	2.83

Source: Compiled from numerous studies and sources reporting price elasticity of demand.

In the short run, people are "stuck" with their present cars and trucks, but with rising gasoline prices they eventually replace them with smaller, more fuel-efficient vehicles.

Table 4.1 shows estimated price-elasticity coefficients for a number of products. Each reflects some combination of the elasticity determinants just discussed.

APPLYING THE ANALYSIS

Price Elasticity of Demand and College Tuition

For some goods and services, for-profit firms or not-for-profit institutions may find it advantageous to determine differences in price elasticity of demand for different groups of customers and then charge different prices to the different groups. Price increases for groups that have inelastic demand will increase total revenue, as will price decreases for groups that have elastic demand.

It is relatively easy to observe differences between group elasticities. Consider tuition pricing by colleges and universities. Prospective students from low-income families generally have more elastic demand for higher education than similar students from high-income families. This is true because tuition is a much larger proportion of household income for a low-income student or family than for his or her high-income counterpart. Desiring a diverse student body, colleges charge different *net* prices (= tuition *minus* financial aid) to the two groups on the basis of elasticity of demand. High-income students pay full tuition, unless they receive merit-based scholarships. Low-income students receive considerable financial aid in addition to merit-based scholarships and, in effect, pay a lower *net* price.

It is common for colleges to announce a large tuition increase and immediately cushion the news by emphasizing that they also are increasing financial aid. In effect, the college is increasing the tuition for students who have inelastic demand by the full amount and raising the *net* tuition of those with elastic demand by some lesser amount or not at all. Through this strategy, colleges boost revenue to cover rising costs while maintaining affordability for a wide range of students.

QUESTION: What are some other examples of charging different prices to different groups of customers on the basis of differences in elasticity of demand? (*Hint:* Think of price discounts based on age or time of purchase.)

APPLYING THE ANALYSIS

Decriminalization of Illegal Drugs

In recent years proposals to legalize drugs have been widely debated. Proponents contend that drugs should be treated like alcohol; they should be made legal for adults and regulated for purity and potency. The current war on drugs, it is argued, has been unsuccessful, and the associated costs—including enlarged police forces, the construction of more prisons, an overburdened court system, and untold human costs—have increased markedly. Legalization would allegedly reduce drug trafficking significantly by taking the profit out of it. Crack cocaine and heroin, for example, are cheap to produce and could be sold at low prices in legal markets. Because the demand of addicts is highly inelastic, the amounts consumed at the lower prices would increase only modestly. Addicts' total expenditures for cocaine and heroin would decline, and so would the street crime that finances those expenditures.

Opponents of legalization say that the overall demand for cocaine and heroin is far more elastic than proponents think. In addition to the inelastic demand of addicts, there is another market segment whose demand is relatively elastic. This segment consists of the occasional users or "dabblers," who use hard drugs when their prices are low but who abstain or substitute, say, alcohol when their prices are high. Thus, the lower prices associated with the legalization of hard drugs would increase consumption by dabblers. Also, removal of the legal prohibitions against using drugs might make drug use more socially acceptable, increasing the demand for cocaine and heroin.

Many economists predict that the legalization of cocaine and heroin would reduce street prices by up to 60 percent, depending on if and how much they were taxed. According to one study, price declines of that size would increase the number of occasional users of heroin by 54 percent and the number of occasional users of cocaine by 33 percent. The total quantity of heroin demanded would rise by an estimated 100 percent, and the quantity of cocaine demanded would rise by 50 percent.* Moreover, many existing and first-time dabblers might in time become addicts. The overall result, say the opponents of legalization, would be higher social costs, possibly including an increase in street crime.

QUESTION: In what ways do drug rehabilitation programs increase the elasticity of demand for illegal drugs?

*Henry Saffer and Frank Chaloupka, "The Demand for Illegal Drugs," *Economic Inquiry*, July 1999, pp. 401–411.

APPLYING THE ANALYSIS

Excise Taxes and Tax Revenue

The government pays attention to elasticity of demand when it selects goods and services on which to levy *excise taxes* (taxes levied on the production of a product or on the quantity of the product purchased). If a $1 tax is levied on a product and 10,000 units are sold, tax revenue will be $10,000 (= $1 × 10,000 units sold). If the government raises the tax to $1.50, but the higher price that results reduces sales (quantity demanded) to 4000 because demand is elastic, tax revenue will decline to $6000 (= $1.50 × 4000 units sold). So a higher tax on a product that has an elastic demand will bring in less tax revenue.

In contrast, if demand is inelastic, the tax increase from $1 to $1.50 will boost tax revenue. For example, if sales fall from 10,000 to 9000, tax revenue will rise from $10,000 to $13,500 (= $1.50 × 9000 units). Little wonder that legislatures tend to seek out products such as liquor, gasoline, cigarettes, and phone service when levying and raising taxes. Those taxes yield high tax revenues.

QUESTION: Under what circumstance might a reduction of an excise tax actually produce more tax revenue?

APPLYING THE ANALYSIS

Fluctuating Farm Income

Inelastic demand for farm products and year-to-year changes in farm supply combine to produce highly volatile farm prices and incomes. Let's see why.

In industrially advanced economies, the price elasticity of demand for agricultural products is low. For farm products in the aggregate, the elasticity coefficient is between .20 and .25. These figures suggest that the prices of agricultural products would have to fall by 40 to 50 percent for consumers to increase their purchases by a mere 10 percent. Consumers apparently put a low value on additional farm output compared with the value they put on additional units of alternative goods.

Why is this so? Recall that a basic determinant of elasticity of demand is substitutability. When the price of one product falls, the consumer tends to substitute that product for other products whose prices have not fallen. But in relatively wealthy societies, this substitution is very modest for food. Although people may eat more, they do not switch from three meals a day to, say, five or six meals a day in response to a decline in the relative prices of farm products. Real biological factors constrain an individual's capacity to substitute food for other products.

Farm supply tends to fluctuate from year to year, mainly because farmers have limited control over their output. Floods, droughts, unexpected frost, insect damage, and similar disasters can mean poor crops, while an excellent growing season means bumper crops (extraordinarily large crops). Such natural phenomena are beyond the control of farmers, yet those phenomena exert an important influence on output.

In addition to natural phenomena, the highly competitive nature of agriculture makes it difficult for farmers to form huge combinations to control production. If the thousands of widely scattered and independent producers happened to plant an unusually large or an abnormally small portion of their land one year, an extra-large or a very small farm output would result even if the growing season were normal.

Combining inelastic demand with the instability of supply, we can see why farm prices and incomes are unstable. Even if the market demand for some crop such as barley remains fixed, its price inelasticity will magnify small changes in output into relatively large changes in farm prices and income. For example, suppose that a "normal" barley crop of 100 million bushels results in a "normal" price per bushel of $3 and a "normal" farm income of $300 million (= $3 × 100 million).

A bumper crop of barley will cause large deviations from these normal prices and incomes because of the inelasticity of demand. Suppose that a good growing season occurs and that the result is a large crop of 110 million bushels. As farmers watch their individual crops mature, little will they realize that their collectively large crop, when harvested, will drive the price per bushel down to, say, $2.50. Their revenue will fall from $300 million in the normal year to $275 million (= $2.50 × 110 million bushels) this year. When demand is inelastic, an increase in the quantity sold will be accompanied by a more-than-proportionate decline in price. The net result is that total revenue, that is, total farm income, will decline disproportionately.

Similarly, a small crop of 90 million bushels, perhaps caused by drought, might boost the price to $3.50. Total farm income will rise to $315 million (= $3.50 × 90 million bushels) from the normal level of $300 million. A decline in supply will cause a more-than-proportionate increase in price and in income when demand is inelastic. Ironically, for farmers as a group, a poor crop may be a blessing and a bumper crop a hardship.

QUESTION: How might government programs that pay farmers to take land out of production in order to achieve conservation goals (such as erosion control and wildlife protection) increase crop prices and farm income?

Price Elasticity of Supply

The concept of price elasticity also applies to supply. If the quantity supplied by producers is relatively responsive to price changes, supply is elastic. If it is relatively insensitive to price changes, supply is inelastic.

We measure the degree of price elasticity or inelasticity of supply with the coefficient E_s, defined almost like E_d except that we substitute "percentage change in quantity supplied" for "percentage change in quantity demanded":

$$E_s = \frac{\text{percentage change in quantity supplied of X}}{\text{percentage change in price of X}}$$

For reasons explained earlier, the averages, or midpoints, of the before and after quantities supplied and the before and after prices are used as reference points for the percentage changes. Suppose an increase in the price of a good from \$4 to \$6 increases the quantity supplied from 10 units to 14 units. The percentage change in price would be 2/5, or 40 percent, and the percentage change in quantity would be 4/12, or 33 percent:

$$E_s = \frac{.33}{.40} = .83$$

price elasticity of supply
A measure of the responsiveness of the quantity of a product supplied by sellers when the product price changes.

In this case, supply is inelastic because the price-elasticity coefficient is less than 1. If E_s is greater than 1, supply is elastic. If it is equal to 1, supply is unit-elastic. Also, E_s is never negative, since price and quantity supplied are directly related. Thus, there are no minus signs to drop, as was necessary with elasticity of demand.

The degree of **price elasticity of supply** depends mainly on how easily and quickly producers can shift resources between alternative uses to alter production of a good. The easier and more rapid the transfers of resources, the greater is the price elasticity of supply. Take the case of a producer of surfboards. The producer's response

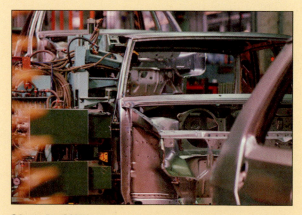

© Royalty-Free/CORBIS

© The Art Archive/Corbis

PHOTO OP Elastic versus Inelastic Supply

The supply of automobiles is elastic, whereas the supply of Monet paintings is inelastic.

to an increase in the price of surfboards depends on its ability to shift resources from the production of other products such as wakeboards, skateboards, and snowboards (whose prices we assume remain constant) to the production of surfboards. And shifting resources takes time: The longer the time, the greater the transferability of resources. So there will be a greater production response, and therefore greater elasticity of supply, the longer a firm has to adjust to a price change.

In analyzing the impact of time on elasticity, economists distinguish among the immediate market period, the short run, and the long run.

Price Elasticity of Supply: The Market Period

The **market period** is the period that occurs when the time immediately after a change in market price is too short for producers to respond with a change in the amount they supply. Suppose a farmer brings to market one truckload of tomatoes that is the entire season's output. The supply curve for the tomatoes is perfectly inelastic (vertical); the farmer will sell the truckload whether the price is high or low. Why? Because the farmer can offer only one truckload of tomatoes even if the price of tomatoes is much higher than anticipated. The farmer might like to offer more tomatoes, but tomatoes cannot be produced overnight. Another full growing season is needed to respond to a higher-than-expected price by producing more than one truckload. Similarly, because the product is perishable, the farmer cannot withhold it from the market. If the price is lower than anticipated, the farmer will still sell the entire truckload.

The farmer's costs of production, incidentally, will not enter into this decision to sell. Though the price of tomatoes may fall far short of production costs, the farmer will nevertheless sell everything brought to market to avoid a total loss through spoilage. In the market period, both the supply of tomatoes and the quantity of tomatoes supplied are fixed. The farmer offers only one truckload, no matter how high or low the price.

Figure 4.4a shows the farmer's vertical supply curve during the market period. Supply is perfectly inelastic because the farmer does not have time to respond to a change in demand, say, from D_1 to D_2. The resulting price increase from P_0 to P_m simply determines which buyers get the fixed quantity supplied; it elicits no increase in output.

However, not all supply curves are perfectly inelastic immediately after a price change. If the product is not perishable and the price rises, producers may choose to increase quantity supplied by drawing down their inventories of unsold, stored goods. This will cause the market supply curve to attain some positive slope. For our tomato farmer, the market period may be a full growing season; for producers of goods that can be inexpensively stored, there may be no market period at all.

Price Elasticity of Supply: The Short Run

The **short run** in microeconomics is a period of time too short to change plant capacity but long enough to use the fixed-size plant more or less intensively. In the short run, our farmer's plant (land and farm machinery) is fixed. But he does have time in the short run to cultivate tomatoes more intensively by applying more labor and more fertilizer and pesticides to the crop. The result is a somewhat greater output in response to a presumed increase in demand; this greater output is reflected in a more elastic supply of tomatoes, as shown by S_s in Figure 4.4b. Note now that the increase in demand from D_1 to D_2 is met by an increase in quantity (from Q_0 to Q_s),

market period
A period in which producers of a product are unable to change the quantity produced in response to a change in price.

short run
A period in which producers are able to change the quantities of some but not all the resources they employ.

FIGURE 4.4 **Time and the elasticity of supply.** The greater the amount of time producers have to adjust to a change in demand, here from D_1 to D_2, the greater will be their output response. In the immediate market period (a) there is insufficient time to change output, and so supply is perfectly inelastic. In the short run (b) plant capacity is fixed, but changing the intensity of its use can alter output; supply is therefore more elastic. In the long run (c) all desired adjustments, including changes in plant capacity, can be made, and supply becomes still more elastic.

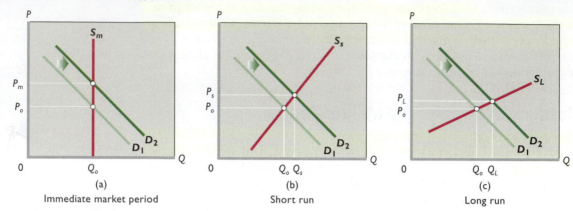

| (a) | (b) | (c) |
| Immediate market period | Short run | Long run |

so there is a smaller price adjustment (from P_0 to P_s) than would be the case in the market period. The equilibrium price is therefore lower in the short run than in the market period.

Price Elasticity of Supply: The Long Run

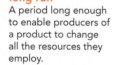

long run
A period long enough to enable producers of a product to change all the resources they employ.

The **long run** in microeconomics is a time period long enough for firms to adjust their plant sizes and for new firms to enter (or existing firms to leave) the industry. In the "tomato industry," for example, our farmer has time to acquire additional land and buy more machinery and equipment. Furthermore, other farmers may, over time, be attracted to tomato farming by the increased demand and higher price. Such adjustments create a larger supply response, as represented by the more elastic supply curve S_L in Figure 4.4c. The outcome is a smaller price rise (P_0 to P_L) and a larger output increase (Q_0 to Q_L) in response to the increase in demand from D_1 to D_2.

There is no total-revenue test for elasticity of supply. Supply shows a positive or direct relationship between price and amount supplied; the supply curve is upsloping. Regardless of the degree of elasticity or inelasticity, price and total revenue always move together.

Antiques and Reproductions

The *Antiques Road Show* is a popular PBS television program in which people bring antiques to a central location for appraisal by experts. Some people are pleased to learn that their old piece of furniture or funky folk art is worth a large amount, say, $30,000 or more.

The high price of a particular antique is due to strong demand and limited, highly inelastic supply. Because a genuine antique can no longer be reproduced, its quantity supplied either does not rise or rises only slightly as its price goes up. The higher price might prompt the discovery of a few more of the remaining originals and thus add to the quantity available for sale, but this quantity response is usually quite small. So the supply of antiques and other collectibles tends to be inelastic. For one-of-a-kind antiques, the supply is perfectly inelastic.

Factors such as increased population, higher income, and greater enthusiasm for collecting antiques have increased the demand for antiques over time. Because the supply of antiques is limited and inelastic, those increases in demand have greatly boosted the prices of antiques.

Contrast the inelastic supply of original antiques with the elastic supply of modern "made-to-look-old" reproductions. Such faux antiques are quite popular and widely available at furniture stores and knickknack shops. When the demand for reproductions increases, the firms making them simply boost production. Because the supply of reproductions is highly elastic, increased demand raises their prices only slightly.

QUESTION: How does the reluctance to sell antiques add to their inelastic supply?

Volatile Gold Prices

The price of gold is quite volatile, sometimes rocketing upward one period and plummeting downward the next. The main sources of these fluctuations are shifts in demand and highly inelastic supply. Gold production is a costly and time-consuming process of exploration, mining, and refining. Moreover, the physical availability of gold is highly limited. For both reasons, increases in gold prices do not elicit substantial increases in quantity supplied. Conversely, gold mining is costly to shut down, and existing gold bars are expensive to store. Price decreases therefore do not produce large drops in the quantity of gold supplied. In short, the supply of gold is inelastic.

The demand for gold is partly derived from the demand for its uses, such as for jewelry, dental fillings, and coins. But people also demand gold as a speculative financial investment. They increase their demand for gold when they fear general inflation or domestic or international turmoil that might undermine the value of currency and more traditional investments. They reduce their demand when events settle down. Because of the inelastic supply of gold, even relatively small changes in demand produce relatively large changes in price.

QUESTION: What is the current price of gold? (See www.goldprices.com.) What were the highest and the lowest prices over the last 12 months?

Income Elasticity of Demand

income elasticity of demand

A measure of the responsiveness of the quantity of a product demanded to changes in consumer income.

Income elasticity of demand measures the degree to which the quantity of a product demanded responds, positively or negatively, to a change in consumers' incomes. The coefficient of income elasticity of demand E_i is determined with the formula

$$E_i = \frac{\text{percentage change in quantity demanded}}{\text{percentage change in income}}$$

Normal Goods

For most goods, the income-elasticity coefficient E_i is positive, meaning that more of them are demanded as income rises. Such goods are called *normal* or *superior goods* (and were first described in Chapter 3). But the value of E_i varies greatly among normal goods. For example, income elasticity of demand for automobiles is about +3, while income elasticity for most farm products is only about +.20.

Inferior Goods

A negative income-elasticity coefficient designates an inferior good. Used mattresses, long-distance bus tickets, used clothing, and some frozen meals are likely candidates. Consumers decrease their purchases of inferior goods as their incomes rise.

APPLYING THE ANALYSIS

Which Consumer Products Suffer the Greatest Demand Decreases during Recessions?

Coefficients of income elasticity of demand provide insights into how recessions impact the sales of different consumer products. A recession is defined as two or more consecutive quarters (six months) of falling real output, and is typically characterized by rising unemployment rates, lower profits for business firms, falling consumer incomes, and weaker demand for products. In December 2007, the U.S. economy entered its tenth recession since 1950. Because of a worsening mortgage debt crisis, the recession continued through 2008 and into 2009. When recessions occur and incomes fall, coefficients of income elasticity of demand help predict which products will experience more rapid declines in demand than other products.

Products with relatively high income elasticity coefficients such as automobiles ($E_i = +3$), housing ($E_i = +1.5$), and restaurant meals ($E_i = +1.4$) are generally hit hardest by recessions. Those with low or negative income elasticity coefficients are much less affected. For example, food products ($E_i = +.20$) respond relatively little to income fluctuations. When incomes drop, purchases of food (and toothpaste and toilet paper) drop little compared to purchases of movie tickets, luxury vacations, and wide-screen TVs. Products we view as essential tend to have lower income elasticity coefficients than products we view as luxuries. When our incomes fall, we cannot easily eliminate or postpone the purchase of essential products.

QUESTION: Why did discount clothing stores (such as Kohl's) suffer less than high-end clothing stores (such as Nordstrom) during the 2007–2009 U.S. recession?

Cross-Elasticity of Demand

Cross-elasticity of demand measures how the quantity of a product demanded (say, X) responds to a change in the price of some other product (say, Y). We calculate the coefficient of cross-elasticity of demand E_{xy} just as we do the coefficient of simple price elasticity, except that we relate the percentage change in the consumption of X to the percentage change in the price of Y:

$$E_{xy} = \frac{\text{percentage change in quantity demanded of product X}}{\text{percentage change in price of product Y}}$$

This cross-elasticity (or cross-price-elasticity) concept allows us to quantify and more fully understand substitute and complementary goods, introduced in Chapter 3.

Substitute Goods

If cross-elasticity of demand is positive, meaning that sales of X move in the same direction as a change in the price of Y, then X and Y are substitute goods. An example is Evian water (X) and Dasani water (Y). An increase in the price of Dasani causes consumers to buy more Evian, resulting in a positive cross-elasticity. The larger the positive cross-elasticity coefficient, the greater is the substitutability between the two products.

Complementary Goods

When cross-elasticity is negative, we know that X and Y "go together"; an increase in the price of one decreases the demand for the other. This indicates that the two are complementary goods. For example, a decrease in the price of digital cameras will increase the number of memory sticks purchased. The larger the negative cross-elasticity coefficient, the greater is the complementarity between the two goods.

Independent Goods

A zero or near-zero cross-elasticity suggests that the two products being considered are unrelated or independent goods. An example is textbooks and plums: We would not expect a change in the price of textbooks to have any effect on purchases of plums, and vice versa.

cross-elasticity of demand
A measure of the responsiveness of the quantity demanded of one product to a change in the price of another product.

APPLYING THE ANALYSIS

Using Cross-Elasticity to Make Business and Regulatory Decisions

The degree of substitutability of products, measured by the cross-elasticity coefficient, is important to businesses and government. For example, suppose that Coca-Cola is considering whether or not to lower the price of its Sprite brand. Not only will it want to know something about the price elasticity of demand for Sprite (will the price cut increase or decrease total revenue?), but it also will be interested in knowing if the increased sales of Sprite will come at the expense of its Coke brand. How sensitive are the sales of one of its products (Coke) to a change in the price of another of its products (Sprite)? By how much will the increased sales of Sprite "cannibalize" the sales of Coke? A low cross-elasticity would indicate that Coke and Sprite are weak substitutes for each other and that a lower price for Sprite would have little effect on Coke sales.

Government also implicitly uses the idea of cross-elasticity of demand in assessing whether a proposed merger between two large firms will substantially reduce competition and therefore violate the antitrust laws. For example, the cross-elasticity between Coke and Pepsi is high, making them strong substitutes for each other. In addition, Coke and Pepsi together sell about 75 percent of all carbonated cola drinks consumed in the United States. Taken together, the high cross-elasticities and the large market shares suggest that the government would likely block a merger between Coke and Pepsi because the merger would substantially lessen competition. In contrast, the cross-elasticity between cola and gasoline is low or zero. A merger between Coke and Shell Oil Company would have a minimal effect on competition. So government would let that merger happen.

QUESTION: Prior to the 2007–2009 recession, why did sales of sport utility vehicles (SUVs) decline dramatically, while sales of hybrid vehicles rose significantly? Relate your answer to cross-elasticity of demand.

Summary

1. Price elasticity of demand measures the responsiveness of the quantity of a product demanded when the price changes. If consumers are relatively sensitive to price changes, demand is elastic. If they are relatively unresponsive to price changes, demand is inelastic.

2. The price-elasticity coefficient E_d measures the degree of elasticity or inelasticity of demand. The coefficient is found by the formula

$$E_d = \frac{\text{percentage change in quantity demanded of X}}{\text{percentage change in price of X}}$$

Economists use the averages of prices and quantities under consideration as reference points in determining percentage changes in price and quantity. If E_d is greater than 1, demand is elastic. If E_d is less than 1, demand is inelastic. Unit elasticity is the special case in which E_d equals 1.

3. Perfectly inelastic demand is graphed as a line parallel to the vertical axis; perfectly elastic demand is shown by a line above and parallel to the horizontal axis.

4. Total revenue (TR) is the total number of dollars received by a firm from the sale of a product in a particular period. It is found by multiplying price times quantity. Graphically, TR is shown as the $P \times Q$ rectangle under a point on a demand curve.

5. If total revenue changes in the opposite direction from prices, demand is elastic. If price and total revenue change in the same direction, demand is inelastic. Where demand is of unit elasticity, a change in price leaves total revenue unchanged.

6. Elasticity varies at different price ranges on a demand curve, tending to be elastic in the upper-left segment and inelastic in the lower-right segment. Elasticity cannot be judged by the steepness or flatness of a demand curve.

7. The number of available substitutes, the size of an item's price relative to one's budget, whether the product is a luxury or a necessity, and the length of time to adjust are all determinants of elasticity of demand.

8. The elasticity concept also applies to supply. The coefficient of price elasticity of supply is found by the formula

$$E_s = \frac{\text{percentage change in quantity supplied of X}}{\text{percentage change in price of X}}$$

The averages of the prices and quantities under consideration are used as reference points for computing percentage changes.

9. Elasticity of supply depends on the ease of shifting resources between alternative uses, which varies directly with the time producers have to adjust to a price change.

10. Income elasticity of demand indicates the responsiveness of consumer purchases to a change in income. The coefficient of income elasticity of demand is found by the formula

$$E_i = \frac{\text{percentage change in quantity demanded}}{\text{percentage change in income}}$$

The coefficient is positive for normal goods and negative for inferior goods.

11. Cross-elasticity of demand indicates the responsiveness of consumer purchases of one product (X) to a change in the price of some other product (Y). The coefficient of cross-elasticity is found by the formula

$$E_{xy} = \frac{\text{percentage change in quantity demanded of product X}}{\text{percentage change in price of product Y}}$$

The coefficient is positive if X and Y are substitute goods and negative if X and Y are complements.

Terms and Concepts

price elasticity of demand	perfectly elastic demand	short run
elastic demand	total revenue (TR)	long run
inelastic demand	total-revenue test	income elasticity of demand
unit elasticity	price elasticity of supply	cross-elasticity of demand
perfectly inelastic demand	market period	

Questions

1. What is the formula for measuring price elasticity of demand? What does it mean (in terms of relative price and quantity changes) if the price-elasticity coefficient is less than 1? Equal to 1? Greater than 1? **LO1**

2. Graph the accompanying demand data, and then use the price-elasticity formula (midpoints approach) for E_d to determine price elasticity of demand for each of the four possible $1 price changes. What can you conclude about the relationship between the slope of a curve and its elasticity? **LO1**

Product Price	Quantity Demanded
$5	1
4	2
3	3
2	4
1	5

3. What are the major determinants of price elasticity of demand? Use those determinants and your own reasoning in judging whether demand for each of the following products is probably elastic or inelastic: (a) bottled water; (b) toothpaste; (c) Crest toothpaste; (d) ketchup; (e) diamond bracelets; (f) Microsoft Windows operating system. **LO1**

4. What effect would a rule stating that university students must live in university dormitories have on the price elasticity of demand for dormitory space? What impact might this in turn have on room rates? **LO1**

5. Calculate total-revenue data from the demand schedule in question 2. Referring to changes in price and total revenue, describe the total-revenue test for elasticity. **LO2**

6. How would the following changes in price affect total revenue? That is, would total revenue increase, decrease, or remain unchanged? **LO2**
   a. Price falls and demand is inelastic.
   b. Price rises and demand is elastic.
   c. Price rises and supply is elastic.
   d. Price rises and supply is inelastic.
   e. Price rises and demand is inelastic.
   f. Price falls and demand is elastic.
   g. Price falls and demand is of unit elasticity.

7. You are chairperson of a state tax commission responsible for establishing a program to raise new revenue through excise taxes. Why would elasticity of demand be important to you in determining the products on which the taxes should be levied? **LO4**

8. In 2006, Willem de Koonig's abstract painting *Woman III* sold for $137.5 million. Portray this sale in a demand and supply diagram, and comment on the elasticity of supply. Comedian George Carlin once mused, "If a painting can be forged well enough to fool some experts, why is the original so valuable?" Provide an answer. **LO4**

9. Because of a legal settlement over state health care claims, in 1999 the U.S. tobacco companies had to raise the average price of a pack of cigarettes from $1.95 to $2.45. The decline in cigarette sales was estimated at 8 percent. What does this imply for the elasticity of demand for cigarettes? Explain. **LO4**

10. The income elasticities of demand for movies, dental services, and clothing have been estimated to be +3.4, +1, and +.5, respectively. Interpret these coefficients. What does it mean if an income-elasticity coefficient is negative? **LO5**

11. Suppose the cross-elasticity of demand for products A and B is +3.6, and for products C and D is −5.4. What can you conclude about how products A and B are related? Products C and D? **LO5**

Problems

1. Look at the demand curve in Figure 4.2a. Use the midpoint formula and points *a* and *b* to calculate the elasticity of demand for that range of the demand curve. Do the same for the demand curves in Figures 4.2b and 4.2c using, respectively, points *c* and *d* for Figure 4.2b and points *e* and *f* for Figure 4.2c. **LO1**

2. Investigate how demand elasticities are affected by increases in demand. Shift each of the demand curves in

Figures 4.2a, 4.2b, and 4.2c to the right by 10 units. For example, point *a* in Figure 4.2a would shift rightward from location (10 units, $2) to (20 units, $2), while point *b* would shift rightward from location (40 units, $1) to (50 units, $1). After making these shifts, apply the midpoint formula to calculate the demand elasticities for the shifted points. Are they larger or smaller than the elasticities you calculated in problem 1 for the original points? In terms of the midpoint formula, what explains the change in elasticities? **LO1**

3. Suppose that the total revenue received by a company selling basketballs is $600 when the price is set at $30 per basketball and $600 when the price is set at $20 per basketball. Without using the midpoint formula, can you tell whether demand is elastic, inelastic, or unit-elastic over this price range? **LO2**

4. Danny "Dimes" Donahue is a neighborhood's 9-year old entrepreneur. His most recent venture is selling homemade brownies that he bakes himself. At a price of $1.50 each, he sells 100. At a price of $1.00 each, he sells 300. Is demand elastic or inelastic over this price range? *If* demand had the same elasticity for a price decline from $1.00 to $0.50 as it does for the decline from $1.50 to $1.00, would cutting the price from $1.00 to $0.50 increase or decrease Danny's total revenue? **LO2**

5. What is the formula for measuring the price elasticity of supply? Suppose the price of apples goes up from $20 to $22 a box. In direct response, Goldsboro Farms supplies 1200 boxes of apples instead of 1000 boxes. Compute the coefficient of price elasticity (midpoints approach) for Goldsboro's supply. Is its supply elastic, or is it inelastic? **LO3**

6. **ADVANCED ANALYSIS** Currently, at a price of $1 each, 100 popsicles are sold per day in the perpetually hot town of Rostin. Consider the elasticity of supply. In the short run, a price increase from $1 to $2 is unit-elastic ($E_s = 1.0$). So how many popsicles will be sold each day in the short run if the price rises to $2 each? In the long run, a price increase from $1 to $2 has an elasticity of supply of 1.50. So how many popsicles will be sold per day in the long run if the price rises to $2 each? (Hint: Apply the midpoints approach to the elasticity of supply.) **LO3**

7. Lorena likes to play golf. The number of times per year that she plays depends on both the price of playing a round of golf as well as Lorena's income and the cost of other types of entertainment—in particular, how much it costs to go see a movie instead of playing golf. The three demand schedules in the table below show how many rounds of golf per year Lorena will demand at each price under three different scenarios. In scenario D_1, Lorena's income is $50,000 per year and movies cost $9 each. In scenario D_2, Lorena's income is also $50,000 per year, but the price of seeing a movie rises to $11. And in scenario D_3, Lorena's income goes up to $70,000 per year, while movies cost $11. **LO5**

	Quantity Demanded		
Price	D_1	D_2	D_3
$50	15	10	15
35	25	15	30
20	40	20	50

a. Using the data under D_1 and D_2, calculate the cross-elasticity of Lorena's demand for golf at all three prices. (To do this, apply the midpoints approach to the cross-elasticity of demand.) Is the cross-elasticity the same at all three prices? Are movies and golf substitute goods, complementary goods, or independent goods?

b. Using the data under D_2 and D_3, calculate the income elasticity of Lorena's demand for golf at all three prices. (To do this, apply the midpoints approach to the income elasticity of demand.) Is the income elasticity the same at all three prices? Is golf an inferior good?

FURTHER TEST YOUR KNOWLEDGE AT
www.mcconnellbrief2e.com

At the text's Online Learning Center, **www.mcconnellbrief2e.com**, you will find one or more web-based questions that require information from the Internet to answer. We urge you to check them out, since they will familiarize you with websites that may be helpful in other courses and perhaps even in your career. The OLC also features multiple-choice quizzes that give instant feedback and provides other helpful ways to further test your knowledge of the chapter.

Visit your mobile app store and download the McConnell Brief Edition: Study Econ app *today*!

5

After reading this chapter, you should be able to:

1 Differentiate between demand-side market failures and supply-side market failures.

2 Explain consumer surplus and producer surplus, and discuss how properly functioning markets maximize their sum while optimally allocating resources.

3 Identify how public goods are distinguished from private goods, and explain the method for determining the optimal quantity of a public good.

4 Explain how positive and negative externalities cause under- and overallocations of resources, and how they might be corrected.

5 Show why we normally won't want to pay what it would cost to eliminate every last bit of a negative externality.

Market Failures: Public Goods and Externalities

Competitive markets usually do a remarkable job of allocating society's scarce resources to their highest-valued uses. But markets have certain limitations. In some circumstances, economically desirable goods are not produced at all. In other situations, they are either overproduced or underproduced. This chapter examines **market failure,** which occurs when the competitive market system (1) does not allocate any resources whatsoever to the production of certain goods or (2) either underallocates or overallocates resources to the production of certain goods.

Where private markets fail, an economic role for government may arise. In this chapter, we will examine that role as it relates to public goods and so-called externalities—situations where market

market failure
The inability of a market to produce a desirable product or produce it in the "right" amount.

failures lead to suboptimal outcomes that the government may be able to improve upon by using its powers to tax, spend, and regulate. We conclude the chapter by noting potential government inefficiencies that can hinder government's economic efforts.

Market Failures in Competitive Markets[1]

Competitive markets usually produce an assignment of resources that is "right" from an economic perspective. Unfortunately, the presence of robust competition involving many buyers and many sellers may not be enough to guarantee that a market will allocate resources correctly. Market failures sometimes happen in competitive markets. The focus of this chapter is to explain how and why such market failures can arise, and how they might be corrected.

Fortunately, the broad picture is simple. Market failures in competitive markets fall into just two categories:

demand-side market failures
Underallocations of resources that occur when private demand curves understate consumers' full willingness to pay for a good or service.

supply-side market failures
Overallocations of resources that occur when private supply curves understate the full cost of producing a good or service.

- **Demand-side market failures** happen when demand curves do not reflect consumers' full willingness to pay for a good or service.
- **Supply-side market failures** occur when supply curves do not reflect the full cost of producing a good or service.

Demand-Side Market Failures

Demand-side market failures arise because it is impossible in certain cases to charge consumers what they are willing to pay for a product. Consider outdoor fireworks displays. People enjoy fireworks and would therefore be *willing* to pay to see a fireworks display if the only way to see it was to have to pay for the right to do so. But because such displays are outdoors and in public, people don't actually *have* to pay to see the display because there is no way to exclude those who haven't paid from also enjoying the show. Private firms will therefore be unwilling to produce outdoor fireworks displays, as it will be nearly impossible for them to raise enough revenue to cover production costs.

Supply-Side Market Failures

Supply-side market failures arise in situations in which a firm does not have to pay the full cost of producing its output. Consider a coal-burning power plant. The firm running the plant will have to pay for all of the land, labor, capital, and entrepreneurship that it uses to generate electricity by burning coal. But if the firm is not charged for the smoke that it releases into the atmosphere, it will fail to pay another set of costs—the costs that its pollution imposes on other people. These include future harm from global warming, toxins that affect wildlife, and possible damage to agricultural crops downwind.

A market failure arises because it is not possible for the market to correctly weigh costs and benefits in a situation in which some of the costs are completely unaccounted for. The coal-burning power plant produces more electricity and generates more pollution than it would if it had to pay for each ton of smoke that it released into the atmosphere. The extra units that are produced are units of output for which the costs are *greater than* the benefits. Obviously, these units should not be produced.

externalities - supply side

---

[1]Other market failures arise when there are not enough buyers or sellers to ensure competition. In those situations, the lack of competition allows either buyers or sellers to restrict purchases or sales below optimal levels for their own benefit. As an example, a monopoly—a firm that is the only producer in its industry—can restrict the amount of output that it supplies in order to drive up the market price and thereby increase its own profit.

Efficiently Functioning Markets

The best way to understand market failure is to first understand how properly functioning competitive markets achieve economic efficiency.

A competitive market not only makes private goods available to consumers but also allocates society's resources efficiently to the particular product. Competition among producers forces them to use the best technology and right mix of productive resources. Otherwise, lower-cost producers will drive them out of business. The result is **productive efficiency**: the production of any particular good in the least costly way. When society produces, say, bottled water at the lowest achievable per-unit cost, it is expending the smallest amount of resources to produce that product and therefore is making available the largest amount of resources to produce other desired goods. Suppose society has only $100 worth of resources available. If it can produce a bottle of water using only $1 of those resources, then it will have available $99 of resources to produce other goods. This is clearly better than producing the bottle of water for $5 and having only $95 of resources available for alternative uses.

Competitive markets also produce **allocative efficiency**: the *particular mix* of goods and services most highly valued by society (minimum-cost production assumed). For example, society wants high-quality mineral water to be used for bottled water, not for gigantic blocks of refrigeration ice. It wants MP3 players (such as iPods), not phonographs and 45-rpm records. Moreover, society does not want to devote all its resources to bottled water and MP3 players. It wants to assign some resources to automobiles and personal computers. Competitive markets make those proper assignments, as we will demonstrate.

Two conditions must hold if a competitive market is to produce efficient outcomes: The demand curve in the market must reflect consumers' full willingness to pay and the supply curve in the market must reflect all the costs of production. If these conditions hold, then the market will produce only units for which benefits are at least equal to costs. It also will maximize the amount of "benefit surpluses" that are shared between consumers and producers.

Consumer Surplus

The benefit surplus received by a consumer or consumers in a market is called **consumer surplus**. It is defined as the difference between the maximum price a consumer is (or consumers are) willing to pay for a product and the actual price that they do pay.

Suppose that the maximum Ted is willing to pay for an apple is $1.25. If Ted is charged any market price less than $1.25, he will receive a consumer surplus equal to the difference between the $1.25 maximum price that he would have been willing to pay and the lower market price. For instance, if the market price is $.50 per apple, Ted will receive a consumer surplus of $.75 per apple (= $1.25 − $.50). In nearly all markets, consumers individually and collectively gain greater total utility or satisfaction in dollar terms from their purchases than the amount of their expenditures (= product price × quantity). This utility surplus arises because each consumer who buys the product only has to pay the equilibrium price even though many of them would have been willing to pay more than the equilibrium price to obtain the product.

The concept of maximum willingness to pay also gives us another way to understand demand curves. Consider Table 5.1, where the first two columns show the maximum amounts that six consumers would each be willing to pay for a bag of oranges. Bob, for instance, would be willing to pay a maximum of $13 for a bag of oranges. Betty, by contrast, would only be willing to pay a maximum of $8 for a bag of oranges.

---

productive efficiency
The production of a good in the least costly way.

allocative efficiency
The production of the "right" mix of goods and services (minimum-cost production assumed).

consumer surplus
The difference between the maximum price a consumer is (or consumers are) willing to pay for a product and the actual price they do pay.

demand side

great deal

pro

TABLE 5.1 Consumer Surplus

(1) Person	(2) Maximum Price Willing to Pay	(3) Actual Price (Equilibrium Price)	(4) Consumer Surplus
Bob	$13	$8	$5 (= $13 − $8)
Barb	12	8	4 (= $12 − $8)
Bill	11	8	3 (= $11 − $8)
Bart	10	8	2 (= $10 − $8)
Brent	9	8	1 (= $9 − $8)
Betty	8	8	0 (= $8 − $8)

The maximum prices that these individuals are willing to pay represent points on a demand curve because the lower the market price, the more bags of oranges will be demanded. At a price of $12.50, for instance, Bob will be the only person listed in the table who will purchase a bag. But at a price of $11.50, both Bob and Barb will want to purchase a bag. The lower the price, the greater the total quantity demanded as the market price falls below the maximum prices of more and more consumers.

Lower prices also imply larger consumer surpluses. When the price is $12.50, Bob only gets $.50 in consumer surplus because his maximum willingness to pay of $13 is only $.50 higher than the market price of $12.50. But if the market price were to fall to $8, then his consumer surplus would be $5 (= $13 − $8). The third and fourth columns of Table 5.1 show how much consumer surplus each of our six consumers will receive if the market price of a bag of oranges is $8. Only Betty receives no consumer surplus because her maximum willingness to pay exactly matches the $8 equilibrium price.

It is easy to show on a graph the consumer surplus received by buyers in a market. Consider Figure 5.1, which shows the market equilibrium price $P_1 = $8 as well as the downsloping demand curve D for bags of oranges. Demand curve D includes not only the six consumers named in Table 5.1 but also every other consumer of oranges in the market. The individual consumer surplus of each particular person who is willing to buy at the $8 market price is simply the vertical distance from the horizontal line that marks the $8 market price up to that particular buyer's maximum willingness to pay. The collective consumer surplus obtained by all of our named and unnamed buyers is found by adding together each of their individual consumer surpluses. To obtain the Q_1 bags of oranges represented, consumers collectively are willing to pay the total

FIGURE 5.1 **Consumer surplus.**
Consumer surplus—shown as the green triangle—is differences between the maximum prices consumers are willing to pay for a product and the lower equilibrium price, here assumed to be $8. For quantity Q_1, consumers are willing to pay the sum of the amounts represented by the green triangle and the yellow rectangle. Because they need to pay only the amount shown as the yellow rectangle, the green triangle shows consumer surplus.

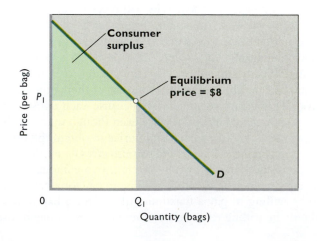

amount shown by the sum of the green triangle and yellow rectangle under the demand curve and to the left of Q_1. But consumers need pay only the amount represented by the yellow rectangle ($= P_1 \times Q_1$). So the green triangle is the consumer surplus in this market. It is the sum of the vertical distances between the demand curve and the $8 equilibrium price at each quantity up to Q_1. Thus, consumer surplus can also be defined as the area that lies below the demand curve and above the price line that extends horizontally from P_1.

Consumer surplus and price are inversely (negatively) related. Given the demand curve, higher prices reduce consumer surplus; lower prices increase it. When price goes up, the gap narrows between the maximum willingness to pay and the actual price; a price decline widens the gap.

Producer Surplus

Like consumers, producers also receive a benefit surplus in markets. This **producer surplus** is the difference between the actual price a producer receives (or producers receive) and the minimum acceptable price that a consumer would have to pay the producer to make a particular unit of output available.

A producer's minimum acceptable price for a particular unit will equal the producer's marginal cost of producing that particular unit. That marginal cost will be the sum of the rent, wages, interest, and profit that the producer will need to pay in order to obtain the land, labor, capital, and entrepreneurship required to produce that particular unit. In this section, we are assuming that the marginal cost of producing a unit will include *all* of the costs of production. Unlike the coal-burning power plant mentioned previously, the producer must pay for all of its costs, including the cost of pollution. In later sections, we will explore the market failures that arise in situations where firms do not have to pay all their costs.

The size of the producer surplus earned on any particular unit will be the difference between the market price that the producer actually receives and the producer's minimum acceptable price. Consider Table 5.2, which shows the minimum acceptable prices of six different orange growers. With a market price of $8, Carlos, for instance, has a producer surplus of $5, which is equal to the market price of $8 minus his minimum acceptable price of $3. Chad, by contrast, receives no producer surplus because his minimum acceptable price of $8 just equals the market equilibrium price of $8.

Carlos's minimum acceptable price is lower than Chad's minimum acceptable price because Carlos is a more efficient producer than Chad, by which we mean that Carlos produces oranges using a less-costly combination of resources than Chad uses. The differences in efficiency between Carlos and Chad are likely due to differences in the type and quality of resources available to them.

ORIGIN OF THE IDEA

O 5.1

Consumer surplus

producer surplus
The difference between the actual price a producer receives (or producers receive) and the minimum acceptable price.

supply side

TABLE 5.2 Producer Surplus

(1) Person	(2) Minimum Acceptable Price	(3) Actual Price (Equilibrium Price)	(4) Producer Surplus
Carlos	$3	$8	$5 (= $8 − $3)
Courtney	4	8	4 (= $8 − $4)
Chuck	5	8	3 (= $8 − $5)
Cindy	6	8	2 (= $8 − $6)
Craig	7	8	1 (= $8 − $7)
Chad	8	8	0 (= $8 − $8)

farther below equilibrium price, more money you make

FIGURE 5.2 Producer surplus.
Producer surplus—shown as the blue triangle—is the differences between the actual price producers receive for a product (here $8) and the lower minimum payments they are willing to accept. For quantity Q_1, producers receive the sum of the amounts represented by the blue triangle plus the yellow area. Because they need receive only the amount shown by the yellow area to produce Q_1, the blue triangle represents producer surplus.

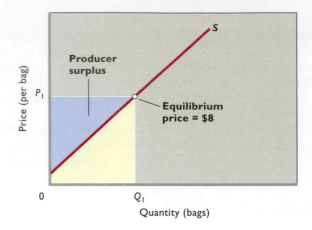

The minimum acceptable prices that producers are willing to accept form points on a supply curve because the higher the price, the more bags of oranges will be supplied. At a price of $3.50, for instance, only Carlos would be willing to supply a bag of oranges. But at a price of $5.50, Carlos, Courtney, and Chuck would all be willing to supply a bag of oranges. The higher the market price, the more oranges will be supplied, as the market price surpasses the marginal costs and minimum acceptable prices of more and more producers. Thus, supply curves shown in this competitive market are both marginal-cost curves and minimum-acceptable-price curves.

The supply curve in Figure 5.2 includes not only the six producers named in Table 5.2 but also every other producer of oranges in the market. At the market price of $8 per bag, Q_1 bags are produced because only those producers whose minimum acceptable prices are less than $8 per bag will choose to produce oranges with their resources. Those lower acceptable prices for each of the units up to Q_1 are shown by the portion of the supply curve lying to the left of and below the assumed $8 market price.

The individual producer surplus of each of these sellers is thus the vertical distance from each seller's respective minimum acceptable price on the supply curve up to the $8 market price. Their collective producer surplus is shown by the blue triangle in Figure 5.2. In that figure, producers collect revenues of $P_1 \times Q_1$, which is the sum of the blue triangle and the yellow area. As shown by the supply curve, however, revenues of only those illustrated by the yellow area would be required to entice producers to offer Q_1 bags of oranges for sale. The sellers therefore receive a producer surplus shown by the blue triangle. That surplus is the sum of the vertical distances between the supply curve and the $8 equilibrium price at each of the quantities to the left of Q_1.

There is a direct (positive) relationship between equilibrium price and the amount of producer surplus. Given the supply curve, lower prices reduce producer surplus; higher prices increase it. The gaps between minimum acceptable payments and actual prices widen when the price increases.

WORKED PROBLEMS

W 5.1

Consumer and producer surplus

Efficiency Revisited

In Figure 5.3 we bring together the demand and supply curves of Figures 5.1 and 5.2 to show the equilibrium price and quantity and the previously described regions of consumer and producer surplus. All markets that have downsloping demand curves and upsloping supply curves yield consumer and producer surplus.

Because we are assuming in Figure 5.3 that the demand curve reflects buyers' full willingness to pay and the supply curve reflects all of the costs facing sellers, the

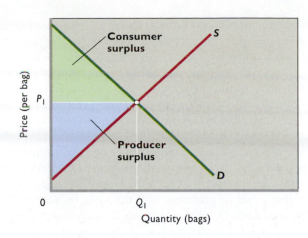

FIGURE 5.3 Efficiency: maximum combined consumer and producer surplus. At quantity Q_1 the combined amount of consumer surplus, shown as the green triangle, and producer surplus, shown as the blue triangle, is maximized. Efficiency occurs because, at Q_1, maximum willingness to pay, indicated by the points on the demand curve, equals minimum acceptable price, shown by the points on the supply curve.

equilibrium quantity in Figure 5.3 reflects both components of economic efficiency: productive efficiency and allocative efficiency.

- *Productive efficiency* is achieved because competition forces orange growers to use the best technologies and combinations of resources available. Doing so minimizes the per-unit cost of the output produced.
- *Allocative efficiency* is achieved because the correct quantity of oranges—Q_1—is produced relative to other goods and services.

There are two ways to understand why Q_1 is the correct quantity of oranges. Both involve realizing that any resources directed toward the production of oranges are resources that could have been used to produce other products. Thus, the only way to justify taking any amount of any resource (land, labor, capital, entrepreneurship) away from the production of other products is if it brings more utility or satisfaction when devoted to the production of oranges than it would if it were used to produce other products.

The first way to see why Q_1 is the allocatively efficient quantity of oranges is to note that demand and supply curves can be interpreted as measuring marginal benefit (MB) and marginal cost (MC). Recall from the discussion relating to Figure 1.3 that optimal allocation is achieved at the output level where MB = MC. We have already seen that supply curves are marginal cost curves. As it turns out, demand curves are marginal benefit curves. This is true because the maximum price that a consumer would be willing to pay for any particular unit is equal to the benefit that she would get if she were to consume that unit. Thus, each point on a demand curve represents both some consumer's maximum willingness to pay as well as the marginal benefit that he or she would get from consuming the particular unit in question.

Combining the fact that supply curves are MC curves with the fact that demand curves are MB curves, we see that points on the demand curve in Figure 5.3 measure the marginal benefit of oranges at each level of output, while points on the supply curve measure the marginal cost of oranges at each level of output. As a result, MB = MC where the demand and supply curves intersect—which means that the equilibrium quantity Q_1 must be allocatively efficient.

The second way to see why Q_1 is the correct quantity of oranges is based on our analysis of consumer and producer surplus and the fact that we can interpret demand and supply curves in terms of maximum willingness to pay and minimum acceptable price. In Figure 5.3, the maximum willingness to pay on the demand curve for each bag of oranges up to Q_1 exceeds the corresponding minimum acceptable price on the supply curve. Thus, each of these bags adds a positive amount (= maximum willingness to pay *minus* minimum acceptable price) to the *total* of consumer and producer surplus.

The fact that maximum willingness to pay exceeds minimum acceptable price for every unit up to Q_1 means that people gain more utility from producing and consuming those units than they would if they produced and consumed anything else that could be made with the resources that went into making those units. Only at the equilibrium quantity Q_1—where the maximum willingness to pay exactly equals the minimum acceptable price—does society exhaust all opportunities to produce units for which benefits exceed costs (including opportunity costs). Producing Q_1 units therefore achieves allocative efficiency because the market is producing and distributing only those units that make people happier with bags of oranges than they would be with anything else that could be produced with the same resources.

Geometrically, producing Q_1 units maximizes the combined area of consumer and producer surplus in Figure 5.3. In this context, the combined area is referred to as *total surplus*. Thus, when Q_1 units are produced, total surplus is equal to the large triangle formed by the green consumer-surplus triangle and the blue producer-surplus triangle.

When demand curves reflect buyers' full willingness to pay and when supply curves reflect all the costs facing sellers, competitive markets produce equilibrium quantities that maximize the sum of consumer and producer surplus. Allocative efficiency occurs at the market equilibrium quantity where three conditions exist simultaneously:

- MB = MC (Figure 1.3).
- Maximum willingness to pay = minimum acceptable price.
- Total surplus (= sum of consumer and producer surplus) is at a maximum.

Economists are enamored of markets because properly functioning markets automatically achieve allocative efficiency. Other methods of allocating resources—such as government central planning—do exist. But because other methods cannot do any better than properly functioning markets—and may in many cases do much worse—economists usually prefer that resources be allocated through markets whenever properly functioning markets are available.

Efficiency Losses (or Deadweight Losses)

efficiency (or deadweight) losses
Reductions in combined consumer and producer surplus caused by an underallocation or overallocation of resources to the production of a good or service.

Figures 5.4a and 5.4b demonstrate that **efficiency losses**—reductions of combined consumer and producer surplus—result from both underproduction and overproduction. First, consider Figure 5.4a, which analyzes the case of underproduction by considering what happens if output falls from the efficient level Q_1 to the smaller amount Q_2. When that happens, the sum of consumer and producer surplus, previously *abc*, falls to *adec*. So the combined consumer and producer surplus declines by the amount of the gray triangle to the left of Q_1. That triangle represents an efficiency loss to buyers and sellers. And because buyers and sellers are members of society, it represents an efficiency loss (or a so-called **deadweight loss**) to society.

For output levels from Q_2 to Q_1, consumers' maximum willingness to pay (as reflected by points on the demand curve) exceeds producers' minimum acceptable price (as reflected by points on the supply curve). By failing to produce units of this product for which a consumer is willing to pay more than a producer is willing to accept, society suffers a loss of net benefits. As a concrete example, consider a particular unit for which a consumer is willing to pay $10 and a producer is willing to accept $6. The $4 difference between those values is a net benefit that will not be realized if this unit is not produced. In addition, the resources that should have gone to producing this unit will go instead to producing other products that will not generate as much utility as if those resources had been used here to produce this unit of this product. The triangle

FIGURE 5.4 Efficiency losses (or deadweight losses). Quantity levels either less than or greater than the efficient quantity Q_1 create efficiency losses. In (a), triangle *dbe* shows the efficiency loss associated with underproduction at output Q_2. Triangle *bfg* in (b) illustrates the efficiency loss associated with overproduction at output level Q_3.

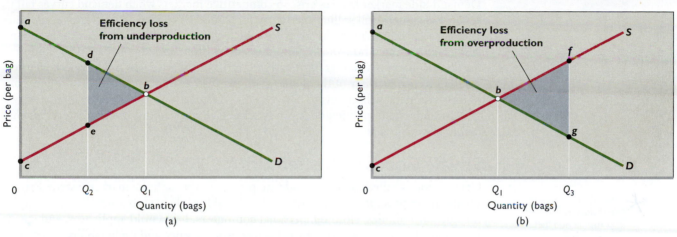

dbe in Figure 5.4a shows the total loss of net benefits that results from failing to produce the units from Q_2 to Q_1.

In contrast, consider the case of overproduction shown in Figure 5.4b, in which the number of oranges produced is Q_3 rather than the efficient level Q_1. In Figure 5.4b the combined consumer and producer surplus therefore declines by *bfg*—the gray triangle to the right of Q_1. This triangle subtracts from the total consumer and producer surplus of *abc* that would occur if the quantity had been Q_1. That is, for all units from 0 to Q_1, benefits exceed costs, so that those units generate the economic surplus shown by triangle *abc*. But the units from Q_1 to Q_3 are such that costs exceed benefits. Thus, they generate an economic loss shown by triangle *bfg*. The total economic surplus for all units from 0 to Q_3 is therefore the economic surplus given by *abc* for the units from 0 to Q_1 minus the economic loss given by *bfg* for the units from Q_1 to Q_3.

Producing any unit beyond Q_1 generates an economic loss because the willingness to pay for such units on the part of consumers is less than the minimum acceptable price to produce such units on the part of producers. As a concrete example, note that producing an item for which the maximum willingness to pay is, say, $7 and the minimum acceptable price is, say, $10 subtracts $3 from society's net benefits. Such production is uneconomical and creates an efficiency loss (or deadweight loss) for society. Because the net benefit of each bag of oranges from Q_1 to Q_3 is negative, we know that the benefits from these units are smaller than the opportunity costs of the other products that could have been produced with the resources that were used to produce these bags of oranges. The resources used to produce the bags from Q_1 to Q_3 could have generated net benefits instead of net losses if they had been directed toward producing other products. The gray triangle *bfg* to the right of Q_1 in Figure 5.4b shows the total efficiency loss from overproduction at Q_3.

The magic of markets is that when demand reflects consumers' full willingness to pay and when supply reflects all costs, the market equilibrium quantity will automatically equal the allocatively efficient output level. Under these conditions, the market equilibrium quantity will ensure that there are neither efficiency losses from underproduction nor efficiency losses from overproduction. As we are about to see, however, such losses do happen when either demand does not reflect consumers' full willingness to pay or supply does not reflect all costs.

Private and Public Goods

Demand-side market failures arise in competitive markets when demand curves fail to reflect consumers' full willingness to pay for a good or service. In such situations, markets fail to produce all of the units for which there are net benefits because demand curves underreport how much consumers are willing and able to pay. This underreporting problem reaches its most extreme form in the case of a public good: Markets may fail to produce *any* of the public good because its demand curve may reflect *none* of its consumers' willingness to pay.

To understand public goods, we first need to understand the characteristics that define private goods.

Private Goods Characteristics

private goods
Goods that people individually buy and consume and that private firms can profitably provide because they keep people who do not pay from receiving the benefits.

Certain goods called **private goods** are produced through the market system. Private goods encompass the full range of goods offered for sale in stores and shops. Examples include automobiles, clothing, personal computers, household appliances, and sporting goods. Private goods have two characteristics: rivalry and excludability.

- *Rivalry* (in consumption) means that when one person buys and consumes a product, it is not available for another person to buy and consume. When Adams purchases and drinks a bottle of mineral water, it is not available for Benson to purchase and consume.
- *Excludability* means that sellers can keep people who do not pay for a product from obtaining its benefits. Only people who are willing and able to pay the market price for bottles of water can obtain these drinks and the benefits they confer.

Profitable Provision

Consumers fully express their personal demands for private goods in the market. If Adams likes bottled mineral water, that fact will be known by her desire to purchase the product. Other things equal, the higher the price of bottled water, the fewer bottles she will buy. So Adams' demand for bottled water will reflect an inverse relationship between the price of bottled water and the quantity of it demanded. This is simply *individual* demand, as described in Chapter 3.

The *market* demand for a private good is the horizontal summation of the individual demand schedules (review Figure 3.2). Suppose there are just two consumers in the market for bottled water and the price is $1 per bottle. If Adams will purchase 3 bottles and Benson will buy 2, the market demand will reflect that consumers demand 5 bottles at the $1 price. Similar summations of quantities demanded at other prices will generate the market demand schedule and curve.

Suppose the equilibrium price of bottled water is $1. Adams and Benson will buy a total of 5 bottles, and the sellers will obtain total revenue of $5 (= $1 × 5). If the sellers' cost per bottle is $.80, their total cost will be $4 (= $.80 × 5). So sellers charging $1 per bottle will obtain $5 of total revenue, incur $4 of total cost, and earn $1 of profits for the 5 bottles sold.

Because firms can profitably "tap market demand" for private goods, they will produce and offer them for sale. Consumers demand private goods, and profit-seeking suppliers produce goods that satisfy the demand. Consumers willing to pay the market price obtain the goods; nonpayers go without. A competitive market not only makes private goods available to consumers but also allocates society's resources efficiently to the particular product. There is neither underproduction nor overproduction of the product.

Public Goods Characteristics

supplied by govt.

Public goods have the opposite characteristics of private goods. Public goods are distinguished by nonrivalry and nonexcludability.

- *Nonrivalry* (in consumption) means that one person's consumption of a good does not preclude consumption of the good by others. Everyone can simultaneously obtain the benefit from a public good such as a global positioning system, national defense, street lighting, and environmental protection.

- *Nonexcludability* means there is no effective way of excluding individuals from the benefit of the good once it comes into existence.

These two characteristics create a **free-rider problem.** Once a producer has provided a public good, everyone including nonpayers can obtain the benefit. Because most people do not voluntarily pay for something that they can obtain for free, most people become free riders. Free riders would be willing to pay for the public good if producers could somehow force them to pay—but nonexcludability means that there is no way for producers to withhold the good from the free riders without also denying it to the few who do pay. As a result, free riding means that the willingness to pay of the free riders is not expressed in the market. From the viewpoint of producers, free riding reduces demand. The more free riding, the less demand. And if all consumers free ride, demand will collapse all the way to zero.

public goods
Goods that everyone can simultaneously consume and from which no one can be excluded, even if they do not pay.

free-rider problem
The inability of a firm to profitably provide a good because everyone, including nonpayers, can obtain the benefit.

© Steven P. Lynch/The McGraw-Hill Companies, Inc.

© S. Solum/PhotoLink/Getty Images

PHOTO OP   Private versus Public Goods

Apples, distinguished by rivalry (in consumption) and excludability, are examples of private goods. In contrast, streetlights, distinguished by nonrivalry (in consumption) and nonexcludability, are examples of public goods.

The low or even zero demand caused by free riding makes it virtually impossible for private firms to profitably provide public goods. With little or no demand, firms cannot effectively "tap market demand" for revenues and profits. As a result, they will not produce public goods. Society will therefore suffer efficiency losses because goods for which marginal benefits exceed marginal costs are not produced. Thus, if society wants a public good to be produced, it will have to direct government to provide it. Because the public good will still feature nonexcludability, the government won't have any better luck preventing free riding or charging people for it. But because the government can finance the provision of the public good through the taxation of other things, the government does not have to worry about profitability. It can therefore provide the public good even when private firms can't.

A significant example of a public good is homeland defense. The vast majority of Americans think this public good is economically justified because they perceive the benefits as exceeding the costs. Once homeland defense efforts are undertaken, however, the benefits accrue to all Americans (nonrivalry). And there is no practical way to exclude any American from receiving those benefits (nonexcludability).

No private firm will undertake overall homeland defense because the free-rider problem means that benefits cannot be profitably sold. So here we have a service that yields substantial net benefits but to which the market system will not allocate sufficient resources. Like national defense in general, homeland defense is a public good. Society signals its desire for such goods by voting for particular political candidates who support their provision. Because of the free-rider problem, government provides these goods and finances them through compulsory charges in the form of taxes.

*greater good –
taxes!!*

Optimal Quantity of a Public Good If consumers need not reveal their true demand for a public good in the marketplace, how can society determine the optimal amount of that good? The answer is that the government has to try to estimate the demand for a public good through surveys or public votes. It can then compare the marginal benefit of an added unit of the good against the government's marginal cost of providing it. Adhering to the $MB = MC$ rule, it can provide the "right" amount of the public good.

ILLUSTRATING THE IDEA

Art for Art's Sake

Suppose an enterprising sculptor creates a piece of art costing $600 and, with permission, places it in the town square. Also suppose that Jack gets $300 of enjoyment from the art and Diane gets $400. Sensing this enjoyment and hoping to make a profit, the sculptor approaches Jack for a donation equal to his satisfaction. Jack falsely says that, unfortunately, he does not particularly like the piece. The sculptor then tries Diane, hoping to get $400 or so. Same deal: Diane professes not to like the piece either. Jack and Diane have become free riders. Although feeling a bit guilty, both reason that it makes no sense to pay for something when anyone can receive the benefits without paying for them. The artist is a quick learner; he vows never to try anything like that again.

QUESTION: What is the rationale for government funding for art placed in town squares and other public spaces?

(1) Quantity of Public Good	(2) Adams' Willingness to Pay (Price)		(3) Benson's Willingness to Pay (Price)		(4) Collective Willingness to Pay (Price)	(5) Marginal Cost
1	$4	+	$5	=	$9	$3
2	3	+	4	=	7	4
3	2	+	3	=	5	5
4	1	+	2	=	3	6
5	0	+	1	=	1	7

TABLE 5.3 Optimal Quantity of a Public Good, Two Individuals

Measuring Demand Suppose that Adams and Benson are the only two people in the society and that their willingness to pay for a public good, this time the war on terrorism, is as shown in columns 1 and 2 and columns 1 and 3 in Table 5.3. Economists might have discovered these schedules through a survey asking hypothetical questions about how much each citizen was willing to pay for various types and amounts of public goods rather than go without them.

Notice that the schedules in the first four columns of Table 5.3 are price-quantity schedules, meaning they are demand schedules. Rather than depicting demand in the usual way—the quantity of a product someone is willing to buy at each possible price—these schedules show the price someone is willing to pay for the extra unit of each possible quantity. That is, Adams is willing to pay $4 for the first unit of the public good, $3 for the second, $2 for the third, and so on.

Suppose the government produces 1 unit of this public good. Because of nonrivalry, Adams' consumption of the good does not preclude Benson from also consuming it, and vice versa. So both people consume the good, and neither volunteers to pay for it. But from Table 5.3 we can find the amount these two people would be willing to pay, together, rather than do without this 1 unit of the good. Columns 1 and 2 show that Adams would be willing to pay $4 for the first unit of the public good, whereas columns 1 and 3 reveal that Benson would be willing to pay $5 for it. Adams and Benson therefore are jointly willing to pay $9 (= $4 + $5) for this first unit.

For the second unit of the public good, the collective price they are willing to pay is $7 (= $3 from Adams + $4 from Benson); for the third unit they will pay $5 (= $2 + $3); and so on. By finding the collective willingness to pay for each additional unit (column 4), we can construct a collective demand schedule (a willingness-to-pay schedule) for the public good. Here we are *not* adding the quantities demanded at each possible price, as with the market demand for a private good. Instead, we are adding the prices that people are willing to pay for the last unit of the public good at each possible quantity demanded.

What does it mean in columns 1 and 4 of Table 5.3 that, for example, Adams and Benson are collectively willing to pay $7 for the second unit of the public good? It means that they jointly expect to receive $7 of extra benefit or utility from that unit. Column 4, in effect, reveals the collective marginal benefit of each unit of the public good.

Comparing Marginal Benefit and Marginal Cost

Now let's suppose the marginal cost of providing the public good is as shown in column 5 of Table 5.3. As explained in Chapter 1, marginal cost tends to rise as more of a good is produced. In view of the marginal-cost data shown, how much of the good

WORKED PROBLEMS

W 5.2

Optimal amount of a public good

should government provide? The optimal amount occurs at the quantity where marginal benefit equals marginal cost. In Table 5.3 that quantity is 3 units, where the collective willingness to pay for the third unit—the $5 marginal benefit—just matches that unit's $5 marginal cost. As we saw in Chapter 1, equating marginal benefit and marginal cost efficiently allocates society's scarce resources.

APPLYING THE ANALYSIS

Cost-Benefit Analysis

cost-benefit analysis
The formal comparison of marginal costs and marginal benefits of a government project to decide whether it is worth doing and to what extent resources should be devoted to it.

The above example suggests a practical means, called **cost-benefit analysis,** for deciding whether to provide a particular public good and how much of it to provide. Like our example, cost-benefit analysis (or marginal-benefit–marginal-cost analysis) involves a comparison of marginal costs and marginal benefits.

Suppose the federal government is contemplating a highway construction plan. Because the economy's resources are limited, any decision to use more resources in the public sector will mean fewer resources for the private sector. There will be both a cost and a benefit. The cost is the loss of satisfaction resulting from the accompanying decline in the production of private goods; the benefit is the extra satisfaction resulting from the output of more public goods. Should the needed resources be shifted from the private to the public sector? The answer is yes if the benefit from the extra public goods exceeds the cost that results from having fewer private goods. The answer is no if the cost of the forgone private goods is greater than the benefit associated with the extra public goods.

Cost-benefit analysis, however, can indicate more than whether a public program is worth doing. It can also help the government decide on the extent to which a project should be pursued. Real economic questions cannot usually be answered simply by "yes" or "no" but, rather, involve questions such as "how much" or "how little."

Roads and highways can be run privately, as excludability is possible with toll gates. However, the federal highway system is almost entirely nonexclusive because anyone with a car can get on and off most federal highways without restriction anytime they want. Federal highways therefore satisfy one characteristic of a public good: nonexcludability. The other characteristic, nonrivalry, is also satisfied by the the fact that unless a highway is already extremely crowded, one person's driving on the highway does not preclude another person's driving on the highway. Thus, the federal highway system is effectively a public good. This leads us to ask: Should the federal government expand the federal highway system? If so, what is the proper size or scope for the overall project?

Table 5.4 lists a series of increasingly ambitious and increasingly costly highway projects: widening existing two-lane highways; building new two-lane highways; building new four-lane highways; building new six-lane highways. The extent to which government should undertake highway construction depends on the costs and benefits. The costs are largely the costs of constructing and maintaining the highways; the benefits are improved flows of people and goods throughout the nation.

The table shows that total annual benefit (column 4) exceeds total annual cost (column 2) for plans A, B, and C, indicating that some highway construction is economically justifiable. We see this directly in column 6, where total costs (column 2) are subtracted from total annual benefits (column 4). Net benefits are positive for plans A, B, and C. Plan D is not economically justifiable because net benefits are negative.

But the question of optimal size or scope for this project remains. Comparing the marginal cost (the change in total cost) and the marginal benefit (the change in total

TABLE 5.4 Cost-Benefit Analysis for a National Highway Construction Project (in Billions)

(1) Plan	(2) Total Cost of Project	(3) Marginal Cost	(4) Total Benefit	(5) Marginal Benefit	(6) Net Benefit (4) − (2)
No new construction	$ 0		$ 0		$ 0
A: Widen existing highways	4	$ 4	5	$ 5	1
B: New 2-lane highways	10	6	13	8	3
C: New 4-lane highways	18	8	23	10	5
D: New 6-lane highways	28	10	26	3	−2

benefit) relating to each plan determines the answer. The guideline is well known to you from previous discussions: Increase an activity, project, or output as long as the marginal benefit (column 5) exceeds the marginal cost (column 3). Stop the activity at, or as close as possible to, the point at which the marginal benefit equals the marginal cost. Do not undertake a project for which marginal cost exceeds marginal benefit.

In this case plan C (building new four-lane highways) is the best plan. Plans A and B are too modest; the marginal benefits exceed the marginal costs. Plan D's marginal cost ($10 billion) exceeds the marginal benefit ($3 billion) and therefore cannot be justified; it overallocates resources to the project. Plan C is closest to the theoretical optimum because its marginal benefit ($10 billion) still exceeds marginal cost ($8 billion) but approaches the MB = MC (or MC = MB) ideal.

This marginal-cost–marginal-benefit rule tells government which plan provides the maximum excess of total benefits over total costs or, in other words, the plan that provides society with the maximum net benefit. You can confirm directly in column 6 that the maximum net benefit ($5 billion) is associated with plan C.

QUESTION: Do you think it is generally easier to measure the costs of public goods or their benefits? Explain your reasoning.

Externalities

In addition to providing public goods, governments also can improve the allocation of resources in the economy by correcting for market failures caused by externalities. An *externality* occurs when some of the costs or the benefits of a good or service are passed onto or "spill over" to someone other than the immediate buyer or seller. Such spillovers are called externalities because they are benefits or costs that accrue to some third party that is external to the market transaction.

Negative Externalities

Production or consumption costs inflicted on a third party without compensation are called **negative externalities** or *spillover costs*. Environmental pollution is an example. When a chemical manufacturer or a meatpacking plant dumps its wastes into a lake or river, water users such as swimmers, fishers, and boaters suffer negative externalities. When a petroleum refinery pollutes the air with smoke or a paper mill creates obnoxious odors, the community experiences negative externalities for which it is not compensated.

negative externalities
Spillover production or consumption costs imposed on third parties without compensation to them.

FIGURE 5.5 Negative externalities and positive externalities. (a) With negative externalities borne by society, the producers' supply curve S is to the right of (below) the total-cost supply curve S_t. Consequently, the equilibrium output Q_e is greater than the optimal output Q_o and the efficiency loss is *abc*. (b) When positive externalities accrue to society, the market demand curve D is to the left of (below) the total-benefit demand curve D_t. As a result, the equilibrium output Q_e is less than the optimal output Q_o and the efficiency loss is *xyz*.

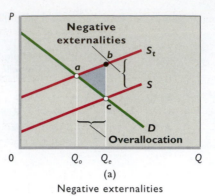

(a)

Negative externalities

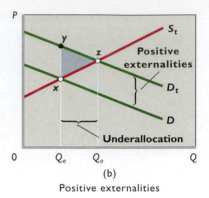

(b)

Positive externalities

Figure 5.5a illustrates how negative externalities affect the allocation of resources. When producers shift some of their costs onto the community as spillover costs, producers' marginal costs are lower than they would be if they had to pay for these costs. So their supply curves do not include or "capture" all the costs legitimately associated with the production of their goods. A supply curve such as S in Figure 5.5a therefore understates the total cost of production for a polluting firm. Its supply curve lies to the right of (or below) the full-cost supply curve S_t, which would include the negative externality. Through polluting and thus transferring cost to society, the firm enjoys lower production costs and has the supply curve S.

The resource allocation outcome is shown in Figure 5.5a, where equilibrium output Q_e is larger than the optimal output Q_o. This is a market failure because resources are *overallocated* to the production of this commodity; too many units of it are produced. In fact, there is a net loss to society for every unit from Q_0 to Q_e because, for those units, the supply curve that accounts for all costs, S_t, lies above the demand curve. Therefore, MC exceeds MB for those units. The resources that went into producing those units should have been used elsewhere in the economy to produce other things.

In terms of our previous analysis, the negative externality results in an efficiency loss represented by triangle *abc*.

Positive Externalities

Sometimes spillovers appear as external benefits. The production or consumption of certain goods and services may confer spillover or external benefits on third parties or on the community at large without compensating payment. Immunization against measles and polio results in direct benefits to the immediate consumer of those vaccines. But it also results in widespread substantial positive externalities to the entire community.

Education is another example of **positive externalities.** Education benefits individual consumers: Better-educated people generally achieve higher incomes than less-well-educated people. But education also benefits society through a more versatile and more productive labor force, on the one hand, and smaller outlays for crime prevention, law enforcement, and welfare programs, on the other.

Figure 5.5b shows the impact of positive externalities on resource allocation. When positive externalities occur, the market demand curve D lies to the left of (or below) the full-benefits demand curve, D_t. That is, D does not include the positive externalities of the product, whereas D_t does. Consider inoculations against a communicable disease. When John gets vaccinated against a disease, this is a benefit not only to himself (because he can no longer contract the disease) but also to everyone else

positive externalities
Spillover production or consumption benefits conferred on third parties without compensation from them.

Underallocation
invention
education
immunization

production cost high

around him (because they know that in the future he will never be able to infect them). These other people would presumably be willing to pay some positive amount of money for the benefit they receive when John is vaccinated. But because there is no way to make them pay, the market demand curve reflects only the direct, private benefits to John. It does not reflect the positive externalities—the spillover benefits—to those around John, which are included in D_t.

The outcome, as shown in Figure 5.5b, is that the equilibrium output Q_e is less than the optimal output Q_o. The market fails to produce enough vaccinations, and resources are *underallocated* to this product. The underproduction implies that society is missing out on potential net benefits. For every unit from Q_e to Q_0, the demand curve that accounts for all benefits, D_t, lies above the supply curve that accounts for all costs—including the opportunity cost of producing other items with the resources that would be needed to produce these units. Therefore, MB exceeds MC for each of these units and society should redeploy some of its resources away from the production of other things in order to produce these units that generate net benefits.

In terms of our previous analysis, the positive externality results in an efficiency loss represented by triangle *xyz*.

Economists have explored several approaches to the problems of negative and positive externalities. Sometimes private parties work out their own solutions to externality problems; other times government intervention is warranted.

ORIGIN OF THE IDEA

O 5.2

Externalities

© Paul Taylor/Photolibrary

© Charles Smith/Corbis

PHOTO OP   Positive and Negative Consumption Externalities

Homeowners create positive externalities when they put up nice holiday lighting displays. Not only does the homeowner benefit from consuming the sight, but so do people who pass by the house. In contrast, when people consume roads (drive) during rush hour, it creates a negative externality. This takes the form of traffic congestion, imposing time and fuel costs on other drivers.

Coase theorem
The idea that externality problems can be resolved through private negotiations by the affected parties when property rights are clearly established.

ORIGIN OF THE IDEA

O 5.3

Coase theorem

Beekeepers and the Coase Theorem

Economist Ronald Coase received the Nobel Prize for his so-called **Coase theorem,** which pointed out that under the right conditions, private individuals could often negotiate their own mutually agreeable solutions to externality problems through *private bargaining* without the need for government interventions like pollution taxes.

This is a very important insight because it means that we shouldn't automatically call for government intervention every time we see a potential externality problem. Consider the positive externalities that bees provide by pollinating farmers' crops. Should we assume that beekeeping will be underprovided unless the government intervenes with, for instance, subsidies to encourage more hives and hence more pollination?

As it turns out, no. Research has shown that farmers and beekeepers long ago used private bargaining to develop customs and payment systems that avoid free riding by farmers and encourage beekeepers to keep the optimal number of hives. Free riding is avoided by the custom that all farmers in an area simultaneously hire beekeepers to provide bees to pollinate their crops. And farmers always pay the beekeepers for their pollination services because if they didn't, then no beekeeper would ever work with them in the future—a situation that would lead to massively reduced crop yields due to a lack of pollination.

The "Fable of the Bees" is a good reminder that it is a fallacy to assume that the government must always get involved to remedy externalities. In many cases, the private sector can solve both positive and negative externality problems on its own.

QUESTIONS: Suppose that in a town a large number of home gardeners need pollination services for their fruit and vegetable crops, but none can individually afford to pay a professional beekeeper. How might that affect the contracting of beekeepers? Would it suggest a possible role for government?

Government Intervention

Government intervention may be called upon to achieve economic efficiency when externalities affect large numbers of people or when community interests are at stake. Government can use direct controls and taxes to counter negative externalities (spillover costs); it may provide subsidies or public goods to deal with positive externalities (spillover benefits).

 Direct Controls   The direct way to reduce negative externalities from a certain activity is to pass legislation limiting that activity. Such direct controls force the offending firms to incur the actual costs of the offending activity. To date, this approach has dominated public policy in the United States. Clean-air legislation has

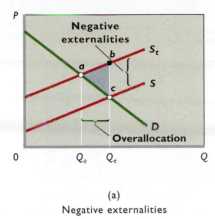

(a)
Negative externalities

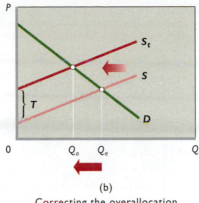

(b)
Correcting the overallocation
of resources via direct controls
or via a tax

FIGURE 5.6 Correcting for negative externalities. (a) Negative externalities (spillover costs) result in an overallocation of resources. (b) Government can correct this overallocation in two ways: (1) using direct controls, which would shift the supply curve from S to S_t and reduce output from Q_e to Q_o, or (2) imposing a specific tax T, which would also shift the supply curve from S to S_t, eliminating the overallocation of resources and thus the efficiency loss.

created uniform emission standards—limits on allowable pollution—and has forced factories and businesses to install "maximum achievable control technology" to reduce emissions of toxic chemicals. It has also mandated reductions in (1) tailpipe emissions from automobiles, (2) use of chlorofluorocarbons (CFCs) that deplete the ozone layer, and (3) emissions of sulfur dioxide by coal-burning utilities to prevent the acid-rain destruction of lakes and forests. Also, clean-water legislation has limited the amounts of heavy metals and detergents that firms can discharge into rivers and bays. Toxic-waste laws dictate special procedures and dump sites for disposing of contaminated soil and solvents. Violating these laws means fines and, in some cases, imprisonment.

Direct controls raise the marginal cost of production because the firms must operate and maintain pollution-control equipment. The supply curve S in Figure 5.6b, which does not reflect the negative externalities, shifts leftward (upward) to the full-cost supply curve, S_t. Product price increases, equilibrium output falls from Q_e to Q_o, and the initial overallocation of resources shown in Figure 5.6a is corrected. Observe that the efficiency loss shown by triangle *abc* in Figure 5.6a disappears after the overallocation is corrected in Figure 5.6b.

Specific Taxes A second policy approach to negative externalities is for government to levy taxes or charges specifically on the related good. For example, the government has placed a manufacturing excise tax on CFCs, which deplete the stratospheric ozone layer protecting the earth from excessive solar ultraviolet radiation. Facing such an excise tax, manufacturers must decide whether to pay the tax or expend additional funds to purchase or develop substitute products. In either case, the tax raises the marginal cost of producing CFCs, shifting the private supply curve for this product leftward (or upward).

In Figure 5.6b, a tax equal to T per unit increases the firm's marginal cost, shifting the supply curve from S to S_t. The equilibrium price rises, and the equilibrium output declines from Q_e to the economically efficient level Q_o. The tax thus eliminates the initial overallocation of resources, and therefore the efficiency loss, associated with the negative externality.

FIGURE 5.7 **Correcting for positive externalities.** (a) Positive externalities (spillover benefits) result in an underallocation of resources. (b) Government can correct this underallocation through a subsidy to consumers, which shifts market demand from D to D_t and increases output from Q_e to Q_o. (c) Alternatively, government can eliminate the underallocation by giving producers a subsidy of U, which shifts their supply curve from S_t to S'_t, increasing output from Q_e to Q_o.

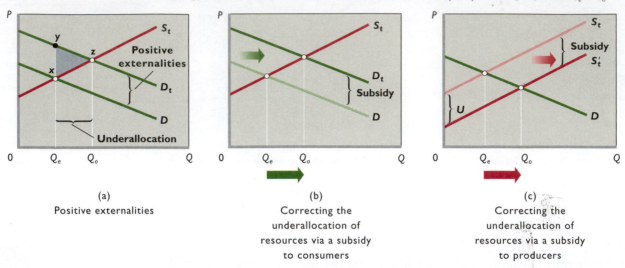

(a)
Positive externalities

(b)
Correcting the
underallocation of
resources via a subsidy
to consumers

(c)
Correcting the
underallocation of
resources via a subsidy
to producers

Subsidies and Government Provision

What policies might be useful in dealing with *positive* externalities? Where positive externalities are large and diffuse, as in our earlier example of inoculations, government has three options for correcting the underallocation of resources:

- **Subsidies to buyers** Figure 5.7a again shows the supply-demand situation for positive externalities. Government could correct the underallocation of resources, for example, to inoculations, by subsidizing consumers of the product. It could give each new mother in the United States a discount coupon to be used to obtain a series of inoculations for her child. The coupon would reduce the "price" to the mother by, say, 50 percent. As shown in Figure 5.7b, this program would shift the demand curve for inoculations from too low D to the appropriate D_t. The number of inoculations would rise from Q_e to the economically optimal Q_o, eliminating the underallocation of resources and efficiency loss shown in Figure 5.7a.

- **Subsidies to producers** A subsidy to producers is a tax in reverse. Taxes impose an extra cost on producers, while subsidies reduce producers' costs. As shown in Figure 5.7c, a subsidy of U per inoculation to physicians and medical clinics would reduce their marginal costs and shift their supply curve rightward from S_t to S'_t. The output of inoculations would increase from Q_e to the optimal level Q_o, correcting the underallocation of resources and efficiency loss shown in Figure 5.7a.

- **Government provision** Finally, where positive externalities are extremely large, the government may decide to provide the product for free or for a minimal charge. Government provides many goods that could be produced and delivered in such a way that exclusion would be possible. Such goods, called **quasi-public goods,** include education, streets and highways, police and fire protection, libraries and museums, preventive medicine, and sewage disposal. They could all be priced and provided by private firms through the market system because the free-rider problem would be minimal. But, because spillover benefits extend well beyond the individual buyer, the market system may underproduce them. Therefore, government often provides quasi-public goods.

quasi-public goods
Goods for which exclusion could occur but which government provides because of perceived widespread and diffuse benefits.

Lojack: A Case of Positive Externalities

Economists Ayres and Levitt point out that some forms of private crime prevention simply redistribute crime rather than reduce it. For example, car alarm systems that have red blinking warning lights may simply divert professional auto thieves to vehicles that do not have such lights and alarms. The owner of a car with such an alarm system benefits through reduced likelihood of theft but imposes a cost on other car owners who do not have such alarms. Their cars are more likely to be targeted for theft by thieves because other cars have visible security systems.

In contrast, some private crime prevention measures actually reduce crime, rather than simply redistribute it. One such measure is installation of a Lojack (or some similar) car retrieval system. Lojack is a tiny radio transmitter that is hidden in one of many possible places within the car. When an owner reports a stolen car, the police can remotely activate the transmitter. Police then can determine the car's precise location and track its subsequent movements.

The owner of the car benefits because the 95 percent retrieval rate on cars with the Lojack system is higher than the 60 percent retrieval rate for cars without the system. But, according to a study by Ayres and Levitt, the benefit to the car owner is only 10 percent of the total benefit. Ninety percent of the total benefit is external; it is a spillover benefit to other car owners in the community.

There are two sources of this positive externality. First, the presence of the Lojack device sometimes enables police to intercept the car while the thief is still driving it. For example, in California the arrest rate for cars with Lojack was three times greater than that for cars without it. The arrest puts the car thief out of commission for a time and thus reduces subsequent car thefts in the community. Second, and far more important, the device enables police to trace cars to "chop shops," where crooks disassemble cars for resale of the parts. When police raid the chop shop, they put the entire theft ring out of business. In Los Angeles alone, Lojack has eliminated 45 chop shops in just a few years. The purging of the chop shop and theft ring reduces auto theft in the community. So auto owners who do not have Lojack devices in their cars benefit from car owners who do. Ayres and Levitt estimate the *marginal social benefit* of Lojack—the marginal benefit to the Lojack car owner *plus* the spillover benefit to other car owners—is 15 times greater than the marginal cost of the device.

We saw in Figure 5.7a that the existence of positive externalities causes an insufficient quantity of a product and thus an underallocation of scarce resources to its production. The two general ways to correct the outcome are to subsidize the consumer, as shown in Figure 5.7b, or to subsidize the producer, as shown in Figure 5.7c. Currently, there is only one form of government intervention in place: state-mandated insurance discounts for people who install auto retrieval systems such as Lojack. In effect, those discounts on insurance premiums subsidize the consumer by lowering the "price" of the system to consumers. The lower price raises the number of systems installed. But, on the basis of their research, Ayres and Levitt contend that the current levels of insurance discounts are far too small to correct the underallocation that results from the positive externalities created by Lojack.

QUESTION: Other than mandating lower insurance premiums for Lojack users, what might government do to increase the use of Lojack devices in automobiles?

Source: Based on Ian Ayres and Steven D. Levitt, "Measuring Positive Externalities from Unobservable Victim Precaution: An Empirical Analysis of Lojack," *Quarterly Journal of Economics*, February 1998, pp. 43–77. The authors point out that Lojack did not fund their work; nor do they have any financial stake in Lojack.

Reducing Greenhouse Gases

Climate change, to the extent it is caused by human-generated greenhouse gases, is a negative externality problem. Suggested policies to reduce carbon emissions, a major greenhouse gas, include carbon taxes and a cap-and-trade program.

A tax imposed on each ton of carbon emitted would increase the marginal cost of production to all firms that release carbon into the air through their production processes. Because of the added marginal cost, the supply curves within affected markets would shift to the left (as illustrated by the move from S to S_t in Figure 5.5). The reduced market supply would increase equilibrium price and reduce equilibrium quantity. With the lower output, carbon emissions in these industries would fall.

A carbon tax would require minimum government interference in the economy once the tax was in place. The federal government could direct the revenues from the tax to research on cleaner production technologies or simply use the new revenues to reduce other taxes. But there would be no free lunch here: According to a 2007 study, a proposed $15 tax per ton of carbon dioxide emitted would add an estimated 14 cents to a gallon of gasoline, 1.63 cents to a kilowatt hour of electricity, $28.50 to a ton of coal, and $6.48 to a barrel of crude oil.

An alternative approach is a cap-and-trade program, which creates a market for the right to discharge a particular pollutant into the air or water. These rights, allocated in the form of a fixed quantity of pollution permits, can be bought or sold in a permit market. Each permit specifies the amount of the pollutant that can be emitted. The decision to buy or sell permits depends on how costly it is for a company to reduce its pollution relative to the market price of the permits. Permit buyers, for example, are those whose costs to reduce emissions exceed the costs of the permits that allow them to pollute.

As it currently does with sulfur dioxide emissions, the federal government could place a cap or lid on total carbon emissions and then either hand out emission rights or auction them off. In ways previously discussed, the cap-and-trade program would reduce society's overall cost of lowering carbon emissions. In that regard, it would be more efficient than direct controls requiring each producer of greenhouse gas to reduce emissions by a fixed percentage amount. Existing cap-and-trade programs—including current European markets for carbon certificates—prove that this program can work. But such programs require considerable government oversight and enforcement of the rules.

QUESTION: Why would rising prices of emission rights increase the incentive for firms to use cleaner production methods?

Table 5.5 lists several methods for correcting externalities, including those we have discussed thus far.

Society's Optimal Amount of Externality Reduction

Negative externalities such as pollution reduce the utility of those affected. These spillovers are not economic goods but economic "bads." If something is bad, shouldn't society eliminate it? Why should society allow firms or municipalities to discharge *any* impure waste into public waterways or to emit *any* pollution into the air?

TABLE 5.5 **Methods for Dealing with Externalities**

Problem	Resource Allocation Outcome	Ways to Correct
Negative externalities (spillover costs)	Overproduction of output and therefore overallocation of resources	1. Private bargaining 2. Liability rules and lawsuits 3. Tax on producers 4. Direct controls 5. Market for externality rights
Positive externalities (spillover benefits)	Underproduction of output and therefore underallocation of resources	1. Private bargaining 2. Subsidy to consumers 3. Subsidy to producers 4. Government provision

Economists answer these questions by pointing out that reducing pollution and negative externalities is not free. There are costs as well as benefits to reducing pollution. As a result, the correct question to ask when it comes to cleaning up negative externalities is not, "Do we pollute a lot or pollute zero?" That is an all-or-nothing question that ignores marginal costs and marginal benefits. Instead, the correct question is, "What is the optimal amount to clean up—the amount that equalizes the marginal cost of cleaning up with the marginal benefit of a cleaner environment?"

Reducing a negative externality has a "price." Society must decide how much of a reduction it wants to "buy." High costs may mean that totally eliminating pollution might not be desirable, even if it is technologically feasible. Because of the law of diminishing returns, cleaning up the second 10 percent of pollutants from an industrial smokestack normally is more costly than cleaning up the first 10 percent. Eliminating the third 10 percent is more costly than cleaning up the second 10 percent, and so on. Therefore, cleaning up the last 10 percent of pollutants is the most costly reduction of all.

The marginal cost (MC) to the firm and hence to society—the opportunity cost of the extra resources used—rises as pollution is reduced more and more. At some point MC may rise so high that it exceeds society's marginal benefit (MB) of further pollution abatement (reduction). Additional actions to reduce pollution will therefore lower society's well-being; total cost will rise more than total benefit.

MC, MB, and Equilibrium Quantity

Figure 5.8 shows both the rising marginal-cost curve, MC, for pollution reduction and the downsloping marginal-benefit curve, MB, for pollution reduction. MB slopes downward because of the law of diminishing marginal utility: The more pollution reduction society accomplishes, the lower the utility (and benefit) of the next unit of pollution reduction.

The **optimal reduction of an externality** occurs when society's marginal cost and marginal benefit of reducing that externality are equal (MC = MB). In Figure 5.8 this optimal amount of pollution abatement is Q_1 units. When MB exceeds MC, additional abatement moves society toward economic efficiency; the added benefit of cleaner air or water exceeds the benefit of any alternative use of the required resources. When MC exceeds MB, additional abatement reduces economic efficiency; there would be greater benefits from using resources in some other way than to further reduce pollution.

In reality, it is difficult to measure the marginal costs and benefits of pollution control. Figure 5.8 demonstrates that some pollution may be economically efficient. This is so not because pollution is desirable but because beyond some level of control,

optimal reduction of an externality
The reduction of a negative externality to the level at which the marginal benefit and marginal cost of reduction are equal.

FIGURE 5.8 **Society's optimal amount of pollution abatement.** The optimal amount of externality reduction—in this case, pollution abatement—occurs at Q_1, where society's marginal cost MC and marginal benefit MB of reducing the spillover are equal.

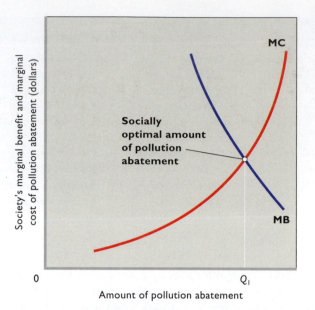

further abatement may reduce society's net well-being. As an example, it would cost the government billions of dollars to clean up every last piece of litter in America. Thus, it would be better to tolerate some trash blowing around if the money saved by picking up less trash would yield larger net benefits when spent on other things.

Shifts in Locations of the Curves   The locations of the marginal-cost and marginal-benefit curves in Figure 5.8 are not forever fixed. They can, and probably do, shift over time. For example, suppose that the technology of pollution-control equipment improved noticeably. We would expect the cost of pollution abatement to fall, society's MC curve to shift rightward, and the optimal level of abatement to rise. Or suppose that society were to decide that it wanted cleaner air and water because of new information about the adverse health effects of pollution. The MB curve in Figure 5.8 would shift rightward, and the optimal level of pollution control would increase beyond Q_1. Test your understanding of these statements by drawing the new MC and MB curves in Figure 5.8.

Government's Role in the Economy

Market failures can be used to justify government interventions in the economy. The inability of private-sector firms to break even when attempting to provide public goods and the over- and underproduction problems caused by positive and negative externalities mean that government can have an important role to play if society's resources are to be efficiently allocated to the goods and services that people most highly desire.

Correcting for market failures is not, however, an easy task. To begin with, government officials must correctly identify the existence and the cause of any given market failure. That by itself may be difficult, time-consuming, and costly. But even if a market failure is correctly identified and diagnosed, government may still fail to take appropriate corrective action due to the fact that government undertakes its economic role in the context of politics.

To serve the public, politicians need to get elected. To stay elected, officials (presidents, senators, representatives, mayors, council members, school board members) need to satisfy their particular constituencies. At best, the political realities complicate government's role in the economy; at worst, they produce undesirable economic outcomes.

In the political context, overregulation can occur in some cases; underregulation, in others. Some public goods and quasi-public goods can be produced not because their benefits exceed their costs but because their benefits accrue to firms located in states served by powerful elected officials. Inefficiency can easily creep into government activities because of the lack of a profit incentive to hold down costs. Policies to correct negative externalities can be politically blocked by the very parties that are producing the spillovers. In short, the economic role of government, although critical to a well-functioning economy, is not always perfectly carried out.

Economists use the term "government failure" to describe economically inefficient outcomes caused by shortcomings in the public sector.

Summary

1. A market failure happens in a particular market when the market produces an equilibrium level of output that either overallocates or underallocates resources to the product being traded in the market. In competitive markets that feature many buyers and many sellers, market failures can be divided into two types: Demand-side market failures occur when demand curves do not reflect consumers' full willingness to pay; supply-side market failures occur when supply curves do not reflect all production costs, including those that may be borne by third parties.

2. Properly functioning competitive markets ensure that private goods are (a) available, (b) produced in the least costly way, and (c) produced and sold in the "right" amounts.

3. Consumer surplus is the difference between the maximum price that a consumer is willing to pay for a product and the lower price actually paid; producer surplus is the difference between the minimum price that a producer is willing to accept for a product and the higher price actually received. Collectively, consumer surplus is represented by the triangle under the demand curve and above the actual price, whereas producer surplus is shown by the triangle above the supply curve and below the actual price.

4. Graphically, the combined amount of producer and consumer surplus is represented by the triangle to the left of the intersection of the supply and demand curves that is below the demand curve and above the supply curve. At the equilibrium price and quantity in competitive markets, marginal benefit equals marginal cost, maximum willingness to pay equals minimum acceptable price, and the combined amount of consumer surplus and producer surplus is maximized.

5. Output levels that are either less than or greater than the equilibrium output create efficiency losses, also called deadweight losses. These losses are reductions in the combined amount of consumer surplus and producer surplus. Underproduction creates efficiency losses because output is not being produced for which maximum willingness to pay exceeds minimum acceptable price. Overproduction creates efficiency losses because output is being produced for which minimum acceptable price exceeds maximum willingness to pay.

6. Public goods are distinguished from private goods. Private goods are characterized by rivalry (in consumption) and excludability. One person's purchase and consumption of a private good precludes others from also buying and consuming it. Producers can exclude nonpayers (free riders) from receiving the benefits. In contrast, public goods are characterized by nonrivalry (in consumption) and nonexcludability. Public goods are not profitable to private firms because nonpayers (free riders) can obtain and consume those goods without paying. Government can, however, provide desirable public goods, financing them through taxation.

7. The collective demand schedule for a particular public good is found by summing the prices that each individual is willing to pay for an additional unit. The optimal quantity of a public good occurs where the society's willingness to pay for the last unit—the marginal benefit of the good—equals the marginal cost of the good.

8. Externalities cause the output of certain goods to vary from society's optimal output. Negative externalities (spillover costs) result in an overallocation of resources to a particular product. Positive externalities (spillover benefits) are accompanied by an underallocation of resources to a particular product.

9. Direct controls and specific taxes can improve resource allocation in situations where negative externalities affect many people and community resources. Both direct controls (for example, smokestack emission standards) and specific taxes (for example, taxes on firms producing toxic chemicals) increase production costs and hence product price. As product price rises, the externality, overallocation

of resources, and efficiency loss are reduced since less of the output is produced.

10. Government can correct the underallocation of resources and therefore the efficiency losses that result from positive externalities in a particular market either by subsidizing consumers (which increases market demand) or by subsidizing producers (which increases market supply). Such subsidies increase the equilibrium output, reducing or eliminating the positive externality and consequent underallocation of resources and efficiency loss.

11. The Coase theorem suggests that under the right circumstances private bargaining can solve externality problems. Thus, government intervention is not always needed to deal with externality problems.

12. The socially optimal amount of externality abatement occurs where society's marginal cost and marginal benefit of reducing the externality are equal. With pollution, for example, this optimal amount of pollution abatement is likely to be less than a 100 percent reduction. Changes in technology or changes in society's attitudes toward pollution can affect the optimal amount of pollution abatement.

13. Market failures present government with opportunities to improve the allocation of society's resources and thereby enhance society's total well-being. But even when government correctly identifies the existence and cause of a market failure, political pressures may make it difficult or impossible for government officials to implement a proper solution.

Terms and Concepts

market failures	producer surplus	negative externality
demand-side market failures	efficiency losses (or deadweight losses)	positive externality
supply-side market failures	private goods	Coase theorem
productive efficiency	public goods	quasi-public goods
allocative efficiency	free-rider problem	optimal reduction of an externality
consumer surplus	cost-benefit analysis	

Questions

1. Explain the two causes of market failures. Given their definitions, could a market be affected by both types of market failures simultaneously? **LO1**

2. Draw a supply and demand graph and identify the areas of consumer surplus and producer surplus. Given the demand curve, what impact will an increase in supply have on the amount of consumer surplus shown in your diagram? Explain why. **LO2**

3. Use the ideas of consumer surplus and producer surplus to explain why economists say competitive markets are efficient. Why are below- or above-equilibrium levels of output inefficient, according to these two sets of ideas? **LO2**

4. Contrast the characteristics of public goods with those of private goods. Why won't private firms produce public goods? **LO3**

5. Draw a production possibilities curve with public goods on the vertical axis and private goods on the horizontal axis. Assuming the economy is initially operating on the curve, indicate how the production of public goods might be increased. How might the output of public goods be increased if the economy is initially operating at a point inside the curve? **LO3**

6. Use the distinction between the characteristics of private and public goods to determine whether the following should be produced through the market system or provided by government: (a) French fries, (b) airport screening, (c) court systems, (d) mail delivery, and (e) medical care. State why you answered as you did in each case. **LO3**

7. What divergences arise between equilibrium output and efficient output when (a) negative externalities and (b) positive externalities are present? How might government correct these divergences? Cite an example (other than the text examples) of an external cost and an external benefit. **LO4**

8. Why are spillover costs and spillover benefits also called negative and positive externalities? Show graphically how a tax can correct for a negative externality and how a subsidy to producers can correct for a positive externality. How does a subsidy to consumers differ from a subsidy to producers in correcting for a positive externality? **LO4**

9. An apple grower's orchard provides nectar to a neighbor's bees, while the beekeeper's bees help the apple grower by pollinating his apple blossoms. Use Figure 5.5b to explain why this situation of dual positive externalities might lead to

an underallocation of resources to both apple growing and beekeeping. How might this underallocation get resolved via the means suggested by the Coase theorem? **LO4**

10. Explain the following statement, using the MB curve in Figure 5.8 to illustrate: "The optimal amount of pollution abatement for some substances, say, dirty water from storm drains, is very low; the optimal amount of abatement for other substances, say, cyanide poison, is close to 100 percent." **LO5**

11. Explain why zoning laws, which allow certain land uses only in specific locations, might be justified in dealing with a problem of negative externalities. Explain why in areas where buildings sit close together tax breaks to property owners for installing extra fire prevention equipment might be justified in view of positive externalities. Explain why excise taxes on beer might be justified in dealing with a problem of external costs. **LO5**

Problems

1. Refer to Table 5.1. If the six people listed in the table are the only consumers in the market and the equilibrium price is $11 (not the $8 shown), how much consumer surplus will the market generate? **LO2**

2. Refer to Table 5.2. If the six people listed in the table are the only producers in the market and the equilibrium price is $6 (not the $8 shown), how much producer surplus will the market generate? **LO2**

3. Look at Tables 5.1 and 5.2 together. What is the total surplus if Bob buys a unit from Carlos? If Barb buys a unit from Courtney? If Bob buys a unit from Chad? If you match up pairs of buyers and sellers so as to maximize the total surplus of all transactions, what is the largest total surplus that can be achieved? **LO2**

4. **ADVANCED ANALYSIS** Assume the following values for Figures 5.4a and 5.4b. Q_1 = 20 bags. Q_2 = 15 bags. Q_3 = 27 bags. The market equilibrium price is $45 per bag. The price at a is $85 per bag. The price at c is $5 per bag. The price at f is $59 per bag. The price at g is $31 per bag. Apply the formula for the area of a triangle (Area = ½ × Base × Height) to answer the following questions. **LO2**

   a. What is the dollar value of the total surplus (producer surplus plus consumer surplus) when the allocatively efficient output level is being produced? How large is the dollar value of the consumer surplus at that output level?

   b. What is the dollar value of the deadweight loss when output level Q_2 is being produced? What is the total surplus when output level Q_2 is being produced?

   c. What is the dollar value of the deadweight loss when output level Q_3 is produced? What is the dollar value of the total surplus when output level Q_3 is produced?

5. The accompanying table relating to a public good provides information on the prices Young and Zorn are willing to pay for various quantities of that public good. These two people are the only members of society. Determine the price that society is willing to pay for the public good at each quantity of output. If the government's marginal cost of providing this public good is constant at $7,

how many units of the public good should government provide? **LO3**

Young		Zorn		Society	
P	**Q_d**	**P**	**Q_d**	**P**	**Q_d**
$8	0	$8	1	$___	1
7	0	7	2	___	2
6	0	6	3	___	3
5	1	5	4	___	4
4	2	4	5	___	5
3	3	3	6	___	6
2	4	2	7	___	7
1	5	1	8	___	8

6. The table below shows the total costs and total benefits in billions for four different antipollution programs of increasing scope. Use cost-benefit analysis to determine which program should be undertaken. **LO3**

Program	Total Cost	Total Benefit
A	$ 3	$ 7
B	7	12
C	12	16
D	18	19

7. On the basis of the three individual demand schedules at the top of the next page, and assuming these three people are the only ones in the society, determine (a) the market demand schedule on the assumption that the good is a private

good and (b) the collective demand schedule on the assumption that the good is a public good. **LO3**

P	$Q_d(D_1)$	$Q_d(D_2)$	$Q_d(D_3)$
$8	0	1	0
7	0	2	0
6	0	3	1
5	1	4	2
4	2	5	3
3	3	6	4
2	4	7	5
1	5	8	6

8. Use your demand schedule for a public good, determined in problem 7, and the following supply schedule to ascertain the optimal quantity of this public good. **LO3**

P	Q_s
$19	10
16	8
13	6
10	4
7	2
4	1

9. Look at Tables 5.1 and 5.2, which show, respectively, the willingness to pay and willingness to accept of buyers and sellers of bags of oranges. For the following questions, assume that the equilibrium price and quantity will depend on the indicated changes in supply and demand. Assume that the only market participants are those listed by name in the two tables. **LO4**
    a. What are the equilibrium price and quantity for the data displayed in the two tables?
    b. What if, instead of bags of oranges, the data in the two tables dealt with a public good like fireworks displays? If all the buyers free ride, what will be the quantity supplied by private sellers?
    c. Assume that we are back to talking about bags of oranges (a private good), but that the government has decided that tossed orange peels impose a negative externality on the public that must be rectified by imposing a $2-per-bag tax on sellers. What are the new equilibrium price and quantity? If the new equilibrium quantity is the optimal quantity, by how many bags were oranges being overproduced before?

FURTHER TEST YOUR KNOWLEDGE AT
www.mcconnellbrief2e.com

At the text's Online Learning Center, **www.mcconnellbrief2e.com**, you will find one or more web-based questions that require information from the Internet to answer. We urge you to check them out, since they will familiarize you with websites that may be helpful in other courses and perhaps even in your career. The OLC also features multiple-choice quizzes that give instant feedback and provides other helpful ways to further test your knowledge of the chapter.

Visit your mobile app store and download the McConnell Brief Edition: Study Econ app *today*!

PRODUCT MARKETS

Businesses and Their Costs

In market economies, a wide variety of businesses produce an even greater variety of goods and services. Each of those businesses needs economic resources in order to produce its product. In obtaining and using resources, a business makes monetary payments to resource owners (for example, workers) and incurs opportunity costs when using resources that it already owns (for example, entrepreneurial talent). Those payments and opportunity costs constitute the firm's *costs of production.*

This chapter describes the U.S. business population and identifies the costs faced by firms in producing products. Then, in the next several chapters, we bring demand, product price, and revenue into the analysis and explain how businesses compare revenues and costs to decide how much to produce. Our ultimate purpose is to show how those comparisons relate to profits, losses, and allocative efficiency.

The Business Population

Like households, businesses are a major element in the circular flow diagram that we discussed in Chapter 2. In discussing businesses, it will be useful to distinguish among a plant, a firm, and an industry:

- A *plant* is an establishment—a factory, farm, mine, store, website, or warehouse—that performs one or more functions in fabricating and distributing goods and services.
- A *firm* is an organization that employs resources to produce goods and services for profit and operates one or more plants.
- An *industry* is a group of firms that produce the same, or similar, products.

The organizational structures of firms are often complex and varied. *Multiplant firms* may be organized horizontally, with several plants performing much the same function. Examples are the multiple bottling plants of Coca-Cola and the many individual Walmart stores. Firms also may be *vertically integrated*, meaning they own plants that perform different functions in the various stages of the production process. For example, oil companies such as Shell own oil fields, refineries, and retail gasoline stations. Some firms are *conglomerates*, so named because they have plants that produce products in several separate industries. For example, Pfizer makes prescription medicines (Lipitor, Viagra) but also chewing gum (Trident, Dentyne), razors (Schick), cough drops (Halls), breath mints (Clorets, Certs), and antacids (Rolaids).

The business population ranges from giant corporations such as Walmart, Exxon, and IBM, with hundreds of thousands of employees and billions of dollars of annual sales, to neighborhood specialty shops with one or two employees and daily sales of only a few hundred dollars. As shown in Figure 2.3 (page 46), only 18 percent of U.S. firms are corporations, yet they account for 82 percent of all sales (output).

Advantages of Corporations

Certain advantages of the corporate form of business enterprise have catapulted it into a dominant sales and profit position in the United States. The corporation is by far the most effective form of business organization for raising money to finance the expansion of its facilities and capabilities. The corporation employs unique methods of finance—the selling of stocks and bonds—that enable it to pool the financial resources of large numbers of people.

A common **stock** represents a share in the ownership of a corporation. The purchaser of a stock certificate has the right to vote for corporate officers and to share in dividends. If you buy 1000 of the 100,000 shares issued by OutTell, Inc. (OT), then you own 1 percent of the company, are entitled to 1 percent of any dividends declared by the board of directors, and control 1 percent of the votes in the annual election of corporate officials.

In contrast, a corporate **bond** does not bestow any corporate ownership on the purchaser. A bond purchaser is simply lending money to a corporation. A bond is an IOU, in acknowledgment of a loan, whereby the corporation promises to pay the holder a fixed amount set forth on the bond at some specified future date and other fixed amounts (interest payments) every year up to the bond's maturity date. For example, you might purchase a 10-year OutTell bond with a face value of $1000 and a 5 percent rate of interest. This means that, in exchange for your $1000, OT promises you a $50 interest payment for each of the next 10 years and then repays your $1000 principal at the end of that period.

Financing through sales of stocks and bonds also provides other advantages to those who purchase these *corporate securities*. An individual investor can spread risks by buying

stocks
Ownership shares of a corporation.

bonds
Certificates indicating obligations to pay the principal and interest on loans at a specific time in the future.

the securities of several corporations. And it is usually easy for holders of corporate securities to sell their holdings. Organized stock exchanges and bond markets simplify the transfer of securities from sellers to buyers. This "ease of sale" increases the willingness of savers to make financial investments in corporate securities. Besides, corporations have easier access to bank credit than do other types of business organizations. Corporations are better risks and are more likely to become profitable clients of banks.

Corporations provide **limited liability** to owners (stockholders), who risk only what they paid for their stock. Their personal assets are not at stake if the corporation defaults on its debts. Creditors can sue the corporation as a legal entity but cannot sue the owners of the corporation as individuals.

Because of their ability to attract financial capital, successful corporations can easily expand the scope of their operations and realize the benefits of expansion. For example, they can take advantage of mass-production technologies and division of labor. A corporation can hire specialists in production, accounting, and marketing functions and thus improve efficiency.

As a legal entity, the corporation has a life independent of its owners and its officers. Legally, at least, corporations are immortal. The transfer of corporate ownership through inheritance or the sale of stock does not disrupt the continuity of the corporation. Corporations have permanence that lends itself to long-range planning and growth.

limited liability
Restriction of the maximum loss to a shareholder to the amount paid for the stock.

The Principal-Agent Problem

Many of the world's corporations are extremely large. In 2010, 128 of the world's corporations had annual sales of more than $20 billion, 46 firms had sales exceeding $50 billion, and 17 firms had sales greater than $100 billion. U.S.-based Walmart alone had sales of nearly $422 billion in 2010.

But large size creates a potential problem. In sole proprietorships and partnerships, the owners of the real and financial assets of the firm enjoy direct control of those assets. But ownership of large corporations is spread over tens or hundreds of thousands of stockholders. The owners of a corporation usually do not manage it—they hire others to do so.

That practice can create a **principal-agent problem.** The *principals* are the stockholders who own the corporation and who hire executives as their *agents* to run the business on their behalf. But the interests of these managers (the agents) and the wishes of the owners (the principals) do not always coincide. The owners typically want maximum company profit and stock price. However, the agents may want the power, prestige, and pay that often accompany control over a large enterprise, independent of its profitability and stock price.

So a conflict of interest may develop. For example, executives may build expensive office buildings, enjoy excessive perks such as corporate jets, and pay too much to acquire other corporations. Consequently, the firm's costs will be excessive, and the firm will fail to maximize profits and stock prices for its owners.

ORIGIN OF THE IDEA

O 6.1

Principal-agent problem

principal-agent problem
A conflict of interest that occurs when agents (managers) pursue their own objectives to the detriment of the principals' (stockholders') goals.

APPLYING THE ANALYSIS

Unprincipled Agents

In the 1990s many corporations addressed the principal-agent problem by providing a substantial part of executive pay either as shares of the firm's stock or as stock options. *Stock options* are contracts that allow executives or other key employees to buy shares of their employers' stock at fixed, lower prices when the stock prices rise. The idea was to align the interest of the executives and other key employees more closely with those of the broader corporate owners. By pursuing high profits and share prices, the executives would enhance their own wealth as well as that of all the stockholders.

This "solution" to the principal-agent problem had an unexpected negative side effect. It prompted a few unscrupulous executives to inflate their firm's share prices by hiding costs, overstating revenues, engaging in deceptive transactions, and, in general, exaggerating profits. These executives then sold large quantities of their inflated stock, making quick personal fortunes. In some cases, "independent" outside auditing firms turned out to be "not so independent" because they held valuable consulting contracts with the firms being audited.

When the stock market bubble of the late 1990s burst, many instances of business manipulations and fraudulent accounting were exposed. Several executives of large U.S. firms were indicted, and a few large firms collapsed, among them Enron (energy trading), WorldCom (communications), and Arthur Andersen (business consulting). General stockholders of those firms were left holding severely depressed or even worthless stock.

In 2002 Congress strengthened the laws and penalties against executive misconduct. Also, corporations have improved their accounting and auditing procedures. But the revelations of recent wrongdoings make it clear that the principal-agent problem is not an easy problem to solve.

QUESTION: Why are accurate accounting and independent auditing so crucial in reducing the principal-agent problem?

Economic Costs

Firms face costs because the resources they need to produce their products are scarce and have alternative uses. Because of scarcity, firms wanting a particular resource have to bid it away from other firms. That process is costly for firms because it requires a payment to the resource owner. This reality causes economists to define **economic cost** as the payment that must be made to obtain and retain the services of a resource. It is the income the firm must provide to resource suppliers to attract resources away from alternative uses.

This section explains how firms incorporate opportunity costs to calculate economic costs. If you need a refresher on opportunity costs, a brief review of the section on opportunity costs in Chapter 1 might be useful before continuing on with the rest of this section.

economic cost
A payment that must be made to obtain and retain the services of a resource.

Explicit and Implicit Costs

To properly calculate a firm's economic costs, you must remember that *all* of the resources used by the firm have an opportunity cost. This is true both for the resources that a firm purchases from outsiders as well as for the resources that it already owns. As a result, *all* of the resources that a firm uses have economic costs. Economists refer to these two types of economic costs as *explicit costs* and *implicit costs*:

- A firm's **explicit costs** are the monetary payments it makes to those from whom it must purchase resources that it does not own. Because these costs involve an obvious cash transaction, they are referred to as explicit costs. Be sure to remember that explicit costs are opportunity costs because every monetary payment used to

explicit costs
The monetary payments a firm must make to an outsider to obtain a resource.

shipping resource books, gas

[handwritten margin note: time away from family, work]

implicit costs
The monetary income a firm sacrifices when it uses a resource it owns rather than supplying the resource in the market.

purchase outside resources necessarily involves forgoing the best alternatives that could have been purchased with the money.

- A firm's **implicit costs** are the opportunity costs of using the resources that it already owns to make the firm's own product rather than selling those resources to outsiders for cash. Because these costs are present but not obvious, they are referred to as implicit costs.

A firm's economic costs are the sum of its explicit costs and its implicit costs:

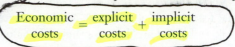

$$\text{Economic costs} = \text{explicit costs} + \text{implicit costs}$$

The following example makes clear how both explicit costs and implicit costs affect firm profits and firm behavior.

Accounting Profit and Normal Profit

Suppose that after working as a sales representative for a large T-shirt manufacturer, you decide to open your own retail T-shirt shop. As we explain in Chapter 2, you will be providing two different economic resources to your new enterprise: labor and entrepreneurial ability. The part of your job that involves providing labor includes routine tasks that help run the business—things like answering customer e-mails, taking inventory, and sweeping the floor. The part of your job that involves providing entrepreneurial ability includes any nonroutine tasks involved with organizing the business and directing its strategy—things like deciding how to promote your business, what to include in your product mix, and how to decorate your store to maximize its appeal to potential customers.

You begin providing entrepreneurial ability to your new firm by making some initial organizational decisions. You decide to work full time at your new business, so you quit your old job that paid you $22,000 per year. You invest $20,000 of savings that has been earning $1000 per year. You decide that your new firm will occupy a small retail space that you own and had been previously renting out for $5000 per year. Finally, you decide to hire one clerk to help you in the store. She agrees to work for you for $18,000 per year.

After a year in business, you total up your accounts and find the following:

Total sales revenue............................	$120,000
Cost of T-shirts................... $40,000	
Clerk's salary 18,000	
Utilities 5000	
Total (explicit) costs............................	63,000
Accounting profit...............................	57,000

accounting profit
The total revenue of a firm less its explicit costs.

These numbers look very good. In particular, you are happy with your $57,000 **accounting profit**, the profit number that accountants calculate by subtracting total explicit costs from total sales revenue. This is the profit (or net income) that would appear on your accounting statement and that you would report to the government for tax purposes.

But don't celebrate yet! Your $57,000 accounting profit overstates the economic success of your business because it ignores your implicit costs. The true measure of success is doing as well as you possibly can—that is, making more money in your new venture selling T-shirts than you could pursuing any other business venture.

To figure out whether you are achieving that goal, you must take into account *all* of your opportunity costs—both your implicit costs as well as your explicit costs. Doing so will indicate whether your new business venture is earning more money than what you could have earned in any other business venture.

To see how these calculations are made, let's continue with our example.

By providing your own financial capital, retail space, and labor, you incurred three different implicit costs during the year: $1000 of forgone interest, $5000 of forgone rent, and $22,000 of forgone wages. But don't forget that there is another implicit cost that you must also take account of—how much income you chose to forgo by applying your entrepreneurial abilities to your current retail T-shirt venture rather than applying them to other potential business ventures.

But what dollar value should we place on the size of the profits that you might have made if you had provided your entrepreneurial ability to one of those other ventures?

The answer is given by estimating a **normal profit**, the typical (or "normal") amount of accounting profit that you would most likely have earned in your next-best-alternative business venture. For the sake of argument, let us assume that with your particular set of skills and talents your entrepreneurial abilities would have on average yielded a normal profit of $5000 in one of the other potential ventures. Knowing that value, we can take all of your implicit costs properly into account by subtracting them from your accounting profit:

normal profit
A payment that must be made by a firm to obtain and retain entrepreneurial ability.

Accounting profit	$57,000
Forgone interest	$ 1000
Forgone rent	5000
Forgone wages	22,000
Forgone entrepreneurial income	5000
Total implicit costs	33,000
Economic profit	24,000

Economic Profit

After subtracting your $33,000 of implicit costs from your accounting profit of $57,000, we are left with an *economic profit* of $24,000.

Please distinguish clearly between accounting profit and economic profit. Accounting profit is the result of subtracting only explicit costs from revenue: *Accounting Profit = Revenue − Explicit Costs*. By contrast, **economic profit** is the result of subtracting all of your economic costs—both explicit costs and implicit costs—from revenue: *Economic Profit = Revenue − Explicit Costs − Implicit Costs*.

By subtracting all of your economic costs from your revenue, you determine how your current business venture compares with your best alternative business venture. In our example, the fact that you are generating an economic profit of $24,000 means that you are making $24,000 more than you could expect to make in your best alternative business venture.

By contrast, suppose that you had instead done poorly in business, so that this year your firm generated an economic loss (a negative economic profit) of $8000. This would mean that you were doing worse in your current venture than you could have done in your best alternative venture. You would, as a result, wish to switch to that alternative.

Generalizing this point, we see that there is an important behavioral threshold at $0 of economic profit. If a firm is breaking even (that is, earning exactly $0 of economic profit), then its entrepreneurs know that they are doing exactly as well as they could

WORKED PROBLEMS

W 6.1
Economic profit

economic profit
A firm's total revenue less its total cost (= explicit cost + implicit cost).

FIGURE 6.1 Economic profit versus accounting profit. Economic profit is equal to total revenue less economic costs. Economic costs are the sum of explicit and implicit costs and include a normal profit to the entrepreneur. Accounting profit is equal to total revenue less accounting (explicit) costs.

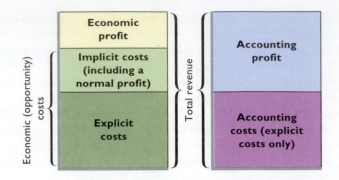

expect to do in their best alternative business venture. They are earning enough to cover all their explicit and implicit costs, including the normal profit that they could expect to earn in other business ventures. Thus, they have no incentive to change. By contrast, entrepreneurs running a positive economic profit know they are doing better than they could in alternative ventures and will want to continue doing what they are doing or maybe even expand their business. And entrepreneurs running an economic loss (a negative economic profit) know that they could do better by switching to something else.

It is for this reason that economists focus on economic profits rather than accounting profits. Simply put, economic profits direct how resources are allocated in the economy. Entrepreneurs running economic losses close their current businesses, thereby freeing up the land, labor, capital, and entrepreneurial ability that they had been using. These resources are freed up to be used by firms that are generating positive economic profits or that are at least breaking even. Resources thus flow from producing goods and services with lower net benefits toward producing goods and services with higher net benefits. Allocative efficiency increases as firms are led by their profit signals to produce more of what consumers want the most.

Figure 6.1 shows the relationship among the various cost and profit concepts that we have just discussed. To test yourself, you might want to enter cost data from our example in the appropriate blocks.

Short Run and Long Run

When the demand for a firm's product changes, the firm's profitability may depend on how quickly it can adjust the amounts of the various resources it employs. It can easily and quickly adjust the quantities employed of many resources such as hourly labor, raw materials, fuel, and power. It needs much more time, however, to adjust its *plant capacity*—the size of the factory building, the amount of machinery and equipment, and other capital resources. In some heavy industries such as aircraft manufacturing, a firm may need several years to alter plant capacity. Because of these differences in adjustment time, economists find it useful to distinguish between two conceptual periods: the short run and the long run. We will discover that costs differ in these two time periods.

Short Run: Fixed Plant   In microeconomics, the **short run** is a period too brief for a firm to alter its plant capacity yet long enough to permit a change in the degree to which the fixed plant is used. The firm's plant capacity is fixed in the short run. However, the firm can vary its output by applying larger or smaller amounts of labor, materials, and other resources to that plant. It can use its existing plant capacity more or less intensively in the short run.

If Boeing hires 1000 extra workers for one of its commercial airline plants or adds an entire shift of workers, we are speaking of the short run. Both are *short-run adjustments*.

short run
A time period in which producers are able to change the quantities of some but not all of the resources they employ.

Nothing Fixed

Long Run: Variable Plant From the viewpoint of an existing firm, the **long run** is a period long enough for it to adjust the quantities of all the resources that it employs, including plant capacity. From the industry's viewpoint, the long run also includes enough time for existing firms to dissolve and leave the industry or for new firms to be created and enter the industry. While the short run is a "fixed-plant" period, the long run is a "variable-plant" period. If Boeing adds a new production facility or merges with a supplier, we are referring to the long run. Both are *long-run adjustments*.

long run
A time period sufficiently long to enable producers to change the quantities of all the resources they employ.

Everything Variable

© Viviane Moos/CORBIS

© Richard Klune/CORBIS

PHOTO OP Long-Run Adjustments by Firms

An apparel manufacturer can make long-run adjustments to add production capacity in a matter of days by leasing another building and ordering and installing extra sewing machines. In contrast, an oil firm may need 2 to 3 years to construct a new refinery to increase its production capacity.

The short run and the long run are conceptual periods rather than calendar time periods. As indicated in the Photo Op, light-manufacturing industries can accomplish changes in plant capacity almost overnight. But for heavy industry the long run is a different matter. A firm may require several years to construct a new facility.

Short-Run Production Relationships

A firm's costs of producing a specific output depend on the prices of the needed resources and the quantities of those resources (inputs) needed to produce that output. Resource supply and demand determine resource prices. The technological aspects of production, specifically the relationships between inputs and output, determine the quantities of resources needed. Our focus will be on the *labor*-output relationship, given a fixed plant capacity. But before examining that relationship, we need to define three terms:

- **Total product (TP)** is the total quantity, or total output, of a particular good or service produced.
- **Marginal product (MP)** is the extra output or added product associated with adding a unit of a variable resource, in this case labor, to the production process. Thus,

total product (TP)
The total output of a particular good or service produced by a firm.

marginal product (MP)
The extra output or added product associated with adding a unit of a variable resource (labor) to the production process.

$$\text{Marginal product} = \frac{\text{change in total product}}{\text{change in labor input}}$$

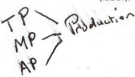

TP
MP → Production
AP

average product (AP)
The total output divided by the quantity of the resource employed (labor).

• **Average product (AP)**, also called *labor productivity*, is output per unit of labor input:

$$\text{Average product} = \frac{\text{total product}}{\text{units of labor}}$$

In the short run, a firm for a time can increase its output by adding units of labor to its fixed plant. But by how much will output rise when it adds the labor? Why do we say "for a time"?

Law of Diminishing Returns

law of diminishing returns
The principle that as successive units of a variable resource are added to a fixed resource, the marginal product of the variable resource will eventually decline.

The answers are provided in general terms by the **law of diminishing returns.** This law assumes that technology is fixed and thus the techniques of production do not change. It states that as successive units of a variable resource (say, labor) are added to a fixed resource (say, capital or land), beyond some point the extra, or marginal, product that can be attributed to each additional unit of the variable resource will decline. For example, if additional workers are hired to work with a constant amount of capital equipment, output will eventually rise by smaller and smaller amounts as more workers are hired. Diminishing returns will eventually occur.

Relevancy for Firms

The law of diminishing returns is highly relevant for production within firms. As producers add successive units of a variable input such as labor to a fixed input such as capital, the marginal product of labor eventually declines. Diminishing returns will occur sooner or later. Total product eventually will rise at a diminishing rate, then reach a maximum, and finally decline.

ORIGIN OF THE IDEA

O 6.2

Law of diminishing returns

ILLUSTRATING THE IDEA

Diminishing Returns from Study

The following noneconomic example of a relationship between "inputs" and "output" may help you better understand the idea. Suppose for an individual that

Total course learning = *f*(intelligence, quality of course materials, instructor effectiveness, class time, and study time)

where *f* means "function of" or "depends on." So this relationship supposes that total course learning depends on intelligence (however defined), the quality of course materials such as the textbook, the effectiveness of the instructor, the amount of class time, and the amount of personal study time outside the class.

For analytical purposes, let's assume that one's intelligence, the quality of course materials, the effectiveness of the instructor, and the amount of class time are *fixed*—meaning they do not change over the length of the course. Now let's add units of study time per day over the length of the course to "produce" greater course learning. The first hour of study time per day increases total course learning. Will the second hour enhance course learning by as much as the first? By how much will the third, fourth, fifth, . . . or fifteenth hour of study per day contribute to total course learning relative to the *immediately previous hour*?

We think you will agree that eventually diminishing returns to course learning will set in as successive hours of study are added each day. At some point the marginal product of an extra hour of study time will decline and, at some further point, become zero.

QUESTION: Given diminishing returns to study time, why devote any extra time to study?

What is true for study time is true for producers. Suppose a farmer has a fixed resource—80 acres of land—planted in corn. If the farmer does not cultivate the corn-fields (clear the weeds) at all, the yield will be 40 bushels per acre. If he cultivates the land once, output may rise to 50 bushels per acre. A second cultivation may increase output to 57 bushels per acre, a third to 61, and a fourth to 63. Succeeding cultivations will add less and less to the land's yield. If this were not so, the world's needs for corn could be fulfilled by extremely intense cultivation of this single 80-acre plot of land. Indeed, if diminishing returns did not occur, the world could be fed out of a flowerpot. Why not? Just keep adding more seed, fertilizer, and harvesters!

The law of diminishing returns also holds true in nonagricultural industries. Assume a wood shop is manufacturing furniture frames. It has a specific amount of equipment such as lathes, planers, saws, and sanders. If this shop hired just one or two workers, total output and productivity (output per worker) would be very low. The workers would have to perform many different jobs, and the advantages of specialization would not be realized. Time would be lost in switching from one job to another, and machines would stand idle much of the time. In short, the plant would be under-staffed, and production would be inefficient because there would be too much capital relative to the amount of labor.

The shop could eliminate those difficulties by hiring more workers. Then the equipment would be more fully used, and workers could specialize in doing a single job. Time would no longer be lost switching from job to job. As more workers were added, production would become more efficient and the marginal product of each succeeding worker would rise.

But the rise could not go on indefinitely. Beyond a certain point, adding more workers would cause overcrowding. Since workers would then have to wait in line to use the machinery, they would be underused. Total output would increase at a diminishing rate because, given the fixed size of the plant, each worker would have less capital equipment to work with as more and more labor was hired. The marginal product of additional workers would decline because there would be more labor in proportion to the fixed amount of capital. Eventually, adding still more workers would cause so much congestion that marginal product would become negative and total product would decline. At the extreme, the addition of more and more labor would exhaust all the standing room, and total product would fall to zero.

Note that the law of diminishing returns assumes that all units of labor are of equal quality. Each successive worker is presumed to have the same innate ability, motor coordination, education, training, and work experience. Less-skilled or less-energetic workers are not the cause of diminishing returns. Rather, marginal product ultimately diminishes because more workers are being used relative to the amount of plant and equipment available.

Tabular and Graphical Representations

The table at the top of Figure 6.2 is a numerical illustration of the law of diminishing returns. Column 2 shows the total product, or total output, resulting from combining each level of a variable input (labor) in column 1 with a fixed amount of capital, using the existing technology.

Column 3 shows the marginal product (MP), the change in total product associated with each additional unit of labor. Note that with no labor input, total product is zero; a plant with no workers will produce no output. The first 3 units of labor reflect increasing marginal returns, with marginal products of 10, 15, and 20 units, respectively. But beginning with the fourth unit of labor, marginal product diminishes

WORKED PROBLEMS

W 6.2

Total, marginal, and average product

FIGURE 6.2 The law of diminishing returns. (a) As a variable resource (labor) is added to fixed amounts of other resources (land or capital), the total product that results will eventually increase by diminishing amounts, reach a maximum, and then decline. (b) Marginal product is the change in total product associated with each new unit of labor. Average product is simply output per labor unit. Note that marginal product intersects average product at the maximum average product.

(1) Units of the Variable Resource (Labor)	(2) Total Product (TP)	(3) Marginal Product (MP), Change in (2)/ Change in (1)		(4) Average Product (AP), (2)/(1)
0	0			—
1	10	10	Increasing marginal returns	10.00
2	25	15		12.50
3	45	20		15.00
4	60	15	Diminishing marginal returns	15.00
5	70	10		14.00
6	75	5		12.50
7	75	0	Negative marginal returns	10.71
8	70	−5		8.75

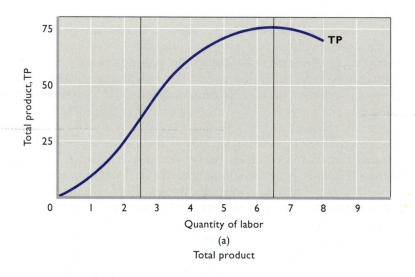

(a)
Total product

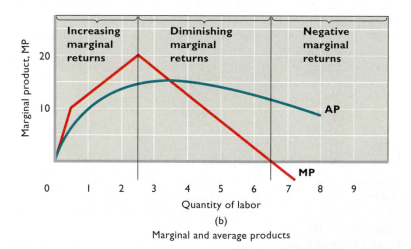

(b)
Marginal and average products

continuously, becoming zero with the seventh unit of labor and negative with the eighth.

Average product, or output per labor unit, is shown in column 4. It is calculated by dividing total product (column 2) by the number of labor units needed to produce it (column 1). At 5 units of labor, for example, AP is 14 (=70/5).

Figure 6.2 also shows the diminishing-returns data graphically and further clarifies the relationships between total, marginal, and average products. (Marginal product in Figure 6.2b is plotted halfway between the units of labor, since it applies to the addition of each labor unit.)

Note first in Figure 6.2a that total product, TP, goes through three phases: It rises initially at an increasing rate; then it increases, but at a diminishing rate; finally, after reaching a maximum, it declines.

Geometrically, marginal product—shown by the MP curve in Figure 6.2b—is the slope of the total-product curve. Marginal product measures the change in total product associated with each succeeding unit of labor. Thus, the three phases of total product are also reflected in marginal product. Where total product is increasing at an increasing rate, marginal product is rising. Here, extra units of labor are adding larger and larger amounts to total product. Similarly, where total product is increasing but at a decreasing rate, marginal product is positive but falling. Each additional unit of labor adds less to total product than did the previous unit. When total product is at a maximum, marginal product is zero. When total product declines, marginal product becomes negative.

Average product, AP (Figure 6.2b), displays the same tendencies as marginal product. It increases, reaches a maximum, and then decreases as more and more units of labor are added to the fixed plant. But note the relationship between marginal product and average product: Where marginal product exceeds average product, average product rises. And where marginal product is less than average product, average product declines. It follows that marginal product intersects average product where average product is at a maximum.

ORIGIN OF THE IDEA

O 6.3

Production relationships

ILLUSTRATING THE IDEA

Exam Scores

The relationship between "marginal" and "average" shown in Figure 6.2b is a mathematical necessity. If you add to a total a number larger than the current average of that total, the average must rise. And if you add to a total a number smaller than the current average of that total, the average must fall. You raise your average examination grade only when your score on an additional (marginal) examination is greater than the average of all your past scores. You lower your average when your grade on an additional exam is below your current average. In our production example, when the amount an extra worker adds to total product exceeds the average product of all workers currently employed, average product will rise. Conversely, when the amount an extra worker adds to total product is less than the current average product, average product will decrease.

QUESTION: Suppose your average exam score for the first three exams is 80 and you receive a 92 on your fourth exam. What is your marginal score? What is your new average score? Why did your average go up?

Short-Run Production Costs

Production information such as that in Figure 6.2 must be coupled with resource prices to determine the total and per-unit costs of producing various levels of output. We know that in the short run, resources associated with the firm's plant are fixed. Other resources, however, are variable in the short run. As a result, short-run costs can be either fixed or variable.

Fixed, Variable, and Total Costs

Let's see what distinguishes fixed costs, variable costs, and total costs from one another.

fixed costs
Costs that do not change in total when the firm changes its output.

Fixed Costs   **Fixed costs** are costs that do not vary with changes in output. Fixed costs are associated with the very existence of a firm's plant and therefore must be paid even if its output is zero. Such costs as rental payments, interest on a firm's debts, a portion of depreciation on equipment and buildings, and insurance premiums are generally fixed costs; they are fixed and do not change even if a firm produces more. In column 2 of Figure 6.3's table, we assume that the firm's total fixed cost is $100. By definition, this fixed cost is incurred at all levels of output, including zero. The firm cannot avoid paying fixed costs in the short run.

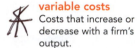

variable costs
Costs that increase or decrease with a firm's output.

Variable Costs   Unlike fixed costs, **variable costs** are costs that change with the level of output. They include payments for materials, fuel, power, transportation services, most labor, and similar variable resources. In column 3 of the table in Figure 6.3, we find that the total of variable costs changes directly with output.

APPLYING THE ANALYSIS

Sunk Costs

Some of a firm's costs are not only *fixed* (recurring, but unrelated to the level of output) but *sunk* (unrecoverable). Such costs are like sunken ships on the ocean floor: Once these costs are incurred, they cannot be recovered. For example, suppose a firm spends $1 million on R&D to bring out a new product, only to discover that the product sells very poorly. Should the firm continue to produce the product at a loss even when there is no realistic hope for future success? Obviously, it should not. In making this decision, the firm realizes that the amount it has spent in developing the product is irrelevant; it should stop production of the product and cut its losses. In fact, many firms have dropped products after spending millions of dollars on their development. For example, in 2007 Pfizer withdrew its novel insulin inhaler from the market because of poor sales and concerns about long-term side effects. The product had cost an estimated $2.8 billion to develop and market.

In short, a firm should ignore any cost that it cannot partly or fully recoup through a subsequent choice. Such costs are sunk costs. They are irrelevant in making future-oriented business decisions. Or, as the saying goes, don't cry over spilt milk.

QUESTION: Which is a sunk cost, rather than simply a recurring fixed cost: (1) a prior expenditure on a business computer that is now outdated or (2) a current monthly payment on an equipment lease that runs for 6 more months? Explain.

FIGURE 6.3 A firm's cost curves. AFC falls as a given amount of fixed costs is apportioned over a larger and larger output. AVC initially falls because of increasing marginal returns but then rises because of diminishing marginal returns. The marginal-cost (MC) curve eventually rises because of diminishing returns and cuts through the average-total-cost (ATC) curve and the average-variable-cost (AVC) curve at their minimum points.

Total-Cost Data				Average-Cost Data			Marginal Cost
(1)	(2)	(3)	(4)	(5)	(6)	(7)	(8)
				Average Fixed Cost (AFC)	Average Variable Cost (AVC)	Average Total Cost (ATC)	Marginal Cost (MC)
Total Product (Q)	Total Fixed Cost (TFC)	Total Variable Cost (TVC)	Total Cost (TC) TC = TFC + TVC	$AFC = \dfrac{TFC}{Q}$	$AVC = \dfrac{TVC}{Q}$	$ATC = \dfrac{TC}{Q}$	$MC = \dfrac{\text{change in TC}}{\text{change in Q}}$
0	$100	$ 0	$ 100				
1	100	90	190	$100.00	$90.00	$190.00	$ 90
2	100	170	270	50.00	85.00	135.00	80
3	100	240	340	33.33	80.00	113.33	70
4	100	300	400	25.00	75.00	100.00	60
5	100	370	470	20.00	74.00	94.00	70
6	100	450	550	16.67	75.00	91.67	80
7	100	540	640	14.29	77.14	91.43	90
8	100	650	750	12.50	81.25	93.75	110
9	100	780	880	11.11	86.67	97.78	130
10	100	930	1030	10.00	93.00	103.00	150

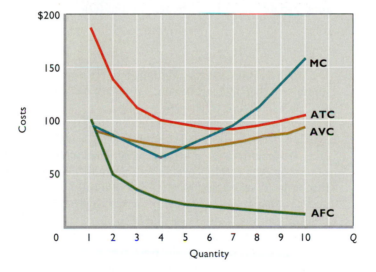

Total Cost

Total cost is the sum of fixed cost and variable cost at each level of output. It is shown in column 4 of the table in Figure 6.3. At zero units of output, total cost is equal to the firm's fixed cost. Then for each unit of the 10 units of production, total cost increases by the same amount as variable cost.

$$TC = TFC + TVC$$

The distinction between fixed and variable costs is significant to the business manager. Variable costs can be controlled or altered in the short run by changing production levels. Fixed costs are beyond the business manager's current control; they are incurred in the short run and must be paid regardless of output level.

total cost
The sum of fixed cost and variable cost.

Per-Unit, or Average, Costs

Producers are certainly interested in their total costs, but they are equally concerned with per-unit, or average, costs. In particular, average-cost data are more meaningful for making comparisons with product price, which is always stated on a per-unit basis. Average fixed cost, average variable cost, and average total cost are shown in columns 5 to 7 of the table in Figure 6.3.

average fixed cost (AFC)
A firm's total fixed cost divided by output.

↓ AFC = ↑
output

AFC **Average fixed cost (AFC)** for any output level is found by dividing total fixed cost (TFC) by that output (Q). That is,

$$AFC = \frac{TFC}{Q}$$

Because the total fixed cost is, by definition, the same regardless of output, AFC must decline as output increases. As output rises, the total fixed cost is spread over a larger and larger output. When output is just 1 unit in Figure 6.3's table, TFC and AFC are the same at $100. But at 2 units of output, the total fixed cost of $100 becomes $50 of AFC or fixed cost per unit; then it becomes $33.33 per unit as $100 is spread over 3 units, and $25 per unit when spread over 4 units. This process is sometimes referred to as "spreading the overhead." Figure 6.3 shows that AFC graphs as a continuously declining curve as total output is increased.

average variable cost (AVC)
A firm's total variable cost divided by output.

AVC **Average variable cost (AVC)** for any output level is calculated by dividing total variable cost (TVC) by that output (Q):

$$AVC = \frac{TVC}{Q}$$

Due to increasing and then diminishing returns, AVC declines initially, reaches a minimum, and then increases again. A graph of AVC is a U-shaped or saucer-shaped curve, as shown in Figure 6.3.

Because total variable cost reflects the law of diminishing returns, so must AVC, which is derived from total variable cost. Because marginal returns increase initially, it takes fewer and fewer additional variable resources to produce each of the first 4 units of output. As a result, variable cost per unit declines. AVC hits a minimum with the fifth unit of output, and beyond that point AVC rises because diminishing returns require more and more variable resources to produce each additional unit of output.

You can verify the U or saucer shape of the AVC curve by returning to the production table in Figure 6.2. Assume the price of labor is $10 per unit. Labor cost per unit of output is then $10 (the price per unit of labor in this example) divided by average product (output per labor unit). Because we have assumed labor to be the only variable input, the labor cost per unit of output is the variable cost per unit of output, or AVC. When average product is initially low, AVC is high. As workers are added, average product rises and AVC falls. When average product is at its maximum, AVC is at its minimum. Then, as still more workers are added and average product declines, AVC rises. The "hump" of the average-product curve is reflected in the saucer or U shape of the AVC curve.

average total cost (ATC)
A firm's total cost (= total fixed costs + total variable costs) divided by output.

ATC **Average total cost (ATC)** for any output level is found by dividing total cost (TC) by that output (Q) or by adding AFC and AVC at that output:

$$ATC = \frac{TC}{Q} = \frac{TFC}{Q} + \frac{TVC}{Q} = AFC + AVC$$

Graphically, we can find ATC by adding vertically the AFC and AVC curves, as in Figure 6.3. Thus, the vertical distance between the ATC and AVC curves measures AFC at any level of output.

Marginal Cost

One final and very crucial cost concept remains: **Marginal cost (MC)** is *the extra, or additional, cost of producing 1 more unit of output.* MC can be determined for each added unit of output by noting the change in total cost which that unit's production entails:

$$MC = \frac{\text{change in TC}}{\text{change in } Q}$$

Calculations   In column 4 of Figure 6.3's table, production of the first unit of output increases total cost from $100 to $190. Therefore, the additional, or marginal, cost of that first unit is $90 (column 8). The marginal cost of the second unit is $80 (= $270 − $190); the MC of the third is $70 (= $340 − $270); and so forth. The MC for each of the 10 units of output is shown in column 8.

MC can also be calculated from the total-variable-cost column because the only difference between total cost and total variable cost is the constant amount of fixed costs ($100). Thus, the change in total cost and the change in total variable cost accompanying each additional unit of output are always the same.

Marginal Decisions   Marginal costs are costs the firm can control directly and immediately. Specifically, MC designates all the cost incurred in producing the last unit of output. Thus, it also designates the cost that can be "saved" by not producing that last unit. Average-cost figures do not provide this information. For example, suppose the firm is undecided whether to produce 3 or 4 units of output. At 4 units the table in Figure 6.3 indicates that ATC is $100. But the firm does not increase its total costs by $100 by producing the fourth unit, nor does it save $100 by not producing that unit. Rather, the change in costs involved here is only $60, as the MC column in the table reveals.

A firm's decisions as to what output level to produce are typically marginal decisions, that is, decisions to produce a few more or a few less units. Marginal cost is the change in costs when 1 more or 1 less unit of output is produced. When coupled with marginal revenue (which, as you will see in Chapter 7, indicates the change in revenue from 1 more or 1 less unit of output), marginal cost allows a firm to determine if it is profitable to expand or contract its production. The analysis in the next three chapters focuses on those marginal calculations.

Graphical Portrayal   Marginal cost is shown graphically in Figure 6.3. Marginal cost at first declines sharply, reaches a minimum, and then rises rather abruptly. This reflects the fact that variable costs, and therefore total cost, increase first by decreasing amounts and then by increasing amounts.

Relation of MC to AVC and ATC   Figure 6.3 shows that the marginal-cost curve MC intersects both the AVC and the ATC curves at their minimum points. As noted earlier, this marginal-average relationship is a mathematical necessity. When the amount (the marginal cost) added to total cost is less than the current average total cost, ATC will fall. Conversely, when the marginal cost exceeds ATC, ATC will rise. This means in Figure 6.3 that as long as MC lies below ATC, ATC will fall, and whenever MC lies above ATC, ATC will rise. Therefore, at the point of intersection where MC equals ATC, ATC has just ceased to fall but has not yet begun to rise. This, by

marginal cost (MC)
The extra or additional cost of producing 1 more unit of output.

WORKED PROBLEMS
W 6.3
Per-unit cost

INTERACTIVE GRAPHS
G 6.1
Production and costs

definition, is the minimum point on the ATC curve. The marginal-cost curve intersects the average-total-cost curve at the ATC curve's minimum point.

Marginal cost can be defined as the addition either to total cost or to total variable cost resulting from 1 more unit of output; thus, this same rationale explains why the MC curve also crosses the AVC curve at the AVC curve's minimum point. No such relationship exists between the MC curve and the average-fixed-cost curve because the two are not related; marginal cost includes only those costs that change with output, and fixed costs by definition are those that are independent of output.

APPLYING THE ANALYSIS

Rising Gasoline Prices

Changes in supply and demand often lead to rapid increases in the price of gasoline. Because gasoline is used to power nearly all motor vehicles, including those used by businesses, increases in the price of gasoline lead to increases in firms' short-run variable costs, marginal costs, and average total costs. In terms of our analysis, their AVC, MC, and ATC curves all shift upward when an increase in the price of gasoline increases their production costs.

The extent of these upward shifts depends upon the relative importance of gasoline as a variable input in the various firms' individual production processes. Package-delivery companies like FedEx that use a lot of gasoline-powered vehicles will see substantial upward shifts while software companies like Symantec (Norton) that mainly deliver their products through Internet downloads may see only small upward shifts.

QUESTION: If rising gasoline prices increase the cost for delivery to firms such as FedEx, how would that affect the cost curves for Internet retailers such as Amazon, that ship a lot of packages?

Long-Run Production Costs

In the long run, an industry and its individual firms can undertake all desired resource adjustments. That is, they can change the amount of all inputs used. The firm can alter its plant capacity; it can build a larger plant or revert to a smaller plant than that assumed in Figures 6.2 and 6.3. The industry also can change its overall capacity; the long run allows sufficient time for new firms to enter or for existing firms to leave an industry. We will discuss the impact of the entry and exit of firms to and from an industry in the next chapter; here we are concerned only with changes in plant capacity made by a single firm. Let's couch our analysis in terms of average total cost (ATC), making no distinction between fixed and variable costs because all resources, and therefore all costs, are variable in the long run.

Firm Size and Costs

Suppose a manufacturer with a single plant begins on a small scale and, as the result of successful operations, expands to successively larger plant sizes with larger output capacities. What happens to average total cost as this occurs? For a time, successively larger plants will reduce average total cost. However, eventually the building of a still larger plant may cause ATC to rise.

[Handwritten margin note: Nothing is fixed in the long run

No law of Diminishing Return - No fixed input?!]

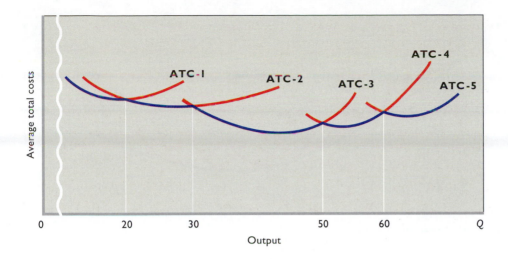

FIGURE 6.4 The long-run average-total-cost curve: five possible plant sizes. The long-run average-total-cost curve is made up of segments of the short-run cost curves (ATC-1, ATC-2, etc.) of the various-size plants from which the firm might choose. Each point on the bumpy planning curve shows the lowest unit cost attainable for any output when the firm has had time to make all desired changes in its plant size.

Figure 6.4 illustrates this situation for five possible plant sizes. ATC-1 is the short-run average-total-cost curve for the smallest of the five plants, and ATC-5, the curve for the largest. Constructing larger plants will lower the minimum average total costs through plant size 3. But then larger plants will mean higher minimum average total costs.

The Long-Run Cost Curve

The vertical lines perpendicular to the output axis in Figure 6.4 indicate the outputs at which the firm should change plant size to realize the lowest attainable average total costs of production. These are the outputs at which the per-unit costs for a larger plant drop below those for the current, smaller plant. For all outputs up to 20 units, the lowest average total costs are attainable with plant size 1. However, if the firm's volume of sales expands beyond 20 units but less than 30, it can achieve lower per-unit costs by constructing a larger plant, size 2. Although total cost will be higher at the expanded levels of production, the cost per unit of output will be less. For any output between 30 and 50 units, plant size 3 will yield the lowest average total costs. From 50 to 60 units of output, the firm must build the size-4 plant to achieve the lowest unit costs. Lowest average total costs for any output over 60 units require construction of the still larger plant, size 5.

Tracing these adjustments, we find that the long-run ATC curve for the enterprise is made up of segments of the short-run ATC curves for the various plant sizes that can be constructed. The long-run ATC curve shows the lowest average total cost at which *any output level* can be produced after the firm has had time to make all appropriate adjustments in its plant size. In Figure 6.4 the red, bumpy curve is the firm's long-run ATC curve or, as it is often called, the firm's *planning curve*.

In most lines of production, the choice of plant size is much wider than in our illustration. In many industries the number of possible plant sizes is virtually unlimited, and in time quite small changes in the volume of output will lead to changes in plant size. Graphically, this implies an unlimited number of short-run ATC curves, one for each output level, as suggested by Figure 6.5. Then, rather than being made up of segments of short-run ATC curves as in Figure 6.4, the long-run ATC curve is made up of all the points of tangency of the unlimited number of short-run ATC curves from which the long-run ATC curve is derived. Therefore, the planning curve is smooth rather than bumpy. Each point on it tells us the minimum ATC of producing the corresponding level of output.

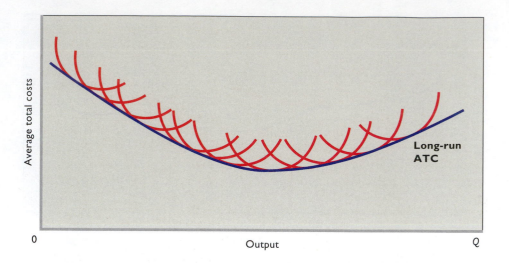

Economies and Diseconomies of Scale

We have assumed that, for a time, larger and larger plant sizes will lead to lower unit costs but that, beyond some point, successively larger plants will mean higher average total costs. That is, we have assumed the long-run ATC curve is U-shaped. But why should this be? It turns out that the U shape is caused by economies and diseconomies of large-scale production, as we explain in a moment. But before we do, please understand that the U shape of the long-run average-total-cost curve *cannot* be the result of rising resource prices or the law of diminishing returns. First, our discussion assumes that resource prices are constant. Second, the law of diminishing returns does not apply to production in the long run. This is true because the law of diminishing returns only deals with situations in which a productive resource or input is held constant. Under our definition of "long run," all resources and inputs are variable.

economies of scale
Reductions in the average total cost of producing a product as the firm expands the size of its operations (output) in the long run.

Economies of Scale   **Economies of scale,** or *economies of mass production*, explain the downsloping part of the long-run ATC curve, as indicated in Figure 6.6, graphs (a), (b), and (c). As plant size increases, a number of factors will, for a time, lead to lower average costs of production.

Labor Specialization   Increased specialization in the use of labor becomes more achievable as a plant increases in size. Hiring more workers means jobs can be divided and subdivided. Each worker may now have just one task to perform instead of five or six. Workers can work full time on the tasks for which they have special skills. By contrast, skilled machinists in a small plant may spend half their time performing unskilled tasks, leading to higher production costs.

Further, by working at fewer tasks, workers become even more proficient at those tasks. The jack-of-all-trades doing five or six jobs is not likely to be efficient in any of them. Concentrating on one task, the same worker may become highly efficient.

Finally, greater labor specialization eliminates the loss of time that occurs whenever a worker shifts from one task to another.

Managerial Specialization   Large-scale production also means better use of, and greater specialization in, management. A supervisor who can handle 20 workers is underused in a small plant that employs only 10 people. The production staff could be doubled with no increase in supervisory costs.

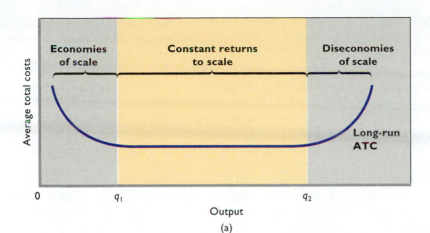

(a)

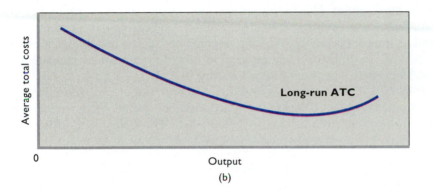

(b)

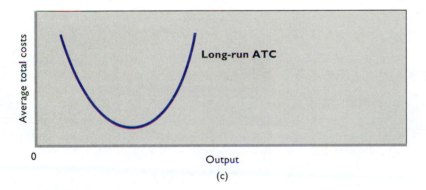

(c)

FIGURE 6.6 Various possible long-run average-total-cost curves. In (a), economies of scale are rather rapidly obtained as plant size rises, and diseconomies of scale are not encountered until a considerably large scale of output has been achieved. Thus, long-run average total cost is constant over a wide range of output. In (b), economies of scale are extensive, and diseconomies of scale occur only at very large outputs. Average total cost therefore declines over a broad range of output. In (c), economies of scale are exhausted quickly, followed immediately by diseconomies of scale. Minimum ATC thus occurs at a relatively low output.

Small firms cannot use management specialists to best advantage. For example, a sales specialist working in a small plant may have to spend some of her time on functions outside of her area of expertise—marketing, personnel, and finance. A larger scale of operations would allow her to supervise marketing full time, while different specialists perform other managerial functions. Greater efficiency and lower unit costs are the net result.

Efficient Capital Small firms often cannot afford the most efficient equipment. In many lines of production, such machinery is available only in very large and extremely expensive units. Furthermore, effective use of the equipment demands a high volume of production, and that again requires large-scale producers.

In the automobile industry the most efficient fabrication method employs robotics and elaborate assembly-line equipment. Effective use of this equipment demands an annual output of perhaps 200,000 to 400,000 automobiles. Only very-large-scale producers can afford to purchase and use this equipment efficiently. The small-scale producer is faced with a dilemma. To fabricate automobiles using other equipment is inefficient and therefore more costly per unit. But so, too, is buying and underutilizing the equipment used by the large manufacturers. Because it cannot spread the high equipment cost over very many units of output, the small-scale producer will be stuck with high costs per unit of output.

Other Factors   Many products entail design and development costs, as well as other "start-up" costs, which must be incurred irrespective of projected sales. These costs decline per unit as output is increased. Similarly, advertising costs decline per auto, per computer, per stereo system, and per box of detergent as more units are produced and sold. Also, the firm's production and marketing expertise usually rises as it produces and sells more output. This *learning by doing* is a further source of economies of scale.

All these factors contribute to lower average total costs for the firm that is able to expand its scale of operations. Where economies of scale are possible, an increase in all resources of, say, 10 percent will cause a more-than-proportionate increase in output of, say, 20 percent. The result will be a decline in ATC.

In many U.S. manufacturing industries, economies of scale have been of great significance. Firms that have expanded their scale of operations to obtain economies of mass production have survived and flourished. Those unable to expand have become relatively high-cost producers, doomed to a struggle to survive.

© Getty Images

© Bryan Mullennix/Getty Images

PHOTO OP   Economies of Scale

Economies of scale are extensive in the automobile industry, where the capital required is large and expensive and many workers are needed to perform the numerous, highly specialized tasks. Economies of scale in copying keys are exhausted at low levels of output; production usually occurs in small shops, the capital involved is relatively small and inexpensive, and a small number of workers (often only one) perform all of the labor and managerial functions of the business. There would be little, if any, cost advantage to establishing a key copying "factory" with hundreds of stations.

The Verson Stamping Machine

In 1996 Verson (a U.S. firm located in Chicago) introduced a 49-foot-tall metal-stamping machine that is the size of a house and weighs as much as 12 locomotives. This $30 million machine, which cuts and sculpts raw sheets of steel into automobile hoods and fenders, enables automakers to make new parts in just 5 minutes compared with 8 hours for older stamping presses. A single machine is designed to make 5 million auto parts per year. So, to achieve the cost saving from the machine, an auto manufacturer must have sufficient auto production to use all these parts. By allowing the use of this cost-saving piece of equipment, large firm size achieves economies of scale.

QUESTION: Do you see any potential problems for a company that relies too heavily on just a few large machines for fabricating millions of its critical product parts?

Diseconomies of Scale   In time the expansion of a firm may lead to diseconomies and therefore higher average total costs.

The main factor causing **diseconomies of scale** is the difficulty of efficiently controlling and coordinating a firm's operations as it becomes a large-scale producer. In a small plant, a single key executive may make all the basic decisions for the plant's operation. Because of the firm's small size, the executive is close to the production line, understands the firm's operations, and can make efficient decisions because the small plant size requires only a relatively small amount of information to be examined and understood in optimizing production.

This neat picture changes as a firm grows. One person cannot assemble, digest, and understand all the information essential to decision making on a large scale. Authority must be delegated to many vice presidents, second vice presidents, and so forth. This expansion of the management hierarchy leads to problems of communication and cooperation, bureaucratic red tape, and the possibility that decisions will not be coordinated. At the same time, each new manager must be paid a salary. Thus, declining efficiency in making and executing decisions goes hand-in-hand with rising average total costs as bureaucracy expands beyond a certain point.

Also, in massive production facilities, workers may feel alienated from their employers and care little about working efficiently. Opportunities to shirk, by avoiding work in favor of on-the-job leisure, may be greater in large plants than in small ones. Countering worker alienation and shirking may require additional worker supervision, which increases costs.

Where diseconomies of scale are operative, an increase in all inputs of, say, 10 percent will cause a less-than-proportionate increase in output of, say, 5 percent. As a consequence, ATC will increase. The rising portion of the long-run cost curves in Figure 6.6 illustrates diseconomies of scale.

Constant Returns to Scale   In some industries there may exist a rather wide range of output between the output at which economies of scale end and the output at which diseconomies of scale begin. That is, there may be a range of **constant returns to scale**

diseconomies of scale
Increases in the average total cost of producing a product as the firm expands the size of its operations (output) in the long run.

constant returns to scale
No changes in the average total cost of producing a product as the firm expands the size of its operations (output) in the long run.

over which long-run average cost does not change. The q_1q_2 output range of Figure 6.6a is an example. Here a given percentage increase in all inputs of, say, 10 percent will cause a proportionate 10 percent increase in output. Thus, in this range ATC is constant.

Minimum Efficient Scale and Industry Structure

minimum efficient scale (MES)
The lowest level of output at which a firm can minimize long-run average total cost.

Economies and diseconomies of scale are an important determinant of an industry's structure. Here we introduce the concept of **minimum efficient scale (MES),** which is the lowest level of output at which a firm can minimize long-run average costs. In Figure 6.6a that level occurs at q_1 units of output. Because of the extended range of constant returns to scale, firms producing substantially greater outputs could also realize the minimum attainable long-run average costs. Specifically, firms within the q_1q_2 range would be equally efficient. So we would not be surprised to find an industry with such cost conditions to be populated by firms of quite different sizes. The apparel, banking, furniture, snowboard, wood products, food processing, and small-appliance industries are examples. With an extended range of constant returns to scale, relatively large and relatively small firms can coexist in an industry and be equally successful.

Compare this with Figure 6.6b, where economies of scale continue over a wide range of outputs and diseconomies of scale appear only at very high levels of output. This pattern of declining long-run average total cost occurs in the automobile, aluminum, steel, and other heavy industries. The same pattern holds in several of the new industries related to information technology, for example, computer microchips, operating system software, and Internet service provision. Given consumer demand, efficient production will be achieved with a few large-scale producers. Small firms cannot realize the minimum efficient scale and will not be able to compete.

Where economies of scale are few and diseconomies come into play quickly, the minimum efficient size occurs at a low level of output, as shown in Figure 6.6c. In such industries, a particular level of consumer demand will support a large number of relatively small producers. Many retail trades and some types of farming fall into this category. So do certain kinds of light manufacturing, such as the baking, clothing, and shoe industries. Fairly small firms are more efficient than larger-scale producers would be if they were present in such industries.

Our point here is that the shape of the long-run average-total-cost curve is determined by technology and the economies and diseconomies of scale that result. The shape of the long-run ATC curve, in turn, can be significant in determining whether an industry is populated by a relatively large number of small firms or is dominated by a few large producers, or lies somewhere in between.

But we must be cautious in our assessment because industry structure does not depend on cost conditions alone. Government policies, the geographic size of markets, managerial strategy and skill, and other factors must be considered in explaining the structure of a particular industry.

ORIGIN OF THE IDEA

O 6.4

Minimum efficient scale

APPLYING THE ANALYSIS

Aircraft Assembly Plants versus Concrete Plants

Why are there only three plants in the United States (all operated by Boeing) that produce large commercial aircraft and thousands of plants (owned by hundreds of firms) that produce ready-mix concrete? The simple answer is that MES is radically different in the two industries. Why is that? First, while economies of scale are extensive in assembling large commercial aircraft, they are only very modest in mixing concrete. Manufacturing airplanes is a complex process that requires huge facilities, thousands of workers, and very expensive, specialized machinery. Economies of scale extend to huge plant sizes. But mixing Portland cement, sand, gravel, and water to produce concrete requires only a handful of workers and relatively inexpensive equipment. Economies of scale are exhausted at relatively small size.

The differing MES also derives from the vastly different sizes of the geographic markets. The market for commercial airplanes is global, and aircraft manufacturers can deliver new airplanes anywhere in the world by flying them there. In contrast, the geographic market for a concrete plant is roughly the 50-mile radius within which the concrete can be delivered before it "sets up." So in the ready-mix concrete industry, thousands of small concrete plants are positioned close to their customers in hundreds of small and large cities.

QUESTION: Speculate as to why the MES of firms in the Portland cement industry is considerably larger than the MES of single ready-mix concrete plants.

Summary

1. Corporations—the dominant form of business organizations—are legal entities, distinct and separate from the individuals who own them. They often have thousands, or even millions, of stockholders who jointly own them. They finance their operations and purchases of new plant and equipment partly through the issuance of stocks and bonds. Stocks are ownership shares of a corporation, and bonds are promises to repay a loan, usually at a set rate of interest.

2. A principal-agent problem may occur in corporations when the agents (managers) hired to represent the interest of the principals (stockholders) pursue their own objectives to the detriment of the objectives of the principals.

3. The economic cost of using a resource to produce a good or service is the value or worth that the resource would have had in its best alternative use. Economic costs include explicit costs, which flow to resources owned and supplied by others, and implicit costs, which are payments for the use of self-owned and self-employed resources. One implicit cost is a normal profit to the entrepreneur. Economic profit occurs when total revenue exceeds total cost (= explicit costs + implicit costs, including a normal profit).

4. In the short run, a firm's plant capacity is fixed. The firm can use its plant more or less intensively by adding or subtracting units of variable resources, but it does not have sufficient time in the short run to alter plant size.

5. The law of diminishing returns describes what happens to output as a fixed plant is used more intensively. As successive units of a variable resource, such as labor, are added to a fixed plant, beyond some point the marginal product associated with each additional unit of a resource declines.

6. Because some resources are variable and others are fixed, costs can be classified as variable or fixed in the short run. Fixed costs are independent of the level of output; variable costs vary with output. The total cost of any output is the sum of fixed and variable costs at that output.

7. Average fixed, average variable, and average total costs are fixed, variable, and total costs per unit of output. Average fixed cost declines continuously as output increases because a fixed sum is being spread over a larger and larger number of units of production. A graph of average variable cost is U-shaped, reflecting the law of diminishing returns. Average total cost is the sum of average fixed and average variable costs; its graph is also U-shaped.

8. Marginal cost is the extra, or additional, cost of producing 1 more unit of output. It is the amount by which total cost and total variable cost change when 1 more or 1 less unit of output is produced. Graphically, the marginal-cost curve intersects the ATC and AVC curves at their minimum points.

9. The long run is a period of time sufficiently long for a firm to vary the amounts of all resources used, including plant size. In the long run, all costs are variable. The long-run ATC, or planning, curve is composed of segments of the short-run ATC curves, and it represents the various plant sizes a firm can construct in the long run.

10. The long-run ATC curve is generally U-shaped. Economies of scale are first encountered as a small firm expands. Greater specialization in the use of labor and management, the ability to use the most efficient equipment, and the spreading of start-up costs among more units of output all contribute to economies of scale. As the firm continues to grow, it will encounter diseconomies of scale stemming from the managerial complexities that accompany large-scale production. The ranges of output over which economies and diseconomies of scale occur in an industry are often an important determinant of the structure of that industry.

11. A firm's minimum efficient scale (MES) is the lowest level of output at which it can minimize its long-run average cost. In some industries, MES occurs at such low levels of output that numerous firms can populate the industry. In other industries, MES occurs at such high output levels that only a few firms can exist in the long run.

Terms and Concepts

stocks	economic profit	total cost
bonds	short run	average fixed cost (AFC)
limited liability	long run	average variable cost (AVC)
principal-agent problem	total product (TP)	average total cost (ATC)
economic cost	marginal product (MP)	marginal cost (MC)
explicit costs	average product (AP)	economies of scale
implicit costs	law of diminishing returns	diseconomies of scale
accounting profit	fixed costs	constant returns to scale
normal profit	variable costs	minimum efficient scale (MES)

Questions

1. Distinguish between a plant, a firm, and an industry. Contrast a vertically integrated firm, a horizontally integrated firm, and a conglomerate. Cite an example of a horizontally integrated firm from which you have recently made a purchase. **LO1**

2. What major advantages of corporations have given rise to their dominance as a form of business organization? **LO1**

3. What is the principal-agent problem as it relates to corporate managers and stockholders? How did firms try to solve this problem in the 1990s? In what way did the "solution" backfire on some firms? **LO1**

4. Distinguish between explicit and implicit costs, giving examples of each. What are some explicit and implicit costs of attending college? **LO2**

5. Distinguish between accounting profit, economic profit, and normal profit. Does accounting profit or economic profit determine how entrepreneurs allocate resources between different business ventures? Explain. **LO2**

6. Which of the following are short-run and which are long-run adjustments? **LO3**
  a. Wendy's builds a new restaurant.
  b. Harley-Davidson Corporation hires 200 more production workers.
  c. A farmer increases the amount of fertilizer used on his corn crop.
  d. An Alcoa aluminum plant adds a third shift of workers.

7. Complete the following table by calculating marginal product and average product from the data given: **LO3**

Inputs of Labor	Total Product	Marginal Product	Average Product
0	0		
1	15	_____	_____
2	34	_____	_____
3	51	_____	_____
4	65	_____	_____
5	74	_____	_____
6	80	_____	_____
7	83	_____	_____
8	82	_____	_____

Explain why marginal product eventually declines and ultimately becomes negative. What bearing does the law of diminishing returns have on marginal costs? Be specific.

8. Why can the distinction between fixed costs and variable costs be made in the short run? Classify the following as fixed or variable costs: advertising expenditures, fuel, interest on company-issued bonds, shipping charges, payments for raw materials, real estate taxes, executive salaries, insurance premiums, wage payments, sales taxes, and rental payments on leased office machinery. **LO4**

9. A firm has fixed costs of $60 and variable costs as indicated in the accompanying table. **LO4**

    Complete the table and check your calculations by referring to question 3 at the end of Chapter 7.

   a. Graph the AFC, ATC, and MC curves. Why does the AFC curve slope continuously downward? Why does the MC curve eventually slope upward? Why does the MC curve intersect the ATC curve at its minimum point?

   b. Explain how the location of each curve graphed in question 9a would be altered if (1) total fixed cost had been $100 rather than $60 and (2) total variable cost had been $10 less at each level of output.

10. Indicate how each of the following would shift the (1) marginal-cost curve, (2) average-variable-cost curve, (3) average-fixed-cost curve, and (4) average-total-cost curve of a manufacturing firm. In each case, specify the direction of the shift. **LO4**

   a. A reduction in business property taxes.

   b. An increase in the hourly wage rates of production workers.

   c. A decrease in the price of electricity.

   d. An increase in transportation costs.

11. Suppose a firm has only three possible plant-size options, represented by the ATC curves shown in the accompanying

figure. What plant size will the firm choose in producing (a) 50, (b) 130, (c) 160, and (d) 250 units of output? Draw the firm's long-run average-cost curve on the diagram and describe this curve. **LO5**

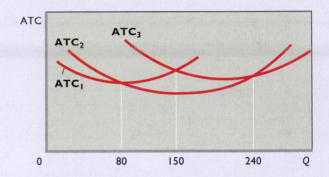

12. Use the concepts of economies and diseconomies of scale to explain the shape of a firm's long-run ATC curve. What is the concept of minimum efficient scale? What bearing can the shape of the long-run ATC curve have on the structure of an industry? **LO5**

Total Product	Total Fixed Cost	Total Variable Cost	Total Cost	Average Fixed Cost	Average Variable Cost	Average Total Cost	Marginal Cost
0	$_____	$ 0	$_____			$_____	$_____
1	_____	45	_____	$_____	$_____	_____	_____
2	_____	85	_____	_____	_____	_____	_____
3	_____	120	_____	_____	_____	_____	_____
4	_____	150	_____	_____	_____	_____	_____
5	_____	185	_____	_____	_____	_____	_____
6	_____	225	_____	_____	_____	_____	_____
7	_____	270	_____	_____	_____	_____	_____
8	_____	325	_____	_____	_____	_____	_____
9	_____	390	_____	_____	_____	_____	_____
10	_____	465	_____	_____	_____	_____	_____

Problems

1. Gomez runs a small pottery firm. He hires one helper at $12,000 per year, pays annual rent of $5000 for his shop, and spends $20,000 per year on materials. He has $40,000 of his own funds invested in equipment (pottery wheels, kilns, and so forth) that could earn him $4000 per year if alternatively invested. He has been offered $15,000 per year to work as a potter for a competitor. He estimates his entrepreneurial talents are worth $3000 per year. Total annual revenue from pottery sales is $72,000. Calculate the accounting profit and the economic profit for Gomez's pottery firm. **LO2**

2. Imagine you have some workers and some handheld computers that you can use to take inventory at a warehouse. There are diminishing returns to taking inventory. If one worker uses one computer, he can inventory 100 items per hour. Two workers sharing a computer can together

inventory 150 items per hour. Three workers sharing a computer can together inventory 160 items per hour. And four or more workers sharing a computer can together inventory fewer than 160 items per hour. Computers cost $100 each and you must pay each worker $25 per hour. If you assign one worker per computer, what is the cost of inventorying a single item? What if you assign two workers per computer? Three? How many workers per computer should you assign if you wish to minimize the cost of inventorying a single item? **LO3**

3. You are a newspaper publisher. You are in the middle of a one-year rental contract for your factory that requires you to pay $500,000 per month, and you have contractual labor obligations of $1 million per month that you can't get out of. You also have a marginal printing cost of $.25 per paper as well as a marginal delivery cost of $.10 per paper. If sales

fall by 20 percent from 1 million papers per month to 800,000 papers per month, what happens to the AFC per paper, the MC per paper, and the minimum amount that you must charge to break even on these costs? **LO4**

4. There are economies of scale in ranching, especially with regard to fencing land. Suppose that barbed-wire fencing costs $10,000 per mile to set up. How much would it cost to fence a single property whose area is one square mile if that property also happens to be perfectly square, with sides that are each one mile long? How much would it cost to fence exactly four such properties, which together would contain four square miles of area? Now, consider how much it would cost to fence in four square miles of ranch land if, instead, it comes as a single large square that is two miles long on each side. Which is more costly—fencing in the four, one-square-mile properties or the single four-square-mile property? **LO5**

After reading this chapter, you should be able to:

1 Give the names and summarize the main characteristics of the four basic market models.

2 List the conditions required for purely competitive markets.

3 Describe how purely competitive firms maximize profits or minimize losses.

4 Explain why the marginal-cost curve and supply curve of competitive firms are identical.

5 Discuss how industry entry and exit produce economic efficiency.

6 Identify the differences between constant-cost, increasing-cost, and decreasing-cost industries.

Pure Competition

In Chapter 4 we examined the relationship between product demand and total revenue, and in Chapter 6 we discussed businesses and their production costs. Now we want to connect revenues and costs to see how a business decides what price to charge and how much output to produce. But a firm's decisions concerning price and production depend greatly on the character of the industry in which it is operating. There is no "average" or "typical" industry. At one extreme is a single producer that dominates the market; at the other extreme are industries in which thousands of firms each produces a tiny fraction of market supply. Between these extremes are many other industries.

Since we cannot examine each industry individually, our approach will be to look at four basic *models* of market structure. Together, these models will help you understand how price, output, and profit are determined in the many product markets in the economy. They also will help you evaluate the efficiency or inefficiency of those markets. Finally, these four models will provide a crucial background for assessing public policies (such as antitrust policy) relating to certain firms and industries.

[handwritten marginalia: What price? Level of output? What point does the company start losing money?]

Four Market Models

Economists group industries into four distinct market structures: pure competition, pure monopoly, monopolistic competition, and oligopoly. These four market models differ in several respects: the number of firms in the industry, whether those firms produce a standardized product or try to distinguish their products from those of other firms, and how easy or how difficult it is for firms to enter the industry.

The four models are as follows, presented in order of degree of competition (most to least):

- *Pure competition* involves a very large number of firms producing a standardized product (that is, a product like cotton for which each producer's output is virtually identical to that of every other producer). New firms can enter or exit the industry very easily.

- *Monopolistic competition* is characterized by a relatively large number of sellers producing differentiated products (clothing, furniture, books). Present in this model is widespread *nonprice competition*, a selling strategy in which one firm tries to distinguish its product or service from all competing products on the basis of attributes such as design and workmanship (an approach called *product differentiation*). Either entry to or exit from monopolistically competitive industries is quite easy.

- *Oligopoly* involves only a few sellers of a standardized or differentiated product, so each firm is affected by the decisions of its rivals and must take those decisions into account in determining its own price and output.

[handwritten margin notes: "Cell phone / T.V. / Computer / Camera" and "Car Production"]

© Getty Images

© PRNewsFoto/Dove

PHOTO OP Standardized versus Differentiated Products

Wheat is an example of a standardized product, whereas Dove shampoo is an example of a differentiated product.

• *Pure monopoly* is a market structure in which one firm is the sole seller of a product or service for which there is no good substitute (for example, a local electric utility or patented medical device). Since the entry of additional firms is blocked, one firm constitutes the entire industry. The pure monopolist produces a single unique product, so product differentiation is not an issue.

Pure Competition: Characteristics and Occurrence

Let's take a fuller look at **pure competition,** the focus of the remainder of this chapter:

• *Very large numbers*   A basic feature of a purely competitive market is the presence of a large number of independently acting sellers, often offering their products in large national or international markets. Examples: markets for farm commodities, the stock market, and the foreign exchange market.

pure competition
A market structure in which a very large number of firms produce a standardized product and there are no restrictions on entry.

• *Standardized product*   Purely competitive firms produce a standardized (identical or homogeneous) product. As long as the price is the same, consumers will be indifferent about which seller to buy the product from. Buyers view the products of firms B, C, D, and E as perfect substitutes for the product of firm A. Because purely competitive firms sell standardized products, they make no attempt to differentiate their products and do not engage in other forms of nonprice competition.

• *"Price takers"*   In a purely competitive market, individual firms do not exert control over product price. Each firm produces such a small fraction of total output that increasing or decreasing its output will not perceptibly influence total supply or, therefore, product price. In short, the competitive firm is a **price taker:** It cannot change market price; it can only adjust to it. That means that the individual competitive producer is at the mercy of the market. Asking a price higher than the market price would be futile. Consumers will not buy from firm A at $2.05 when its 9999 competitors are selling an identical product, and therefore a perfect substitute, at $2 per unit. Conversely, because firm A can sell as much as it chooses at $2 per unit, it has no reason to charge a lower price, say, $1.95. Doing that would shrink its profit.

price taker
A competitive firm that cannot change the market price, but can only accept it as "given" and adjust to it.

• *Free entry and exit*   New firms can freely enter and existing firms can freely leave purely competitive industries. No significant legal, technological, financial, or other obstacles prohibit new firms from selling their output in any competitive market.

Although pure competition is somewhat rare in the real world, this market model is highly relevant to several industries. In particular, we can learn much about markets for agricultural goods, fish products, foreign exchange, basic metals, and stock shares by studying the pure-competition model. Also, pure competition is a meaningful starting point for any discussion of how prices and output are determined. Moreover, the operation of a purely competitive economy provides a norm for evaluating the efficiency of the real-world economy.

Demand as Seen by a Purely Competitive Seller

To develop a model of pure competition, we first examine demand from a purely competitive seller's viewpoint and see how it affects revenue. This seller might be a wheat farmer, a strawberry grower, a sheep rancher, a foreign-currency broker, or some other pure competitor. Because each purely competitive firm offers only a negligible fraction of total market supply, it must accept the price predetermined by the market. Pure competitors are price takers, not price makers.

FIGURE 7.1 **A purely competitive firm's demand and revenue curves.** The demand curve (*D*) of a purely competitive firm is a horizontal line (perfectly elastic) because the firm can sell as much output as it wants at the market price (here, $131). Because each additional unit sold increases total revenue by the amount of the price, the firm's total-revenue curve (TR) is a straight upward-sloping line and its marginal-revenue curve (MR) coincides with the firm's demand curve. The average-revenue curve (AR) also coincides with the demand curve.

Firm's Demand Schedule		Firm's Revenue Data	
(1) Product Price (P) (Average Revenue)	(2) Quantity Demanded (Q)	(3) Total Revenue (TR), (1) × (2)	(4) Marginal Revenue (MR)
$131	0	$ 0	
131	1	131	$131
131	2	262	131
131	3	393	131
131	4	524	131
131	5	655	131
131	6	786	131
131	7	917	131
131	8	1048	131
131	9	1179	131
131	10	1310	131

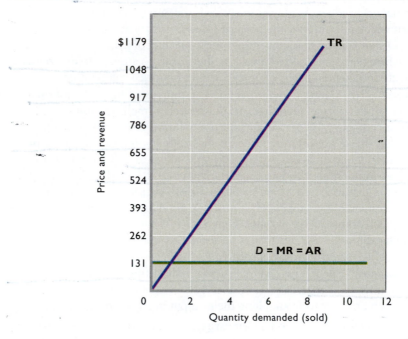

Perfectly Elastic Demand

The demand schedule faced by the *individual firm* in a purely competitive industry is perfectly elastic at the market price, as demonstrated in Figure 7.1. As shown in column 1 of the table in Figure 7.1, the market price is $131. The firm represented cannot obtain a higher price by restricting its output, nor does it need to lower its price to increase its sales volume. Columns 1 and 2 show that the firm can produce and sell as many or as few units as it likes at the market price of $131.

We are *not* saying that *market* demand is perfectly elastic in a competitive market. Rather, market demand graphs as a downsloping curve. An entire industry (all firms producing a particular product) can affect price by changing industry output. For example, all firms, acting independently but simultaneously, can increase price by reducing output. But the individual competitive firm cannot do that because its output represents such a small fraction of its industry's total output. For the individual competitive firm, the market price is therefore a fixed value at which it can sell as many or as few units as it cares to. Graphically, this implies that the individual competitive firm's demand curve will plot as a straight, horizontal line such as *D* in Figure 7.1.

Average, Total, and Marginal Revenue

The firm's demand schedule is also its average-revenue schedule. Price per unit to the purchaser is also revenue per unit, or average revenue, to the seller. To say that all buyers must pay $131 per unit is to say that the revenue per unit, or **average revenue**, received by the seller is $131. Price and average revenue are the same thing.

The **total revenue** for each sales level is found by multiplying price by the corresponding quantity the firm can sell. (Column 1 multiplied by column 2 in the table in Figure 7.1 yields column 3.) In this case, total revenue increases by a constant amount, $131, for each additional unit of sales. Each unit sold adds exactly its constant price to total revenue.

When a firm is pondering a change in its output, it will consider how its total revenue will change as a result. **Marginal revenue** is the change in total revenue (or the extra revenue) that results from selling 1 more unit of output. In column 3 of the table in Figure 7.1, total revenue is zero when zero units are sold. The first unit of output sold increases total revenue from zero to $131, so marginal revenue for that unit is $131. The second unit sold increases total revenue from $131 to $262, and marginal revenue is again $131. Note in column 4 that marginal revenue is a constant $131, as is price. *In pure competition, marginal revenue and price are equal.*

Figure 7.1 shows the purely competitive firm's total-revenue, demand, marginal-revenue, and average-revenue curves. Total revenue (TR) is a straight line that slopes upward to the right. Its slope is constant because each extra unit of sales increases TR by $131. The demand curve (*D*) is horizontal, indicating perfect price elasticity. The marginal-revenue curve (MR) coincides with the demand curve because the product price (and hence MR) is constant. The average revenue equals price and therefore also coincides with the demand curve.

Profit Maximization in the Short Run

Because the purely competitive firm is a price taker, it cannot attempt to maximize its profit by raising or lowering the price it charges. With its price set by supply and demand in the overall market, the only variable that the firm can control is its output. As a result, the purely competitive firm attempts to maximize its economic profit (or minimize its economic loss) by adjusting its *output*. And, in the short run, the firm has a fixed plant. Thus, it can adjust its output only through changes in the amount of variable resources (materials, labor) it uses. It adjusts its variable resources to achieve the output level that maximizes its profit.

More specifically, the firm compares the amounts that each *additional* unit of output would add to total revenue and to total cost. In other words, the firm compares the *marginal revenue* (MR) and the *marginal cost* (MC) of each successive unit of output. Assuming that producing is preferable to shutting down, the firm should produce any unit of output whose marginal revenue exceeds its marginal cost because the firm would gain more in revenue from selling that unit than it would add to its costs by producing it. Conversely, if the marginal cost of a unit of output exceeds its marginal revenue, the firm should not produce that unit. Producing it would add more to costs than to revenue, and profit would decline or loss would increase.

In the initial stages of production, where output is relatively low, marginal revenue will usually (but not always) exceed marginal cost. So it is profitable to produce through this range of output. But at later stages of production, where output is relatively high, rising marginal costs will exceed marginal revenue. Obviously, a profit-maximizing firm

average revenue
Total revenue from the sale of a product divided by the quantity of the product sold.

total revenue
The total number of dollars received by a firm from the sale of a product.

marginal revenue
The change in total revenue that results from selling 1 more unit of a firm's product.

will want to avoid output levels in that range. Separating these two production ranges is a unique point at which marginal revenue equals marginal cost. This point is the key to the output-determining rule: *In the short run, the firm will maximize profit or minimize loss by producing the output at which marginal revenue equals marginal cost (as long as producing is preferable to shutting down).* This profit-maximizing guide is known as the **MR = MC rule.** (For most sets of MR and MC data, MR and MC will be precisely equal at a fractional level of output. In such instances the firm should produce the last complete unit of output for which MR exceeds MC.)

Keep in mind these three features of the MR = MC rule:

- As noted, the rule applies only if producing is preferable to shutting down. We will show shortly that if marginal revenue does not equal or exceed average variable cost, the firm will shut down rather than produce the amount of output at which MR = MC.

- The rule is an accurate guide to profit maximization for all firms whether they are purely competitive, monopolistic, monopolistically competitive, or oligopolistic.

- We can restate the rule as $P = MC$ when applied to a purely competitive firm. Because the demand schedule faced by a competitive seller is perfectly elastic at the going market price, product price and marginal revenue are equal. So under pure competition (and only under pure competition), we may substitute P for MR in the rule: *When producing is preferable to shutting down, the competitive firm that wants to maximize its profit or minimize its loss should produce at that point where price equals marginal cost ($P = MC$).*

Now let's apply the MR = MC rule or, because we are considering pure competition, the $P = MC$ rule.

Profit Maximization

The first five columns in the table in Figure 7.2 reproduce the AFC, AVC, ATC, and MC data derived for our product in Chapter 6. Here, we will compare the marginal-cost data of column 5 with price (equals marginal revenue) for each unit of output. Suppose first that the market price, and therefore marginal revenue, is $131, as shown in column 6.

What is the profit-maximizing output? Every unit of output up to and including the ninth unit represents greater marginal revenue than marginal cost of output. Each of the first 9 units therefore adds to the firm's profit and should be produced. The firm, however, should not produce the tenth unit. It would add more to cost ($150) than to revenue ($131).

We can calculate the economic profit realized by producing 9 units from the average-total-cost data. Price ($131) multiplied by output (9) yields total revenue of $1179. Multiplying average total cost ($97.78) by output (9) gives us total cost of $880.[1] The difference of $299 (= $1179 − $880) is the economic profit. Clearly, this firm will prefer to operate rather than shut down.

An alternative, and perhaps easier, way to calculate the economic profit is to determine the profit per unit by subtracting the average total cost ($97.78) from the product price ($131). Then multiply the difference (a per-unit profit of $33.22) by output (9). Take some time now to verify the numbers in column 7. You will find that any output other than that which adheres to the MR = MC rule will yield either profits below $299 or losses.

---

[1]Most of the unit-cost data are rounded figures from the total-cost figures presented in the previous chapter. Therefore, economic profits calculated from the unit-cost figures will typically vary by a few cents from the profits determined by subtracting actual total cost from total revenue. Here we simply ignore the few-cents differentials.

MR = MC rule
A method of determining the total output at which economic profit is at a maximum (or losses at a minimum).

WORKED PROBLEMS

W 7.1

Profit maximization: MR = MC

[Handwritten margin notes: Exceptions to Rule; Produce at level P = MC; Purely competitive market; Most money we can; P = MC; P > ATC good; P < ATC bad]

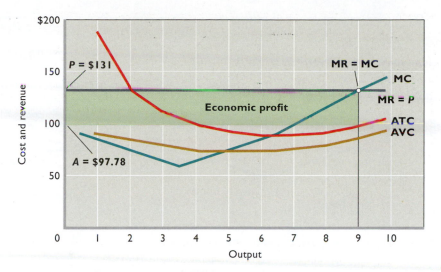

FIGURE 7.2 Short-run profit maximizing for a purely competitive firm. The MR = MC output enables the purely competitive firm to maximize profits or to minimize losses. In this case MR (= *P* in pure competition) and MC are equal at 9 units of output, *Q*. There *P* exceeds the average total cost *A* = $97.78, so the firm realizes an economic profit of *P* − *A* per unit. The total economic profit is represented by the green rectangle and is 9 × (*P* − *A*).

(1) Total Product (Output)	(2) Average Fixed Cost (AFC)	(3) Average Variable Cost (AVC)	(4) Average Total Cost (ATC)	(5) Marginal Cost (MC)	(6) $131 Price = Marginal Revenue (MR)	(7) Total Economic Profit (+) or Loss (−)
0						$−100
1	$100.00	$90.00	$190.00	$ 90	$131	−59
2	50.00	85.00	135.00	80	131	−8
3	33.33	80.00	113.33	70	131	+53
4	25.00	75.00	100.00	60	131	+124
5	20.00	74.00	94.00	70	131	+185
6	16.67	75.00	91.67	80	131	+236
7	14.29	77.14	91.43	90	131	+277
8	12.50	81.25	93.75	110	131	+298
9	11.11	86.67	97.78	130	131	+299
10	10.00	93.00	103.00	150	131	+280

Figure 7.2 also shows price (= MR) and marginal cost graphically. Price equals marginal cost at the profit-maximizing output of 9 units. There the per-unit economic profit is *P* − *A*, where *P* is the market price and *A* is the average total cost of 9 units of output. The total economic profit is 9 × (*P* − *A*), shown by the green rectangular area.

Loss Minimization and Shutdown

Now let's assume that the market price is $81 rather than $131. Should the firm still produce? If so, how much? And what will be the resulting profit or loss? The answers, respectively, are "Yes," "Six units," and "A loss of $64."

The first five columns of the table in Figure 7.3 are the same as the first five columns of the table in Figure 7.2. But column 6 of the table in Figure 7.3 shows the new price (equal to MR) of $81. Looking at columns 5 and 6, notice that the first unit of output adds $90 to total cost but only $81 to total revenue. One might conclude: "Don't produce—close down!" But that would be hasty. Remember that in the very early stages of production, marginal product is low, making marginal cost unusually high. The price–marginal cost relationship improves with increased production. For units 2 through 6, price exceeds marginal cost. Each of these 5 units adds more to revenue than to cost, and as shown in column 7, they decrease the total loss. Together

FIGURE 7.3 Short-run loss minimization for a purely competitive firm. If price P exceeds the minimum AVC (here, $74 at $Q = 5$) but is less than ATC, the MR = MC output (here, 6 units) will permit the firm to minimize its losses. In this instance the loss is $A - P$ per unit, where A is the average total cost at 6 units of output. The total loss is shown by the red area and is equal to $6 \times (A - P)$.

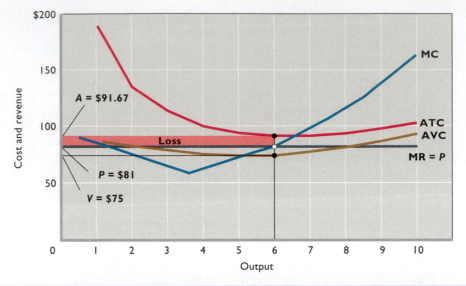

(1)	(2)	(3)	(4)	(5)	(6)	(7)
Total Product (Output)	Average Fixed Cost (AFC)	Average Variable Cost (AVC)	Average Total Cost (ATC)	Marginal Cost (MC)	$81 Price = Marginal Revenue (MR)	Profit (+) or Loss (−), $81 Price
0						$−100
1	$100.00	$90.00	$190.00	$ 90	$81	−109
2	50.00	85.00	135.00	80	81	−108
3	33.33	80.00	113.33	70	81	− 97
4	25.00	75.00	100.00	60	81	− 76
5	20.00	74.00	94.00	70	81	− 65
6	16.67	75.00	91.67	80	81	−64
7	14.29	77.14	91.43	90	81	− 73
8	12.50	81.25	93.75	110	81	−102
9	11.11	86.67	97.78	130	81	−151
10	10.00	93.00	103.00	150	81	−220

they more than compensate for the "loss" taken on the first unit. Beyond 6 units, however, MC exceeds MR (= P). The firm should therefore produce 6 units. In general, the profit-seeking producer should always compare marginal revenue (or price under pure competition) with the rising portion of the marginal-cost schedule or curve.

Loss Minimization Will production be profitable? No, because at 6 units of output the average total cost of $91.67 exceeds the price of $81 by $10.67 per unit. If we multiply that by the 6 units of output, we find the firm's total loss is $64. Alternatively, comparing the total revenue of $486 (= $6 \times$ $81) with the total cost of $550 (= $6 \times$ $91.67), we see again that the firm's loss is $64.

Then why produce? Because this loss is less than the firm's $100 of fixed costs, which is the $100 loss the firm would incur in the short run by closing down. The firm receives enough revenue per unit ($81) to cover its average variable costs of $75 and also provide $6 per unit, or a total of $36, to apply against fixed costs. Therefore, the firm's loss is only $64 (= $100 − $36), not $100.

This loss-minimizing case is illustrated in the graph in Figure 7.3. Wherever price P exceeds AVC but is less than ATC, the firm can pay part, but not all, of its fixed costs by producing. The firm minimizes its loss by producing the output at which MC = MR (here, 6 units). At that output, each unit contributes $P - V$ to covering fixed cost, where V is the AVC at 6 units of output. The per-unit loss is $A - P = \$10.67$, and the total loss is $6 \times (A - P)$, or $64, as shown by the red area.

Shutdown Suppose now that the market yields a price of only $71. Should the firm produce? No, because at every output level the firm's average variable cost is greater than the price (compare columns 3 and 6 of the table in Figure 7.4). The smallest loss the firm can incur by producing is greater than the $100 fixed cost it will lose by shutting down (as shown by column 7). The best action is to shut down.

You can see this shutdown situation in the graph in Figure 7.4, where the MR = P line lies below AVC at all points. The $71 price comes closest to covering average

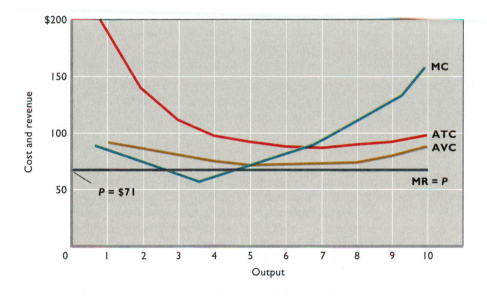

FIGURE 7.4 The short-run shutdown case for a purely competitive firm. If price P (here, $71) falls below the minimum AVC (here, $74 at Q = 5), the competitive firm will minimize its losses in the short run by shutting down. There is no level of output at which the firm can produce and realize a loss smaller than its total fixed cost.

(1) Total Product (Output)	(2) Average Fixed Cost (AFC)	(3) Average Variable Cost (AVC)	(4) Average Total Cost (ATC)	(5) Marginal Cost (MC)	(6) $71 Price = Marginal Revenue (MR)	(7) Profit (+) or Loss (−), $81 Price
0						$−100
1	$100.00	$90.00	$190.00	$ 90	$71	−119
2	50.00	85.00	135.00	80	71	−128
3	33.33	80.00	113.33	70	71	−127
4	25.00	75.00	100.00	60	71	−116
5	20.00	74.00	94.00	70	71	−115
6	16.67	75.00	91.67	80	71	−124
7	14.29	77.14	91.43	90	71	−143
8	12.50	81.25	93.75	110	71	−182
9	11.11	86.67	97.78	130	71	−241
10	10.00	93.00	103.00	150	71	−320

variable costs at the MR (= P) = MC output of 5 units. But even here, the table reveals that price or revenue per unit would fall short of average variable cost by $3 (= $74 − $71). By producing at the MR (= P) = MC output, the firm would lose its $100 worth of fixed cost plus $15 (= $3 of variable cost on each of the 5 units), for a total loss of $115. This compares unfavorably with the $100 fixed-cost loss the firm would incur by shutting down and producing no output. So it will make sense for the firm to shut down rather than produce at a $71 price—or at any price less than the minimum average variable cost of $74.

The shutdown case reminds us of the qualifier to our MR (= P) = MC rule. A competitive firm will maximize profit or minimize loss in the short run by producing that output at which MR (= P) = MC, *provided that market price exceeds minimum average variable cost.*

APPLYING THE ANALYSIS

The Still There Motel

Have you ever driven by a poorly maintained business facility and wondered why the owner does not either fix up the property or go out of business? The somewhat surprising reason is that it may be unprofitable to improve the facility yet profitable to continue for a time to operate the business as it deteriorates. Seeing why will aid your understanding of the "stay open or shut down" decision facing firms experiencing declining demand.

Consider the Still There Motel on Old Highway North, Anytown, USA. The owner built the motel on the basis of traffic patterns and competition existing several decades ago. But as interstate highways were built, the motel found itself located on a relatively untraveled stretch of road. Also, it faced severe competition from "chain" motels located much closer to the interstate highway.

As demand and revenue fell, Still There moved from profitability to loss ($P <$ ATC). But at first its room rates and annual revenue were sufficient to cover its total variable costs and contribute some to the payment of fixed costs such as insurance and property taxes ($P >$ AVC). By staying open, Still There lost less than it would have if it shut down. But since its total revenue did not cover its total costs (or $P <$ ATC), the owner realized that something must be done in the long run. The owner decided to lower average total costs by reducing annual maintenance. In effect, the owner opted to allow the motel to deteriorate as a way of regaining temporary profitability.

This renewed profitability of Still There cannot last because in time no further reduction in maintenance costs will be possible. The further deterioration of the motel structure will produce even lower room rates, and therefore even less total revenue. The owner of Still There knows that sooner or later total revenue will again fall below total cost (or P will again fall below ATC), even with an annual maintenance expense of zero. When that occurs, the owner will close down the business, tear down the structure, and sell the vacant property. But, in the meantime, the motel is still there—open, deteriorating, and profitable.

QUESTION: Why might even a well-maintained, profitable motel shut down in the long run if the land on which it is located becomes extremely valuable due to surrounding economic development?

Marginal Cost and Short-Run Supply

In the preceding section, we simply selected three different prices and asked what quantity the profit-seeking competitive firm, faced with certain costs, would choose to offer in the market at each price. This set of product prices and corresponding quantities supplied constitutes part of the supply schedule for the competitive firm.

Table 7.1 summarizes the supply schedule data for those three prices ($131, $81, and $71) and four others. This table confirms the direct relationship between product price and quantity supplied that we identified in Chapter 3. Note first that the firm will not produce at price $61 or $71 because both are less than the $74 minimum AVC. Then note that quantity supplied increases as price increases. Observe finally that economic profit is higher at higher prices.

Generalized Depiction

Figure 7.5 generalizes the MR = MC rule and the relationship between short-run production costs and the firm's supply behavior. The ATC, AVC, and MC curves are shown, along with several marginal-revenue lines drawn at possible market prices. Let's observe quantity supplied at each of these prices:

- Price P_1 is below the firm's minimum average variable cost, so at this price the firm won't operate at all. Quantity supplied will be zero, as it will be at all other prices below P_2.
- Price P_2 is just equal to the minimum average variable cost. The firm will supply Q_2 units of output (where $MR_2 = MC$) and just cover its total variable cost. Its loss will equal its total fixed cost. (Actually, the firm would be indifferent as to shutting down or supplying Q_2 units of output, but we assume it produces.)
- At price P_3 the firm will supply Q_3 units of output to minimize its short-run losses. At any other price between P_2 and P_4 the firm will minimize its losses by producing and supplying the MR = MC quantity.
- The firm will just break even at price P_4. There it will supply Q_4 units of output (where $MR_4 = MC$), earning a normal profit but not an economic profit. (Recall that a normal profit is a cost and included in the cost curves.) Total revenue will just cover total cost, including a normal profit, because the revenue per unit ($MR_4 = P_4$) and the total cost per unit (ATC) are the same.
- At price P_5 the firm will realize an economic profit by producing and supplying Q_5 units of output. In fact, at any price above P_4, the firm will obtain economic profit by producing to the point where MR (= P) = MC.

Note that each of the MR (= P) = MC intersection points labeled *b*, *c*, *d*, and *e* in Figure 7.5 indicates a possible product price (on the vertical axis) and the corresponding quantity that the firm would supply at that price (on the horizontal axis). Thus,

Price	Quantity Supplied	Maximum Profit (+) or Minimum Loss (−)
$151	10	$+480
131	9	+299
111	8	+138
91	7	−3
81	6	−64
71	0	−100
61	0	−100

TABLE 7.1
The Supply Schedule of a Competitive Firm Confronted with the Cost Data in the Table in Figure 7.2

FIGURE 7.5 The *P* = MC rule and the competitive firm's short-run supply curve. Application of the *P* = MC rule, as modified by the shutdown case, reveals that the (solid) segment of the firm's MC curve that lies above AVC is the firm's short-run supply curve.

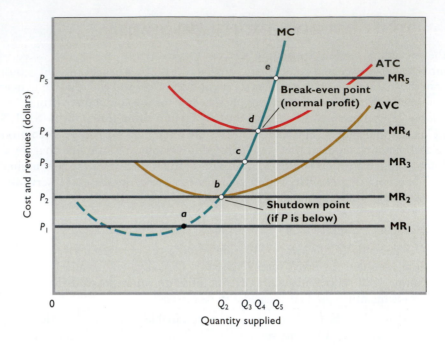

points such as these are on the upsloping supply curve of the competitive firm. Note too that quantity supplied would be zero at any price below the minimum average variable cost (AVC). *We can conclude that the portion of the firm's marginal-cost curve lying above its average-variable-cost curve is its short-run supply curve.* In Figure 7.5, the solid segment of the marginal-cost curve MC *is* this firm's **short-run supply curve.** It tells us the amount of output the firm will supply at each price in a series of prices. It slopes upward because of the law of diminishing returns.

Table 7.2 summarizes the MR = MC approach to determining the competitive firm's profit-maximizing output level. It also shows the conditions under which a firm should decide to produce, and the circumstances that will generate economic profits.

short-run supply curve

A curve that shows the quantity of a product a firm in a purely competitive industry will offer to sell at various prices in the short run.

Firm and Industry: Equilibrium Price

In the preceding section we established the competitive firm's short-run supply curve by applying the MR (= *P*) = MC rule. But which of the various possible prices will actually be the market equilibrium price?

From Chapter 3 we know that the market equilibrium price will be the price at which the total quantity supplied of the product equals the total quantity demanded. So to determine the equilibrium price, we first need to obtain a total supply schedule and a total demand schedule. We find the total supply schedule by assuming a particular

TABLE 7.2 Output Determination in Pure Competition in the Short Run

Question	Answer
Should this firm produce?	Yes, if price is equal to, or greater than, minimum average variable cost. This means that the firm is profitable or that its losses are less than its fixed cost.
What quantity should this firm produce?	Produce where MR (= *P*) = MC; there, profit is maximized (TR exceeds TC by a maximum amount) or loss is minimized.
Will production result in economic profit?	Yes, if price exceeds average total cost (so that TR exceeds TC). No, if average total cost exceeds price (so that TC exceeds TR).

(1) Quantity Supplied, Single Firm	(2) Total Quantity Supplied, 1000 Firms	(3) Product Price	(4) Total Quantity Demanded
10	10,000	$151	4,000
9	9,000	131	6,000
8	**8,000**	**111**	**8,000**
7	7,000	91	9,000
6	6,000	81	11,000
0	0	71	13,000
0	0	61	16,000

TABLE 7.3
Firm and Market Supply and Market Demand

number of firms in the industry and supposing that each firm has the same individual supply schedule as the firm represented in Figure 7.5. Then we sum the quantities supplied at each price level to obtain the total (or market) supply schedule. Columns 1 and 3 in Table 7.3 repeat the supply schedule for the individual competitive firm, as derived in Table 7.1. Suppose 1000 firms compete in this industry, all having the same total and unit costs as the single firm we discussed. This lets us calculate the market supply schedule (columns 2 and 3) by multiplying the quantity-supplied figures of the single firm (column 1) by 1000.

Market Price and Profits To determine the equilibrium price and output, we must compare these total-supply data with total-demand data. Let's assume that total demand is as shown in columns 3 and 4 in Table 7.3. By comparing the total quantity supplied and the total quantity demanded at the seven possible prices, we determine that the equilibrium price is $111 and the equilibrium quantity is 8000 units for the industry—8 units for each of the 1000 identical firms.

Will these conditions of market supply and demand make this a profitable or unprofitable industry? Multiplying product price ($111) by output (8 units), we find that the total revenue of each firm is $888. The total cost is $750, found by looking at column 4 of the table in Figure 6.3. The $138 difference is the economic profit of each firm. For the industry, total economic profit is $138,000. This, then, is a profitable industry.

Another way of calculating economic profit is to determine per-unit profit by subtracting average total cost ($93.75) from product price ($111) and multiplying the difference (per-unit profit of $17.25) by the firm's equilibrium level of output (8). Again we obtain an economic profit of $138 per firm and $138,000 for the industry.

Figure 7.6 shows this analysis graphically. The individual supply curves of each of the 1000 identical firms—one of which is shown as s = MC in Figure 7.6a—are summed horizontally to get the total-supply curve S = ΣMC's of Figure 7.6b. With total-demand curve D, it yields the equilibrium price $111 and equilibrium quantity (for the industry) 8000 units. This equilibrium price is given and unalterable to the individual firm; that is, each firm's demand curve is perfectly elastic at the equilibrium price, as indicated by d in Figure 7.6a. Because the individual firm is a price taker, the marginal-revenue curve coincides with the firm's demand curve d. This $111 price exceeds the average total cost at the firm's equilibrium MR = MC output of 8 units, so the firm earns an economic profit represented by the green area in Figure 7.6a.

Assuming no changes in costs or market demand, these diagrams reveal a genuine equilibrium in the short run. There are no shortages or surpluses in the market to cause price or total quantity to change. Nor can any firm in the industry increase its profit by altering its output. Note, however, that weaker market demand or stronger

WORKED PROBLEMS

W 7.2

Short-run competitive equilibrium

FIGURE 7.6 **Short-run competitive equilibrium for (a) a firm and (b) the industry.** The horizontal sum of the 1000 firms' individual supply curves (*s*) determines the industry (market) supply curve (*S*). Given industry (market) demand (*D*), the short-run equilibrium price and output for the industry are $111 and 8000 units. Taking the equilibrium price as given, the individual firm establishes its profit-maximizing output at 8 units and, in this case, realizes the economic profit represented by the green area.

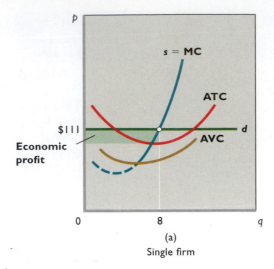

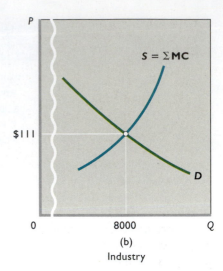

(a)
Single firm

(b)
Industry

market supply (and therefore lower prices) could shift the line *d* downward and change the situation to losses (*P* < ATC) or even to shutdown (*P* < AVC).

Firm versus Industry   Figure 7.6 underscores a point made earlier: Product price is a given fact to the individual competitive firm, but the supply plans of all competitive producers as a group are a basic determinant of product price. There is no inconsistency here. One firm, supplying a negligible fraction of total supply, cannot affect price. But the sum of the supply curves of all the firms in the industry constitutes the market supply curve, and that curve (along with demand) does have an important bearing on equilibrium price.

Profit Maximization in the Long Run

The entry and exit of firms in our market models can only take place in the long run. In the short run, the industry is composed of a specific number of firms, each with a plant size that is fixed and unalterable in the short run. Firms may shut down in the sense that they can produce zero units of output in the short run, but they do not have sufficient time to liquidate their assets and go out of business.

In the long run, by contrast, the firms already in an industry have sufficient time to either expand or contract their capacities. More important, the number of firms in the industry may either increase or decrease as new firms enter or existing firms leave.

The length of time constituting the long run varies substantially by industry, however, so that you should not fix in your mind any specific number of years, months, or days. Instead, focus your attention on the incentives provided by profits and losses for the entry and exit of firms into any purely competitive industry and, later in the chapter, on how those incentives lead to productive and allocative efficiency. The time horizons are far less important than how these long-run adjustments affect price, quantity, and profits, and the process by which profits and losses guide business managers toward the efficient use of society's resources.

Assumptions

We make three simplifying assumptions, none of which alters our conclusions:

- *Entry and exit only* The only long-run adjustment in our graphical analysis is caused by the entry or exit of firms. Moreover, we ignore all short-run adjustments in order to concentrate on the effects of the long-run adjustments.
- *Identical costs* All firms in the industry have identical cost curves. This assumption lets us discuss an "average," or "representative," firm, knowing that all other firms in the industry are similarly affected by any long-run adjustments that occur.
- *Constant-cost industry* The industry is a constant-cost industry. This means that the entry and exit of firms does not affect resource prices or, consequently, the locations of the average-total-cost curves of individual firms.

Goal of Our Analysis

The basic conclusion we seek to explain is this: After all long-run adjustments are completed in a purely competitive industry, product price will be exactly equal to, and production will occur at, each firm's minimum average total cost.

This conclusion follows from two basic facts: (1) Firms seek profits and shun losses and (2) under pure competition, firms are free to enter and leave an industry. If market price initially exceeds minimum average total costs, the resulting economic profits will attract new firms to the industry. But this industry expansion will increase supply until price is brought back down to equality with minimum average total cost. Conversely, if price is initially less than minimum average total cost, resulting losses will cause firms to leave the industry. As they leave, total supply will decline, bringing the price back up to equality with minimum average total cost.

Long-Run Equilibrium

Consider the average firm in a purely competitive industry that is initially in long-run equilibrium. This firm is represented in Figure 7.7a, where MR = MC and price and minimum average total cost are equal at $50. Economic profit here is zero; the industry is in equilibrium or "at rest" because there is no tendency for firms to enter or to leave. The existing firms are just covering the explicit and implicit costs that are represented by their cost curves. Recall that the firm's cost curves include the normal profits that owners could expect to receive in their best alternative business ventures. The $50 market price is

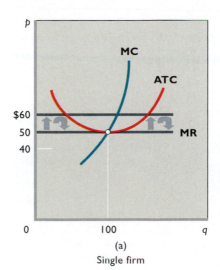

(a)
Single firm

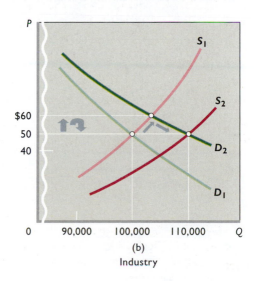

(b)
Industry

FIGURE 7.7 Temporary profits and the reestablishment of long-run equilibrium in (a) a representative firm and (b) the industry. A favorable shift in demand (D_1 to D_2) will upset the original industry equilibrium and produce economic profits. But those profits will entice new firms to enter the industry, increasing supply (S_1 to S_2) and lowering product price until economic profits are once again zero.

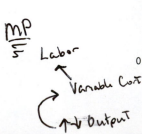

determined in Figure 7.7b by market or industry demand D_1 and supply S_1. (S_1 is a short-run supply curve; we will develop the long-run industry supply curve in our discussion.)

As shown on the quantity axes of the two graphs, equilibrium output in the industry is 100,000 while equilibrium output for the single firm is 100. If all firms in the industry are identical, there must be 1000 firms (=100,000/100).

Entry Eliminates Economic Profits

Let's upset the long-run equilibrium in Figure 7.7 and see what happens. Suppose a change in consumer tastes increases product demand from D_1 to D_2. Price will rise to $60, as determined at the intersection of D_2 and S_1, and the firm's marginal-revenue curve will shift upward to $60. This $60 price exceeds the firm's average total cost of $50 at output 100, creating an economic profit of $10 per unit. This economic profit will lure new firms into the industry. Some entrants will be newly created firms; others will shift from less-prosperous industries.

As firms enter, the market supply of the product increases and the product price falls below $60. Economic profits persist, and entry continues until short-run supply increases to S_2. Market price falls to $50, as does marginal revenue for the firm. Price and minimum average total cost are again equal at $50. The economic profits caused by the boost in demand have been eliminated, and, as a result, the previous incentive for more firms to enter the industry has disappeared because the firms that remain are earning only a normal profit (zero economic profit). Entry ceases and a new long-run equilibrium is reached.

Observe in Figure 7.7a and 7.7b that total quantity supplied is now 110,000 units and each firm is producing 100 units. Now 1100 firms rather than the original 1000 populate the industry. Economic profits have attracted 100 more firms.

Exit Eliminates Losses

Now let's consider a shift in the opposite direction. We begin in Figure 7.8b with curves S_1 and D_1 setting the same initial long-run equilibrium situation as in our previous analysis, including the $50 price.

Suppose consumer demand declines from D_1 to D_3. This forces the market price and marginal revenue down to $40, making production unprofitable at the minimum ATC of $50. In time the resulting economic losses will induce firms to leave the industry. Their owners will seek a normal profit elsewhere rather than accept the below-normal profits (losses) now confronting them. As this exodus of firms proceeds, however, industry supply decreases, pushing the price up from $40 toward $50. Losses continue and more firms leave the industry until the supply curve shifts to S_3. Once this happens, price is again $50, just equal to the minimum average total cost. Losses have been eliminated so that the

FIGURE 7.8 **Temporary losses and the reestablishment of long-run equilibrium in (a) a representative firm and (b) the industry.** An unfavorable shift in demand (D_1 to D_3) will upset the original industry equilibrium and produce losses. But those losses will cause firms to leave the industry, decreasing supply (S_1 to S_3) and increasing product price until all losses have disappeared.

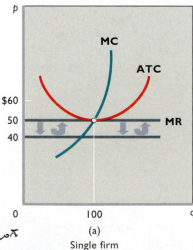

(a)
Single firm

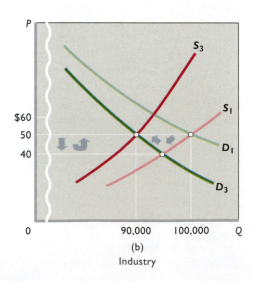

(b)
Industry

firms that remain are earning only a normal profit (zero economic profit). Since this is no better or worse than entrepreneurs could expect to earn in other business ventures, there is no longer any incentive to exit the industry. Long-run equilibrium is restored.

In Figure 7.8a and 7.8b, total quantity supplied is now 90,000 units and each firm is producing 100 units. Only 900 firms, not the original 1000, populate the industry. Losses have forced 100 firms out.

You may have noted that we have sidestepped the question of which firms will leave the industry when losses occur by assuming that all firms have identical cost curves. In the "real world," of course, managerial talents differ. Even if resource prices and technology are the same for all firms, less skillfully managed firms tend to incur higher costs and therefore are the first to leave an industry when demand declines. Similarly, firms with less-productive labor forces or higher transportation costs will be higher-cost producers and likely candidates to quit an industry when demand decreases.

APPLYING THE ANALYSIS

The Exit of Farmers from U.S. Agriculture

The U.S. agricultural industry serves as a good example of how losses resulting from declining prices received by individual producers create an exit of producers from an industry.

A rapid rate of technological advance has significantly increased the *supply* of U.S. agricultural products over time. This technological progress has many roots: the mechanization of farms, improved techniques of land management, soil conservation, irrigation, development of hybrid crops, availability of improved fertilizers and insecticides, polymer-coated seeds, and improvements in the breeding and care of livestock. In 1950 each farmworker produced enough food and fiber to support about a dozen people. By 2011 that figure had increased to more than 100 people!

Increases in *demand* for agricultural products, however, have failed to keep pace with technologically created increases in the supply of the products. The demand for farm products in the United States is *income-inelastic*. Estimates indicate that a 10 percent increase in real per capita after-tax income produces about a 2 percent increase in consumption of farm products. Once consumers' stomachs are filled, they turn to the amenities of life that manufacturing and services, not agriculture, provide. So, as the incomes of Americans rise, the demand for farm products increases far less rapidly than the demand for products in general.

The consequences of the long-run supply and demand conditions just outlined have been those predicted by the long-run pure-competition model. Financial losses in agriculture have triggered a large decline in the number of farms and a massive exit of workers to other sectors of the economy. In 1950 there were about 5.4 million farms in the United States employing 9.3 million people. Today there are just over 2 million farms employing 1.8 million people. Since 1950, farm employment has declined from 15.8 percent of the U.S. workforce to just 1.2 percent. Moreover, the exodus of farmers would have been even larger in the absence of government subsidies that have enabled many farmers to remain in agriculture. Such subsidies were traditionally in the form of government price supports (price floors) but have more recently evolved to direct subsidy payments to farmers. Such payments have averaged more than $16 billion annually over the last decade.

QUESTION: Why is the exit of farmers from U.S. agriculture bad for the farmers who must leave but good for the farmers who remain?

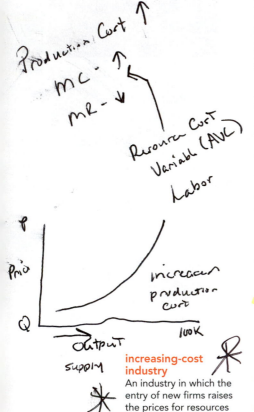

long-run supply curve
A curve that shows the prices at which a purely competitive industry will make various quantities of the product available in the long run.

constant-cost industry
An industry in which the entry of new firms has no effect on resource prices and thus no effect on production costs.

increasing-cost industry
An industry in which the entry of new firms raises the prices for resources and thus increases their production costs.

Long-Run Supply for a Constant-Cost Industry

We have established that changes in market supply through entry and exit create a long-run equilibrium in purely competitive markets. Although our analysis has dealt with the long run, we have noted that the market supply curves in Figures 7.7b and 7.8b are short-run curves. What then is the character of the **long-run supply curve** of a competitive industry? Our analysis points us toward an answer. The crucial factor here is the effect, if any, that changes in the number of firms in the industry will have on costs of the individual firms in the industry.

In our discussion of long-run competitive equilibrium, we assumed that the industry under discussion was a **constant-cost industry.** This means that industry expansion or contraction will not affect resource prices and therefore production costs. Graphically, it means that the entry or exit of firms does not shift the long-run ATC curves of individual firms. This is the case when the industry's demand for resources is small in relation to the total demand for those resources. Then the industry can expand or contract without significantly affecting resource prices and costs.

What does the long-run supply curve of a constant-cost industry look like? The answer is contained in our previous analysis. There we saw that the entry and exit of firms changes industry output but always brings the product price back to its original level, where it is just equal to the constant minimum ATC. Specifically, we discovered that the industry would supply 90,000, 100,000, or 110,000 units of output, all at a price of $50 per unit. In other words, the long-run supply curve of a constant-cost industry is perfectly elastic.

Figure 7.9a demonstrates this graphically. Suppose industry demand is originally D_1, industry output is Q_1 (100,000 units), and product price is P_1 ($50). This situation, from Figure 7.7, is one of long-run equilibrium. We saw that when demand increases to D_2, upsetting this equilibrium, the resulting economic profits attract new firms. Because this is a constant-cost industry, entry continues and industry output expands until the price is driven back down to the level of the unchanged minimum ATC. This is at price P_2 ($50) and output Q_2 (110,000).

From Figure 7.8, we saw that a decline in market demand from D_1 to D_3 causes an exit of firms and ultimately restores equilibrium at price P_3 ($50) and output Q_3 (90,000 units). The points Z_1, Z_2, and Z_3 in Figure 7.9a represent these three price-quantity combinations. A line or curve connecting all such points shows the various price-quantity combinations that firms would produce if they had enough time to make all desired adjustments to changes in demand. This line or curve is the industry's long-run supply curve. In a constant-cost industry, this curve (straight line) is horizontal, as in Figure 7.9a, thus representing perfectly elastic supply.

Long-Run Supply for an Increasing-Cost Industry

Constant-cost industries are a special case. Most industries are **increasing-cost industries,** in which firms' ATC curves shift upward as the industry expands and downward as the industry contracts. The construction industry and medical care industries are examples.

Usually, the entry of new firms will increase resource prices, particularly in industries using specialized resources whose long-run supplies do not readily increase in response to increases in resource demand. Higher resource prices result in higher long-run average total costs for all firms in the industry. These higher costs cause upward shifts in each firm's long-run ATC curve.

Thus, when an increase in product demand results in economic profits and attracts new firms to an increasing-cost industry, a two-way squeeze works to eliminate those

FIGURE 7.9 Long-run supply: constant-cost industry versus increasing-cost industry. (a) In a constant-cost industry, the entry of firms does not affect resource prices or, therefore, unit costs. So an increase in demand (D_1 to D_2) or a decrease in demand (D_1 to D_3) causes a change in industry output (Q_1 to Q_2 or Q_1 to Q_3) but no alteration in price ($50). This means that the long-run industry supply curve (S) is horizontal through points Z_3, Z_1, and Z_2. (b) In an increasing-cost industry, the entry of new firms in response to an increase in demand (D_3 to D_1 to D_2) will bid up resource prices and thereby increase unit costs. As a result, an increased industry output (Q_3 to Q_1 to Q_2) will be forthcoming only at higher prices ($45 to $50 to $55). The long-run industry supply curve (S) therefore slopes upward through points Y_3, Y_1, and Y_2.

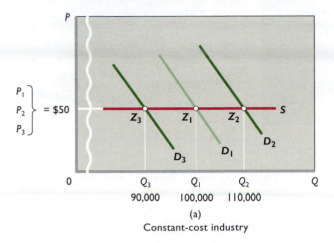

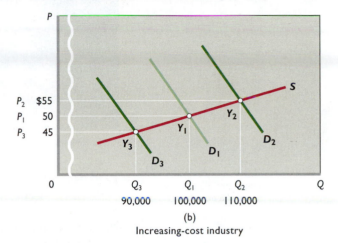

profits. As before, the entry of new firms increases market supply and lowers the market price. But now each firm's ATC curve also shifts upward. The overall result is a higher-than-original equilibrium price. ==The industry produces a larger output at a higher product price because the industry expansion has increased resource prices and the minimum average total cost.==

Since greater output will be supplied at a higher price, the long-run industry supply curve is upsloping. Instead of supplying 90,000, 100,000, or 110,000 units at the same price of $50, an increasing-cost industry might supply 90,000 units at $45, 100,000 units at $50, and 110,000 units at $55. A higher price is required to induce more production because costs per unit of output increase as production increases.

Figure 7.9b nicely illustrates the situation. Original market demand is D_1 and industry price and output are P_1 ($50) and Q_1 (100,000 units), respectively, at equilibrium point Y_1. An increase in demand to D_2 upsets this equilibrium and leads to economic profits. New firms enter the industry, increasing both market supply and production costs of individual firms. A new price is established at point Y_2, where P_2 is $55 and Q_2 is 110,000 units.

Conversely, a decline in demand from D_1 to D_3 makes production unprofitable and causes firms to leave the industry. The resulting decline in resource prices reduces the minimum average total cost of production for firms that stay. A new equilibrium price is established at some level below the original price, say, at point Y_3, where P_3 is $45 and Q_3 is 90,000 units. Connecting these three equilibrium positions, we derive the upsloping long-run supply curve S in Figure 7.9b.

Long-Run Supply for a Decreasing-Cost Industry

In **decreasing-cost industries,** ==firms experience lower costs as their industry expands.== The personal computer industry is an example. As demand for personal computers increased, new manufacturers of computers entered the industry and greatly increased the resource demand for the components used to build them (for example, memory chips, hard drives, monitors, and operating software). The expanded production of the components enabled the producers of those items to achieve substantial economies of

decreasing-cost industry
An industry in which the entry of new firms lowers the prices of resources and thus decreases production costs.

© Craig Aurness/CORBIS

© Compassionate Eye Foundation/Getty Images

PHOTO OP Increasing-Cost versus Decreasing-Cost Industries

Mining is an example of an increasing-cost industry, whereas electronics is an example of a decreasing-cost industry.

scale. The decreased production costs of the components reduced their prices, which greatly lowered the computer manufacturers' average costs of production. The supply of personal computers increased by more than demand, and the price of personal computers declined. Although not shown in Figure 7.9, the long-run supply curve of a decreasing-cost industry is *downsloping*.

Unfortunately, the industries that show decreasing costs also show increasing costs if output contracts. A decline in demand (say from foreign competition) makes production unprofitable and causes firms to leave the industry. Firms that remain face a greater minimum average total cost of production, implying a higher long-run equilibrium price in the market.

Pure Competition and Efficiency

Our final goal in this chapter is to examine the efficiency aspects of pure competition. Assuming a constant- or increasing-cost industry, the final long-run equilibrium positions of all firms have the same basic efficiency characteristics. As shown in Figure 7.10, price (and marginal revenue) will settle where it is equal to minimum average total cost: P (and MR) = minimum ATC. Moreover, since the marginal-cost curve intersects the average-total-cost curve at its minimum point, marginal cost and average total cost are equal: MC = minimum ATC. So in long-run equilibrium, a multiple equality occurs: P (and MR) = MC = minimum ATC. Thus, in long-run equilibrium, each firm produces at the output level that is associated with this triple equality.[2]

The triple equality tells us two very important things about long-run equilibrium. First, it tells us that although a competitive firm may realize economic profit or loss in the short run, it will earn only a normal profit by producing in accordance with the MR (= P) = MC rule in the long run. Second, the triple equality tells us that in long-run

---

[2]This triple equality does not hold for decreasing-cost industries because MC always remains below ATC if average costs are decreasing. We will discuss this situation of "natural monopoly" in Chapter 8.

FIGURE 7.10 Long-run equilibrium: a competitive firm and market. (a) The equality of price (*P*), marginal cost (MC), and minimum average total cost (ATC) at output Q_f indicates that the firm is achieving productive efficiency and allocative efficiency. It is using the most efficient technology, charging the lowest price, and producing the greatest output consistent with its costs. It is receiving only a normal profit, which is incorporated into the ATC curve. The equality of price and marginal cost indicates that society allocated its scarce resources in accordance with consumer preferences. (b) In the purely competitive market, allocative efficiency occurs at the market equilibrium output Q_e. The sum of consumer surplus (green area) and producer surplus (blue area) is maximized.

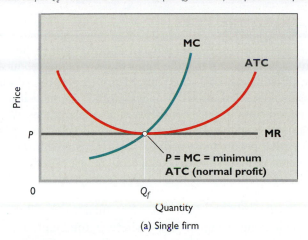

(a) Single firm

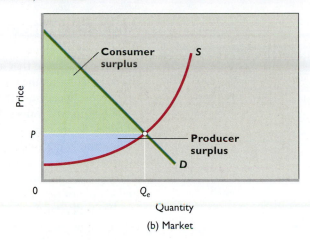

(b) Market

equilibrium, the profit-maximizing decision rule that leads each firm to produce the quantity at which *P* = MR also implies that each firm will produce at the output level that is associated with the minimum point on each identical firm's ATC curve.

This is very important because it suggests that pure competition leads to the most efficient possible use of society's resources. Indeed, subject only to Chapter 5's qualifications relating to public goods and externalities, an idealized purely competitive market economy composed of constant- or increasing-cost industries will generate both productive efficiency and allocative efficiency.

Productive efficiency requires that goods be produced in the least costly way. Allocative efficiency requires that resources be apportioned among firms and industries so as to yield the mix of products and services that is most wanted by society (least-cost production assumed). Allocative efficiency has been realized when it is impossible to alter the combination of goods produced and achieve a net gain for society. Let's look at how productive and allocative efficiency would be achieved under purely competitive conditions.

Productive Efficiency: *P* = Minimum ATC

In the long run, pure competition forces firms to produce at the minimum average total cost of production and to charge a price that is just consistent with that cost. This is true because firms that do not use the best-available (least-cost) production methods and combinations of inputs will not survive.

To see why that is true, let's suppose that Figure 7.10 has to do with pure competition in the cucumber industry. In the final equilibrium position shown in Figure 7.10, suppose each firm in the cucumber industry is producing 100 units (say, pickup truckloads) of output by using $5000 (equal to average total cost of $50 × 100 units) worth of resources. If any firm produced that same amount of output at any higher total cost, say $7000, it would be wasting resources because all of the other firms in the industry are able to produce that same amount of output using only $5000 worth of resources. Society would be faced with a net loss of $2000 worth of alternative products. But this cannot happen in pure competition; this firm would incur a loss of $2000, requiring it either to reduce its costs or go out of business.

Note, too, that consumers benefit from productive efficiency by paying the lowest product price possible under the prevailing technology and cost conditions. And the firm receives only a normal profit, which is part of its economic costs and thus incorporated in its ATC curve.

Allocative Efficiency: $P = MC$

Productive efficiency alone does not ensure the efficient allocation of resources. It does not guarantee that anyone will want to buy the items that are being produced in the least-cost manner. For all we know, consumers might prefer that the resources used to produce those items be redirected toward producing other products instead.

Fortunately, long-run equilibrium in pure competition also guarantees *allocative efficiency,* so we can be certain that society's scarce resources are directed toward producing the goods and services that people most want to consume. Stated formally, allocative efficiency occurs when it is impossible to produce any net gains for society by altering the combination of goods and services that are produced from society's limited supply of resources.

To understand how pure competition leads to allocative efficiency, recall the concept of opportunity cost while looking at Figure 7.10b, where Q_e total units are being produced in equilibrium by the firms in a purely competitive industry. For every unit up to Q_e, market demand curve D lies above market supply curve S. Recall from Chapter 5 what this means in terms of marginal benefits and marginal costs.

- For each unit of output on the horizontal axis, the point directly above it on demand curve D shows how many dollars' worth of other goods and services consumers are willing to give up to obtain that unit of output. Consequently, the demand curve shows the dollar value of the marginal benefit that consumers place on each unit.

- For each unit of output on the horizontal axis, the point directly above it on supply curve S shows how many dollars' worth of other products have to be sacrificed in order to direct the underlying resources toward producing each unit of this product. Consequently, the supply curve shows the dollar value of the marginal opportunity cost of each unit.

Keeping these definitions in mind, the fact that the demand curve lies above the supply curve for every unit up to Q_e means that marginal benefit exceeds marginal cost for every one of these units. It also implies that redirecting the necessary resources toward producing anything else would make people less happy.

The fact that pure competition yields allocative efficiency can also be understood by looking at the situation facing each individual firm in long-run equilibrium. To see this, take the market equilibrium price P that is determined in Figure 7.10b and see how it affects the behavior of the individual firm shown in Figure 7.10a. This profit-maximizing firm takes P as fixed and produces Q_f units, the output level at which $P = MC$.

By comparing the horizontal line at P with the upsloping MC curve, it is clear that for every unit up to Q_f, the price at which each unit can be sold exceeds the marginal cost of producing it. That is equivalent to saying that these units are worth more to consumers than they cost to make. Why? Because consumers are willing to forgo P dollars' worth of other goods and services when they pay P dollars for these units, but the firm uses less than P dollars' worth of resources to produce them. Thus, if these units are produced and consumed, there are net benefits and society comes out ahead. Allocative efficiency obtains because by spending their P dollars per unit on these units rather than anything else, consumers are indicating that they would rather have the necessary resources directed toward producing these units rather than anything else.

Maximum Consumer and Producer Surplus

We confirm the existence of allocative efficiency in Figure 7.10b, where we see that pure competition maximizes the sum of the "benefit surpluses" to consumers and producers. Recall from Chapter 5 that *consumer surplus* is the difference between the maximum prices that consumers are willing to pay for a product (as shown by the demand curve) and the market price of that product. In Figure 7.10b, consumer surplus is the green triangle, which is the sum of the vertical distances between the demand curve and equilibrium price. In contrast, *producer surplus* is the difference between the minimum prices that producers are willing to accept for a product (as shown by the supply curve) and the market price of the product. Producer surplus is the sum of the vertical distances between the equilibrium price and the supply curve. Here producer surplus is the blue area.

At the equilibrium quantity Q_e, the combined amount of consumer surplus and producer surplus is maximized. Allocative efficiency occurs because, at Q_e, marginal benefit, reflected by points on the demand curve, equals marginal cost, reflected by the points on the supply curve. At any output less than Q_e, the sum of consumer and producer surplus—the combined size of the green and blue area—would be less than that shown. At any output greater than Q_e, an efficiency loss (deadweight loss) would subtract from the combined consumer and producer surplus shown by the green and blue area.

After long-run adjustments, pure competition produces both productive and allocative efficiency. It yields a level of output at which $P = MC = $ lowest ATC, marginal benefit = marginal cost, maximum willingness to pay for the last unit = minimum acceptable price for that unit, and combined consumer and producer surplus are maximized.

Dynamic Adjustments A further attribute of purely competitive markets is their ability to restore efficiency when disrupted by changes in the economy. A change in consumer tastes, resource supplies, or technology will automatically set in motion the appropriate realignments of resources. For example, suppose that cucumbers and pickles become dramatically more popular. First, the price of cucumbers will increase, and so, at current output, the price of cucumbers will exceed their marginal cost. At this point efficiency will be lost, but the higher price will create economic profits in the cucumber industry and stimulate its expansion. The profitability of cucumbers will permit the industry to bid resources away from now less-pressing uses, say, watermelons. Expansion of the industry will end only when the price of cucumbers and their marginal cost are equal—that is, when allocative efficiency has been restored.

Similarly, a change in the supply of a particular resource—for example, the field laborers who pick cucumbers—or in a production technique will upset an existing price–marginal-cost equality by either raising or lowering marginal cost. The resulting inequality will cause business managers, in either pursuing profit or avoiding loss, to reallocate resources until price once again equals marginal cost. In so doing, they will correct any inefficiency in the allocation of resources that the original change may have temporarily imposed on the economy.

"Invisible Hand" Revisited The highly efficient allocation of resources that a purely competitive economy promotes comes about because businesses and resource suppliers seek to further their self-interest. For private goods with no externalities (Chapter 5), the "invisible hand" (Chapter 2) is at work. The competitive system not only maximizes profits for individual producers but also, at the same time, creates a pattern of resource allocation that maximizes consumer satisfaction. The invisible hand thus organizes the private interests of producers in a way that is fully in sync with society's interest in using scarce resources efficiently. Striving for profit (and avoiding losses) produces highly desirable economic outcomes.

Summary

1. Economists group industries into four models based on their market structures: (a) pure competition, (b) monopolistic competition, (c) oligopoly, and (d) pure monopoly.

2. A purely competitive industry consists of a large number of independent firms producing a standardized product. Pure competition assumes that firms and resources are mobile among different industries.

3. In a competitive industry, no single firm can influence market price. This means that the firm's demand curve is perfectly elastic and price equals both marginal revenue and average revenue.

4. Provided price exceeds minimum average variable cost, a competitive firm maximizes profit or minimizes loss in the short run by producing the output at which price or marginal revenue equals marginal cost.

5. If price is less than minimum average variable cost, a competitive firm minimizes its loss by shutting down. If price is greater than average variable cost but is less than average total cost, a competitive firm minimizes its loss by producing the $P = MC$ amount of output. If price also exceeds average total cost, the firm maximizes its economic profit at the $P = MC$ amount of output.

6. Applying the MR ($= P$) $= MC$ rule at various possible market prices leads to the conclusion that the segment of the firm's short-run marginal-cost curve that lies above the firm's average-variable-cost curve is its short-run supply curve.

7. In the long run, the market price of a product will equal the minimum average total cost of production. At a higher price, economic profits would entice firms to enter the industry until those profits had been competed away. At a lower price, losses would force firms to exit the industry until the product price rose to equal average total cost.

8. The long-run supply curve is horizontal for a constant-cost industry, upsloping for an increasing-cost industry, and downsloping for a decreasing-cost industry.

9. The long-run equality of price and minimum average total cost means that competitive firms will use the most efficient known technology and charge the lowest price consistent with their production costs. That is, purely competitive firms will achieve productive efficiency.

10. The long-run equality of price and marginal cost implies that resources will be allocated in accordance with consumer tastes. Allocative efficiency will occur. In the market, the combined amount of consumer surplus and producer surplus will be at a maximum.

11. The competitive price system will reallocate resources in response to a change in consumer tastes, in technology, or in resource supplies and will thereby maintain allocative efficiency over time.

Terms and Concepts

pure competition	marginal revenue	constant-cost industry
price taker	MR = MC rule	increasing-cost industry
average revenue	short-run supply curve	decreasing-cost industry
total revenue	long-run supply curve	

Questions

1. Briefly state the basic characteristics of pure competition, pure monopoly, monopolistic competition, and oligopoly. Under which of these market classifications does each of the following most accurately fit? (a) a supermarket in your hometown; (b) the steel industry; (c) a Kansas wheat farm; (d) the commercial bank in which you or your family has an account; (e) the automobile industry. In each case, justify your classification. **LO1**

2. Use the demand schedule to the right to determine total revenue and marginal revenue for each possible level of sales: **LO2**

    a. What can you conclude about the structure of the industry in which this firm is operating? Explain.

Product Price	Quantity Demanded	Total Revenue	Marginal Revenue
$2	0	$_____	
2	1	_____	$_____
2	2	_____	_____
2	3	_____	_____
2	4	_____	_____
2	5	_____	_____

    b. Graph the demand, total-revenue, and marginal-revenue curves for this firm.

c. Why do the demand, marginal-revenue, and average-revenue curves coincide?

d. "Marginal revenue is the change in total revenue associated with additional units of output." Explain verbally and graphically, using the data in the table.

3. "Even if a firm is losing money, it may be better to stay in business in the short run." Is this statement ever true? Under what condition(s)? **LO3**

4. Why is the equality of marginal revenue and marginal cost essential for profit maximization in all market structures? Explain why price can be substituted for marginal revenue in the MR = MC rule when an industry is purely competitive. **LO3**

5. "That segment of a competitive firm's marginal-cost curve that lies above its average-variable-cost curve constitutes the short-run supply curve for the firm." Explain using a graph and words. **LO4**

6. Explain: "The short-run rule for operating or shutting down is $P > AVC$, operate; $P < AVC$, shut down. The long-run rule for continuing in business or exiting the industry is $P \geq ATC$, continue; $P < ATC$, exit." **LO5**

7. Using diagrams for both the industry and a representative firm, illustrate competitive long-run equilibrium. Assuming constant costs, employ these diagrams to show how (a) an increase and (b) a decrease in market demand will upset that long-run equilibrium. Trace graphically and describe verbally the adjustment processes by which long-run equilibrium is restored. Now rework your analysis for increasing- and decreasing-cost industries, and compare the three long-run supply curves. **LO6**

8. In long-run equilibrium, P = minimum ATC = MC. What is the significance of the equality of P and minimum ATC for society? The equality of P and MC? Distinguish between productive efficiency and allocative efficiency in your answer. **LO5**

9. Suppose that purely competitive firms producing cashews discover that P exceeds MC. Will their combined output of cashews be too little, too much, or just right to achieve allocative efficiency? In the long run, what will happen to the supply of cashews and the price of cashews? Use a supply-and-demand diagram to show how that response will change the combined amount of consumer surplus and producer surplus in the market for cashews. **LO5**

Problems

1. A purely competitive firm finds that the market price for its product is $20. It has a fixed cost of $100 and a variable cost of $10 per unit for the first 50 units and then $25 per unit for all successive units. Does price exceed average variable cost for the first 50 units? What about for the first 100 units? What is the marginal cost per unit for the first 50 units? What about for units 51 and higher? For each of the first 50 units, does MR exceed MC? What about for units 51 and higher? What output level will yield the largest possible profit for this purely competitive firm? **LO3**

2. A purely competitive wheat farmer can sell any wheat he grows for $10 per bushel. His five acres of land show diminishing returns because some are better suited for wheat production than others. The first acre can produce 1000 bushels of wheat, the second acre 900, the third 800, and so on. Draw a table with multiple columns to help you answer the following questions. How many bushels will each of the farmer's five acres produce? How much revenue will each acre generate? What are the TR and MR for each acre? If the marginal cost of planting and harvesting an acre is $7000 per acre for each of the five acres, how many acres should the farmer plant and harvest? **LO3**

3. Karen runs a print shop that makes posters for large companies. It is a very competitive business. The market price is currently $1 per poster. She has fixed costs of $250. Her variable costs are $1000 for the first thousand posters, $800 for the second thousand, and then $750 for each additional thousand posters. What is her AFC per poster (not per thousand!) if she prints 1000 posters? 2000? 10,000? What is her ATC per poster if she prints 1000? 2000? 10,000? If the market price fell to 70 cents per poster, would there be *any* output level at which Karen would *not* shut down production immediately? **LO3**

4. Assume that the cost data in the table below are for a purely competitive producer: **LO3**

Total Product	Average Fixed Cost	Average Variable Cost	Average Total Cost	Marginal Cost
0				
				$45
1	$60.00	$45.00	$105.00	
				40
2	30.00	42.50	72.50	
				35
3	20.00	40.00	60.00	
				30
4	15.00	37.50	52.50	
				35
5	12.00	37.00	49.00	
				40
6	10.00	37.50	47.50	
				45
7	8.57	38.57	47.14	
				55
8	7.50	40.63	48.13	
				65
9	6.67	43.33	50.00	
				75
10	6.00	46.50	52.50	

a. At a product price of $56, will this firm produce in the short run? If it is preferable to produce, what will be the profit-maximizing or loss-minimizing output? What economic profit or loss will the firm realize per unit of output?

b. Answer the questions of 4a assuming product price is $41.

c. Answer the questions of 4a assuming product price is $32.

d. In the table below, complete the short-run supply schedule for the firm (columns 1 and 2) and indicate the profit or loss incurred at each output (column 3).

(1) Price	(2) Quantity Supplied, Single Firm	(3) Profit (+) or Loss (−)	(4) Quantity Supplied 1500 Firms
$26	_____	$_____	_____
32	_____	_____	_____
38	_____	_____	_____
41	_____	_____	_____
46	_____	_____	_____
56	_____	_____	_____
66	_____	_____	_____

e. Now assume that there are 1500 identical firms in this competitive industry; that is, there are 1500 firms, each of which has the cost data shown in the table. Complete the industry supply schedule (column 4).

f. Suppose the market demand data for the product are as follows:

Price	Total Quantity Demanded
$26	17,000
32	15,000
38	13,500
41	12,000
46	10,500
56	9500
66	8000

What will be the equilibrium price? What will be the equilibrium output for the industry? For each firm? What will profit or loss be per unit? Per firm? Will this industry expand or contract in the long run?

After reading this chapter, you should be able to:

1 List the characteristics of pure monopoly and discuss several barriers to entry that relate to monopoly.

2 Explain how a pure monopoly sets its profit-maximizing output and price.

3 Discuss the economic effects of monopoly.

4 Describe why a monopolist might prefer to charge different prices in different markets.

5 Identify the antitrust laws that are used to deal with monopoly.

Pure Monopoly

We turn now from pure competition to pure monopoly (a single seller). You deal with monopolies—or near-monopolies—more often than you might think. This happens when you see the Microsoft Windows logo after you turn on your computer and when you swallow a prescription drug that is under patent. Depending on where you live, you may be patronizing a local or regional monopoly when you make a local telephone call, turn on your lights, or subscribe to cable TV.

What precisely do we mean by "pure monopoly," and what conditions enable it to arise and survive? How does a pure monopolist determine what price to charge? Does a pure monopolist achieve the efficiency associated with pure competition? If not, what should the government try to do about it? A model of pure monopoly will help us answer these questions.

pure monopoly
An industry in which one firm is the sole producer or seller of a product or service for which there are no close substitutes.

ORIGIN OF THE IDEA

O 8.1

Monopoly

barriers to entry
Any conditions that prevent the entry of firms into an industry.

An Introduction to Pure Monopoly

Pure monopoly exists when a single firm is the sole producer of a product for which there are no close substitutes. Here are the main characteristics of **pure monopoly:**

- *Single seller* A pure, or absolute, monopoly is an industry in which a single firm is the sole producer of a specific good or the sole supplier of a service; the firm and the industry are synonymous.
- *No close substitutes* A pure monopoly's product is unique in that there are no close substitutes. The consumer who chooses not to buy the monopolized product must do without it.
- *Price maker* The pure monopolist controls the total quantity supplied and thus has considerable control over price; it is a *price maker*. (Unlike a pure competitor, which has no such control and therefore is a *price taker*.) The pure monopolist confronts the usual downward-sloping product demand curve. It can change its product price by changing the quantity of the product it produces. The monopolist will use this power whenever it is advantageous to do so.
- *Blocked entry* A pure monopolist faces no immediate competition because certain barriers keep potential competitors from entering the industry. Those barriers may be economic, technological, legal, or of some other type. But entry is totally blocked in pure monopoly.

Examples of *pure* monopoly are relatively rare, but there are excellent examples of less pure forms. In many cities, government-owned or government-regulated public utilities—natural gas and electric companies, the water company, the cable TV company, and the local telephone company—are all monopolies or virtually so.

There are also many "near-monopolies" in which a single firm has the bulk of sales in a specific market. Intel, for example, produces 80 percent of the central microprocessors used in personal computers. First Data Corporation, via its Western Union subsidiary, accounts for 80 percent of the market for money order transfers. Brannock Device Company has an 80 percent market share of the shoe-sizing devices found in shoe stores. Wham-O, through its Frisbee brand, sells 90 percent of plastic throwing disks. The De Beers diamond syndicate effectively controls 55 percent of the world's supply of rough-cut diamonds.

Professional sports teams are, in a sense, monopolies because they are the sole suppliers of specific services in large geographic areas. With a few exceptions, a single major-league team in each sport serves each large American city. If you want to see a live major-league baseball game in St. Louis or Seattle, you must patronize the Cardinals or the Mariners, respectively. Other geographic monopolies exist. For example, a small town may be served by only one airline or railroad. In a small, extremely isolated community, the local barber shop, dry cleaner, or grocery store may approximate a monopoly.

Of course, there is almost always some competition. Satellite television is a substitute for cable, and amateur softball is a substitute for professional baseball. The Linux operating system can substitute for Windows, and so on. But such substitutes are typically in some way less appealing.

Barriers to Entry

The factors that prohibit firms from entering an industry are called **barriers to entry.** In pure monopoly, strong barriers to entry effectively block all potential competition. Somewhat weaker barriers may permit *oligopoly*, a market structure dominated by a few firms. Still weaker barriers may permit the entry of a fairly large number of competing firms, giving rise to *monopolistic competition*. And the absence of any effective entry barriers permits the entry of a very large number of firms, which provide the basis of pure competition. So barriers to entry are pertinent not only to the extreme case of pure monopoly but also to other market structures in which there are monopoly-like characteristics or monopoly-like behavior.

We will now discuss the four most prominent barriers to entry.

Economies of Scale

Modern technology in some industries is such that economies of scale—declining average total cost with added firm size—are extensive. In such cases, a firm's long-run average-cost schedule will decline over a wide range of output. Given market demand, only a few large firms or, in the extreme, only a single large firm can achieve low average total costs.

If a pure monopoly exists in such an industry, economies of scale will serve as an entry barrier and will protect the monopolist from competition. New firms that try to enter the industry as small-scale producers cannot realize the cost economies of the monopolist. They therefore will be undercut and forced out of business by the monopolist, which can sell at a much lower price and still make a profit because of its lower per-unit cost associated with its economies of scale. A new firm might try to start out big, that is, to enter the industry as a large-scale producer so as to achieve the necessary economies of scale. But the massive plant facilities required would necessitate huge amounts of financing, which a new and untried enterprise would find difficult to secure. In most cases, the financial obstacles and risks to "starting big" are prohibitive. This explains why efforts to enter such industries as automobiles, computer operating software, commercial aircraft, and basic steel are so rare.

In the extreme circumstance, in which the market demand curve cuts the long-run ATC curve where average total costs are still declining, the single firm is called a **natural monopoly.** It might seem that a natural monopolist's lower unit cost would enable it to charge a lower price than if the industry were more competitive. But that won't necessarily happen. As with any monopolist, a natural monopolist may, instead, set its price far above ATC and obtain substantial economic profit. In that event, the lowest-unit-cost advantage of a natural monopolist would accrue to the monopolist as profit and not as lower prices to consumers.

natural monopoly
An industry in which economies of scale are so great that only a single firm can achieve minimum efficient scale.

Legal Barriers to Entry: Patents and Licenses

Government also creates legal barriers to entry by awarding patents and licenses.

Patents   A *patent* is the exclusive right of an inventor to use, or to allow another to use, her or his invention. Patents and patent laws aim to protect the inventor from rivals who would use the invention without having shared in the effort and expense of developing it. At the same time, patents provide the inventor with a monopoly position for the life of the patent. The world's nations have agreed on a uniform patent length of 20 years from the time of application. Patents have figured prominently in the growth of modern-day giants such as IBM, Pfizer, Kodak, Xerox, Intel, General Electric, and DuPont.

Research and development (R&D) is what leads to most patentable inventions and products. Firms that gain monopoly power through their own research or by purchasing the patents of others can use patents to strengthen their market position. The profit from one patent can finance the research required to develop new patentable products. In the pharmaceutical industry, patents on prescription drugs have produced large monopoly profits that have helped finance the discovery of new patentable medicines. So monopoly power achieved through patents may well be self-sustaining, even though patents eventually expire and generic drugs then compete with the original brand.

Licenses   Government may also limit entry into an industry or occupation through *licensing*. At the national level, the Federal Communications Commission licenses only so many radio and television stations in each geographic area. In many large cities, one of a limited number of municipal licenses is required to drive a taxicab. The consequent restriction of the supply of cabs creates economic profit for cab owners and drivers. New cabs cannot enter the industry to drive down prices and profits. In a few instances, the government might "license" itself to provide some product and thereby create a public monopoly. For example, in some states only state-owned retail outlets can sell liquor. Similarly, many states have "licensed" themselves to run lotteries.

Ownership or Control of Essential Resources

A monopolist can use private property as an obstacle to potential rivals. For example, a firm that owns or controls a resource essential to the production process can prohibit the entry of rival firms. At one time the International Nickel Company of Canada (now called Inco) controlled a large percentage of the world's known nickel reserves. A local firm may own all the nearby deposits of sand and gravel. And it is very difficult for new sports leagues to be created because existing professional sports leagues have contracts with the best players and have long-term leases on the major stadiums and arenas.

Pricing and Other Strategic Barriers to Entry

Even if a firm is not protected from entry by, say, extensive economies of scale or ownership of essential resources, entry may effectively be blocked by the way the monopolist responds to attempts by rivals to enter the industry. Confronted with a new entrant, the monopolist may "create an entry barrier" by slashing its price, stepping up its advertising, or taking other strategic actions to make it difficult for the entrant to succeed.

Examples of entry deterrence: In 2005 Dentsply, the dominant American maker of false teeth (70 percent market share) was found to have unlawfully precluded independent distributors of false teeth from carrying competing brands. The lack of access to the distributors deterred potential foreign competitors from entering the U.S. market. As another example, in 2001 a U.S. court of appeals upheld a lower court's finding that Microsoft used a series of illegal actions to maintain its monopoly in Intel-compatible PC operating systems (95 percent market share). One such action was charging higher prices for its Windows operating system to computer manufacturers that featured Netscape's Navigator rather than Microsoft's Internet Explorer.

Monopoly Demand

Now that we have explained the sources of monopoly, we want to build a model of pure monopoly so that we can analyze its price and output decisions. Let's start by making three assumptions:

- Patents, economies of scale, or resource ownership secure our firm's monopoly.
- No unit of government regulates the firm.
- The firm is a single-price monopolist; it charges the same price for all units of output.

Price set by firm

The crucial difference between a pure monopolist and a purely competitive seller lies on the demand side of the market. The purely competitive seller faces a perfectly elastic demand at the price determined by market supply and demand. It is a price taker that can sell as much or as little as it wants at the going market price. Each additional unit sold will add the amount of the constant product price to the firm's total revenue. That means that marginal revenue for the competitive seller is constant and equal to product price. (Review Figure 7.1 for price, marginal-revenue, and total-revenue relationships for the purely competitive firm.)

The demand curve for the monopolist (or oligopolist or monopolistic competitor) is quite different from that of the pure competitor. Because the pure monopolist *is* the industry, its demand curve is *the market demand curve*. And because market demand is not perfectly elastic, the monopolist's demand curve is downsloping. Columns 1 and 2 in the table in Figure 8.1 illustrate this fact. Note that quantity demanded increases as price decreases.

In Chapter 7 we drew separate demand curves for the purely competitive industry and for a single firm in such an industry. But only a single demand curve is needed in pure monopoly because the firm and the industry are one and the same. We have graphed part of the demand data in the table in Figure 8.1 as demand curve *D* in Figure 8.1a. This is the monopolist's demand curve *and* the market demand curve. The downward-sloping demand curve has two implications that are essential to understanding the monopoly model.

Marginal Revenue Is Less Than Price

With a fixed downsloping demand curve, the pure monopolist can increase sales only by charging a lower price. Consequently, marginal revenue is less than price (average revenue) for every unit of output except the first. Why so? The reason is that the lower price of the extra unit of output also applies to all prior units of output. The monopolist could have sold these prior units at a higher price if it had not produced and sold the extra output. Each additional unit of output sold increases total revenue by an amount equal to its own price less the sum of the price cuts that apply to all prior units of output.

Figure 8.1a confirms this point. There, we have highlighted two price-quantity combinations from the monopolist's demand curve. The monopolist can sell 1 more unit at $132 than it can at $142 and that way obtain $132 of extra revenue (the blue area). But to sell that fourth unit for $132, the monopolist must also sell the first 3 units at $132 rather than $142. The $10 reduction in revenue on 3 units results in a $30 revenue loss (the red area). The net difference in total revenue from selling a fourth unit is $102: the $132 gain from the fourth unit minus the $30 forgone on the first 3 units. This net gain (marginal revenue) of $102 from the fourth unit is clearly less than the $132 price of the fourth unit.

Column 4 in the table shows that marginal revenue is always less than the corresponding product price in column 2, except for the first unit of output. We show the relationship between the monopolist's demand curve and marginal-revenue curve in Figure 8.1b. For this figure, we extended the demand and marginal-revenue data of columns 1, 2, and 4 in the table, assuming that successive $10 price cuts each elicits 1 additional unit of sales. That is, the monopolist can sell 11 units at $62, 12 units at $52, and so on. Note that the monopolist's MR curve lies below the demand curve, indicating that marginal revenue is less than price at every output quantity except the very first unit.

The Monopolist Is a Price Maker

All imperfect competitors, whether they are pure monopolists, oligopolists, or monopolistic competitors, face downsloping demand curves. As a result, any change in quantity produced causes a movement along their respective demand curves and a change in the price they can charge for their respective products. Economists summarize this fact by saying that firms with downsloping demand curves are *price makers*.

FIGURE 8.1 Demand, price, and marginal revenue in pure monopoly. (a) A pure monopolist (or any other imperfect competitor) must set a lower price in order to sell more output. Here, by charging $132 rather than $142, the monopolist sells an extra unit (the fourth unit) and gains $132 from that sale. But from this gain $30 is subtracted, which reflects the $10 less the monopolist received for each of the first 3 units. Thus, the marginal revenue of the fourth unit is $102 (= $132 − $30), considerably less than its $132 price. (b) Because a monopolist must lower the price on all units sold in order to increase its sales, its marginal-revenue curve (MR) lies below its downsloping demand curve (D).

	Revenue Data		
(1) Quantity of Output	(2) Price (Average Revenue)	(3) Total Revenue, (1) × (2)	(4) Marginal Revenue
0	$172	$ 0	
1	162	162	$162
2	152	304	142
3	142	426	122
4	132	528	102
5	122	610	82
6	112	672	62
7	102	714	42
8	92	736	22
9	82	738	2
10	72	720	−18

Qty increase
Price decrease

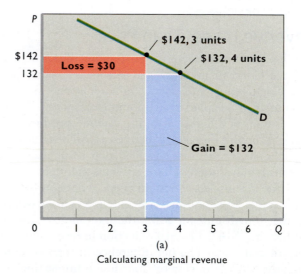

(a)
Calculating marginal revenue

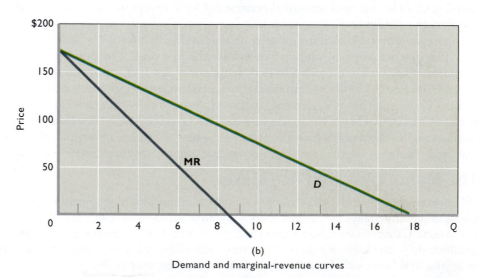

(b)
Demand and marginal-revenue curves

This is most evident in pure monopoly, where an industry consists of a single monopoly firm so that total industry output is exactly equal to whatever the single monopoly firm chooses to produce. As we just mentioned, the monopolist faces a downsloping demand curve in which each amount of output is associated with some unique price. Thus, in deciding on the quantity of output to produce, the monopolist is also indirectly determining the price it will charge. Through control of output, it can "make the price." From columns 1 and 2 in the table in Figure 8.1 we find that the monopolist can charge a price of $72 if it produces and offers for sale 10 units, a price of $82 if it produces and offers for sale 9 units, and so forth.

Output and Price Determination

At what specific price-quantity combination will a profit-maximizing monopolist choose to operate? To answer this question, we must add production costs to our analysis.

Cost Data

On the cost side, we will assume that although the firm is a monopolist in the product market, it hires resources competitively and employs the same technology and, therefore, has the same cost structure as the purely competitive firm that we studied in Chapter 7. By using the same cost data that we developed in Chapter 6 and applied to the competitive firm in Chapter 7, we will be able to directly compare the price and output decisions of a pure monopoly with those of a pure competitor. Columns 5 through 7 in the table in Figure 8.2 restate the pertinent cost data from the table in Figure 7.2.

MR = MC Rule

A monopolist seeking to maximize total profit will employ the same rationale as a profit-seeking firm in a competitive industry. If producing is preferable to shutting down, it will produce up to the output at which marginal revenue equals marginal cost (MR = MC).

A comparison of columns 4 and 7 in the table in Figure 8.2 indicates that the profit-maximizing output is 5 units because the fifth unit is the last unit of output whose marginal revenue exceeds its marginal cost. What price will the monopolist charge? The demand schedule shown as columns 1 and 2 in the table indicates there is only one price at which 5 units can be sold: $122.

This analysis is shown in Figure 8.2, where we have graphed the demand, marginal-revenue, average-total-cost, and marginal-cost data from the table. The profit-maximizing output occurs at 5 units of output (Q_m), where the marginal-revenue (MR) and marginal-cost (MC) curves intersect. There, MR = MC.

To find the price the monopolist will charge, we extend a vertical line from Q_m up to the demand curve D. The unique price P_m at which Q_m units can be sold is $122. In this case, $122 is the profit-maximizing price. So the monopolist sets the quantity at Q_m to charge its profit-maximizing price of $122.

Columns 2 and 5 of the table show that at 5 units of output, the product price ($122) exceeds the average total cost ($94). The monopolist thus obtains an economic profit of $28 per unit, and the total economic profit is then $140 (= 5 units × $28). In the graph in Figure 8.2, per-unit profit is $P_m - A$, where A is the average total cost of producing Q_m units. Total economic profit of $140 (the green rectangle) is found by multiplying this per-unit profit by the profit-maximizing output Q_m.

WORKED PROBLEMS

W 8.1

Monopoly price and output

INTERACTIVE GRAPHS

G 8.1

Monopoly

FIGURE 8.2 Profit maximization by a pure monopolist. The pure monopolist maximizes profit by producing the MR = MC output, here Q_m = 5 units. Then, as seen from the demand curve, it will charge price P_m = $122. Average total cost is A = $94, so per-unit profit is $P_m − A$ and total profit is $5 × (P_m − A)$. Total economic profit is thus $140, as shown by the green rectangle.

	Revenue Data				Cost Data		
(1) Quantity of Output	(2) Price (Average Revenue)	(3) Total Revenue, (1) × (2)	(4) Marginal Revenue	(5) Average Total Cost	(6) Total Cost, (1) × (5)	(7) Marginal Cost	(8) Profit [+] or Loss [−]
0	$172	$ 0		$ 100			$−100
1	162	162	$162	$190.00	190	$ 90	−28
2	152	304	142	135.00	270	80	+34
3	142	426	122	113.33	340	70	+86
4	132	528	102	100.00	400	60	+128
5	122	610	82	94.00	470	70	+140
6	112	672	62	91.67	550	80	+122
7	102	714	42	91.43	640	90	+74
8	92	736	22	93.75	750	110	−14
9	82	738	2	97.78	880	130	−142
10	72	720	−18	103.00	1030	150	−310

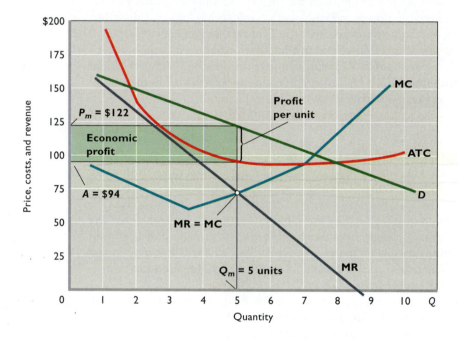

Misconceptions Concerning Monopoly Pricing

Our analysis exposes three fallacies concerning monopoly behavior.

Not Highest Price Because a monopolist can manipulate output and price, people often believe it "will charge the highest price possible." That is incorrect. There are many prices above P_m in Figure 8.2, but the monopolist shuns them because they yield a smaller-than-maximum total profit. The monopolist seeks maximum total profit, not maximum price. Some high prices that could be charged would reduce sales and total revenue too severely to offset any decrease in total cost.

2) *Total, Not Unit, Profit*   The monopolist seeks maximum *total* profit, not maximum *unit* profit. In Figure 8.2 a careful comparison of the vertical distance between average total cost and price at various possible outputs indicates that per-unit profit is greater at a point slightly to the left of the profit-maximizing output Q_m. This is seen in the table, where unit profit at 4 units of output is $32 (= $132 − $100) compared with $28 (= $122 − $94) at the profit-maximizing output of 5 units. Here the monopolist accepts a lower-than-maximum per-unit profit because additional sales more than compensate for the lower unit profit. A profit-seeking monopolist would rather sell 5 units at a profit of $28 per unit (for a total profit of $140) than 4 units at a profit of $32 per unit (for a total profit of only $128).

3) *Possibility of Losses*   The likelihood of economic profit is greater for a pure monopolist than for a pure competitor. In the long run, the pure competitor is destined to have only a normal profit, whereas barriers to entry mean that any economic profit realized by the monopolist can persist. In pure monopoly there are no new entrants to increase supply, drive down price, and eliminate economic profit.

Profitability is not assured

   But pure monopoly does not guarantee profit. Despite dominance in its market (as, say, a seller of home sewing machines), a monopoly enterprise can suffer a loss because of weak demand and relatively high costs. If the demand and cost situation faced by the monopolist is far less favorable than that in Figure 8.2, the monopolist can incur losses. Like the pure competitor, the monopolist will not persist in operating at a loss in the long run. Faced with continuing losses, the firm's owners will move their resources to alternative industries that offer better profit opportunities. Like any firm, a monopolist must obtain a minimum of a normal profit in the long run or it will go out of business.

Economic Effects of Monopoly

Let's now evaluate pure monopoly from the standpoint of society as a whole. Our reference for this evaluation will be the outcome of long-run efficiency in a purely competitive market, identified by the triple equality $P = MC = $ minimum ATC.

Price, Output, and Efficiency

Figure 8.3 graphically contrasts the price, output, and efficiency outcomes of pure monopoly and a purely competitive *industry*. The $S = MC$ curve in Figure 8.3a reminds us that the market supply curve S for a purely competitive industry is the horizontal sum of the marginal-cost curves of all the firms in the industry. Suppose there are 1000 such firms. Comparing their combined supply curve S with market demand D, we see that the purely competitive price and output are P_c and Q_c.

   Recall that this price-output combination results in both productive efficiency and allocative efficiency. *Productive efficiency* is achieved because free entry and exit force firms to operate where their average total cost is at a minimum. The sum of the minimum-ATC outputs of the 1000 pure competitors is the industry output, here, Q_c. Product price is at the lowest level consistent with minimum average total cost. The *allocative efficiency* of pure competition results because production occurs up to that output at which price (the measure of a product's value or marginal benefit to society) equals marginal cost (the worth of the alternative products forgone by society in producing any given commodity). In short: $P = MC = $ minimum ATC.

*Purely competitive
→ Production = lowest cost
→ Allocative = right mix of goods determined by consumers.*

   Now let's suppose that this industry becomes a pure monopoly (Figure 8.3b) as a result of one firm acquiring all its competitors. We also assume that no changes in costs or market demand result from this dramatic change in the industry structure.

FIGURE 8.3 Inefficiency of pure monopoly relative to a purely competitive industry. (a) In a purely competitive industry, entry and exit of firms ensure that price (P_c) equals marginal cost (MC) and that the minimum average-total-cost output (Q_c) is produced. Both productive efficiency (P = minimum ATC) and allocative efficiency (P = MC) are obtained. (b) In pure monopoly, the MR curve lies below the demand curve. The monopolist maximizes profit at output Q_m, where MR = MC, and charges price P_m. Thus, output is lower (Q_m rather than Q_c) and price is higher (P_m rather than P_c) than they would be in a purely competitive industry. Monopoly is inefficient, since output is less than that required for achieving minimum ATC (here, at Q_c) and because the monopolist's price exceeds MC. Monopoly creates an efficiency loss (here, of triangle abc). There is also a transfer of income from consumers to the monopoly (here, of rectangle P_cP_mbd).

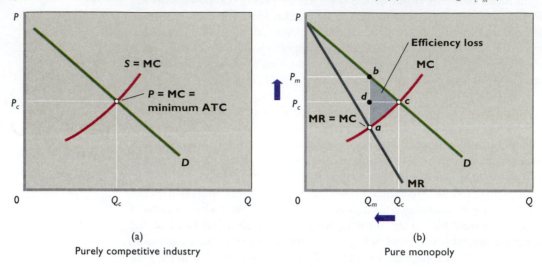

(a)
Purely competitive industry

(b)
Pure monopoly

What formerly were 1000 competing firms are now a single pure monopolist consisting of 1000 noncompeting branches.

The competitive market supply curve S has become the marginal-cost curve (MC) of the monopolist, the summation of the individual marginal-cost curves of its many branch plants. The important change, however, is on the demand side. From the viewpoint of each of the 1000 individual competitive firms, demand was perfectly elastic, and marginal revenue was therefore equal to the market equilibrium price P_c. So each firm equated its marginal revenue of P_c dollars per unit with its individual marginal cost curve to maximize profits. But market demand and individual demand are the same to the pure monopolist. The firm *is* the industry, and thus the monopolist sees the downsloping demand curve D shown in Figure 8.3b.

This means that marginal revenue is less than price, that graphically the MR curve lies below demand curve D. In using the MR = MC rule, the monopolist selects output Q_m and price P_m. A comparison of both graphs in Figure 8.3 reveals that the monopolist finds it profitable to sell a smaller output at a higher price than do the competitive producers.

Monopoly yields neither productive nor allocative efficiency. The lack of productive efficiency can be understood most directly by noting that the monopolist's output Q_m is less than Q_c, the output at which average total cost is lowest. In addition, the monopoly price P_m is higher than the competitive price P_c that we know in long-run equilibrium in pure competition equals minimum average total cost. Thus, the monopoly price exceeds minimum average total cost, thereby demonstrating in another way that the monopoly will not be productively efficient.

The monopolist's underproduction also implies allocative inefficiency. One way to see this is to note that at the monopoly output level Q_m, the monopoly price P_m that consumers are willing to pay exceeds the marginal cost of production. This means that consumers value additional units of this product more highly than they do the alternative products that could be produced from the resources that would be necessary to make more units of the monopolist's product.

The monopolist's allocative inefficiency can also be understood by noting that for every unit between Q_m and Q_c, marginal benefit exceeds marginal cost because the demand curve lies above the supply curve. By choosing not to produce these units, the monopolist reduces allocative efficiency because the resources that should have been used to make these units will be redirected instead toward producing items that bring lower net benefits to society. The total dollar value of this efficiency loss (or *deadweight loss*) is equal to the area of the gray triangle labeled *abc* in Figure 8.3b.

Income Transfer

In general, a monopoly transfers income from consumers to the owners of the monopoly. The income is received by the owners as revenue. Because a monopoly has market power, it can charge a higher price than would a purely competitive firm with the same costs. So the monopoly in effect levies a "private tax" on consumers. This private tax can often generate substantial economic profits that can persist because entry to the industry is blocked.

The transfer from consumers to the monopolist is evident in Figure 8.3b. For the Q_m units of output demanded, consumers pay price P_m rather than the price P_c that they would pay to a pure competitor. The total amount of income transferred from consumers to the monopolist is $P_m - P_c$ multiplied by the number of units sold, Q_m. So the total transfer is the dollar amount of rectangle $P_c P_m bd$. What the consumer loses, the monopolist gains. In contrast, the efficiency loss *abc* is a *deadweight* loss—society totally loses the net benefits of the Q_c minus Q_m units that are not produced.

Cost Complications

Our conclusion has been that, given identical costs, a purely monopolistic industry will charge a higher price, produce a smaller output, and allocate economic resources less efficiently than a purely competitive industry. These inferior results are rooted in the entry barriers present in monopoly.

Now we must recognize that costs may not be the same for purely competitive and monopolistic producers. The unit cost incurred by a monopolist may be either larger or smaller than that incurred by a purely competitive firm. There are four reasons why costs may differ: (1) economies of scale, (2) a factor called "X-inefficiency," (3) the need for monopoly-preserving expenditures, and (4) the "very long run" perspective, which allows for technological advance.

Economies of Scale Once Again
Where economies of scale are extensive, market demand may not be sufficient to support a large number of competing firms, each producing at minimum efficient scale (MES). In such cases, an industry of one or two firms would have a lower average total cost than would the same industry made up of numerous competitive firms. At the extreme, only a single firm—a natural monopoly—might be able to achieve the lowest long-run average total cost.

Some firms relating to new information technologies—for example, computer software, Internet service, and wireless communications—have displayed extensive economies of scale. As these firms have grown, their long-run average total costs have declined because of greater use of specialized inputs, the spreading of product development costs, and learning by doing. Also, *simultaneous consumption* and *network effects* have reduced costs.

A product's ability to satisfy a large number of consumers at the same time is called **simultaneous consumption.** Dell Inc. needs to produce a personal computer for each customer, but Microsoft needs to produce its Windows program only once. Then, at very low marginal cost, Microsoft delivers its program by disk or Internet to

simultaneous consumption
A product's ability to satisfy a large number of consumers at the same time.

millions of consumers. Others able to deliver to additional consumers at low cost include Internet service providers, music producers, and wireless communication firms. Because marginal costs are so low, the average total cost of output typically declines as more customers are added.

network effects
Increases in the value of a product to each user as the total number of users rises.

Network effects are present if the value of a product to each user, including existing users, increases as the total number of users rises. Good examples are computer software, cell phones, and websites like Facebook where the content is provided by users. When other people have Internet service and devices to access it, a person can conveniently send e-mail messages to them. And when they have similar software, then documents, spreadsheets, and photos can be attached to the e-mail messages. The greater the number of persons connected to the system, the greater are the benefits of the product to each person.

Such network effects may drive a market toward monopoly because consumers tend to choose standard products that everyone else is using. The focused demand for these products permits their producers to grow rapidly and thus achieve economies of scale. Smaller firms, which have either higher-cost "right" products or "wrong" products, get acquired or go out of business.

Economists generally agree that some new information firms have not yet exhausted their economies of scale. But most economists question whether such firms are truly natural monopolies. Most firms eventually achieve their minimum efficient scale at less than the full size of the market. That means competition among firms is possible.

But even if natural monopoly develops, it's unlikely that the monopolist will pass cost reductions along to consumers as price reductions. So, with perhaps a handful of exceptions, economies of scale do not change the general conclusion that monopoly industries are inefficient relative to competitive industries.

ORIGIN OF THE IDEA

O 8.3
X-inefficiency

X-Inefficiency In constructing all the average-total-cost curves used in this book, we have assumed that the firm uses the most efficient existing technology. This assumption is only natural because firms cannot maximize profits unless they are minimizing costs. **X-inefficiency** occurs when a firm produces output at a higher cost than is necessary to produce it. For example, in Figure 8.2 the ATC and MC curves might be located above those shown, indicating higher costs at each level of output.

X-inefficiency
The production of output, whatever its level, at higher than the lowest average (and total) cost possible.

In monopolies

Sloppy, no comp.

Why is X-inefficiency allowed to occur if it reduces profits? The answer harks back to our early discussion of the principal-agent problem. Managers may have goals, such as expanding power, having an easier work life, avoiding business risk, or giving jobs to incompetent relatives, that conflict with cost minimization. Or X-inefficiency may arise because a firm's workers are poorly motivated or ineffectively supervised. Or a firm may simply become lethargic and inert, relying on rules of thumb or intuition in decision making as opposed to relevant calculations of costs and revenues.

Presumably, monopolistic firms tend more toward X-inefficiency than competitive producers do. Firms in competitive industries are continually under pressure from rivals, forcing them to be internally efficient to survive. But monopolists are sheltered from such competitive forces by entry barriers, and that lack of pressure may lead to X-inefficiency.

rent-seeking behavior
Any action designed to gain special benefits from government at taxpayers' or someone else's expense.

USAF

Rent-Seeking Expenditures Economists define **rent-seeking behavior** as any activity designed to transfer income or wealth to a particular firm or resource supplier at someone else's, or even society's, expense. We have seen that a monopolist can obtain an economic profit even in the long run. Therefore, it is no surprise that a firm may go to great expense to acquire or maintain a monopoly granted by government through legislation or an exclusive license. Such rent-seeking expenditures add nothing to the firm's output, but they clearly increase its costs. Taken alone, rent-seeking implies that monopoly involves higher costs and less efficiency than suggested in Figure 8.3b.

Technological Advance   In the very long run, firms can reduce their costs through the discovery and implementation of new technology. If monopolists are more likely than competitive producers to develop more efficient production techniques over time, then the inefficiency of monopoly might be overstated. The general view of economists is that a pure monopolist will not be technologically progressive. Although its economic profit provides ample means to finance research and development, it has little incentive to implement new techniques (or products). The absence of competitors means that there is no external pressure for technological advance in a monopolized market. Because of its sheltered market position, the pure monopolist can afford to be inefficient and lethargic; there is no major penalty for not being more efficient.

One caveat: Recall that entirely new products and new methods of production can suddenly supplant existing monopoly through the process of creative destruction (Chapter 2). Recognizing this threat, the monopolist may continue to engage in R&D and seek technological advance to avoid falling prey to future rivals. In this case technological advance is essential to the maintenance of monopoly. But forestalling creative destruction means that it is *potential* competition, not the monopoly market structure, that is driving the technological advance. By assumption, no such competition exists in the pure-monopoly model because entry is entirely blocked.

APPLYING THE ANALYSIS

Is De Beers' Diamond Monopoly Forever?

De Beers, a Swiss-based company controlled by a South African corporation, produces about 45 percent of the world's rough-cut diamonds and purchases for resale a sizable number of the rough-cut diamonds produced by other mines worldwide. As a result, De Beers markets about 55 percent of the world's diamonds to a select group of diamond cutters and dealers. But that percentage has declined from 80 percent in the mid-1980s. Therein lies the company's problem.

De Beers' past monopoly behavior is a classic example of the monopoly model illustrated in Figure 8.2. No matter how many diamonds it mined or purchased, it sold only the quantity of diamonds that would yield an "appropriate" (monopoly) price. That price was well above production costs, and De Beers and its partners earned monopoly profits.

When demand fell, De Beers reduced its sales to maintain price. The excess of production over sales was then reflected in growing diamond stockpiles held by De Beers. It also attempted to bolster demand through advertising ("Diamonds are forever"). When demand was strong, it increased sales by reducing its diamond inventories.

De Beers used several methods to control the production of many mines it did not own. First, it convinced a number of independent producers that "single-channel" or monopoly marketing through De Beers would maximize their profit. Second, mines that circumvented De Beers often found their market suddenly flooded with similar diamonds from De Beers' vast stockpiles. The resulting price decline and loss of profit often would encourage a "rogue" mine into the De Beers fold. Finally, De Beers simply purchased and stockpiled diamonds produced by independent mines to keep their added supplies from undercutting the market.

Several factors have come together to unravel the monopoly. New diamond discoveries resulted in a growing leakage of diamonds into world markets outside De Beers' control. For example, significant prospecting and trading in Angola occurred.

Recent diamond discoveries in Canada's Northwest Territories posed another threat. Although De Beers is a participant in that region, a large uncontrolled supply of diamonds has begun to emerge. Another challenge has been technological improvements that now allow chemical firms to manufacture flawless artificial diamonds. To prevent consumers from switching to synthetic diamonds, De Beers had to launch a costly campaign to promote "mined diamonds" over synthetics.

Moreover, the international media began to focus heavily on the role that diamonds play in financing bloody civil wars in Africa. Fearing a consumer boycott of diamonds, De Beers pledged that it would not buy these "conflict" diamonds or do business with any firms that did. These diamonds, however, continue to find their way into the marketplace, eluding De Beers' control.

In mid-2000 De Beers abandoned its attempt to control the supply of diamonds. Since then it has tried to transform itself from a diamond cartel to a modern international corporation selling "premium" diamonds under the De Beers label. It has gradually reduced its $4 billion stockpile of diamonds and turned its efforts to increasing the demand for its "branded" diamonds through advertising. De Beers' new strategy is to establish itself as "the diamond supplier of choice."

Diamonds may be forever, but the De Beers diamond monopoly was not. Nevertheless, with its high market share and ability to control its own production levels, De Beers continues to wield considerable influence over the price of rough-cut diamonds.

QUESTION: De Beers' advertising is trying to establish the tradition of giving diamond anniversary rings. What is the logic behind its efforts? Use Figure 8.2 to demonstrate this graphically.

Price Discrimination

We have thus far assumed that the monopolist charges a single price to all buyers. But under certain conditions the monopolist can increase its profit by charging different prices to different buyers. In so doing, the monopolist is engaging in **price discrimination,** the practice of selling a specific product at more than one price when the price differences are not justified by cost differences.

Price discrimination is a common business practice that rarely reduces competition and therefore is rarely challenged by government. The exception occurs when a firm engages in price discrimination as part of a strategy to block entry or drive out competitors.

price discrimination
The selling of a product to different buyers at different prices when the price differences are not justified by differences in costs.

ORIGIN OF THE IDEA

O 8.4

Price discrimination

Conditions

The opportunity to engage in price discrimination is not readily available to all sellers. Price discrimination is possible when the following conditions are met:

1) • *Monopoly power* The seller must be a monopolist or, at least, must possess some degree of monopoly power, that is, some ability to control output and price.

2) • *Market segregation* At relatively low cost to itself, the seller must be able to segregate buyers into distinct classes, each of which has a different willingness or ability to pay for the product. This separation of buyers is usually based on different price elasticities of demand, as the examples below will make clear.

3) • *No resale* The original purchaser cannot resell the product or service. If buyers in the low-price segment of the market could easily resell in the high-price

segment, the monopolist's price-discrimination strategy would create competition in the high-price segment. This competition would reduce the price in the high-price segment and undermine the monopolist's price-discrimination policy. This condition suggests that service industries such as the transportation industry or legal and medical services, where resale is impossible, are candidates for price discrimination.

Examples

Price discrimination is widely practiced in the U.S. economy. For example, airlines charge high fares to business travelers, whose demand for travel is inelastic, and offer lower highly restricted, nonrefundable fares to attract vacationers and others whose demands are more elastic.

Health Care

Electric utilities frequently segment their markets by end uses, such as lighting and heating. The absence of reasonable lighting substitutes means that the demand for electricity for illumination is inelastic and that the price per kilowatt-hour for such use is high. But the availability of natural gas and petroleum for heating makes the demand for electricity for this purpose less inelastic and the price lower.

Movie theaters and golf courses vary their charges on the basis of time (for example, higher evening and weekend rates) and age (for example, lower rates for children, senior discounts). Railroads vary the rate charged per ton-mile of freight according to the market value of the product being shipped. The shipper of 10 tons of television sets or refrigerators is charged more than the shipper of 10 tons of gravel or coal.

The issuance of discount coupons, redeemable at purchase, is a form of price discrimination. It enables firms to give price discounts to their most price-sensitive customers who have elastic demand. Less price-sensitive consumers who have less elastic demand are not as likely to take the time to clip and redeem coupons. The firm thus makes a larger profit than if it had used a single-price, no-coupon strategy.

Finally, price discrimination often occurs in international trade. A Russian aluminum producer, for example, might sell aluminum for less in the United States than in Russia. In the United States, this seller faces an elastic demand because several substitute suppliers are available. But in Russia, where the manufacturer dominates the market and trade barriers impede imports, consumers have fewer choices and thus demand is less elastic.

Graphical Analysis

Figure 8.4 demonstrates price discrimination graphically. The two graphs are for a single pure monopolist selling its product, say, software, in two segregated parts of the market. For example, one segment might be small-business customers and the other students. Student versions of the software are identical to the versions sold to businesses but are available (1 per person) only to customers with a student ID. Presumably, students have lower ability to pay for the software and are charged a discounted price.

The demand curve D_b, in Figure 8.4a, represents the relatively inelastic demand for the product of business customers. The demand curve D_s, in Figure 8.4b, reflects the elastic demand of students. The marginal revenue curves (MR_b and MR_s) lie below their respective demand curves, reflecting the demand–marginal revenue relationship previously described.

For visual clarity, we have assumed that average total cost (ATC) is constant. Therefore, marginal cost (MC) equals average total cost (ATC) at all quantities of output. These costs are the same for both versions of the software and therefore appear as the single straight line labeled "MC = ATC."

What price will the pure monopolist charge to each set of customers? Using the MR = MC rule for profit maximization, the firm will offer Q_b units of the software for

FIGURE 8.4 Price discrimination to different groups of buyers. The price-discriminating monopolist represented here maximizes its total profit by dividing the market into two segments based on differences in elasticity of demand. It then produces and sells the MR = MC output in each market segment. (For visual clarity, average total cost (ATC) is assumed to be constant. Therefore, MC equals ATC at all output levels.) (a) The firm charges a higher price (here, P_b) to customers who have a less elastic demand curve and (b) a lower price (here, P_s) to customers with a more elastic demand. The price discriminator's total profit is larger than it would be with no discrimination and therefore a single price.

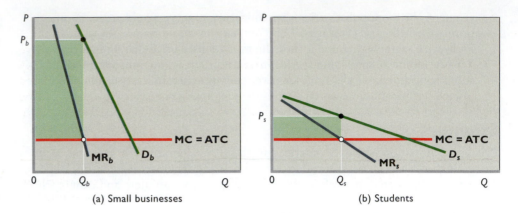

(a) Small businesses   (b) Students

WORKED PROBLEMS

W 8.2

Price discrimination

sale to small businesses. It can sell that profit-maximizing output by charging price P_b. Again using the MR = MC rule, the monopolist will offer Q_s units of software to students. To sell those Q_s units, the firm will charge students the lower price P_s.

Firms engage in price discrimination because it enhances their profit. The numbers (not shown) behind the curves in Figure 8.4 would reveal that the sum of the two profit rectangles shown in green exceeds the single profit rectangle the firm would obtain from a single monopoly price. How do consumers fare? In this case, students clearly benefit by paying a lower price than they would if the firm charged a single monopoly price; in contrast, the price discrimination results in a higher price for business customers. Therefore, compared to the single-price situation, students buy more of the software and small businesses buy less.

APPLYING THE ANALYSIS

Price Discrimination at the Ballpark

Professional baseball teams earn substantial revenues through ticket sales. To maximize profit, they offer significantly lower ticket prices for children (whose demand is elastic) than for adults (whose demand is inelastic). This discount may be as much as 50 percent.

If this type of price discrimination increases revenue and profit, why don't teams also price-discriminate at the concession stands? Why don't they offer half-price hot dogs, soft drinks, peanuts, and Cracker Jack to children? The answer involves the three requirements for successful price discrimination. All three requirements are met for game tickets: (1) The team has monopoly power; (2) it can segregate ticket buyers by age group, each group having a different elasticity of demand; and (3) children cannot resell their discounted tickets to adults.

It's a different situation at the concession stands. Specifically, the third condition is *not* met. If the team had dual prices, it could not prevent the exchange or "resale" of the concession goods from children to adults. Many adults would send children to buy food and soft drinks for them: "Here's some money, Billy. Go buy *10* hot dogs for all of us." In this case, price discrimination would reduce, not increase, team profit. Thus, children and adults are charged the same high prices at the concession stands.

QUESTION: Why are the prices for concessions at the games quite high compared to prices for the same or similar items at the local convenience store?

Monopoly and Antitrust Policy

Monopoly is a legitimate concern. Monopolists can charge higher-than-competitive prices that result in an underallocation of resources to the monopolized product. They can stifle innovation, engage in rent-seeking behavior, and foster X-inefficiency. Even when their costs are low because of economies of scale, there is no guarantee that the price they charge will reflect those low costs. The cost savings may simply accrue to the monopoly as greater economic profit.

Not Widespread

Fortunately, however, monopoly is not widespread in the United States. Barriers to entry are seldom completely successful. Although research and technological advances may strengthen the market position of a monopoly, technology may also undermine monopoly power. Over time, the creation of new technologies may work to destroy monopoly positions (creative destruction). For example, the development of courier delivery, fax machines, and e-mail has eroded the monopoly power of the U.S. Postal Service. Cable television monopolies are now challenged by satellite TV and by new technologies that permit the transmission of audio and visual signals over the Internet.

Similarly, patents eventually expire; and even before they do, the development of new and distinct substitutable products often circumvents existing patent advantages. New sources of monopolized resources sometimes are found, and competition from foreign firms may emerge. (See Global Snapshot 8.1.) Finally, if a monopoly is

GLOBAL SNAPSHOT 8.1

Competition from Foreign Multinational Corporations

Competition from foreign multinational corporations diminishes the market power of firms in the United States. Here are just a few of the hundreds of foreign multinational corporations that compete strongly with U.S. firms in certain American markets.

Company (Country)	Main Products
Bayer (Germany)	chemicals
BP Amoco (United Kingdom)	gasoline
Michelin (France)	tires
NEC (Japan)	computers
Nestlé (Switzerland)	food products
Nokia (Finland)	wireless phones
Royal Dutch/Shell (Netherlands)	gasoline
Royal Philips (Netherlands)	electronics
Sony (Japan)	electronics
Toyota (Japan)	automobiles
Unilever (Netherlands)	food products

Source: Compiled from "Global 500," *Fortune*, July 26, 2010. © Time Inc., used under license.

sufficiently fearful of future competition from new products, it may keep its prices relatively low so as to discourage rivals from developing such products. If so, consumers may pay nearly competitive prices even though competition is currently lacking.

Antitrust Policy

What should government do about monopoly when it arises and persists in the real world? Economists agree that government needs to look carefully at monopoly on a case-by-case basis. If the monopoly appears to be unsustainable over a long period of time, say, because of emerging new technology, society can simply choose to ignore it. In contrast, the government may want to file charges against a monopoly under the antitrust laws if the monopoly was achieved through anticompetitive actions, creates substantial economic inefficiency, and appears to be long-lasting. (Monopolies were once called "trusts.") The relevant antitrust law is the Sherman Act of 1890, which has two main provisions:

- *Section 1* "Every contract, combination in the form of a trust or otherwise, or conspiracy, in restraint of trade or commerce among the several States, or with foreign nations is declared to be illegal."
- *Section 2* "Every person who shall monopolize, or attempt to monopolize, or combine or conspire with any person or persons, to monopolize any part of the trade or commerce among the several States, or with foreign nations, shall be deemed guilty of a felony . . ." (as later amended from "misdemeanor").

In the 1911 Standard Oil case, the Supreme Court found Standard Oil guilty of monopolizing the petroleum industry through a series of abusive and anticompetitive actions. The Court's remedy was to divide Standard Oil into several competing firms. But the Standard Oil case left open an important question: Is every monopoly in violation of Section 2 of the Sherman Act or just those created or maintained by anticompetitive actions?

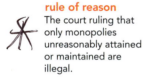

rule of reason
The court ruling that only monopolies unreasonably attained or maintained are illegal.

In the 1920 U.S. Steel case, the courts established a **rule of reason** interpretation of Section 2, saying that it is not illegal to be a monopoly. Only monopolies that "unreasonably" restrain trade violate Section 2 of the Sherman Act and are subject to antitrust action. Size alone was not an offense. Although U.S. Steel clearly possessed monopoly power, it was innocent of "monopolizing" because it had not resorted to illegal acts against competitors in obtaining that power nor had it unreasonably used its monopoly power. Unlike Standard Oil, which was a "bad trust," U.S. Steel was a "good trust" and therefore not in violation of the law. The rule of reason was attacked and once reversed by the courts, but today it is the accepted legal interpretation of the Sherman Act's monopoly provisions.

Today, the U.S. Department of Justice, the Federal Trade Commission, injured private parties, or state attorney generals can file antitrust suits against alleged violators of the Sherman Act. The courts can issue injunctions to prohibit anticompetitive practices (a behavioral remedy) or, if necessary, break up monopolists into competing firms (a structural remedy). Courts also can fine and imprison violators. Also, parties injured by monopolies can sue for *treble damages*—an award of three times the amount of the monetary injury done to them. In some cases, these damages have summed to millions or even billions of dollars.

The largest and most significant monopoly case of recent times is the Microsoft case, which is the subject of the application that follows.

United States v. Microsoft

In May 1998 the U.S. Justice Department, 19 individual states, and the District of Columbia (hereafter, "the government") filed antitrust charges against Microsoft under the Sherman Antitrust Act. The government charged that Microsoft had violated Section 2 of the act through a series of unlawful actions designed to maintain its "Windows" monopoly. It also charged that some of that conduct violated Section 1 of the Sherman Act, which prohibits actions that restrain trade or commerce.

Microsoft denied the charges, arguing it had achieved its success through product innovation and lawful business practices. Microsoft contended it should not be penalized for its superior foresight, business acumen, and technological prowess. It also insisted that its monopoly was highly transitory because of rapid technological advance.

In June 2000 the district court ruled that the relevant market was software used to operate Intel-compatible personal computers (PCs). Microsoft's 95 percent share of that market clearly gave it monopoly power. The court pointed out, however, that being a monopoly is not illegal. The violation of the Sherman Act occurred because Microsoft used anticompetitive means to maintain its monopoly power.

According to the court, Microsoft feared that the success of Netscape's Navigator, which allowed people to browse the Internet, might allow Netscape to expand its software to include a competitive PC operating system—software that would threaten the Windows monopoly. It also feared that Sun's Internet applications of its Java programming language might eventually threaten Microsoft's Windows monopoly.

To counter these and similar threats, Microsoft illegally signed contracts with PC makers that required them to feature its Internet Explorer on the PC desktop and penalized companies that promoted software products that competed with Microsoft products. Moreover, it gave friendly companies coding that linked Windows to software applications and withheld such coding from companies featuring Netscape. Finally, under license from Sun, Microsoft developed Windows-related Java software that made Sun's own software incompatible with Windows.

The district court ordered Microsoft to split into two competing companies, one initially selling the Windows operating system and the other initially selling Microsoft applications (such as Word, Hotmail, MSN, PowerPoint, and Internet Explorer). Both companies would be free to develop new products that compete with each other, and both could derive those products from the intellectual property embodied in the common products existing at the time of divestiture.

In late 2000 Microsoft appealed the district court decision to a U.S. court of appeals. In 2001 the higher court affirmed that Microsoft illegally maintained its monopoly, but tossed out the district court's decision to break up Microsoft. It agreed with Microsoft that the company was denied due process during the penalty phase of the trial and concluded that the district court judge had displayed an appearance of bias by holding extensive interviews with the press. The appeals court sent the remedial phase of the case to a new district court judge to determine appropriate remedies. The appeals court also raised issues relating to the wisdom of a structural remedy.

At the urging of the new district court judge, the federal government and Microsoft negotiated a proposed settlement. With minor modification, the settlement became the final court order in 2002. The breakup was rescinded and replaced with a behavioral remedy. It (1) prevents Microsoft from retaliating against any firm that is developing, selling, or using software that competes with Microsoft Windows or

Internet Explorer or is shipping a personal computer that includes both Windows and a non-Microsoft operating system; (2) requires Microsoft to establish uniform royalty and licensing terms for computer manufacturers wanting to include Windows on their PCs; (3) requires that manufacturers be allowed to remove Microsoft icons and replace them with other icons on the Windows desktop; and (4) calls for Microsoft to provide technical information to other companies so those firms can develop programs that work as well with Windows as Microsoft's own products.

Microsoft's actions and conviction have indirectly resulted in billions of dollars of fines and payouts by Microsoft. Main examples: To AOL Time Warner (Netscape), $750 million; to the European Commission, $600 million in 2004 and $1.35 billion in 2008; to Sun Microsystems, $1.6 billion; to Novell, $536 million; to Brust.com, $60 million; to Gateway; $150 million; to interTrust, $440 million; to RealNetworks, $761 million; and to IBM, $850 million.

QUESTION: Why is the 2002 Microsoft settlement a behavioral remedy rather than a structural remedy?

Source: *United States v. Microsoft* (District Court Conclusions of Law), April 2000; *United States v. Microsoft* (court of appeals), June 2001; *United States v. Microsoft* (Final Judgment), November 2002; and Reuters and Associated Press news services.

Summary

1. A pure monopolist is the sole producer of a good or service for which there are no close substitutes.

2. The existence of pure monopoly is explained by barriers to entry in the form of (a) economies of scale, (b) patent ownership and research, (c) ownership or control of essential resources, and (d) pricing and other strategic behavior.

3. The pure monopolist's market situation differs from that of a competitive firm in that the monopolist's demand curve is downsloping, causing the marginal-revenue curve to lie below the demand curve. Like the competitive seller, the pure monopolist will maximize profit by equating marginal revenue and marginal cost. Barriers to entry may permit a monopolist to acquire economic profit even in the long run. However, (a) the monopolist does not charge "the highest price possible"; (b) the price that yields maximum total profit to the monopolist rarely coincides with the price that yields maximum unit profit; and (c) high costs and a weak demand may prevent the monopolist from realizing any profit at all.

4. With the same costs, the pure monopolist will find it profitable to restrict output and charge a higher price than would sellers in a purely competitive industry. This restriction of output causes a misallocation of resources, as is evidenced by the fact that price exceeds marginal cost in monopolized markets.

5. Monopoly transfers income from consumers to monopolists because monopolists can charge a higher price than would a purely competitive firm with the same costs. So monopolists, in effect, levy a "private tax" on consumers and, if demand is strong enough, obtain substantial economic profits.

6. The costs monopolists and competitive producers face may not be the same. On the one hand, economies of scale may make lower unit costs available to monopolists but not to competitors. Also, pure monopoly may be more likely than pure competition to reduce costs via technological advance because of the monopolist's ability to realize economic profit, which can be used to finance research. On the other hand, X-inefficiency—the failure to produce with the least costly combination of inputs—is more common among monopolists than among competitive firms. Also, monopolists may make costly expenditures to maintain monopoly privileges that are conferred by government. Finally, the blocked entry of rival firms weakens the monopolist's incentive to be technologically progressive.

7. A firm can increase its profit through price discrimination provided it (a) has monopoly pricing power, (b) can segregate buyers on the basis of elasticities of demand, and (c) can prevent its product or service from being readily transferred between the segregated markets.

8. The cornerstone of antimonopoly law is the Sherman Act of 1890, particularly Section 2. According to the rule of reason, possession of monopoly power is not illegal. But monopoly that is unreasonably gained or unreasonably maintained is a violation of the law.

9. If a company is found guilty of violating the Sherman Act, the government can either break up the monopoly into competing firms (a structural remedy) or prohibit it from engaging in specific anticompetitive business practices (a behavioral remedy).

Terms and Concepts

pure monopoly	simultaneous consumption	rent-seeking behavior
barriers to entry	network effects	price discrimination
natural monopoly	X-inefficiency	rule of reason

Questions

1. "No firm is completely sheltered from rivals; all firms compete for consumer dollars. If that is so, then pure monopoly does not exist." Do you agree? Explain. LO1

✳ 2. Discuss the major barriers to entry into an industry. Explain how each barrier can foster either monopoly or oligopoly. Which barriers, if any, do you feel give rise to monopoly that is socially justifiable? LO1

✳ 3. How does the demand curve faced by a purely monopolistic seller differ from that confronting a purely competitive firm? Why does it differ? Of what significance is the difference? Why is the pure monopolist's demand curve typically not perfectly inelastic? LO2

4. Use the following demand schedule for a pure monopolist to calculate total revenue and marginal revenue at each quantity. Plot the monopolist's demand curve and marginal-revenue curve, and explain the relationships between them. Explain why the marginal revenue of the fourth unit of output is $3.50, even though its price is $5. What generalization can you make as to the relationship between the monopolist's demand and its marginal revenue? Suppose the marginal cost of successive units of output was zero. What output would the single-price monopolist produce, and what price would it charge? LO2

Price (P)	Quantity Demanded (Q)	Price (P)	Quantity Demanded (Q)
$7.00	0	$4.50	5
6.50	1	4.00	6
6.00	2	3.50	7
5.50	3	3.00	8
5.00	4	2.50	9

5. Assume a monopolistic publisher has agreed to pay an author 10 percent of the total revenue from the sales of a text. Will the author and the publisher want to charge the same price for the text? Explain. LO2

6. Assume that a pure monopolist and a purely competitive firm have the same unit costs. Contrast the two with respect to (a) price, (b) output, (c) profits, (d) allocation of resources, and (e) impact on the distribution of income. Since both monopolists and competitive firms follow the MR = MC rule in maximizing profits, how do you account for the different results? Why might the costs of a purely competitive firm and those of a monopolist be different? What are the implications of such a cost difference? LO3

7. Critically evaluate and explain each statement: LO3
   a. Because they can control product price, monopolists are always assured of profitable production by simply charging the highest price consumers will pay.
   b. The pure monopolist seeks the output that will yield the greatest per-unit profit.
   c. An excess of price over marginal cost is the market's way of signaling the need for more production of a good.
   d. The more profitable a firm, the greater its monopoly power.
   e. The monopolist has a pricing policy; the competitive producer does not.
   f. With respect to resource allocation, the interests of the seller and of society coincide in a purely competitive market but conflict in a monopolized market.

8. U.S. pharmaceutical companies charge different prices for prescription drugs to buyers in different nations, depending on elasticity of demand and government-imposed price ceilings. Explain why these companies, for profit reasons, oppose laws allowing reimportation of their drugs back into the United States. LO4

9. How was De Beers able to control the world price of diamonds over the past several decades even though it produced only 45 percent of the diamonds? What factors ended its monopoly? What is its new profit strategy? LO5

✳ 10. Under what law and on what basis did the federal district court find Microsoft guilty of violating the Sherman Act? What was the initial district court's remedy? How did Microsoft fare with its appeal to the court of appeals? What was the final negotiated remedy? LO5

Problems

1. Assume that the most efficient production technology available for making vitamin pills has the cost structure given in the following table. Note that output is measured as the number of bottles of vitamins produced per day and that costs include a normal profit. LO1

Output	TC	MC
25,000	$100,000	$0.50
50,000	150,000	1.00
75,000	187,500	2.50
100,000	275,500	3.00

a. What is ATC per unit for each level of output listed in the table?

b. Is this a decreasing-cost industry? (Answer yes or no).

c. Suppose that the market price for a bottle of vitamins is $2.50 and that at that price the total market quantity demanded is 75,000,000 bottles. How many firms will there be in this industry?

d. Suppose that, instead, the market quantity demanded at a price of $2.50 is only 75,000. How many firms do you expect there to be in this industry?

e. Review your answers to parts b, c, and d. Does the level of demand determine this industry's market structure?

2. A new production technology for making vitamins is invented by a college professor who decides not to patent it. Thus, it is available for anybody to copy and put into use. The TC per bottle for production up to 100,000 bottles per day is given in the following table. LO1

Output	TC
25,000	$50,000
50,000	70,000
75,000	75,000
100,000	80,000

a. What is ATC for each level of output listed in the table?

b. Suppose that for each 25,000-bottle-per-day increase in production above 100,000 bottles per day, TC increases by $5000 (so that, for instance, 125,000 bottles per day would generate total costs of $85,000 and 150,000 bottles per day would generate total costs of $90,000). Is this a decreasing-cost industry?

c. Suppose that the price of a bottle of vitamins is $1.33 and that at that price the total quantity demanded by consumers is 75,000,000 bottles. How many firms will there be in this industry?

d. Suppose that, instead, the market quantity demanded at a price of $1.33 is only 75,000. How many firms do you expect there to be in this industry?

e. Review your answers to parts b, c, and d. Does the level of demand determine this industry's market structure?

f. Compare your answer to part d of this problem with your answer to part d of problem 1. Do both production technologies show constant returns to scale?

3. Suppose a pure monopolist is faced with the demand schedule shown below and the same cost data as the competitive producer discussed in problem 4 at the end of Chapter 7. Calculate the missing total-revenue and marginal-revenue amounts, and determine the profit-maximizing price and profit-maximizing output for this monopolist. What is the monopolist's profit? Verify your answer graphically and by comparing total revenue and total cost. LO2

Price	Quantity Demanded	Total Revenue	Marginal Revenue
$115	0	$_____	
100	1	_____	$_____
83	2	_____	_____
71	3	_____	_____
63	4	_____	_____
55	5	_____	_____
48	6	_____	_____
42	7	_____	_____
37	8	_____	_____
33	9	_____	_____
29	10	_____	_____

4. Suppose that a price-discriminating monopolist has segregated its market into two groups of buyers. The first group is described by the demand and revenue data that you developed for problem 3. The demand and revenue data for the second group of buyers is shown in the table. Assume that MC is $13 in both markets and MC = ATC at all output levels. What price will the firm charge in each market? Based solely on these two prices, which market has the higher price elasticity of demand? What will be this monopolist's total economic profit? LO4

Price	Quantity Demanded	Total Revenue	Marginal Revenue
$71	0	$ 0	
63	1	63	$63
55	2	110	47
48	3	144	34
42	4	168	24
37	5	185	17
33	6	198	13
29	7	203	5

FURTHER TEST YOUR KNOWLEDGE AT
www.mcconnellbrief2e.com

At the text's Online Learning Center, **www.mcconnellbrief2e.com**, you will find one or more web-based questions that require information from the Internet to answer. We urge you to check them out, since they will familiarize you with websites that may be helpful in other courses and perhaps even in your career. The OLC also features multiple-choice quizzes that give instant feedback and provides other helpful ways to further test your knowledge of the chapter.

Visit your mobile app store and download the McConnell Brief Edition: Study Econ app *today*!

Monopolistic Competition and Oligopoly

In the United States, most industries have a market structure that falls somewhere between the two poles of pure competition (Chapter 7) and pure monopoly (Chapter 8). To begin with, most real-world industries usually have fewer than the large number of producers required for pure competition but more than the single producer that defines pure monopoly. In addition, most firms in most industries have both distinguishable rather than standardized products as well as some discretion over the prices they charge. As a result, competition often occurs on the basis of price, quality, location, service, and advertising. Finally, entry to most real-world industries ranges from easy to very difficult but is rarely completely blocked.

This chapter examines two models that more closely approximate these widespread industry structures. You will discover that *monopolistic competition* mixes a small amount of monopoly power with a large amount of competition. *Oligopoly,* in contrast, blends a large amount of monopoly power with both considerable rivalry among existing firms and the threat of increased future competition due to foreign firms and new technologies.

Monopolistic Competition

Let's begin by examining **monopolistic competition,** which is characterized by (1) a relatively large number of sellers, (2) differentiated products (often promoted by heavy advertising), and (3) easy entry into, and exit from, the industry. The first and third characteristics provide the "competitive" aspect of monopolistic competition; the second characteristic provides the "monopolistic" aspect. In general, however, monopolistically competitive industries are much more competitive than they are monopolistic.

no collusion

monopolistic competition
A market structure in which many firms sell a differentiated product and entry into and exit from the market are relatively easy.

Relatively Large Number of Sellers

Monopolistic competition is characterized by a fairly large number of firms, say, 25, 35, 60, or 70, not by the hundreds or thousands of firms in pure competition. Consequently, monopolistic competition involves:

- ***Small market shares*** Each firm has a comparatively small percentage of the total market and consequently has limited control over market price. *large # of sellers Price taker*

© Robert Landau/CORBIS

© Royalty-Free/CORBIS

PHOTO OP Monopolistic Competition versus Oligopoly

Furniture is produced in a monopolistically competitive industry, whereas refrigerators are produced in an oligopolistic industry.

- *No collusion*   The presence of a relatively large number of firms ensures that collusion by a group of firms to restrict output and set prices is unlikely.
- *Independent action*   With numerous firms in an industry, there is no feeling of interdependence among them; each firm can determine its own pricing policy without considering the possible reactions of rival firms. A single firm may realize a modest increase in sales by cutting its price, but the effect of that action on competitors' sales will be nearly imperceptible and will probably trigger no response.

Differentiated Products

product differentiation
A form of nonprice competition in which a firm tries to distinguish its product or service from all competing ones on the basis of attributes such as design and quality.

In contrast to pure competition, in which there is a standardized product, monopolistic competition is distinguished by **product differentiation**. Monopolistically competitive firms turn out variations of a particular product. They produce products with slightly different physical characteristics, offer varying degrees of customer service, provide varying amounts of locational convenience, or proclaim special qualities, real or imagined, for their products.

These aspects of product differentiation require more attention.

Product Attributes   Product differentiation may entail physical or qualitative differences in the products themselves. Real differences in functional features, materials, design, and workmanship are vital aspects of product differentiation. Personal computers, for example, differ in terms of storage capacity, speed, graphic displays, and included software. There are dozens of competing principles of economics textbooks that differ in content, organization, presentation and readability, pedagogical aids, and graphics and design. Most cities have a variety of retail stores selling men's and women's clothes that differ greatly in styling, materials, and quality of work. Similarly, one pizza place may feature its thin crust Neapolitan style pizza, while another may tout its thick-crust Chicago-style pizza.

Service   Service and the conditions surrounding the sale of a product are forms of product differentiation too. One shoe store may stress the fashion knowledge and helpfulness of its clerks. A competitor may leave trying on shoes and carrying them to the register to its customers but feature lower prices. Customers may prefer 1-day over 3-day dry cleaning of equal quality. The prestige appeal of a store, the courteousness and helpfulness of clerks, the firm's reputation for servicing or exchanging its products, and the credit it makes available are all service aspects of product differentiation.

Location   Products may also be differentiated through the location and accessibility of the stores that sell them. Small convenience stores manage to compete with large supermarkets, even though these minimarts have a more limited range of products and charge higher prices. They compete mainly on the basis of location—being close to customers and situated on busy streets. A motel's proximity to an interstate highway gives it a locational advantage that may enable it to charge a higher room rate than nearby motels in less convenient locations.

Brand Names and Packaging   Product differentiation may also be created through the use of brand names and trademarks, packaging, and celebrity connections. Most aspirin tablets are very much alike, but many headache sufferers believe that one brand—for example, Bayer, Anacin, or Bufferin—is superior and worth a higher price than a generic substitute. A celebrity's name associated with watches, perfume, or athletic apparel may enhance the appeal of those products for some buyers. Many customers prefer one style of ballpoint pen to another. Packaging that touts "natural spring" bottled water may attract additional customers.

Some Control over Price Despite the relatively large number of firms, monopolistic competitors do have some control over their product prices because of product differentiation. If consumers prefer the products of specific sellers, then within limits they will pay more to satisfy their preferences. Sellers and buyers are not linked randomly, as in a purely competitive market. But the monopolistic competitor's control over price is quite limited since there are numerous potential substitutes for its product.

Easy Entry and Exit

Entry into monopolistically competitive industries is relatively easy compared to oligopoly or pure monopoly. Because monopolistic competitors are typically small firms, both absolutely and relatively, economies of scale are few and capital requirements are low. On the other hand, compared with pure competition, financial barriers may result from the need to develop and advertise a product that differs from rivals' products. Some firms may have trade secrets relating to their products or hold trademarks on their brand names, making it difficult and costly for other firms to imitate them.

Exit from monopolistically competitive industries is relatively easy. Nothing prevents an unprofitable monopolistic competitor from holding a going-out-of-business sale and shutting down.

Advertising

The expense and effort involved in product differentiation would be wasted if consumers were not made aware of product differences. Thus, monopolistic competitors advertise their products, often heavily. The goal of product differentiation and advertising—so-called **nonprice competition**—is to make price less of a factor in consumer purchases and make product differences a greater factor. If successful, the demand for the firm's product will increase. The firm's demand may also become less elastic because of the greater loyalty to the firm's product.

nonprice competition
A selling strategy in which one firm tries to distinguish its product or service from all competing ones on the basis of attributes other than price.

Monopolistically Competitive Industries

Several manufacturing industries approximate monopolistic competition. Examples of manufactured goods produced in monopolistically competitive industries are jewelry, asphalt, wood pallets, commercial signs, leather goods, plastic pipes, textile bags, and kitchen cabinets. In addition, many retail establishments in metropolitan areas are monopolistically competitive, including grocery stores, gasoline stations, hair salons, dry cleaners, clothing stores, and restaurants. Also, many providers of professional services such as medical care, legal assistance, real estate sales, and basic bookkeeping are monopolistic competitors.

Price and Output in Monopolistic Competition

How does a monopolistically competitive firm decide what quantity to produce and what price to charge? Initially, we assume that each firm in the industry is producing a specific differentiated product and engaging in a particular amount of advertising. Later we'll see how changes in the product and in the amount of advertising modify our conclusions.

The Firm's Demand Curve

Our explanation is based on Figure 9.1, which shows that the demand curve faced by a monopolistically competitive seller is highly, but not perfectly, elastic. It is precisely this feature that distinguishes monopolistic competition from both pure monopoly and pure competition. The monopolistic competitor's demand is more elastic than the demand faced by a pure monopolist because the monopolistically competitive seller has many competitors producing closely substitutable goods. The pure monopolist has no rivals at all. Yet, for two reasons, the monopolistic competitor's demand is not perfectly elastic like that of the pure competitor. First, the monopolistic competitor has fewer rivals; second, its products are differentiated, so they are not perfect substitutes.

The price elasticity of demand faced by the monopolistically competitive firm depends on the number of rivals and the degree of product differentiation. The larger the number of rivals and the weaker the product differentiation, the greater the price elasticity of each seller's demand, that is, the closer monopolistic competition will be to pure competition.

FIGURE 9.1 **A monopolistically competitive firm: short run and long run.** The monopolistic competitor maximizes profit or minimizes loss by producing the output at which MR = MC. The economic profit shown in (a) will induce new firms to enter, eventually eliminating economic profit. The loss shown in (b) will cause an exit of firms until normal profit is restored. After such entry and exit, the price will settle in (c) to where it just equals average total cost at the MR = MC output. At this price P_3 and output Q_3, the monopolistic competitor earns only a normal profit, and the industry is in long-run equilibrium.

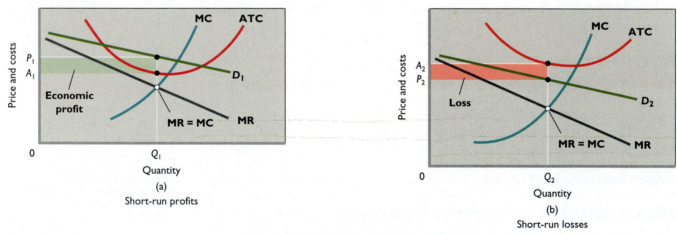

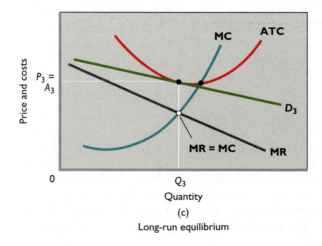

The Short Run: Profit or Loss

In the short run, monopolistically competitive firms maximize profit or minimize loss using exactly the same strategy as pure competitors and monopolists: They produce the level of output at which marginal revenue equals marginal cost (MR = MC). Thus, the monopolistically competitive firm in Figure 9.1a produces output Q_1, where MR = MC. As shown by demand curve D_1, it then can charge price P_1. It realizes an economic profit, shown by the green area [= $(P_1 - A_1) \times Q_1$].

[handwritten: May profit, minimize loss Produce at level MR = MC]

But with less favorable demand or costs, the firm may incur a loss in the short run. We show this possibility in Figure 9.1b, where the firm's best strategy is to minimize its loss. It does so by producing output Q_2 (where MR = MC) and, as determined by demand curve D_2, by charging price P_2. Because price P_2 is less than average total cost A_2, the firm incurs a per-unit loss of $A_2 - P_2$ and a total loss represented as the red area [= $(A_2 - P_2) \times Q_2$].

The Long Run: Only a Normal Profit

In the long run, firms will enter a profitable monopolistically competitive industry and leave an unprofitable one. So a monopolistic competitor will earn only a normal profit in the long run or, in other words, will only break even. (Remember that the cost curves include both explicit and implicit costs, including a normal profit.)

Profits: Firms Enter In the case of short-run profit (Figure 9.1a), economic profits attract new rivals because entry to the industry is relatively easy. As new firms enter, the demand curve faced by the typical firm shifts to the left (falls). Why? Because each firm has a smaller share of total demand and now faces a larger number of close-substitute products. This decline in the firm's demand reduces its economic profit. When entry of new firms has reduced demand to the extent that the demand curve is tangent to the average-total-cost curve at the profit-maximizing output, the firm is just making a normal profit. This situation is shown in Figure 9.1c, where demand is D_3 and the firm's long-run equilibrium output is Q_3. As Figure 9.1c indicates, any greater or lesser output will entail an average total cost that exceeds product price P_3, meaning a loss for the firm. At the tangency point between the demand curve and ATC, total revenue equals total costs. With the economic profit gone, there is no further incentive for additional firms to enter.

Losses: Firms Leave When the industry suffers short-run losses, as in Figure 9.1b, some firms will exit in the long run. Faced with fewer substitute products and blessed with an expanded share of total demand, the surviving firms will see their demand curves shift to the right (rise), as to D_3. Their losses will disappear and give way to normal profits (Figure 9.1c). (For simplicity we have assumed a constant-cost industry; shifts in the cost curves as firms enter or leave would complicate our discussion slightly but would not alter our conclusions.)

INTERACTIVE GRAPHS

G 9.1

Monopolistic competition

Monopolistic Competition and Efficiency

We know from Chapter 7 that economic efficiency requires each firm to produce the amount of output at which P = MC = minimum ATC. The equality of P and ATC yields *productive efficiency*. The good is being produced in the least costly way, and the price is just sufficient to cover average total cost, including a normal profit. The equality of P and MC yields *allocative efficiency*. The right amount of output is being produced, and thus the right amount of society's scarce resources is being devoted to this specific use.

How efficient is monopolistic competition, as measured against this triple equality? In particular, do monopolistically competitive firms produce the efficient output level associated with P = MC = minimum ATC?

FIGURE 9.2 The inefficiency of monopolistic competition. In long-run equilibrium a monopolistic competitor achieves neither productive nor allocative efficiency. Productive efficiency is not realized because production occurs where the average total cost A_3 exceeds the minimum average total cost A_4. Allocative efficiency is not achieved because the product price P_3 exceeds the marginal cost M_3. The results are an underallocation of resources as well as an efficiency loss and excess production capacity at every firm in the industry. This firm's efficiency loss is area acd and its excess production capacity is $Q_4 - Q_3$.

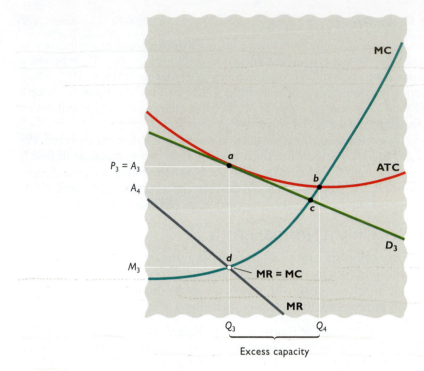

Neither Productive nor Allocative Efficiency

In monopolistic competition, neither productive nor allocative efficiency occurs in long-run equilibrium. Figure 9.2 enlarges part of Figure 9.1c and clearly shows this. First note that the profit-maximizing price P_3 slightly exceeds the lowest average total cost, A_4. In producing the profit-maximizing output Q_3, the firm's average total cost therefore is slightly higher than optimal from society's perspective—productive efficiency is not achieved. Also note that the profit-maximizing price P_3 exceeds marginal cost (here M_3), meaning that monopolistic competition causes an underallocation of resources. To measure the size of this inefficiency, note that the allocatively optimal amount of output is determined by point c, where demand curve D intersects the MC curve. So for all units between Q_3 and the level of output associated with point c, marginal benefits exceed marginal costs. Consequently, by producing only Q_3 units, this monopolistic competitor creates an efficiency loss (deadweight loss) equal in size to area acd. The total efficiency loss for the industry as a whole will be the sum of the individual efficiency losses generated by each of the firms in the industry.

Excess Capacity

excess capacity
Plant or equipment that is underused because the firm is producing less than the minimum-ATC output.

In monopolistic competition, the gap between the minimum-ATC output and the profit-maximizing output identifies **excess capacity:** plant and equipment that are underused because firms are producing less than the minimum-ATC output. This gap is shown as the distance between Q_4 and Q_3 in Figure 9.2. Note in the figure that the minimum ATC is at point b. If each monopolistic competitor could profitably produce at this point on its ATC curve, the lower average total cost would enable a lower price than P_3. More importantly, if each firm produced at b rather than at a, fewer firms would be needed to produce the industry output. But because monopolistically competitive firms produce at a in long-run equilibrium, monopolistically competitive industries are overpopulated with firms, each operating below its optimal capacity. This situation is typified by many kinds of retail establishments. For example, in most cities there is an abundance of small motels and restaurants that operate well below half capacity.

Product Variety and Improvement

But monopolistic competition also has two notable virtues. It promotes product variety and product improvement. A monopolistic competitor is rarely satisfied with the situation portrayed in Figure 9.1c because it means only a normal profit. Instead, it may try to regain its economic profit through further product differentiation and better advertising. By developing or improving its product, it may be able to re-create, at least for a while, the profit outcome of Figure 9.1a.

The product variety and product improvement that accompany the drive to regain economic profit in monopolistic competition are benefits for society—ones that may offset the cost of the inefficiency associated with monopolistic competition. Consumers have a wide diversity of tastes: Some people like Italian salad dressing, others prefer French dressing; some people like contemporary furniture, others prefer traditional furniture. If a product is differentiated, then at any time the consumer will be offered a wide range of types, styles, brands, and quality gradations of that product. Compared with pure competition, this provides an advantage to the consumer. The range of choice is widened, and producers more fully meet the wide variation in consumer tastes.

The product improvement promoted by monopolistic competition further differentiates products and expands choices. And a successful product improvement by one firm obligates rivals to imitate or improve on that firm's temporary market advantage or else lose business. So society benefits from new and improved products.

Oligopoly

In terms of competitiveness, the spectrum of market structures reaches from pure competition, to monopolistic competition, to oligopoly, to pure monopoly. We now direct our attention to **oligopoly**, a market dominated by a few large producers of a homogeneous or differentiated product. Because of their "fewness," oligopolists have considerable control over their prices, but each must consider the possible reaction of rivals to its own pricing, output, and advertising decisions.

Auto Industry!

oligopoly
A market structure dominated by a few large producers of homogeneous or differentiated products.

A Few Large Producers

The phrase "a few large producers" is necessarily vague because the market model of oligopoly covers much ground, ranging between pure monopoly, on the one hand, and monopolistic competition, on the other. Oligopoly encompasses the U.S. aluminum industry, in which three huge firms dominate an entire national market, and the situation in which four or five much smaller auto-parts stores enjoy roughly equal shares of the market in a medium-size town. Generally, however, when you hear a term such as "Big Three," "Big Four," or "Big Six," you can be sure it refers to an oligopolistic industry. Examples of U.S. industries that are oligopolies are tires, beer, cigarettes, copper, greeting cards, lightbulbs, aircraft, motor vehicles, gypsum products, and breakfast cereals. There are numerous others.

homogeneous oligopoly   *Standardized*
An oligopoly in which the firms produce a standardized product.

differentiated oligopoly
An oligopoly in which the firms produce a differentiated product.   *Differentiated*

Either Homogeneous or Differentiated Products

An oligopoly may be either a **homogeneous oligopoly** or a **differentiated oligopoly**, depending on whether the firms in the oligopoly produce standardized (homogeneous) or differentiated products. Many industrial products (steel, zinc, copper, aluminum, lead, cement, industrial alcohol) are virtually standardized products that are produced in oligopolies. Alternatively, many consumer goods industries (automobiles, tires, household appliances, electronic equipment, breakfast cereals, cigarettes, and many sporting goods) are differentiated oligopolies. These differentiated oligopolies typically engage in considerable nonprice competition supported by heavy advertising.

Control over Price, but Mutual Interdependence

strategic behavior
Self-interested behavior that takes into account the reactions of others.

mutual interdependence
A situation in which a change in strategy (usually price) by one firm will affect the sales and profits of other firms.

Because firms are few in oligopolistic industries, each firm is a "price maker"; like the monopolist, it can set its price and output levels to maximize its profit. But unlike the monopolist, which has no rivals, the oligopolist must consider how its rivals will react to any change in its price, output, product characteristics, or advertising. Oligopoly is thus characterized by *strategic behavior* and *mutual interdependence*. By **strategic behavior**, we simply mean self-interested behavior that takes into account the reactions of others. Firms develop and implement price, quality, location, service, and advertising strategies to "grow their business" and expand their profits. But because rivals are few, there is **mutual interdependence:** a situation in which each firm's profit depends not just on its own price and sales strategies but also on those of the other firms in its highly concentrated industry. So oligopolistic firms base their decisions on how they think rivals will react. Example: In deciding whether to increase the price of its cosmetics, L'Oreal will try to predict the response of the other major producers, such as Clinique. Second example: In deciding on its advertising strategy, Burger King will take into consideration how McDonald's might react.

ILLUSTRATING THE IDEA

Creative Strategic Behavior

The following story, offered with tongue in cheek, illustrates a localized market that exhibits some characteristics of oligopoly, including strategic behavior.

Tracy Martinez's Native American Arts and Crafts store is located in the center of a small tourist town that borders on a national park. In its early days, Tracy had a minimonopoly. Business was brisk, and prices and profits were high.

To Tracy's annoyance, two "copycat" shops opened adjacent to her store, one on either side of her shop. Worse yet, the competitors named their shops to take advantage of Tracy's advertising. One was "Native Arts and Crafts"; the other, "Indian Arts and Crafts." These new sellers drew business away from Tracy's store, forcing her to lower her prices. The three side-by-side stores in the small, isolated town constituted a localized oligopoly for Native American arts and crafts.

Tracy began to think strategically about ways to boost profit. She decided to distinguish her shop from those on either side by offering a greater mix of high-quality, expensive products and a lesser mix of inexpensive souvenir items. The tactic worked for a while, but the other stores eventually imitated her product mix.

Then, one of the competitors next door escalated the rivalry by hanging up a large sign proclaiming "We Sell for Less!" Shortly thereafter, the other shop put up a large sign stating "We Won't Be Undersold!"

Not to be outdone, Tracy painted a colorful sign of her own and hung it above her door. It read "Main Entrance."

QUESTION: How do you think the two rivals will react to Tracy's strategy?

Entry Barriers

The same barriers to entry that create pure monopoly also contribute to the creation of oligopoly. Economies of scale are important entry barriers in a number of oligopolistic industries, such as the aircraft, rubber, and copper industries. In those industries, three or four firms might each have sufficient sales to achieve economies of scale, but new firms would have such a small market share that they could not do so. They would then be high-cost producers, and as such they could not survive. A closely related barrier is the large expenditure for capital—the cost of obtaining necessary plant and equipment—required for entering certain industries. The jet engine, automobile, commercial aircraft, and petroleum-refining industries, for example, are all characterized by very high capital requirements.

The ownership and control of raw materials help explain why oligopoly exists in many mining industries, including gold, silver, and copper. In the computer, chemicals, consumer electronics, and pharmaceutical industries, patents have served as entry barriers. Moreover, oligopolists can sometimes preclude the entry of new competitors through preemptive and retaliatory pricing and advertising strategies.

Mergers

Some oligopolies have emerged mainly through the growth of the dominant firms in a given industry (examples: breakfast cereals, chewing gum, candy bars). But for other industries the route to oligopoly has been through mergers (examples: steel, in its early history; and, more recently, airlines, banking, and entertainment). Section 7 of the Clayton Act (1914) outlaws mergers that *substantially* lessen competition. But the implied "rule of reason" leaves room for considerable interpretation. As a result, many mergers between firms in the same industry go unchallenged by government.

The combining of two or more firms in the same industry may significantly increase their market share, which may allow the new firm to achieve greater economies of scale. The merger also may increase the firm's monopoly power (pricing power) through greater control over market supply. Finally, because the new firm is a larger buyer of inputs, it may be able to obtain lower prices (costs) on its production inputs.

Oligopoly Behavior: A Game-Theory Overview

Oligopoly pricing behavior has the characteristics of certain games of strategy, such as poker, chess, and bridge. The best way to play such a game depends on the way one's opponent plays. Players (and oligopolists) must pattern their actions according to the actions and expected reactions of rivals. The study of how people or firms behave in strategic situations is called **game theory.**

game theory
The study of how people or firms behave in strategic situations.

ILLUSTRATING THE IDEA

The Prisoner's Dilemma

Games come in different forms, with many possible strategies and outcomes, and have numerous business, political, and personal applications. One frequently observed type of game is known as a *prisoner's dilemma game* because it is similar to a situation in which two people—let's call them Betty and Al—have committed a diamond heist and are being detained by the police as prime suspects. Unknown to the two, the evidence against them is weak so that the best hope that the police have for getting a conviction is if one or both of the thieves confess to the crime. The police place Betty and Al in separate holding cells and offer each the same deal: Confess to the crime and receive a lighter prison sentence.

Each detainee therefore faces a dilemma. If Betty remains silent and Al confesses, Betty will end up with a long prison sentence. If Betty confesses and Al says nothing, Al will receive a long prison sentence. What happens? Fearful that the other person will confess, both confess, even though they each would be better off saying nothing. In business, a form of the "confess–confess outcome" can occur when two oligopolists escalate their advertising budgets to high levels, even though both would earn higher profits at agreed-upon lower levels. In politics, it occurs when two candidates engage in negative advertising, despite claiming that, in principle, they are opposed to its use.

QUESTION: How might the prisoners' strategies or decisions be affected if the general prison population tends to punish those who are known to "rat out" (confess against) their partners?

Now let's look at a more detailed prisoner's dilemma game, using the tools of game theory to analyze the pricing behavior of oligopolists. We assume that a duopoly, or two-firm oligopoly, is producing athletic shoes. Each of the two firms—for example, RareAir and Uptown—has a choice of two pricing strategies: price high or price low. The profit each firm earns will depend on the strategy it chooses *and* the strategy its rival chooses.

There are four possible combinations of strategies for the two firms, and a lettered cell in Figure 9.3 represents each combination. For example, cell C represents a low-price strategy for Uptown along with a high-price strategy for RareAir. Figure 9.3 is called a *payoff matrix* because each cell shows the payoff (profit) to each firm that would result from each combination of strategies. Cell C shows that if Uptown adopts a low-price strategy and RareAir a high-price strategy, then Uptown will earn $15 million (yellow portion) and RareAir will earn $6 million (blue portion).

ORIGIN OF THE IDEA

O 9.2
Game theory

FIGURE 9.3 Profit payoff (in millions) for a two-firm oligopoly. Each firm has two possible pricing strategies. RareAir's strategies are shown in the top margin, and Uptown's in the left margin. Each lettered cell of this four-cell payoff matrix represents one combination of a RareAir strategy and an Uptown strategy and shows the profit that combination would earn for each firm. Assuming no collusion, the outcome of this game is cell D, with both parties using low-price strategies and earning $8 million of profits.

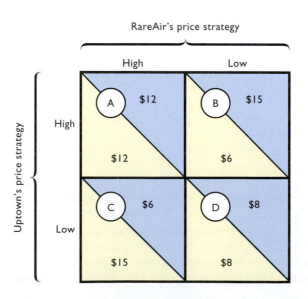

Mutual Interdependence Revisited

The data in Figure 9.3 are hypothetical, but their relationships are typical of real situations. Recall that oligopolistic firms can increase their profits, and influence their rivals' profits, by changing their pricing strategies. Each firm's profit depends on its own pricing strategy and that of its rivals. This mutual interdependence of oligopolists is the most obvious point demonstrated by Figure 9.3. If Uptown adopts a high-price strategy, its profit will be $12 million provided that RareAir also employs a high-price strategy (cell A). But if RareAir uses a low-price strategy against Uptown's high-price strategy (cell B), RareAir will increase its market share and boost its profit from $12 million to $15 million. RareAir's higher profit will come at the expense of Uptown, whose profit will fall from $12 million to $6 million. Uptown's high-price strategy is a good strategy only if RareAir also employs a high-price strategy.

Collusion

Figure 9.3 also suggests that oligopolists often can benefit from **collusion**—that is, cooperation with rivals. Collusion occurs whenever firms in an industry reach an agreement to fix prices, divide up the market, or otherwise restrict competition among them. To see the benefits of collusion, first suppose that both firms in Figure 9.3 are acting independently and following high-price strategies. Each realizes a $12 million profit (cell A).

Note that either RareAir or Uptown could increase its profit by switching to a low-price strategy (cell B or C). The low-price firm would increase its profit to $15 million, and the profit of the high-price firm would fall to $6 million. The high-price firm would be better off if it, too, adopted a low-price policy because its profit would rise from $6 million to $8 million (cell D). The effect of all this independent strategy shifting would be the reduction of both firms' profits from $12 million (cell A) to $8 million (cell D).

In real situations, too, independent action by oligopolists may lead to mutually "competitive" low-price strategies: Independent oligopolists compete with respect to price, and this leads to lower prices and lower profits. This outcome is clearly beneficial to consumers but not to the oligopolists, whose profits decrease.

How could oligopolists avoid the low-profit outcome of cell D? The answer is that they could collude, rather than establish prices competitively or independently. In our example, the two firms could agree to establish and maintain a high-price policy. So each firm will increase its profit from $8 million (cell D) to $12 million (cell A).

Incentive to Cheat

The payoff matrix also explains why an oligopolist might be strongly tempted to cheat on a collusive agreement. Suppose Uptown and RareAir agree to maintain high-price policies, with each earning $12 million in profit (cell A). Both are tempted to cheat on this collusive pricing agreement because either firm can increase its profit to $15 million by lowering its price. For instance, if Uptown secretly cheats and sells at the low price while RareAir keeps on charging the high price, the payoff would move from cell A to cell C so that Uptown's profit would rise to $15 million while RareAir's profit would fall to $6 million. On the other hand, if RareAir cheats and sets a low price while Uptown keeps the agreement and charges the high price, the payoff matrix would move from cell A to cell B so that RareAir would get $15 million while Uptown would get only $6 million. As you can see, cheating is both very lucrative to the cheater as well as very costly to the firm that gets cheated on. As a result, both firms will probably cheat so that the game will settle back to cell D, with each firm using its low-price strategy. This is another example of the prisoner's dilemma illustrated previously.

collusion
A situation in which firms act together and in agreement to fix prices, divide markets, or otherwise restrict competition.

INTERACTIVE GRAPHS

G 9.2

Game theory

Kinked-Demand Model

Our game-theory discussion is helpful in understanding more traditional, graphical oligopoly models. We begin by examining a model in which rivals do not overtly collude to fix a common price. Such collusion is, in fact, illegal in the United States. Specifically, Section 1 of the Sherman Act of 1890 outlaws conspiracies to restrain trade. In antitrust law, these violations are known as **per se violations;** they are "in and of themselves" illegal, and therefore not subject to the rule of reason (Chapter 8). To gain a conviction, the government needs to show only that there was a conspiracy to fix prices, rig bids, or divide up markets, not that the conspiracy succeeded or caused serious damage to other parties.

Kinked-Demand Curve

Imagine an oligopolistic industry made up of three law-abiding firms (Arch, King, and Dave's), each having about one-third of the total market for a differentiated product. The question is, "What does each firm's demand curve look like?"

Let's focus on Arch, understanding that the analysis is applicable to each firm. Assume that the going price for the product is P_0 and Arch is currently selling output Q_0, as shown in Figure 9.4. Suppose Arch is considering a price increase. But if Arch raises its price above P_0 and its rivals ignore the price increase, Arch will lose sales significantly to its two rivals, who will be underpricing it. If that is the case, the demand and marginal-revenue curves faced by Arch will resemble the straight lines D_2 and MR_2 in Figure 9.4. Demand in this case is quite elastic: Arch's total revenue will fall. Because of product differentiation, however, Arch's sales and total revenue will not fall to zero when it raises its price; some of Arch's customers will pay the higher price because they have a strong preference for Arch's product.

And what about a price cut? It is reasonable to expect that King and Dave's will exactly match any price cut to prevent Arch from gaining an advantage over them. Arch's sales will increase only modestly. The small increase in sales that Arch (and its

per se violation
A collusive action, such as an attempt to fix prices or divide a market, that violates the antitrust laws, even if the action is unsuccessful.

FIGURE 9.4 **The kinked-demand curve.** In all likelihood an oligopolist's rivals will ignore a price increase above the going price P_0 but follow a price cut below P_0. This causes the oligopolist's demand curve (D_2eD_1) to be kinked at e (price P_0) and the marginal-revenue curve to have a vertical break, or gap (fg). The firm will be highly reluctant to raise or lower its price. Moreover, any shift in marginal costs between MC_1 and MC_2 will cut the vertical (dashed) segment of the marginal-revenue curve and produce no change in price P_0 or output Q_0.

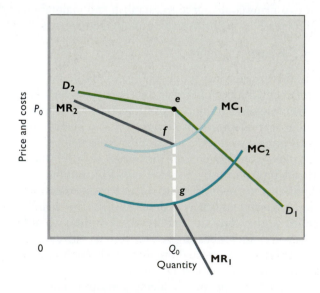

two rivals) will realize is at the expense of other industries; Arch will gain no sales from King and Dave's. So Arch's demand and marginal-revenue curves below price P_0 will look like the straight lines labeled D_1 and MR_1 in Figure 9.4.

Graphically, the D_2e "rivals ignore" segment of Arch's demand curve seems relevant for price increases, and the D_1e "rivals match" segment of demand seems relevant for price cuts. It is logical, then, or at least a reasonable assumption, that the noncollusive oligopolist faces the **kinked-demand curve** D_2eD_1, as shown in Figure 9.4. Demand is highly elastic above the going price P_0 but much less elastic or even inelastic below that price.

Note also that if rivals ignore a price increase but match a price decrease, the marginal-revenue curve of the oligopolist also will have an odd shape. It, too, will be made up of two segments: the left-hand marginal-revenue curve MR_2f in Figure 9.4 and the right-hand marginal-revenue curve MR_1g. Because of the sharp difference in elasticity of demand above and below the going price, there is a gap, or what we can simply treat as a vertical segment, in the marginal-revenue curve. This gap is the dashed segment fg in the combined marginal-revenue curve MR_2fgMR_1.

Price Inflexibility

This analysis helps explain why prices are generally stable in noncollusive oligopolistic industries. There are both demand and cost reasons.

On the demand side, the kinked-demand curve gives each oligopolist reason to believe that any change in price will be for the worse. If it raises its price, many of its customers will desert it. If it lowers its price, its sales will increase very modestly since rivals will match the lower price. Even if a price cut increases the oligopolist's total revenue somewhat, its costs may increase by a greater amount, depending on the price elasticity of demand. For instance, if its demand is inelastic to the right of Q_0, as it may well be, then the firm's profit will surely fall. Its total revenue will decline at the same time that the production of a larger output increases its total cost.

On the cost side, the broken marginal-revenue curve suggests that even if an oligopolist's costs change substantially, the firm may have no reason to change its price. In particular, all positions of the marginal-cost curve between MC_1 and MC_2 in Figure 9.4 will result in the firm's deciding on exactly the same price and output. For all those positions, MR equals MC at output Q_0; at that output, it will charge price P_0.

Price Leadership

The uncertainties of the reactions of rivals create a major problem for oligopolists. There are times when wages and other input prices rise beyond the marginal costs associated with MC_1 in Figure 9.4. If no oligopolist dare raise its price, profits for all rivals will be severely squeezed. In many industries, a pattern of price leadership has emerged to handle these situations. **Price leadership** involves an implicit understanding by which oligopolists can coordinate prices without engaging in outright collusion based on formal agreements and secret meetings. Rather, a practice evolves whereby the "dominant firm"—usually the largest or most efficient in the industry—initiates price changes and all other firms more or less automatically follow the leader. Many industries, including farm machinery, cement, copper, newsprint, glass containers, steel, beer, fertilizer, cigarettes, and tin, practice, or have in the recent past practiced, price leadership.

kinked-demand curve
A demand curve based on the assumption that rivals will ignore a price increase and follow a price decrease.

price leadership
An implicit understanding that other firms will follow the lead when a certain firm in the industry initiates a price change.

An examination of price leadership in a variety of industries suggests that the price leader is likely to observe the following tactics.

- *Infrequent price changes*   Because price changes always carry the risk that rivals will not follow the lead, price adjustments are made only infrequently. The price leader does not respond to minuscule day-to-day changes in costs and demand. Price is changed only when cost and demand conditions have been altered significantly and on an industry basis as the result of, for example, industry wage increases, an increase in excise taxes, or an increase in the price of some basic input such as energy. In the automobile industry, price adjustments traditionally have been made when new models are introduced each fall.
- *Communications*   The price leader often communicates impending price adjustments to the industry through speeches by major executives, trade publication interviews, or press releases. By publicizing "the need to raise prices," the price leader seeks agreement among its competitors regarding the actual increase.
- *Avoidance of price wars*   Price leaders try to prevent price wars that can damage industry profits. Such wars can lead to successive rounds of price cuts as rivals attempt to maintain their market shares.

APPLYING THE ANALYSIS

Challenges to Price Leadership

Despite attempts to maintain orderly price leadership, price wars occasionally break out in oligopolistic industries. Sometimes price wars result from attempts to establish new price leaders; other times, they result from attempts to "steal" business from rivals.

Consider the breakfast cereal industry, in which Kellogg traditionally had been the price leader. General Mills countered Kellogg's leadership in 1995 by reducing the prices of its cereals by 11 percent. In 1996, another rival, Post, responded to General Mills' action with a 20 percent price cut. Kellogg then followed with a 20 percent cut of its own. Not to be outdone, Post reduced its prices by another 11 percent. In short, a full-scale price war broke out between General Mills, Post, and Kellogg.

As another example, in October 2009 with the Christmas shopping season just getting underway, Walmart cut its price on 10 highly anticipated new books to just $10 each. Within hours, Amazon.com matched the price cut. Walmart then retaliated by cutting its price for the books to just $9 each. Amazon.com matched that reduction—at which point Walmart went to $8.99! Then, out of nowhere, Target jumped in at $8.98, a price that Amazon.com and Walmart immediately matched. And that is where the price finally came to rest—at a level so low that each company was losing money on each book it sold.

Most price wars eventually run their course. After a period of low or negative profits, they again yield price leadership to one of the industry's dominant firms. That firm then begins to raise prices back to their previous levels, and the other firms willingly follow. Orderly pricing is then restored.

QUESTION: How might a low-cost price leader "enforce" its leadership through implied threats to rivals?

Collusion

The disadvantages and uncertainties of kinked-demand oligopolies and price leader-ship make collusion tempting. By controlling price through collusion, oligopolists may be able to reduce uncertainty, increase profits, and perhaps even prohibit the entry of new rivals. Collusion may assume a variety of forms. The most comprehen-sive form is the **cartel,** a group of producers that typically creates a formal written agreement specifying how much each member will produce and charge. The cartel members must control output—divide up the market—in order to maintain the agreed-upon price. The collusion is *overt,* or open to view, and typically involves a group of foreign nations or foreign producers. More common forms of collusion are *covert,* or hidden from view. They include conspiracies to fix prices, rig bids, and divide up markets. Such conspiracies sometimes occur even though they are illegal.

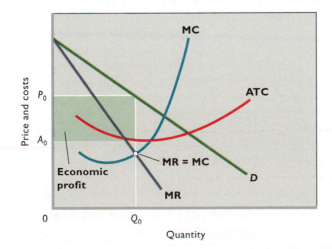

cartel
A formal agreement among producers to set the price and the individual firm's output levels of a product.

Joint-Profit Maximization

To see the benefits of a cartel or other form of collusion, assume there are three hypo-thetical oligopolistic firms (Gypsum, Sheetrock, and GSR) producing, in this instance, gypsum drywall panels for finishing interior walls. Suppose all three firms produce a homogeneous product and have identical cost, demand, and marginal-revenue curves. Figure 9.5 represents the position of each of our three oligopolistic firms.

   What price and output combination should, say, Gypsum select? If Gypsum were a pure monopolist, the answer would be clear: Establish output at Q_0, where marginal rev-enue equals marginal cost; charge the corresponding price P_0; and enjoy the maximum profit attainable. However, Gypsum does have two rivals selling identical products, and if Gypsum's assumption that its rivals will match its price of P_0 proves to be incorrect, the consequences could be disastrous for Gypsum. Specifically, if Sheetrock and GSR actually charge prices below P_0, then Gypsum's demand curve D will shift sharply to the left as its potential customers turn to its rivals, which are now selling the same product at a lower price. Of course, Gypsum can retaliate by cutting its price too, but this will move all three firms down their demand curves, lowering their profits. It may even drive them to a point where average total cost exceeds price and losses are incurred.

   So the question becomes, "Will Sheetrock and GSR want to charge a price below P_0?" Under our assumptions, and recognizing that Gypsum has little choice except to match any price they may set below P_0, the answer is no. Faced with the same demand and cost circumstances, Sheetrock and GSR will find it in their interest to produce Q_0

FIGURE 9.5 Collusion and the tendency toward joint-profit maximization. If oligopolistic firms face identical or highly similar demand and cost conditions, they may collude to limit their joint output and to set a single, common price. Thus, each firm acts as if it were a pure monopolist, setting output at Q_0 and charging price P_0. This price and output combination maximizes each firm's profit (green area) and thus the joint profits of all.

and charge P_0. This is a curious situation; each firm finds it most profitable to charge the same price, P_0, but only if its rivals actually do so! How can the three firms ensure the price P_0 and quantity Q_0 solution in which each is keenly interested? How can they avoid the less profitable outcomes associated with either higher or lower prices?

The answer is evident: They can collude. They can get together, talk it over, and agree to charge the same price, P_0. In addition to reducing the possibility of price wars, this will give each firm the maximum profit. For society, the result will be the same as would occur if the industry were a pure monopoly composed of three identical plants.

APPLYING THE ANALYSIS

Cartels and Collusion

Undoubtedly the most significant international cartel is the Organization of Petroleum Exporting Countries (OPEC), comprising 12 oil-producing nations (Saudi Arabia, Iran, Venezuela, UAE, Nigeria, Kuwait, Libya, Algeria, Angola, Ecuador, Qatar, and Iraq). OPEC produces about 41 percent of the world's oil and supplies about 43 percent of all oil traded internationally. OPEC has in some cases been able to drastically alter oil prices by increasing or decreasing supply. In the late 1990s, for instance, it caused oil prices to rise from $11 per barrel to $34 per barrel over a 15-month period.

That being said, most increases in the price of oil are not caused by OPEC. Between 2005 and 2008, for example, oil prices went from $40 per barrel to $140 per barrel due to rapidly rising demand from China and supply uncertainties related to armed conflict in the Middle East. But as the recession that began in December 2007 took hold, demand slumped and oil prices collapsed back down to about $40 per barrel. OPEC was largely a non-factor in this rise and fall in the price of oil. But in those cases where OPEC can effectively enforce its production agreements, there is little doubt that it can hold the price of oil substantially above the marginal cost of production.

Because cartels among domestic firms are illegal in the United States, any collusion that exists is covert or secret. Yet there are numerous examples of collusion, as shown by evidence from antitrust (antimonopoly) cases. In 1993 Borden, Pet, and Dean Food, among others, either pleaded guilty to or were convicted of rigging bids on the prices of milk products sold to schools and military bases. By phone or at luncheons, company executives agreed in advance on which firm would submit the low bid for each school district or military base. In 1996 American agribusiness Archer Daniels Midland and three Japanese and South Korean firms were found to have conspired to fix the world-wide price and sales volume of a livestock feed additive. Executives for the firms secretly met in Hong Kong, Paris, Mexico City, Vancouver, and Zurich to discuss their plans.

There are many other relatively recent examples of price fixing: ConAgra and Hormel agreed to pay more than $21 million to settle their roles in a nationwide price-fixing case involving catfish. The U.S. Justice Department fined UCAR International $110 million for scheming with rivals to fix prices and divide the world market for graphite electrodes used in steel mills. The auction houses Sotheby's and Christy's were found guilty of conspiring over a 6-year period to set the same commission rates for sellers at auctions. Bayer AG pleaded guilty to, and was fined $66 million for, taking part in a conspiracy to divide up the market and set prices for chemicals used in rubber manufacturing.

QUESTION: In what way might mergers be an alternative to illegal collusion? In view of your answer, why is it important to enforce laws that outlaw mergers that substantially reduce competition?

Obstacles to Collusion

Normally, cartels and similar collusive arrangements are difficult to establish and maintain. Below are several barriers to collusion beyond the antitrust laws.

1) *Demand and Cost Differences* When oligopolists face different costs and demand curves, it is difficult for them to agree on a price. This is particularly the case in industries where products are differentiated and change frequently. Even with highly standardized products, firms usually have somewhat different market shares and operate with differing degrees of productive efficiency. Thus, it is unlikely that even homogeneous oligopolists would have the same demand and cost curves.

In either case, differences in costs and demand mean that the profit-maximizing price will differ among firms; no single price will be readily acceptable to all, as we assumed was true in Figure 9.5. So price collusion depends on compromises and concessions that are not always easy to obtain and hence act as an obstacle to collusion.

2) *Number of Firms* Other things equal, the larger the number of firms, the more difficult it is to create a cartel or some other form of price collusion. Agreement on price by three or four producers that control an entire market may be relatively easy to accomplish. But such agreement is more difficult to achieve where there are, say, 10 firms, each with roughly 10 percent of the market, or where the Big Three have 70 percent of the market while a competitive fringe of 8 or 10 smaller firms battles for the remainder.

3) *Cheating* As the game-theory model makes clear, there is a temptation for collusive oligopolists to engage in secret price cutting to increase sales and profit. The difficulty with such cheating is that buyers who are paying a high price for a product may become aware of the lower-priced sales and demand similar treatment. Or buyers receiving a price concession from one producer may use the concession as a wedge to get even larger price concessions from a rival producer. Buyers' attempts to play producers against one another may precipitate price wars among the producers. Although secret price concessions are potentially profitable, they threaten collusive oligopolies over time. Collusion is more likely to succeed when cheating is easy to detect and punish. Then the conspirators are less likely to cheat on the price agreement.

4) *Recession* Long-lasting recession usually serves as an enemy of collusion because slumping markets increase average total cost. In technical terms, as the oligopolists' demand and marginal-revenue curves shift to the left in Figure 9.5 in response to a recession, each firm moves leftward and upward to a higher operating point on its average-total-cost curve. Firms find they have substantial excess production capacity, sales are down, unit costs are up, and profits are being squeezed. Under such conditions, businesses may feel they can avoid serious profit reductions (or even losses) by cutting price and thus gaining sales at the expense of rivals.

increase excess capacity strengthen incentive to cheat

5) *Potential Entry* The greater prices and profits that result from collusion may attract new entrants, including foreign firms. Since that would increase market supply and reduce prices and profits, successful collusion requires that colluding oligopolists block the entry of new producers.

Oligopoly and Advertising

We have noted that oligopolists would rather not compete on the basis of price and may become involved in price collusion. Nonetheless, each firm's share of the total market is typically determined through product development and advertising, for two reasons:

- Product development and advertising campaigns are less easily duplicated than price cuts. Price cuts can be quickly and easily matched by a firm's rivals to cancel any potential gain in sales derived from that strategy. Product improvements and successful advertising, however, can produce more permanent gains in market share because they cannot be duplicated as quickly and completely as price reductions.
- Oligopolists have sufficient financial resources to engage in product development and advertising. For most oligopolists, the economic profits earned in the past can help finance current advertising and product development.

In 2010, U.S. firms spent an estimated $131 billion on advertising in the United States. *Advertising is prevalent in both monopolistic competition and oligopoly*. Table 9.1 lists the 10 leading U.S. advertisers in 2010.

Advertising may affect prices, competition, and efficiency either positively or negatively, depending on the circumstances. While our focus here is on advertising by oligopolists, the analysis is equally applicable to advertising by monopolistic competitors.

Positive Effects of Advertising

In order to make rational (efficient) decisions, consumers need information about product characteristics and prices. Media advertising may be a low-cost means for consumers to obtain that information. Suppose you are in the market for a high-quality camera and there is no advertising of such a product in newspapers or magazines. To make a rational choice, you may have to spend several days visiting stores to determine the availability, prices, and features of various brands. This search entails both direct costs (gasoline, parking fees) and indirect costs (the value of your time). By providing information about the available options, advertising reduces your search time and minimizes these direct and indirect costs.

By providing information about the various competing goods that are available, advertising diminishes monopoly power. In fact, advertising is frequently associated with the introduction of new products designed to compete with existing brands. Could Toyota and Honda have so strongly challenged U.S. auto producers without advertising? Could FedEx have sliced market share away from UPS and the U.S. Postal Service without advertising?

TABLE 9.1 The Largest U.S. Advertisers, 2010

Company	Advertising Spending Millions of $
Procter & Gamble	$3124
General Motors	2131
AT&T	2093
Verizon	1823
News Corp	1368
Pfizer	1229
Time Warner	1194
Johnson & Johnson	1140
Ford Motor	1132
L'Oréal	1112

Source: Kantar Media, **www.kantarmediana.com**

Viewed this way, advertising is an efficiency-enhancing activity. It is a relatively inexpensive means of providing useful information to consumers and thus lowering their search costs. By enhancing competition, advertising results in greater economic efficiency. By facilitating the introduction of new products, advertising speeds up technological progress. By increasing sales and output, advertising can reduce long-run average total cost by enabling firms to obtain economies of scale.

Potential Negative Effects of Advertising

Not all the effects of advertising are positive, of course. Much advertising is designed simply to manipulate or persuade consumers—that is, to alter their preferences in favor of the advertiser's product. A television commercial that indicates that a popular personality drinks a particular brand of soft drink—and therefore that you should too—conveys little or no information to consumers about price or quality. In addition, advertising is sometimes based on misleading and extravagant claims that confuse consumers rather than enlighten them. Indeed, in some cases advertising may well persuade consumers to pay high prices for much-acclaimed but inferior products, forgoing better but unadvertised products selling at lower prices. Example: *Consumer Reports* has found that heavily advertised premium motor oils and fancy additives provide no better engine performance and longevity than do cheaper brands.

Firms often establish substantial brand-name loyalty and thus achieve monopoly power via their advertising (see Global Snapshot 9.1). As a consequence, they are able to increase their sales, expand their market shares, and enjoy greater profits. Larger profits permit still more advertising and further enlargement of the firm's market share and profit. In time, consumers may lose the advantages of competitive markets and face the disadvantages of monopolized markets. Moreover, new entrants to the industry need to incur large advertising costs in order to establish their products in the marketplace; thus, advertising costs may be a barrier to entry.

GLOBAL SNAPSHOT 9.1

The World's Top 10 Brand Names

Here are the world's top 10 brands, based on four criteria: the brand's market share within its category, the brand's world appeal across age groups and nationalities, the loyalty of customers to the brand, and the ability of the brand to "stretch" to products beyond the original product.

World's Top 10 Brands

- Coca-Cola
- IBM
- Microsoft
- Google
- General Electric
- McDonald's
- Intel
- Apple
- Disney
- Hewlett-Packard

Source: Interbrand's Top 100 Best Global Brands, 2011, **www.BestGlobalBrands.com.** Used with permission of Interbrand.

Advertising can also be self-canceling. The advertising campaign of one fast-food hamburger chain may be offset by equally costly campaigns waged by rivals, so each firm's demand actually remains unchanged. Few, if any, extra burgers will be purchased, and all firms will experience higher costs, and either their profits will fall or, through successful price leadership, their product prices will rise.

When advertising either leads to increased monopoly power or is self-canceling, economic inefficiency results.

Oligopoly and Efficiency

Is oligopoly, then, an efficient market structure from society's standpoint? How do the price and output decisions of the oligopolist measure up to the triple equality $P = \text{MC} = $ minimum ATC that occurs in pure competition?

Inefficiency

Many economists believe that the outcome of some oligopolistic markets is approximately as shown in Figure 9.5. This view is bolstered by evidence that many oligopolists sustain sizable economic profits year after year. In that case, the oligopolist's production occurs where price exceeds marginal cost and average total cost. Moreover, production is below the output at which average total cost is minimized. In this view, neither productive efficiency ($P = $ minimum ATC) nor allocative efficiency ($P = \text{MC}$) is likely to occur under oligopoly. A few observers assert that oligopoly is actually less desirable than pure monopoly because government usually regulates pure monopoly in the United States to guard against abuses of monopoly power. Informal collusion among oligopolists may yield price and output results similar to those under pure monopoly yet give the outward appearance of competition involving independent firms.

Qualifications

We should note, however, three qualifications to this view:

- **Increased foreign competition** In recent decades foreign competition has increased rivalry in a number of oligopolistic industries—steel, automobiles, video games, electric shavers, outboard motors, and copy machines, for example. This has helped to break down such cozy arrangements as price leadership and to stimulate much more competitive pricing.
- **Limit pricing** Recall that some oligopolists may purposely keep prices below the short-run profit-maximizing level in order to bolster entry barriers. In essence, consumers and society may get some of the benefits of competition— prices closer to marginal cost and minimum average total cost—even without the competition that free entry would provide.
- **Technological advance** Over time, oligopolistic industries may foster more rapid product development and greater improvement of production techniques than would be possible if they were purely competitive. Oligopolists have large economic profits from which they can fund expensive research and development (R&D). Moreover, the existence of barriers to entry may give the oligopolist some assurance that it will reap the rewards of successful R&D. Oligopolists account for the bulk of the more than $200 billion that U.S. businesses spend on R&D each year. Thus, the short-run economic inefficiencies of oligopolists may be partly or wholly offset by the oligopolists' contributions to better products, lower prices, and lower costs over time.

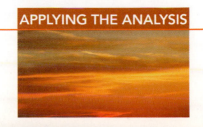

Oligopoly in the Beer Industry

The beer industry serves as a good case study for oligopoly. This industry was once populated by hundreds of firms and an even larger number of brands. But it now is an oligopoly dominated by a handful of producers.

Since the Second World War, profound changes have increased the level of concentration in the U.S. beer industry. In 1947 more than 400 independent brewing companies resided in the United States. By 1967, the number had declined to 124 and by 1980 it had dropped to just 33. In 1947 the largest five brewers sold only 19 percent of the nation's beer. In 2007, the Big Three brewers (Anheuser-Busch, SABMiller, and Molson/Coors) sold 76 percent. In 2007, Anheuser-Bush (48 percent) and SABMiller (18 percent) alone combined for 66 percent of industry sales. And, in late 2007, SABMiller acquired the U.S. operations of Molson/Coors, thus creating MillerCoors and turning the Big Three into the Big Two. In 2008, Belgian brewer InBev purchased Anheuser-Busch, thereby forming international brewing giant A-B. The U.S. beer industry clearly meets all the criteria of oligopoly.

Changes on the demand side of the market have contributed to the "shakeout" of small brewers from the industry. First, consumer tastes in the mass market have generally shifted from the stronger-flavored beers of the small brewers to the light products of the larger brewers. Second, there has been a shift from the consumption of beer in taverns to consumption of it in the home. The beer consumed in taverns was mainly "draft" or "tap" beer from kegs, supplied by local and regional brewers that could deliver the kegs in a timely fashion at relatively low transportation cost. But the large increase in the demand for beer consumed at home opened the door for large brewers that sold their beer in bottles and aluminum cans. The large brewers could ship their beer by truck or rail over long distances and compete directly with the local brewers.

Developments on the supply side of the market have been even more profound. Technological advances speeded up the bottling and canning lines. Today, large brewers can fill and close 2000 cans per line per minute. Large plants are also able to reduce labor costs through the automating of brewing and warehousing. Furthermore, plant construction costs per barrel of production capacity are about one-third less for a 4.5-million-barrel plant than for a 1.5-million-barrel plant. As a consequence of these and other factors, the minimum efficient scale in brewing is a plant size of about 4.5 million barrels. Additionally, studies indicate that further cost savings are available to brewing firms that have two or more separate large breweries in different regions of the country. Between the economies of scale from plant size and these cost savings from multiple plants, cost considerations deter entry to the mainline beer industry.

"Blindfold" taste tests confirm that most mass-produced American beers taste alike. Undaunted, brewers spend large amounts of money touting the supposed differences between their brands in order to build brand loyalty. And here Anheuser-Busch InBev and MillerCoors, which sell national brands, enjoy major cost advantages over producers such as Pabst that have many regional brands (for example, Lonestar, Rainer, Schaefer, and Schmidts). The reason is that national television advertising is less costly *per viewer* than local TV advertising.

Up until the recent combination of Molson/Coors and SABMiller, mergers had not been the dominant factor in explaining the industry consolidation. Rather, that was largely caused by failing smaller breweries' (such as Heileman's) selling out. Dominant firms have expanded by heavily advertising their main brands and by creating new brands such as Miller Lite, Bud Light, Genuine Draft, Keystone, and Icehouse rather than acquiring other brewers. This has sustained significant product differentiation, despite the declining number of major brewers.

The story of the last three decades has been Anheuser-Busch InBev (A-B), which has greatly expanded its market share. A-B now makes the nation's top two brands: Bud Light and Budweiser account for nearly half the beer sold in the United States. Part of A-B's success owes to the demise of regional competitors. But part also is the result of A-B's competitive prowess. It has constructed state-of-the-art breweries, created effective advertising campaigns, and forged strong relationships with regional distributors. Meanwhile, Miller's market share has declined slightly in recent years. In 2002 Philip Morris sold Miller to London-based SAB. SABMiller, as the combined firm was called, redesigned Miller's labeling to enhance its appeal both domestically and overseas. Perhaps of greater importance, SABMiller's acquisition of Coors to form MillerCoors immediately expanded its U.S. market share from 18 percent to 29 percent. MillerCoors thus became the number two brewer in the United States after A-B, which controls 49 percent of the market.

Imported beers such as Heineken, Corona, and Guinness constitute about 9 percent of the market, with individual brands seeming to wax and wane in popularity. Some local or regional microbreweries such as Samuel Adams and Pyramid, which brew "craft" or specialty beers and charge super-premium prices, have whittled into the sales of the major brewers. Craft and specialty beers account for only 6 percent of beer consumed in the United States, but they are the fastest-growing segment of the U.S. industry. A-B and and MillerCoors have taken notice, responding with specialty brands of their own (for example, Red Wolf, Red Dog, Killarney's, Icehouse, and Blue Moon) and buying stakes in microbrewers Redhook Ale and Celis.

Source: Based on Kenneth G. Elzinga, "Beer," in Walter Adams and James Brock (eds.), *The Structure of American Industry*, 10th ed. (Upper Saddle River, N.J.: Prentice-Hall, 2001), pp. 85–113; and Douglas F. Greer, "Beer: Causes of Structural Change," in Larry Duetsch (ed.), *Industry Studies*, 2d ed. (New York: M. E. Sharpe, 1998), pp. 28–64. Updated data and information are mainly from *Beer Marketer's Insights*, **www.beerinsights.com**, and the Association of Brewers, **www.beertown.com**.

Summary

1. The distinguishing features of monopolistic competition are (a) there are enough firms in the industry to ensure that each firm has only limited control over price, mutual interdependence is absent, and collusion is nearly impossible; (b) products are characterized by real or perceived differences so that economic rivalry entails both price and nonprice competition; and (c) entry to the industry is relatively easy. Many aspects of retailing, and some manufacturing industries in which economies of scale are few, approximate monopolistic competition.

2. Monopolistically competitive firms may earn economic profits or incur losses in the short run. The easy entry and exit of firms result in only normal profits in the long run.

3. The long-run equilibrium position of the monopolistically competitive producer is less efficient than that of the pure competitor. Under monopolistic competition, price exceeds marginal cost, suggesting an underallocation of resources to the product, and price exceeds minimum average total cost, indicating that consumers do not get the product at the lowest price that cost conditions might allow.

4. Nonprice competition provides a way that monopolistically competitive firms can offset the long-run tendency for economic profit to fall to zero. Through product differentiation, product development, and advertising, a firm may strive to increase the demand for its product more than enough to cover the added cost of such nonprice competition. Consumers benefit from the wide diversity of product choice that monopolistic competition provides.

5. In practice, the monopolistic competitor seeks the specific combination of price, product, and advertising that will maximize profit.

6. Oligopolistic industries are characterized by the presence of few firms, each having a significant fraction of the market.

Firms thus situated engage in strategic behavior and are mutually interdependent: The behavior of any one firm directly affects, and is affected by, the actions of rivals. Products may be either virtually uniform or significantly differentiated. Various barriers to entry, including economies of scale, underlie and maintain oligopoly.

7. Game theory (a) shows the interdependence of oligopolists' pricing policies, (b) reveals the tendency of oligopolists to collude, and (c) explains the temptation of oligopolists to cheat on collusive arrangements.

8. Noncollusive oligopolists may face a kinked-demand curve. This curve and the accompanying marginal-revenue curve help explain the price rigidity that often characterizes oligopolies; they do not, however, explain how the actual prices of products were first established.

9. Price leadership is an informal means of overcoming difficulties relating to kinked-demand curves whereby one firm, usually the largest or most efficient, initiates price changes and the other firms in the industry follow the leader.

10. Collusive oligopolists such as cartels maximize joint profits—that is, they behave like pure monopolists. Demand and cost differences, a "large" number of firms, cheating through secret price concessions, recessions, and the antitrust laws are all obstacles to collusive oligopoly.

11. Market shares in oligopolistic industries are usually determined on the basis of product development and advertising. Oligopolists emphasize nonprice competition because (a) advertising and product variations are less easy for rivals to match and (b) oligopolists frequently have ample resources to finance nonprice competition.

12. Advertising may affect prices, competition, and efficiency either positively or negatively. Positive: It can provide consumers with low-cost information about competing products, help introduce new competing products into concentrated industries, and generally reduce monopoly power and its attendant inefficiencies. Negative: It can promote monopoly power via persuasion and the creation of entry barriers. Moreover, it can be self-canceling when engaged in by rivals; then it boosts costs and creates inefficiency while accomplishing little else.

13. Neither productive nor allocative efficiency is realized in oligopolistic markets, but oligopoly may be superior to pure competition in promoting research and development and technological progress.

Terms and Concepts

monopolistic competition	oligopoly	mutual interdependence	kinked-demand curve
product differentiation	homogeneous oligopoly	game theory	price leadership
nonprice competition	differentiated oligopoly	collusion	cartel
excess capacity	strategic behavior	per se violation	

Questions

1. How does monopolistic competition differ from pure competition in its basic characteristics? How does it differ from pure monopoly? Explain fully what product differentiation may involve. Explain how the entry of firms into its industry affects the demand curve facing a monopolistic competitor and how that, in turn, affects its economic profit. **LO1**

2. Compare the elasticity of the monopolistic competitor's demand with that of a pure competitor and a pure monopolist. Assuming identical long-run costs, compare graphically the prices and outputs that would result in the long run under pure competition and under monopolistic competition. Contrast the two market structures in terms of productive and allocative efficiency. Explain: "Monopolistically competitive industries are characterized by too many firms, each of which produces too little." **LO2**

3. "Monopolistic competition is monopolistic up to the point at which consumers become willing to buy close-substitute products and competitive beyond that point." Explain. **LO1, LO2**

4. "Competition in quality and service may be just as effective as price competition in giving buyers more for their money." Do you agree? Why? Explain why monopolistically competitive firms frequently prefer nonprice competition to price competition. **LO2**

5. Why do oligopolies exist? List five or six oligopolists whose products you own or regularly purchase. What distinguishes oligopoly from monopolistic competition? **LO3**

6. Explain the general meaning of the following profit payoff matrix for oligopolists X and Y. All profit figures are in thousands. **LO4**

a. Use the payoff matrix to explain the mutual interdependence that characterizes oligopolistic industries.

b. Assuming no collusion between X and Y, what is the likely pricing outcome?

c. In view of your answer to part b, explain why price collusion is mutually profitable. Why might there be a temptation to cheat on the collusive agreement?

7. Construct a game-theory matrix to illustrate the text example of two firms and their decisions on high versus low advertising budgets and the effects of each on profits. Show a circumstance in which both firms select high advertising budgets even though both would be more profitable with low advertising budgets. Why won't they unilaterally cut their advertising budgets? Explain why this is an example of the prisoner's dilemma. **LO4, LO7**

8. What assumptions about a rival's response to price changes underlie the kinked-demand curve for oligopolists? Why is there a gap in the oligopolist's marginal-revenue curve? How does the kinked-demand curve explain price rigidity in oligopoly? **LO5**

9. Why might price collusion occur in oligopolistic industries? Assess the economic desirability of collusive pricing. What are the main obstacles to collusion? Speculate as to why price leadership is legal in the United States, whereas price fixing is not. **LO6**

10. Why is there so much advertising in monopolistic competition and oligopoly? How does such advertising help consumers and promote efficiency? Why might it be excessive at times? **LO7**

11. What firm dominates the beer industry? What demand and supply factors have contributed to "fewness" in this industry? **LO3**

Problems

1. Assume that in short-run equilibrium, a particular monopolistically competitive firm charges $12 for each unit of its output and sells 52 units of output per day. How much revenue will it take in each day? If its average total cost (ATC) for those 52 units is $10, will the firm (a) earn a short-run economic profit, (b) break even with only a normal profit, or (c) suffer an economic loss? If a profit or loss, what will be the amount? Next, suppose that entry or exit occurs in this monopolistic industry and establishes a long-run equilibrium. If the firm's daily output remains at 52 units, what price will it be able to charge? What will be its economic profit? **LO2**

2. Suppose that a restaurant in an oligopolistic part of that industry is currently serving 230 meals per day (the output where MR = MC). At that output level, ATC per meal is $10 and consumers are willing to pay $12 per meal. What is the size of this firm's profit or loss? Will there be entry or exit? Will this restaurant's demand curve shift left or right?

In long-run equilibrium, suppose that this restaurant charges $11 per meal for 180 meals and that the marginal cost of the 180th meal is $8. What is the size of the firm's profit? Suppose that the allocatively efficient output level in long-run equilibrium is 200 meals. Is the deadweight loss for this firm greater than or less than $60? **LO3**

3. Suppose than an oligopolist is charging $21 per unit of output and selling 31 units each day. What is its daily total revenue? Also suppose that previously it had lowered its price from $21 to $19, rivals matched the price cut, and the firm's sales increased from 31 to 32 units. It also previously raised its price from $21 to $23, rivals ignored the price hike, and the firm's daily total revenue came in at $482. Which of the following is most logical to conclude? The firm's demand curve is (a) inelastic over the $21 to $23 price range, (b) elastic over the $19 to $21 price range, (c) a linear (straight) downsloping line, or (d) a curve with a kink in it? **LO5**

RESOURCE MARKETS AND GOVERNMENT

10

After reading this chapter, you should be able to:

1 Explain why the firm's marginal revenue product curve is its labor demand curve.

2 List the factors that increase or decrease labor demand.

3 Discuss the determinants of elasticity of labor demand.

4 Demonstrate how wage rates are determined in competitive and monopsonistic labor markets.

5 Show how unions increase wage rates and how minimum wage laws affect labor markets.

6 Identify the major causes of wage differentials.

Wage Determination

We now turn from the pricing and production of *goods and services* to the pricing and employment of *resources*. Although firms come in various sizes and operate under highly different market conditions, each has a demand for productive resources. They obtain those resources from households—the direct or indirect owners of land, labor, capital, and entrepreneurial resources. So, referring to the circular flow diagram (Figure 2.2, page 44), we shift our attention from the bottom loop (where businesses supply products that households demand) to the top loop (where businesses demand resources that households supply).

A Focus on Labor

The basic principles we develop in this chapter apply to land, labor, and capital resources, but we will emphasize the pricing and employment of labor. About 70 percent of all income in the United States flows to households in the form of wages and salaries. More than 146 million of us go to work each day in the United States. We have an amazing variety of jobs with thousands of different employers and receive large differences in pay. What determines our hourly wage or annual salary? Why is the salary of, say, a topflight major-league baseball player $15 million or more a year, whereas the pay for a first-rate schoolteacher is $50,000? Why are starting salaries for college graduates who major in engineering and accounting so much higher than those for graduates majoring in journalism and sociology?

Demand and supply analysis helps us answer these questions. We begin by examining labor demand and labor supply in a **purely competitive labor market.** In such a market,

- Numerous employers compete with one another in hiring a specific type of labor.
- Each of many workers with identical skills supplies that type of labor.
- Individual employers and individual workers are "wage takers" because neither can control the market wage rate.

purely competitive labor market
A labor market in which a large number of similarly qualified workers independently offer their labor services to a large number of employers, none of whom can set the wage rate.

Labor Demand

Labor demand is the starting point for any discussion of wages and salaries. Labor demand is a schedule or a curve showing the amounts of labor that buyers are willing and able to purchase at various price levels (hourly wages) over some period of time. As with all resources, labor demand is a **derived demand**, meaning that the demand for labor is derived from the demand for the products that labor helps to produce. This is true because labor resources usually do not directly satisfy customer wants but do so indirectly through their use in producing goods and services. Almost nobody wants to directly consume the labor services of a software engineer, but millions of people do want to use the software that the engineer helps create.

derived demand
The demand for a resource that results from the demand for the products it helps produce.

Marginal Revenue Product

Because resource demand is derived from product demand, the strength of the demand will depend on the productivity of the labor—its ability to produce goods and services—and the price of the good or service it helps produce. Other things equal, a resource that is highly productive in turning out a highly valued commodity will be in great demand. In contrast, a relatively unproductive resource that is capable of producing only a minimally valued commodity will be in little demand. And no demand whatsoever will exist for a resource that is phenomenally efficient in producing something that no one wants to buy.

Consider the table in Figure 10.1, which shows the roles of marginal productivity and product price in determining labor demand.

Productivity Columns 1 and 2 give the number of units of labor employed and the resulting total product (output). Column 3 provides the marginal product (MP), or additional output, resulting from using each additional unit of labor. Columns 1 through 3 remind us that the law of diminishing returns applies here, causing the marginal product of labor to fall beyond some point. For simplicity, we assume that these diminishing marginal returns—these declines in marginal product—begin with the second worker hired.

FIGURE 10.1 The purely competitive seller's demand for labor. The MRP-of-labor curve is the labor demand curve; each of its points relates a particular wage rate (= MRP when profit is maximized) with a corresponding quantity of labor demanded. The downward slope of the D = MRP curve results from the law of diminishing marginal returns.

(1) Units of Labor	(2) Total Product (Output)	(3) Marginal Product (MP)	(4) Product Price	(5) Total Revenue, (2) × (4)	(6) Marginal Revenue Product (MRP)
0	0		$2	$ 0	
		7			$14
1	7		2	14	
		6			12
2	13		2	26	
		5			10
3	18		2	36	
		4			8
4	22		2	44	
		3			6
5	25		2	50	
		2			4
6	27		2	54	
		1			2
7	28		2	56	

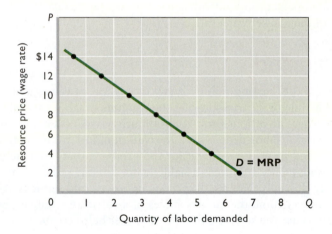

marginal revenue product (MRP)
The change in a firm's total revenue when it employs 1 more unit of labor.

Product Price The derived demand for labor depends also on the market value (product price) of the good or service. Column 4 in the table in Figure 10.1 adds this price information to the mix. Because we are assuming a competitive product market, product price equals marginal revenue. The firm is a price taker and can sell units of output only at this market price. And this price will also be the firm's marginal revenue. In this case, both price and marginal revenue are a constant $2.

Multiplying column 2 by column 4 provides the total-revenue data of column 5. These are the amounts of revenue the firm realizes from the various levels of employment. From these total-revenue data we can compute the **marginal revenue product (MRP)** of labor—the change in total revenue resulting from the use of each additional unit of labor. In equation form,

$$\text{Marginal revenue product} = \frac{\text{change in total revenue}}{\text{unit change in labor}}$$

The MRPs are listed in column 6 in the table.

Rule for Employing Labor: MRP = MRC

The MRP schedule, shown as columns 1 and 6, is the firm's demand schedule for labor. To understand why, you must first know the rule that guides a profit-seeking firm in hiring any resource: To maximize profit, a firm should hire additional units of labor as long as each successive unit adds more to the firm's total revenue than to the firm's total cost.

Economists use special terms to designate what each additional unit of labor (or any other variable resource) adds to total revenue and what it adds to total cost. We have seen that MRP measures how much each successive unit of labor adds to total revenue. The amount that each additional unit of labor adds to the firm's total cost is called its **marginal resource cost (MRC).** In equation form,

$$\begin{array}{c} \text{Marginal} \\ \text{resource} \\ \text{cost} \end{array} = \frac{\text{change in total (labor) cost}}{\text{unit change in labor}}$$

So we can restate our rule for hiring resources as follows: It will be profitable for a firm to hire additional units of labor up to the point at which labor's MRP is equal to its MRC. If the number of workers a firm is currently hiring is such that the MRP of the last worker exceeds his or her MRC, the firm can profit by hiring more workers. But if the number being hired is such that the MRC of the last worker exceeds his or her MRP, the firm is hiring workers who are not "paying their way" and it can increase its profit by discharging some workers. You may have recognized that this **MRP = MRC rule** is similar to the MR = MC profit-maximizing rule employed throughout our discussion of price and output determination. The rationale of the two rules is the same, but the point of reference is now *inputs* of a resource, not *outputs* of a product.

MRP as Labor Demand Schedule

In a competitive labor market, market supply and market demand establish the wage rate. Because each firm hires such a small fraction of the market supply of labor, an individual firm cannot influence the market wage rate; it is a wage taker, not a wage maker. This means that for each additional unit of labor hired, each firm's total labor cost increases by exactly the amount of the constant market wage rate. More specifically, the MRC of labor exactly equals the market wage rate. Thus, resource "price" (the market wage rate) and resource "cost" (marginal resource cost) are equal for a firm that hires labor in a competitive labor market. As a result, the MRP = MRC rule tells us that a competitive firm will hire units of labor up to the point at which the market *wage rate* (its MRC) is equal to its MRP.

In terms of the data in columns 1 and 6 of Figure 10.1's table, if the market wage rate is, say, $13.95, the firm will hire only one worker. This is the outcome because only the hiring of the first worker results in an increase in profits. To see this, note that for the first worker, MRP (= $14) exceeds MRC (= $13.95). Thus, hiring the first worker is profitable. For each successive worker, however, MRC (= $13.95) exceeds MRP (= $12 or less), indicating that it will not be profitable to hire any of those workers. If the wage rate is $11.95, by the same reasoning we discover that it will pay the firm to hire both the first and second workers. Similarly, if the wage rate is $9.95, three will be hired; if it is $7.95, four; if it is $5.95, five; and so forth. *The MRP schedule therefore constitutes the firm's demand for labor because each point on this schedule (or curve) indicates the quantity of labor units the firm would hire at each possible wage rate.* In the graph in Figure 10.1, we show the *D* = MRP curve based on the data in the table. The competitive firm's labor demand curve identifies an inverse relationship between the wage

marginal resource cost (MRC)
The change in a firm's total cost when it employs 1 more unit of labor.

MRP = MRC rule
The principle that to maximize profit a firm should expand employment until the marginal revenue product (MRP) of labor equals the marginal resource cost (MRC) of labor.

rate and the quantity of labor demanded, other things equal. The curve slopes downward because of diminishing marginal returns.[1]

Market Demand for Labor

We have now explained the individual firm's demand curve for labor. Recall that the total, or market, demand curve for a *product* is found by summing horizontally the demand curves of all individual buyers in the market. The market demand curve for a particular *resource* is derived in essentially the same way. Economists sum horizontally the individual labor demand curves of all firms hiring a particular kind of labor to obtain the market demand for that labor.

Changes in Labor Demand

What will alter the demand for labor (shift the labor demand curve)? The fact that labor demand is derived from *product demand* and depends on *resource productivity* suggests two "resource demand shifters." Also, our analysis of how changes in the prices of other products can shift a product's demand curve (Chapter 3) suggests another factor: changes in the *prices of other resources*.

Changes in Product Demand

Other things equal, an increase in the demand for a product will increase the demand for a resource used in its production, whereas a decrease in product demand will decrease the demand for that resource.

Let's see how this works. The first thing to recall is that a change in the demand for a product will normally change its price. In the table in Figure 10.1, let's assume that an increase in product demand boosts product price from $2 to $3. You should calculate the new labor demand schedule (columns 1 and 6) that would result, and plot it in the graph to verify that the new labor demand curve lies to the right of the old demand curve. Similarly, a decline in the product demand (and price) will shift the labor demand curve to the left. The fact that labor demand changes along with product demand demonstrates that labor demand is derived from product demand.

Example: With no offsetting change in supply, a decrease in the demand for new houses will drive down house prices. Those lower prices will decrease the MRP of construction workers, and therefore the demand for construction workers will fall. The labor demand curve will shift to the left.

Changes in Productivity

Other things equal, an increase in the productivity of a resource will increase the demand for the resource and a decrease in productivity will reduce the demand for the resource. If we doubled the MP data of column 3 in the table in Figure 10.1, the MRP data of column 6 also would double, indicating a rightward shift of the labor demand curve in the graph.

---

[1]Note that we plot the points in Figure 10.1 halfway between succeeding numbers of labor units. For example, we plot the MRP of the second unit ($12) not at 1 or 2 but at 1½. This "smoothing" enables us to sketch a continuously downsloping curve rather than one that moves downward in discrete steps as each new unit of labor is hired.

The productivity of any resource may be altered over the long run in several ways:

- **Quantities of other resources** The marginal productivity of any resource will vary with the quantities of the other resources used with it. The greater the amount of capital and land resources used with labor, the greater will be labor's marginal productivity and, thus, labor demand.

- **Technological advance** Technological improvements that increase the quality of other resources, such as capital, have the same effect. The better the *quality* of capital, the greater the productivity of labor used with it. Dockworkers employed with a specific amount of capital in the form of unloading cranes are more productive than dockworkers with the same amount of capital embodied in older conveyor-belt systems.

- **Quality of labor** Improvements in the quality of labor will increase its marginal productivity and therefore its demand. In effect, there will be a new demand curve for a different, more skilled, kind of labor.

Changes in the Prices of Other Resources

Changes in the prices of other resources may change the demand for labor.

Substitute Resources Suppose that labor and capital are substitutable in a certain production process. A firm can produce some specific amount of output using a relatively small amount of labor and a relatively large amount of capital, or vice versa. What happens if the price of machinery (capital) falls? The effect on the demand for labor will be the net result of two opposed effects: the substitution effect and the output effect.

- **Substitution effect** The decline in the price of machinery prompts the firm to substitute machinery for labor. This allows the firm to produce its output at lower cost. So at the fixed wage rate, smaller quantities of labor are now employed. This **substitution effect** decreases the demand for labor. More generally, the substitution effect indicates that a firm will purchase more of an input whose relative price has declined and, conversely, use less of an input whose relative price has increased.

- **Output effect** Because the price of machinery has declined, the costs of producing various outputs also must decline. With lower costs, the firm can profitably produce and sell a greater output. The greater output increases the demand for all resources, including labor. So this **output effect** increases the demand for labor. More generally, the output effect means that the firm will purchase more of one particular input when the price of the other input falls and less of that particular input when the price of the other input rises.

- **Net effect** The substitution and output effects are both present when the price of an input changes, but they work in opposite directions. For a decline in the price of capital, the substitution effect decreases the demand for labor and the output effect increases it. The net change in labor demand depends on the relative sizes of the two effects: If the substitution effect outweighs the output effect, a decrease in the price of capital decreases the demand for labor. If the output effect exceeds the substitution effect, a decrease in the price of capital increases the demand for labor.

Complementary Resources Resources may be complements rather than substitutes in the production process; an increase in the quantity of one of them also requires an increase in the amount of the other used, and vice versa. Suppose a small design firm does computer-assisted design (CAD) with relatively expensive personal computers as its basic piece of capital equipment. Each computer requires exactly one

substitution effect
The replacement of labor by capital when the price of capital falls.

output effect
An increase in the use of labor that occurs when a decline in the price of capital reduces a firm's production costs and therefore enables it to sell more output.

design engineer to operate it; the machine is not automated—it will not run itself—and a second engineer would have nothing to do.

Now assume that these computers substantially decline in price. There can be no substitution effect because labor and capital must be used in *fixed proportions:* one person for one machine. Capital cannot be substituted for labor. But there *is* an output effect. Other things equal, the reduction in the price of capital goods means lower production costs. It will therefore be profitable to produce a larger output. In doing so, the firm will use both more capital and more labor. When labor and capital are complementary, a decline in the price of capital increases the demand for labor through the output effect.

We have cast our analysis of substitute resources and complementary resources mainly in terms of a decline in the price of capital. Obviously, an *increase* in the price of capital causes the opposite effects on labor demand.

© Photodisc/Getty Images

© Royalty-Free/CORBIS

PHOTO OP Substitute Resources versus Complementary Resources

Automatic teller machines (ATMs) and human tellers are substitute resources, whereas construction equipment and their operators are complementary resources.

APPLYING THE ANALYSIS

Occupational Employment Trends

Changes in labor demand are of considerable significance because they affect employment in specific occupations. Other things equal, increases in labor demand for certain occupational groups result in increases in their employment; decreases in labor demand result in decreases in their employment. For illustration, let's look at occupations that are growing and declining in demand.

Table 10.1 lists the 10 fastest-growing and 10 most rapidly declining U.S. occupations (in percentage terms) for 2008–2018, as projected by the Bureau of Labor Statistics. Notice that service occupations dominate the fastest-growing list. In general, the demand for service workers is rapidly outpacing the demand for manufacturing, construction, and mining workers in the United States.

TABLE 10.1 The 10 Fastest-Growing and Most Rapidly Declining U.S. Occupations, in Percentage Terms, 2008–2018

Occupation	Employment, Thousands of Jobs		Percentage Change*
	2008	2018	
Fastest Growing			
Biomedical engineers	16	28	72.0
Network systems and data communications analysts	292	448	53.4
Home health aides	922	1383	50.0
Personal and home care aides	817	1193	46.0
Financial examiners	27	38	41.2
Medical scientists, except epidemiologists	109	154	40.4
Physician assistants	75	104	39.0
Skin care specialists	39	54	37.9
Biochemists and biophysicists	23	32	37.4
Athletic trainers	16	22	37.0
Most Rapidly Declining			
Textile machine operators	35	21	−40.7
Sewing machine operators	212	141	−33.7
Postal service workers	180	125	−30.3
Lathe operators	56	41	−26.7
Order clerks	246	182	−26.1
Photographic processing machine operators	51	39	−24.3
File clerks	212	163	−23.4
Machine feeders and offbearers	141	110	−22.2
Paper goods machine setters, operators, tenders	103	81	−21.5
Computer operators	110	90	−18.6

*Percentages may not correspond with employment numbers due to rounding of the employment data and the percentages.

Source: Bureau of Labor Statistics, "Employment Projections," **www.bls.gov.**

Of the 10 fastest-growing occupations in percentage terms, over half are related to health care services, research, and medical technology. The rising demands for these types of labor are derived from the growing demand for health services, caused by several factors. The aging of the U.S. population has brought with it more medical problems, rising incomes have led to greater expenditures on health care, and the growing presence of private and public insurance has allowed people to buy more health care than most could afford individually.

The increase in the demand for network systems and data communication analysts arises from the rapid rise in the demand for computers, computer services, and the Internet. It also results from the rising marginal revenue productivity of these particular workers, given the vastly improved quality of the computer and communications equipment they work with. Moreover, price declines on such equipment have had stronger output effects than substitution effects, increasing the demand for these kinds of labor.

Table 10.1 also lists the 10 U.S. occupations with the greatest projected job loss (in percentage terms) between 2008 and 2018. These occupations are more diverse than the fastest-growing occupations. Several of the occupations owe their declines mainly to "labor-saving" technological change. For example, automated or computerized equipment has greatly reduced the need for order clerks, file clerks, and various machine operators. The advent of digital photography explains the projected decline in the employment of people operating photographic processing equipment.

Three of the occupations in the declining-employment list are related to textiles and apparel. The U.S. demand for these goods is increasingly being filled through imports. Those jobs are therefore rapidly disappearing in the United States.

QUESTION: Name some occupation (other than those listed) that you think will grow in demand over the next decade. Name an occupation that you think will decline in demand. In each case, explain your reasoning.

Elasticity of Labor Demand

The employment changes we have just discussed have resulted from shifts in the locations of labor demand curves. Such changes in demand must be distinguished from changes in the quantity of labor demanded caused by a change in the wage rate. Such a change is caused not by a shift of the demand curve but, rather, by a movement from one point to another on a fixed labor demand curve. Example: In Figure 10.1 we note that an increase in the wage rate from $5 to $7 will reduce the quantity of labor demanded from 5 units to 4 units. This is a change in the *quantity of labor demanded* as distinct from a *change in the demand for labor*.

elasticity of labor demand
A measure of the responsiveness of labor quantity to a change in the wage rate.

The sensitivity of labor quantity to changes in wage rates along a fixed labor demand curve is measured by the **elasticity of labor demand** (or *wage elasticity of demand*). In coefficient form,

$$E_w = \frac{\text{percentage change in labor quantity demanded}}{\text{percentage change in wage rate}}$$

When E_w is greater than 1, labor demand is elastic; when E_w is less than 1, labor demand is inelastic; and when E_w equals 1, labor demand is unit-elastic. Several factors interact to determine the wage elasticity of demand.

ORIGIN OF THE IDEA

O 10.1

Elasticity of resource demand

Ease of Resource Substitutability

The greater the substitutability of other resources for labor, the more elastic is the demand for labor. As an example, the high degree to which computerized voice recognition systems are substitutable for human beings implies that the demand for human beings answering phone calls at call centers is quite elastic. In contrast, there are few good substitutes for physicians, so demand for them is less elastic or even inelastic.

Time can play a role in the input substitution process. For example, a firm's truck drivers may obtain a substantial wage increase with little or no immediate decline in employment. But over time, as the firm's trucks wear out and are replaced, that wage increase may motivate the company to purchase larger trucks and in that way deliver the same total output with fewer drivers.

Elasticity of Product Demand

The greater the elasticity of product demand, the greater is the elasticity of labor demand. The derived nature of resource demand leads us to expect this relationship. A small rise in the price of a product (caused by a wage increase) will sharply reduce output if product demand is elastic. So a relatively large decline in the amount of labor demanded will result. This means that the demand for labor is elastic.

Ratio of Labor Cost to Total Cost

The larger the proportion of total production costs accounted for by labor, the greater is the elasticity of demand for labor. In the extreme, if labor cost is the only production cost, then a 20 percent increase in wage rates will increase marginal cost and average total cost by 20 percent. If product demand is elastic, this substantial increase in costs will cause a relatively large decline in sales and a sharp decline in the amount of labor demanded. So labor demand is highly elastic. But if labor cost is only 50 percent of production cost, then a 20 percent increase in wage rates will increase costs by only 10 percent. With the same elasticity of product demand, this will cause a relatively small decline in sales and therefore in the amount of labor demanded. In this case the demand for labor is much less elastic.

Market Supply of Labor

Let's now turn to the supply side of a purely competitive labor market. The supply curve for each type of labor slopes upward, indicating that employers as a group must pay higher wage rates to obtain more workers. Employers must do this to bid workers away from other industries, occupations, and localities. Within limits, workers have alternative job opportunities. For example, they may work in other industries in the same locality, or they may work in their present occupations in different cities or states, or they may work in other occupations.

Firms that want to hire these workers must pay higher wage rates to attract them away from the alternative job opportunities available to them. They also must pay higher wages to induce people who are not currently in the labor force—who are perhaps doing household activities or enjoying leisure—to seek employment. In short, assuming that wages are constant in other labor markets, higher wages in a particular labor market entice more workers to offer their labor services in that market. This fact results in a direct relationship between the wage rate and the quantity of labor supplied, as represented by the upward-sloping market supply-of-labor curve S in Figure 10.2a.

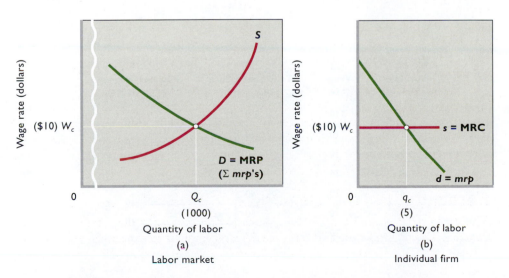

FIGURE 10.2 A purely competitive labor market. In a purely competitive labor market (a), market labor supply S and market labor demand D determine the equilibrium wage rate W_c and the equilibrium number of workers Q_c. Each individual competitive firm (b) takes this competitive wage W_c as given. Thus, the individual firm's labor supply curve $s = $ MRC is perfectly elastic at the going wage W_c. Its labor demand curve, d, is its MRP curve (here labeled mrp). The firm maximizes its profit by hiring workers up to the point where MRP = MRC.

Wage and Employment Determination

What determines the market wage rate and how do firms respond to it? Suppose 200 firms demand a particular type of labor, say, carpenters. These firms need not be in the same industry; industries are defined according to the products they produce and not the resources they employ. Thus, firms producing wood-framed furniture, wood windows and doors, houses and apartment buildings, and wood cabinets will demand carpenters. To find the total, or market, labor demand curve for a particular labor service, we sum horizontally the labor demand curves (the marginal revenue product curves) of the individual firms, as indicated in Figure 10.2. The horizontal summing of the 200 labor demand curves like d in Figure 10.2b yields the market labor demand curve D in Figure 10.2a.

The intersection of the market labor demand curve D and the market labor supply curve S in Figure 10.2a determines the equilibrium wage rate and the level of employment in this purely competitive labor market. Observe that the equilibrium wage rate is W_c ($10) and the number of workers hired is Q_c (1000).

To the individual firm (Figure 10.2b) the market wage rate W_c is given at $10. Each of the many firms employs such a small fraction of the total available supply of this type of labor that no single firm can influence the wage rate. As shown by the horizontal line s in Figure 10.2b, the supply of labor faced by an individual firm is perfectly elastic. It can hire as many or as few workers as it wants to at the market wage rate. This fact is clarified in Table 10.2, where we see that the marginal cost of labor MRC is constant at $10 and is equal to the wage rate. Each additional unit of labor employed adds precisely its own wage rate (here, $10) to the firm's total resource cost.

Each individual firm will apply the MRP = MRC rule to determine its profit-maximizing level of employment. So the competitive firm maximizes its profit by hiring units of labor to the point at which its wage rate (= MRC) equals MRP. In Figure 10.2b the employer will hire q_c (5) units of labor, paying each worker the market wage rate W_c ($10). The other 199 firms (not shown) in this labor market will also each employ 5 workers and pay $10 per hour. The workers will receive pay based on their contribution to the firm's output and thus revenues.

INTERACTIVE GRAPHS

G 10.1

Competitive labor market

TABLE 10.2 The Supply of Labor: Pure Competition in the Hire of Labor

(1) Units of Labor	(2) Wage Rate	(3) Total Labor Cost (Wage Bill)	(4) Marginal Resource (Labor) Cost
0	$10	$ 0	
			$10
1	10	10	
			10
2	10	20	
			10
3	10	30	
			10
4	10	40	
			10
5	10	50	
			10
6	10	60	

Monopsony

In the purely competitive labor market, each firm can hire as little or as much labor as it needs at the market wage rate, as reflected in its horizontal labor supply curve. The situation is strikingly different when the labor market is a **monopsony**, a market structure in which there is only a single buyer. Labor market monopsony has the following characteristics:

- There is only a single buyer of a particular type of labor.
- The workers providing this type of labor have few employment options other than working for the monopsony either because they are geographically immobile or because finding alternative employment would mean having to acquire new skills.
- The firm is a "wage maker" because the wage rate it must pay varies directly with the number of workers it employs.

As is true of monopoly power, there are various degrees of monopsony power. In *pure* monopsony, such power is at its maximum because only a single employer hires labor in the labor market. The best real-world examples are probably the labor markets in towns that depend almost entirely on one major firm. For example, a silver-mining company may be almost the only source of employment in a remote Idaho town. A Wisconsin paper mill, a Colorado ski resort, or an Iowa food processor may provide most of the employment in its locale. In other cases, three or four firms may each hire a large portion of the supply of labor in a certain market and therefore have some monopsony power. Moreover, if they illegally act in concert in hiring labor, they greatly enhance their monopsony power.

Upward-Sloping Labor Supply to Firm

When a firm hires most of the available supply of a certain type of labor, its decision to employ more or fewer workers affects the wage rate it pays to those workers. Specifically, if a firm is large in relation to the size of the labor market, it will have to pay a higher wage rate to obtain more labor. Suppose that there is only one employer of a particular type of labor in a certain geographic area. In this pure monopsony situation, the labor supply curve for the *firm* and the total labor supply curve for the *labor market* are identical. The monopsonist's supply curve—represented by curve S in Figure 10.3—is upsloping because the firm must pay higher wage rates if it wants to attract and hire additional workers. This same curve is also the monopsonist's average-cost-of-labor curve. Each point on curve S indicates the wage rate (cost) per worker that must be paid to attract the corresponding number of workers.

monopsony
A market structure in which only a single buyer of a good, service, or resource is present.

ORIGIN OF THE IDEA

O 10.2

Monopsony

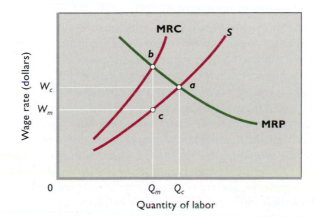

FIGURE 10.3 Monopsony. In a monopsonistic labor market, the employer's marginal resource (labor) cost curve (MRC) lies above the labor supply curve S. Equating MRC with MRP at point b, the monopsonist hires Q_m workers (compared with Q_c under competition). As indicated by point c on S, it pays only wage rate W_m (compared with the competitive wage W_c).

TABLE 10.3 The Supply of Labor: Monopsony in the Hiring of Labor

(1) Units of Labor	(2) Wage Rate	(3) Total Labor Cost (Wage Bill)	(4) Marginal Resource (Labor) Cost
0	$ 5	$ 0	
			$ 6
1	6	6	
			8
2	7	14	
			10
3	8	24	
			12
4	9	36	
			14
5	10	50	
			16
6	11	66	

MRC Higher Than the Wage Rate

When a monopsonist pays a higher wage to attract an additional worker, it must pay that higher wage not only to the additional worker, but to all the workers it is currently employing at a lower wage. If not, labor morale will deteriorate, and the employer will be plagued with labor unrest because of wage-rate differences existing for the same job. Paying a uniform wage to all workers means that the cost of an extra worker—the marginal resource (labor) cost (MRC)—is the sum of that worker's wage rate and the amount necessary to bring the wage rate of all current workers up to the new wage level.

Table 10.3 illustrates this point. One worker can be hired at a wage rate of $6. But hiring a second worker forces the firm to pay a higher wage rate of $7. The marginal resource cost of the second worker is $8—the $7 paid to the second worker plus a $1 raise for the first worker. From another viewpoint, total labor cost is now $14 (= 2 × $7), up from $6 (= 1 × $6). So the MRC of the second worker is $8 (= $14 − $6), not just the $7 wage rate paid to that worker. Similarly, the marginal labor cost of the third worker is $10—the $8 that must be paid to attract this worker from alternative employment plus $1 raises, from $7 to $8, for the first two workers.

Here is the key point: Because the monopsonist is the only employer in the labor market, its marginal resource (labor) cost exceeds the wage rate. Graphically, the monopsonist's MRC curve lies above the average-cost-of-labor curve, or labor supply curve S, as is clearly shown in Figure 10.3.

Equilibrium Wage and Employment

How many units of labor will the monopsonist hire, and what wage rate will it pay? To maximize profit, the monopsonist will employ the quantity of labor Q_m in Figure 10.3 because at that quantity MRC and MRP are equal (point *b*). The monopsonist next determines how much it must pay to attract these Q_m workers. From the supply curve S, specifically point *c*, it sees that it must pay wage rate W_m. Clearly, it need not pay a wage equal to MRP; it can attract and hire exactly the number of workers it wants (Q_m) with wage rate W_m. And that is the wage that it will pay.

Contrast these results with those that would prevail in a competitive labor market. With competition in the hiring of labor, the level of employment would be greater (at Q_c) and the wage rate would be higher (at W_c). Other things equal, the monopsonist maximizes its profit by hiring a smaller number of workers and thereby paying a less-than-competitive wage rate. Society obtains a smaller output, and workers get a wage rate that is less by *bc* than their marginal revenue product.

WORKED PROBLEMS

W 10.2

Labor markets: competition and monopsony

INTERACTIVE GRAPHS

G 10.2

Monopsony

Monopsony Power

Fortunately, monopsonistic labor markets are uncommon in the United States. In most labor markets, several potential employers compete for most workers, particularly for workers who are occupationally and geographically mobile. Also, where monopsony labor market outcomes might have otherwise occurred, unions have often sprung up to counteract that power by forcing firms to negotiate wages. Nevertheless, economists have found some evidence of monopsony power in such diverse labor markets as the markets for nurses, professional athletes, public school teachers, newspaper employees, and some building-trade workers.

In the case of nurses, the major employers in most locales are a relatively small number of hospitals. Further, the highly specialized skills of nurses are not readily transferable to other occupations. It has been found, in accordance with the monopsony model, that, other things equal, the smaller the number of hospitals in a town or city (that is, the greater the degree of monopsony), the lower the beginning salaries of nurses.

Professional sports leagues also provide a good example of monopsony, particularly as it relates to the pay of first-year players. The National Football League, the National Basketball Association, and Major League Baseball assign first-year players to teams through "player drafts." That device prohibits other teams from competing for a player's services, at least for several years, until the player becomes a "free agent." In this way each league exercises monopsony power, which results in lower salaries than would occur under competitive conditions.

QUESTION: The salaries of star players often increase substantially when they become free agents. How does that fact relate to monopsony power?

Union Models

Our assumption thus far has been that workers compete with one another in selling their labor services. In some labor markets, however, workers unionize and sell their labor services collectively. In the United States, about 12 percent of wage and salary workers belong to unions. (As shown in Global Snapshot 10.1, this percentage is low relative to some other nations.)

Union efforts to raise wage rates are mainly concentrated on the supply side of the labor market.

Exclusive or Craft Union Model

Unions can boost wage rates by reducing the supply of labor, and over the years organized labor has favored policies to do just that. For example, labor unions have supported legislation that has (1) restricted permanent immigration, (2) reduced child labor, (3) encouraged compulsory retirement, and (4) enforced a shorter workweek.

GLOBAL SNAPSHOT 10.1

Union Density, Selected Nations

The percentage of workers unionized varies considerably across countries, but sometimes this is due to differences in international practices, including some nations' legal restrictions preventing unionization in certain occupations. To adjust for these differences, alternative measures such as "union density," the rate of "actual" to "potential" membership, are used. Compared with most other industrialized nations, the percentage of potential wage and salary earners belonging to unions in the United States is small.

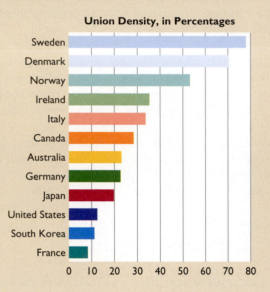

Union Density, in Percentages

Source: U.S. Bureau of Labor Statistics, *Union Membership Statistics in 24 Countries*, 2006, **www.bls.gov**.

Moreover, certain types of workers have adopted techniques designed to restrict the number of workers who can join their union. This is especially true of *craft unions*, whose members possess a particular skill, such as carpenters or brick masons or plumbers. Craft unions have frequently forced employers to agree to hire only union members, thereby gaining virtually complete control of the labor supply. Then, by following restrictive membership policies—for example, long apprenticeships, very high initiation fees, and limits on the number of new members admitted—they have artificially restricted labor supply. As indicated in Figure 10.4, such practices result in higher wage rates and constitute what is called **exclusive unionism.** By excluding workers from unions and therefore from the labor supply, craft unions succeed in elevating wage rates.

This craft union model is also applicable to many professional organizations, such as the American Medical Association, the National Education Association, the American Bar Association, and hundreds of others. Such groups seek to prohibit competition for their services from less-qualified labor suppliers. One way to accomplish that is through **occupational licensing.** Here, a group of workers in a given occupation pressure federal, state, or municipal government to pass a law that says that some occupational group (for example, barbers, physicians, lawyers, plumbers, cosmetologists, egg graders, pest controllers) can practice their trade only if they meet certain requirements. Those requirements might include level of education, amount of work experience, and the passing of an examination. Members of the licensed occupation typically

exclusive unionism
The union practice of restricting the supply of skilled union labor to increase the wage rate received by union members.

occupational licensing
Government laws that require a worker to satisfy certain specified requirements and obtain a license from a licensing board before engaging in a particular occupation.

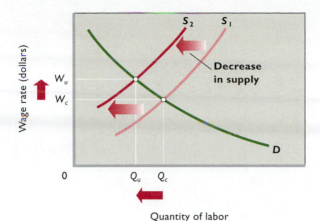

FIGURE 10.4 Exclusive or craft unionism. By reducing the supply of labor (say, from S_1 to S_2) through the use of restrictive membership policies, exclusive unions achieve higher wage rates (W_c to W_u). However, restriction of the labor supply also reduces the number of workers employed (Q_c to Q_u).

dominate the licensing board that administers such laws. The result is self-regulation, which can lead to policies that restrict entry to the occupation and reduce labor supply.

The expressed purpose of licensing is to protect consumers from incompetent practitioners—surely a worthy goal. But such licensing, if abused, simply results in above-competitive wages and earnings for those in the licensed occupation (Figure 10.4). Moreover, licensing requirements often include a residency requirement, which inhibits the interstate movement of qualified workers. Some 600 occupations are now licensed in the United States.

Inclusive or Industrial Union Model

Instead of trying to limit their membership, however, most unions seek to organize all available workers. This is especially true of the *industrial unions*, such as those of the automobile workers and steelworkers. Such unions seek as members all available unskilled, semiskilled, and skilled workers in an industry. It makes sense for a union to be exclusive when its members are skilled craft workers for whom the employer has few substitutes. But it does not make sense for a union to be exclusive when trying to organize unskilled and semiskilled workers. To break a strike, employers could then easily substitute unskilled or semiskilled nonunion workers for the unskilled or semiskilled union workers.

By contrast, an industrial union that includes virtually all available workers in its membership can put firms under great pressure to agree to its wage demands. Because of its legal right to strike, such a union can threaten to deprive firms of their entire labor supply. And an actual strike can do just that. Further, with virtually all available workers in the union, it will be difficult in the short run for new nonunion firms to emerge and thereby undermine what the union is demanding from existing firms.

We illustrate such **inclusive unionism** in Figure 10.5. Initially, the competitive equilibrium wage rate is W_c and the level of employment is Q_c. Now suppose an industrial union is formed that demands a higher, above-equilibrium wage rate of, say, W_u. That wage rate W_u would create a perfectly elastic labor supply over the range *ae* in Figure 10.5. If firms wanted to hire any workers in this range, they would have to pay the union-imposed wage rate. If they decide against meeting this wage demand, the union will supply no labor at all, and the firms will be faced with a strike. If firms decide it is better to pay the higher wage rate than to suffer a strike, they will cut back on employment from Q_c to Q_u.

By agreeing to the union's W_u wage demand, individual employers become wage takers at the union wage rate W_u. Because labor supply is perfectly elastic over range *ae*,

inclusive unionism
The union practice of including as members all workers employed in an industry.

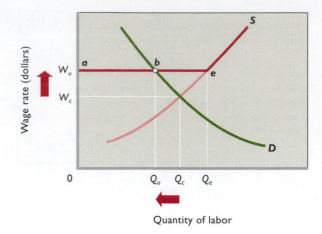

FIGURE 10.5 Inclusive or industrial unionism. By organizing virtually all available workers in order to control the supply of labor, inclusive industrial unions may impose a wage rate, such as W_u, that is above the competitive wage rate W_c. In effect, this changes the labor supply curve from S to aeS. At wage rate W_u, employers will cut employment from Q_c to Q_u.

the marginal resource (labor) cost is equal to the union wage rate W_u over this range. The Q_u level of employment is the result of employers' equating this MRC (now equal to the union wage rate) with MRP, according to our profit-maximizing rule.

Note from point e on labor supply curve S that Q_e workers desire employment at wage W_u. But as indicated by point b on labor demand curve D, only Q_u workers are employed. The result is a surplus of labor of $Q_e - Q_u$ (also shown by distance eb). In a purely competitive labor market without the union, the effect of a surplus of unemployed workers would be lower wages. Specifically, the wage rate would fall to the equilibrium level W_c where the quantity of labor supplied equals the quantity of labor demanded (each, Q_c). But this drop in wages does not happen because workers are acting collectively through their union. Individual workers cannot offer to work for less than W_u nor can employers pay less than that.

Wage Increases and Job Loss

Evidence suggests that union members on average achieve a 15-percent wage advantage over nonunion workers. But when unions are successful in raising wages, their efforts also have another major effect. As Figures 10.4 and 10.5 suggest, the wage-raising actions achieved by both exclusive and inclusive unionism reduce employment in unionized firms. Simply put, a union's success in achieving above-equilibrium wage rates thus tends to be accompanied by a decline in the number of workers employed. That result acts as a restraining influence on union wage demands. A union cannot expect to maintain solidarity within its ranks if it seeks a wage rate so high that 20–30 percent of its members lose their jobs.

Wage Differentials

wage differentials
The differences between the wage received by one worker or group of workers and that received by another worker or group of workers.

Hourly wage rates and annual salaries differ greatly among occupations. In Table 10.4 we list average annual salaries for a number of occupations to illustrate such **wage differentials.** For example, observe that aircraft pilots on average earn nearly five times as much as retail salespersons. Not shown, there are also large wage differentials within some of the occupations listed. For example, some highly experienced pilots earn several times as much income as pilots just starting their careers. And, although average wages for retail salespersons are relatively low, some top salespersons selling on commission make several times the average wages listed for their occupation.

TABLE 10.4 Average Annual Wages in Selected Occupations, 2010

Occupation	Average Annual Wages
Surgeons	$225,390
Petroleum engineers	127,970
Financial managers	116,970
Aircraft pilots	115,300
Law professors	107,990
Chemical engineers	94,590
Dental hygienists	68,680
Registered nurses	67,720
Police officers	55,620
Electricians	51,810
Travel agents	33,950
Barbers	27,930
Recreation workers	25,270
Retail salespersons	25,000
Teacher aides	24,880
Fast-food cooks	18,540

Source: Bureau of Labor Statistics, **www.bls.gov.**

What explains wage differentials such as these? Once again, the forces of demand and supply are highly revealing. As we demonstrate in Figure 10.6, wage differentials can arise on either the supply or the demand side of labor markets. Panels (a) and (b) in Figure 10.6 represent labor markets for two occupational groups that have identical *labor supply curves*. Labor market (a) has a relatively high equilibrium wage (W_a) because labor demand is very strong. In labor market (b) the equilibrium wage is relatively low (W_b) because labor demand is weak. Clearly, the wage differential between occupations (a) and (b) results solely from differences in the magnitude of labor demand.

Contrast that situation with panels (c) and (d) in Figure 10.6, where the *labor demand curves* are identical. In labor market (c) the equilibrium wage is relatively high (W_c) because labor supply is low. In labor market (d) labor supply is highly abundant, so the equilibrium wage (W_d) is relatively low. The wage differential between (c) and (d) results solely from the differences in the magnitude of labor supply.

Although Figure 10.6 provides a good starting point for understanding wage differentials, we need to know *why* demand and supply conditions differ in various labor markets. There are several reasons.

Marginal Revenue Productivity

The strength of labor demand—how far rightward the labor demand curve is located—differs greatly among occupations due to differences in how much various occupational groups contribute to the revenue of their respective employers. This revenue contribution, in turn, depends on the workers' productivity and the strength of the demand for the products they are helping to produce. Where labor is highly productive and product demand is strong, labor demand also is strong and, other things equal, pay is high. Top professional athletes, for example, are highly productive at producing sports entertainment, for which millions of people are willing to pay billions of dollars over the course of a season. Because the marginal revenue productivity of these players is so high, they are in very high demand by sports teams. This high demand leads to their extremely high salaries (as in Figure 10.6a). In contrast, most workers generate much

FIGURE 10.6 Labor demand, labor supply, and wage differentials. The wage differential between labor markets (a) and (b) results solely from differences in labor demand. In labor markets (c) and (d), differences in labor supply are the sole cause of the wage differential.

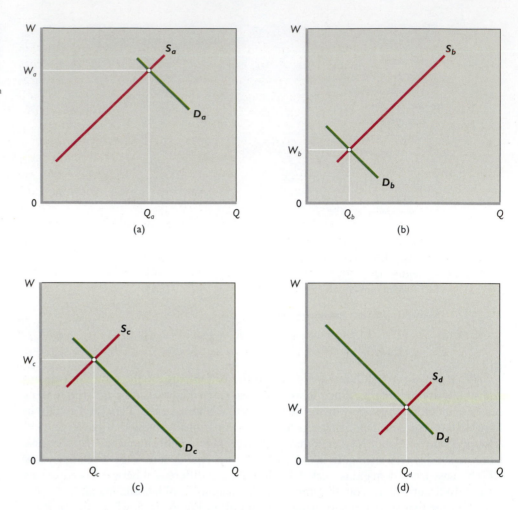

more modest revenue for their employers. This results in much lower demand for their labor and, consequently, much lower wages (as in Figure 10.6b).

Noncompeting Groups

On the supply side of the labor market, workers are not homogeneous; they differ in their mental and physical capacities and in their education and training. At any given time the labor force is made up of many noncompeting groups of workers, each representing several occupations for which the members of that particular group qualify. In some groups qualified workers are relatively few, whereas in others they are plentiful. And workers in one group do not qualify for the occupations of other groups.

Ability   Only a few workers have the ability or physical attributes to be brain surgeons, concert violinists, top fashion models, research chemists, or professional athletes. Because the supply of these particular types of labor is very small in relation to labor demand, their wages are high (as in Figure 10.6c). The members of these and similar groups do not compete with one another or with other skilled or semiskilled workers. The violinist does not compete with the surgeon, nor does the surgeon compete with the violinist or the fashion model.

Education and Training Another source of wage differentials is differing amounts of **human capital,** which is the personal stock of knowledge, know-how, and skills that enables a person to be productive and thus to earn income. Such stocks result from investments in human capital. Like expenditures on machinery and equipment, productivity-enhancing expenditures on education or training are investments. In both cases, people incur *present costs* with the intention that those expenditures will lead to a greater flow of *future earnings*.

Figure 10.7 indicates that workers who have made greater investments in education achieve higher incomes during their careers. The reason is twofold: (1) There are fewer such workers, so their supply is limited relative to less-educated workers, and (2) more educated workers tend to be more productive and thus in greater demand. Figure 10.7 also indicates that the incomes of better-educated workers generally rise more rapidly than those of poorly educated workers. The primary reason is that employers provide more on-the-job training to the better-educated workers, boosting their marginal revenue productivity and therefore their earnings.

Although education yields higher incomes, it carries substantial costs. A college education involves not only direct costs (tuition, fees, books) but indirect or opportunity costs (forgone earnings) as well. Does the higher pay received by better-educated workers compensate for these costs? The answer is yes. Rates of return are estimated to be 10 to 13 percent for investments in secondary education and 8 to 12 percent for investments in college education. One generally accepted estimate is that each year of schooling raises a worker's wage by about 8 percent. Currently, college graduates on average earn about $1.70 for each $1 earned by high school graduates.

human capital
The personal stock of knowledge, know-how, and skills that enables a person to be productive and thus to earn income.

ORIGIN OF THE IDEA

O 10.3

Human capital

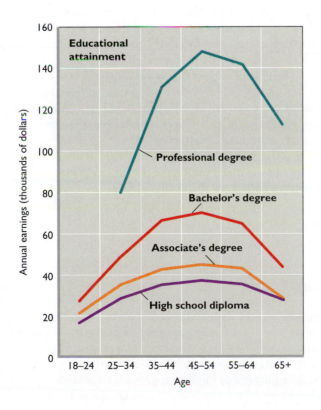

FIGURE 10.7 Education levels and average annual income.
Annual income by age is higher for workers with more education. Investment in education yields a return in the form of earnings differences enjoyed over one's work life.

Source: U.S. Bureau of the Census, **www. census.gov.** Data are for 2008 and include both men and women.

My Entire Life

For some people, high earnings have little to do with actual hours of work and much to do with their tremendous skill, which reflects their accumulated stock of human capital. The point is demonstrated in the following story: It is said that a tourist once spotted the famous Spanish artist Pablo Picasso (1881–1973) in a Paris café. The tourist asked Picasso if he would do a sketch of his wife for pay. Picasso sketched the wife in a matter of minutes and said, "That will be 10,000 francs [roughly $2000]." Hearing the high price, the tourist became irritated, saying, "But that took you only a few minutes."

"No," replied Picasso, "it took me my entire life!"

QUESTION: In general, how do the skill requirements of the highest-paying occupations in Table 10.4 compare with the skill requirements of the lowest-paying occupations?

Compensating Differences

If the workers in a particular noncompeting group are equally capable of performing several different jobs, you might expect the wage rates to be identical for all these jobs. Not so. A group of high school graduates may be equally capable of becoming sales-clerks or general construction workers, but these jobs pay different wages. In virtually all locales, construction laborers receive much higher wages than salesclerks. These wage differentials are called **compensating differences** because they must be paid to compensate for nonmonetary differences in various jobs.

The construction job involves dirty hands, a sore back, the hazard of accidents, and irregular employment, both seasonally and during recessions (the economywide economic slowdowns that periodically affect the economy). The retail sales job means clean clothing, pleasant air-conditioned surroundings, and little fear of injury or layoff. Other things equal, it is easy to see why workers would rather pick up a credit card than a shovel. So the amount of labor that is supplied to construction firms (as in Figure 10.6c) is smaller than that which is supplied to retail shops (as in Figure 10.6d). Construction firms must pay higher wages than retailers to compensate for the unattractive nonmonetary aspects of construction jobs.

Compensating differences play an important role in allocating society's scarce labor resources. If very few workers want to be garbage collectors, then society must pay high wages to garbage collectors to get the garbage collected. If many more people want to be salesclerks, then society need not pay them as much as it pays garbage collectors to get those services performed.

compensating differences
Wage differentials received by workers to compensate them for nonmonetary disparities in their jobs.

The Minimum Wage

Since the passage of the Fair Labor Standards Act in 1938, the United States has had a federal minimum wage. That wage has ranged between 35 and 50 percent of the average wage paid to manufacturing workers and was most recently raised to $7.25 in July 2009. Numerous states, however, have minimum wages considerably above the federal mandate. The purpose of minimum wages is to provide a "wage floor" that will help less-skilled workers earn enough income to escape poverty.

Critics, reasoning in terms of Figure 10.5, contend that an above-equilibrium minimum wage (say, W_u) will simply cause employers to hire fewer workers. Downsloping labor demand curves are a reality. The higher labor costs may even force some firms out of business. In either case, some of the poor, low-wage workers whom the minimum wage was designed to help will find themselves out of work. Critics point out that a worker who is *unemployed* and desperate to find a job at a minimum wage of $7.25 per hour is clearly worse off than he or she would be if *employed* at a market wage rate of, say, $6.50 per hour.

A second criticism of the minimum wage is that it is "poorly targeted" to reduce household poverty. Critics point out that much of the benefit of the minimum wage accrues to workers, including many teenagers, who do not live in impoverished households.

Advocates of the minimum wage say that critics analyze its impact in an unrealistic context, specifically a competitive labor market (Figure 10.2). But in a less-competitive, low-pay labor market where employers possess some monopsony power (Figure 10.3), the minimum wage can increase wage rates without causing significant unemployment. Indeed, a higher minimum wage may even produce more jobs by eliminating the motive that monopsonistic firms have for restricting employment. For example, a minimum-wage floor of W_c in Figure 10.3 would change the firm's labor supply curve to $W_c aS$ and prompt the firm to increase its employment from Q_m workers to Q_c workers.

Moreover, even if the labor market is competitive, the higher wage rate might prompt firms to find more productive tasks for low-paid workers, thereby raising their productivity. Alternatively, the minimum wage may reduce *labor turnover* (the rate at which workers voluntarily quit). With fewer low-productive trainees, the *average* productivity of the firm's workers would rise. In either case, the alleged negative employment effects of the minimum wage might not occur.

Which view is correct? Unfortunately, there is no clear answer. All economists agree that firms will not hire workers who cost more per hour than the value of their hourly output. So there is some minimum wage so high that it would severely reduce employment. Consider $30 an hour, as an absurd example. Because the majority of U.S. workers earn far less than $30 per hour, a minimum wage that high would render the majority of workers unemployable because the minimum wage that they would have to be paid would far exceed their marginal revenue products.

It has to be remembered, though, that a minimum wage will only cause unemployment in labor markets where the minimum wage exceeds the equilibrium wage. Jobs in these labor markets are typically filled by unskilled or low-skilled workers. For members of such groups, recent research suggests that a 10 percent increase in the minimum wage will reduce employment of unskilled workers by about 1 to 3 percent. However, estimates of the employment effects of minimum wage laws vary from study to study, so significant controversy remains.

The overall effect of the minimum wage is thus uncertain. There seems to be a consensus emerging that, on the one hand, the employment and unemployment effects of the minimum wage are not as great as many critics fear. On the other hand, because a large part of its effect is dissipated on nonpoverty families, the minimum wage is not as strong an antipoverty tool as many supporters contend.

Voting patterns and surveys make it clear, however, that the minimum wage has strong political support. Perhaps this stems from two realities: (1) More workers are believed to be helped than hurt by the minimum wage and (2) the minimum wage gives society some assurance that employers are not "taking undue advantage" of vulnerable, low-skilled workers.

QUESTION: Have you ever worked for the minimum wage? If so, for how long? Would you favor increasing the minimum wage by $1? By $2? By $5? Explain your reasoning.

Summary

1. The demand for labor is derived from the product it helps produce. That means the demand for labor will depend on its productivity and on the market value (price) of the good it is producing.

2. Because the firm equates the wage rate and MRP in determining its profit-maximizing level of employment, the marginal revenue product curve is the firm's labor demand curve. Thus, each point on the MRP curve indicates how many labor units the firm will hire at a specific wage rate.

3. The competitive firm's labor demand curve slopes downward because of the law of diminishing returns. Summing horizontally the demand curves of all the firms hiring that resource produces the market demand curve for labor.

4. The demand curve for labor will shift as the result of (a) a change in the demand for, and therefore the price of, the product the labor is producing; (b) changes in the productivity of labor; and (c) changes in the prices of substitutable and complementary resources.

5. The elasticity of demand for labor measures the responsiveness of labor quantity to a change in the wage rate. The coefficient of the elasticity of labor demand is

$$E_w = \frac{\text{percentage change in labor quantity demanded}}{\text{percentage change in wage rate}}$$

When E_w is greater than 1, labor demand is elastic; when E_w is less than 1, labor demand is inelastic; and when E_w equals 1, labor demand is unit-elastic.

6. The elasticity of labor demand will be greater (a) the greater the ease of substituting other resources for labor, (b) the greater the elasticity of demand for the product, and (c) the larger the proportion of total production costs attributable to labor.

7. Specific wage rates depend on the structure of the particular labor market. In a competitive labor market, the equilibrium wage rate and level of employment are determined at the intersection of the labor supply curve and labor demand curve. For the individual firm, the market wage rate establishes a horizontal labor supply curve, meaning that the wage rate equals the firm's constant marginal resource cost. The firm hires workers to the point where its MRP equals its MRC.

8. Under monopsony, the marginal resource cost curve lies above the resource supply curve because the monopsonist must bid up the wage rate to hire extra workers and must pay that higher wage rate to all workers. The monopsonist hires fewer workers than are hired under competitive conditions, pays less-than-competitive wage rates (has lower labor costs), and thus obtains greater profit.

9. A union may raise competitive wage rates by (a) restricting the supply of labor through exclusive unionism or (b) directly enforcing an above-equilibrium wage rate through inclusive unionism. On average, unionized workers realize wage rates 15 percent higher than those of comparable nonunion workers.

10. Wage differentials are largely explainable in terms of (a) marginal revenue productivity of various groups of workers; (b) noncompeting groups arising from differences in the capacities and education of different groups of workers; and (c) compensating wage differences, that is, wage differences that must be paid to offset nonmonetary differences in jobs.

11. Economists disagree about the desirability of the minimum wage. While it raises the income of some workers, it reduces the income of other workers whose skills are not sufficient to justify being paid the mandated wage.

Terms and Concepts

purely competitive labor market	substitution effect	occupational licensing
derived demand	output effect	inclusive unionism
marginal revenue product (MRP)	elasticity of labor demand	wage differentials
marginal resource cost (MRC)	monopsony	human capital
MRP = MRC rule	exclusive unionism	compensating differences

Questions  ECONOMICS

1. Explain the meaning and significance of the fact that the demand for labor is a derived demand. Why do labor demand curves slope downward? LO1

2. On the following page, complete the labor demand table for a firm that is hiring labor competitively and selling its product in a purely competitive market. LO1

a. How many workers will the firm hire if the market wage rate is $27.95? $19.95? Explain why the firm will not hire a larger or smaller number of units of labor at each of these wage rates.

b. Show in schedule form and graphically the labor demand curve of this firm.

Units of Labor	Total Product	Marginal Product	Product Price	Total Revenue	Marginal Revenue Product
0	0		$2	$ _____	$ _____
1	17	_____	2	_____	_____
2	31	_____	2	_____	_____
3	43	_____	2	_____	_____
4	53	_____	2	_____	_____
5	60	_____	2	_____	_____
6	65	_____	2	_____	_____

3. In 2009 General Motors (GM) announced that it would reduce employment by 21,000 workers. What does this decision reveal about how GM viewed its marginal revenue product (MRP) and marginal resource cost (MRC)? Why didn't GM reduce employment by more than 21,000 workers? By less than 21,000 workers? **LO2**

4. How will each of the following affect the demand for resource A, which is being used to produce commodity Z? Where there is any uncertainty as to the outcome, specify the causes of that uncertainty. **LO2**
    a. An increase in the demand for product Z.
    b. An increase in the price of substitute resource B.
    c. A technological improvement in the capital equipment with which resource A is combined.
    d. A fall in the price of complementary resource C.
    e. A decline in the elasticity of demand for product Z due to a decline in the competitiveness of product market Z.

5. What effect would each of the following factors have on elasticity of demand for resource A, which is used to produce product Z? **LO3**
    a. There is an increase in the number of resources substitutable for A in producing Z.

    b. Due to technological change, much less of resource A is used relative to resources B and C in the production process.
    c. The elasticity of demand for product Z greatly increases.

6. Florida citrus growers say that the recent crackdown on illegal immigration is increasing the market wage rates necessary to get their oranges picked. Some are turning to $100,000 to $300,000 mechanical harvesting machines known as "trunk, shake, and catch" pickers, which vigorously shake oranges from the trees. If widely adopted, how will this substitution affect the demand for human orange pickers? What does that imply about the relative strengths of the substitution and output effects? **LO2**

7. Why is a firm in a purely competitive labor market a *wage taker?* What would happen if it decided to pay less than the going market wage rate? **LO4**

8. Contrast the methods used by inclusive unions and exclusive unions to raise union wage rates. **LO5**

9. What is meant by the terms "investment in human capital" and "compensating wage differences"? Use these concepts to explain wage differentials. **LO6**

10. Why might an increase in the minimum wage in the United States simply send some jobs abroad? Relate your answer to elasticity of labor demand. **LO5**

Problems

1. Suppose that marginal product tripled while product price fell by one-half in Table 10.1. What would be the new MRP values in Table 10.1? What would be the net impact on the location of the resource demand curve in Figure 10.1? **LO2**

2. Complete the following labor supply table for a firm hiring labor competitively: **LO4**
    a. Show graphically the labor supply and marginal resource (labor) cost curves for this firm. Are the curves the same or different? If they are different, which one is higher?
    b. Plot the labor demand data of question 2 on the graph used in part *a* above. What are the equilibrium wage rate and level of employment?

Units of Labor	Wage Rate	Total Labor Cost	Marginal Resource (Labor) Cost
0	$14	$ _____	$ _____
1	14	_____	_____
2	14	_____	_____
3	14	_____	_____
4	14	_____	_____
5	14	_____	_____
6	14	_____	

3. Assume a firm is a monopsonist that can hire its first worker for $6 but must increase the wage rate by $3 to attract each successive worker (so that the second worker must be paid $9, the third $12, and so on). **LO4**

   a. Draw the firm's labor supply and marginal resource cost curves. Are the curves the same or different? If they are different, which one is higher?

   b. On the same graph, plot the labor demand data of question 2. What are the equilibrium wage rate and level of employment?

   c. Compare these answers with those you found in problem 2. By how much does the monoposonist reduce wages below the competitive wage? By how much does the monopsonist reduce employment below the competitive level?

4. Suppose that low-skilled workers employed in clearing woodland can each clear one acre per month if they are each equipped with a shovel, a machete, and a chainsaw. Clearing one acre brings in $1000 in revenue. Each worker's equipment costs the worker's employer $150 per month to rent and each worker toils 40 hours per week for four weeks each month. **LO5**

   a. What is the marginal revenue product of hiring one low-skilled worker to clear woodland for one month?

   b. How much revenue per hour does each worker bring in?

   c. If the minimum wage were $6.20, would the revenue per hour in part *b* exceed the minimum wage? If so, by how much per hour?

   d. Now consider the employer's total costs. These include the equipment costs as well as a normal profit of $50 per acre. If the firm pays workers the minimum wage of $6.20 per hour, what will the firm's economic profit or loss be per acre?

   e. At what value would the minimum wage have to be set so that the firm would make zero economic profit from employing an additional low-skilled worker to clear woodland?

FURTHER TEST YOUR KNOWLEDGE AT
www.mcconnellbrief2e.com

At the text's Online Learning Center, **www.mcconnellbrief2e.com**, you will find one or more web-based questions that require information from the Internet to answer. We urge you to check them out, since they will familiarize you with websites that may be helpful in other courses and perhaps even in your career. The OLC also features multiple-choice quizzes that give instant feedback and provides other helpful ways to further test your knowledge of the chapter.

Visit your mobile app store and download the McConnell Brief Edition: Study Econ app *today*!

11

Income Inequality and Poverty

Evidence that suggests wide income disparity in the United States is easy to find. In 2009 talk-show host Oprah Winfrey earned an estimated $270 million, golfer Tiger Woods earned $110 million, and singer Beyoncé Knowles earned $87 million. In contrast, the salary of the president of the United States is $400,000, and the typical schoolteacher earns $49,000. A full-time minimum-wage worker at a fast-food restaurant makes about $15,000. Cash welfare payments to a mother with two children average $5000.

In 2009 about 43.6 million Americans—or 14.3 percent of the population—lived in poverty. An estimated 643,000 people were homeless in that year, with about 1.56 million spending at least one night in a shelter. The richest fifth of American households received about 50.3 percent of total income, while the poorest fifth received about 3.4 percent.

What are the sources of income inequality? Is income inequality rising or falling? Is the United States making progress against poverty? What are the major income-maintenance programs in the United States? Is the current welfare system effective? These are some of the questions we will answer in this chapter.

Facts about Income Inequality

Average household income in the United States is among the highest in the world; in 2009, it was $68,827 per household (one or more persons occupying a housing unit). But that average tells us nothing about income inequality. To learn about that, we must examine how income is distributed around the average.

Distribution by Income Category

income inequality
The unequal distribution of an economy's total income among households or families.

One way to measure **income inequality** is to look at the percentages of households in a series of income categories. Table 11.1 shows that about 25 percent of all households had annual before-tax incomes of less than $25,000 in 2009, while another 20.2 percent had annual incomes of $100,000 or more. The data in the table suggest a wide dispersion of household income in the United States.

Distribution by Quintiles (Fifths)

A second way to measure income inequality is to divide the total number of individuals, households, or families (two or more persons related by birth, marriage, or adoption) into five numerically equal groups, or *quintiles*, and examine the percentage of total personal (before-tax) income received by each quintile. We do this for households in the table in Figure 11.1, where we also provide the upper income limit for each quintile. Any amount of income greater than that listed in each row of column 3 would place a household into the next-higher quintile.

Lorenz curve
A curve that shows an economy's distribution of income by measuring the cumulated percentage of income receivers along the horizontal axis and the cumulated percentage of income they receive along the vertical axis.

The Lorenz Curve and Gini Ratio

We can display the quintile distribution of personal income through a **Lorenz curve.** In Figure 11.1, we plot the cumulative percentage of households on the horizontal axis and the cumulative percentage of income they obtain on the vertical axis. The diagonal line

TABLE 11.1 **The Distribution of U.S. Income by Households, 2009**

(1) Personal Income Category	(2) Percentage of All Households in This Category
Under $10,000	7.3
$10,000–$14,999	5.8
$15,000–$24,999	11.9
$25,000–$34,999	11.0
$35,000–$49,999	14.1
$50,000–$74,999	18.1
$75,000–$99,999	11.5
$100,000 and above	20.2
	100.0

Source: Bureau of the Census, **www.census.gov**. Numbers do not add to 100 percent due to rounding.

FIGURE 11.1 The Lorenz curve and Gini ratio. The Lorenz curve is a convenient way to show the degree of income inequality (here, household income by quintile in 2009). The area between the diagonal (the line of perfect equality) and the Lorenz curve represents the degree of inequality in the distribution of total income. This inequality is measured numerically by the Gini ratio—area A (shown in blue) divided by area A + B (the blue + green area). The Gini ratio for the distribution shown is 0.468.

(1) Quintile	(2) Percentage of Total Income*	(3) Upper Income Limit
Lowest 20%	3.4	$ 20,453
Second 20%	8.6	38,550
Third 20%	14.6	61,801
Fourth 20%	23.2	100,000
Highest 20%	50.3	No limit
Total	100.0	

*Numbers do not add to 100 percent due to rounding.

Source: Bureau of the Census, **www.census.gov**.

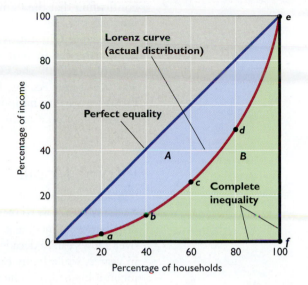

0*e* represents a *perfectly equal distribution of income* because each point along that line indicates that a particular percentage of households receive the same percentage of income. In other words, points representing 20 percent of all households receiving 20 percent of total income, 40 percent receiving 40 percent, 60 percent receiving 60 percent, and so on, all lie on the diagonal line.

By plotting the quintile data from the table in Figure 11.1, we obtain the Lorenz curve for 2009. Observe from point *a* that the bottom 20 percent of all households received 3.4 percent of the income; the bottom 40 percent received 12 percent (= 3.4 + 8.6), as shown by point *b*; and so forth. The blue area between the diagonal line and the Lorenz curve is determined by the extent that the Lorenz curve sags away from the diagonal and indicates the degree of income inequality. If the actual income distribution were perfectly equal, the Lorenz curve and the diagonal would coincide and the blue area would disappear.

At the opposite extreme is complete inequality, where all households but one have zero income. In that case, the Lorenz curve would coincide with the horizontal axis from 0 to point *f* (at 0 percent of income) and then would move immediately up from *f* to point *e* along the vertical axis (indicating that a single household has 100 percent of the total income). The entire area below the diagonal line (triangle 0*ef*) would indicate this extreme degree of inequality. So the farther the Lorenz curve sags away from the diagonal, the greater is the degree of income inequality.

We can easily transform the visual measurement of income inequality described by the Lorenz curve into the **Gini ratio**—a numerical measure of the overall dispersion of income:

$$\text{Gini ratio} = \frac{\text{area between Lorenz curve and diagonal}}{\text{total area below the diagonal}}$$

$$= \frac{A \text{ (blue area)}}{A + B \text{ (blue + green area)}}$$

WORKED PROBLEMS

W 11.1

Lorenz curve

Gini ratio
A numerical measure of the overall dispersion of income among an economy's income receivers.

For the distribution of household income shown in Figure 11.1, the Gini ratio is 0.468. As the area between the Lorenz curve and the diagonal gets larger, the Gini ratio rises to reflect greater inequality. (Test your understanding of this idea by confirming that the Gini ratio for complete income equality is zero and for complete inequality is 1.)

Because Gini ratios are numerical, they are easier to use than Lorenz curves for comparing the income distributions of different ethnic groups and countries. For example, in 2009 the Gini ratio of U.S. household income for African Americans was 0.481; for Asians, 0.488; for whites, 0.455; and for Hispanics, 0.456.[1] Gini ratios for various nations range from 0.230 (Sweden) to 0.707 (Namibia). Examples within this range include Denmark, 0.290; Italy, 0.320; Mexico, 0.482; and South Aftrica, 0.650.[2]

Income Mobility: The Time Dimension

The income data used so far have a major limitation: The income accounting period of 1 year is too short to be very meaningful. Because the Census Bureau data portray the distribution of income in only a single year, they may conceal a more equal distribution over a few years, a decade, or even a lifetime. If Brad earns $1000 in year 1 and $100,000 in year 2, while Jenny earns $100,000 in year 1 and only $1000 in year 2, do we have income inequality? The answer depends on the period of measurement. Annual data would reveal great income inequality, but there would be complete equality over the 2-year period.

income mobility
The extent to which income receivers move from one part of the income distribution to another over some period of time.

This point is important because evidence suggests considerable "churning around" in the distribution of income over time. Such movement of individuals or households from one income quintile to another over time is called **income mobility**. For most income receivers, income starts at a relatively low level during youth, reaches a peak during middle age, and then declines. It follows that if all people receive exactly the same stream of income over their lifetimes, considerable income inequality would still exist in any specific year because of age differences. In any single year, the young and the old would receive low incomes while the middle-aged receive high incomes.

If we change from a "snapshot" view of income distribution in a single year to a "time exposure" portraying incomes over much longer periods, we find considerable movement of income receivers among income classes. For instance, one study showed that between 1996 and 2005, half of the individuals in the lowest quintile of the U.S. income distribution in 1996 were in a higher income quintile in 2005. Almost 25 percent made it to the middle fifth and 5 percent achieved the top quintile. The income mobility moved in both directions. About 57 percent of the top 1 percent of income receivers in 1996 had dropped out of that category by 2005. Overall, income mobility between 1996 and 2005 was the same as it was the previous 10 years. All this correctly suggests that income is more equally distributed over a 5–, 10–, or 20–year period than in any single year.[3]

In short, there is significant individual and household income mobility over time; for many people, "low income" and "high income" are not permanent conditions.

---

[1]U.S. Census Bureau, *Historical Income Tables*, **www.census.gov**.
[2]*CIA World Factbook, 2010*, **www.cia.gov**.
[3]U.S. Department of the Treasury, *Income Mobility in the U.S. from 1996–2005*, November 13, 2007, pp. 1–22.

Effect of Government Redistribution

The income data in the table in Figure 11.1 include wages, salaries, dividends, and interest. They also include all cash transfer payments such as Social Security, unemployment compensation benefits, and welfare assistance to needy households. The data are before-tax data and therefore do not take into account the effects of personal income and payroll (Social Security) taxes that are levied directly on income receivers. Nor do they include government-provided in-kind or **noncash transfers**, which make available specific goods or services rather than cash. Noncash transfers include such things as medical care, housing subsidies, subsidized school lunches, and food stamps. Such transfers are much like income because they enable recipients to "purchase" goods and services.

One economic function of government is to redistribute income, if society so desires. Figure 11.2 and its table reveal that government significantly redistributes income from higher- to lower-income households through taxes and transfers. Note that the U.S. distribution of household income before taxes and transfers are taken into account (dark red Lorenz curve) is substantially less equal than the distribution after taxes and transfers (light red Lorenz curve). Without government redistribution, the lowest 20 percent of households in 2008 would have received only 0.9 percent of total income. *With* redistribution, they received 4.2 percent, or 4.7 times as much.[4]

Which contributes more to redistribution, government taxes or government transfers? The answer is transfers. Because the U.S. tax system is only modestly progressive, nearly all of the reduction in income inequality is attributable to transfer payments. Together with job opportunities, transfer payments have been the most important means of alleviating poverty in the United States.

noncash transfers Government transfer payments in the form of goods and services (or vouchers to obtain them) rather than money.

---

[4] The data in this table are for 2008, whereas the data in Figure 11.1 are for 2009. Even if contemporaneous, the "before" data would differ from the data in Figure 11.1 because the latter include cash transfers. Also, the "after" data in Figure 11.2 are based on a broader concept of income than are the data in Figure 11.1.

FIGURE 11.2 The impact of taxes and transfers on U.S. income inequality. The distribution of income is significantly more equal after taxes and transfers are taken into account than before. Transfers account for most of the lessening of inequality and provide most of the income received by the lowest quintile of households.

	Percentage of Total Income Received, 2008*	
	(1)	(2)
Quintile	**Before Taxes and Transfers**	**After Taxes and Transfers**
Lowest 20 percent	0.9	4.2
Second 20 percent	7.0	10.5
Third 20 percent	14.5	16.4
Fourth 20 percent	24.2	24.1
Highest 20 percent	53.5	44.8

*The data include all money income from private sources, including realized capital gains and employer-provided health insurance. The "after taxes and transfers" data include the value of noncash transfers as well as cash transfers. Numbers may not add to 100 percent due to rounding.

Source: Bureau of the Census, **www.census.gov**.

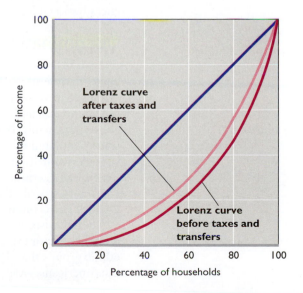

Causes of Income Inequality

There are several causes of income inequality in the United States. In general, the market system is permissive of a high degree of income inequality because it rewards individuals on the basis of the contributions that they, or the resources that they own, make in producing society's output.

More specifically, the factors that contribute to income inequality are the following.

Ability

People have different mental, physical, and aesthetic talents. Some have inherited the exceptional mental qualities that are essential to such high-paying occupations as medicine, corporate finance, and law. Others are blessed with the physical capacity and coordination to become highly paid professional athletes. A few have the talent to become great artists or musicians or have the beauty to become top fashion models. Others have very weak mental endowments and may work in low-paying occupations or may be incapable of earning any income at all. The intelligence and skills of most people fall somewhere in between.

Education and Training

Native ability alone rarely produces high income; people must develop and refine their capabilities through education and training. Individuals differ significantly in the amount of education and training they obtain and thus in their capacity to earn income. Such differences may be a matter of choice: Chin enters the labor force after graduating from high school, while Rodriguez takes a job only after earning a college degree. Other differences may be involuntary: Chin and her parents may simply be unable to finance a college education.

People also receive varying degrees of on-the-job training, which also contributes to income inequality. Some workers learn valuable new skills each year on the job and therefore experience significant income growth over time; others receive little or no on-the-job training and earn no more at age 50 than they did at age 30. Moreover, firms tend to select for advanced on-the-job training the workers who have the most formal education. That added training magnifies the education-based income differences between less-educated and better-educated individuals.

Discrimination

Discrimination in education, hiring, training, and promotion undoubtedly causes some income inequality. If discrimination confines certain racial, ethnic, or gender groups to lower-pay occupations, the supply of labor in those occupations will increase relative to demand and hourly wages and income in those lower-paying jobs will decline. Conversely, labor supply will be artificially reduced in the higher-pay occupations populated by "preferred" workers, raising their wage rates and income. In this way, discrimination can add to income inequality. In fact, economists cannot account for all racial, ethnic, and gender differences in work earnings on the basis of differences in years of education, quality of education, occupations, and annual hours of work. Many economists attribute the unexplained residual to discrimination.

Economists, however, do not see discrimination by race, gender, and ethnicity as a dominant factor explaining income inequality. The income distributions *within* racial or ethnic groups that historically have been targets of discrimination—for example, African Americans—are similar to the income distribution for whites. Other factors besides discrimination are obviously at work. Nevertheless, discrimination is an important concern since it harms individuals and reduces society's overall output and income.

Preferences and Risks

Incomes also differ because of differences in preferences for market work relative to leisure, market work relative to work in the household, and types of occupations. People who choose to stay home with children, work part-time, or retire early usually have less income than those who make the opposite choices. Those who are willing to take arduous, unpleasant jobs (for example, underground mining or heavy construction), to work long hours with great intensity, or to "moonlight" will tend to earn more.

Individuals also differ in their willingness to assume risk. We refer here not only to the race-car driver or the professional boxer but also to the entrepreneur. Although many entrepreneurs fail, many of those who develop successful new products or services realize very substantial incomes. That contributes to income inequality.

Unequal Distribution of Wealth

Income is a *flow*; it represents a stream of wage and salary earnings, along with rent, interest, and profits, as depicted in Chapter 2's circular flow diagram. In contrast, wealth is a *stock*, reflecting at a particular moment the financial and real assets an individual has accumulated over time. A retired person may have very little income and yet own a home, mutual fund shares, and a pension plan that add up to considerable wealth. A new college graduate may be earning a substantial income as an accountant, middle manager, or engineer but have yet to accumulate significant wealth.

The ownership of wealth in the United States is more unequal than the distribution of income. According to the most recent (2004) Federal Reserve wealth data, the wealthiest 10 percent of families owned 70 percent of the total wealth and the top 1 percent owned 33 percent. The bottom 90 percent held only 30 percent of the total wealth. This wealth inequality leads to inequality in rent, interest, and dividends, which in turn contributes to income inequality. Those who own more machinery, real estate, farmland, and stocks and bonds, and who have more money in savings accounts obviously receive greater income from that ownership than people with less or no such wealth.

Market Power

The ability to "rig the market" on one's own behalf also contributes to income inequality. For example, in *resource* markets, certain unions and professional groups have adopted policies that limit the supply of their services, thereby boosting the incomes of those "on the inside." Also, legislation that requires occupational licensing for, say, doctors, dentists, and lawyers can bestow market power that favors the licensed groups. In *product* markets, "rigging the market" means gaining or enhancing monopoly power, which results in greater profit and thus greater income to the firms' owners.

Luck, Connections, and Misfortune

Other forces also play a role in producing income inequality. Luck and "being in the right place at the right time" have helped individuals stumble into fortunes. Discovering oil on a ranch, owning land along a major freeway interchange, and hiring the right press agent have accounted for some high incomes. Personal contacts and political connections are other potential routes to attaining high income.

In contrast, economic misfortunes such as prolonged illness, serious accident, the death of the family breadwinner, or unemployment may plunge a family into the low range of income. The burden of such misfortune is borne very unevenly by the population and thus contributes to income inequality.

Income inequality of the magnitude we have described is not exclusively an American phenomenon. Global Snapshot 11.1 compares income inequality in the United States (here by individuals, not by households) with that in several other nations. Income inequality tends to be greatest in South American nations, where land and capital resources are highly concentrated in the hands of very wealthy families.

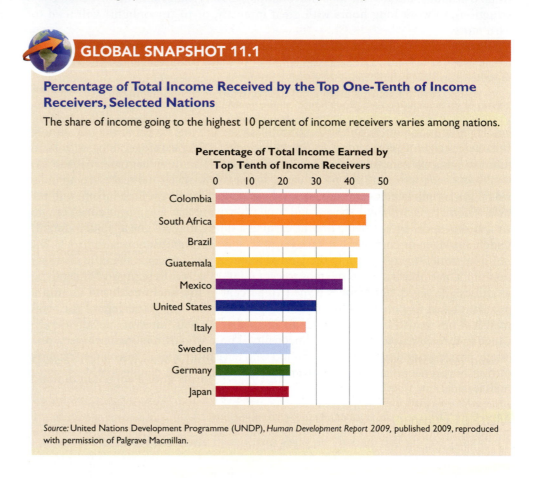

GLOBAL SNAPSHOT 11.1

Percentage of Total Income Received by the Top One-Tenth of Income Receivers, Selected Nations

The share of income going to the highest 10 percent of income receivers varies among nations.

Percentage of Total Income Earned by Top Tenth of Income Receivers

Source: United Nations Development Programme (UNDP), *Human Development Report 2009,* published 2009, reproduced with permission of Palgrave Macmillan.

Income Inequality over Time

Over a period of years, economic growth has raised incomes in the United States: In *absolute* dollar amounts, the entire distribution of income has been moving upward. But incomes may move up in *absolute* terms while leaving the *relative* distribution of income less equal, more equal, or unchanged. Table 11.2 shows how the distribution of household income has changed since 1970. This income is "before tax" and includes cash transfers but not noncash transfers.

Rising Income Inequality since 1970

It is clear from Table 11.2 that the distribution of income by quintiles has become more unequal since 1970. In 2009 the lowest 20 percent of households received

Quintile	1970	1975	1980	1985	1990	1995	2000	2009
Lowest 20%	4.1	4.4	4.3	4.0	3.9	3.7	3.6	3.4
Second 20%	10.8	10.5	10.3	9.7	9.6	9.1	8.9	8.6
Third 20%	17.4	17.1	16.9	16.3	15.9	15.2	14.8	14.6
Fourth 20%	24.5	24.8	24.9	24.6	24.0	23.3	23.0	23.2
Highest 20%	43.3	43.2	43.7	45.3	46.6	48.7	49.8	50.3
Total	100.0	100.0	100.0	100.0	100.0	100.0	100.0	100.0
Top 5%	16.6	15.9	15.8	17.0	18.6	21.0	22.1	21.7

TABLE 11.2 Percentage of Total Before-Tax Income Received by Each One-Fifth and by the Top 5 percent of Households, Selected Years*

*Numbers may not add to 100 percent due to rounding.

Source: Bureau of the Census, **www.census.gov**.

3.4 percent of total before-tax income, compared with 4.1 in 1970. Meanwhile, the income share received by the highest 20 percent rose from 43.3 in 1970 to 50.3 percent in 2009. Also, the percentage of income received by the top 5 percent of households rose significantly over the 1970–2009 period.

Causes of Growing Inequality

Economists suggest several major explanations for the growing U.S. income inequality of the past several decades.

Greater Demand for Highly Skilled Workers Perhaps the most significant contributor to the growing income inequality has been an increasing demand by many firms for workers who are highly skilled and well educated. Moreover, several industries requiring highly skilled workers have either recently emerged or expanded greatly, such as the computer software, business consulting, biotechnology, health care, and Internet industries. Because highly skilled workers remain relatively scarce, their wages have been bid up. Consequently, the wage differences between them and less-skilled workers have increased. In fact, between 1980 and 2007, the wage difference between college graduates and high school graduates rose from 28 percent to 49 percent for women and from 22 percent to 44 percent for men.

The rising demand for skill also has shown up in rapidly rising pay for chief executive officers (CEOs), sizable increases in income from stock options, substantial increases in income for professional athletes and entertainers, and huge fortunes for successful entrepreneurs. This growth of "superstar" pay also has contributed to rising income inequality.

Demographic Changes The entrance of large numbers of less-experienced and less-skilled "baby boomers" into the labor force during the 1970s and 1980s may have contributed to greater income inequality in those two decades. Because younger workers tend to earn less income than older workers, their growing numbers contributed to income inequality. There also has been a growing tendency for men and women with high earnings potential to marry each other, thus increasing family income among the highest income quintiles. Finally, the number of households headed by single or divorced women has increased greatly. That trend has increased income inequality because such households lack a second major wage earner and also because the poverty rate for female-headed households is very high.

International Trade, Immigration, and Decline in Unionism Other factors are probably at work as well. Stronger international competition from imports has reduced the demand for and employment of less-skilled (but highly paid) workers in such industries as the automobile and steel industries. The decline in such jobs has reduced the average wage for less-skilled workers. It also has swelled the ranks of workers in already low-paying industries, placing further downward pressure on wages there.

Similarly, the transfer of jobs to lower-wage workers in developing countries has exerted downward wage pressure on less-skilled workers in the United States. Also, an upsurge in immigration of unskilled workers has increased the number of low-income households in the United States. Finally, the decline in unionism in the United States has undoubtedly contributed to wage inequality since unions tend to equalize pay within firms and industries.

Two cautions: First, when we note growing income inequality, we are not saying that the "rich are getting richer and the poor are getting poorer" in terms of absolute income. Both the rich and the poor are experiencing rises in real income. Rather, what has happened is that, while incomes have risen in all quintiles, income growth has been fastest in the top quintile. Second, increased income inequality is not solely a U.S. phenomenon. The recent rise of inequality also has occurred in several other industrially advanced nations.

The Lorenz curve can be used to contrast the distribution of income at different points in time. If we plotted Table 11.2's data as Lorenz curves, we would find that the curve shifted away from the diagonal between 1970 and 2009. The Gini ratio rose from 0.394 in 1970 to 0.468 in 2009.

APPLYING THE ANALYSIS

Laughing at Shrek

Some economists say that the distribution of annual *consumption* is more meaningful for examining inequality of well-being than is the distribution of annual *income*. In a given year, people's consumption of goods and services may be above or below their income because they can save, draw down past savings, use credit cards, take out home mortgages, spend from inheritances, give money to charities, and so on. A recent study of the distribution of consumption finds that annual consumption inequality is less than income inequality. Moreover, consumption inequality has remained relatively constant over several decades, even though income inequality has increased.*

The Economist magazine extends the argument even further, pointing out that despite the recent increase in income inequality, the products consumed by the rich and the poor are far closer in functionality today than at any other time in history:

> More than 70 percent of Americans under the official poverty line own at least one car. And the distance between driving a used Hyundai Elantra and new Jaguar XJ is well nigh undetectable compared with the difference between motoring and hiking through the muck . . . A wide screen plasma television is lovely, but you do not need one to laugh at "Shrek". . .
>
> Those intrepid souls who make vast fortunes turning out ever higher-quality goods at ever lower prices widen the income gap while reducing the differences that really matter.[†]

Economists generally agree that products and experiences once reserved exclusively for the rich in the United States have, in fact, become more commonplace for nearly all income classes. But skeptics argue that *The Economist*'s argument is too simplistic. Even though both are water outings, there is a fundamental difference between yachting among the Greek isles on your private yacht and paddling on a local pond in your kayak.

QUESTION: How do the ideas of income inequality, consumption inequality, and wealth inequality differ?

*Dirk Krueger and Fabrizio Perri, "Does Income Inequality Lead to Consumption Inequality?" *Review of Economic Studies*, 2006, pp. 163–193.

†*The Economist*, "Economic Focus: The New (Improved) Gilded Age," December 22, 2007, p. 122. © The Economist Newspaper Limited, London.

© Royalty-Free/CORBIS

© Richard Bickel/CORBIS

PHOTO OP The Rich and the Poor in America

Wide disparities of income and wealth exist in the United States.

Equality versus Efficiency

The main policy issue concerning income inequality is how much is necessary and justified. While there is no general agreement on the justifiable amount, we can gain insight by exploring the economic cases for and against greater equality.

The Case for Equality: Maximizing Total Utility

The basic economic argument for an equal distribution of income is that income equality maximizes the total consumer satisfaction (utility) from any particular level of output and income. The rationale for this argument is shown in Figure 11.3, in which we assume that the money incomes of two individuals, Anderson and Brooks, are

FIGURE 11.3 The utility-maximizing distribution of income. With identical marginal-utility-of-income curves MU_A and MU_B, Anderson and Brooks will maximize their combined utility when any amount of income (say, $10,000) is equally distributed. If income is unequally distributed (say, $2500 to Anderson and $7500 to Brooks), the marginal utility derived from the last dollar will be greater for Anderson than for Brooks, and a redistribution toward equality will result in a net increase in total utility. The utility gained by equalizing income at $5000 each, shown by the blue area below curve MU_A in panel (a), exceeds the utility lost, indicated by the red area below curve MU_B in (b).

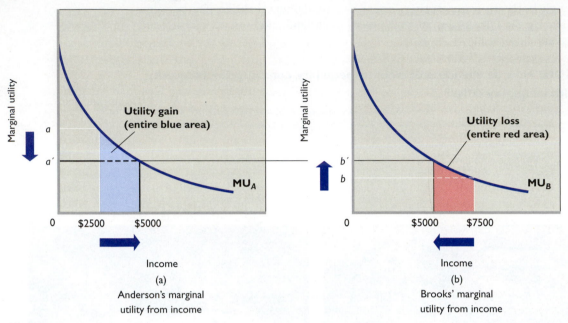

(a)
Anderson's marginal
utility from income

(b)
Brooks' marginal
utility from income

law of diminishing marginal utility

The principle that the amount of extra satisfaction (marginal utility) from consuming a product declines as more of it is consumed.

subject to the **law of diminishing marginal utility.** In any time period, income receivers spend the first dollars received on the products they value most—products whose marginal utility (extra satisfaction) is high. As a consumer's most-pressing wants become satisfied, he or she then spends additional dollars of income on less-important, lower-marginal-utility goods. So marginal-utility-from-income curves slope downward, as in Figure 11.3. The identical diminishing curves (MU_A and MU_B) reflect the assumption that Anderson and Brooks have the same capacity to derive utility from income. Each point on one of the curves measures the marginal utility of the last dollar of a particular level of income.

Now suppose that there is $10,000 worth of income (output) to be distributed between Anderson and Brooks. According to proponents of income equality, the optimal distribution is an equal distribution, which causes the marginal utility of the last dollar spent to be the same for both persons. We can confirm this by demonstrating that if the income distribution is initially unequal, then distributing income more equally can increase the combined utility of the two individuals.

Suppose that the $10,000 of income initially is distributed such that Anderson gets $2500 and Brooks $7500. The marginal utility, *a*, from the last dollar received by Anderson is high and the marginal utility, *b*, from Brooks' last dollar of income is low. If a single dollar of income is shifted from Brooks to Anderson—that is, toward greater equality—then Anderson's utility increases by *a* and Brooks' utility decreases by *b*. The combined utility then increases by *a* minus *b* (Anderson's large gain minus Brooks' small loss). The transfer of another dollar from Brooks to Anderson again increases their combined utility, this time by a slightly smaller amount. Continued transfer of dollars from Brooks to Anderson increases their combined utility until the income is evenly distributed and both receive $5000. At that time their marginal utilities from the last dollar of income are equal (at a' and b'), and any further income redistribution beyond the $2500 already transferred would begin to create inequality and decrease their combined utility.

The area under the MU curve and to the left of the individual's particular level of income represents the total utility (the sum of the marginal utilities) of that income. Therefore, as a result of the transfer of the $2500, Anderson has gained utility represented by the blue area below curve MU_A and Brooks has lost utility represented by the red area below curve MU_B. The blue area exceeds the red area, so income equality yields greater combined total utility than does the initial income inequality.

The Case for Inequality: Incentives and Efficiency

Although the logic of the argument for equality is sound, critics attack its fundamental assumption that there is some fixed amount of output produced and therefore income to be distributed. Critics of income equality argue that the way in which income is distributed is an important determinant of the amount of output or income that is produced and is available for distribution.

Suppose once again in Figure 11.3 that Anderson earns $2500 and Brooks earns $7500. In moving toward equality, society (the government) must tax away some of Brooks' income and transfer it to Anderson. This tax and transfer process diminishes the income rewards of high-income Brooks and raises the income rewards of low-income Anderson; in so doing, it reduces the incentives of both to earn high incomes. Why should high-income Brooks work hard, save and invest, or undertake entrepreneurial risks when the rewards from such activities will be reduced by taxation? And why should low-income Anderson be motivated to increase his income through market activities when the government stands ready to transfer income to him? Taxes are a reduction in the rewards from increased productive effort; redistribution through transfers is a reward for diminished effort.

In the extreme, imagine a situation in which the government levies a 100 percent tax on income and distributes the tax revenue equally to its citizenry. Why would anyone work hard? Why would anyone work at all? Why would anyone assume business risk? Or why would anyone save (forgo current consumption) in order to invest? The economic incentives to "get ahead" will have been removed, greatly reducing society's total production and income. That is, the way income is distributed affects the size of that income. The basic argument for income inequality is that inequality is an unavoidable consequence of maintaining the incentives needed to motivate people to produce output and income year after year.

The Equality-Efficiency Trade-off

At the essence of the income equality-inequality debate is a fundamental trade-off between equality and efficiency. In this **equality-efficiency trade-off,** greater income equality (achieved through redistribution of income) comes at the opportunity cost of reduced production and income. And greater production and income (through reduced redistribution) come at the expense of less equality of income. The trade-off obligates society to choose how much redistribution it wants, in view of the costs. If society decides it wants to redistribute income, it needs to determine methods that minimize the adverse effects on economic efficiency.

equality-efficiency trade-off
The decrease in economic efficiency that may accompany an increase in income equality.

ILLUSTRATING THE IDEA

Slicing the Pizza

The equality-efficiency trade-off might better be understood through an analogy. Assume that society's income is a huge pizza, baked year after year, *with the sizes of the pieces going to people on the basis of their contribution to making it*. Now suppose that, for fairness reasons, society decides some people are getting pieces that are too large and others are getting pieces too small. But when society redistributes the pizza to make the sizes more equal, they discover the result is a smaller pizza than before. Why participate in making the pizza if you get a decent-size piece without contributing?

The shrinkage of the pizza represents the efficiency loss—the loss of output and income—caused by the harmful effects of the redistribution on incentives to work, to save and invest, and to accept entrepreneurial risk. The shrinkage also reflects the resources that society must divert to the bureaucracies that administer the redistribution system.

How much pizza shrinkage will society accept while continuing to agree to the redistribution? If redistributing pizza to make it less unequal reduces the size of the pizza, what amount of pizza loss will society tolerate? Is a loss of 10 percent acceptable? 25 percent? 75 percent? This is the basic question in any debate over the ideal size of a nation's income redistribution program.

QUESTION: Why might "equality of opportunity" be a more realistic and efficient goal than "equality of income outcome"?

The Economics of Poverty

We now turn from the broader issue of income distribution to the more specific issue of very low income, or "poverty." A society with a high degree of income inequality can have a high, moderate, or low amount of poverty. In fact, it could have no poverty at all. We therefore need a separate examination of poverty.

Definition of Poverty

Poverty is a condition in which a person or family does not have the means to satisfy basic needs for food, clothing, shelter, and transportation. The means include currently earned income, transfer payments, past savings, and property owned. The basic needs have many determinants, including family size and the health and age of its members.

The federal government has established minimum income thresholds below which a person or a family is "in poverty." In 2009 an unattached individual receiving less than $10,956 per year was said to be living in poverty. For a family of four, the poverty line was $21,954; for a family of six, it was $29,405. Based on these thresholds, in 2009 about 43.6 million Americans lived in poverty. In 2009 the **poverty rate**—the percentage of the population living in poverty—was 14.3 percent.

poverty rate
The percentage of the population with incomes below the official poverty income levels established by the federal government.

Incidence of Poverty

The poor are heterogeneous: They can be found in all parts of the nation; they are whites and nonwhites, rural and urban, young and old. But as Figure 11.4 indicates, poverty is far from randomly distributed. For example, the poverty rate for African

Population group

Percentage in poverty, 2009

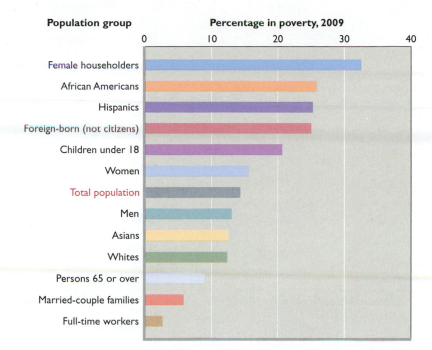

FIGURE 11.4 Poverty rates among selected population groups, 2009. Poverty is disproportionately borne by African Americans, Hispanics, children, foreign-born residents who are not citizens, and families headed by women. People who are employed full-time or are married tend to have low poverty rates.
Source: Bureau of the Census.

Americans is above the national average, as is the rate for Hispanics, while the rate for whites and Asians is below the average. In 2009 the poverty rates for African Americans and Hispanics were 25.9 and 25.3 percent, respectively; the rates for whites and Asians were 12.3 percent and 12.4 percent, respectively.

Figure 11.4 shows that female-headed households, foreign-born noncitizens, and children under 18 years of age have very high incidences of poverty. Marriage and full-time, year-round work are associated with low poverty rates, and, because of the Social Security system, the incidence of poverty among the elderly is less than that for the population as a whole.

The high poverty rate for children is especially disturbing because poverty tends to breed poverty. Poor children are at greater risk for a range of long-term problems, including poor health and inadequate education, crime, drug use, and teenage pregnancy. Many of today's impoverished children will reach adulthood unhealthy and illiterate and unable to earn above-poverty incomes.

As many as half of people in poverty are poor for only 1 or 2 years before climbing out of poverty. But poverty is much more long-lasting among some groups than among others. In particular, African-American and Hispanic families, families headed by women, persons with little education and few labor market skills, and people who are dysfunctional because of drug use, alcoholism, or mental illness are more likely than others to remain in poverty. Also, long-lasting poverty is heavily present in depressed areas of cities, parts of the Deep South, and some Native American reservations.

Poverty Trends

As Figure 11.5 shows, the total poverty rate fell significantly between 1959 and 1969, stabilized at 11 to 13 percent over the next decade, and then rose in the early 1980s. In 1993 the rate was 15.1 percent, the highest since 1983. Between 1993 and 2000 the rate turned downward, falling to 11.3 percent in 2000. Because of recession and slow recovery, the rate rose to 11.7 percent in 2001, 12.1 percent in 2002, and 12.7 percent

FIGURE 11.5 Poverty-rate trends, 1959–2009. Although the national poverty rate declined sharply between 1959 and 1969, it stabilized in the 1970s only to increase significantly in the early 1980s. Between 1993 and 2000 it substantially declined, before rising slightly again in the immediate years following the 2001 recession. Although poverty rates for African Americans and Hispanics are much higher than the average, they significantly declined during the 1990s. Poverty rates rose in 2008 and 2009 in response to the recession that began in December 2007.

Source: Bureau of the Census, **www.census.gov.**

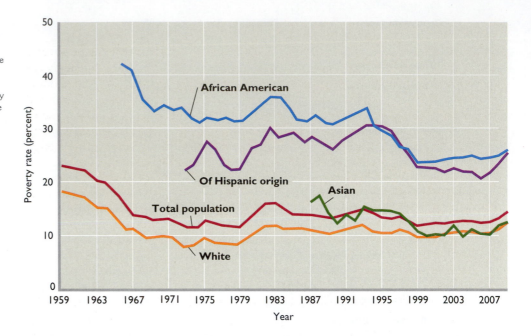

in 2004. During the second half of the 1990s, poverty rates plunged for African Americans, Hispanics, and Asians. Nevertheless, in 2006 African Americans and Hispanics still had poverty rates that were roughly double the rates for whites.

The recession that began in December 2007 increased poverty rates for all groups with, for instance, the Asian poverty rate rising from 10.2 percent in 2007 to 12.4 percent in 2009. As data become available for 2010 and 2011, many economists expect to see poverty rates rise further in response to the widespread and lingering unemployment caused by the so-called Great Recession.

Measurement Issues

The poverty rates and trends in Figures 11.4 and 11.5 need to be interpreted cautiously. The official income thresholds for defining poverty are necessarily arbitrary and therefore may inadequately measure the true extent of poverty in the United States.

Some observers say that the high cost of living in major metropolitan areas means that the official poverty thresholds exclude millions of families whose income is slightly above the poverty level but clearly inadequate to meet basic needs for food, housing, and medical care. These observers use city-by-city studies on "minimal income needs" to show there is much more poverty in the United States than is officially measured and reported.

In contrast, some economists point out that using income to measure poverty understates the standard of living of many of the people who are officially poor. When individual, household, or family *consumption* is considered rather than family *income*, some of the poverty in the United States disappears. Some low-income families maintain their consumption by drawing down past savings, borrowing against future income, or selling homes. Moreover, many poverty families receive substantial noncash benefits such as food stamps and rent subsidies that boost their living standards. Such "in-kind" benefits are not included in determining a family's official poverty status.

The U.S. Income-Maintenance System

Regardless of how poverty is measured, economists agree that considerable poverty exists in the United States. Helping those who have very low income is a widely accepted goal of public policy. A wide array of antipoverty programs, including education and training programs, subsidized employment, minimum-wage laws, and antidiscrimination policies, are designed to increase the earnings of the poor. In addition, there are a number of income-maintenance programs devised to reduce poverty, the most important of which are listed in Table 11.3. These programs involve large expenditures and numerous beneficiaries.

The U.S. income-maintenance system consists of two kinds of programs: (1) social insurance and (2) public assistance or "welfare." Both are known as **entitlement programs** because all eligible persons are legally entitled to receive the benefits set forth in the programs.

Social Insurance Programs

Social insurance programs partially replace earnings that have been lost due to retirement, disability, or temporary unemployment; they also provide health insurance for the elderly. The main social insurance programs are Social Security, unemployment compensation, and Medicare. Benefits are viewed as earned rights and do not carry the stigma of public charity. These programs are financed primarily out of federal payroll taxes. In these programs the entire population shares the risk of an individual's losing

entitlement programs
Government programs that guarantee particular levels of transfer payments or noncash benefits to all who fit the programs' critieria.

TABLE 11.3 Characteristics of Major Income-Maintenance Programs

Program	Basis of Eligibility	Source of Funds	Form of Aid	Expenditures,* Billions	Beneficiaries, Millions
Social Insurance Programs					
Social Security	Age, disability, or death of parent or spouse; lifetime work earnings	Federal payroll tax on employers and employees	Cash	$676	53
Medicare	Age or disability	Federal payroll tax on employers and employees	Subsidized health insurance	$502	47
Unemployment compensation	Unemployment	State and federal payroll taxes on employers	Cash	$43	10
Public Assistance Programs					
Supplemental Security Income (SSI)	Age or disability; income	Federal revenues	Cash	$47	8
Temporary Assistance for Needy Families (TANF)	Certain families with children; income	Federal-state-local revenues	Cash and services	$15	5
Supplemental Nutrition Assistance Program (SNAP)	Income	Federal revenues	Cash via EBT cards	$65	40
Medicaid	Persons eligible for TANF or SSI and medically indigent	Federal-state-local revenues	Subsidized medical services	$297	59
Earned-income tax credit (EITC)	Low-wage working families	Federal revenues	Refundable tax credit, cash	$58	26

*Expenditures by federal, state, and local governments; excludes administrative expenses.

Source: Social Security Administration, *Annual Statistical Supplement, 2010,* **www.socialsecurity.gov**; U.S. Department of Agriculture, **www.fns.usda.gov**; Internal Revenue Service, **www.irs.gov/taxstats**; and other government sources. Latest data.

income because of retirement, unemployment, disability, or illness. Workers (and employers) pay a part of their wages to the government while they are working. The workers then receive benefits when they retire or face specified misfortunes.

Social Security and Medicare

Social Security
A federal pension program (financed by payroll taxes on employers and employees) that replaces part of the earnings lost when workers retire, become disabled, or die.

The major social insurance program known as **Social Security** replaces earnings lost when workers retire, become disabled, or die. This gigantic program ($676 billion in 2009) is financed by compulsory payroll taxes levied on both employers and employees. Workers currently may retire at age 65 and receive full retirement benefits or retire early at age 62 with reduced benefits. When a worker dies, benefits accrue to his or her family survivors. Special provisions provide benefits for disabled workers.

Social Security covers over 90 percent of the workforce; some 50 million people receive Social Security benefits averaging about $1082 per month. In 2011, those benefits were financed with a combined Social Security and Medicare payroll tax of 13.3 percent, with the worker and the employer paying 5.65 percent and 7.65 percent, respectively, on the worker's first $106,800 of earnings. The 5.65 and 7.65 percent taxes comprise 4.2 and 6.2 percent for Social Security and 1.45 percent for Medicare. Self-employed workers pay the full 13.3 percent.

Medicare
A federal insurance program (financed by payroll taxes on employers and employees) that provides health insurance benefits to those 65 or older.

Medicare provides hospital insurance for the elderly and disabled and is financed out of the payroll tax. This overall 2.9 percent tax is paid on all work income, not just on the first $106,800. Medicare also makes available a supplementary low-cost insurance program that helps pay doctor fees.

The number of retirees drawing Social Security and Medicare benefits is rapidly rising relative to the number of workers paying payroll taxes. As a result, Social Security and Medicare face serious long-term funding problems. These fiscal imbalances have spawned calls to reform the programs.

Unemployment Compensation

unemployment compensation
A federal-state social insurance program (financed by payroll taxes on employers) that makes income available to workers who are unemployed.

All 50 states sponsor unemployment insurance programs called **unemployment compensation,** a federal-state program that makes income available to unemployed workers. This insurance is financed by a relatively small payroll tax, paid by employers, that varies by state and by the size of the firm's payroll. After a short waiting period, eligible wage and salary workers who become unemployed can receive benefit payments. The size of the payments varies from state to state. Generally, benefits approximate 33 percent of a worker's wages up to a certain maximum weekly payment, and last for a maximum of 26 weeks. In 2010 benefits averaged about $304 weekly. During recessions—when unemployment soars—Congress often provides supplemental funds to the states to extend the benefits for additional weeks.

Public Assistance Programs

Supplemental Security Income (SSI)
A federal program (financed by general tax revenues) that provides a uniform nationwide minimum income for the aged, blind, and disabled who do not qualify for benefits under the Social Security program in the United States.

Public assistance programs (welfare) provide benefits for those who are unable to earn income because of permanent disabilities or have no or very low income and also have dependent children. These programs are financed out of general tax revenues and are regarded as public charity. They include "means tests," which require that individuals and families demonstrate low incomes in order to qualify for aid. The federal government finances about two-thirds of the welfare program expenditures, and the rest is paid for by the states.

Many needy persons who do not qualify for social insurance programs are assisted through the federal government's **Supplemental Security Income (SSI)** program. The purpose of SSI is to establish a uniform, nationwide minimum income for the aged, blind, and disabled who are unable to work and who do not qualify for Social Security aid. Over half the states provide additional income supplements to the aged, blind, and disabled.

The **Temporary Assistance for Needy Families (TANF)** is the basic welfare program for low-income families in the United States. The program is financed through general federal tax revenues and consists of lump-sum payments of federal money to states to operate their own welfare and work programs. These lump-sum payments are called TANF funds, and in 2009 about 4.4 million people (including children) received TANF assistance. TANF expenditures in 2009 were about $15 billion.

In 1996 TANF replaced the six-decade-old Aid for Families with Dependent Children (AFDC) program. Unlike that welfare program, TANF established work requirements and placed limits on the length of time a family can receive welfare payments. Specifically, the TANF program

- Set a lifetime limit of 5 years on receiving TANF benefits and required able-bodied adults to work after receiving assistance for 2 years.
- Ended food-stamp eligibility for able-bodied persons age 18 to 50 (with no dependent children) who are not working or engaged in job-training programs.
- Tightened the definition of "disabled children" as it applies for eligibilty of low-income families for SSI assistance.
- Established a 5-year waiting period on public assistance for new legal immigrants who have not become citizens.

In 1996 about 12.6 million people were welfare recipients, including children, or 4.8 percent of the U.S. population. By the middle of 2007, those totals had declined to 4.5 million and 2 percent of the population. The recession that began in December 2007 pushed the number of welfare recipients up to about 4.4 million by December 2009. These recipients accounted for about 1.4 percent of the population in December 2009.

The welfare program has greatly increased the employment rate (= employment/population) for single mothers with children under age 6—a group particularly prone to welfare dependency. Today, that rate is about 13 percentage points higher than it was in 1996.

The **Supplemental Nutrition Assistance Program (SNAP)** was formerly known as the food-stamp program. SNAP is designed to provide all low-income Americans with a "nutritionally adequate diet." Under the program, eligible households receive monthly deposits of spendable electronic money on specialized debit cards known as Electronic Benefit Transfer (EBT) cards. The EBT cards are designed so that the deposits can only be spent on food. The amount deposited onto a family's EBT card varies inversely with the family's earned income.

Medicaid helps finance the medical expenses of individuals participating in the SSI and the TANF programs.

The **earned-income tax credit (EITC)** is a tax credit for low-income working families, with or without children. The credit reduces the federal income taxes that such families owe or provides them with cash payments if the credit exceeds their tax liabilities. The purpose of the credit is to offset Social Security taxes paid by low-wage earners and thus keep the federal government from "taxing families into poverty." In essence, EITC is a wage subsidy from the federal government that works out to be as much as $2 per hour for the lowest-paid workers with families. Under the program, many people owe no income tax and receive direct checks from the federal government once a year. According to the Internal Revenue Service, 26 million taxpayers received $58 billion in payments from the EITC in 2009.

Several other welfare programs are not listed in Table 11.3. Most provide help in the form of noncash transfers. Head Start provides education, nutrition, and social services to economically disadvantaged 3- and 4-year-olds. Housing assistance in the form of rent subsidies and funds for construction is available to low-income families. Pell grants provide assistance to college students from low-income families.

Temporary Assistance for Needy Families (TANF)
The basic welfare program (financed through general tax revenues) for low-income families in the United States.

Supplemental Nutrition Assistance Program (SNAP)
A government program that provides food money to low-income recipients by depositing electronic money onto special debit cards.

Medicaid
A federal program (financed by general tax revenues) that provides medical benefits to people covered by the Supplemental Security Income (SSI) and Temporary Assistance for Needy Families (TANF) programs.

earned-income tax credit (EITC)
A refundable federal tax credit provided to low-income wage earners to supplement their families' incomes and encourage work.

© Royalty-Free/CORBIS

© Jack Star/PhotoLink/Getty Images

PHOTO OP   Social Insurance versus Public Assistance Programs

Beneficiaries of social insurance programs such as Social Security have typically paid for at least a portion of that insurance through payroll taxes. Food stamps and other public assistance are funded from general tax revenue and are generally seen as public charity.

Summary

1. The distribution of income in the United States reflects considerable inequality. The richest 20 percent of families receive 50.3 percent of total income, while the poorest 20 percent receive 3.4 percent.

2. The Lorenz curve shows the percentage of total income received by each percentage of households. The extent of the gap between the Lorenz curve and a line of total equality illustrates the degree of income inequality.

3. The Gini ratio measures the overall dispersion of the income distribution and is found by dividing the area between the diagonal and the Lorenz curve by the entire area below the diagonal. The Gini ratio ranges from zero to 1; higher ratios signify greater degrees of income inequality.

4. Recognizing that the positions of individual families in the distribution of income change over time and incorporating the effects of noncash transfers and taxes would reveal less income inequality than do standard census data. Government transfers (cash and noncash) greatly lessen the degree of income inequality; taxes also reduce inequality, but not by nearly as much as transfers.

5. Causes of income inequality include differences in abilities, in education and training, and in job tastes, along with dis-

crimination, inequality in the distribution of wealth, and an unequal distribution of market power.

6. Census data show that income inequality has increased significantly since 1970. The major cause of recent increases in income inequality is a rising demand for highly skilled workers, which has boosted their earnings significantly.

7. The basic argument for income equality is that it maximizes consumer satisfaction (total utility) from a particular level of total income. The main argument for income inequality is that it provides the incentives to work, invest, and assume risk and is necessary for the production of output, which, in turn, creates income that is then available for distribution.

8. Current statistics reveal that 14.3 percent of the U.S. population lived in poverty in 2009. Poverty rates are particularly high for female-headed families, young children, African Americans, and Hispanics.

9. The present income-maintenance program in the United States consists of social insurance programs (Social Security, Medicare, and unemployment compensation) and public assistance programs (SSI, TANF, SNAP, Medicaid, and earned-income tax credit).

10. In 1996 Congress established the Temporary Assistance for Needy Families (TANF) program, which shifted responsibility for welfare from the federal government to the states. Among its provisions are work requirements for adults receiving welfare and a 5-year lifelong limit on welfare benefits.

11. A generally strong economy and TANF have reduced the U.S. welfare rolls by more than one-half since 1996.

Terms and Concepts

income inequality

Lorenz curve

Gini ratio

income mobility

noncash transfers

law of diminishing marginal utility

equality-efficiency trade-off

poverty rate

entitlement programs

Social Security

Medicare

unemployment compensation

Supplemental Security Income (SSI)

Temporary Assistance for Needy Families (TANF)

Supplemental Nutrition Assistance Program (SNAP)

Medicaid

earned-income tax credit (EITC)

Questions

1. Use quintiles to briefly summarize the degree of income inequality in the United States. How and to what extent does government reduce income inequality? **LO1**

2. Assume that Al, Beth, Carol, David, and Ed receive incomes of $500, $250, $125, $75, and $50, respectively. Construct and interpret a Lorenz curve for this five-person economy. What percentages of total income are received by the richest quintile and by the poorest quintile? **LO1**

3. How does the Gini ratio relate to the Lorenz curve? Why can't the Gini ratio exceed 1? What is implied about the direction of income inequality if the Gini ratio declines from 0.42 to 0.35? How would one show that change of inequality in the Lorenz diagram? **LO1**

4. Why is the lifetime distribution of income more equal than the distribution in any specific year? **LO2**

5. Briefly discuss the major causes of income inequality. What factors have contributed to greater income inequality since 1970? **LO2, LO3**

6. Should a nation's income be distributed to its members according to their contributions to the production of that total income or according to the members' needs? Should society attempt to equalize income or economic opportunities? Are the issues of equity and equality in the distribution of income synonymous? To what degree, if any, is income inequality equitable? **LO4**

7. Comment on or explain: **LO4**
   a. Endowing everyone with equal income will make for very unequal enjoyment and satisfaction.
   b. Equality is a "superior good"; the richer we become, the more of it we can afford.

   c. The mob goes in search of bread, and the means it employs is generally to wreck the bakeries.
   d. Some freedoms may be more important in the long run than freedom from want on the part of every individual.
   e. Capitalism and democracy are really a most improbable mixture. Maybe that is why they need each other—to put some rationality into equality and some humanity into efficiency.
   f. The incentives created by the attempt to bring about a more equal distribution of income are in conflict with the incentives needed to generate increased income.

8. How do government statisticians determine the poverty rate? How could the poverty rate fall while the number of people in poverty rises? Which group in each of the following pairs has the higher poverty rate: (a) children or people age 65 or over? (b) African Americans or foreign-born noncitizens? (c) Asians or Hispanics? **LO5**

9. What are the essential differences between social insurance and public assistance programs? Why is Medicare a social insurance program whereas Medicaid is a public assistance program? Why is the earned-income tax credit considered to be a public assistance program? **LO6**

10. Prior to the implementation of welfare reforms through the Temporary Assistance for Needy Families (TANF) program, the old system (AFDC) was believed to be creating dependency, robbing individuals and family members of motivation and dignity. How did this reform (TANF) try to address those criticisms? Do you agree with the general thrust of the reform and with its emphasis on work requirements and time limits on welfare benefits? Has the reform reduced U.S. welfare rolls or increased them? **LO6**

Problems

1. In 2010 *Forbes* magazine listed Bill Gates, the founder of Microsoft, as the richest person in the United States. His personal wealth was estimated to be $53 billion. Given that there were about 309 million people living in the United States that year, how much could each person have received if Gates' wealth had been divided equally among the population of the United States? (Hint: A billion is a 1 followed by 9 zeros, while a million is a 1 followed by six zeros.) **LO1**

2. Imagine an economy with only two people. Larry earns $20,000 per year, while Roger earns $80,000 per year. As shown in the following figure, the Lorenz curve for this two-person economy consists of two line segments. The first runs from the origin to point *a*, while the second runs from point *a* to point *b*. **LO1**

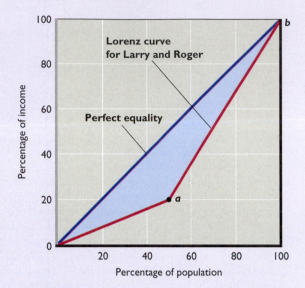

a. Calculate the Gini ratio for this two-person economy using the geometric formulas for the area of a triangle (= ½ × base × height) and the area of a rectangle (= base × height). (Hint: The area under the line segment from point *a* to point *b* can be thought of as the sum of the area of a particular triangle and the area of a particular rectangle.)

b. What would the Gini ratio be if the government taxed $20,000 away from Roger and gave it to Larry? (Hint: The figure will change.)

c. Start again with Larry earning $20,000 per year and Roger earning $80,000 per year. What would the Gini

ratio be if both their incomes doubled? How much has the Gini ratio changed from before the doubling in incomes to after the doubling in incomes?

3. In 2010, many unskilled workers in the United States earned the federal minimum wage of $7.25 per hour. By contrast, average earnings in 2010 were about $22 per hour, and certain highly skilled professionals, such as doctors and lawyers, earned $100 or more per hour. **LO6**

a. If we assume that wage differences are caused solely by differences in productivity, how many times more productive was the average worker than a worker being paid the federal minimum wage? How many times more productive was a $100-per-hour lawyer compared to a worker earning minimum wage?

b. Assume that there are 20 minimum-wage workers in the economy for each $100-per-hour lawyer. Also assume that both lawyers and minimum-wage workers work the same number of hours per week. If everyone works 40 hours per week, how much does a $100-per-hour lawyer earn a week? How much does a minimum-wage worker earn a week?

c. Suppose that the government pairs each $100-per-hour lawyer with 20 nearby minimum-wage workers. If the government taxes 25 percent of each lawyer's income each week and distributes it equally among the 20 minimum-wage workers with whom each lawyer is paired, how much will each of those minimum-wage workers receive each week? If we divide by the number of hours worked each week, how much does each minimum-wage worker's weekly transfer amount to on an hourly basis?

d. What if instead the government taxed each lawyer 100 percent before dividing the money equally among the 20 minimum-wage workers with whom each lawyer is paired—how much per week will each minimum-wage worker receive? And how much is that on an hourly basis?

After reading this chapter, you should be able to:

1 Identify the main categories of government spending and the main sources of government revenue.

2 Summarize the different philosophies regarding the distribution of a nation's tax burden.

3 Explain the principles relating to tax shifting, tax incidence, and the efficiency losses caused by taxes.

4 Demonstrate how the distribution of income between rich and poor is affected by government taxes, transfers, and spending.

Public Finance: Expenditures and Taxes

As discussed in Chapter 2, the U.S. economy relies heavily on the private sector (households and businesses) and the market system to decide what gets produced, how it gets produced, and who gets the output. But the private sector is not the only entity in the decision process. The public sector (federal, state, and local government) also affects these economic decisions.

Government influences what gets produced and how it gets produced through laws that regulate the activities of private firms and also by directly producing certain goods and services, such as national defense and education. As discussed in Chapter 5, many of these government-produced goods and services are *public goods* that the private sector has trouble producing because of free-rider problems. Also, as seen in Chapter 11, government influences who receives society's output of goods and services through various taxes and through welfare and income-transfer payments that redistribute income from the rich to the poor.

Government-provided goods, services, and transfer payments are funded by taxes, borrowing, and *proprietary income*—the income that governments receive from running government-owned enterprises such as hospitals, utilities, toll roads, and lotteries.

Public finance is the subdiscipline of economics that studies the various ways in which governments raise and expend money. In this chapter we view the economy through the lens of public finance. Our main goal is to understand how taxes and income transfers not only pay for government-produced goods and services but also affect the distribution of income between rich and poor.

Government and the Circular Flow

In Figure 12.1 we integrate government into the circular flow model first shown in Figure 2.2. Here flows (1) through (4) are the same as the corresponding flows in that figure. Flows (1) and (2) show business expenditures for the resources provided by households. These expenditures are costs to businesses but represent wage, rent, interest, and profit income to households. Flows (3) and (4) show household expenditures for the goods and services produced by businesses.

FIGURE 12.1 Government within the circular flow diagram. Government buys products from the product market and employs resources from the resource market to provide goods and services to households and businesses. Government finances its expenditures through the net taxes (taxes minus transfer payments) it receives from households and businesses.

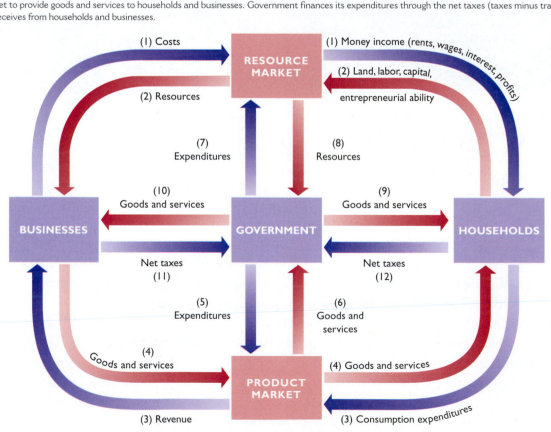

Now consider what happens when we add government. Flows (5) through (8) illustrate that government makes purchases in both product and resource markets. Flows (5) and (6) represent government purchases of such products as paper, computers, and military hardware from private businesses. Flows (7) and (8) represent government purchases of resources. The federal government employs and pays salaries to members of Congress, the armed forces, Justice Department lawyers, meat inspectors, and so on. State and local governments hire and pay teachers, bus drivers, police, and firefighters. The federal government might also lease or purchase land to expand a military base and a city might buy land on which to build a new elementary school.

Government then provides goods and services to both households and businesses, as shown by flows (9) and (10). Governments rely on three revenue sources to finance those goods and services: taxes, borrowing, and the proprietary income generated by government-run or government-sponsored businesses like public utilities and state lotteries. These revenues flowing from households and businesses to government are included in flows (11) and (12), which are labeled as "net taxes" for two reasons. First, the vast majority of the money raised by these three revenue sources comes from taxes; thus, it is sensible to have these labels refer to taxes. Second, the labels refer to *net taxes* to indicate that they also include "taxes in reverse" in the form of transfer payments to households and subsidies to businesses. Thus, flow (11) entails various subsidies to farmers, shipbuilders, and airlines as well as income, sales, and excise taxes paid by businesses to government. Most subsidies to business are "concealed" in the form of low-interest loans, loan guarantees, tax concessions, or public facilities provided at prices below their cost. Similarly, flow (12) includes not only taxes (personal income taxes, payroll taxes) collected by government from households but also transfer payments made by government to households. These include welfare payments and Social Security benefits.

Government Finance

How large is the U.S. public sector? What are the main expenditure categories of federal, state, and local governments? How are these expenditures financed?

Government Purchases and Transfers

We can get an idea of the size of government's economic role by examining government purchases of goods and services and government transfer payments. There is a significant difference between these two kinds of outlays:

- **Government purchases** are *exhaustive;* the products purchased directly absorb (require the use of) resources and are part of the domestic output. For example, the purchase of a missile absorbs the labor of physicists and engineers along with steel, explosives, and a host of other inputs.

- **Transfer payments** are *nonexhaustive;* they do not directly absorb resources or create output. Social Security benefits, welfare payments, veterans' benefits, and unemployment compensation are examples of transfer payments. Their key characteristic is that recipients make no current contribution to domestic output in return for them.

Federal, state, and local governments spent $5332 billion (roughly $5.3 trillion) in 2010. Of that total, government purchases were $3000 billion and government transfers were $2332 billion. Figure 12.2 shows these amounts as percentages of U.S. domestic output for 2010 and compares them to percentages for 1960. Government purchases have declined from about 22 to 20 percent of output since 1960. But transfer payments have tripled as a percentage of output—from 5 percent in 1960 to about 15 percent in 2010.

government purchases
Expenditures by government for goods and services that government consumes in providing public goods and for public capital.

transfer payments
Payments of money (or goods or services) by a government to a household or firm for which the payer receives no good or service directly in return.

FIGURE 12.2 Government purchases, transfers, and total spending as percentages of U.S. output, 1960 and 2010. Government purchases have declined as a percentage of U.S. output since 1960. Transfer payments, however, have increased by more than this drop, raising total government spending (purchases plus transfers) from 27 percent of U.S. GDP in 1960 to about 36 percent today.

Source: Compiled from Bureau of Economic Analysis data, **www.bea.gov**.

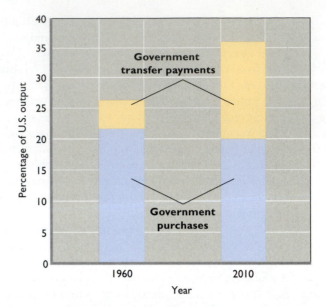

Relative to U.S. output, total government spending is thus higher today than it was 50 years earlier. This means that the tax revenues required to finance government expenditures are also higher. Today, government spending and the tax revenues needed to finance it are about 36 percent of U.S. output. While it is not unusual to hear U.S. politicians and their constituents complain about high taxes, Global Snapshot 12.1 reveals that the tax burden in the United States is relatively low compared to many industrialized nations.

GLOBAL SNAPSHOT 12.1

Total Tax Revenue as a Percentage of Total Output, Selected Nations, 2009*

A nation's "tax burden" is its tax revenue from all levels of government as a percentage of its total output (GDP). Among the world's industrialized nations, the United States has a very moderate tax burden.

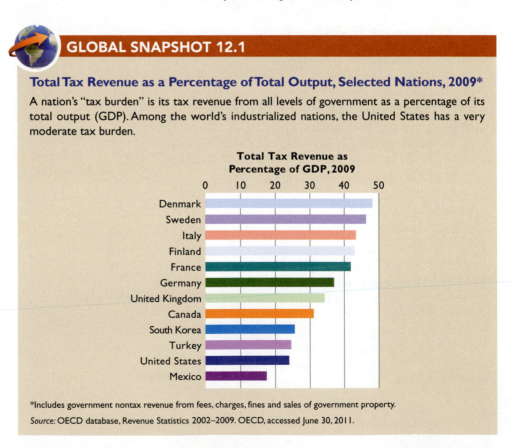

*Includes government nontax revenue from fees, charges, fines and sales of government property.

Source: OECD database, Revenue Statistics 2002–2009. OECD, accessed June 30, 2011.

Government Revenues

The funds used to pay for government purchases and transfers come from three sources: taxes, proprietary income, and funds that are borrowed by selling bonds to the public.

Government Borrowing and Deficit Spending The ability to borrow allows a government to spend more in a given time period than it collects in tax revenues and proprietary income during that period. This flexibility is useful during an economic downturn because a government can use borrowed funds to maintain high levels of spending on goods, services, and transfer payments even if tax revenues and proprietary income are falling due to the slowing economy.

Any money borrowed by a government, however, is money that cannot be put to other uses. During an economic downturn, this opportunity cost is likely to be small because any funds that the government does not borrow are likely to sit idle and unused by other parties due to the lack of economic activity during the downturn. But if the government borrows when the economy is doing well, many economists worry that the opportunity cost may be high. In particular, the government's borrowing may "crowd out" private-sector investment. As an example, a billion dollars borrowed and spent by the federal government on roads is a billion dollars that was not lent to private companies to fund the expansion of factories or the development of new technologies.

Government spending that is financed by borrowing is often referred to as *deficit spending* because a government's budget is said to be "in deficit" if the government's spending in a given time period exceeds the money that it collects from taxes and proprietary income during that period.

Federal Finance

Now let's look separately at each of the federal, state, and local units of government in the United States and compare their expenditures and taxes. Figure 12.3 tells the story for the federal government.

Federal Expenditures

Four areas of federal spending stand out: (1) pensions and income security, (2) national defense, (3) health, and (4) interest on the public debt. The *pensions and income security*

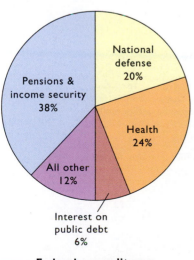

Federal expenditures:
$3456 billion

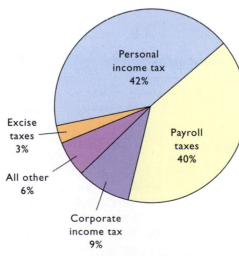

Federal tax revenues:
$2162 billion

FIGURE 12.3 Federal expenditures and tax revenues, 2010. Federal expenditures are dominated by spending for pensions and income security, health, and national defense. A full 82 percent of federal tax revenue is derived from just two sources: the personal income tax and payroll taxes. The $1294 billion difference between expenditures and revenues reflects a budget deficit.

Source: U.S. Treasury, *Combined Statement of Receipts*, Outlays, and Balances, 2010, **fms.treas.gov**.

category includes the many income-maintenance programs for the aged, persons with disabilities or handicaps, the unemployed, the retired, and families with no breadwinner. This category—dominated by the $707 billion pension portion of the Social Security program—accounts for 38 percent of total federal expenditures. *National defense* accounts for about 20 percent of the federal budget, underscoring the high cost of military preparedness. *Health* reflects the cost of government health programs for the retired (Medicare) and poor (Medicaid). *Interest on the public debt* accounts for 5 percent of federal spending.

Federal Tax Revenues

The revenue side of Figure 12.3 shows that the personal income tax, payroll taxes, and the corporate income tax are the largest revenue sources, accounting respectively for 42, 40, and 9 cents of each dollar collected.

personal income tax
A tax levied on the taxable income of individuals, households, and unincorporated firms.

Personal Income Tax The **personal income tax** is the kingpin of the federal tax system and merits special comment. This tax is levied on *taxable income*, that is, on the incomes of households and unincorporated businesses after certain exemptions ($3700 for each household member) and deductions (business expenses, charitable contributions, home mortgage interest payments, certain state and local taxes) are taken into account.

The federal personal income tax is a *progressive tax*, meaning that people with higher incomes pay a larger percentage of their incomes as taxes than do people with lower incomes. The progressivity is achieved by applying higher tax rates to successive layers or brackets of income.

Columns 1 and 2 in Table 12.1 show the mechanics of the income tax for a married couple filing a joint return in 2011. Note that a 10 percent tax rate applies to all taxable income up to $17,000 and a 15 percent rate applies to additional income up to $69,000. The rates on additional layers of income then go up to 25, 28, 33, and 35 percent.

marginal tax rate
The tax rate paid on each additional dollar of income.

The tax rates shown in column 2 in Table 12.1 are marginal tax rates. A **marginal tax rate** is the rate at which the tax is paid on each *additional* unit of taxable income. Thus, if a couple's taxable income is $80,000, they will pay the marginal rate of 10 percent on each dollar from $1 to $17,000, 15 percent on each dollar from $17,000 to $69,000, and 25 percent on each dollar from $69,001 to $80,000. You should confirm that their total income tax is $12,250.

TABLE 12.1 Federal Personal Income Tax Rates, 2011*

(1) Total Taxable Income	(2) Marginal Tax Rate, %	(3) Total Tax on Highest Income in Bracket	(4) Average Tax Rate on Highest Income in Bracket, % (3) ÷ (1)
$1–$17,000	10	$ 1700	10
$17,001–$69,000	15	9500	14
$69,001–$139,500	25	27,125	19
$139,501–$212,300	28	47,509	22
$212,301–$379,150	33	102,570	27
Over $379,150	35		

*For a married couple filing a joint return.

The marginal tax rates in column 2 overstate the personal income tax bite because the rising rates in that column apply only to the income within each successive tax bracket. To get a better idea of the tax burden, we must consider **average tax rates.** The average tax rate is the total tax paid divided by total taxable income. The couple in our previous example is in the 25 percent tax bracket because they pay a top marginal tax rate of 25 percent on the highest dollar of their income. But their *average tax rate* is 15 percent (= $12,250/$80,000).

As we will discuss in more detail shortly, a tax whose average rate rises as income increases is said to be a *progressive tax* because it claims both a progressively larger absolute amount of income as well as a progressively larger proportion of income as income rises. Thus we can say that the federal personal income tax is progressive.

Payroll Taxes   Social Security contributions are **payroll taxes**—taxes based on wages and salaries—used to finance two compulsory federal programs for retired workers: Social Security (an income-enhancement program) and Medicare (which pays for medical services). Employers and employees pay these taxes equally. In 2011, employees and employers paid 5.65 percent and 7.65 percent, respectively, on the first $106,800 of an employee's annual earnings and 1.45 percent on all additional earnings.

Corporate Income Tax   The federal government also taxes corporate income. The **corporate income tax** is levied on a corporation's profit—the difference between its total revenue and its total expenses. For almost all corporations, the tax rate is 35 percent.

Excise Taxes   Taxes on commodities or on purchases take the form of **sales and excise taxes.** The two differ primarily in terms of coverage. Sales taxes fall on a wide range of products, whereas excises are levied individually on a small, select list of commodities. An additional difference is that sales taxes are calculated as a percentage of the price paid for a product, whereas excise taxes are levied on a per-unit basis—for example, $2 per pack of cigarettes or $.50 per gallon of gasoline.

As Figure 12.3 suggests, the federal government collects excise taxes of various rates (on the sale of such commodities as alcoholic beverages, tobacco, and gasoline) but does not levy a general sales tax; sales taxes are, however, the primary revenue source of most state governments.

State and Local Finance

State and local governments have different mixes of revenues and expenditures than the federal government has.

State Finances

The primary source of tax revenue for state governments is sales and excise taxes, which account for about 48 percent of all their tax revenue. State personal and corporate income taxes, which have much lower rates than the federal income tax, are the second most important source of state tax revenue. They bring in about 40 percent of total state tax revenue. License fees and other taxes account for most of the remainder of state tax revenue.

Education expenditures account for about 37 percent of all state spending. State expenditures on public welfare are next in relative weight, at about 28 percent of the total. States also spend heavily on health and hospitals (8 percent), and highway maintenance and construction (7 percent). That leaves about 20 percent of all state spending for public safety and a variety of other purposes.

average tax rate
The total tax paid divided by total taxable income, as a percentage.

payroll taxes
Taxes levied on employers and employees equal to a percentage of the wages and salaries paid to the employees.

corporate income tax
A tax levied on the net income (accounting profit) of corporations.

sales tax
A tax levied on the retail cost of a broad group of products.

excise tax
A tax levied on the production of a specific product or on the quantity of the product purchased.

APPLYING THE ANALYSIS

State Lotteries: A Good Bet?

State lotteries generated about $77.3 billion in revenue in 2008. Of that amount, $56.7 billion went to prizes and $2.4 billion went to administrative costs. That left $18.2 billion that could be spent by the states as they saw fit.

Though nowadays common, state lotteries are still controversial. Critics argue that (1) it is morally wrong for states to sponsor gambling; (2) lotteries generate compulsive gamblers who impoverish themselves and their families; (3) low-income families spend a larger portion of their incomes on lotteries than do high-income families; (4) as a cash business, lotteries attract criminals and other undesirables; and (5) lotteries send the message that luck and fate—rather than education, hard work, and saving—are the route to wealth.

Defenders contend that (1) lotteries are preferable to taxes because they are voluntary rather than compulsory; (2) they are a relatively painless way to finance government services such as education, medical care, and welfare; and (3) lotteries compete with illegal gambling and are thus socially beneficial in curtailing organized crime.

As a further point for debate, also note that state lotteries are monopolies, with states banning competing private lotteries. The resulting lack of competition allows many states to restrict prizes to only about half the money wagered. These payout rates are substantially lower than the 80–95 percent payout rates typically found in private betting operations such as casinos.

Thus, while lotteries are indeed voluntary, they are overpriced and underprovided relative to what would happen if there were a free market in lotteries. But, then again, a free market in lotteries would eliminate monopoly profits for state lotteries and possibly add government costs for regulation and oversight. Consequently, the alternative of allowing a free market in lottery tickets and then taxing the firms selling lottery tickets would probably net very little additional revenue to support state spending programs.

QUESTION: Lottery programs often warn potential participants that lottery games should only be played for entertainment and not as a form of financial investment. How do these warnings apply to the arguments both for and against lotteries?

These tax and expenditure percentages combine data from all the states, so they reveal little about the finances of individual states. States vary significantly in the taxes levied. Thus, although personal income taxes are a major source of revenue for all state governments combined, seven states do not levy a personal income tax. Also, there are great variations in the sizes of tax revenues and disbursements among the states, both in the aggregate and as percentages of personal income.

Forty-three states augment their tax revenues with state-run lotteries to help close the gap between their tax receipts and expenditures. Individual states also receive large intergovernmental grants from the federal government. In fact, about 32 percent of their total revenue is in that form. States also take in revenue from miscellaneous sources such as state-owned utilities and liquor stores.

Local Finances

The local levels of government include counties, municipalities, townships, and school districts as well as cities and towns. Local governments obtain about 71 percent of their

© Digital Vision/Getty Images

© Ariel Skelley/Getty Images

PHOTO OP   Federal versus State and Local Spending

Spending priorities vary across the different levels of government. The federal government spends the majority of its budget on national defense, and pensions and income security. State and local governments spend heavily on education and public welfare.

tax revenue from **property taxes.** Sales and excise taxes contribute about 17 percent of all local government tax revenue.

About 44 percent of local government expenditures go to education. Welfare, health, and hospitals (12 percent); public safety (11 percent); housing, parks, and sewerage (11 percent); and streets and highways (6 percent) are also major spending categories.

The tax revenues of local government cover less than one-half of their expenditures. The bulk of the remaining revenue comes from intergovernmental grants from the federal and state governments. Also, local governments receive considerable amounts of proprietary income, for example, revenue from government-owned utilities providing water, electricity, natural gas, and transportation.

property tax
A tax on the value of property (capital, land, stocks and bonds, and other assets) owned by firms and households.

Local, State, and Federal Employment

In 2008, U.S. governments (local, state, and federal) employed about 19.4 million workers, or about 13 percent of the U.S. labor force. The types of jobs done by government workers depend on the level of government. Over half of state and local government employment is focused on education. The next largest sector is hospitals and health care, which accounts for about 9 percent of state and local government employment. Police and corrections make up another 10 percent. Smaller categories like highways, public welfare, and judicial together combine for less than 10 percent of state and local employment. The remaining employees work in areas such as parks and recreation, fire fighting, transit, and libraries.

Just over half of federal government jobs are in national defense or the postal service. A further 12 percent of government jobs are in hospitals or health care. Jobs in natural resources, police, and financial administration each accounts for between 4 and 7 percent of federal employment. The remaining 19 percent of federal employees work in areas such as justice and law, corrections, air transportation, and social insurance administration.

Apportioning the Tax Burden

Taxes are the major source of funding for the goods and services provided by government and the wages and salaries paid to government workers. Without taxes, there would be no public schools, no national defense, no public highways, no courts, no police, and no other government-provided public and quasi-public goods. As stated by Supreme Court Justice Oliver Wendell Holmes, "Taxes are the price we pay for civilization."

Once government has decided on the total tax revenue it needs to finance its activities, including the provision of public and quasi-public goods, it must determine how to apportion the tax burden among the citizens. (By "tax burden" we mean the total cost of taxes imposed on society.) This apportionment question affects each of us. The overall level of taxes is important, but the average citizen is much more concerned with his or her share of taxes.

Benefits Received versus Ability to Pay

Two basic philosophies coexist on how the economy's tax burden should be apportioned.

benefits-received principle
The idea that people who receive the benefits from government-provided goods and services should pay the taxes required to finance them.

Benefits-Received Principle The **benefits-received principle** of taxation asserts that households should purchase the goods and services of government in the same way they buy other commodities. Those who benefit most from government-supplied goods or services should pay the taxes necessary to finance them. A few public goods are now financed on this basis. For example, money collected as gasoline taxes is typically used to finance highway construction and repairs. Thus people who benefit from good roads pay the cost of those roads. Difficulties immediately arise, however, when we consider widespread application of the benefits-received principle:

- How will the government determine the benefits that individual households and businesses receive from national defense, education, the court system, and police and fire protection? Recall from Chapter 5 that public goods are characterized by nonrivalry and nonexcludability. So benefits from public goods are especially widespread and diffuse. Even in the seemingly straightforward case of highway financing it is difficult to measure benefits. Good roads benefit owners of cars in different degrees. But others also benefit. For example, businesses benefit because good roads bring them workers and customers.
- The benefits-received principle cannot logically be applied to income redistribution programs. It would be absurd and self-defeating to ask poor families to pay the taxes needed to finance their welfare payments. It would also be self-defeating to tax only unemployed workers to finance the unemployment benefits they receive.

ability-to-pay principle
The idea that people who have greater income should pay a greater proportion of it as taxes than those who have less income.

Ability-to-Pay Principle The **ability-to-pay principle** of taxation asserts that the tax burden should be apportioned according to taxpayers' income and wealth. In practice, this means that individuals and businesses with larger incomes should pay more taxes in both absolute and relative terms than those with smaller incomes.

In justifying the ability-to-pay principle, proponents contend that each additional dollar of income received by a household yields a smaller amount of satisfaction or marginal utility when it is spent. Because consumers act rationally, the first dollars of income received in any time period will be spent on high-urgency goods that yield the greatest marginal utility. Successive dollars of income will go for less urgently needed goods and finally for trivial goods and services. This means that a dollar taken through taxes from a poor person who has few dollars represents a greater utility sacrifice than a dollar taken through taxes from a rich person who has many dollars. To balance the sacrifices that taxes impose on income receivers, taxes should be apportioned according to the amount of income a taxpayer receives.

This argument is appealing, but application problems arise here too. Although we might agree that the household earning $100,000 per year has a greater ability to pay taxes than a household receiving $10,000, we don't know exactly how much more ability to pay the first family has. Should the wealthier family pay the *same* percentage of its larger income, and hence a larger absolute amount, as taxes? Or should it be made to pay a *larger* percentage of its income as taxes? And how much larger should that percentage be? Who is to decide?

There is no scientific way of making utility comparisons among individuals and thus of measuring someone's relative ability to pay taxes. That is the main problem. In practice, the solution hinges on guesswork, the tax views of the political party in power, expediency, and how urgently the government needs revenue.

Progressive, Proportional, and Regressive Taxes

Any discussion of taxation leads ultimately to the question of tax rates. Taxes are classified as progressive, proportional, or regressive, depending on the relationship between average tax rates and taxpayer incomes. We focus on incomes because all taxes—whether on income, a product, a building, or a parcel of land—are ultimately paid out of someone's income.

- A tax is **progressive** if its average rate increases as income increases. Such a tax claims not only a larger absolute (dollar) amount but also a larger percentage of income as income increases.
- A tax is **regressive** if its average rate declines as income increases. Such a tax takes a smaller proportion of income as income increases. A regressive tax may or may not take a larger absolute amount of income as income increases. (You may want to derive an example to substantiate this fact.)
- A tax is **proportional** if its average rate *remains the same* regardless of the size of income. Proportional income taxes are often referred to as *flat taxes* or *flat-rate taxes* because their average rates do not vary with (are flat with respect to) income levels.

We can illustrate these ideas with the personal income tax. Suppose tax rates are such that a household pays 10 percent of its income in taxes regardless of the size of its income. This is a *proportional* income tax. Now suppose the rate structure is such that a household with an annual taxable income of less than $10,000 pays 5 percent in income taxes; a household with an income of $10,000 to $20,000 pays 10 percent; one with a $20,000 to $30,000 income pays 15 percent; and so forth. This is a *progressive* income tax. Finally, suppose the rate declines as taxable income rises: You pay 15 percent if you earn less than $10,000; 10 percent if you earn $10,000 to $20,000; 5 percent if you earn $20,000 to $30,000; and so forth. This is a *regressive* income tax.

In general, progressive taxes are those that fall relatively more heavily on people with high incomes; regressive taxes are those that fall relatively more heavily on the poor.

Applications Let's examine the progressivity, or regressivity, of several taxes.

Personal Income Tax As noted earlier, the federal personal income tax is progressive, with marginal tax rates (those assessed on additional income) ranging from 10 to 35 percent in 2011. Rules that allow individuals to deduct from income interest on home mortgages and property taxes and that exempt interest on state and local bonds from taxation tend to make the tax less progressive than these marginal rates suggest. Nevertheless, average tax rates rise with income.

progressive tax
A tax whose average tax rate increases as the taxpayer's income increases.

regressive tax
A tax whose average tax rate decreases as the taxpayer's income increases.

proportional tax
A tax whose average tax rate remains constant as the taxpayer's income increases.

Sales Taxes At first thought, a general sales tax with, for example, a 5 percent rate would seem to be proportional. But in fact it is regressive with respect to income. A larger portion of a low-income person's income is exposed to the tax than is the case for a high-income person; the rich pay no tax on the part of income that is saved, whereas the poor are unable to save. Example: "Low-income" Smith has an income of $15,000 and spends it all. "High-income" Jones has an income of $300,000 but spends only $200,000 and saves the rest. Assuming a 5 percent sales tax applies to all expenditures of each individual, we find that Smith pays $750 (5 percent of $15,000) in sales taxes and Jones pays $10,000 (5 percent of $200,000). But Smith pays $750/$15,000, or 5 percent of income as sales taxes while Jones pays $10,000/$300,000, or 3.3 percent of income. The general sales tax therefore is regressive.

Corporate Income Tax The federal corporate income tax is essentially a proportional tax with a flat 35 percent tax rate. In the short run, the corporate owners (shareholders) bear the tax through lower dividends and share values. In the long run, workers may bear some of the tax since it reduces the return on investment and therefore slows capital accumulation. It also causes corporations to relocate to other countries that have lower tax rates. With less capital per worker, U.S. labor productivity may decline and wages may fall. To the extent this happens, the corporate income tax may be somewhat regressive.

Payroll Taxes Payroll taxes are taxes levied upon wages and salaries by certain states as well as by the federal government. The federal payroll tax is known as the FICA tax after the Federal Insurance Contributions Act, which mandated one payroll tax to fund the Social Security program and another to fund the Medicare program.

Both taxes are split between employer and employee. Of the 10.4 percent Social Security tax (as of 2011), 4.2 percent is paid by employees and an additional 6.2 percent is paid by employers. The 2.9 percent Medicare tax is split in half, with 1.45 percent paid by employees and 1.45 percent paid by employers.

Crucially, however, only the Medicare tax applies to all wage and salary income without limit. The Social Security tax, by contrast, is "capped," meaning that it applies only up to a certain limit, or cap. In 2011, the cap was $106,800.

The fact that the Social Security tax applies only on income below the cap implies that the FICA tax is regressive. To see this, consider a person with $106,800 in wage income. He would pay $6034.20, or 5.65 percent (= 4.2 percent + 1.45 percent) of his wages in FICA taxes. By contrast, someone with twice that income, or $213,600, would pay $7582.80 (= $6034.20 on the first $106,800 + $1548.60 on the second $106,800), which is only 3.6 percent of his wage income. Thus, the average FICA tax falls as income rises, thereby confirming that the FICA tax is regressive.

But payroll taxes are even more regressive than suggested by this example because they only apply to wage and salary income. People earning high incomes tend to derive a higher percentage of their total incomes from nonwage sources like rents and dividends than do people who have incomes below the $106,800 cap on which Social Security taxes are paid. Thus, if our individual with the $213,600 of wage income also received $213,600 of nonwage income, his $7582.80 of FICA tax would be only 1.8 percent of his total income of $427,200.

Property Taxes Most economists conclude that property taxes on buildings are regressive for the same reasons as are sales taxes. First, property owners add the tax to the rents that tenants are charged. Second, property taxes, as a percentage of income, are higher for low-income families than for high-income families because the poor must spend a larger proportion of their incomes for housing.

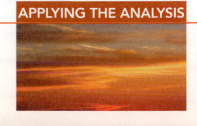

The VAT: A Very Alluring Tax?

A value-added tax (VAT) is like a retail sales tax except that it applies only to the *difference* between the value of a firm's sales and the value of its purchases from other firms. For instance, Intel would pay the VAT—say, 7 percent—only on the difference between the value of the microchips it sells and the value of the materials used to make them. Dell, Lenovo, and other firms that buy chips and other components to make computers would subtract the value of their materials from the value of their sales of personal computers. They would pay the 7 percent tax on that difference—on the value that *they* added.

Economists reason that because the VAT would apply to all firms, sellers could shift their VATs to buyers in the form of higher prices without having to worry that their higher prices might cause them to lose sales to competitors. Final consumers, who cannot shift the tax, would be the ones who ultimately end up paying the full VAT as 7 percent higher prices. So the VAT would amount to a national sales tax on consumer goods.

Most other nations besides the United States have a VAT in addition to other taxes. Why the attraction? Proponents argue that it encourages savings and investment because it penalizes consumption. Unlike income taxes and profits taxes, which reduce the returns to working and investing, the VAT only taxes consumption. Thus, people might be expected to save and invest more if the government switched from taxing income and profits to taxing consumption via a VAT.

Opponents counter, however, that the VAT discourages savings and investment just as much as do income and profit taxes because the whole point of working hard, saving, and investing is the ability to reward yourself in the future with increased consumption. By making consumption more expensive, the VAT reduces this future reward. Also, because VATs are regressive, opponents argue that VATs lead to higher and more progressive income taxes as governments try to use the progressivity of income taxes to counter the regressivity of the VAT. Finally, critics note that the VAT is deeply buried within product prices and therefore is a *hidden tax*. Such taxes are usually easier to increase than other taxes and therefore can result in excessively large government.

QUESTION: Would you rather pay an income tax or a value-added tax? Explain your reasoning.

Tax Incidence and Efficiency Loss

Determining whether a particular tax is progressive, proportional, or regressive is complicated because those on whom taxes are levied do not always pay the taxes. This is true because some or all of the value of the tax may be passed on to others. We therefore need an understanding of **tax incidence,** the degree to which a tax falls on a particular person or group. The tools of elasticity of supply and demand will help. Let's focus on a hypothetical excise tax levied on wine producers. Do the producers really pay this tax, or is some fraction of the tax shifted to wine consumers?

tax incidence
The degree to which a tax falls on a particular person or group.

Elasticity and Tax Incidence

In Figure 12.4, *S* and *D* represent the pretax market for a certain domestic wine; the no-tax equilibrium price and quantity are $8 per bottle and 15 million bottles. Suppose that government levies an excise tax of $2 per bottle at the winery. Who will actually pay this tax?

FIGURE 12.4 The incidence of an excise tax. An excise tax of a specified amount (here, $2 per unit) shifts the supply curve upward by the amount of the tax per unit: the vertical distance between S and S_t. This results in a higher price (here, $9) to consumers and a lower after-tax price (here, $7) to producers. Thus consumers and producers share the burden of the tax in some proportion (here, equally at $1 per unit).

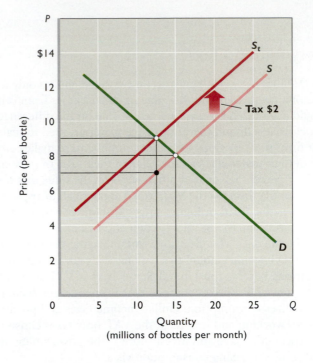

Quantity
(millions of bottles per month)

Division of Burden Since the government imposes the tax on the sellers (suppliers), we can view the tax as an addition to the marginal cost of the product. Now sellers must get $2 more for each bottle to receive the same per-unit profit they were getting before the tax. While sellers are willing to offer, for example, 5 million bottles of un-taxed wine at $4 per bottle, they must now receive $6 per bottle (= $4 + $2 tax) to offer the same 5 million bottles. The tax shifts the supply curve upward (leftward) as shown in Figure 12.4, where S_t is the "after-tax" supply curve.

The after-tax equilibrium price is $9 per bottle, whereas the before-tax equilibrium price was $8. So, in this case, consumers pay half the $2 tax as a higher price; producers pay the other half in the form of a lower after-tax per-unit revenue. That is, after remitting the $2 tax per unit to government, producers receive $7 per bottle, or $1 less than the $8 before-tax price. So, in this case, consumers and producers share the burden of the tax equally: Half of the $2 per-bottle tax is shifted to consumers in the form of a higher price and half is paid by producers.

Note also that the equilibrium quantity declines because of the tax levy and the higher price that it imposes on consumers. In Figure 12.4 that decline in quantity is from 15 million bottles to 12.5 million bottles per month.

Elasticities If the elasticities of demand and supply were different from those shown in Figure 12.4, the incidence of tax would also be different. Two generalizations are relevant.

With a specific supply, the more inelastic the demand for the product, the larger is the portion of the tax shifted to consumers. To verify this, sketch graphically the extreme cases in which demand is perfectly elastic and perfectly inelastic. In the first case, the incidence of the tax is entirely on sellers; in the second, the tax is shifted entirely to consumers.

Figure 12.5 contrasts the more usual cases where demand is either relatively elastic or relatively inelastic in the relevant price range. With elastic demand (Figure 12.5a), a small portion of the tax ($P_2 - P_1$) is shifted to consumers and most of the

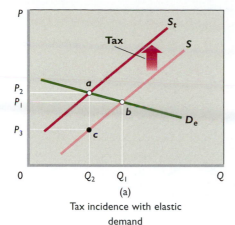

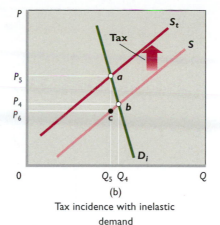

(a)
Tax incidence with elastic
demand

(b)
Tax incidence with inelastic
demand

FIGURE 12.5 Demand elasticity and the incidence of an excise tax. (a) If demand is elastic in the relevant price range, price rises modestly (P_1 to P_2) when an excise tax is levied. Hence, the producers bear most of the tax burden. (b) If demand is inelastic, the price increases substantially (P_4 to P_5) and most of the tax is borne by consumers.

tax ($P_1 - P_3$) is borne by the producers. With inelastic demand (Figure 12.5b), most of the tax ($P_5 - P_4$) is shifted to consumers and only a small amount ($P_4 - P_6$) is paid by producers. In both graphs the per-unit tax is represented by the vertical distance between S_t and S.

Note also that the decline in equilibrium quantity (from Q_1 to Q_2 in Figure 12.5a and from Q_4 to Q_5 in Figure 12.5b) is smaller when demand is more inelastic. This is the basis of our previous applications of the elasticity concept to taxation in earlier chapters: Revenue-seeking legislatures place heavy excise taxes on liquor, cigarettes, automobile tires, telephone service, and other products whose demand is thought to be inelastic. Since demand for these products is relatively inelastic, the tax does not reduce sales by much, so the tax revenue stays high.

The second generalization is that, with a specific demand, the more inelastic the supply, the larger is the portion of the tax borne by producers. When supply is elastic (Figure 12.6a), consumers bear most of the tax ($P_2 - P_1$) while producers bear only a small portion ($P_1 - P_3$) themselves. But where supply is inelastic (Figure 12.6b), the reverse is true: The major portion of the tax ($P_4 - P_6$) falls on sellers, and a relatively small amount ($P_5 - P_4$) is shifted to buyers. The equilibrium quantity also declines less with an inelastic supply than it does with an elastic supply.

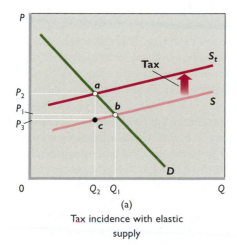

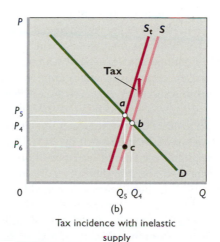

(a)
Tax incidence with elastic
supply

(b)
Tax incidence with inelastic
supply

FIGURE 12.6 Supply elasticity and the incidence of an excise tax. (a) With elastic supply, an excise tax results in a large price increase (P_1 to P_2) and the tax is therefore paid mainly by consumers. (b) If supply is inelastic, the price rise is small (P_4 to P_5) and sellers bear most of the tax.

FIGURE 12.7 Efficiency loss (or deadweight loss) of a tax. The levy of a $2 tax per bottle of wine increases the price per bottle from $8 to $9 and reduces the equilibrium quantity from 15 million to 12.5 million. Tax revenue to the government is $25 million (area *efac*). The efficiency loss of the tax arises from the 2.5 million decline in output; the amount of that loss is shown as triangle *abc*.

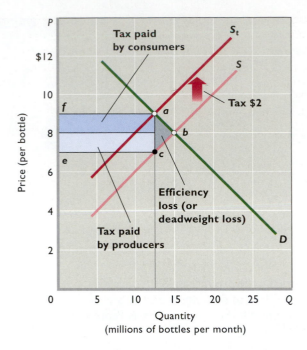

Gold is an example of a product with an inelastic supply and therefore one where the burden of an excise tax (such as an extraction tax) would mainly fall on producers. On the other hand, because the supply of baseballs is relatively elastic, producers would pass on to consumers much of an excise tax on baseballs.

Efficiency Loss of a Tax

We just observed that producers and consumers typically each bears part of an excise tax levied on producers. Let's now look more closely at the overall economic effect of the excise tax. Consider Figure 12.7, which is identical to Figure 12.4 but contains the additional detail we need for our discussion.

Tax Revenues In our example, a $2 excise tax on wine increases its market price from $8 to $9 per bottle and reduces the equilibrium quantity from 15 million bottles to 12.5 million. Government tax revenue is $25 million (= $2 × 12.5 million bottles), an amount shown as the rectangle *efac* in Figure 12.7. The elasticities of supply and demand in this case are such that consumers and producers each pays half this total amount, or $12.5 million apiece (= $1 × 12.5 million bottles). The government uses this $25 million of tax revenue to provide public goods and services. So this transfer of dollars from consumers and producers to government involves no loss of well-being to society.

Efficiency Loss The $2 tax on wine does more than require consumers and producers to pay $25 million of taxes; it also reduces the equilibrium amount of wine produced and consumed by 2.5 million bottles. The fact that consumers and producers demanded and supplied 2.5 million more bottles of wine before the tax means that those 2.5 million bottles provided benefits in excess of their production costs. This is clear from the following analysis.

Segment *ab* of demand curve *D* in Figure 12.7 indicates the willingness to pay—the marginal benefit—associated with each of the 2.5 million bottles consumed before (but not after) the tax. Segment *cb* of supply curve *S* reflects the marginal cost of each of the bottles of wine. For all but the very last one of these 2.5 million bottles, the marginal benefit (shown by a point on *ab*) exceeds the marginal cost (shown by a point on *cb*). Not producing these 2.5 million bottles of wine reduces well-being by an amount represented by the triangle *abc*. The area of this triangle identifies the **efficiency loss of the tax** (also called the *deadweight loss of the tax*). This loss is society's sacrifice of net benefit because the tax reduces production and consumption of the product below their levels of economic efficiency, where marginal benefit and marginal cost are equal.

efficiency (deadweight) loss of a tax
The loss of net benefits to society because a tax reduces the production and consumption of a taxed good below the level of allocative efficiency.

Role of Elasticities   Most taxes create some degree of efficiency loss, but just how much depends on the supply and demand elasticities. Glancing back at Figure 12.5, we see that the efficiency loss area *abc* is greater in Figure 12.5a, where demand is relatively elastic, than in Figure 12.5b, where demand is relatively inelastic. Similarly, area *abc* is greater in Figure 12.6a than in Figure 12.6b, indicating a larger efficiency loss where supply is more elastic. Other things equal, the greater the elasticities of supply and demand, the greater the efficiency loss of a particular tax.

Two taxes yielding equal revenues do not necessarily impose equal costs on society. The government must keep this fact in mind in designing a tax system to finance beneficial public goods and services. In general, it should minimize the efficiency loss of the tax system in raising any specific dollar amount of tax revenue.

Qualifications   We must acknowledge, however, that other tax goals may be as important as, or even more important than, minimizing efficiency losses from taxes. Here are two examples:

- *Redistributive goals*   Government may wish to impose progressive taxes as a way to redistribute income. The 10 percent excise tax the federal government placed on selected luxuries in 1990 was an example. Because the demand for luxuries is elastic, substantial efficiency losses from this tax were to be expected. However, Congress apparently concluded that the benefits from the redistribution effects of the tax would exceed the efficiency losses.

   Ironically, in 1993 Congress repealed the luxury taxes on personal airplanes and yachts, mainly because the taxes had reduced quantity demanded so much that widespread layoffs of workers were occurring in those industries. But the 10 percent tax on luxury automobiles remained in place until it expired in 2003.

- *Reducing negative externalities*   Our analysis of the efficiency loss of a tax assumes no negative externalities arising from either the production or consumption of the product in question. Where such spillover costs occur, an excise tax on producers might actually improve allocative efficiency by reducing output and thus lessening the negative externality. For example, the $2 excise tax on wine in our example might be part of a broader set of excise taxes on alcoholic beverages. The government may have concluded that the consumption of these beverages produces certain negative externalities. Therefore, it might have purposely levied this $2 tax to shift the market supply curve in Figure 12.7 to increase the price of wine, decrease alcohol consumption, and reduce the amount of resources devoted to wine.

Excise taxes that are intended to reduce the production and consumption of products with negative externalities are sometimes referred to as *sin taxes*. This name captures the idea that governments are motivated to impose these taxes to discourage activities that are perceived to be harmful or sinful. Excise taxes on cigarettes and alcohol in particular are commonly referred to as sin taxes.

Probable Incidence of U.S. Taxes

Let's look now at the probable incidence of each of the major sources of tax revenue in the United States.

The incidence of the *personal income tax* generally is on the individual because there is little chance for shifting it. For every dollar paid to the tax, individuals have one less dollar in their pocketbooks. The same ordinarily holds true for inheritance taxes.

As discussed earlier, employees and employers in 2011 paid 5.65 and 7.65 percent, respectively, in *payroll taxes* on a worker's annual earnings up to the 2011 Social Security cap of $106,800 and then 1.45 percent on any additional earnings.

Workers bear the full burden of their share of the Social Security and Medicare payroll taxes. As is true for the income tax, they cannot shift the payroll taxes that they pay to anyone else.

But what about the portion of the FICA tax that is levied on employers? Who pays that? The consensus view is that part of the employers' share of the FICA tax gets shifted to workers in the form of lower before-tax wages. By making it more costly to hire workers, the payroll tax reduces the demand for labor relative to supply. That reduces the market wages that employers pay workers. In a sense, employers "collect" some of the payroll tax they owe from their workers.

In the short run, the incidence of the *corporate income tax* falls on the company's stockholders (owners), who bear the burden of the tax through lower dividends or smaller amounts of retained corporate earnings. A firm currently charging the profit-maximizing price and producing the profit-maximizing output will have no reason to change product price, output, or wages when a tax on corporate income (profit) is imposed. The price and output combination yielding the greatest profit before the tax will still yield the greatest profit after a fixed percentage of the firm's profit is removed by a corporate income tax. So, the company's stockholders will not be able to shift the tax to consumers or workers.

The situation may be different in the long run. Workers, in general, may bear a significant part of the corporate income tax in the form of lower wage growth. Because it reduces the return on investment, the corporate income tax may slow the accumulation of capital (plant and equipment). It also may prompt some U.S. firms to relocate abroad in countries that have lower corporate tax rates. In either case, the tax may slow the growth of U.S. labor productivity, which depends on American workers having access to more and better equipment. The growth of labor productivity is the main reason labor demand grows over time. If the corporate income tax reduces the growth of labor productivity, then labor demand and wages may rise less rapidly. In this indirect way—and over long periods of time—workers may bear part of the corporate income tax.

A *sales tax* is a general excise tax levied on a full range of consumer goods and services, whereas a *specific excise tax* is one levied only on a particular product. Sales taxes are usually transparent to the buyer, whereas excise taxes are often "hidden" in the price of the product. But whether they are hidden or clearly visible, both are often partly or largely shifted to consumers through higher equilibrium product prices (as in Figures 12.4 through 12.6). Sales taxes and excise taxes may get shifted to different extents, however. Because a sales tax covers a much wider range of products than an excise tax, there is little chance for consumers to avoid the price boosts that sales taxes entail. They cannot reallocate their expenditures to untaxed, lower-priced products. Therefore, sales taxes tend to be shifted in their entirety from producers to consumers.

Excise taxes, however, fall on a select list of goods. Therefore, the possibility of consumers turning to substitute goods and services is greater. An excise tax on theater tickets that does not apply to other types of entertainment might be difficult to pass on to consumers via price increases. Why? The answer is provided in Figure 12.5a, where demand is elastic. A price boost to cover the excise tax on theater tickets might cause consumers to substitute alternative types of entertainment. The higher price would reduce sales so much that a seller would be better off to bear all, or a large portion of, the excise tax.

With other products, modest price increases to cover taxes may have smaller effects on sales. The excise taxes on gasoline, cigarettes, and alcoholic beverages provide examples. Here consumers have few good substitute products to which they can turn as prices rise. For these goods, the seller is better able to shift nearly all the excise tax to consumers. Example: Prices of cigarettes have gone up nearly in lockstep with the recent, substantial increases in excise taxes on cigarettes.

As indicated in Global Snapshot 12.2, the United States depends less on sales and excise taxes for tax revenue than do several other nations.

Many *property taxes* are borne by the property owner because there is no other party to whom they can be shifted. This is typically true for taxes on land, personal property, and owner-occupied residences. Even when land is sold, the property tax is not likely to be shifted. The buyer will understand that future taxes will have to be paid on it, and this expected taxation would be reflected in the price the buyer is willing to offer for the land.

GLOBAL SNAPSHOT 12.2

Taxes on General Consumption as a Percentage of GDP, Selected Nations

A number of advanced industrial nations rely much more heavily on consumption taxes—sales taxes, specific excise taxes, and value-added taxes—than does the United States. A value-added tax, which the United States does not have, applies only to the difference between the value of a firm's sales and the value of its purchases from other firms. As a percentage of GDP, the highest tax rates on consumption are in countries that have value-added taxes.

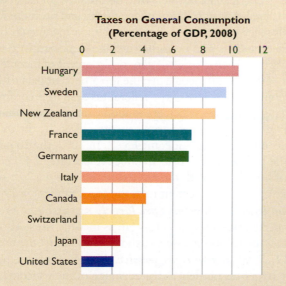

Taxes on General Consumption
(Percentage of GDP, 2008)

Source: OECD database, "Consumption Tax Trends, 2008 Edition." OECD, accessed October 30, 2011.

TABLE 12.2 The Probable Incidence of Taxes

Type of Tax	Probable Incidence
Personal income tax	The household or individual on which it is levied.
Payroll taxes	Workers pay the full tax levied on their earnings and part of the tax levied on their employers.
Corporate income tax	In the short run, the full tax falls on owners of the businesses. In the long run, some of the tax may be borne by workers through lower wages.
Sales tax	Consumers who buy the taxed products.
Specific excise taxes	Consumers, producers, or both, depending on elasticities of demand and supply.
Property taxes	Owners in the case of land and owner-occupied residences; tenants in the case of rented property; consumers in the case of business property.

Taxes on rented and business property are a different story. Taxes on rented property can be, and usually are, shifted wholly or in part from the owner to the tenant by the process of boosting the rent. Business property taxes are treated as a business cost and are taken into account in establishing product price; hence such taxes are ordinarily shifted to the firm's customers.

Table 12.2 summarizes this discussion of the shifting and incidence of taxes.

The U.S. Tax Structure

Is the overall U.S. tax structure—federal, state, and local taxes combined—progressive, proportional, or regressive? The question is difficult to answer. Estimates of the distribution of the total tax burden depend on the extent to which the various taxes are shifted to others, and who bears the burden is subject to dispute. But the majority view of economists who study taxes is as follows:

- *The federal tax system is progressive.* Overall, higher-income groups pay larger percentages of their income as federal taxes than do lower-income groups. Although federal payroll taxes and excise taxes are regressive, the federal income tax is sufficiently progressive to make the overall federal tax system progressive. About one-third of federal income tax filers owe no tax at all. In fact, because of fully refundable tax credits designed to reduce poverty and promote work, millions of households receive tax rebates even though their income tax bill is zero. Most of the federal income tax is paid by higher-income taxpayers. In 2007 (the latest year for which data have been compiled), the top 1 percent of income-tax filers paid 39.5 percent of the federal income tax; the top 5 percent paid 61.0 percent of the tax.

  The overall progressivity of the federal tax system is confirmed by comparing effective (average) tax rates, which are found by dividing the total of federal income, payroll, and excise taxes paid at various income levels by the total incomes earned by the people at those various income levels. In 2007, the 20 percent of the households with the lowest income paid an effective tax rate of 4.0 percent. The 20 percent of households with the highest income paid a 25.1 percent rate. The top 10 percent paid a 26.7 percent rate; the top 1 percent, a 29.5 percent rate.[1]

- *The state and local tax structures are largely regressive.* As a percentage of income, property taxes and sales taxes fall as income rises. Also, state income taxes are generally less progressive than the federal income tax.

- *The overall U.S. tax system is progressive.* Higher-income people carry a substantially larger tax burden, as a percentage of their income, than do lower-income people.

[1] *Average Federal Tax Rates in 2007*, Congressional Budget Office, June 2010.

The income tax system cannot be relied upon by itself to substantially alter the distribution of income because the government might choose to spend the taxes collected from the rich to pay for things that are used more by the rich than the poor. In actual fact, however, this does not happen in the United States because the government uses a large portion of the tax revenues collected from the rich to make income transfer payments to the poor and to pay for the provision of goods and services that are utilized more by the poor than the rich. The transfer payments by themselves are so large that they almost quadruple the incomes of the poorest fifth of U.S. households. Thus, the combined tax-transfer system levels the income distribution by much more than the tax system does on its own.

Summary

1. The funds used to pay for government purchases and transfers come from taxes, proprietary income, and borrowing. The ability to borrow allows governments to maintain high spending during economic downturns, but government borrowing when the economy is doing well may "crowd out" private-sector investment.

2. Government purchases exhaust (use up or absorb) resources; transfer payments do not. Government purchases have declined from about 22 percent of domestic output in 1960 to 20 percent today. Transfer payments, however, have grown rapidly. As a percentage of GDP, total government spending (purchases plus transfers) now stands at about 36 percent, up from 27 percent in 1960.

3. The main categories of federal spending are pensions and income security, national defense, health, and interest on the public debt; federal revenues come primarily from personal income taxes, payroll taxes, and corporate income taxes.

4. States derive their revenue primarily from sales and excise taxes and personal income taxes; major state expenditures go to education, public welfare, health and hospitals, and highways. Local communities derive most of their revenue from property taxes; education is their most important expenditure. State and local tax revenues are supplemented by sizable revenue grants from the federal government.

5. Slightly over half of state and local government employees work in education. Just over half of federal government employees work either for the postal service or in national defense.

6. The benefits-received principle of taxation states that those who receive the benefits of goods and services provided by government should pay the taxes required to finance them. The ability-to-pay principle states that those who have greater income should be taxed more, absolutely and relatively, than those who have less income.

7. The federal personal income tax is progressive. The corporate income tax is roughly proportional. General sales, excise, payroll, and property taxes are regressive.

8. Excise taxes affect supply and therefore equilibrium price and quantity. The more inelastic the demand for a product, the greater is the portion of an excise tax that is borne by consumers. The greater the inelasticity of supply, the larger is the portion of the tax that is borne by the seller.

9. Taxation involves the loss of some output whose marginal benefit exceeds its marginal cost. The more elastic the supply and demand curves, the greater is the efficiency loss (or deadweight loss) resulting from a particular tax.

10. Some taxes are borne by those taxed; other taxes are shifted to someone else. The income tax, the payroll tax levied on workers, and the corporate income tax (in the short run) are borne by those taxed. In contrast, sales taxes are shifted to consumers, part of the payroll tax levied on employers is shifted to workers, and, in the long run, part of the corporate income tax is shifted to workers. Specific excise taxes may or may not be shifted to consumers, depending on the elasticities of demand and supply. Property taxes on owner-occupied property are borne by the owner; those on rental property are borne by tenants.

11. The federal tax structure is progressive; the state and local tax structure is regressive; and the overall tax structure is progressive.

Terms and Concepts

government purchases	corporate income tax	regressive tax
transfer payments	sales and excise taxes	proportional tax
personal income tax	property taxes	tax incidence
marginal tax rate	benefits-received principle	efficiency loss of a tax
average tax rate	ability-to-pay principle	
payroll taxes	progressive tax	

Questions ![McGraw-Hill]connect™ ECONOMICS

1. Use a circular flow diagram to show how the allocation of resources and the distribution of income are affected by each of the following government actions. **LO1**
   a. The construction of a new high school.
   b. A 2-percentage-point reduction of the corporate income tax.
   c. An expansion of preschool programs for disadvantaged children.
   d. The levying of an excise tax on polluters.

2. What do economists mean when they say government purchases are "exhaustive" expenditures whereas government transfer payments are "nonexhaustive" expenditures? Cite an example of a government purchase and a government transfer payment. **LO1**

3. What is the most important source of revenue and the major type of expenditure at the federal level? At the state level? At the local level? **LO1**

4. Distinguish between the benefits-received and the ability-to-pay principles of taxation. Which philosophy is more evident in our present tax structure? Justify your answer. To which principle of taxation do you subscribe? Why? **LO2**

5. What is meant by a progressive tax? A regressive tax? A proportional tax? Comment on the progressivity or regressivity of each of the following taxes, indicating in each case where you think the tax incidence lies: (a) the federal personal income tax, (b) a 4 percent state general sales tax, (c) a federal excise tax on automobile tires, (d) a municipal property tax

on real estate, (e) the federal corporate income tax, (f) the portion of the payroll tax levied on employers. **LO3**

6. What is the tax incidence of an excise tax when demand is highly inelastic? Highly elastic? What effect does the elasticity of supply have on the incidence of an excise tax? What is the efficiency loss of a tax, and how does it relate to elasticity of demand and supply? **LO3**

7. Given the inelasticity of cigarette demand, discuss an excise tax on cigarettes in terms of efficiency loss and tax incidence. **LO3**

8. **ADVANCED ANALYSIS** Suppose the equation for the demand curve for some product X is $P = 8 - .6Q$ and the supply curve is $P = 2 + .4Q$. What are the equilibrium price and quantity? Now suppose an excise tax is imposed on X such that the new supply equation is $P = 4 + .4Q$. How much tax revenue will this excise tax yield the government? Graph the curves, and label the area of the graph that represents the tax collection "TC" and the area that represents the efficiency loss of the tax "EL." Briefly explain why area EL is the efficiency loss of the tax but TC is not. **LO3**

9. Is it possible for a country with a regressive tax system to have a tax-spending system that transfers resources from the rich to the poor? **LO4**

10. Does a progressive tax system by itself guarantee that resources will be redistributed from the rich to the poor? Explain. Is the *tax* system in the United States progressive, regressive, or proportional? **LO4**

Problems

1. Suppose a tax is such that an individual with an income of $10,000 pays $2000 of tax, a person with an income of $20,000 pays $3000 of tax, a person with an income of $30,000 pays $4000 of tax, and so forth. What is each person's average tax rate? Is this tax regressive, proportional, or progressive? **LO3**

2. Suppose in Fiscalville there is no tax on the first $10,000 of income, but a 20 percent tax on earnings between $10,000 and $20,000 and a 30 percent tax on income between $20,000 and $30,000. Any income above $30,000 is taxed at 40 percent. If your income is $50,000, how much will you pay in taxes? Determine your marginal and average tax rates. Is this a progressive tax? **LO3**

3. For tax purposes, "gross income" is all the money a person receives in a given year from any source. But income taxes are levied on "taxable income" rather than gross income. The difference between the two is the result of many exemptions and deductions. To see how they work, suppose you made $50,000 last year in wages and $10,000 from

investments, and were given $5000 as a gift by your grandmother. Also assume that you are a single parent with one small child living with you. **LO3**
   a. What is your gross income?
   b. Gifts of up to $13,000 per year from any person are not counted as taxable income. Also, the "personal exemption" allows you to reduce your taxable income by $3700 for each member of your household. Given these exemptions, what is your taxable income?
   c. Next, assume you paid $700 in interest on your student loans last year, put $2000 into a health savings account (HSA), and deposited $4000 into an individual retirement account (IRA). These expenditures are all *tax exempt*, meaning that any money spent on them reduces taxable income dollar-for-dollar. Knowing that fact, what is now your taxable income?
   d. Next, you can either take the so-called standard deduction or apply for itemized deductions (which involve a lot of tedious paperwork). You opt for the standard

deduction that allows you as head of your household to exempt another $8500 from your taxable income. Taking that into account, what is your taxable income?

e. Apply the tax rates shown in Table 12.1 to your taxable income. How much federal tax will you owe? What is the marginal tax rate that applies to your last dollar of taxable income?

f. As the parent of a dependent child, you qualify for the government's $1000-per-child "tax credit." Like all tax credits, this $1000 credit "pays" for $1000 of whatever amount of tax you owe. Given this credit, how much money will you actually have to pay in taxes? Using that actual amount, what is your average tax rate relative to your taxable income? What about your average tax rate relative to your gross income?

FURTHER TEST YOUR KNOWLEDGE AT
www.mcconnellbrief2e.com

At the text's Online Learning Center, **www.mcconnellbrief2e.com**, you will find one or more web-based questions that require information from the Internet to answer. We urge you to check them out, since they will familiarize you with websites that may be helpful in other courses and perhaps even in your career. The OLC also features multiple-choice quizzes that give instant feedback and provides other helpful ways to further test your knowledge of the chapter.

Visit your mobile app store and download the McConnell Brief Edition: Study Econ app *today!*

PART FIVE

13 **INTERNATIONAL TRADE AND EXCHANGE RATES**

INTERNATIONAL ECONOMICS

After reading this chapter, you should be able to:

1 List and discuss several key facts about U.S. international trade.

2 Define comparative advantage and demonstrate how specialization and trade add to a nation's output.

3 Explain how exchange rates are determined in currency markets.

4 Analyze the validity of the most frequently presented arguments for protectionism.

5 Discuss the role played by free-trade zones and the World Trade Organization (WTO) in promoting international trade.

International Trade and Exchange Rates

Backpackers in the wilderness like to think they are "leaving the world behind," but, like Atlas, they carry the world on their shoulders. Much of their equipment is imported—knives from Switzerland, rain gear from South Korea, cameras from Japan, aluminum pots from England, sleeping bags from China, and compasses from Finland. Moreover, they may have driven to the trailheads in Japanese-made Toyotas or German-made BMWs, sipping coffee from Brazil or snacking on bananas from Honduras.

International trade and the global economy affect all of us daily, whether we are hiking in the wilderness, driving our cars, listening to music, or working at our jobs. We cannot "leave the world behind." We are enmeshed in a global web of economic relationships—trading of goods and services, multinational corporations, cooperative ventures among the world's firms, and ties among the world's financial markets.

Trade Facts

The following facts provide an "executive summary" of U.S. international trade:

- A *trade deficit* occurs when imports exceed exports. The United States has a trade deficit in goods. In 2010, U.S. imports of goods exceeded U.S. exports of goods by $646 billion.
- A *trade surplus* occurs when exports exceed imports. The United States has a trade surplus in services (such as air transportation services and financial services). In 2010, U.S. exports of services exceeded U.S. imports of services by $146 billion.
- Principal U.S. exports include chemicals, agricultural products, consumer durables, semiconductors, and aircraft; principal imports include petroleum, automobiles, metals, household appliances, and computers.
- Canada is the United States' most important trading partner quantitatively. In 2010, 19 percent of U.S. exported goods were sold to Canadians, who in turn provided 14 percent of the U.S. imports of goods.
- The United States has a sizable trade deficit with China. In 2010, U.S. imports of goods from China exceeded exports of goods to China by $273 billion.
- The U.S. dependence on foreign oil is reflected in its trade with members of OPEC. In 2010, the United States imported $150 billion of goods (mainly oil) from OPEC members, while exporting $54 billion of goods to those countries.
- The United States leads the world in the combined volume of exports and imports, as measured in dollars. China, Germany, the United States, Japan, and the Netherlands were the top five exporters by dollar in 2009. Currently, the United States provides about 8.5 percent of the world's exports. (See Global Snapshot 13.1.)

GLOBAL SNAPSHOT 13.1

Shares of World Exports, Selected Nations

China has the largest share of world exports, followed by Germany and the United States. The eight largest export nations account for about 46 percent of world exports.

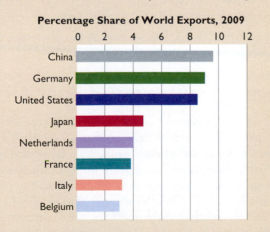

Percentage Share of World Exports, 2009

Source: International Trade Statistics, WTO Publications. Used with permission of the World Trade Organization, www.wto.org.

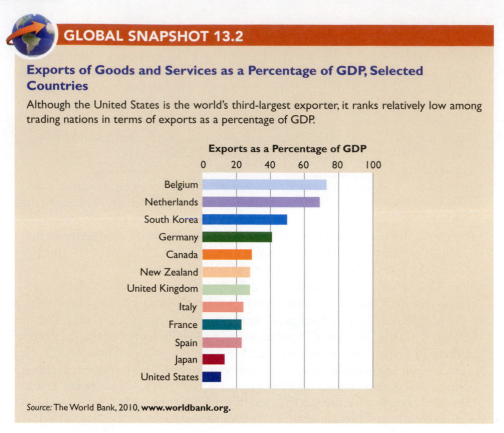

GLOBAL SNAPSHOT 13.2

Exports of Goods and Services as a Percentage of GDP, Selected Countries

Although the United States is the world's third-largest exporter, it ranks relatively low among trading nations in terms of exports as a percentage of GDP.

Exports as a Percentage of GDP

Belgium
Netherlands
South Korea
Germany
Canada
New Zealand
United Kingdom
Italy
France
Spain
Japan
United States

Source: The World Bank, 2010, **www.worldbank.org.**

- Exports of goods and services make up about 14 percent of total U.S. output. That percentage is much lower than the percentage in many other nations, including Canada, Italy, France, and the United Kingdom (see Global Snapshot 13.2).
- China has become a major international trader, with an estimated $1.2 trillion of exports in 2009. Other Asian economies—including South Korea, Taiwan, and Singapore—are also active in international trade. Their combined exports exceed those of France, Britain, or Italy.
- International trade and finance are often at the center of economic policy.

With this information in mind, let's look more closely at the economics of international trade.

Comparative Advantage and Specialization

Given the presence of an *open economy*—one that includes the international sector—the United States produces more of certain goods (exports) and fewer of other goods (imports) than it would otherwise. Thus, U.S. labor and other resources are shifted toward export industries and away from import industries. For example, the United States uses more resources to make computers and to grow wheat and less to make sporting goods and clothing. So we ask: "Do shifts of resources like these make economic sense? Do they enhance U.S. total output and thus the U.S. standard of living?"

The answers are affirmative. Specialization and international trade increase the productivity of a nation's resources and allow for greater total output than would otherwise be possible. This idea is not new. Adam Smith had this to say in 1776:

> It is the maxim of every prudent master of a family, never to attempt to make at home what it will cost him more to make than to buy. The taylor does not attempt to make his own shoes, but buys them of the shoemaker. The shoemaker does not attempt to make his own clothes, but employs a taylor. The farmer attempts to make neither the one nor the other, but employs those different artificers. . . .
>
> What is prudence in the conduct of every private family, can scarce be folly in that of a great kingdom. If a foreign country can supply us with a commodity cheaper than we can make it, better buy it of them with some part of the produce of our own industry, employed in a way in which we have some advantage.[1]

Nations specialize and trade for the same reasons that individuals do: Specialization and exchange result in greater overall output and income. In the early 1800s British economist David Ricardo expanded on Smith's idea by observing that it pays for a person or a country to specialize and trade even if a nation is more productive than a potential trading partner in *all* economic activities. We demonstrate Ricardo's principle in the examples that follow.

ILLUSTRATING THE IDEA

A CPA and a House Painter

Consider the certified public accountant (CPA) who is also a skilled house painter. Suppose the CPA is a swifter painter than the professional painter she is thinking of hiring. Also suppose that she can earn $50 per hour as an accountant but would have to pay the painter $15 per hour. And say it would take the accountant 30 hours to paint her house but the painter would take 40 hours.

Should the CPA take time from her accounting to paint her own house, or should she hire the painter? The CPA's opportunity cost of painting her house is $1500 (= 30 hours of sacrificed CPA time × $50 per CPA hour). The cost of hiring the painter is only $600 (= 40 hours of painting × $15 per hour of painting). Although the CPA is better at both accounting and painting, she will get her house painted at lower cost by specializing in accounting and using some of her earnings from accounting to hire a house painter.

Similarly, the house painter can reduce his cost of obtaining accounting services by specializing in painting and using some of his income to hire the CPA to prepare his income tax forms. Suppose it would take the painter 10 hours to prepare his tax return, while the CPA could handle the task in 2 hours. The house painter would sacrifice $150 of income (= 10 hours of painting time × $15 per hour) to do something he could hire the CPA to do for $100 (= 2 hours of CPA time × $50 per CPA hour). By specializing in painting and hiring the CPA to prepare his tax return, the painter lowers the cost of getting his tax return prepared.

We will see that what is true for our CPA and house painter is also true for nations. Specializing on the basis of comparative advantage enables nations to reduce the cost of obtaining the goods and services they desire.

QUESTION: How might the specialization described above change once the CPA retires? What generalization about the permanency of a particular pattern of specialization can you draw from your answer?

---

[1]Adam Smith, *The Wealth of Nations* (New York: Modern Library, 1937), p. 424. (Originally published in 1776.)

Comparative Advantage: Production Possibilities Analysis

Our simple example shows that the reason specialization is economically desirable is that it results in more efficient production. Now let's put specialization into the context of trading nations and use the familiar concept of the production possibilities table for our analysis.

Assumptions and Comparative Costs Suppose the production possibilities for one product in Mexico and for one product in the United States are as shown in Tables 13.1 and 13.2. Both tables reflect constant costs. Each country must give up a constant amount of one product to secure a certain increment of the other product. (This assumption simplifies our discussion without impairing the validity of our conclusions. Later we will allow for increasing costs.)

Also for simplicity, suppose that the labor forces in the United States and Mexico are of equal size. The data then tell us that the United States has an *absolute advantage* in producing both products. If the United States and Mexico use their entire (equal-size) labor forces to produce avocados, the United States can produce 90 tons compared with Mexico's 60 tons. Similarly, the United States can produce 30 tons of soybeans compared to Mexico's 15 tons. There are greater production possibilities in the United States, using the same number of workers as in Mexico. So labor productivity (output per worker) in the United States exceeds that in Mexico in producing both products.

Although the United States has an absolute advantage in producing both goods, gains from specialization and trade are possible. Specialization and trade are mutually beneficial or "profitable" to the two nations if the *comparative* costs of producing the two products within the two nations differ. What are the comparative costs of avocados and soybeans in Mexico? By comparing production alternatives A and B in Table 13.1, we see that Mexico must sacrifice 5 tons of soybeans (= 15 − 10) to produce 20 tons of avocados (= 20 − 0). Or, more simply, in Mexico it costs 1 ton of soybeans (S) to produce 4 tons of avocados (A); that is, 1S ≡ 4A. (The "≡" sign simply means "equivalent to.") Because we assumed constant costs, this domestic opportunity cost will not change as Mexico expands the output of either product. This is evident from production possibilities B and C, where we see that 4 more tons of avocados (= 24 − 20) cost 1 unit of soybeans (= 10 − 9).

TABLE 13.1 Mexico's Production Possibilities Table (in Tons)

Product	Production Alternatives				
	A	B	C	D	E
Avocados	0	20	24	40	60
Soybeans	15	10	9	5	0

TABLE 13.2 U.S. Production Possibilities Table (in Tons)

Product	Production Alternatives				
	R	S	T	U	V
Avocados	0	30	33	60	90
Soybeans	30	20	19	10	0

Similarly, in Table 13.2, comparing U.S. production alternatives R and S reveals that in the United States it costs 10 tons of soybeans (= 30 − 20) to obtain 30 tons of avocados (= 30 − 0). That is, the domestic (internal) comparative-cost ratio for the two products in the United States is 1S ≡ 3A. Comparing production alternatives S and T reinforces this conclusion: an extra 3 tons of avocados (= 33 − 30) comes at the sacrifice of 1 ton of soybeans (= 20 − 19).

The comparative costs of the two products within the two nations are obviously different. Economists say that the United States has a **comparative advantage** over Mexico in soybeans. The United States must forgo only 3 tons of avocados to get 1 ton of soybeans, but Mexico must forgo 4 tons of avocados to get 1 ton of soybeans. In terms of opportunity costs, soybeans are relatively cheaper in the United States. *A nation has a comparative advantage in some product when it can produce that product at a lower opportunity cost than can a potential trading partner.* Mexico, in contrast, has a comparative advantage in avocados. While 1 ton of avocados costs $\frac{1}{3}$ ton of soybeans in the United States, it costs only $\frac{1}{4}$ ton of soybeans in Mexico. Comparatively speaking, avocados are cheaper in Mexico. We summarize the situation in Table 13.3. Be sure to give it a close look.

Because of these differences in comparative costs, Mexico should produce avocados and the United States should produce soybeans. If both nations specialize according to their comparative advantages, each can achieve a larger total output with the same total input of resources. Together they will be using their scarce resources more efficiently.

Terms of Trade

The United States can shift production between soybeans and avocados at the rate of 1S for 3A. Thus, the United States would specialize in soybeans only if it could obtain *more than* 3 tons of avocados for 1 ton of soybeans by trading with Mexico. Similarly, Mexico can shift production at the rate of 4A for 1S. So it would be advantageous to Mexico to specialize in avocados if it could get 1 ton of soybeans for *less than* 4 tons of avocados.

Suppose that through negotiation the two nations agree on an exchange rate of 1 ton of soybeans for $3\frac{1}{2}$ tons of avocados. These **terms of trade** are mutually beneficial to both countries, since each can "do better" through such trade than through domestic production alone. The United States can get $3\frac{1}{2}$ tons of avocados by sending 1 ton of soybeans to Mexico, while it can get only 3 tons of avocados by shifting its own resources domestically from soybeans to avocados. Mexico can obtain 1 ton of soybeans at a lower cost of $3\frac{1}{2}$ tons of avocados through trade with the United States, compared to the cost of 4 tons if Mexico produced the 1 ton of soybeans itself.

comparative advantage
A lower relative or comparative opportunity cost than that of another person, producer, or country.

ORIGIN OF THE IDEA
O 13.1
Absolute and comparative advantage

terms of trade
The rate at which units of one product can be exchanged for units of another product.

Soybeans	Avocados
Mexico: Must give up 4 tons of avocados to get 1 ton of soybeans	**Mexico:** Must give up $\frac{1}{4}$ ton of soybeans to get 1 ton of avocados
United States: Must give up 3 tons of avocados to get 1 ton of soybeans	**United States:** Must give up $\frac{1}{3}$ ton of soybeans to get 1 ton of avocados
Comparative advantage: United States	**Comparative advantage:** Mexico

TABLE 13.3 Comparative-Advantage Example: A Summary

Gains from Specialization and Trade Let's pinpoint the gains in total output from specialization and trade. Suppose that, before specialization and trade, production alternative C in Table 13.1 and alternative T in Table 13.2 were the optimal product mixes for the two countries. That is, Mexico preferred 24 tons of avocados and 9 tons of soybeans (Table 13.1) and the United States preferred 33 tons of avocados and 19 tons of soybeans (Table 13.2) to all other available domestic alternatives. These outputs are shown in column 1 in Table 13.4.

Now assume that both nations specialize according to their comparative advantages, with Mexico producing 60 tons of avocados and no soybeans (alternative E) and the United States producing no avocados and 30 tons of soybeans (alternative R). These outputs are shown in column 2 in Table 13.4. Using our $1S \equiv 3\frac{1}{2} A$ terms of trade, assume that Mexico exchanges 35 tons of avocados for 10 tons of U.S. soybeans. Column 3 in Table 13.4 shows the quantities exchanged in this trade, with a minus sign indicating exports and a plus sign indicating imports. As shown in column 4, after the trade Mexico has 25 tons of avocados and 10 tons of soybeans, while the United States has 35 tons of avocados and 20 tons of soybeans. Compared with their optimal product mixes before specialization and trade (column 1), *both* nations now enjoy more avocados and more soybeans! Specifically, Mexico has gained 1 ton of avocados and 1 ton of soybeans. The United States has gained 2 tons of avocados and 1 ton of soybeans. These gains are shown in column 5.

Specialization based on comparative advantage improves global resource allocation. The same total inputs of world resources and technology result in a larger global output. If Mexico and the United States allocate all their resources to avocados and soybeans, respectively, the same total inputs of resources can produce more output between them, indicating that resources are being allocated more efficiently.

Through specialization and international trade a nation can overcome the production constraints imposed by its domestic production possibilities table and curve. Our discussion of Tables 13.1, 13.2, and 13.4 has shown just how this is done. The domestic production possibilities data (Tables 13.1 and 13.2) of the two countries have not changed, meaning that neither nation's production possibilities curve has shifted. But specialization and trade mean that citizens of both countries can enjoy increased consumption (column 5 of Table 13.4).

Trade with Increasing Costs

To explain the basic principles underlying international trade, we simplified our analysis in several ways. For example, we limited discussion to two products and two nations. But multiproduct and multinational analysis yields the same conclusions.

WORKED PROBLEMS

W 13.1

Gains from specialization

TABLE 13.4 Specialization According to Comparative Advantage and the Gains from Trade (in Tons)

Country	(1) Outputs before Specialization	(2) Outputs after Specialization	(3) Amounts Traded	(4) Outputs Available after Trade	(5) Gains from Specialization and Trade (4) − (1)
Mexico	24 avocados	60 avocados	−35 avocados	25 avocados	1 avocados
	9 soybeans	0 soybeans	+10 soybeans	10 soybeans	1 soybeans
United States	33 avocados	0 avocados	+35 avocados	35 avocados	2 avocados
	19 soybeans	30 soybeans	−10 soybeans	20 soybeans	1 soybeans

We also assumed constant opportunity costs, which is a more substantive simplification. Let's consider the effect of allowing increasing opportunity costs to enter the picture.

As before, suppose that comparative advantage indicates that the United States should specialize in soybeans and Mexico in avocados. But now, as the United States begins to expand soybean production, its cost of soybeans will rise. It will eventually have to sacrifice more than 3 tons of avocados to get 1 additional ton of soybeans. Resources are no longer perfectly substitutable between alternative uses, as our constant-cost assumption implied. Resources less and less suitable to soybean production must be allocated to the U.S. soybean industry in expanding soybean output, and that means increasing costs—the sacrifice of larger and larger amounts of avocados for each additional ton of soybeans.

© Getty Images

© Photolink/Getty Images

PHOTO OP The Fruits of Free Trade*

Because of specialization and exchange, fruits and vegetables from all over the world appear in our grocery stores. For example, apples may be from New Zealand; bananas, from Ecuador; coconuts, from the Philippines; pineapples, from Costa Rica; avocados, from Mexico; plums, from Chile; and potatoes, from Peru.

*This example is from "The Fruits of Free Trade," 2002 Annual Report, by W. Michael Cox and Richard Alm, p. 3, Federal Reserve Bank of Dallas.

Similarly, Mexico will find that its cost of producing an additional ton of avocados will rise beyond 4 tons of soybeans as it produces more avocados. Resources transferred from soybean to avocado production will eventually be less suitable to avocado production.

At some point the differing domestic cost ratios that underlie comparative advantage will disappear, and further specialization will become uneconomical. And, most importantly, this point of equal cost ratios may be reached while the United States is still producing some avocados along with its soybeans and Mexico is producing some soybeans along with its avocados. The primary effect of increasing opportunity costs is less-than-complete specialization. For this reason we often find domestically produced products competing directly against identical or similar imported products within a particular economy.

The Foreign Exchange Market

Buyers and sellers (whether individuals, firms, or nations) use money to buy products or to pay for the use of resources. Within the domestic economy, prices are stated in terms of the domestic currency and buyers use that currency to purchase domestic products. In Mexico, for example, buyers have pesos, and that is what sellers want.

International markets are different. Sellers set their prices in terms of their domestic currencies, but buyers often possess entirely different currencies. How many dollars does it take to buy a truckload of Mexican avocados selling for 3000 pesos, a German automobile selling for 50,000 euros, or a Japanese motorcycle priced at 300,000 yen? Producers in Mexico, Germany, and Japan want payment in pesos, euros, and yen, respectively, so that they can pay their wages, rent, interest, dividends, and taxes.

A **foreign exchange market,** a market in which various national currencies are exchanged for one another, serves this need. The equilibrium prices in such currency markets are called **exchange rates.** An exchange rate is the rate at which the currency of one nation can be exchanged for the currency of another nation. (See Global Snapshot 13.3.)

The market price or exchange rate of a nation's currency is an unusual price; it links all domestic prices with all foreign prices. Exchange rates enable consumers in one country to translate prices of foreign goods into units of their own currency: They need only multiply the foreign product price by the exchange rate. If the U.S. dollar–yen exchange rate is $.01 (1 cent) per yen, a Sony television set priced at ¥20,000 will cost $200 (= 20,000 × $.01) in the United States. If the exchange rate rises to $.02 (2 cents) per yen, the television will cost $400 (= 20,000 × $.02) in the United States. Similarly, all other Japanese products would double in price to U.S. buyers in response to the altered exchange rate.

foreign exchange market
A market in which foreign currencies are exchanged and relative currency prices are established.

exchange rates
The rates at which national currencies trade for one another.

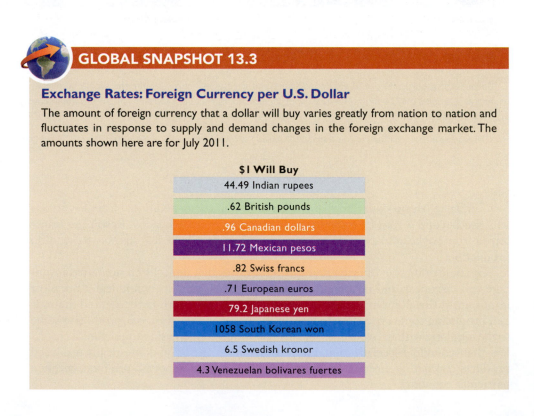

GLOBAL SNAPSHOT 13.3

Exchange Rates: Foreign Currency per U.S. Dollar

The amount of foreign currency that a dollar will buy varies greatly from nation to nation and fluctuates in response to supply and demand changes in the foreign exchange market. The amounts shown here are for July 2011.

$1 Will Buy

44.49 Indian rupees
.62 British pounds
.96 Canadian dollars
11.72 Mexican pesos
.82 Swiss francs
.71 European euros
79.2 Japanese yen
1058 South Korean won
6.5 Swedish kronor
4.3 Venezuelan bolivares fuertes

PHOTO OP Foreign Currencies

The world is awash with hundreds of national currencies. Currency markets determine the rates of exchange between them.

Exchange Rates

Let's examine the rate, or price, at which U.S. dollars might be exchanged for British pounds. In Figure 13.1 we show the dollar price of 1 pound on the vertical axis and the quantity of pounds on the horizontal axis. The demand for pounds is D_1 and the supply of pounds is S_1 in this market for British pounds.

The *demand-for-pounds curve* is downward-sloping because all British goods and services will be cheaper to the United States if pounds become less expensive to the United States. That is, at lower dollar prices for pounds, the United States can obtain more pounds for each dollar and therefore buy more British goods and services per dollar. To buy those cheaper British goods, U.S. consumers will increase the quantity of pounds they demand.

INTERACTIVE GRAPHS

G 13.1

Exchange rates

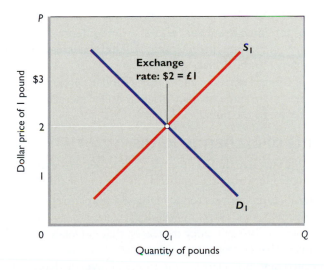

Quantity of pounds

FIGURE 13.1 The market for foreign currency (pounds) The intersection of the demand-for-pounds curve D_1 and the supply-of-pounds curve S_1 determines the equilibrium dollar price of pounds, here, $2. That means that the exchange rate is $2 = £1. Not shown, an increase in demand for pounds or a decrease in the supply of pounds will increase the dollar price of pounds and thus cause the pound to appreciate. Also not shown, a decrease in demand for pounds or an increase in the supply of pounds will reduce the dollar price of pounds, meaning that the pound has depreciated.

The *supply-of-pounds curve* is upsloping because the British will purchase more U.S. goods when the dollar price of pounds rises (that is, as the pound price of dollars falls). When the British buy more U.S. goods, they supply a greater quantity of pounds to the foreign exchange market. In other words, they must exchange pounds for dollars to purchase U.S. goods. So, when the dollar price of pounds rises, the quantity of pounds supplied goes up.

The intersection of the supply curve and the demand curve will determine the dollar price of pounds. In Figure 13.1, that price (exchange rate) is $2 for £1. At this exchange rate, the quantity of pounds supplied and demanded are equal; neither a shortage nor a surplus of pounds occurs.

Depreciation and Appreciation

depreciation (of a currency)
A decrease in the value of a currency relative to another currency.

appreciation (of a currency)
An increase in the value of a currency relative to another currency.

An exchange rate determined by market forces can, and often does, change daily like stock and bond prices. These price changes result from changes in the supply of, or demand for, a particular currency. When the dollar price of pounds *rises*, for example, from $2 = £1 to $3 = £1, the dollar has *depreciated* relative to the pound (and the pound has appreciated relative to the dollar). A **depreciation** of a currency means that more units of it (dollars) are needed to buy a single unit of some other currency (a pound).

When the dollar price of pounds *falls*, for example, from $2 = £1 to $1 = £1, the dollar has *appreciated* relative to the pound. An **appreciation** of a currency means that it takes fewer units of it (dollars) to buy a single unit of some other currency (a pound). For example, the dollar price of pounds might decline from $2 to $1. Each British product becomes less expensive in terms of dollars, so people in the United States purchase more British goods. In general, U.S. imports from the United Kingdom rise. Meanwhile, because it takes more pounds to get a dollar, U.S. exports to the United Kingdom fall.

The central point is this: When the dollar depreciates (dollar price of foreign currencies rises), U.S. exports rise and U.S. imports fall; when the dollar appreciates (dollar price of foreign currencies falls), U.S. exports fall and U.S. imports rise.

In our U.S.-Britain illustrations, depreciation of the dollar means an appreciation of the pound, and vice versa. When the dollar price of a pound jumps from $2 = £1 to $3 = £1, the pound has appreciated relative to the dollar because it takes fewer pounds to buy $1. At $2 = £1, it took £1/2 to buy $1; at $3 = £1, it takes only £1/3 to buy $1. Conversely, when the dollar appreciates relative to the pound, the pound depreciates relative to the dollar. More pounds are needed to buy a U.S. dollar.

In general, the relevant terminology and relationships between the U.S. dollar and another currency are as follows.

- Dollar price of foreign currency increases ≡ dollar depreciates relative to the foreign currency ≡ foreign currency price of dollar decreases ≡ foreign currency appreciates relative to the dollar.
- Dollar price of foreign currency decreases ≡ dollar appreciates relative to the foreign currency ≡ foreign currency price of dollar increases ≡ foreign currency depreciates relative to the dollar.

Determinants of Exchange Rates

What factors would cause a nation's currency to appreciate or depreciate in the market for foreign exchange? Here are three generalizations (other things equal):

- If the demand for a nation's currency increases, that currency will appreciate; if the demand declines, that currency will depreciate.
- If the supply of a nation's currency increases, that currency will depreciate; if the supply decreases, that currency will appreciate.
- If a nation's currency appreciates, some foreign currency depreciates relative to it.

With these generalizations in mind, let's examine the determinants of exchange rates—the factors that shift the demand or supply curve for a certain currency. As we do so, keep in mind that the other-things-equal assumption is always in force. Also note that we are discussing factors *that change the exchange rate*, not things that change *as a result of* a change in the exchange rate.

Tastes Any change in consumer tastes or preferences for the products of a foreign country may alter the demand for that nation's currency and change its exchange rate. If technological advances in U.S. MP3 players make them more attractive to British consumers and businesses, then the British will supply more pounds in the exchange market in order to purchase more U.S. MP3 players. The supply-of-pounds curve will shift to the right, causing the pound to depreciate and the dollar to appreciate.

In contrast, the U.S. demand-for-pounds curve will shift to the right if British woolen apparel becomes more fashionable in the United States. So the pound will appreciate and the dollar will depreciate.

Relative Income A nation's currency is likely to depreciate if its growth of national income is more rapid than that of other countries. Here's why: A country's imports vary directly with its income level. As total income rises in the United States, people there buy both more domestic goods and more foreign goods. If the U.S. economy is expanding rapidly and the British economy is stagnant, U.S. imports of British goods, and therefore U.S. demands for pounds, will increase. The dollar price of pounds will rise, so the dollar will depreciate.

Relative Inflation Rate Changes Other things equal, changes in the relative rates of inflation of two nations change their relative price levels and alter the exchange rate between their currencies. The currency of the nation with the higher inflation rate—the more rapidly rising price level—tends to depreciate. Suppose, for example, that inflation is zero percent in Great Britain and 5 percent in the United States so that prices, on average, are rising by 5 percent per year in the United States while, on average, remaining unchanged in Great Britain. U.S. consumers will seek out more of the now relatively lower-priced British goods, increasing the demand for pounds. British consumers will purchase less of the now relatively higher-priced U.S. goods, reducing the supply of pounds. This combination of increased demand for pounds and reduced supply of pounds will cause the pound to appreciate and the dollar to depreciate.

Relative Interest Rates Changes in relative interest rates between two countries may alter their exchange rate. Suppose that real interest rates rise in the United States but stay constant in Great Britain. British citizens will then find the United States a more attractive place in which to loan money directly or loan money indirectly by buying bonds. To make these loans, they will have to supply pounds in the foreign exchange market to obtain dollars. The increase in the supply of pounds results in depreciation of the pound and appreciation of the dollar.

Changes in Relative Expected Returns on Stocks, Real Estate, and Production Facilities International investing extends beyond buying foreign bonds. It includes international investments in stocks and real estate as well as foreign purchases of factories and production facilities. Other things equal, the extent of this foreign investment depends on relative expected returns. To make the investments, investors in one country must sell their currencies to purchase the foreign currencies needed for the foreign investments.

For instance, suppose that investing in England suddenly becomes more popular due to a more positive outlook regarding expected returns on stocks, real estate, and production facilities there. U.S. investors therefore will sell U.S. assets to buy more assets in England. The U.S. assets will be sold for dollars, which will then be brought to the foreign exchange market and exchanged for pounds, which will in turn be used to purchase British assets. The increased demand for pounds in the foreign exchange market will cause the pound to appreciate and the dollar to depreciate.

Speculation Currency speculators are people who buy and sell currencies with an eye toward reselling or repurchasing them at a profit. Suppose that, as a group, speculators anticipate that the pound will appreciate and the dollar will depreciate. Speculators holding dollars will therefore try to convert them into pounds. This effort will increase the demand for pounds and cause the dollar price of pounds to rise (that is, cause the dollar to depreciate). A self-fulfilling prophecy occurs: The pound appreciates and the dollar depreciates because speculators act on the belief that these changes will in fact take place. In this way, speculation can cause changes in exchange rates.

Government and Trade

If people and nations benefit from specialization and international exchange, why do governments sometimes try to restrict the free flow of imports or encourage exports? What kinds of world trade barriers can governments erect, and why would they do so?

Trade Protections and Subsidies

Trade interventions by government take several forms. Excise taxes on imported goods are called **tariffs.** A *protective tariff* is implemented to shield domestic producers from foreign competition. These tariffs impede free trade by increasing the prices of imported goods and therefore shifting sales toward domestic producers. Although protective tariffs are usually not high enough to stop the importation of foreign goods, they put foreign producers at a competitive disadvantage. A tariff on imported shoes, for example, would make domestically produced shoes more attractive to consumers.

Import quotas are limits on the quantities or total value of specific items that may be imported in some period. Once a quota is "filled," further imports of that product are choked off. Import quotas are more effective than tariffs in impeding international trade. With a tariff, a product can go on being imported in large quantities; with an import quota, however, all imports are prohibited once the quota is filled.

Nontariff barriers (NTBs) include onerous licensing requirements, unreasonable standards pertaining to product quality, or excessive bureaucratic hurdles and delays in customs procedures. Some nations require that importers of foreign goods obtain licenses. By restricting the issuance of licenses, imports can be restricted. Although many nations carefully inspect imported agricultural products to prevent the introduction of potentially harmful insects, some countries use lengthy inspections to impede imports.

A **voluntary export restriction (VER)** is a trade barrier by which foreign firms "voluntarily" limit the amount of their exports to a particular country. Exporters agree to a VER, which has the effect of an import quota, to avoid more stringent trade barriers. In the late 1990s, for example, Canadian producers of softwood lumber (fir, spruce, cedar, pine) agreed to a VER on exports to the United States under the threat of a permanently higher U.S. tariff.

tariffs
Taxes imposed by a nation on imported goods.

import quotas
Limits imposed by nations on the quantities (or total values) of goods that may be imported during some period of time.

nontariff barriers (NTBs)
All impediments other than protective tariffs that nations establish to impede imports, including import quotas, licensing requirements, unreasonable product-quality standards, and unnecessary bureaucratic detail in customs procedures.

voluntary export restriction (VER)
An agreement by countries or foreign firms to limit their exports to a certain foreign nation to avoid enactment of formal trade barriers by that nation.

Export subsidies consist of government payments to domestic producers of export goods. By reducing production costs, the subsidies enable producers to charge lower prices and thus to sell more exports in world markets. Example: The United States and other nations have subsidized domestic farmers to boost the domestic food supply. Such subsidies have lowered the market price of agricultural commodities and have artificially lowered their export prices.

export subsidies
Government payments to domestic producers to enable them to reduce the price of a product to foreign buyers.

Economic Impact of Tariffs

Tariffs, quotas, and other trade restrictions have a series of economic effects predicted by supply and demand analysis and observed in reality. These effects vary somewhat by type of trade protection. So to keep things simple, we will focus on the effects of tariffs.

Direct Effects   Because tariffs raise the price of goods imported to the United States, U.S. consumption of those goods declines. Higher prices reduce quantity demanded, as indicated by the law of demand. A tariff prompts consumers to buy fewer of the imported goods and reallocate a portion of their expenditures to less desired substitute products. U.S. consumers are clearly injured by the tariff.

ORIGIN OF THE IDEA

O 13.2
Mercantilism

U.S. producers—who are not subject to the tariff—receive the higher price (pretariff foreign price + tariff) on the imported product. Because this new price is higher than before, the domestic producers respond by producing more. Higher prices increase quantity supplied, as indicated by the law of supply. So domestic producers increase their output. They therefore enjoy both a higher price and expanded sales; this explains why domestic producers lobby for protective tariffs. But from a social point of view, the greater domestic production means the tariff allows domestic producers to bid resources away from other, more efficient, U.S. industries.

Foreign producers are hurt by tariffs. Although the sales price of the imported good is higher, that higher amount accrues to the U.S. government as tariff revenues, not to foreign producers. The after-tariff price, or the per-unit revenue to foreign producers, remains as before, but the volume of U.S. imports (foreign exports) falls.

Government gains revenue from tariffs. This revenue is a transfer of income from consumers to government and does not represent any net change in the nation's economic well-being. The result is that government gains a portion of what consumers lose by paying more for imported goods.

Indirect Effects   Tariffs have a subtle effect beyond those just mentioned. They also hurt domestic firms that use the protected goods as inputs in their production process. For example, a tariff on imported steel boosts the price of steel girders, thus hurting firms that build bridges and office towers. Also, tariffs reduce competition in the protected industries. With less competition from foreign producers, domestic firms may be slow to design and implement cost-saving production methods and introduce new products.

Because foreigners sell fewer imported goods in the United States, they earn fewer dollars and so must buy fewer U.S. exports. U.S. export industries must then cut production and release resources. These are highly efficient industries, as we know from their comparative advantage and their ability to sell goods in world markets.

Tariffs directly promote the expansion of inefficient industries that do not have a comparative advantage; they also indirectly cause the contraction of relatively efficient industries that do have a comparative advantage. Put bluntly, tariffs cause resources to be shifted in the wrong direction—and that is not surprising. We know that specialization and world trade lead to more efficient use of world resources and greater world output. But protective tariffs reduce world trade. Therefore, tariffs also reduce efficiency and the world's real output.

Net Costs of Tariffs

Tariffs impose costs on domestic consumers but provide gains to domestic producers and revenue to the federal government. The consumer costs of trade restrictions are calculated by determining the effect the restrictions have on consumer prices. Protection raises the price of a product in three ways: (1) The price of the imported product goes up; (2) the higher price of imports causes some consumers to shift their purchases to higher-priced domestically produced goods; and (3) the prices of domestically produced goods rise because import competition has declined.

Study after study finds that the costs to consumers substantially exceed the gains to producers and government. A sizable net cost or efficiency loss to society arises from trade protection. Furthermore, industries employ large amounts of economic resources to influence Congress to pass and retain protectionist laws. Because these efforts divert resources away from more socially desirable purposes, trade restrictions also impose that cost on society.

Conclusion: The gains that U.S. trade barriers produce for protected industries and their workers come at the expense of much greater losses for the entire economy. The result is economic inefficiency, reduced consumption, and lower standards of living.

So Why Government Trade Protections?

In view of the benefits of free trade, what accounts for the impulse to impede imports and boost exports through government policy? There are several reasons—some legitimate, most not.

Misunderstanding the Gains from Trade

It is a commonly accepted myth that the greatest benefit to be derived from international trade is greater domestic sales and employment in the export sector. This suggests that exports are "good" because they increase domestic sales and employment, whereas imports are "bad" because they reduce domestic sales and deprive people of jobs at home. Actually, the true benefit created by international trade is the extra output obtained from abroad—the imports obtained for a lower opportunity cost than if they were produced at home.

A recent study suggests that the elimination of trade barriers since the Second World War has increased the income of the average U.S. household by at least $7000 and perhaps by as much as $13,000. These income gains are recurring; they happen year after year.[2]

Political Considerations

While a nation as a whole gains from trade, trade may harm particular domestic industries and particular groups of resource suppliers. In our earlier comparative-advantage example, specialization and trade adversely affected the U.S. avocado industry and the Mexican soybean industry. Understandably, those industries might seek to preserve their economic positions by persuading their respective governments to protect them from imports—perhaps through tariffs.

Those who directly benefit from import protection are relatively few in number but have much at stake. Thus, they have a strong incentive to pursue political activity to achieve their aims. Moreover, because the costs of import protection are buried in the price of goods and spread out over millions of citizens, the cost borne by each individual citizen is quite small. However, the full cost of tariffs and quotas typically greatly exceeds the benefits. It is not uncommon to find that it costs the public $250,000 or more a year to protect a domestic job that pays less than one-fourth that amount.

---

[2]Scott C. Bradford, Paul L.E. Grieco, and Gary C. Hufbauer, "The Payoff to America from Globalization," *The World Economy*, July 2006, pp. 893–916.

In the political arena, the voice of the relatively few producers and unions demanding *protectionism* is loud and constant, whereas the voice of those footing the bill is soft or nonexistent. When political deal making is added in—"You back tariffs for the apparel industry in my state, and I'll back tariffs for the steel industry in your state"—the outcome can be a network of protective tariffs.

ILLUSTRATING THE IDEA

Buy American?

Will "buying American" make Americans better off? No, says Dallas Federal Reserve economist W. Michael Cox:

> A common myth is that it is better for Americans to spend their money at home than abroad. The best way to expose the fallacy of this argument is to take it to its logical extreme. If it is better for me to spend my money here than abroad, then it is even better yet to buy in Texas than in New York, better yet to buy in Dallas than in Houston . . . in my own neighborhood . . . within my own family . . . to consume only what I can produce. Alone and poor.[*]

[*]"The Fruits of Free Trade," 2002 Annual Report, by W. Michael Cox and Richard Alm, p. 16, Federal Reserve Bank of Dallas. Used with permission.

Three Arguments for Protection

Arguments for trade protection are many and diverse. Some—such as tariffs to protect "infant industries" or to create "military self-sufficiency"—have some legitimacy. But other arguments break down under close scrutiny. Three protectionist arguments, in particular, have persisted decade after decade in the United States.

Increased-Domestic-Employment Argument

Arguing for a tariff to "save U.S. jobs" becomes fashionable when the economy encounters a recession (such as the severe recession of 2007–2009 in the United States). In an economy that engages in international trade, exports involve spending on domestic output and imports reflect spending to obtain part of another nation's output. So, in this argument, reducing imports will divert spending on another nation's output to spending on domestic output. Thus domestic output and employment will rise. But this argument has several shortcomings.

While imports may eliminate some U.S. jobs, they create others. Imports may have eliminated the jobs of some U.S. steel and textile workers in recent years, but other workers have gained jobs unloading ships, flying imported aircraft, and selling imported electronic equipment. Import restrictions alter the composition of employment, but they may have little or no effect on the volume of employment.

The *fallacy of composition*—the false idea that what is true for the part is necessarily true for the whole—is also present in this rationale for tariffs. All nations cannot simultaneously succeed in restricting imports while maintaining their exports; what is true for one nation is not true for all nations. The exports of one nation must be the imports of another nation. To the extent that one country is able to expand its economy through an excess of exports over imports, the resulting excess of imports over exports worsens another economy's unemployment problem. It is no wonder that tariffs and import quotas meant to achieve domestic full employment are called "beggar my neighbor" policies: They achieve short-run domestic goals by making trading partners poorer.

Moreover, nations adversely affected by tariffs and quotas are likely to retaliate, causing a "trade-barrier war" that will choke off trade and make all nations worse off. The **Smoot-Hawley Tariff Act** of 1930 is a classic example. Although that act was meant to reduce imports and stimulate U.S. production, the high tariffs it authorized prompted adversely affected nations to retaliate with tariffs equally high. International trade fell, lowering the output and income of all nations. Economic historians generally agree that the Smoot-Hawley Tariff Act was a contributing cause of the Great Depression.

Finally, forcing an excess of exports over imports cannot succeed in raising domestic employment over the long run. It is through U.S. imports that foreign nations earn dollars for buying U.S. exports. In the long run a nation must import in order to export. The long-run impact of tariffs is not an increase in domestic employment but, at best, a reallocation of workers away from export industries and to protected domestic industries. This shift implies a less efficient allocation of resources.

Cheap-Foreign-Labor Argument

The cheap-foreign-labor argument says that government must shield domestic firms and workers from the ruinous competition of countries where wages are low. If protection is not provided, cheap imports will flood U.S. markets and the prices of U.S. goods—along with the wages of U.S. workers—will be pulled down. That is, the domestic living standards in the United States will be reduced.

This argument can be rebutted at several levels. The logic of the argument suggests that it is not mutually beneficial for rich and poor persons to trade with one another. However, that is not the case. A relatively low-income mechanic may fix the Mercedes owned by a wealthy lawyer, and both may benefit from the transaction. And both U.S. consumers and Chinese workers gain when they "trade" a pair of athletic shoes priced at $30 as opposed to U.S. consumers being restricted to a similar shoe made in the United States for $60.

Also, recall that gains from trade are based on comparative advantage, not on absolute advantage. Again, think back to our U.S.-Mexico (soybean-avocado) example in which the United States had greater labor productivity than Mexico in producing both soybeans and avocados. Because of that greater productivity, wages and living standards will be higher for U.S. labor. Mexico's less productive labor will receive lower wages.

The cheap-foreign-labor argument suggests that, to maintain American living standards, the United States should not trade with low-wage Mexico. Suppose it forgoes trade with Mexico. Will wages and living standards rise in the United States as a result? Absolutely not! To obtain avocados, the United States will have to reallocate a portion of its labor from its relatively more-efficient soybean industry to its relatively less-efficient avocado industry. As a result, the average productivity of U.S. labor will fall, as will real wages and living standards for American workers. The labor forces of both countries will have diminished standards of living because without specialization and trade they will have less output available to them. Compare column 4 with column 1 in Table 13.4 to confirm this point.

Protection-against-Dumping Argument

The protection-against-dumping argument contends that tariffs are needed to protect domestic firms from "dumping" by foreign producers. **Dumping** is the sale of a product in a foreign country at prices either below cost or below the prices commonly charged at home.

Smoot-Hawley Tariff Act
Legislation passed in 1930 that established very high U.S. tariffs designed to reduce imports and stimulate the domestic economy. Instead, the law resulted only in retaliatory tariffs by other nations and a decline in trade worldwide.

dumping
The sale of products in a foreign country at prices either below costs or below the prices charged at home.

Economists cite two plausible reasons for this behavior. First, with regard to below-cost dumping, firms in country A may dump goods at below cost into country B in an attempt to drive their competitors in country B out of business. If the firms in country A succeed in driving their competitors in country B out of business, they will enjoy monopoly power and monopoly prices and profits on the goods they subsequently sell in country B. Their hope is that the longer-term monopoly profits will more than offset the losses from below-cost sales that must take place while they are attempting to drive their competitors in country B out of business.

Second, dumping that involves selling abroad at a price that is below the price commonly charged in the home country (but which is still at or above production costs) may be a form of price discrimination, which is charging different prices to different customers. As an example, a foreign seller that has a monopoly in its home market may find that it can maximize its overall profit by charging a high price in its monopolized domestic market while charging a lower price in the United States, where it must compete with U.S. producers. Curiously, it may pursue this strategy even if it makes no profit at all from its sales in the United States, where it must charge the competitive price. So why bother selling in the United States? Because the increase in overall production that comes about by exporting to the United States may allow the firm to obtain the per unit cost savings often associated with large-scale production. These cost savings imply even higher profits in the monopolized domestic market.

Because dumping is an "unfair trade practice," most nations prohibit it. For example, where dumping is shown to injure U.S. firms, the federal government imposes tariffs called *antidumping duties* on the goods in question. But relatively few documented cases of dumping occur each year, and specific instances of unfair trade do not justify widespread, permanent tariffs. Moreover, antidumping duties can be abused. Often, what appears to be dumping is simply comparative advantage at work.

Trade Adjustment Assistance

A nation's comparative advantage in the production of a certain product is not forever fixed. As national economies evolve, the size and quality of their labor forces may change, the volume and composition of their capital stocks may shift, new technologies may develop, and even the quality of land and the quantity of natural resources may be altered. As these changes take place, the relative efficiency with which a nation can produce specific goods will also change. Also, new trade agreements can suddenly leave formerly protected industries highly vulnerable to major disruption or even collapse.

Shifts in patterns of comparative advantage and removal of trade protection can hurt specific groups of workers. For example, the erosion of the United States' once strong comparative advantage in steel has caused production plant shutdowns and layoffs in the U.S. steel industry. The textile and apparel industries in the United States face similar difficulties. Clearly, not everyone wins from free trade (or freer trade). Some workers lose.

The **Trade Adjustment Assistance Act** of 2002 introduced some innovative policies to help those hurt by shifts in international trade patterns. The law provides cash assistance (beyond unemployment insurance) for up to 78 weeks for workers displaced by imports or plant relocations abroad. To obtain the assistance, workers must participate in job searches, training programs, or remedial education. There also are relocation allowances to help displaced workers move geographically to new jobs within the United States. Refundable tax credits for health insurance serve as payments to help workers maintain their insurance coverage during the retraining and job search period. Also, workers who are 50 years of age or older are eligible for "wage insurance," which replaces some of the difference in pay (if any) between their old and new jobs.

Trade Adjustment Assistance Act
A U.S. law passed in 2002 that provides cash assistance, education and training benefits, health care subsidies, and wage subsidies (for persons age 50 or more) to workers displaced by imports or plant relocations abroad.

Many economists support trade adjustment assistance because it not only helps workers hurt by international trade but also helps create the political support necessary to reduce trade barriers and export subsidies.

But not all economists are keen on trade adjustment assistance. Loss of jobs from imports or plant relocations abroad is only a small fraction (about 4 percent in recent years) of total job loss in the economy each year. Many workers also lose their jobs because of changing patterns of demand, changing technology, bad management, and other dynamic aspects of a market economy. Some critics ask, "What makes losing one's job to international trade worthy of such special treatment, compared to losing one's job to, say, technological change or domestic competition?" There is no totally satisfying answer.

APPLYING THE ANALYSIS

offshoring
The practice of shifting work previously done by American workers to workers located in other nations.

Is Offshoring of Jobs Bad?

Not only are some U.S. jobs lost because of international trade, but some are lost because of globalization of resource markets. In recent years U.S. firms have found it increasingly profitable to outsource work abroad. Economists call this business activity **offshoring:** shifting work previously done by American workers to workers located in other nations. Offshoring is not a new practice but traditionally has involved components for U.S. manufacturing goods. For example, Boeing has long offshored the production of major airplane parts for its "American" aircraft.

Recent advances in computer and communications technology have enabled U.S. firms to offshore service jobs such as data entry, book composition, software coding, call-center operations, medical transcription, and claims processing to countries such as India. Where offshoring occurs, some of the value added in the production process occurs in foreign countries rather than the United States. So part of the income generated from the production of U.S. goods is paid to foreigners, not to American workers.

Offshoring is obviously costly to Americans who lose their jobs, but it is not generally bad for the economy. Offshoring simply reflects a growing international trade in services, or, more descriptively, "tasks." That trade has been made possible by recent trade agreements and new information and communication technologies. As with trade in goods, trade in services reflects comparative advantage and is beneficial to both trading parties. Moreover, the United States has a sizable trade surplus with other nations in services. The United States gains by specializing in high-valued services such as transportation services, accounting services, legal services, and advertising services, where it still has a comparative advantage. It then "trades" to obtain lower-valued services such as call-center and data entry work, for which comparative advantage has gone abroad.

Offshoring also increases the demand for complementary jobs in the United States. Jobs that are close substitutes for existing U.S. jobs are lost, but complementary jobs in the United States are expanded. For example, the lower price of offshore maintenance of aircraft and reservation centers reduces the price of airline tickets. That means more domestic and international flights by American carriers, which in turn means more jobs for U.S.-based pilots, flight attendants, baggage handlers, and check-in personnel. Moreover, offshoring encourages domestic investment and expansion of firms in the United States by reducing their costs and keeping them competitive worldwide. Some observers equate "offshoring jobs" to "importing competitiveness."

QUESTION: What has enabled white-collar labor services to become the world's newest export and import commodity even though such labor itself remains in place?

Multilateral Trade Agreements and Free-Trade Zones

Being aware of the overall benefits of free trade, nations have worked to lower tariffs worldwide. Their pursuit of free trade has been aided by the growing power of free-trade interest groups: Exporters of goods and services, importers of foreign components used in "domestic" products, and domestic sellers of imported products all strongly support lower tariffs. And, in fact, tariffs have generally declined during the past half-century.

General Agreement on Tariffs and Trade

Following the Second World War, the major nations of the world set upon a general course of liberalizing trade. In 1947 some 23 nations, including the United States, signed the **General Agreement on Tariffs and Trade (GATT).** GATT was based on the principles of equal, nondiscriminatory trade treatment for all member nations and the reduction of tariffs and quotas by multilateral negotiation. Basically, GATT provided a continuing forum for the negotiation of reduced trade barriers on a multilateral basis among nations.

Since 1947, member nations have completed eight "rounds" of GATT negotiations to reduce trade barriers. The *Uruguay Round* agreement of 1993 phased in trade liberalizations between 1995 and 2005.

World Trade Organization

The Uruguay Round of 1993 established the **World Trade Organization (WTO)** as GATT's successor. In 2011, 153 nations belonged to the WTO, which oversees trade agreements and rules on disputes relating to them. It also provides forums for further rounds of trade negotiations. The ninth and latest round of negotiations—the **Doha Round**—was launched in Doha, Qatar, in late 2001. (The trade rounds occur over several years in several geographic venues but are named after the city or country of origination.) The negotiations are aimed at further reducing tariffs and quotas, as well as agricultural subsidies that distort trade.

GATT and the WTO have been positive forces in the trend toward liberalized world trade. The trade rules agreed upon by the member nations provide a strong and necessary bulwark against the protectionism called for by the special-interest groups in the various nations. For that reason and because current WTO agreements lack strong labor standards and environmental protections, the WTO is controversial.

European Union

Countries have also sought to reduce tariffs by creating regional *free-trade zones*—also called *trade blocs*. The most dramatic example is the **European Union (EU).** In 2007, the addition of Bulgaria and Romania expanded the EU to its present size of 27 nations.[3]

The EU has abolished tariffs and import quotas on nearly all products traded among the participating nations and established a common system of tariffs applicable to all goods received from nations outside the EU. It has also liberalized the movement of capital and labor within the EU and has created common policies in other economic matters of joint concern, such as agriculture, transportation, and business practices. The EU is now a strong **trade bloc:** a group of countries having common identity, economic interests, and trade rules. Of the 27 EU countries, 17 used the **euro** as a common currency in 2011.

---

[3]The other 25 are France, Germany, United Kingdom, Italy, Belgium, the Netherlands, Luxembourg, Denmark, Ireland, Greece, Spain, Portugal, Austria, Finland, Sweden, Poland, Hungary, Czech Republic, Slovakia, Lithuania, Latvia, Estonia, Slovenia, Malta, and Cyprus.

General Agreement on Tariffs and Trade (GATT)
An international accord reached in 1947 in which 23 nations agreed to give equal and nondiscriminatory treatment to one another, to reduce tariffs through multinational negotiations, and to eliminate import quotas.

World Trade Organization (WTO)
An organization of 153 nations (as of 2008) that oversees the provisions of the current world trade agreement, resolves disputes stemming from it, and holds forums for further rounds of trade negotiations.

Doha Round
The latest, uncompleted (as of 2011) sequence of trade negotiations by members of the World Trade Organization; named after Doha, Qatar, where the set of negotiations began.

European Union (EU)
An association of 27 European nations that has eliminated tariffs and quotas among them, established common tariffs for imported goods from outside the member nations, reduced barriers to the free movement of capital, and created other common economic policies.

trade bloc
A group of nations that lower or abolish trade barriers among themselves.

euro
The common currency unit used by 17 (as of 2011) European nations in the European Union.

EU integration has achieved for Europe what the U.S. constitutional prohibition on tariffs by individual states has achieved for the United States: increased regional specialization, greater productivity, greater output, and faster economic growth. The free flow of goods and services has created large markets for EU industries. The resulting economies of large-scale production have enabled those industries to achieve much lower costs than they could have achieved in their small, single-nation markets.

North American Free Trade Agreement

North American Free Trade Agreement (NAFTA)

A 1993 agreement establishing, over a 15-year period, a free-trade zone composed of Canada, Mexico, and the United States.

In 1993 Canada, Mexico, and the United States formed a major trade bloc. The **North American Free Trade Agreement (NAFTA)** established a free-trade zone that has about the same combined output as the EU but encompasses a much larger geographic area. NAFTA has eliminated tariffs and other trade barriers between Canada, Mexico, and the United States for most goods and services.

Critics of NAFTA feared that it would cause a massive loss of U.S. jobs as firms moved to Mexico to take advantage of lower wages and weaker regulations on pollution and workplace safety. Also, there was concern that Japan and South Korea would build plants in Mexico and transport goods tariff-free to the United States, further hurting U.S. firms and workers.

In retrospect, critics were much too pessimistic. Since the passage of NAFTA in 1993, employment in the United States has increased by more than 20 million workers. Increased trade between Canada, Mexico, and the United States has enhanced the standard of living in all three countries.

Not all aspects of trade blocs are positive. By giving preferences to countries within their free-trade zones, trade blocs such as the EU and NAFTA tend to reduce their members' trade with non-bloc members. Thus, the world loses some of the benefits of a completely open global trading system. Eliminating that disadvantage has been one of the motivations for liberalizing global trade through the World Trade Organization. Its liberalizations apply equally to all 153 nations that belong to the WTO.

Recent U.S. Trade Deficits

As shown in Figure 13.2 the United States has experienced large and persistent trade deficits in recent years. These deficits rose rapidly between 2002 and 2006 before declining when consumers and businesses greatly curtailed their purchase of imports

FIGURE 13.2 U.S. trade deficits, 2002–2010.

The United States experienced large deficits in *goods* and in *goods and services* between 2002 and 2010. These deficits steadily increased until the recession of 2007–2009. Despite the decline, large trade deficits are expected to continue for many years to come.

Source: Bureau of Economic Analysis, **www.bea.gov.**

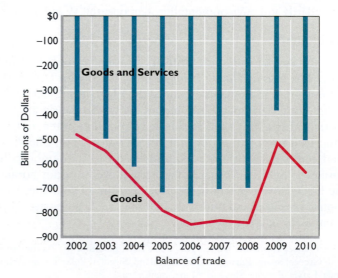

during the recession of 2007–2009. Even in 2009, however, the trade deficit on goods was still at $517 billion and the trade deficit on goods and services was $379 billion. As the economy began to recover, the trade deficit on goods rose to $646 billion in 2010, and the trade deficit on goods and services rose to $500 billion. Economists expect the trade deficits to continue to expand, absolutely and relatively, toward prerecession levels when the economic recovery strengthens and U.S. income and imports rise at a faster pace.

Causes of the Trade Deficits

The large U.S. trade deficits have several causes. First, the U.S. economy expanded more rapidly between 2001 and 2007 than the economies of several U.S. trading partners. The strong U.S. income growth that accompanied that economic growth enabled Americans to greatly increase their purchases of imported products. In contrast, Japan and some European nations suffered recession or experienced relatively slow income growth over that same period. So consumers in those countries increased their purchases of U.S. exports much less rapidly than Americans increased their purchases of foreign imports.

Another factor explaining the large trade deficits is the enormous U.S. trade imbalance with China. In 2007 the United States imported $257 billion more of goods and services than it exported to China. Even in the recession year 2009, the trade deficit with China was $220 billion. That deficit was double the combined deficits with Mexico ($43 billion), Germany ($37 billion), and Japan ($28 billion). The United States is China's largest export market, and although China has greatly increased its imports from the United States, its standard of living has not yet risen sufficiently for its households to afford large quantities of U.S. products. Adding to the problem, China's government has fixed the exchange rate of it currency, the yuan, to a basket of currencies that includes the U.S. dollar. Therefore, China's large trade surpluses with the United States have not caused the yuan to appreciate much against the U.S. dollar. Greater appreciation of the yuan would have made Chinese goods more expensive in the United States and reduced U.S. imports from China. In China a stronger yuan would have reduced the dollar price of U.S. goods and increased Chinese purchases of U.S. exports. That combination—reduced U.S. imports from China and increased U.S. exports to China—would have reduced the large U.S. trade imbalance.

Another factor underlying the large U.S. trade deficits is a continuing trade deficit with oil-exporting nations. For example, in 2010 the United States had a $96 billion trade deficit with the OPEC countries.

Finally, a declining U.S. saving rate (= saving/total income) also contributed to the large U.S. trade deficits. Up until the recession of 2007–2009, the U.S. saving rate declined substantially, while its investment rate (= investment/total income) increased. The gap between U.S. investment and U.S. saving was filled by foreign purchases of U.S. real and financial assets. Because foreign savers were willing to finance a large part of U.S. investment, Americans were able to save less and consume more. Part of that added consumption spending was on imported goods. That is, the inflow of funds from abroad may be one cause of the trade deficits, not just a result of those deficits.

Implications of U.S. Trade Deficits

The prerecession U.S. trade deficits were the largest ever run by a major industrial nation. Whether the large trade deficits should be of significant concern to the United States and the rest of the world is debatable. Most economists see both benefits and costs to trade deficits.

Increased Current Consumption At the time a trade deficit or a current account deficit is occurring, American consumers benefit. A trade deficit means that the United States is receiving more goods and services as imports from abroad than it is sending out as exports. Taken alone, a trade deficit allows the United States to consume outside its production possibilities curve. It augments the domestic standard of living. But here is a catch: The gain in present consumption may come at the expense of reduced future consumption.

Increased U.S. Indebtedness A trade deficit is considered "unfavorable" because it must be financed by borrowing from the rest of the world, selling off assets, or dipping into foreign currency reserves. Trade deficits are financed primarily by net inpayments of foreign currencies to the United States. When U.S. exports are insufficient to finance U.S. imports, the United States increases both its debt to people abroad and the value of foreign claims against assets in the United States. Financing of the U.S. trade deficit has resulted in a larger foreign accumulation of claims against U.S. financial and real assets than the U.S. claim against foreign assets. In 2008, foreigners owned about $3.5 trillion more of U.S. assets (corporations, land, stocks, bonds, loan notes) than U.S. citizens and institutions owned of foreign assets.

If the United States wants to regain ownership of these domestic assets, at some future time it will have to export more than it imports. At that time, domestic consumption will be lower because the United States will need to send more of its output abroad than it receives as imports. Therefore, the current consumption gains delivered by U.S. current account deficits may mean permanent debt, permanent foreign ownership, or large sacrifices of future consumption.

We say "may mean" above because the foreign lending to U.S. firms and foreign investment in the United States increase the stock of American capital. U.S. production capacity might increase more rapidly than otherwise because of a large inflow of funds to offset the trade deficits. We know that faster increases in production capacity and real GDP enhance the economy's ability to service foreign debt and buy back real capital, if that is desired.

Downward Pressure on the Dollar Finally, the large U.S. trade deficits place downward pressure on the exchange value of the U.S. dollar. The surge of imports requires the United States to supply dollars in the currency market in order to obtain the foreign currencies required for purchasing the imported goods. That flood of dollars into the currency market causes the dollar to depreciate relative to other currencies. Between 2002 and 2008, the dollar depreciated against most other currencies, including 43 percent against the European euro, 27 percent against the British pound, 37 percent against the Canadian dollar, 15 percent against the Chinese yuan, and 25 percent against the Japanese yen. Since 2008, the U.S. dollar has continued to depreciate against the Canadian dollar, the Chinese yuan, and the Japanese yen but has appreciated relative to the euro and the pound. Some of this depreciation was fueled by the expansionary monetary policy (reduced real interest rates) undertaken by the Fed beginning in 2007 and carrying into 2011. The subsequent appreciation of the U.S. dollar relative to the European euro and British pound is largely attributed to continued economic weakness in part of the euro zone and the United Kingdom.

Economists feared that the decline in the dollar would contribute to inflation as imports became more expensive to Americans in dollar terms. Traditionally the Fed would need to react to that inflation with a tight monetary policy that raises real interest rates in the United States. However, because of the financial crisis and recession that began in 2007, the Fed chose to aggressively reduce interest rates, hoping to halt the downturn in the economy. In effect, it gambled that its actions would not ignite inflation because of the dampening effect of the severe economic recession on rising prices.

Summary

1. The United States leads the world in the volume of international trade, but trade is much larger as a percentage of GDP in many other nations.

2. Mutually advantageous specialization and trade are possible between any two nations if they have different domestic opportunity-cost ratios for any two products. By specializing on the basis of comparative advantage, nations can obtain larger real incomes with fixed amounts of resources. The terms of trade determine how this increase in world output is shared by the trading nations. Increasing costs lead to less-than-complete specialization for many tradable goods.

3. The foreign exchange market establishes exchange rates between currencies. Each nation's purchases from abroad create a supply of its own currency and a demand for foreign currencies. The resulting supply-demand equilibrium sets the exchange rate that links the currencies of all nations. Depreciation of a nation's currency reduces its imports and increases its exports; appreciation increases its imports and reduces its exports.

4. Currencies will depreciate or appreciate as a result of changes in their supply or demand, which in turn depend on changes in tastes for foreign goods, relative changes in national incomes, relative changes in inflation rates, changes in interest rates, and the extent and direction of currency speculation.

5. Trade barriers and subsidies take the form of protective tariffs, quotas, nontariff barriers, voluntary export restrictions, and export subsidies. Protective tariffs increase the prices and reduce the quantities demanded of the affected goods. Sales by foreign exporters diminish; domestic producers, however, gain higher prices and enlarged sales. Consumer losses from trade restrictions greatly exceed producer and government gains, creating an efficiency loss to society.

6. Three recurring arguments for free trade—increased domestic employment, cheap foreign labor, and protection against dumping—are either fallacies or overstatements that do not hold up under careful economic analysis.

7. Not everyone benefits from free (or freer) trade. The Trade Adjustment Assistance Act of 2002 provides cash assistance, education and training benefits, health care subsidies, and wage subsidies (for persons 50 years old or more) to workers who are displaced by imports or plant relocations abroad. But less than 4 percent of all job losses in the United States each year result from imports, plant relocations, or the offshoring of service jobs.

8. In 1947 the General Agreement on Tariffs and Trade (GATT) was formed to encourage nondiscriminatory treatment for all member nations, to reduce tariffs, and to eliminate import quotas. The Uruguay Round of GATT negotiations (1993) reduced tariffs and quotas, liberalized trade in services, reduced agricultural subsidies, reduced pirating of intellectual property, and phased out quotas on textiles.

9. GATT's successor, the World Trade Organization (WTO), had 153 member nations in 2011. It implements WTO agreements, rules on trade disputes between members, and provides forums for continued discussions on trade liberalization. The latest round of trade negotiations—the Doha Development Agenda—began in late 2001 and as of 2011 was still in progress.

10. Free-trade zones (trade blocs) liberalize trade within regions but may at the same time impede trade with non-bloc members. Two examples of free-trade arrangements are the 27-member European Union (EU) and the North American Free Trade Agreement (NAFTA), comprising Canada, Mexico, and the United States. Seventeen of the EU nations (as of 2011) have abandoned their national currencies for a common currency called the euro.

11. U.S. trade deficits have produced current increases in the living standards of U.S. consumers. But the deficits have also increased U.S. debt to the rest of the world and increased foreign ownership of assets in the United States. This greater foreign investment in the United States, however, has undoubtedly increased U.S. production possibilities. The trade deficits also place extreme downward pressure on the international value of the U.S. dollar.

Terms and Concepts

comparative advantage

terms of trade

foreign exchange market

exchange rates

depreciation

appreciation

tariffs

import quotas

nontariff barriers (NTBs)

voluntary export restriction (VER)

export subsidies

Smoot-Hawley Tariff Act

dumping

Trade Adjustment Assistance Act

offshoring

General Agreement on Tariffs and Trade (GATT)

World Trade Organization (WTO)

Doha Round

European Union (EU)

trade bloc

euro

North American Free Trade Agreement (NAFTA)

Questions

1. Quantitatively, how important is international trade to the United States relative to its importance to other nations? What country is the United States' most important trading partner, quantitatively? With what country does the United States have the largest current trade deficit? **LO1**

2. What effect do rising costs (rather than constant costs) have on the extent of specialization and trade? Explain. **LO2**

3. What is offshoring of white-collar service jobs, and how does it relate to international trade? Why has it recently increased? Why do you think more than half of all offshored jobs have gone to India? Give an example (other than that in the textbook) of how offshoring can eliminate some U.S. jobs while creating other U.S. jobs. **LO2**

4. Explain why the U.S. demand for Mexican pesos is downsloping and the supply of pesos to Americans is upsloping. Indicate whether each of the following would cause the Mexican peso to appreciate or depreciate: **LO3**
   a. The United States unilaterally reduces tariffs on Mexican products.
   b. Mexico encounters severe inflation.
   c. Deteriorating political relations reduce American tourism in Mexico.
   d. The U.S. economy moves into a severe recession.
   e. The United States engages in a high-interest-rate monetary policy.
   f. Mexican products become more fashionable to U.S. consumers.
   g. The Mexican government encourages U.S. firms to invest in Mexican oil fields.

5. Explain why you agree or disagree with the following statements: **LO3**
   a. A country that grows faster than its major trading partners can expect the international value of its currency to depreciate.
   b. A nation whose interest rate is rising more rapidly than interest rates in other nations can expect the international value of its currency to appreciate.
   c. A country's currency will appreciate if its inflation rate is less than that of the rest of the world.

6. If the European euro were to depreciate relative to the U.S. dollar in the foreign exchange market, would it be easier or harder for the French to sell their wine in the United States? Suppose you were planning a trip to Paris. How would depreciation of the euro change the dollar cost of your trip? **LO3**

7. What measures do governments take to promote exports and restrict imports? Who benefits and who loses from protectionist policies? What is the net outcome for society? **LO4**

8. Speculate as to why some U.S. firms strongly support trade liberalization while other U.S. firms favor protectionism. Speculate as to why some U.S. labor unions strongly support trade liberalization while other U.S. labor unions strongly oppose it. **LO4**

9. Explain: "Free-trade zones such as the EU and NAFTA lead a double life: They can promote free trade among members, but they pose serious trade obstacles for nonmembers." Do you think the net effects of trade blocs are good or bad for world trade? Why? How do the efforts of the WTO relate to these trade blocs? **LO5**

Problems

1. Assume that the comparative-cost ratios of two products—baby formula and tuna fish—are as follows in the nations of Canswicki and Tunata:

   Canswicki: 1 can baby formula ≡ 2 cans tuna fish
   Tunata: 1 can baby formula ≡ 4 cans tuna fish

   In what product should each nation specialize? Which of the following terms of trade would be acceptable to both nations: (a) 1 can baby formula ≡ $2\frac{1}{2}$ cans tuna fish; (b) 1 can baby formula ≡ 1 can tuna fish; (c) 1 can baby formula ≡ 5 cans tuna fish? **LO2**

2. The accompanying hypothetical production possibilities tables are for New Zealand and Spain. Each country can produce apples and plums. Plot the production possibilities data for each of the two countries separately. Referring to your graphs, answer the following: **LO2**

New Zealand's Production Possibilities Table (Millions of Bushels)

Product	Production Alternatives			
	A	B	C	D
Apples	0	20	40	60
Plums	15	10	5	0

Spain's Production Possibilities Table (Millions of Bushels)

Product	Production Alternatives			
	R	S	T	U
Apples	0	20	40	60
Plums	60	40	20	0

a. What is each country's cost ratio of producing plums and apples?

b. Which nation should specialize in which product?

c. Show the trading possibilities lines for each nation if the actual terms of trade are 1 plum for 2 apples. (Plot these lines on your graph.)

d. Suppose the optimum product mixes before specialization and trade were alternative B in New Zealand and alternative S in Spain. What would be the gains from specialization and trade?

3. The following hypothetical production possibilities tables are for China and the United States. Assume that before specialization and trade the optimal product mix for China is alternative B and for the United States is alternative U. **LO2**

	China Production Possibilities					
Product	**A**	**B**	**C**	**D**	**E**	**F**
Apparel (in thousands)	30	24	18	12	6	0
Chemicals (in tons)	0	6	12	18	24	30

	U.S. Production Possibilities					
Product	**R**	**S**	**T**	**U**	**V**	**W**
Apparel (in thousands)	10	8	6	4	2	0
Chemicals (in tons)	0	4	8	12	16	20

a. Are comparative-cost conditions such that the two areas should specialize? If so, what product should each produce?

b. What is the total gain in apparel and chemical output that would result from such specialization?

c. What are the limits of the terms of trade? Suppose that the actual terms of trade are 1 unit of apparel for $1\frac{1}{2}$ units

of chemicals and that 4 units of apparel are exchanged for 6 units of chemicals. What are the gains from specialization and trade for each nation?

4. Refer to the following table, in which Q_d is the quantity of yen demanded, P is the dollar price of yen, Q_s is the quantity of yen supplied in year 1, and Q_s' is the quantity of yen supplied in year 2. All quantities are in billions and the dollar-yen exchange rate is fully flexible. **LO3**

Q_d	P	Q_s	Q_s'
10	125	30	20
15	120	25	15
20	115	20	10
25	110	15	5

a. What is the equilibrium dollar price of yen in year 1?

b. What is the equilibrium dollar price of yen in year 2?

c. Did the yen appreciate or did it depreciate relative to the dollar between years 1 and 2?

d. Did the dollar appreciate or did it depreciate relative to the yen between years 1 and 2?

e. Which one of the following could have caused the change in relative values of the dollar and yen between years 1 and 2: (1) more rapid inflation in the United States than in Japan, (2) an increase in the real interest rate in the United States but not in Japan, or (3) faster income growth in the United States than in Japan.

5. Suppose that the current Canadian dollar (CAD) to U.S. dollar exchange rate is $.85 CAD = $1 US and that the U.S. dollar price of an Apple iPhone is $300. What is the Canadian dollar price of an iPhone? Next, suppose that the CAD to U.S. dollar exchange rate moves to $.96 CAD = $1 US. What is the new Canadian dollar price of an iPhone? Other things equal, would you expect Canada to import more or fewer iPhones at the new exchange rate? **LO3**

FURTHER TEST YOUR KNOWLEDGE AT
www.mcconnellbrief2e.com

At the text's Online Learning Center, **www.mcconnellbrief2e.com**, you will find one or more web-based questions that require information from the Internet to answer. We urge you to check them out, since they will familiarize you with websites that may be helpful in other courses and perhaps even in your career. The OLC also features multiple-choice quizzes that give instant feedback and provides other helpful ways to further test your knowledge of the chapter.

Visit your mobile app store and download the McConnell Brief Edition: Study Econ app today!

ability-to-pay principle   The idea that those who have greater income (or wealth) should pay a greater proportion of it as taxes than those who have less income (or wealth).

accounting profit   The total revenue of a firm less its explicit costs.

advertising   A seller's activities in communicating its message about its product to potential buyers.

aggregate   A collection of specific economic units treated as if they were one. For example, all prices of individual goods and services are combined into a price level, or all the units of output are aggregated into gross domestic product.

allocative efficiency   The apportionment of resources among firms and industries to obtain the production of the products most wanted by society (consumers); the output of each product at which its marginal cost and price or marginal benefit are equal.

antitrust laws   Legislation (including the Sherman Act) that prohibits anticompetitive business activities such as price fixing, bid rigging, monopolization, and tying contracts.

appreciation (of the dollar)   An increase in the value of the dollar relative to the currency of another nation, so a dollar buys a larger amount of the foreign currency and thus of foreign goods.

asset   Anything of monetary value owned by a firm or individual.

average fixed cost   A firm's total fixed cost divided by output (the quantity of product produced).

average product   The total output produced per unit of a resource employed (total product divided by the quantity of that employed resource).

average revenue   Total revenue from the sale of a product divided by the quantity of the product sold (demanded); equal to the price at which the product is sold when all units of the product are sold at the same price.

average tax rate   Total tax paid divided by total (taxable) income, as a percentage.

average total cost   A firm's total cost divided by output (the quantity of product produced); equal to average fixed cost plus average variable cost.

average variable cost   A firm's total variable cost divided by output (the quantity of product produced).

barrier to entry   Anything that artificially prevents the entry of firms into an industry.

barter   The exchange of one good or service for another good or service.

benefits-received principle   The idea that those who receive the benefits of goods and services provided by government should pay the taxes required to finance them.

bond   A financial device through which a borrower (a firm or government) is obligated to pay the principal and interest on a loan at a specific date in the future.

budget constraint   The limit that the size of a consumer's income (and the prices that must be paid for goods and services) imposes on the ability of that consumer to obtain goods and services.

budget line   A line that shows the different combinations of two products a consumer can purchase with a specific money income, given the products' prices.

business   A firm that purchases resources and provides goods and services to the economy.

business firm   (See **firm.**)

capital   Human-made resources (buildings, machinery, and equipment) used to produce goods and services; goods that do not directly satisfy human wants; also called *capital goods* and *investment goods*.

capital gain   The gain realized when securities or properties are sold for a price greater than the price paid for them.

capital goods   (See **capital.**)

capitalism   An economic system in which property resources are privately owned and markets and prices are used to direct and coordinate economic activities.

capital stock   The total available capital in a nation.

cartel   A formal agreement among firms (or countries) in an industry to set the price of a product and establish the outputs of the individual firms (or countries) or to divide the market for the product geographically.

ceiling price   (See **price ceiling.**)

central economic planning   Government determination of the objectives of the economy and how resources will be directed to attain those goals.

***ceteris paribus* assumption**   (See **other-things-equal assumption.**)

change in demand   A change in the quantity demanded of a good or service at every price; a shift of the demand curve to the left or right.

change in quantity demanded   A change in the amount of a product that consumers are willing and able to purchase because of a change in the product's price; a movement from one point to another on a fixed demand curve.

change in quantity supplied   A change in the amount of a product that producers offer for sale because of a change in the product's price.

change in supply   A change in the quantity supplied of a good or service at every price; a shift of the supply curve to the left or right.

circular flow diagram The flow of resources from households to firms and of products from firms to households. These flows are accompanied by reverse flows of money from firms to households and from households to firms.

Coase theorem The idea, first stated by economist Ronald Coase, that externality problems may be resolved through private negotiations of the affected parties.

coincidence of wants A situation in which the good or service that one trader desires to obtain is the same as that which another trader desires to give up and an item that the second trader wishes to acquire is the same as that which the first trader desires to surrender.

collusion A situation in which firms act together and in agreement (collude) to fix prices, divide a market, or otherwise restrict competition.

command system A method of organizing an economy in which property resources are publicly owned and government uses central economic planning to direct and coordinate economic activities; command economy; communism.

communism (See **command system.**)

comparative advantage A situation in which a person or country can produce a specific product at a lower opportunity cost than some other person or country; the basis for specialization and trade.

compensating differences Differences in the wages received by workers in different jobs to compensate for nonmonetary differences in the jobs.

competition The presence in a market of independent buyers and sellers competing with one another along with the freedom of buyers and sellers to enter and leave the market.

competitive industry's short-run supply curve The horizontal summation of the short-run supply curves of the firms in a purely competitive industry (see **pure competition**); a curve that shows the total quantities offered for sale at various prices by the firms in an industry in the short run.

competitive labor market (See **purely competitive labor market.**)

complementary goods Products and services that are used together. When the price of one falls, the demand for the other increases (and conversely).

constant-cost industry An industry in which expansion by the entry of new firms has no effect on the prices firms in the industry must pay for resources and thus no effect on production costs.

constant opportunity cost An opportunity cost that remains the same for each additional unit as a consumer (or society) shifts purchases (production) from one product to another along a straight-line budget line (production possibilities curve).

constant returns to scale Unchanging average total cost of producing a product as the firm expands the size of its plan (its output) in the long run.

consumer goods Products and services that satisfy human wants directly.

consumer sovereignty Determination by consumers of the types and quantities of goods and services that will be produced with the scarce resources of the economy; consumers' direction of production through their dollar votes.

consumer surplus The difference between the maximum price a consumer is (or consumers are) willing to pay for a product and the actual price paid.

corporate income tax A tax levied on the net income (accounting profit) of corporations.

corporation A legal entity ("person") chartered by a state or the federal government that is distinct and separate from the individuals who own it.

cost-benefit analysis A comparison of the marginal costs of a government project or program with the marginal benefits to decide whether or not to employ resources in that project or program and to what extent.

craft union A labor union that limits its membership to workers with a particular skill (craft).

creative destruction The hypothesis that the creation of new products and production methods simultaneously destroys the market power of existing monopolies.

cross-elasticity of demand The ratio of the percentage change in *quantity demanded* of one good to the percentage change in the price of some other good. A positive coefficient indicates the two products are *substitute goods;* a negative coefficient indicates they are *complementary goods.*

decreasing-cost industry An industry in which expansion through the entry of firms lowers the prices that firms in the industry must pay for resources and therefore decreases their production costs.

demand A schedule showing the amounts of a good or service that buyers (or a buyer) wish to purchase at various prices during some time period.

demand curve A curve illustrating demand.

demand-side market failures Underallocations of resources that occur when private demand curves understate consumers' full willingness to pay for a good or service.

dependent variable A variable that changes as a consequence of a change in some other (independent) variable; the "effect" or outcome.

depreciation (of a currency) A decrease in the value of the dollar relative to another currency, so a dollar buys a smaller amount of the foreign currency and therefore of foreign goods.

derived demand The demand for a resource that depends on the demand for the products it helps to produce.

determinants of demand Factors other than price that locate the position of the demand curve.

determinants of supply Factors other than price that locate the position of the suppy curve.

differentiated oligopoly An oligopoly in which the firms produce a differentiated product.

differentiated product A product that differs physically or in some other way from similar products produced by other firms; a product such that buyers are not indifferent to the seller when the price charged by all sellers is the same.

diminishing marginal returns (See **law of diminishing returns.**)

direct relationship The relationship between two variables that change in the same direction, for example, product price and quantity supplied.

discrimination The practice of according individuals or groups inferior treatment in hiring, occupational access, education and training, promotion, wage rates, or working conditions even though they have the same abilities, education, skills, and work experience as other workers.

diseconomies of scale Increases in the average total cost of producing a product as the firm expands the size of its plant (its output) in the long run.

dividends Payments by a corporation of all or part of its profit to its stockholders (the corporate owners).

division of labor The separation of the work required to produce a product into a number of different tasks that are performed by different workers; specialization of workers.

Doha Round The latest, uncompleted (as of 2011) sequence of trade negotiations by members of the World Trade Organization; named after Doha, Qatar, where the set of negotiations began.

dollar votes The "votes" that consumers and entrepreneurs cast for the production of consumer and capital goods, respectively, when they purchase those goods in product and resource markets.

dumping The sale of products in a foreign country at prices either below costs or below the prices charged at home.

durable good A consumer good with an expected life (use) of 3 or more years.

earned-income tax credit A refundable federal tax credit for low-income working people designed to reduce poverty and encourage labor-force participation.

earnings The money income received by a worker; equal to the wage (rate) multiplied by the amount of time worked.

economic cost A payment that must be made to obtain and retain the services of a resource; the income a firm must provide to a resource supplier to attract the resource away from an alternative use; equal to the quantity of other products that cannot be produced when resources are instead used to make a particular product.

economic efficiency The use of the minimum necessary resources to obtain the socially optimal amounts of goods and services; entails both productive efficiency and allocative efficiency.

economic growth (1) An outward shift in the production possibilities curve that results from an increase in resource supplies or quality or an improvement in technology; (2) an increase of real output (gross domestic product) or real output per capita.

economic law An economic principle that has been tested and retested and has stood the test of time.

economic model A simplified picture of economic reality; an abstract generalization.

economic perspective A viewpoint that envisions individuals and institutions making rational decisions by comparing the marginal benefits and marginal costs associated with their actions.

economic policy A course of action intended to correct or avoid a problem.

economic principle A widely accepted generalization about the economic behavior of individuals or institutions.

economic problem The choices necessitated because society's economic wants for goods and services are unlimited but the resources available to satisfy these wants are limited (scarce).

economic profit The total revenue of a firm less its economic costs (which include both explicit costs and implicit costs); also called *pure profit* and *above-normal profit.*

economic resources The land, labor, capital, and entrepreneurial ability that are used in the production of goods and services; productive agents; factors of production.

economics The study of how people, institutions, and society make economic choices under conditions of scarcity.

economic system A particular set of institutional arrangements and a coordinating mechanism for solving the economizing problem; a method of organizing an economy, of which the market system and the command system are the two general types.

economic theory A statement of a cause-effect relationship; when accepted by nearly all economists, an economic principle.

economies of scale Reductions in the average total cost of producing a product as the firm expands the size of plant (its output) in the long run; the economies of mass production.

efficiency (deadweight) loss A reduction in combined consumer and producer surplus caused by an underallocation or overallocation of resources to the production of a good or service.

efficiency (deadweight) loss of a tax The loss of net benefits to society because a tax reduces the production and consumption of a taxed good below the level of allocative efficiency.

efficient allocation of resources That allocation of an economy's resources among the production of different products that leads to the maximum satisfaction of consumers' wants, thus producing the socially optimal mix of output with society's scarce resources.

elastic demand Product or resource demand whose price elasticity is greater than 1. This means the resulting change in quantity demanded is greater than the percentage change in price.

elasticity coefficient The number obtained when the percentage change in quantity demanded (or supplied) is divided by the percentage change in the price of the commodity.

elasticity formula   (See **price elasticity of demand.**)

elasticity of labor demand   A measure of the responsiveness of labor quantity to a change in the wage rate; the percentage change in labor quantity divided by the percentage change in the wage rate.

elastic supply   Product or resource supply whose price elasticity is greater than 1. This means the resulting change in quantity supplied is greater than the percentage change in price.

entitlement programs   Government programs such as social insurance, SNAP, Medicare, and Medicaid that guarantee particular levels of transfer payments or noncash benefits to all who fit the programs' criteria.

entrepreneurial ability   The human resource that combines the other resources to produce a product, makes nonroutine decisions, innovates, and bears risks.

equality-efficiency trade-off   The decrease in economic efficiency that may accompany a decrease in income inequality; the presumption that some income inequality is required to achieve economic efficiency.

equilibrium price   The price in a competitive market at which the quantity demanded and the quantity supplied are equal, there is neither a shortage nor a surplus, and there is no tendency for price to rise or fall.

equilibrium quantity   (1) The quantity demanded and supplied at the equilibrium price in a competitive market; (2) the profit-maximizing output of a firm.

euro   The common currency unit used by 17 European nations as of 2011 (Austria, Belgium, Cyprus, Estonia, Finland, France, Germany, Greece, Ireland, Italy, Luxembourg, Malta, the Netherlands, Portugal, Slovakia, Slovenia, and Spain).

European Union (EU)   An association of 27 European nations (as of 2011) that has eliminated tariffs and quotas among them, established common tariffs for imported goods from outside the member nations, eliminated barriers to the free movement of capital, and created other common economic policies.

excess capacity   Plant resources that are underused when imperfectly competitive firms produce less output than that associated with achieving minimum average total cost.

exchange rate   The rate of exchange of one nation's currency for another nation's currency.

exchange-rate appreciation   An increase in the value of a nation's currency in foreign exchange markets; an increase in the rate of exchange for foreign currencies.

exchange-rate depreciation   A decrease in the value of a nation's currency in foreign exchange markets; a decrease in the rate of exchange for foreign currencies.

excise tax   A tax levied on the production of a specific product or on the quantity of the product purchased.

exclusive unionism   The practice of a labor union of restricting the supply of skilled union labor to increase the wages received by union members; the policies typically employed by a craft union.

expectations   The anticipations of consumers, firms, and others about future economic conditions.

explicit cost   The monetary payment a firm must make to an outsider to obtain a resource.

exports   Goods and services produced in a nation and sold to buyers in other nations.

export subsidies   Government payments to domestic producers to enable them to reduce the price of a good or service to foreign buyers.

external benefit   A benefit obtained without compensation by third parties from the production or consumption of sellers or buyers. Example: A beekeeper benefits when a neighboring farmer plants clover.

external cost   A cost imposed without compensation on third parties by the production or consumption of sellers or buyers. Example: A manufacturer dumps toxic chemicals into a river, killing the fish sought by sport fishers.

externality   A benefit or cost from production or consumption, accruing without compensation to nonbuyers and nonsellers of the product (see **external benefit** and **external cost**).

factors of production   Economic resources: land, capital, labor, and entrepreneurial ability.

fallacy of composition   The false idea that what is true for the individual (or part) is necessarily true for the group (or whole).

federal government   The government of the United States, as distinct from the state and local governments.

financial capital   Money available to purchase capital; simply money, as defined by economists.

firm   An organization that employs resources to produce a good or service for profit and owns and operates one or more plants.

fixed cost   Any cost that in total does not change when the firm changes its output; the cost of fixed resources.

fixed resource   Any resource whose quantity cannot be changed by a firm in the short run.

flexible prices   Product prices that freely move upward or downward when product demand or supply changes.

foreign exchange market   A market in which the money (currency) of one nation can be used to purchase (can be exchanged for) the money of another nation.

foreign exchange rate   (See **exchange rate.**)

freedom of choice   The freedom of owners of property resources to employ or dispose of them as they see fit, of workers to enter any line of work for which they are qualified, and of consumers to spend their incomes in a manner that they think is appropriate.

freedom of enterprise   The freedom of firms to obtain economic resources, to use those resources to produce products of the firm's own choosing, and to sell their products in markets of their choice.

free-rider problem   The inability of a firm to profitably provide a good because everyone, including nonpayers, can obtain the benefit.

free trade   The absence of artificial (government-imposed) barriers to trade among individuals and firms in different nations.

full employment   The use of all available resources to produce want-satisfying goods and services.

gains from trade   The extra output that trading partners obtain through specialization of production and exchange of goods and services.

game theory   A means of analyzing the business behavior of oligopolists that uses the theory of strategy associated with games such as chess and bridge.

GDP   (See **gross domestic product.**)

General Agreement on Tariffs and Trade (GATT)   The international agreement reached in 1947 in which 23 nations agreed to give equal and nondiscriminatory treatment to one another, to reduce tariff rates by multinational negotiations, and to eliminate import quotas. It now includes most nations and has become the World Trade Organization.

Gini ratio   A numerical measure of the overall dispersion of income among households, families, or individuals; found graphically by dividing the area between the diagonal line and the Lorenz curve by the entire area below the diagonal line.

government purchases   Expenditures by government for goods and services that government consumes in providing public goods and for public (or social) capital that has a long lifetime; the expenditures of all governments in the economy for those final goods and services.

government transfer payment   The disbursement of money (or goods and services) by government for which government receives no currently produced good or service in return.

gross domestic product (GDP)   The total market value of all final goods and services produced annually within the boundaries of the United States, whether by U.S.- or foreign-supplied resources.

homogeneous oligopoly   An oligopoly in which the firms produce a standardized product.

household   An economic unit (of one or more persons) that provides the economy with resources and uses the income received to purchase goods and services that satisfy economic wants.

human capital   The accumulation of knowledge and skills that make a worker productive.

human capital investment   Any expenditure undertaken to improve the education, skills, health, or mobility of workers, with an expectation of greater productivity and thus a positive return on the investment.

hypothesis   A tentative explanation of cause and effect that requires testing.

immobility   The inability or unwillingness of a worker to move from one geographic area or occupation to another or from a lower-paying job to a higher-paying job.

imperfect competition   Any market structure except pure competition; includes monopoly, monopolistic competition, and oligopoly.

implicit cost   The monetary income a firm sacrifices when it uses a resource it owns rather than supplying the resource in the market; equal to what the resource could have earned in the best-paying alternative employment; includes a normal profit.

import quota   A limit imposed by a nation on the quantity (or total value) of a good that may be imported during some period of time.

imports   Spending by individuals, firms, and governments for goods and services produced in foreign nations.

inclusive unionism   The practice of a labor union of including as members all workers employed in an industry.

income   A flow of dollars (or purchasing power) per unit of time derived from the use of human or property resources.

income elasticity of demand   The ratio of the percentage change in the quantity demanded of a good to a percentage change in consumer income; measures the responsiveness of consumer purchases to income changes.

income inequality   The unequal distribution of an economy's total income among households or families.

income-maintenance system   A group of government programs designed to eliminate poverty and reduce inequality in the distribution of income.

income mobility   The extent to which income receivers move from one part of the income distribution to another over some period of time.

increase in demand   An increase in the quantity demanded of a good or service at every price; a shift of the demand curve to the right.

increase in supply   An increase in the quantity supplied of a good or service at every price; a shift of the supply curve to the right.

increasing-cost industry   An industry in which expansion through the entry of new firms raises the prices firms in the industry must pay for resources and therefore increases their production costs.

increasing marginal returns   An increase in the marginal product of a resource as successive units of the resource are employed.

increasing returns   An increase in a firm's output by a larger percentage than the percentage increase in its inputs.

independent goods   Products or services for which there is little or no relationship between the price of one and the demand for the other. When the price of one rises or falls, the demand for the other tends to remain constant.

independent variable   The variable causing a change in some other (dependent) variable.

industrial union   A labor union that accepts as members all workers employed in a particular industry (or by a particular firm).

industry   A group of (one or more) firms that produce identical or similar products.

inelastic demand   Product or resource demand for which the elasticity coefficient for price is less than 1. This means the resulting percentage change in quantity demanded is less than the percentage change in price.

inelastic supply   Product or resource supply for which the price elasticity coefficient is less than 1. The percentage change in quantity supplied is less than the percentage change in price.

inferior good   A good or service whose consumption declines when income rises, prices held constant.

information technology   New and more efficient methods of delivering and receiving information through use of computers, fax machines, wireless phones, and the Internet.

infrastructure   The capital goods usually provided by the public sector for the use of its citizens and firms (for example, highways, bridges, transit systems, wastewater treatment facilities, municipal water systems, and airports).

in-kind transfer   The distribution by government of goods and services to individuals for which the government receives no currently produced good or service in return; a government transfer payment made in goods or services rather than in money; also called *noncash transfer.*

interest   The payment made for the use of money (of borrowed funds).

interest rate   The annual rate at which interest is paid; a percentage of the borrowed amount.

inventories   Goods that have been produced but remain unsold.

inverse relationship   The relationship between two variables that change in opposite directions, for example, product price and quantity demanded.

investment   Spending for the production and accumulation of capital and additions to inventories.

investment goods   (See **capital**.)

investment in human capital   (See **human capital investment**.)

"invisible hand"   The tendency of firms and resource suppliers that seek to further their own self-interests in competitive markets to also promote the interest of society.

kinked-demand curve   The demand curve for a noncollusive oligopolist, which is based on the assumption that rivals will match a price decrease and will ignore a price increase.

labor   People's physical and mental talents and efforts that are used to help produce goods and services.

labor productivity   Total output divided by the quantity of labor employed to produce it; the average product of labor or output per hour of work.

labor union   A group of workers organized to advance the interests of the group (to increase wages, shorten the hours worked, improve working conditions, and so on).

land   Natural resources ("free gifts of nature") used to produce goods and services.

law of demand   The principle that, other things equal, an increase in a product's price will reduce the quantity of it demanded, and conversely for a decrease in price.

law of diminishing marginal utility   The principle that as a consumer increases the consumption of a good or service, the marginal utility obtained from each additional unit of the good or service decreases.

law of diminishing returns   The principle that as successive increments of a variable resource are added to a fixed resource, the marginal product of the variable resource will eventually decrease.

law of increasing opportunity costs   The principle that as the production of a good increases, the opportunity cost of producing an additional unit rises.

law of supply   The principle that, other things equal, as price rises, the quantity supplied rises, and as price falls, the quantity supplied falls.

learning by doing   Achieving greater productivity and lower average total cost through gains in knowledge and skill that accompany repetition of a task; a source of economies of scale.

liability   A debt with a monetary value; an amount owed by a firm or an individual.

limited liability   Restriction of the maximum loss to a predetermined amount for the owners (stockholders) of a corporation. The maximum loss is the amount they paid for their shares of stock.

long run   In microeconomics, a period of time long enough to enable producers of a product to change the quantities of all the resources they employ; period in which all resources and costs are variable and no resources or costs are fixed.

long-run competitive equilibrium   The price at which firms in pure competition neither obtain economic profit nor suffer losses in the long run and the total quantity demanded and supplied are equal; a price equal to the minimum long-run average total cost of producing the product.

long-run supply   A schedule or curve showing the prices at which a purely competitive industry will make various quantities of the product available in the long run.

long-run supply curve   A curve showing the prices at which a purely competitive industry will make various quantities of the product available in the long run.

Lorenz curve   A curve showing the distribution of income in an economy. The cumulated percentage of families (income receivers) is measured along the horizontal axis, and cumulated percentage of income is measured along the vertical axis.

macroeconomics The part of economics concerned with the economy as a whole; with such major aggregates as the household, business, and government sectors; and with measures of the total economy.

marginal analysis The comparison of marginal ("extra" or "additional") benefits and marginal costs, usually for decision making.

marginal benefit The extra (additional) benefit of consuming 1 more unit of some good or service; the change in total benefit when 1 more unit is consumed.

marginal cost The extra (additional) cost of producing 1 more unit of output; equal to the change in total cost divided by the change in output (and, in the short run, to the change in total variable cost divided by the change in output).

marginal product The additional output produced when 1 additional unit of a resource is employed (the quantity of all other resources employed remaining constant); equal to the change in total product divided by the change in the quantity of a resource employed.

marginal resource cost The amount the total cost of employing a resource increases when a firm employs 1 additional unit of the resource (the quantity of all other resources employed remaining constant); equal to the change in the total cost of the resource divided by the change in the quantity of the resource employed.

marginal revenue The change in total revenue that results from the sale of 1 additional unit of a firm's product; equal to the change in total revenue divided by the change in the quantity of the product sold.

marginal revenue product The change in a firm's total revenue when it employs 1 additional unit of a resource (the quantity of all other resources employed remaining constant); equal to the change in total revenue divided by the change in the quantity of the resource employed.

marginal tax rate The tax rate paid on an additional dollar of income.

marginal utility The extra utility a consumer obtains from the consumption of 1 additional unit of a good or service; equal to the change in total utility divided by the change in the quantity consumed.

market Any institution or mechanism that brings together buyers (demanders) and sellers (suppliers) of a particular good or service.

market economy An economy in which only the private decisions of consumers, resource suppliers, and firms determine how resources are allocated; the market system.

market failure The inability of a market to bring about the allocation of resources that best satisfies the wants of society; in particular, the overallocation or underallocation of resources to the production of a particular good or service because of spillovers or informational problems or because markets do not provide desired public goods.

market for externality rights A market in which firms can buy rights to discharge pollutants. The price of such rights is determined by the demand for the right to discharge pollutants and a perfectly inelastic supply of such rights (the latter determined by the quantity of discharges that the environment can assimilate).

market period A period in which producers of a product are unable to change the quantity produced in response to a change in its price and in which there is a perfectly inelastic supply.

market system All the product and resource markets of a market economy and the relationships among them; a method that allows the prices determined in those markets to allocate the economy's scarce resources and to communicate and coordinate the decisions made by consumers, firms, and resource suppliers.

Medicaid A federal program that helps finance the medical expenses of individuals covered by the Supplemental Security Income (SSI) and Temporary Assistance for Needy Families (TANF) programs.

Medicare A federal program that is financed by payroll taxes and provides for (1) compulsory hospital insurance for senior citizens, (2) low-cost voluntary insurance to help older Americans pay physicians' fees, and (3) subsidized insurance to buy prescription drugs.

microeconomics The part of economics concerned with such individual units as a household, a firm, or an industry and with individual markets, specific goods and services, and product and resource prices.

minimum efficient scale The lowest level of output at which a firm can minimize long-run average total cost.

minimum wage The lowest wage employers may legally pay for an hour of work.

money Any item that is generally acceptable to sellers in exchange for goods and services.

monopolistic competition A market structure in which many firms sell a differentiated product, into which entry is relatively easy, in which the firm has some control over its product price, and in which there is considerable nonprice competition.

monopoly A market structure in which the number of sellers is so small that each seller is able to influence the total supply and the price of the good or service. (Also see **pure monopoly**.)

monopsony A market structure in which only a single buyer of a good, service, or resource is present.

MR = MC rule The principle that a firm will maximize its profit (or minimize its losses) by producing the output at which marginal revenue and marginal cost are equal, provided product price is equal to or greater than average variable cost.

MRP = MRC rule The principle that to maximize profit (or minimize losses), a firm should employ the quantity of a resource at which its marginal revenue product (MRP) is equal to its marginal resource cost (MRC), the latter being the wage rate in pure competition.

mutual interdependence   A situation in which a change in price strategy (or in some other strategy) by one firm will affect the sales and profits of another firm (or other firms). Any firm that makes such a change can expect the other rivals to react to the change.

natural monopoly   An industry in which economies of scale are so great that a single firm can produce the product at a lower average total cost than would be possible if more than one firm produced the product.

negative externalities   A cost imposed without compensation on third parties by the production or consumption of sellers or buyers. Example: A manufacturer dumps toxic chemicals into a river, killing the fish sought by sports fishers; an external cost or a spillover cost.

negative relationship   (See **inverse relationship.**)

net exports   Exports minus imports.

net taxes   The taxes collected by government less government transfer payments.

network effects   Increases in the value of a product to each user, including existing users, as the total number of users rises.

net worth   The total assets less the total liabilities of a firm or an individual; for a firm, the claims of the owners against the firm's total assets; for an individual, his or her wealth.

noncash transfer   A government transfer payment in the form of goods and services rather than money, for example, SNAP stamps, housing assistance, and job training; also called *in-kind transfer*.

noncollusive oligopoly   An oligopoly in which the firms do not act together and in agreement to determine the price of the product and the output that each firm will produce.

noncompeting groups   Collections of workers in the economy who do not compete with each other for employment because the skill and training of the workers in one group are substantially different from those of the workers in other groups.

nondurable good   A consumer good with an expected life (use) of less than 3 years.

nonexcludability   The inability to keep nonpayers (free riders) from obtaining benefits from a certain good; a public goods characteristic.

nonprice competition   Competition based on distinguishing one's product by means of product differentiation and then advertising the distinguished product to consumers.

nonrivalry   The idea that one person's benefit from a certain good does not reduce the benefit available to others; a public goods characteristic.

nontariff barriers   All barriers other than protective tariffs that nations erect to impede international trade, including import quotas, licensing requirements, unreasonable product-quality standards, and unnecessary bureaucratic detail in customs procedures.

normal good   A good or service whose consumption increases when income increases and falls when income decreases, price remaining constant.

normal profit   The payment made by a firm to obtain and retain entrepreneurial ability; the minimum income entrepreneurial ability must receive to induce it to perform entrepreneurial functions for a firm.

North American Free Trade Agreement (NAFTA)   A 1993 agreement establishing, over a 15-year period, a free-trade zone composed of Canada, Mexico, and the United States.

occupational licensing   State and local laws that require a worker to satisfy certain specific requirements and obtain a license from a licensing board before engaging in a particular occupation.

offshoring   The practice of shifting work previously done by American workers to workers located abroad.

oligopoly   A market structure in which a few firms sell either a standardized or a differentiated product, into which entry is difficult, in which the firm has limited control over product price because of mutual interdependence (except when there is collusion among firms), and in which there is typically nonprice competition.

OPEC   (See **Organization of Petroleum Exporting Countries.**)

opportunity cost   The value of the good, service, or time forgone to obtain something else.

optimal reduction of an externality   The reduction of a negative externality such as pollution to a level at which the marginal benefit and marginal cost of reduction are equal.

Organization of Petroleum Exporting Countries (OPEC)   A cartel of oil-producing countries (Algeria, Angola, Ecuador, Indonesia, Iran, Iraq, Kuwait, Libya, Nigeria, Qatar, Saudi Arabia, Venezuela, and the UAE) that attempts to control the quantity and price of crude oil exported by its members and that accounts for 60 percent of the world's export of oil.

other-things-equal assumption   The assumption that factors other than those being considered are held constant; *ceteris paribus* assumption.

output effect   An increase in the use of labor that occurs when a decline in the price of capital reduces a firm's production costs and therefore enables it to sell more output.

$P = MC$ rule   The principle that a purely competitive firm will maximize its profit or minimize its loss by producing that output at which the price of the product is equal to marginal cost, provided that price is equal to or greater than average variable cost in the short run and equal to or greater than average total cost in the long run.

partnership   An unincorporated firm owned and operated by two or more persons.

patent An exclusive right given to inventors to produce and sell a new product or machine for 20 years from the time of patent application.

payroll tax A tax levied on employers of labor equal to a percentage of all or part of the wages and salaries paid by them and on employees equal to a percentage of all or part of the wages and salaries received by them.

per capita GDP Gross domestic product (GDP) per person; the average GDP of a population.

per capita income A nation's total income per person; the average income of a population.

perfectly elastic demand Product or resource demand in which quantity demanded can be of any amount at a particular product price; graphs as a horizontal demand curve.

perfectly elastic supply Product or resource supply in which quantity supplied can be of any amount at a particular product or resource price; graphs as a horizontal supply curve.

perfectly inelastic demand Product or resource demand in which price can be of any amount at a particular quantity of the product or resource demanded; quantity demanded does not respond to a change in price; graphs as a vertical demand curve.

perfectly inelastic supply Product or resource supply in which price can be of any amount at a particular quantity of the product or resource demanded; quantity supplied does not respond to a change in price; graphs as a vertical supply curve.

per se violations Collusive actions, such as attempts to fix prices or divide markets, that are violations of the antitrust laws, even if the actions are unsuccessful.

personal income tax A tax levied on the taxable income of individuals, households, and unincorporated firms.

per-unit production cost The average production cost of a particular level of output; total input cost divided by units of output.

positive relationship A direct relationship between two variables.

poverty A situation in which the basic needs of an individual or family exceed the means to satisfy them.

poverty rate The percentage of the population with incomes below the official poverty income levels that are established by the federal government.

price The amount of money needed to buy a particular good, service, or resource.

price ceiling A legally established maximum price for a good or service.

price discrimination The selling of a product to different buyers at different prices when the price differences are not justified by differences in cost.

price elasticity of demand The ratio of the percentage change in quantity demanded of a product or resource to the percentage change in its price; a measure of the responsiveness of buyers to a change in the price of a product or resource.

price elasticity of supply The ratio of the percentage change in quantity supplied of a product or resource to the percentage change in its price; a measure of the responsiveness of producers to a change in the price of a product or resource.

price fixing The conspiring by two or more firms to set the price of their products; an illegal practice under the Sherman Act.

price floor A legally determined price above the equilibrium price.

price leadership An informal method that firms in an oligopoly may employ to set the price of their product: One firm (the leader) is the first to announce a change in price, and the other firms (the followers) soon announce identical or similar changes.

price maker A seller (or buyer) that is able to affect the product or resource price by changing the amount it sells (or buys).

price support A minimum price that government allows sellers to receive for a good or service; a legally established or maintained minimum price.

price taker A seller (or buyer) that is unable to affect the price at which a product or resource sells by changing the amount it sells (or buys).

price war Successive and continued decreases in the prices charged by firms in an oligopolistic industry. Each firm lowers its price below rivals' prices, hoping to increase its sales and revenues at its rivals' expense.

principal-agent problem A conflict of interest that occurs when agents (workers or managers) pursue their own objectives to the detriment of the principals' (stockholders') goals.

principles Statements about economic behavior that enable predictions of the probable effects of certain actions.

private good A good or service that is individually consumed and that can be profitably provided by privately owned firms because they can exclude nonpayers from receiving the benefits.

private property The right of private persons and firms to obtain, own, control, employ, dispose of, and bequeath land, capital, and other property.

private sector The households and business firms of the economy.

producer surplus The difference between the actual price a producer receives (or producers receive) and the minimum acceptable price.

product differentiation A strategy in which one firm's product is distinguished from competing products by means of its design, related services, quality, location, or other attributes (except price).

production possibilities curve A curve showing the different combinations of two goods or services that can be produced in a full-employment, full-production economy where the available supplies of resources and technology are fixed.

productive efficiency The production of a good in the least costly way; occurs when production takes place at the output at which average total cost is a minimum and marginal product per dollar's worth of input is the same for all inputs.

productivity A measure of average output or real output per unit of input. For example, the productivity of labor is determined by dividing real output by hours of work.

product market A market in which products are sold by firms and bought by households.

profit The return to the resource entrepreneurial ability (see **normal profit**); total revenue minus total cost (see **economic profit**).

progressive tax A tax whose average tax rate increases as the taxpayer's income increases and decreases as the taxpayer's income decreases.

property tax A tax on the value of property (capital, land, stocks and bonds, and other assets) owned by firms and households.

proportional tax A tax whose average tax rate remains constant as the taxpayer's income increases or decreases.

proprietor's income The net income of the owners of unincorporated firms (proprietorships and partnerships).

protective tariff A tariff designed to shield domestic producers of a good or service from the competition of foreign producers.

public assistance programs Government programs that pay benefits to those who are unable to earn income (because of permanent disabilities or because they have very low income and dependent children); financed by general tax revenues and viewed as public charity (rather than earned rights).

public good A good or service that is characterized by nonrivalry and nonexcludability; a good or service with these characteristics provided by government.

public investments Government expenditures on public capital (such as roads, highways, bridges, mass-transit systems, and electric power facilities) and on human capital (such as education, training, and health).

public sector The part of the economy that contains all government entities; government.

pure competition A market structure in which a very large number of firms sell a standardized product, into which entry is very easy, in which the individual seller has no control over the product price, and in which there is no nonprice competition; a market characterized by a very large number of buyers and sellers.

purely competitive labor market A labor market in which a large number of similarly qualified workers independently offer their labor services to a large number of employers, none of whom can set the wage rate.

pure monopoly A market structure in which one firm sells a unique product, into which entry is blocked, in which the single firm has considerable control over product price, and in which nonprice competition may or may not be found.

quantity demanded The amount of a good or service that buyers (or a buyer) desire to purchase at a particular price during some period.

quantity supplied The amount of a good or service that producers (or a producer) offer to sell at a particular price during some period.

quasi-public good A good or service to which excludability could apply but that has such a large spillover benefit that government sponsors its production to prevent an underallocation of resources.

rational behavior Human behavior based on comparison of marginal costs and marginal benefits; behavior designed to maximize total utility.

recession A period of declining real GDP, accompanied by lower real income and higher unemployment.

regressive tax A tax whose average tax rate decreases as the taxpayer's income increases and increases as the taxpayer's income decreases.

rent-seeking behavior The actions by persons, firms, or unions to gain special benefits from government at the taxpayers' or someone else's expense.

resource A natural, human, or manufactured item that helps produce goods and services; a productive agent or factor of production.

resource market A market in which households sell and firms buy resources or the services of resources.

rule of reason The rule stated and applied in the U.S. Steel case that only combinations and contracts unreasonably restraining trade are subject to actions under the antitrust laws and that size and possession of monopoly power are not illegal.

sales tax A tax levied on the cost (at retail) of a broad group of products.

scarce resources The limited quantities of land, capital, labor, and entrepreneurial ability that are never sufficient to satisfy people's virtually unlimited economic wants.

scientific method The procedure for the systematic pursuit of knowledge involving the observation of facts and the formulation and testing of hypotheses to obtain theories, principles, and laws.

self-interest The most-advantageous outcome as viewed by each firm, property owner, worker, or consumer.

service An (intangible) act or use for which a consumer, firm, or government is willing to pay.

Sherman Act The federal antitrust act of 1890 that makes monopoly and conspiracies to restrain trade criminal offenses.

shortage The amount by which the quantity demanded of a product exceeds the quantity supplied at a particular (below-equilibrium) price.

short run In microeconomics, a period of time in which producers are able to change the quantities of some but not all of the resources they employ; a period in which some resources (usually plant) are fixed and some are variable.

short-run competitive equilibrium The price at which the total quantity of a product supplied in the short run in a purely competitive industry equals the total quantity of the product demanded and that is equal to or greater than average variable cost.

short-run supply curve A supply curve that shows the quantity of a product a firm in a purely competitive industry will offer to sell at various prices in the short run; the portion of the firm's short-run marginal cost curve that lies above its average-variable-cost curve.

shutdown case The circumstance in which a firm would experience a loss greater than its total fixed cost if it were to produce any output greater than zero; alternatively, a situation in which a firm would cease to operate when the price at which it can sell its product is less than its average variable cost.

simultaneous consumption A product's ability to satisfy a large number of consumers at the same time.

slope of a straight line The ratio of the vertical change (the rise or fall) to the horizontal change (the run) between any two points on a line. The slope of an upward-sloping line is positive, reflecting a direct relationship between two variables; the slope of a downward-sloping line is negative, reflecting an inverse relationship between two variables.

Smoot-Hawley Tariff Act Legislation passed in 1930 that established very high tariffs. Its objective was to reduce imports and stimulate the domestic economy, but it resulted only in retaliatory tariffs by other nations.

social insurance programs Programs that replace a portion of the earnings lost when people retire or are temporarily unemployed, that are financed by payroll taxes, and that are viewed as earned rights (rather than charity).

Social Security The federal program, financed by compulsory payroll taxes, that partially replaces earnings lost when workers retire, become disabled, or die.

Social Security trust fund A federal fund that saves excessive Social Security tax revenues received in one year to meet Social Security benefit obligations that exceed Social Security tax revenues in some subsequent year.

sole proprietorship An unincorporated firm owned and operated by one person.

special-interest effect Any result of government promotion of the interests (goals) of a small group at the expense of a much larger group.

specialization The use of the resources of an individual, a firm, a region, or a nation to concentrate production on one or a small number of goods and services.

speculation The activity of buying or selling with the motive of later reselling or rebuying for profit.

SSI (See **Supplemental Security Income.**)

standardized product A product whose buyers are indifferent to the seller from whom they purchase it as long as the price charged by all sellers is the same; a product all units of which are identical and thus are perfect substitutes for each other.

Standard Oil case A 1911 antitrust case in which Standard Oil was found guilty of violating the Sherman Act by illegally monopolizing the petroleum industry. As a remedy the company was divided into several competing firms.

start-up (firm) A new firm focused on creating and introducing a particular new product or employing a specific new production or distribution method.

stock (corporate) An ownership share in a corporation.

strategic behavior Self-interested economic actions that take into account the expected reactions of others.

strike The withholding of labor services by an organized group of workers (a labor union).

subsidy A payment of funds (or goods and services) by a government, firm, or household for which it receives no good or service in return. When made by a government, it is a government transfer payment.

substitute goods Products or services that can be used in place of each other. When the price of one falls, the demand for the other product falls; conversely, when the price of one product rises, the demand for the other product rises.

substitution effect The effect of a change in the price of a resource on the quantity of the resource employed by a firm, assuming no change in its output.

sunk cost A cost that has been incurred and cannot be recovered.

Supplemental Nutrition Assistance Program (SNAP) A government program that provides food money to low-income recipients by depositing electronic money onto special debit cards.

Supplemental Security Income (SSI) A federally financed and administered program that provides a uniform nationwide minimum income for the aged, blind, and disabled who do not qualify for benefits under Social Security in the United States.

supply A schedule showing the amounts of a good or service that sellers (or a seller) will offer at various prices during some period.

supply curve A curve illustrating the direct relationship between the price of a product and the quantity of it supplied, other things equal.

supply-side market failures Overallocations of resources that occur when private supply curves understate the full cost of producing a good or service.

surplus The amount by which the quantity supplied of a product exceeds the quantity demanded at a specific (above-equilibrium) price.

tacit collusion Any method used by an oligopolist to set prices and outputs that does not involve outright (or overt) collusion. Price leadership is a frequent example.

TANF   (See **Temporary Assistance for Needy Families.**)

tariff   A tax imposed by a nation on an imported good.

tax   An involuntary payment of money (or goods and services) to a government by a household or firm for which the household or firm receives no good or service directly in return.

tax incidence   The degree to which a tax falls on a particular person or group.

technological advance   New and better goods and services and new and better ways of producing or distributing them.

technology   The body of knowledge and techniques that can be used to combine economic resources to produce goods and services.

Temporary Assistance for Needy Families (TANF)   A state-administered and partly federally funded program in the United States that provides financial aid to poor families; the basic welfare program for low-income families in the United States; contains time limits and work requirements.

terms of trade   The rate at which units of one product can be exchanged for units of another product; the price of a good or service; the amount of one good or service that must be given up to obtain 1 unit of another good or service.

total cost   The sum of fixed cost and variable cost.

total product   The total output of a particular good or service produced by a firm (or a group of firms or the entire economy).

total revenue   The total number of dollars received by a firm (or firms) from the sale of a product; equal to the total expenditures for the product produced by the firm (or firms); equal to the quantity sold (demanded) multiplied by the price at which it is sold.

total-revenue test   A test to determine elasticity of demand between any two prices: Demand is elastic if total revenue moves in the opposite direction from price; it is inelastic when it moves in the same direction as price; and it is of unitary elasticity when it does not change when price changes.

total utility   The total amount of satisfaction derived from the consumption of a single product or a combination of products.

Trade Adjustment Assistance Act   A U.S. law passed in 2002 that provides cash assistance, education and training benefits, health care subsidies, and wage subsidies (for persons age 50 or more) to workers displaced by imports or plant relocations.

trade balance   The export of goods (or goods and services) of a nation less its imports of goods (or goods and services).

trade bloc   A group of nations that lower or abolish trade barriers among members. Examples include the European Union and the nations of the North American Free Trade Agreement.

trade deficit   The amount by which a nation's imports of goods (or goods and services) exceed its exports of goods (or goods and services).

trademark   A legal protection that gives the originators of a product an exclusive right to use the brand name.

trade-off   The sacrifice of some or all of one economic goal, good, or service to achieve some other goal, good, or service.

trade surplus   The amount by which a nation's exports of goods (or goods and services) exceed its imports of goods (or goods and services).

transfer payment   A payment of money (or goods and services) by a government to a household or firm for which the payer receives no good or service directly in return.

unemployment   The failure to use all available economic resources to produce desired goods and services; the failure of the economy to fully employ its labor force.

unemployment compensation   (See **unemployment insurance.**)

unemployment insurance   The social insurance program that in the United States is financed by state payroll taxes on employers and makes income available to workers who become unemployed and are unable to find jobs.

unit elasticity   Demand or supply for which the elasticity coefficient is equal to 1; means that the percentage change in the quantity demanded or supplied is equal to the percentage change in price.

unlimited wants   The insatiable desire of consumers for goods and services that will give them satisfaction or utility.

U.S. Steel case   The antitrust action brought by the federal government against the U.S. Steel Corporation in which the courts ruled (in 1920) that only unreasonable restraints of trade were illegal and that size and the possession of monopoly power were not violations of the antitrust laws.

usury laws   State laws that specify the maximum legal interest rate at which loans can be made.

utility   The want-satisfying power of a good or service; the satisfaction or pleasure a consumer obtains from the consumption of a good or service (or from the consumption of a collection of goods and services).

utility-maximizing rule   The principle that to obtain the greatest utility, the consumer should allocate money income so that the last dollar spent on each good or service yields the same marginal utility.

variable cost   A cost that in total increases when the firm increases its output and decreases when the firm reduces its output.

vertical integration   A group of plants engaged in different stages of the production of a final product and owned by a single firm.

voluntary export restrictions   Voluntary limitations by countries or firms of their exports to a particular foreign nation to avoid enactment of formal trade barriers by that nation.

wage (or wage rate) The price paid for the use or services of labor per unit of time (per hour, per day, and so on).

wage differential The difference between the wage received by one worker or group of workers and that received by another worker or group of workers.

wealth Anything that has value because it produces income or could produce income. Wealth is a stock; income is a flow. Assets less liabilities; net worth.

World Trade Organization (WTO) An organization of 153 nations (as of 2011) that oversees the provisions of the current world trade agreement, resolves trade disputes stemming from it, and holds forums for further rounds of trade negotiations.

X-inefficiency The production of output, whatever its level, at higher than the lowest average (and total) cost.

Index

Sur le vif

SIXTH EDITION

Clare Tufts
Duke University

Hannelore Jarausch
University of North Carolina, Chapel Hill

Australia • Brazil • Japan • Korea • Mexico • Singapore • Spain • United Kingdom • United States

Sur le vif: Niveau intermédiaire, Sixième édition
Clare Tufts, Hannelore Jarausch

Vice President, Editorial Director:
  P.J. Boardman

Publisher: Beth Kramer

Senior Acquisitions Editor: Nicole Morinon

Development Editor: Catharine Thomson

Editorial Assistant: Greg Madan

Senior Media Editor: Morgen Gallo

Executive Brand Manager: Ben Rivera

Market Development Manager: Courtney
  Wolstoncroft

Senior Marketing Communications
  Manager: Linda Yip

Senior Content Project Manager:
  Tiffany Kayes

Art Director: Linda Jurras

Manufacturing Planner: Betsy Donaghey

Rights Acquisition Specialist: Jessica Elias

Production Service/Compositor:
  PreMediaGlobal

Text Designer: Alisa Aronson

Cover Designer: Bill Reuter

Cover Image: Bruno Ottenheimer

For product information and technology assistance, contact us at
Cengage Learning Customer & Sales Support, 1-800-354-9706

For permission to use material from this text or product,
submit all requests online at **www.cengage.com/permissions**.
Further permissions questions can be emailed to
permissionrequest@cengage.com.

Library of Congress Control Number: 2012949340

ISBN-13: 978-1-133-31126-3

ISBN-10: 1-133-31126-1

Heinle
20 Channel Center Street
Boston, MA 02210
USA

Cengage Learning is a leading provider of customized learning solutions with office locations around the globe, including Singapore, the United Kingdom, Australia, Mexico, Brazil and Japan. Locate your local office at **international.cengage.com/region**

Cengage Learning products are represented in Canada by Nelson Education, Ltd.

For your course and learning solutions, visit **www.cengage.com.**

Purchase any of our products at your local college store or at our preferred online store **www.cengagebrain.com.**

Instructors: Please visit **login.cengage.com** and log in to access instructor-specific resources.

Printed in the United States of America
6 7 8 9 10 11 20 19 18 17 16

Table des matières

	VOCABULAIRE	LECTURES	STRUCTURES
PRELUDE Le français dans le monde p. 2		Lynda Lemay: «Les maudits Français» p. 5	
CHAPITRE I Les études p. 8	les lieux, les gens, les choses, les activités p. 8	Faïza Guène: *Kiffe kiffe demain* p. 12 L'étudiant: *J'ai étudié un an à Vancouver* p. 17	Verb review: *payer, s'ennuyer* **Present indicative** **Infinitives** **Imperatives** *Faire causatif* p. 144
CHAPITRE 2 Les jeunes p. 22	le corps, le caractère, les vêtements et les accessoires, les activités et les passe-temps quotidiens p. 22	Le Figaro: *Les jeunes plébiscitent le service civique* p. 26 Diam's: «Jeune demoiselle» p. 31	Verb review: *décrire, s'asseoir* **Descriptive adjectives** **Comparative and superlative of adjectives** *Tout* **Interrogatives** *Il (Elle) est* vs. *C'est* p. 153

VOCABULAIRE	LECTURES	STRUCTURES

POSTLUDE
Les Cajuns
p. 140

Bruce Daigrepont:
«Disco et fais-do-do»
p. 142

Student Preface

Welcome to *Sur le vif,* Sixth Edition. The title of this one-semester intermediate textbook means "from (real) life"—as in *faire un reportage sur le vif* (to do a live or on-the-spot broadcast). With its current and often provocative topics for reading and discussion, this text will further develop your skills in French, while deepening your knowledge of the complexity of France and the Francophone world. Now that you have completed the introductory sequence, you are ready to move beyond grocery shopping, weather forecasts, and describing your room, to comparing systems of education, expressing your opinions about youth culture, debating issues of immigration, explaining your attitudes towards the media, and changing family structures. You will also talk about the pros and cons of the automobile, enjoy learning about folk traditions, and reflect on environmental issues. You discover how these topics are seen in the French and Francophone world, and make comparisons with the North-American perspective.

To improve your control of French grammar so that you can speak, read, and write about the above topics with greater confidence, *Sur le vif* provides a systematic review of the fundamental structures of the language, giving you many opportunities to practice through form-focused oral activities, reading, and more open discussions in class. Similarly, the listening and the writing exercises in the Student Activities Manual (SAM), which you can use either in print form or on-line through the **eSAM,** will improve your command of the language and build your vocabulary.

LEARNING WITH *SUR LE VIF*

FORMAT

Understanding how *Sur le vif* is organized will help you make the best use of the program, since it may be somewhat different from the language textbook(s) you are familiar with. The first part of the book (and the longest) contains nine chapters plus four shorter units (prelude, two interludes, postlude) with readings and activities for classroom use. Parts of these may, of course, be assigned for homework, but most will be done under the guidance of your instructor. Grammar is not explained in this section, but marginal notes, labeled **Préparation grammaticale,** refer you to the grammar structures to review for each part of a chapter. The **Rappel** boxes, in English, give a brief statement of the rule that applies to activities you are about to do. Both of these point you to the grammar explanations in the second part of the book, called **Structures**; its nine chapters, which correspond to those of the first section of the book, provide a comprehensive grammar review. This part of *Sur le vif* is meant for outside-of-class preparation. Here you will find explanations in English of the structures you are learning and reviewing. Examples that illustrate the grammar rules are based on the readings of the corresponding chapters in the first section to give you more exposure to the chapter theme and vocabulary. After a structure has been explained, you are referred to exercises in the SAM so that you can practice the forms and check your own answers to verify that you have learned how to apply the rule.

The final section of the book, the **Appendices,** contains a brief presentation of preposition usage and present participles followed by verb conjugation charts. At the very end of *Sur le vif* is a French-English glossary, with words defined as they are used in the context of the book. This will help you with readings and activities, but you should be aware that a glossary will not substitute for a good paper or online dictionary.

THE STUDENT'S ROLE

By the end of the elementary sequence, you will have studied most of the fundamental structures of French, but you may not be able to use all of them accurately all the time. You may be stronger in reading than in speaking, or understand more than you can write. This is a perfectly normal phenomenon in second language acquisition, but it makes the intermediate course more complex. Each student will have slightly different needs due to varying levels of proficiency. You are in the best position to know what your strengths and weaknesses are. Therefore, you should assume an active role in your learning. By studying the grammar outside of class you can concentrate on points that are more difficult or new to you and move more quickly when you are reasonably confident of your understanding. The self-check exercises in the SAM (printed workbook or online through the **eSAM**) will show if you can use the structures correctly and allow you to focus on those that still pose problems for you. You will also find additional grammar and vocabulary practice on the Premium Website for the book, at www.cengagebrain.com/login.

In class, your instructor will ask you to apply the vocabulary and structures you have studied to activities relating to chapter themes and discussion of readings. When you have prepared the grammar, you will be ready to practice the forms, demonstrate your understanding of the readings, talk about your personal reactions to the topics, and participate in role-plays and debates. Oral work is central to *Sur le vif* and you will be expected to produce more than single-sentence responses. Being able to elaborate on your answers or paraphrase as needed will make you a more sophisticated speaker of French.

You, your instructor, and *Sur le vif* are partners in this course. You study grammar outside of class so that you are ready to use the structures to communicate. Your instructor creates opportunities for speaking in class that check your preparation and understanding and help you build your skills. The textbook provides French and Francophone cultural information, reading selections, and activities to encourage development of your listening, speaking, reading, and writing proficiency. Exercises in the SAM help you first to practice the forms, then to use them to communicate your own ideas, and finally, to write compositions in which you apply the grammar and vocabulary you have reviewed in more extended essays related to the theme of the chapter.

ADDITIONAL STUDENT COMPONENTS

Student Activities Manual (SAM)

The SAM (either in hard copy or on-line through **eSAM**) is divided into two sections: The *Cahier d'exercices écrits* is for written work, to practice the grammar rules reviewed in the **Structures** section of the textbook. The *Exercices de laboratoire* are to be used for pronunciation and listening practice in tandem with the audio program.

Each chapter of the *Cahier d'exercices écrits* portion of the Student Activities Manual (SAM) has four sections. The first focuses on vocabulary exercises to help you learn the new words in each chapter, understand words families, and use the expressions in context. The second section has both self-check and open-ended grammar exercises for each of the structures presented in the text. By completing the self-check exercises (**Entraînement**), you will see immediately if you have understood the grammar explanations and can apply them. The **Développement** activities continue your practice of the rules but do not have one correct answer. You will be using the structures you are studying to express your personal opinions or reactions; therefore, you should write more than a one-sentence answer whenever possible. The final section of the grammar part of the workbook, **Expression,** focuses on writing and contains a choice of topics for longer (one to three paragraphs) compositions and provides pre-writing instruction to help you prepare your text. In the fourth section, there are pre-, during and post-viewing activities relating to the accompanying video segment in which French speakers comment on the topic of the chapter.

The *Exercices de laboratoire* portion of the SAM is used with the audio materials on the Premium Website or through the **eSAM**. Each chapter takes about thirty minutes to complete and includes pronunciation practice followed by a passage for listening comprehension and a short dictation. Actively practicing the expressions or sentences according to the prompts will help you improve not only your pronunciation but also your comprehension of spoken French.

Premium Website

On the Premium website for *Sur le vif* (www.cengagebrain.com/login), you will find a wide variety of helpful activities and study tools. The complimentary resources include tutorial quizzes, web search activities, Google Earth™ coordinates, and an iTunes™ playlist. You will also find recordings of the chapter vocabulary lists that allow you to hear how the word is pronounced when you click on it. Additionally, the self-check grammar and vocabulary exercises can be used as a diagnostic tool to find out if you need to spend more time studying certain structures, or as additional practice of the forms you worked on in the textbook and Student Activities Manual. Premium password-protected resources on the website include the complete audio program, the video clips to accompany the video activities from the SAM, grammar and pronunciation podcasts, grammar tutorial videos, and audio-enhanced flash cards.

Acknowledgments

We would like to express our gratitude to the colleagues who participated in reviewing the materials for the Sixth Edition:

Eileen Angelini	*Canisius College*
Diane Beckman	*North Carolina State University*
Elizabeth Blood	*Salem State University*
Julien Carrière	*Bellarmine University*
Culley Carson-Grefe	*Austin Peay State University*
Matthieu Chan Tsin	*Coastal Carolina University*
Olivia Choplin	*Elon University*
Susan Clay	*Clemson University*
Donna Coulet du Gard	*University of Delaware*
Claudia Esposito	*University of Massachusetts Boston*
Charles Fleis	*Bridgewater College*
Karen Fowler	*Valencia College*
Françoise Fregnac-Clave	*Washington and Lee University*
Pascale Hubert-Leibler	*Columbia University*

Carrie Klaus	*DePauw University*
Michèle Magnin	*University of San Diego*
Jack Marcus	*Gannon University*
Mihaela Marin	*University of South Alabama*
Antoine Matondo	*University of Missouri*
Alix Mazuet	*University of Central Oklahoma*
Maria Gloria Melgarejo	*St. Cloud State University*
Jessica Miller	*University of Wisconsin-Eau Claire*
Christine Moritz	*University of Northern Colorado*
Shawn Morrison	*College of Charleston*
Lynn Palermo	*Susquehanna University*
Désirée Pries	*University of California, Berkeley*
Suzanne Roos	*Johns Hopkins University*
Peggy Schaller	*Georgia C & State University*
Beatriz Schleppe	*University of Texas at Austin*
Janet Starmer	*Guilford College*
Bernadette Takano	*University of Oklahoma*
Timothy Tomasik	*Valparaiso University*
William L. White	*State University of New York College at Buffalo*
Rachel Williams	*McNeese State University*

Their suggestions and criticisms guided our revisions and provided us with invaluable perspective.

Our thanks also go to those who supported us through this process of revision, most particularly all those instructors and graduate teaching fellows whose comments and suggestions as they taught the Fifth Edition provided ideas for improvements. French exchange students in our two universities provided invaluable assistance. Of course all those third semester French students at Duke University and the University of North Carolina at Chapel Hill need mention, since their responses to the previous editions have guided our revisions. Our respective study abroad programs in Montpellier and Paris allowed us time in France, where we could gather material and stay **"sur le vif"**. Many of our wonderful photos were taken by Clare during her travels in the French speaking world. We are also grateful to Françoise and Alain Planchot, who responded with good humor and endless patience to linguistic and cultural queries, involving their friends and families in debates on their own language and also provided many family pictures. Claire and Jean-Michel Thibault graciously made photos of their children available. It is with our deepest gratitude that we acknowledge the generosity of the artist Bruno Ottenheimer whose painting graces our cover, and of his wife Sylvia, who put so much time and effort into getting us the perfect, high resolution image to facilitate reproduction of Bruno's work.

At Cengage Learning, we would like to express our appreciation first to Nicole Morinon, Acquisitions Editor, who encouraged us with her openness to new ideas and interest in giving a fresh look to this sixth edition. The constructive editing of Cat Thomson, Development Editor, kept us moving along and caught painful slips in attention. Diane Harwood provided tactful native reader commentary, not to mention astute questions to confirm our information. Julie Low searched photo databases for just the right image. Stacy Drew, our project manager, oversaw all of those endless, final details of the production process. The Cengage team's eye for linguistic accuracy and pedagogical insights significantly improved *Sur le vif.* We also extend our thanks to Tiffany Kayes, Greg Madan, Beth Kramer, Morgen Gallo, Courtney Wollstoncroft, and Ben Rivera for their work on this edition.

And finally, we thank each other for laughter, support and encouragement. We are grateful to Konrad for his tolerance of our ups and downs, and to Pierre for his endless and enthusiastic support, including "on the ground" assistance whenever we asked.

H.J.

C.T.

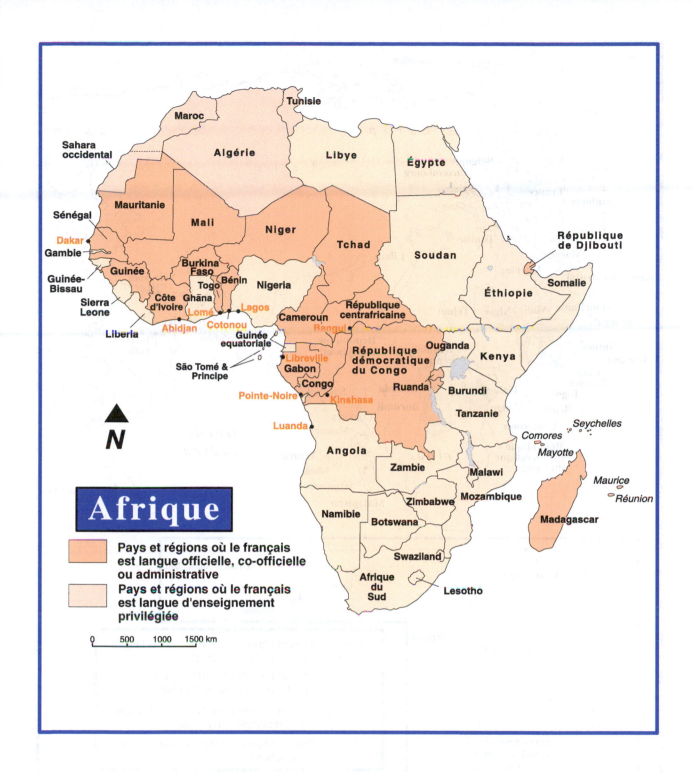

Afrique

Pays et régions où le français est langue officielle, co-officielle ou administrative

Pays et régions où le français est langue d'enseignement privilégiée

0   500   1000   1500 km

Sahara occidental
Maroc
Tunisie
Algérie
Libye
Égypte
Mauritanie
Sénégal
Dakar
Gambie
Guinée-Bissau
Guinée
Sierra Leone
Liberia
Mali
Niger
Tchad
Soudan
République de Djibouti
Burkina Faso
Togo
Bénin
Ghāna
Côte d'Ivoire
Lomé
Abidjan
Cotonou
Lagos
Nigeria
Cameroun
Guinée equatoriale
São Tomé & Principe
Libreville
Gabon
Congo
Pointe-Noire
Kinshasa
Luanda
République centrafricaine
Bangui
République démocratique du Congo
Ouganda
Ruanda
Burundi
Éthiopie
Somalie
Kenya
Tanzanie
Angola
Zambie
Malawi
Mozambique
Zimbabwe
Namibie
Botswana
Swaziland
Afrique du Sud
Lesotho
Madagascar
Comores
Mayotte
Seychelles
Maurice
Réunion

N

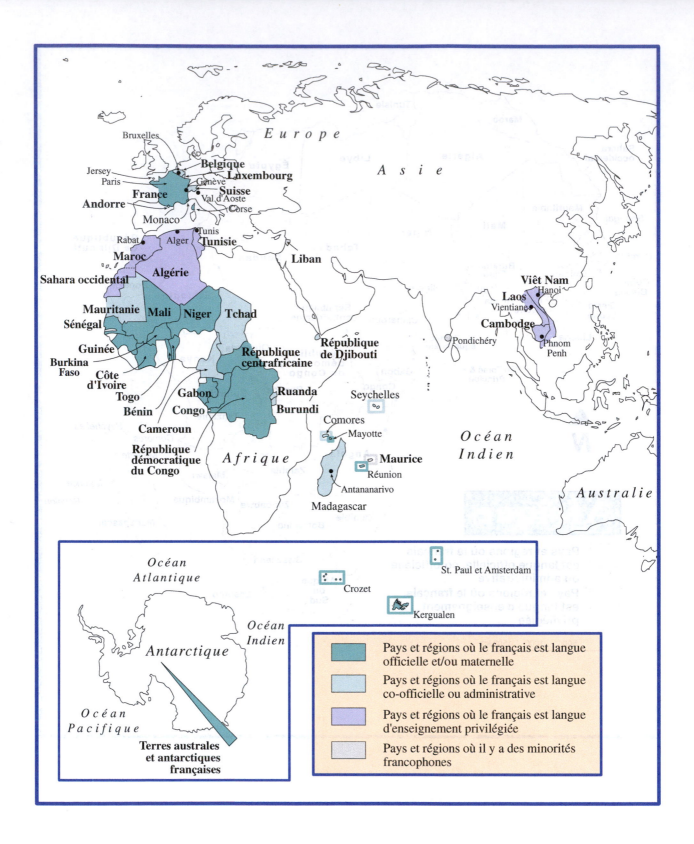

Pays et régions où le français est langue officielle et/ou maternelle

Pays et régions où le français est langue co-officielle ou administrative

Pays et régions où le français est langue d'enseignement privilégiée

Pays et régions où il y a des minorités francophones

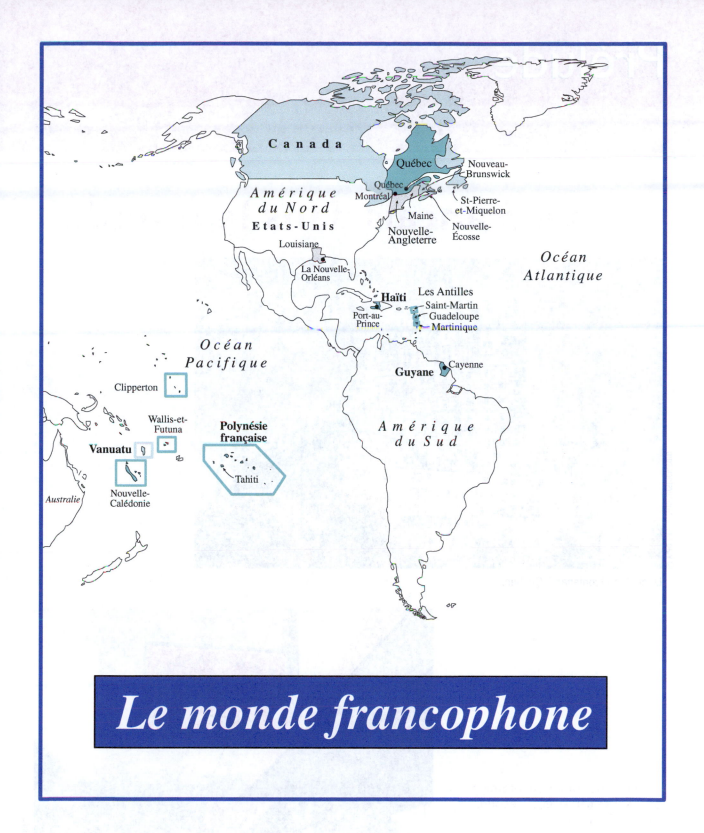

Canada

Québec

Nouveau-
Brunswick

Amérique
du Nord

Québec

Montréal

St-Pierre-
et-Miquelon

Etats-Unis

Maine

Nouvelle-
Écosse

Louisiane

Nouvelle-
Angleterre

Océan
Atlantique

La Nouvelle-
Orléans

Les Antilles

Haïti

Saint-Martin

Port-au-
Prince

Guadeloupe

Martinique

Océan
Pacifique

Guyane

Cayenne

Clipperton

Amérique
du Sud

Wallis-et-
Futuna

Polynésie
française

Vanuatu

Tahiti

Australie

Nouvelle-
Calédonie

Le monde francophone

Le français dans le monde

Le château Frontenac à Québec.

« Pour tout homme, le premier pays est sa patrie, et le second, c'est la France ».

Thomas Jefferson

(Discours inaugural de 1801)

Un café de l'Île de la Réunion

VOS CAMARADES DE CLASSE ET LE FRANÇAIS

Mettez-vous par groupes de deux ou trois (choisissez des camarades de classe que vous ne connaissez pas encore). Posez-vous d'abord les trois premières questions pour faire connaissance, puis parlez de vos idées sur le français et de vos expériences avec cette langue. Prenez des notes, puis choisissez quelques détails intéressants et présentez-les à la classe.

A. Faisons connaissance

1. Comment t'appelles-tu? D'où viens-tu?
2. Qu'est-ce que tu étudies? Quels cours préfères-tu?
3. Choisis deux ou trois adjectifs pour te décrire.

B. Parlons du français et du monde francophone

4. Depuis quand est-ce que tu apprends le français?
5. Pour quelles raisons as-tu choisi d'apprendre le français?
6. As-tu déjà visité la France ou une autre région francophone? Si oui, où es-tu allé(e)?
7. Est-ce que tu connais des films ou des acteurs français? Lesquels?
8. Quelles entreprises *(companies)*, quelles marques *(brands)* ou quels produits français connais-tu?
9. A ton avis, pourquoi y a-t-il souvent des inscriptions en français sur les produits que l'on achète aux Etats-Unis ou au Canada?
10. Qu'est-ce que tu voudrais apprendre ce semestre en cours de français?

Lecture

AVANT DE LIRE

Selon vous, quelle langue étrangère la plupart des élèves français choisissent-ils d'apprendre? Pourquoi? Dans votre pays, à part l'anglais, quelle(s) langues(s) vivante(s) apprend-on à l'école? Pourquoi? A quel âge commence-t-on à apprendre une langue étrangère dans votre pays?

Enseignement des langues étrangères en France

Le système scolaire français prévoit l'enseignement de deux à trois langues vivantes dans le cursus des petits Français: l'anglais, l'allemand et l'espagnol, mais aussi l'italien, le portugais et d'autres encore. Quelles langues sont aujourd'hui populaires? En 6ème, vers l'âge de 11 ans, les écoliers choisissent une première langue étrangère, typiquement l'anglais ou l'allemand. Neufs écoliers sur dix optent pour l'anglais. En 4ème, il y a un nouveau choix. Les options sont quasi invariablement anglais-allemand-espagnol. C'est l'espagnol qui remporte le plus de succès auprès de 70% des collégiens. 13% choisissent l'allemand et 11% de ceux qui avaient pris l'allemand en première langue choisissent l'anglais. La troisième langue, choisie par un faible pourcentage de lycéens à 15 ans (4%) offre un choix plus éclectique, uniquement dans certains établissements. Autrefois

Saviez-vous que... ?

La voix de la diversité: Il y a 220 millions de francophones dans le monde. Le français est la 9ème langue la plus parlée sur la planète et la seule, avec l'anglais, à l'être sur les cinq continents. Dans l'Union européenne, le français est la 2ème langue maternelle la plus parlée (16%), après l'allemand (23%) et devant l'anglais (15,9%). Dans l'Union européenne, le français est la 2ème langue étrangère la plus pratiquée (19%), après l'anglais (41%) et devant l'allemand (10%) ou l'espagnol (7%).

Pourtant l'Afrique est le continent où l'on trouve le plus grand nombre de francophones. Dans la majorité des pays membres de la francophonie, 60% de la population a moins de 30 ans. Le français est la 3ème langue utilisée sur Internet avec 5% des pages après l'anglais (45%) et l'allemand (7%) et devant l'espagnol (4,5%).

Source: www.francophonie.org

concurrencé par l'italien, le portugais est devenu le choix le plus populaire ces 20 dernières années avec près de 70%. L'italien demeure bon second avec 20%, loin derrière arrivent le russe, le chinois et autres.

www.lexiophiles.com

A DISCUTER

Pourquoi, selon vous, les jeunes Français choisissent-ils d'apprendre l'espagnol et l'allemand? Dans quelles régions de France les élèves choisiraient-ils ces langues? Pourquoi apprendre d'autres langues telles l'italien, le chinois, le japonais, l'arabe, le russe ou le swahili? Donnez quelques raisons pour ces choix.

POUR MIEUX S'EXPRIMER

There are several French expressions that allow you to express the idea of causality *(because)*. The three most common are **parce que** + *subject* + *verb*, **car** + *subject* + *verb*, and **à cause de** + *noun*. In English we use the same word, *because,* for all constructions.

Compare: Je voudrais visiter le Québec **parce qu'on** y **parle** français**.**
Il ne veut pas y vivre **car les hivers** y **sont** trop durs.
Les Québécois se moquent des Français **à cause de** leur **cuisine**.

Lecture

La chanson que vous allez lire et écouter est de Lynda Lemay, auteur-compositeur-interprète, née à Portneuf, au Québec, en 1966. Lynda Lemay commence à chanter en 1988 et son premier album sort en 1990. Depuis, avec plus de seize albums en vingt-quatre ans de carrière, elle fait des tournées en Europe et au Canada. Elle a remporté de nombreux prix, dont le prix Montfort du Rayonnement de la francophonie sur la scène internationale en 2004. La chanson suivante est tirée de son album *Du coq à l'âme*[1], sorti en 2000.

AVANT DE LIRE

Quelles images stéréotypées les Nord-Américains anglophones ont-ils des Français? Et existe-t-il des stéréotypes concernant le Canada (climat, nature, cuisine, habitudes, langues, etc.)?

POUR MIEUX COMPRENDRE

Dans cette chanson, Lynda Lemay reproduit un peu le français parlé au Québec (registre familier). Il s'agit surtout de différences de prononciation (les lettres qui ne sont pas prononcées: **y = ils, à tout bout d'champ = à tout bout de champ, s'donnent des bis = se donnent des bises, pis = puis**) et de vocabulaire québécois (**dîner / souper, toilettes / salle de bains**). Parcourez les paroles de la chanson pour trouver d'autres exemples de cette façon de parler et donnez l'équivalent en français standard. Remarquez tous les vers qui commencent par « Y » [Ils]. De qui s'agit-il?

[1] Jeu de mots, de l'expression **passer du coq à l'âne**: passage sans transition d'un sujet à l'autre *(abrupt change of subject)*. **l'âme** = *soul*

Les maudits° Français

maudits *accursed, damned*

Y parlent avec des mots précis
Puis y prononcent toutes leurs syllabes
A tout bout d'champ°, y s'donnent des bis°
Y passent leurs grandes journées à table

 CD 1, Track 2

A... A tout instant /
s'donnent... s'embrassent

5　Y ont des menus qu'on comprend pas
Y boivent du vin comme si c'était d'l'eau
Y mangent du pain pis° du foie gras
En trouvant l'moyen d'pas être gros

pis puis

Y font des manifs° aux quarts d'heure
10　A tous les maudits coins d'rue
Tous les taxis ont des chauffeurs
Qui roulent en fous, qui collent au cul°

manifs manifestations
(demonstrations)

collent... (très fam.) *are right on your tail*

Et quand y parlent de venir chez nous
C'est pour l'hiver ou les Indiens
15　Les longues promenades en Ski-doo°
Ou encore en traîneau° à chiens

Ski-doo *brand of snowmobile*
traîneau *sled*

Ils ont des tasses minuscules
Et des immenses cendriers°
Y font du vrai café d'adulte
20　Ils avalent ça en deux gorgées°

cendriers *ashtrays*

gorgées *gulps*

On trouve leurs gros bergers allemands
Et leurs petits caniches° chéris
Sur les planchers° des restaurants
Des épiceries, des pharmacies

caniches *poodles*
planchers *floors*

25　Y disent qu'y dînent quand y soupent
Et y est deux heures quand y déjeunent[2]
Au petit matin, ça sent l'yaourt
Y connaissent pas les œufs-bacon

En fin d'soirée, c'est plus choucroute°
30　Magret d'canard° ou escargots
Tout s'déroule bien jusqu'à c'qu'on goûte
A leur putain de° tête de veau[3]

choucroute *sauerkraut*
magret... *duck breast*

putain de (très fam.) *(here) damned*

---

[2] Au Québec, on dit « **le déjeuner** » pour « **le petit déjeuner** », « **le dîner** » pour le repas de midi et "**le souper**" pour le repas du soir.

[3] La « **tête de veau** » est un plat fait avec la tête d'un veau; dans la strophe qui suit Lynda Lemay énumère les parties de la tête qui sont utilisées.

paupière *eyelid* / **gencive** *gum*	Un bout d'paupière°, un bout d'gencive°
museau *snout*	Un bout d'oreille, un bout d'museau°
papilles... *taste buds*	35 Pour des papilles gustatives°
	De Québécois, c'est un peu trop
	Puis, y nous prennent pour un martien
	Quand on commande un verre de lait
	Ou quand on demande: La salle de bain
	40 Est à quelle place, s'il vous plaît?[4]
	Et quand ils arrivent chez nous
tuque bonnet de laine	Y s'prennent une tuque° et un Kanuk°
Kanuk marque d'anorak	Se mettent à chercher des igloos
	Finissent dans une cabane à sucre
tombent... tombent	45 Y tombent en amour° sur le coup
amoureux de	Avec nos forêts et nos lacs
	Et y s'mettent à parler comme nous
	Apprennent à dire: Tabarnak°
Tabarnak *swear word in Quebec, comes from "Tabarnacle"*	
	Et bien saoulés° au caribou°
saoulés *drunk* / **caribou**	50 A la Molson et au gros gin
boisson composée de vin	Y s'extasient sur nos ragoûts°
rouge et d'alcool fort	D'pattes° de cochon et nos plats d'binnes°
ragoûts *stews* / **pattes** pieds	
d'un animal **binnes** *beans*	
	Vu qu'on n'a pas d'fromages qui puent°
puent *stink*	Y s'accommodent d'un vieux cheddar
	55 Et y se plaignent pas trop non plus
bâtard dilué et insipide	De notre petit café bâtard°
	Quand leur séjour tire à sa fin
	Ils ont compris qu'ils ont plus l'droit
	De nous appeler les Canadiens
	60 Alors que l'on est Québécois
trempés *wet (with tears)*	Y disent au revoir, les yeux tout trempés°
érable *maple*	L'sirop d'érable° plein les bagages
	On réalise qu'on leur ressemble
	On leur souhaite bon voyage
On... On a accepté **donne...**	65 On est rendu qu'°on donne des becs°
se fait la bise	Comme si on l'avait toujours fait
	Y a comme un trou dans le Québec
	Quand partent les maudits Français

---

[4] Les Français disent « **toilettes** » ou « **W.-C**. » au lieu de « **salle de bains** » et « **endroit** » au lieu de « **place** ».

COMPRENEZ-VOUS?

A **Français ou Québécois?** Dans la chanson, à quelle nationalité Lynda Lemay associe-t-elle les caractéristiques suivantes?

1. parler très clairement
2. souper le soir
3. être mince mais manger et boire beaucoup
4. boire de la Molson
5. conduire de manière agressive
6. amener des chiens partout
7. passer beaucoup de temps à table
8. manger des haricots blancs et du porc
9. s'embrasser en arrivant et en partant

B **La couleur locale.** Avec un(e) partenaire, faites les activités suivantes, basées sur les paroles de la chanson. Comparez vos listes à celles de vos camarades de classe.

1. Énumérez les plats et les boissons associés aux Français dans ce texte. Ensuite, faites la même chose pour les plats (ou aliments) et les boissons associés aux Québécois.
2. Selon l'auteur, pourquoi les Français visitent-ils le Québec?

C **Des stéréotypes.** En groupes de deux ou trois, parcourez encore une fois la chanson pour trouver les réponses aux questions suivantes.

1. De quels aspects de la France et des Français la chanson se moque-t-elle? Quelles images stéréotypées des Français trouve-t-on dans la chanson?
2. Quelles images stéréotypées les Français ont-ils du Canada?

D **Le message.** Avec un(e) partenaire, discutez du message de cette chanson en répondant aux questions suivantes.

1. Pourquoi Lynda Lemay insiste-t-elle sur le fait que les gens décrits dans la chanson sont québécois et non pas canadiens?
2. Quel est le message des deux dernières strophes de la chanson?

ALLEZ PLUS LOIN

Avec deux ou trois camarades de classe, imaginez un clip vidéo pour cette chanson. Créez un plan pour le scénario. Quelles images choisiriez-vous? Allez sur *www.youtube.fr* pour voir s'il y a un clip pour la chanson. Comparez-le à votre scénario.

© Philippe Renault

Les études

A LES LIEUX

l'école maternelle *f.*	*preschool*
l'école primaire *f.*	*elementary school*
le collège	*middle school*
le lycée	*high school*
l'université *f.*	*college, university*
la salle de classe	*classroom*
la faculté, la fac *(fam.)*	*school within university*
la fac de médecine	*the medical school*
la fac de droit	*the law school*
l'amphithéâtre *m.*, l'amphi *(fam.)*	*lecture hall*

B LES GENS

l'élève *m.f.*	*primary and secondary school student*
le (la) lycéen(ne)	*high school student*
l'étudiant(e)	*university student*
l'instituteur(-trice), le (la) maître (maîtresse)	*elementary school teacher*
un(e) nul(le) *(fam.)*, un zéro	*poor student*
une tête *(fam.)*	*very bright student*

© Ian Hanning/REA/Redux

Pour obtenir des exercices et activités supplémentaires
sur le contenu de ce chapitre, rendez-vous sur le site
www.cengagebrain.com

C LES CHOSES

la bourse	scholarship, fellowship
l'enseignement m.	education, instruction
les matières f. (obligatoires)	(required) courses
le cursus	curriculum
la filière	area of concentration
la rentrée	return to school (in fall or after school break)
les droits m. d'inscription	registration fees
la note[1]	grade
la moyenne	grade average
l'UE[2] f.	course credit
le relevé de notes	student record in elementary and secondary school
le dossier	student record (university) including grades
la rédaction	composition
la dissertation, la dissert (fam.)	essay, paper (English, history, etc.)
la thèse	thesis
le (les) cours magistral(-aux)	lecture course(s)
les travaux dirigés, (les TD) m. pl.	discussion section, lab
l'interrogation f. l'interro (fam.), le contrôle	test, quiz
le partiel	midterm exam
l'examen m.	exam
l'examen blanc	practice test
les heures de permanence f.pl.	office hours
le stage	internship

[1] En France, les notes vont de 0 à 20. Au lycée comme à l'université, on utilise le système suivant: 18–20: *excellent*; 16–18: *très bien*; 14–16: *bien*; 12–14: *assez bien*; 10–12: *passable*; 0–9: *insuffisant*. Les notes 18–20 sont plutôt rares. Certains disent que 19 est réservé pour le professeur et 20 pour le bon Dieu.

[2] l'unité d'enseignement

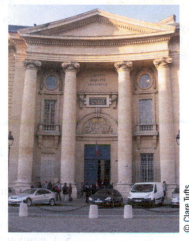

La Faculté de Droit, Paris

© Clare Tufts

D LES ACTIVITES

se débrouiller to get along	to manage, to cope,
s'inscrire	to register
suivre un cours	to take a class
réviser	to review
redoubler (une année) (un cours)	to repeat (a year) (a course)
sécher un cours (fam.)	to skip a class
rendre (un devoir)	to turn in (a homework assignment)
passer un examen	to take a test
réussir (à) un examen	to pass a test
échouer à un examen, rater un examen	to fail a test
bosser (fam.)	to study hard
bosser à la dernière minute	to cram
tricher, pomper (fam.)	to cheat
se spécialiser en	to major in
obtenir son diplôme	to receive a diploma, to graduate (American system)

Vocabulaire

A **L'âge et l'enseignement.** Quels établissements scolaires fréquentent les Français aux âges indiqués ci-dessous? (Référez-vous à la liste A du vocabulaire au début du chapitre.) Qu'est-ce que les élèves/étudiants aiment faire dans ces établissements scolaires?

Modèle: 5 ans

A l'âge de 5 ans, les Français fréquentent l'école maternelle. A cet âge-là, les élèves aiment dessiner.

1. 16 ans
2. 7 ans
3. 20 ans
4. 4 ans
5. 12 ans

PREPARATION GRAMMATICALE

Avant de continuer, révisez l'usage et la formation du présent, pages 145–148.

B **Comment dit-on?** Donnez l'infinitif du verbe de la liste D du vocabulaire qui correspond à chacune des situations suivantes.

1. Ce qu'on doit faire avant de suivre un cours.
2. Ce que font beaucoup d'étudiants la veille *(the night before)* d'un examen.
3. Ce que fait un étudiant qui est trop fatigué ou qui est malade.
4. Ce qu'on est obligé de faire en France quand on a de très mauvaises notes.
5. Ce qui arrive quand on ne peut pas répondre aux questions pendant un examen.
6. Ce qu'on fait pour être sûr d'avoir une très bonne note dans un cours.
7. Ce qui se passe pour l'étudiant qui a assez d'UE à l'université.
8. Ce que font les mauvais élèves pour avoir une meilleure note.
9. Ce que les étudiants font de leurs devoirs une fois qu'ils les ont finis.
10. Ce que font les étudiants qui se sont bien préparés pour un examen.

C **Positive ou négative?** Lisez les mots suivants. Est-ce qu'ils provoquent chez vous une réaction positive ou négative? Pourquoi?

Modèle: mon dossier

J'ai une réaction positive parce que je suis toujours content(e) de mon travail.

1. la rentrée
2. l'école maternelle
3. un cours magistral
4. une dissertation
5. une tête
6. les matières obligatoires

Saviez-vous que... ?

Depuis 2006 le cursus universitaire, dit LMD, s'organise autour de trois diplômes: la licence (six semestres), le master (quatre semestres supplémentaires) et le doctorat (généralement trois ans après le master). Ce cursus européen permet aux étudiants de faire des études dans d'autres pays avec le même système de diplômes et de passer plus facilement d'une discipline à une autre, et d'une formation générale à une formation professionnelle.

Source: cursus universitaire

Maintenant, trouvez un(e) partenaire et comparez vos réactions. Si vous n'avez pas les mêmes réactions à chaque mot, essayez de découvrir pourquoi. Expliquez vos réactions par rapport à celles des autres membres de la classe.

D **Une tête ou un nul?** Avec un(e) camarade de classe, rédigez deux portraits: celui du (de la) meilleur(e) et celui du (de la) plus mauvais(e) étudiant(e) dans une classe typique au lycée ou à l'université. Pour chacune des descriptions, écrivez quatre ou cinq phrases et utilisez autant de mots des listes de vocabulaire que possible.

une tête

un nul

© Cengage Learning

E **Le cours idéal.** Parmi les matières suivantes, choisissez-en une. Ensuite, trouvez un(e) autre étudiant(e) qui a fait le même choix.

> **Matières:** la biologie, l'histoire, les langues étrangères, les mathématiques, la psychologie, la musique, l'art

1. Avec votre partenaire, décrivez le cours idéal dans cette matière du point de vue du professeur. Comment sont les étudiants? Qu'est-ce qu'ils font? Que doit faire le professeur?
2. Décrivez maintenant le cours idéal dans cette même matière du point de vue de l'étudiant. Que fait le professeur? Que font les étudiants? Comment sont les devoirs et les examens?
3. Comparez vos descriptions à celles de vos camarades de classe.

Lecture

Le passage que vous allez lire est tiré du roman *Kiffe kiffe demain*, de Faïza Guène, publié en 2004 quand l'auteur n'avait que dix-neuf ans. Ce premier roman a été l'une des meilleures ventes de 2004 et a été traduit dans 26 pays. Guène, fille d'immigrés algériens, a grandi en banlieue parisienne. Elle a publié deux autres romans depuis la sortie de ce premier et elle a aussi réalisé plusieurs films. Dans l'extrait suivant, Doria, une fille d'origine marocaine qui a quinze ans, parle de son travail à l'école.

Faïza Guène

© Le Livre de Poche

ENTRONS EN MATIERE

Avez-vous souvent reçu des commentaires écrits sur la qualité de votre travail dans un cours? Est-ce que vous en recevez à l'université? Vous en avez reçu au lycée? Avez-vous jamais reçu des commentaires que vous trouviez injustes, ou que vous aviez peur de montrer à vos parents? Préférez-vous recevoir de vos profs des commentaires écrits ou juste une note finale?

AVANT DE LIRE

Dans le système éducatif en France, les professeurs indiquent les notes des élèves à la fin de chaque trimestre dans le bulletin de notes, et à la fin de l'année académique dans le relevé des notes. Ils y mettent aussi leurs « appréciations » — c'est-à-dire, des commentaires pour expliquer les notes données. Ces commentaires ont pour but d'informer les parents, mais cela n'est pas toujours le cas. Pourquoi, à votre avis?

Extrait de *Kiffe kiffe demain*

Du côté du lycée, le trimestre s'est achevé aussi mal qu'il avait commencé. Heureusement que ma mère ne sait pas lire. Enfin, je dis ça surtout par rapport au bulletin... S'il y a bien un truc qui m'énerve, ce sont les profs qui font un concours d'originalité pour les appréciations. Résultat: elle sont toutes aussi connes° les unes que les autres... La

connes stupides

5 pire que j'aie jamais eue, c'est Nadine Benbarchiche, la prof de physique-chimie, qui l'a écrite: « Affligeant°, désespérant, élève qui incite à la démission° ou au suicide... »

affligeant lamentable **démission** acte par lequel on abandonne son travail

Elle pensait certainement faire de l'humour. J'avoue là, elle a fait fort. C'est vrai que je suis nulle mais bon, faut pas exagérer. [...] Sinon, ce que je retrouve toujours et que j'appelle les appréciations récurrentes, c'est: « semble perdue » ou bien « semble ail-
10 leurs » ou, pire, des trucs qui font pitié, style:

« Redescendez sur terre »! La seule qui m'a écrit un truc sympa, c'est Mme Lemoine, la prof de dessin, enfin pardon, d'arts plastiques. Elle a marqué: « Des qualités plastiques »... Bon, OK, ça veut rien dire mais c'est sympa quand même.

Malgré mes qualités plastiques, une copine de Maman a proposé que son fils vienne
15 m'aider à faire mes devoirs. D'après elle, j'aurai plus que des bonnes notes parce que
son fils Nabil c'est un génie. J'ai remarqué que les mères arabes pensent souvent ça de
leurs fils. [...]

Depuis quelques semaines, Nabil vient donc chez moi de temps en temps pour
m'aider dans mes devoirs. Ce type, il se la raconte trop! Il croit qu'il connaît tout sur
20 tout. La dernière fois, il s'est foutu de ma gueule° parce que je croyais que *Zadig*[3],
c'était une marque de pneus. Il a rigolé pendant trois quarts d'heure rien que pour
ça... Un moment, en voyant que ça ne me faisait pas rire du tout, il a dit: « Nan,° mais
t'inquiète pas, je plaisante, tu sais c'est pas grave, dans la vie, y a les intellectuels et y a
les autres... »

s'est foutu... s'est moqué de moi

nan ici: non

« KIFFE KIFFE DEMAIN » de Faïza GUENE © Librairie Arthème Fayard, 2004

COMPRENEZ VOUS?

A. Globalement

Faites le portrait de Doria, en vous basant sur les détails du texte qui révèlent son
caractère, ses intérêts, etc.

B. En détail

1. Doria est-elle vraiment contente que sa mère ne sache pas lire?
2. Cette année scolaire est-elle différente des précédentes pour Doria? Comment le
   savez-vous?
3. Si la mère de Doria ne sait pas lire, comment sa copine sait-elle que Doria a
   besoin de l'aide de son fils?
4. Quel mot du vocabulaire de ce chapitre peut-on utiliser pour décrire Nabil?
5. Pensez-vous que Nabil réussira à aider Doria dans son travail? Pourquoi?

CHERCHEZ LA FORME

1. Au début de cet extrait il y a un exemple d'un verbe qui a une orthographe
   pour les formes *je, tu, il (elle), ils (elles)* et une autre orthographe pour les
   formes *nous* et *vous*. Identifiez ce verbe, et conjuguez-le au présent à la forme
   non-pronominale.
2. Plus loin dans l'extrait il y a un exemple d'un verbe qui double une consonne
   pour les formes *je, tu, il (elle), ils (elles)*. Identifiez-le et mettez-le aux trois
   formes de l'impératif.
3. La dernière phrase de l'extrait est grammaticalement incorrecte. Ecrivez ce que
   dit Nabil « en bon français ».

[3] *Zadig* est un conte philosophique de Voltaire, publié en 1747.

ALLEZ PLUS LOIN

Quels conseils Dora peut-elle donner à Nabil pour qu'il puisse vraiment l'aider à faire ses devoirs? Imaginez que vous êtes Doria et que vous parlez à Nabil. Mettez vos conseils à la forme impérative.

PRÉPARATION GRAMMATICALE

Avant de continuer, révisez l'usage de l'infinitif, de l'impératif et du faire causatif, pages 148–152.

Applications

A Les études. Parlez de ce qu'on fait dans vos cours cette année à l'aide des verbes suivants. Utilisez les sujets donnés et ajoutez des objets directs et indirects, des adverbes, des négations, etc. afin de créer des phrases intéressantes.

1. lire (nous)
2. sécher (je)
3. réussir (ma meilleure amie)
4. rendre (les étudiants)
5. obtenir (vous)
6. préférer (tu)
7. choisir (vous)
8. partager (nous)
9. dormir (les nuls)
10. répondre (je)
11. offrir (les profs)
12. suivre (ce garçon)

RAPPEL   In pronominal (reflexive) constructions, the reflexive pronoun agrees with the subject of the reflexive verb (**je/me, tu/te,** etc.). NOTE: the impersonal subject pronoun **on** takes the pronominal pronoun **se**. For more details, see pages 147–148.

B S'inscrire en fac. Vous faites la queue avec beaucoup d'autres étudiants frustrés le jour des inscriptions. Vous bavardez avec eux. En utilisant les éléments donnés, imaginez quelques commentaires.

Modèles: Je / se demander
> Je me demande pourquoi on fait la queue.
> Ce jeune homme / s'endormir
> Regarde! Ce jeune homme s'endort debout!

1. Je / s'inscrire (en cours...)
2. Tu / s'appeler?
3. Ces garçons / se fâcher
4. Cette fille-là / s'intéresser (à...)
5. Les gens de ce groupe / ne pas se parler
6. Toi et ton ami, vous / s'inquiéter (de... / parce que...)
7. Tout le monde / se disputer
8. Enfin on / se débrouiller
9. Nous / se calmer

La Sorbonne

C **Les adultes et les jeunes.** Quelquefois, les jeunes se plaignent de l'autorité de leurs parents et de leurs professeurs. Ils disent qu'on est toujours en train de leur donner des ordres. Complétez les phrases suivantes en vous basant sur votre propre expérience, ou inventez une réponse logique.

Modèle: Si je veux aller au cinéma, mes parents me font...
Si je veux aller au cinéma, mes parents me font finir tous mes devoirs avant de partir.

1. Quand j'ai une mauvaise note, mon père me fait...
2. Si je ne sais pas répondre à une question, le professeur me fait...
3. Tous les soirs, ma mère me fait...
4. Juste avant les examens, tous les profs me font...
5. Pendant la semaine des examens, mes parents me font...
6. Si je sèche un cours, mon père me fait...
7. Si je ne rends pas un devoir, le professeur me fait...
8. Quand j'échoue à un examen, ma mère me fait...

D **Encore des ordres!** M. Dupont, le prof de français, n'a pas bien dormi, alors il est de mauvaise humeur. Il ne parle pas à ses élèves; il leur donne des ordres! Réfléchissez à votre propre expérience dans un cours de langue pour vous aider à compléter les ordres que M. Dupont donne à ces pauvres élèves. (Notez que M. Dupont tutoie ces jeunes gens.)

> **Modèle:** Camille / ne pas s'arrêter... !
> Camille, ne t'arrête pas de travailler!

1. Samia / se tenir bien!
2. Rachid / répondre... !
3. Julia / s'asseoir... !
4. Madjid / ne pas dormir... !
5. Aline / répéter... !
6. Stéphanie et Kevin / faire... !
7. Audrey et Souleymane / finir... !
8. (A la classe) / savoir... !
9. (A ceux qui ne font pas attention) / se taire... !
10. (A la classe, à la fin de l'heure) / ne pas oublier... !

RAPPEL *Infinitives* have many different uses. When one verb follows another, the first verb is conjugated and the second verb remains in the infinitive form. Additionally, a verb that follows a preposition usually remains in its infinitive form. For more details, see pages 148–150.

E **Les idées sur le travail.** Les étudiants ne travaillent pas tous de la même façon. Comparez vos méthodes de travail avec un(e) autre étudiant(e).

- Dites si vous êtes d'accord avec chacune des phrases suivantes.
- Trouvez ensemble deux autres techniques qui peuvent faciliter vos études.

1. Il faut travailler au moins deux heures par jour pour chaque cours que l'on suit.
2. Il vaut mieux lire chaque livre deux fois.
3. Il ne faut jamais prêter ses notes aux autres étudiants.
4. On ne réussit pas si on ne dort pas au moins huit heures par nuit.
5. On travaille mieux dans sa chambre qu'à la bibliothèque.
6. Il faut poser beaucoup de questions en cours.
7. Pour obtenir une meilleure note, il faut s'asseoir au premier rang, devant le prof.
8. En cours de langue, il faut apprendre par cœur tous les mots de vocabulaire.
9. En cours de biologie, il faut passer deux fois plus de temps au laboratoire que ce que le prof suggère.
10. Il vaut mieux passer beaucoup de temps dans le bureau de ses profs.

F **Les études: On n'a pas les mêmes idées.** Mettez-vous par groupes de trois ou quatre. Un(e) d'entre vous joue le rôle d'un(e) étudiant(e) qui entre en première année de fac. Les autres, des anciens, sont là pour le/la guider et l'aider à réussir. Les anciens choisissent ensemble un des points de vue suivants et essaient de convaincre le (la) nouveau (nouvelle) que leur suggestion est essentielle pour réussir à l'université. Celui-ci / Celle-ci leur pose des questions.

1. Le plus important, c'est d'avoir les meilleures notes possibles dans tous tes cours.
2. L'essentiel, ce sont les copains. Il faut se faire beaucoup d'amis.
3. L'important, c'est de suivre des cours intéressants, même s'ils sont difficiles ou qu'ils ne sont pas dans ta filière.
4. L'engagement politique ou humanitaire, c'est ça qui compte.

Lecture

Agathe Demarais, 21 ans, étudiante en quatrième année à Sciences Po[4], a passé l'année scolaire 2006–2007 à l'University of British Columbia (UBC), à Vancouver. Une année entre études et voyages!

Vancouver, British Columbia

© Andreas Hub/laif/Redux

ENTRONS EN MATIERE

Pour quelle(s) raison(s) décide-t-on de quitter sa propre université pour aller étudier dans un pays étranger? Comment choisit-on où aller? Qu'est-ce qu'on gagne et qu'est-ce qu'on perd quand on quitte son milieu habituel pour vivre dans un autre pays?

AVANT DE LIRE

Pour vous aider à mieux comprendre les idées, lisez d'abord les questions qui précèdent chaque paragraphe. De quoi s'agira-t-il dans chaque partie? Faites une liste des idées principales.

« J'ai étudié un an à Vancouver »

PREMIÈRE PARTIE

Dans quel cadre° êtes-vous partie?

cadre ici: programme

Je suis partie à l'UBC (University of British Columbia) à Vancouver, sur la côte ouest du Canada dans le cadre d'un échange avec Sciences Po. J'ai été accueillie dans le programme *undergraduate* (premier cycle) où j'ai suivi des cours de premier, deuxième, troisième et quatrième semestre de *Bachelor*. J'ai passé un an sur place, de septembre
5 à la fin juin, car même si l'année universitaire s'est terminée fin avril, j'ai profité de mon séjour pour beaucoup voyager. J'ai terminé mon année par un *roadtrip* entre les Rocheuses canadiennes, le Yukon, l'Alaska et la côte Pacifique de l'Alaska à Vancouver en ferry, après avoir voyagé en mai à Washington DC, Philadelphie, San Francisco et Las Vegas.

10 *Pourquoi avoir choisi cette destination?*

Pour plusieurs raisons, les principales étant la beauté des paysages de la côte ouest canadienne, très méconnue° en France, et les opportunités de ski extraordinaires.

méconnue peu connue

---

[4] L'institut d'Etudes Politiques (= sciences politiques) est une des grandes écoles à Paris. Pour pouvoir y faire des études, les étudiants doivent réussir à un concours, un examen très compétitif, pour lequel ils suivent deux ans de cours préparatoires (prépas) après le bac.

Whistler, qui accueillera les JO° de 2010, n'est qu'à 1h30 de bus de UBC, et il y a
un départ chaque vendredi, samedi et dimanche. Ensuite, il y a la qualité des études:
15 UBC est une excellente université, particulièrement renommée en économie, en anthropologie et en sciences. Enfin, choisir le Canada, c'était aussi faire l'expérience de
la vie nord-américaine, sur un campus splendide (avec plage et parc régional), bref,
le rêve...

Quelles sont les principales différences entre les systèmes d'études français et canadiens?

20 D'abord, il y a beaucoup moins de cours qu'en France, une douzaine d'heures par semaine en fait, mais beaucoup de lectures à faire chez soi... et nécessaires pour pouvoir
participer à la discussion! En effet, les cours sont vraiment interactifs, avec une forte
participation des étudiants, même dans des amphis de 120 personnes. Mais s'il ne fallait retenir qu'une différence, j'insisterais sur cette participation orale des étudiants, et
25 sur les rapports privilégiés avec les professeurs. Par exemple, ils répondent à vos e-mails
en une heure ou ils ont des heures de permanence pour répondre à vos questions...

COMPRENEZ-VOUS?

1. Dans quelle école Agathe Demarais fait-elle ses études en France?
2. Pendant combien de temps est-elle restée en Amérique du Nord?
3. Pourquoi n'est-elle pas rentrée en France à la fin du semestre?
4. Quelles sont les raisons les plus importantes pour lesquelles elle a choisi UBC?
   Distinguez entre les raisons scolaires et les raisons « qualité de vie ».
5. Résumez les principales différences entre le système français et le système
   nord-américain, selon Agathe.

CHERCHEZ LA FORME

1. Passé → présent: Dans le premier paragraphe, mettez tous les verbes conjugués
   au passé composé au présent de l'indicatif.
2. Dans le troisième paragraphe, trouvez tous les infinitifs et expliquez leur usage
   (infinitif après une préposition, deuxième verbe après un verbe conjugué, etc.).

« J'ai étudié un an à Vancouver »

Sur place, qu'est-ce qui vous a le plus surprise?

Je pense que c'est l'immense décontraction° des habitants de Vancouver, qui sont vraiment très cool et zen... et la qualité de vie sur le campus, qui est immense: 40 000
5 étudiants y vivent. Il est ainsi réellement possible d'y passer une année entière sans en sortir. On y trouve tout: des piscines et des centres de sport, des coiffeurs, des commerces, des agences de voyages, des banques, un hôpital, la plage, et même un accélérateur de particules!

Combien d'heures de cours avez-vous par semaine?

10 J'avais une douzaine d'heures de cours par semaine, et très peu de travail personnel par rapport à Sciences Po! J'ai en fait passé mon année à voyager, étant donné que mes cours étaient le mardi, le mercredi et le jeudi. J'ai passé mon hiver à Whistler, et sinon j'ai bourlingué° en Amérique du Nord: Seattle, la Colombie-Britannique, New York, Montréal, Ottawa... En ce qui concerne le travail personnel, j'en avais au maximum
15 cinq heures par semaine! J'étais aussi professeur assistant de français à l'université, ce qui me prenait quatre heures par semaine et ce qui m'a permis de financer mes voyages!

Avez-vous connu des difficultés particulières, par exemple pour trouver un logement ou vous adapter à la vie quotidienne?

Pas du tout: l'université prend tout en charge, un logement est garanti à l'arrivée
20 de l'étudiant, et on vient même vous chercher à l'aéroport! Il y a plein de journées d'accueil pour rencontrer des gens et connaître les formalités à accomplir... impossible d'avoir des difficultés! Pour le financement du séjour, le coût de la vie à Vancouver est TRÈS inférieur à celui de Paris, et j'ai pu vivre vraiment de façon princière avec mon budget d'étudiante en France. Concernant l'adaptation à la vie quotidienne, tout s'est
25 très bien passé.

Quels conseils donneriez-vous aux Français qui veulent étudier au Canada?

Foncez°! C'est une opportunité unique, dont vous reviendrez vraiment profondément changé et grandi. C'est par ailleurs une excellente occasion de rentrer bilingue, tout en découvrant des matières auxquelles vous n'auriez pas pensé. Le système éducatif
30 nord-américain est en effet très libre, et il est tout à fait possible de prendre des cours d'astronomie ou d'anthropologie en plus de ses cours obligatoires.

décontraction *laid-back attitude*

bourlingué mené une vie aventureuse

Foncez! *Go for it!*

COMPRENEZ-VOUS?

1. Qu'est-ce qu'Agathe apprécie à Vancouver et sur le campus?
2. Avait-elle un emploi du temps très chargé? Expliquez.
3. Comment Agathe a-t-elle eu assez d'argent pour voyager?
4. Comment l'université aide-t-elle les étudiants qui viennent d'arriver?
5. Qu'est-ce qu'Agathe conseille aux étudiants français? Pourquoi?

CHERCHEZ LA FORME

1. Dans le premier paragraphe de cette deuxième partie, quels adjectifs renforcent l'idée de la décontraction des habitants de Vancouver? Expliquez-les.
2. Dans le deuxième et le troisième paragraphes, donnez l'infinitif de chaque verbe conjugué.

ALLEZ PLUS LOIN

Quelle sorte d'étudiante est Agathe Demarais, selon vous? Donnez beaucoup de détails tirés du texte pour justifier votre opinion.

Activités d'expansion

Rendez-vous sur le site web de *Sur le vif* pour regardez la vidéo de Chapitre 1, puis complétez les activités à la page 17 du **Student Activities Manual**.

A **Le débat: les parents et les études.** La classe est divisée en trois groupes qui vont débattre du rôle que les parents doivent jouer dans la scolarité de leurs enfants. Voici les questions:

1. Qui choisit l'université?
2. Qui choisit les cours à suivre?
3. Qui décide de la profession / carrière de l'enfant?

GROUPE A: Vous pensez que les parents ont le droit de prendre ces décisions pour leur enfant. Expliquez pourquoi.

GROUPE B: Vous êtes opposé(e) à ce que les parents prennent la décision pour leur enfant. Expliquez pourquoi.

GROUPE C: Selon vous, la meilleure solution est de prendre les décisions ensemble. Expliquez comment cela peut se faire.

NOTE: N'oubliez pas qu'en français on **prend** une décision et on **fait** un choix.

Si vous êtes d'accord, vous pouvez dire:
Oui, c'est vrai. De plus,...
Moi aussi, je pense que...
C'est une bonne idée de...
Je dois avouer que tu as raison. En plus,...
C'est vrai ce que tu dis, parce que...

Si vous n'êtes pas d'accord, vous pouvez répondre:
Non, je ne crois pas que...
Je suis en total désaccord avec...
Je regrette, mais tu as tort de dire que...
A mon avis...
Au contraire...

B **L'importance des études dans la vie ordinaire.** A votre avis, les études à l'université sont-elles étroitement liées à la vie de tous les jours? En quoi? Connaissez-vous des gens qui ne partagent pas votre avis? Qui sont-ils? Pouvez-vous comprendre leur point de vue?

C **Des systèmes d'éducation bien différents.** En seconde, les élèves français suivent des enseignements communs et choisissent deux enseignements de détermination et une option facultative. En fin de seconde, ces choix les aident à opter pour un bac général ou technologique. Les élèves de première et terminale générale choisissent certaines matières qui déterminent la spécialité de leur baccalauréat: le Bac S (scientifique), le Bac L (littéraire), le Bac ES (sciences économiques et sociales), ou un des bacs technologiques. Au niveau universitaire, les étudiants suivent peu de cours en dehors de leur spécialisation. La situation aux Etats-Unis est très différente. Quels sont les avantages et les inconvénients des deux systèmes?

© Plantu

Les jeunes

A LE CORPS

être beau (belle)	*to be handsome, beautiful*
joli(e), laid(e)	*pretty, ugly*
fort(e), gros(se)	*strong, fat*
costaud	*robust*
mince, maigre	*thin, skinny*
avoir les cheveux...	*to have . . . hair*
longs, courts	*long, short*
fins, épais	*thin, thick*
raides, ondulés, frisés	*straight, wavy, curly*
ébouriffés, en bataille	*uncombed*
teints	*dyed*
être chauve	*to be bald*
avoir...	*to have . . .*
des dreads	*dreadlocks*
des tresses africaines	*corn rows*
la tête rasée	*a shaved head*
une barbe	*a beard*
... de trois jours	*"designer stubble"*
une moustache	*a moustache*
avoir le visage...	*to have a (an) . . . face*
ovale, rond	*oval, round*
carré	*square*
pointu	*pointed*
joufflu	*fat-cheeked*
avoir le nez...	*to have a . . . nose*
droit, busqué	*straight, hooked*
avoir les lèvres...	*to have . . . lips*
charnues, fines, pincées	*full, thin, pinched*
être...	*to be . . . (coloring)*
bronzé(e)	*tanned*
pâle, blême	*pale, sick-looking*
avoir le teint...	*to have a . . . complexion*
clair, mat	*light, dark*
avoir des taches de rousseur	*to have freckles*

© Clare Tufts

B LE CARACTERE

être, avoir l'air...	*to be . . . , to look . . . (to be . . . looking)*
franc (franche)	*honest*
éveillé(e), endormi(e)	*awake, sleepy*
malin (maligne)	*smart, shrewd*
dur(e), doux (douce), froid(e)	*hard, sweet, cold*
gentil(le)	*nice, kind*
sympathique, sympa	*friendly*
poli(e), impoli(e)	*polite, impolite*
discret(-ète)	*discreet*
sensible, insensible	*sensitive, insensitive*
rêveur(-euse)	*dreamer*
drôle	*funny*
désagréable	*unpleasant*
rouspéteur(-euse)	*grouchy*
paresseux(-euse)	*lazy*
énergique	*energetic*
décontracté(e)	*relaxed*
tendu(e)	*tense*
débrouillard(e)	*resourceful*
maladroit(e)	*awkward, clumsy*

Pour obtenir des exercices et activités supplémentaires sur le contenu de ce chapitre, rendez-vous sur le site www.cengagebrain.com

C LES VETEMENTS ET LES ACCESSOIRES

les vêtements...	. . . clothes
chic(s)[1]	stylish
démodés	out-of-style
vintage (*invariable*)	vintage
propres, sales	clean, dirty
le pantalon	pants
le jean (délavé)	(faded) jeans
le short[2]	shorts
le tee-shirt	T-shirt
le costume	suit (men)
le tailleur	suit (women)
le chemisier	blouse
le pull	sweater
l'imperméable (imper)	raincoat
le manteau	coat
le blouson (en cuir)	(leather) jacket
le maillot de bain	swimsuit
le chapeau	hat
le bracelet	bracelet
le collier	necklace
le vernis à ongles	nail polish
le maquillage	make-up
le piercing	body piercing
au nez, au nombril	nose ring, navel ring
le tatouage	tattoo
les baskets	athletic shoes
la chemise, la cravate	shirt (men), tie

la jupe, la robe	skirt, dress
la veste	suit jacket (men/women)
les chaussures, les bottes	shoes, boots
les sandales	sandals
la casquette	cap
la (les) boucle(s) d'oreille(s)	earring(s)

D LES ACTIVITES ET LES PASSE-TEMPS QUOTIDIENS

s'habiller	to dress
se coiffer	to comb one's hair
se couper les cheveux	to cut one's hair
se faire couper les cheveux	to have one's hair cut
se maquiller	to put on make-up
jouer (à) + sports et jeux	to play . . .
au tennis	tennis
au basket	basketball
au foot	soccer
au football américain	football
à des jeux vidéo	video games
jouer (de) + instruments de musique	to play . . .
du piano	piano
de la guitare	guitar
faire (de) + sports/activités	to go / to do . . .
du jogging	jogging
du lèche-vitrines	window-shopping
des courses	shopping
être...	to be . . .
musicien(-enne)	a musician
dans un groupe (de musique)	in a band
sportif(-ive)	athletic
membre d'une équipe	on a team

---

[1] Although technically an invariable adjective, it has become common to see it written with an -s in the plural; there is no alternate feminine spelling.

[2] Note that **pantalon, jean,** and **short** are all singular in French, whereas they are plural in English: **J'aime ton pantalon gris. Il porte un jean. Elle s'achète un short kaki.**

Vocabulaire

PRÉPARATION GRAMMATICALE

Avant de continuer, révisez la formation et le placement des adjectifs qualificatifs, pages 154–158.

A Vive les différences! Anne et Philippe sont de très bons amis, mais ils ne se ressemblent pas du tout—ni physiquement, ni de caractère. Décrivez Anne, en changeant les éléments nécessaires dans la description de Philippe.

Philippe est un homme costaud et plutôt laid. Il a les cheveux courts et frisés, le visage rond, le nez busqué et les lèvres charnues. Il a l'air endormi, et ses amis le trouvent insensible, rouspéteur et paresseux. Il porte toujours des vêtements sales et démodés. Il passe son temps à jouer à des jeux vidéo.

B Comment dit-on? Trouvez l'adjectif de la liste B du vocabulaire qui correspond à chacune des définitions suivantes.

1. qui s'exprime ouvertement, en toute honnêteté
2. qui n'attire pas l'attention
3. qui manque d'humanité, d'indulgence
4. qui évite l'effort
5. qui ne ressent pas d'émotions
6. qui ne se met pas en colère
7. qui est plein de vie, de vivacité
8. qui sait se tirer facilement d'affaire

RAPPEL In French, descriptive adjectives agree in *gender* (masculine / feminine) and in *number* (singular / plural) with the nouns or pronouns they modify. Although descriptive adjectives usually follow the nouns they modify, some short ones come before. A few adjectives change meaning depending on whether they precede or follow the noun they modify. For more details, see pages 154–158.

C Comment sont-ils? Décrivez en détail l'apparence de chacune des quatre personnes suivantes, en utilisant les listes A et C du vocabulaire.

1.

2.

3.

4.

© Monkey Business Images/Shutterstock.com

© Kevin Dodge/Corbis

D **Les « people ».** Choisissez une des personnes de la liste suivante et décrivez-la. Utilisez au moins trois adjectifs qui décrivent l'apparence et le caractère de cette personne.

1. Michelle Obama
2. Homer Simpson
3. Kate Middleton
4. le Prince Harry
5. Beyoncé
6. le président de la République française
7. Angelina Jolie
8. David Beckham

E **Pour faire le portrait...** Travaillez avec un(e) camarade de classe. Votre camarade va faire votre portrait et vous allez faire le sien.

1. Décrivez en détail l'apparence de votre partenaire en utilisant les listes A et C du vocabulaire.
2. Ensuite, essayez de deviner son caractère (toujours par écrit) en vous basant sur son apparence. Cette fois, utilisez le vocabulaire de la liste B.
3. Finalement, lisez à tour de rôle la description que vous avez faite de votre partenaire et réagissez à ce que vous entendez.
4. Dites à la classe si vous trouvez que votre partenaire vous a bien décrit(e) et justifiez votre opinion.

F **Les différences.** De temps en temps, nous voyons ou rencontrons des gens qui nous semblent bien différents, ou qui ont simplement l'air bizarre. Prenez quelques minutes pour réfléchir à la personne la plus « étrange » que vous ayez jamais vue. Faites-en une description précise en répondant aux questions suivantes.

1. Où était cette personne?
2. Que portait-elle?
3. Comment était cette personne, physiquement?
4. Du point de vue du caractère, comment vous imaginez-vous cette personne?
5. Que faisait cette personne?

Lecture

L'Agence du Service Civique, Groupement d'Intérêt Public, a été créée en France le 12 mai 2010. Toute personne de 16 à 25 ans peut effectuer son service civique, et les missions durent de 6 à 12 mois. Au total, selon les situations, les volontaires sont payés entre 548,14 € et 649,82 €/mois et ils bénéficient d'une protection sociale intégrale.

ENTRONS EN MATIERE

Avez-vous jamais fait du service civique? Si oui, racontez ce que vous avez fait. Est-ce que cela vous a plu? Si vous n'en avez jamais fait, voudriez-vous en faire un un jour? Quelle sorte de service civique vous intéresserait?

E. Perriot/Secours Catholique

Les jeunes plébiscitent le service civique

Lors de sa création, en mars 2010, rien ne garantissait que le service civique allait séduire les jeunes Français. Un an après, une étude TNS Sofres[3] révèle que cette nouvelle forme d'engagement rémunérée attire un public varié, qui y trouve surtout un intérêt personnel. 76% des jeunes inscrits sur le site Internet de l'Agence du
5   service civique estiment ainsi que cette expérience sera avant tout valorisante pour leur parcours professionnel et enrichira dans un premier temps leur curriculum vitae. Ce bénéfice individuel est cité comme le principal atout° de la formule, devant la satisfaction de pouvoir se rendre utile aux autres.

    En 2011, 15 000 jeunes pourront effectuer une mission d'intérêt général, en France
10   ou à l'étranger, dans les domaines de la solidarité°, de la santé, de l'environnement ou de la culture. Or° ils sont près de 45 000 à avoir déjà déposé, à ce jour, une candidature sur

atout avantage

solidarité action humanitaire / **or** *but*

[3] Sondage réalisé par Internet du 1er au 17 mars, auprès d'un échantillon de 2 143 jeunes, pour l'Agence du service civique.

Internet. Le niveau scolaire des candidats est, lui, très varié: 28% ont le bac, 20% sont même diplômés et possèdent une licence ou un master, 27% ont un brevet ou un BEP[4] Ils sont aussi 18% à n'avoir aucune qualification. On retrouve dans ce public une plus
15 large proportion de filles (elles sont 61%), mais tous les âges, de 16 à 25 ans, sont représentés de manière équilibrée. « 18% des inscrits ont moins de 18 ans », remarque Martin Hirsch, président de l'Agence.

Les témoignages des jeunes engagés attestent du bénéfice personnel retiré de cette expérience. En mission au Mémorial de la Shoah[5], David, 20 ans, estime avoir ac-
20 quis des compétences en communication qu'il utilisera plus tard, lorsqu'il aura repris ses études. « J'ai le sentiment d'être devenu plus adulte et de m'être enrichi », ajoute cet étudiant notamment chargé d'accueillir les descendants de déportés venus confier leurs documents personnels au Mémorial. « Ce genre de parcours° interpelle et marque les esprits des employeurs », remarque de son côté Lina, diplômée de
25 HEC[6], qui a effectué une mission au sein du groupe SOS, association spécialisée dans l'accompagnement des exclus°, avant son premier emploi. « C'est une façon de montrer qu'on sort du lot° ».

parcours ici: travail

exclus les pauvres, les SDF, les vieux, etc. / **sortir du lot** *to stand out*

Adapté de: © Delphine Chayet / Lefigaro.fr / 22.04.2011

COMPRENEZ-VOUS?

1. Pour quelle(s) raison(s) les jeunes Français s'intéressent-ils aux missions offertes par l'Agence du Service Civique?
2. Quelle sorte de travail peut-on faire pour cette agence?
3. Dans sa première année, quel pourcentage des candidats a été engagé par cette agence pour un service civique?
4. Est-ce que la majorité des participants font ce service immédiatement après être sortis du lycée?
5. En quoi le bénéfice personnel retiré par David diffère-t-il de celui de Lina, selon leurs propres explications?

CHERCHEZ LA FORME

1. Dans le premier paragraphe on trouve le mot « tout » (ligne 5) et dans le deuxième paragraphe on trouve « tous » (ligne 15). Expliquez les fonctions de ces deux mots dans le contexte.
2. Dans la deuxième phrase du texte (lignes 2-4), on trouve l'exemple d'un adjectif qui précède le nom qu'il qualifie. Lequel? Quelles sont les autres formes de cet adjectif (masculin singulier, masculin et féminin pluriel)?

ALLEZ PLUS LOIN

Pourquoi, à votre avis, y a-t-il plus de filles que de garçons qui s'intéressent au service civique en France?

[4] Abréviation de Brevet d'Etudes Professionnelles
[5] http://www.memorialdelashoah.org/
[6] Hautes Etudes Commerciales (une des Grandes Ecoles en France)

Applications

Avant de continuer, révisez le comparatif et le superlatif de l'adjectif qualificatif, pages 158–159.

PREPARATION GRAMMATICALE

A **Vous et les autres.** Comparez-vous aux personnes suivantes.

Modèle: sensible, votre meilleur(e) ami(e)
Je suis (plus / moins / aussi) sensible que mon (ma) meilleur(e) ami(e).

1. sportif, votre meilleur(e) ami(e)
2. discret, Lady Gaga
3. paresseux, votre professeur de français
4. impoli, votre grand-mère
5. décontracté, vos parents
6. rouspéteur, votre voisin
7. conservateur, le président des États-Unis
8. travailleur, votre camarade de chambre
9. intelligent, Albert Einstein
10. riche, Bill Gates

PREPARATION GRAMMATICALE

Avant de continuer, révisez les formes interrogatives, pages 160–163.

B **Quelle curiosité!** Un jeune Français va passer les vacances d'été chez vous, et il veut vous connaître un peu mieux avant d'arriver. Il vous pose beaucoup de questions! Voici vos réponses. Quelles sont ses questions?

1. Je suis grand et mince, avec les yeux marron et le nez droit. J'ai la tête rasée.
2. J'habite tout près de la ville de San Francisco.
3. Ma maison est très spacieuse, avec beaucoup de lumière.
4. Il y a quatre personnes dans ma famille.
5. Ces quatre personnes sont ma mère, mon père, mon frère et moi.
6. Ma mère s'appelle Alice, mon père s'appelle Tom et mon frère s'appelle Bob.
7. Mes sports préférés sont le tennis et la natation.
8. Nous partirons à la plage une semaine après ton arrivée.
9. Le soir, je vais souvent au cinéma.
10. Nous t'invitons chez nous parce que nous aimons rencontrer des gens d'autres cultures.

C **L'interrogation continue!** Le jeune Français de l'exercice B est arrivé chez vous, et il veut tout savoir sur vos amis, vos études, vos passe-temps, etc. Avec un(e) camarade de classe, jouez cette scène. Une personne joue le rôle du jeune Français et pose trois questions auxquelles l'autre personne répond. Utilisez les mots et expressions interrogatifs suivants. Après trois questions, changez de rôle.

Mots et expressions interrogatifs:

qu'est-ce qui	lequel (laquelle, etc.)	comment
quand	pourquoi	que

D « Turbo-Dating »… la version française de *Speed Dating.*

Avez-vous déjà participé à une soirée « speed dating »? Savez-vous comment ces rencontres se déroulent? En France, le site web de l'organisation « Turbo-Dating » (http://www.turbo-dating.com) annonce la date et le lieu des soirées à venir et explique les règles du jeu. Informez-vous en lisant les phrases suivantes, et complétez chaque phrase avec la forme de **tout** qui convient.

1. Turbo-Dating est ouvert à _____ les personnes, sans restriction.
2. Ces rendez-vous sont parfaits pour _____ ceux qui veulent élargir leur cercle de connaissances.
3. _____ ces soirées ont lieu dans un restaurant ou un club, et on doit payer l'entrée et le prix d'une consommation.
4. _____ ceux qui sont inscrits reçoivent un badge avec un numéro dessus.
5. _____ commence quand à chaque table il y a un homme et une femme l'un en face de l'autre.
6. _____ les dix minutes, il faut que les hommes se déplacent pour parler avec une femme différente.
7. On peut parler de _____ les sujets sauf son nom, son adresse, son travail, ou son salaire.
8. Après huit à dix rencontres, les participants sont _____ invités à remplir un formulaire afin de savoir s'ils aimeraient revoir une ou plusieurs des personnes avec qui ils ont parlé.
9. Pour indiquer son choix, on note _____ simplement le numéro du badge.
10. S'il y a réciprocité dans le choix, l'homme et la femme recevront _____ les deux l'e-mail de l'autre.

E   Généralisation ou vérité? Quand on parle de groupes de personnes
(comment ils sont, ce qu'ils font, etc.), on a tendance à ignorer des différences subtiles mais importantes entre les personnes du groupe. Faites un commentaire sur un des groupes suivants, en utilisant une forme de **tout** et le vocabulaire du chapitre dans votre phrase. Puis, demandez à la classe d'évaluer l'exactitude de votre observation.

     les étudiant(e)s de votre âge
     les chanteurs de rap
     les professeurs
     les parents
     les Français(es)
     les Américain(e)s

F Qui est Carla Bruni?

1. Complétez ce texte avec **il/elle** ou **c'.**

Carla Bruni est l'épouse du sixième président de la Vᵉ République française, Nicolas Sarkozy. (1) _____ est svelte, a les yeux bleus et de longs cheveux bruns et raides. (2) _____ est une femme qui mesure 1m76 *(5'9")* et qui semble encore plus grande à côté de son mari, puisque Sarkozy, (3) _____ est un homme qui ne mesure qu' 1m68 *(5'6")*. Née en Italie, Carla Bruni est la fille d'un compositeur et industriel et d'une pianiste et actrice, bien que son père biologique soit un homme d'affaires italien vivant au Brésil. (4) _____ est une famille très riche, qui s'est installée en France quand Carla avait cinq ans. (5) _____ est intéressant de lire la biographie de Mme Bruni-Sarkozy parce que (6) _____ est une femme qui a déjà vécu une vie personnelle et professionnelle pleine de changements et pourtant (7) _____ est relativement jeune, ayant fêté ses 44 ans en décembre 2011. (8) _____ est une chanteuse qui a sorti son troisième album en juillet 2008, cinq mois après son mariage avec Sarkozy. (9) _____ est aussi connue pour sa carrière de mannequin de 1987 à 1997. La vie privée de Carla Bruni, (10) _____ est loin de celle qu'on imagine pour une première dame. (11) _____ est une femme séduisante qui a eu de nombreuses liaisons avec des hommes célèbres avant son mariage (Eric Clapton, Mick Jagger, Donald Trump, Kevin Costner, l'acteur français Charles Berling, le chanteur français Jean-Jacques Goldman, entre autres). (12) _____ est aussi une mère de famille, car elle a eu un fils en 2001 avec le philosophe Raphaël Enthoven, et une fille en 2011 avec Sarkozy.

2. Continuez cet exercice avec un(e) partenaire. En vous basant sur le paragraphe décrivant Carla Bruni, rédigez une description et une biographie de Michelle Obama, l'épouse du 44ᵉ président des États-Unis, Barack Obama. Suivez le même format, en mettant dans ce portrait autant de phrases que possible avec la construction **il/elle** ou **c'est.**

Lecture

ENTRONS EN MATIERE

Aujourd'hui les nouvelles technologies facilitent les rencontres virtuelles. Faites une liste de ces technologies et des genres de rencontre possibles. Quels en sont les avantages et les inconvénients? Y a-t-il des dangers? Connaissez-vous des gens qui se sont connus virtuellement avant de se rencontrer en personne? Comment leur relation a-t-elle évolué?

AVANT DE LIRE

Le texte que vous allez lire est la transcription des paroles d'une chanson de la rappeuse française Diam's (de son vrai nom Mélanie Georgiades), née en 1980 d'une mère française et d'un père cypriote. Elle raconte qu'à 14 ans elle a pris son pseudonyme après avoir appris qu'un diamant « ne peut être brisé que par un autre diamant et qu'il n'est fait que d'éléments naturels ».[7] En 2005, son second album, *Brut de femme*,

---

[7] Interview (http://www.zicline.com/dossiers/diams/diams.htm)

devient un double disque d'or avec plus de 200 000 exemplaires vendus; et en 2007 Diam's reçoit le MTV « European music award » de l'artiste française de l'année. Diam's est une chanteuse engagée politiquement, ayant milité pour Amnesty International et pour un vote des jeunes contre le Front national.

Une chanson, par définition, existe pour être entendue, pas pour être lue. Alors, avant de passer à la lecture de « Jeune demoiselle », faites un petit exercice d'écoute, en notant en même temps sur une feuille de papier toutes les références aux personnes et aux choses que vous reconnaissez. Ensuite, mettez-vous avec un ou plusieurs camarades de classe, comparez les références que vous avez notées, et organisez-les dans les catégories suivantes: musique, cinéma, télévision, sports. Quelles conclusions tirez-vous de ces références?

Après ce premier exercice d'écoute, lisez les paroles, puis répondez aux questions qui suivent.

Jeune demoiselle

Jeune demoiselle recherche un mec° mortel
Un mec qui pourrait me donner des ailes°
Un mec fidèle et qui n'a pas peur qu'on l'aime
Donc si t'as les critères babe laisse-moi ton e-mail
5 Jeune demoiselle recherche un mec mortel
Un mec qui pourrait me donner des ailes
Un mec qui rêve de famille et de toucher le ciel
Donc si t'as les critères babe laisse-moi ton e-mail

Dans mes rêves mon mec à moi a la voix de Musiq Soulchild[8]
10 Il a du charme et du style à la Beckham
Il a la classe et le feeling tout droit sorti d'un film
Le charisme de Jay-Z[9] et le sourire de Brad Pitt
Mon mec à moi n'aime pas les bimbo
Non, il aime les formes de J-Lo
15 Il a le torse de D'Angelo[10]
Dans mes rêves mon mec me fait rire comme Jamel[11]
Et me fait la cour sur du Cabrel[12]

mec homme (*familier*)
ailes *wings*

---

[8] (Taalib Johnson); artiste afro-américain de nu-soul, R&B, hip-hop, funk; né en 1977
[9] (Shawn Corey Carter); rappeur et entrepreneur afro-américain; né en 1969
[10] Prononcé "Di-Angelo" (Michael D'Angelo Archer); chanteur, pianiste, guitariste, compositeur et producteur afro-américain; né en 1974.
[11] Jamel Debbouze; comique et acteur français; né en France (1975) de parents marocains
[12] Francis Cabrel; auteur, compositeur, chanteur français très marqué par la musique de Bob Dylan; né en 1953

Refrain

Pom pom pom pom
20 Dans mes rêves mon mec m'enlève et m'emmène
Pom pom pom pom
Dans mes rêves mon mec m'aime et me rend belle
Pom pom pom pom
Dans mes rêves mon mec m'enlève et m'emmène
Pom pom pom pom
25 Si t'as les critères babe laisse-moi ton e-mail

Dans mes rêves mon mec me parle tout bas
Quand il m'écrit des lettres il a la plume de Booba[13]
Mon mec a des valeurs et du respect pour ses sœurs
Il a du cœur et quand il danse mon mec c'est Usher[14]
30 Pom pom pom pom

un peu barge un peu fou   Un peu barge° dans sa tête à la Dave Chappelle[15]
Il m'appelle tout le temps car il m'aime
Mon mec regarde Scarface,[16] les Affranchis[17]
Casino mais aussi Friends, Lost et les Sopranos
35 Mon mec est clean mais au-delà du style
Mon mec c'est une encyclopédie car il se cultive

ouais oui / **beau gosse** beau   Bah ouais° mon mec est top entre l'intello et le beau gosse°
garçon   Et peu m'importe qu'il se balade en Porsche

Refrain

Pom pom pom pom
40 Dans mes rêves mon mec m'enlève et m'emmène
Pom pom pom pom
Dans mes rêves mon mec m'aime et me rend belle
Pom pom pom pom
Dans mes rêves mon mec m'enlève et m'emmène
45 Pom pom pom pom
Si t'as les critères babe laisse-moi ton e-mail

---

[13] (Elie Yaffa); compositeur, et rappeur français; né en 1976
[14] (Usher Raymond IV); chanteur de R&B, danseur, parolier, et acteur afro-américain; né en 1978
[15] acteur comique, scénariste et producteur afro-américain; né en 1973
[16] 1983 film policier de Brian De Palma
[17] 1990 film policier de Martin Scorsese

Dans mes rêves mon mec a la carrière d'Eminem[18]
Il a des airs de minet° quand il m'emmène en week-end
Mon mec fait mal au crâne il a le calme de Zidane[19]
50 Et le regard de Method Man[20]
Mon mec c'est Hitch[21] il insiste
Mon mec sait prendre des risques et ne regarde pas les bitches
Non mon mec connaît les femmes et sait bien qu'on est chiante°
Qu'on gueule° tout le temps pour savoir quand il rentre
55 Mon mec est bon ouais mon mec est complet
Mon mec c'est un peu de mon ex mélangé à mon père
Dans la vie mon mec est digne à la Mohamed Ali[22]
Et ses potes° me font rire à la Éric et Ramzy[23]

Refrain

Pom pom pom pom
60 Dans mes rêves mon mec m'enlève et m'emmène
Pom pom pom pom
Dans mes rêves mon mec m'aime et me rend belle
Pom pom pom pom
Dans mes rêves mon mec m'enlève et m'emmène
65 Pom pom pom pom
Si t'as les critères babe laisse-moi ton e-mail

Hein j' t'ai pas trouvé sur la planète
J'te trouverais p't être sur Internet qui sait?
Diam's victime de l'an 2000
70 Tous les moyens sont bons pour trouver l'homme de sa vie

PS: l'adresse e-mail c'est jeunedemoisellerecherche@hotmail.fr
Si vous pouvez joindre 2 photos
Parce qu'une, on sait qu' c'est d' la triche°

----

minet jeune homme vêtu à la mode; terme d'affection ou terme péjoratif

chiante ennuyeuse *(familier)*
gueuler *to yell at (familier)*

pote copain *(familier)*

tricher *to cheat*

JEUNE DEMOISELLE
Paroles : Mélanie Georgiades
Musique : Mélanie Georgiades / Michel Fleurent / Luc Ollivier / Yann Le Men
© Universal Music Publishing (catalogue Universal Music Publishing MGB France)
« Avec l'aimable autorisation d'Universal Music Publishing »

----

[18] (Marshall Bruce Mathers III); musicien, producteur de rap, producteur; né en 1972
[19] Footballeur français; né en 1972 à Marseille, de parents berbères
[20] (Clifford Smith); rappeur afro-américain; né en 1971
[21] Nom du personnage principal du film américain du même nom sorti en 2005; joué par Will Smith; c'est un « expert en séduction »
[22] Boxeur américain; né en 1942
[23] Éric Judor (1969) et Ramzy Bédia (1972); duo d'humoristes français

COMPRENEZ-VOUS?

1. À votre avis, quel est le sens du mot « mortel » dans le contexte des deux premières strophes (vers 1–17)?
2. En vous basant sur ce que vous savez des personnes mentionnées dans les vers 9–17, commencez à faire le portrait de l'homme idéal de Diam's en notant quatre de ses caractéristiques.
3. Dans la même strophe, expliquez le sens des vers 13–14.
4. Comment expliquez-vous « avoir du cœur », troisième strophe, vers 29?
5. Comment expliquez-vous « mon mec est clean », troisième strophe, vers 35?
6. En vous basant sur ce que vous savez des personnes et des choses mentionnées aux vers 26–38 de la troisième strophe, donnez quatre autres précisions en ce qui concerne l'homme idéal de Diam's.
7. À votre avis, cet homme doit-il être riche? Justifiez votre réponse en citant le texte.
8. En vous basant sur ce que vous savez des personnes mentionnées aux vers 47–58 de la quatrième strophe, ajoutez encore quatre détails concernant cet homme idéal.
9. Pourquoi pourrait-on dire que le refrain donne l'impression que Diam's est une fille très romantique?
10. Pourquoi pourrait-on dire que la dernière partie de la chanson (vers 67–73) donne l'image d'une fille très pratique?
11. En vous référant aux trois mini-portraits que vous avez faits pour répondre aux questions 2, 4 et 8, esquissez maintenant un portrait complet et détaillé de ce « mec mortel ».

CHERCHEZ LA FORME

1. Dans les paroles de cette chanson, il y a trois verbes qui font partie de ce groupe de verbes qui changent d'accent ou qui doublent une consonne selon la forme utilisée: [il] m'enlève [il] m'emmène [il] m'appelle.

   Imaginez que Diam's utilise ces trois verbes en parlant directement à son prince charmant—de façon familière (**tu**) et de façon formelle (**vous).** Faites les changements nécessaires.

2. Dans ce texte, trouvez deux exemples du faire causatif—le premier au singulier et le deuxième au pluriel. Indiquez à quels vers se trouvent ces exemples.

ALLEZ PLUS LOIN

Imaginez que Diam's décide de refaire cette chanson du point de vue d'un homme qui cherche sa femme idéale, et qu'elle intitule cette nouvelle version *Jeune homme cherche nana canon.* Rédigez la première strophe et le refrain (vers 1–25) en vous servant de noms de personnes, de choses et d'endroits de votre choix.

Activités d'expansion

 Rendez-vous sur le site web de *Sur le vif* pour regardez la vidéo du Chapitre 2, puis complétez les activités à la page 33 du **Student Activities Manual**.

A **Les «mecs» de Diam's** Trouvez une personne mentionnée par Diam's dans sa chanson « Jeune demoiselle » que vous ne connaissez pas. Informez-vous sur cette personne, et trouvez sa photo sur le web. Ensuite, écrivez une description physique de cette personne à partager avec les autres membres de la classe. Servez-vous du vocabulaire du chapitre pour rendre votre portrait très riche et détaillé.

B **Se faire remarquer**

1. Est-ce qu'il y a des looks particuliers que l'on adopte sur votre campus? Lesquels? Avec un(e) partenaire, choisissez un look que vous avez tous (toutes) les deux remarqué. Est-ce que vous avez réagi à ce look de la même façon que votre partenaire? Comparez vos réactions et essayez de les analyser.
2. Il y a des gens qui veulent se faire remarquer *(make a statement)* par leur façon de s'habiller, de se coiffer, de se maquiller, etc. Trouvez un(e) partenaire et discutez des gens que vous connaissez qui veulent se faire remarquer. Qui sont-ils? Que font-ils pour se distinguer des autres? Pourquoi, à votre avis, veulent-ils être « différents »?

© Clare Tufts

C **Un savoir-vivre mobile?**

Tout le monde se sert d'un téléphone portable, quel que soit son âge, mais chacun a ses propres idées sur l'usage que l'on peut en faire dans un lieu public. Est-il convenable, par exemple, de dire à quelqu'un qu'il parle trop fort au téléphone dans un lieu public? Est-ce qu'il vaut mieux ne pas répondre à un appel si vous vous trouvez dans une salle d'attente, un bus ou un autre lieu où les autres personnes présentes seraient obligées d'écouter votre conversation? Est-ce une mauvaise idée de répondre à un appel, ou de recevoir ou d'envoyer des SMS pendant un repas avec d'autres personnes (votre famille ou des amis, par exemple)? Est-il admissible d'écouter les messages, de lire les SMS ou de consulter le journal d'appels dans le téléphone mobile de quelqu'un d'autre (de ses parents, de ses enfants ou de ses amis)? Êtes-vous pour ou contre l'accès au téléphone mobile dans un avion pendant le vol? Pourquoi?

Vocabulaire utile:

allumer/éteindre
prendre un appel/mettre en mode vibreur/laisser un message

Les immigrés

🔊 A PRESENT OU PASSE?

Pour parler du présent	Pour parler du passé
aujourd'hui	hier
à notre époque	à cette époque-là
	en ce temps-là[1]
de nos jours	il y a... heure(s)
actuellement	... jour(s)
à l'heure actuelle	... an(s)
maintenant	autrefois

© Clare Tufts

© Clare Tufts

B L'IMMIGRATION

Mots apparentés: l'immigré(e), immigrer, l'intégration f., s'intégrer (à, dans), le passeport, le visa, le (la) réfugié(e), ethnique, la colonie, coloniser

accueillir	*to welcome, to greet*
l'accueil[2] m.	*welcome, reception*
accueillant(e)	*welcoming*
la carte de séjour	*residence permit*
les papiers m.	*identity papers*
la cité	*(here) high-rise public housing*
l'immigration f. clandestine	*illegal immigration*
le sans-papiers	*illegal immigrant (person without proper identity papers)*
l'ethnie f.	*ethnic group*

[1] Pour parler d'un moment dans le passé on peut choisir entre **à cette époque-là** et **en ce temps-là**. Le sens est le même.

[2] The word **accueil** means how something or someone is received. To say "Welcome!" as a greeting: **Soyez le (la) bienvenu(e)!**

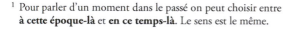

Pour obtenir des exercices et activités supplémentaires sur le contenu de ce chapitre, rendez-vous sur le site
www.cengagebrain.com

C QUESTIONS SOCIALES

Mots apparentés: la tolérance, tolérant(e), l'égalité *f.*, l'inégalité *f.*, les inégalités sociales, le racisme, le (la) raciste, la pauvreté, le (la) pauvre, la richesse, le (la) riche, la bourgeoisie, le (la) bourgeois(e), le (la) propriétaire

le chômage	unemployment
être au chômage	to be unemployed
le (la) chômeur(-euse)	unemployed person
le (la) sans-abri, le (la) SDF[3]	homeless person
mendier	to beg
le préjugé	prejudice

D LA VIE ACTIVE

QUOI?

faire une demande (d'emploi), poser sa candidature	to apply (for a job)
le formulaire	form, application
remplir un formulaire	to fill out a form
la lettre de candidature, la lettre de motivation	cover letter, application letter
le CV	curriculum vitae, job résumé
l'entretien *m.*	interview
passer un entretien (d'embauche)	to be interviewed (for a job)
le boulot *(fam.)*	job, work
le poste	position, job
le CDI (contrat à durée indéterminée)	open-ended contract
le CDD (contrat à durée déterminée)	fixed-term contract
le métier	trade, job
les travaux domestiques *m. pl.*	domestic work
les petits travaux *m. pl.*	odd jobs
embaucher	to hire
gagner sa vie	to earn one's living

[3] sans domicile fixe (invariable au pluriel, comme « sans abri »).

le salaire	salary
travailler	to work
à plein temps	full-time
à mi-temps	half-time
à temps partiel	part-time
comme bénévole	as a volunteer
faire grève	to go on strike
faire de l'intérim	to temp
une agence d'intérim	temp agency
faire un stage	to do an internship
le (la) stagiaire	intern
licencier	to lay off
renvoyer	to fire

QUI?

Mots apparentés: l'employé(e), l'employeur(-euse)

le (la) salarié(e)	wage-earner
l'ouvrier(-ière)	blue-collar worker
saisonnier(-ière)	seasonal worker
non qualifié(e)	unskilled
le (la) patron(ne)	boss
le PDG[4]	CEO
le (la) bénévole	volunteer
l'association *f.* caritative	charitable organization

OÙ?

l'usine *f.*	factory
le chantier	construction site
l'atelier *m.*	workshop
textile	textile mill
d'artiste	artist's studio
le bureau	office
le champ	field
l'entreprise *f.*	business, company

[4] président-directeur général

© Clare Tufts

Vocabulaire

A **Réactions personnelles.** Choisissez un mot des listes B ou C du vocabulaire. Circulez dans la classe et demandez à trois camarades de classe ce qu'ils associent au mot que vous avez choisi, puis partagez ces associations de pensée avec le reste de la classe.

> **Modèle:** **Vous:** A quoi penses-tu quand je dis « chômage »?
> **Autre Etudiant(e):** **Je pense à la pauvreté, au travail, au malheur…**

B **Trouvez le mot.** Voici les définitions de dix mots de la liste D du vocabulaire. Trouvez les mots définis.

1. chef d'une entreprise industrielle ou commerciale
2. engager des salariés
3. renvoyer des employés pour des raisons économiques
4. une personne qui fait un travail gratuitement
5. rendez-vous entre une personne qui cherche des employés et une personne qui cherche du travail
6. feuille comportant des questions auxquelles il faut répondre
7. document sur lequel le candidat à un poste décrit sa formation et son expérience
8. personne qui travaille pendant une période limitée, le plus souvent dans le secteur agricole
9. travail de durée limitée, souvent sans salaire, effectué dans le but d'acquérir de l'expérience professionnelle
10. faire le travail de quelqu'un d'autre pendant une période de temps limité

C **Le contraire.** Trouvez l'antonyme (le contraire) des mots ou expressions de la liste ci-dessous.

1. avoir un emploi
2. la richesse
3. une personne qui a un endroit fixe où habiter
4. la supériorité ou l'infériorité
5. une personne qui a une carte de séjour
6. embaucher
7. un CDI

D **Positive ou négative?** Dans les listes de vocabulaire, choisissez cinq mots à connotation positive et cinq mots à connotation négative. Comparez votre liste avec celle d'un(e) camarade de classe et échangez vos points de vue.

E **Un reportage.** En groupes de trois ou quatre étudiants, choisissez l'un des sujets de la liste suivante. Ensemble, préparez cinq questions pour faire un reportage.

Modèle: l'immigration
D'où viennent la plupart des immigrés?

1. l'immigration
2. le racisme
3. les inégalités sociales
4. le chômage

© Jean-Paul Pelissier/Reuters/Landov

PRÉPARATION GRAMMATICALE

Avant de continuer, révisez la formation et l'usage du passé composé et de l'imparfait, pages 165–169.

Lecture

Dans ce texte sans titre, Francis Bebey (1929–2001), chanteur, musicien, musicologue, et aussi conteur, poète et romancier originaire du Cameroun, présente les sentiments d'un homme qui doit quitter sa patrie pour chercher du travail en France.

POUR MIEUX COMPRENDRE

Lisez la première strophe. Qui parle? De quoi s'agit-il?

A la recherche d'un travail

 CD 1, track 3

lointain à une grande distance

Je suis venu chercher du travail
J'espère qu'il y en aura
Je suis venu de mon lointain° pays
Pour travailler chez vous

5 J'ai tout laissé, ma femme, mes amis
Au pays tout là-bas
J'espère les retrouver tous en vie
Le jour de mon retour

En… Quand elle m'a vu

Ma pauvre mère était bien désolée
10 En me voyant° partir
Je lui ai dit qu'un jour je reviendrai
Mettre fin à sa misère

parcouru fait

J'ai parcouru° de longs jours de voyage
Pour venir jusqu'ici
15 Ne m'a-t-on pas assuré d'un accueil
Qui vaudrait bien cette peine°

vaudrait… would be worth so much trouble

Regardez-moi, je suis fatigué
D'aller par les chemins
Voici des jours que je n'ai rien mangé
20 Auriez-vous un peu de pain?

déchiré torn

Mon pantalon est tout déchiré°
Mais je n'en ai pas d'autre
Ne criez pas, ce n'est pas un scandale
Je suis seulement pauvre

25 Je suis venu chercher du travail
J'espère qu'il y en aura
Je suis venu de mon lointain pays
Pour travailler chez vous.

Francis BEBEY - Je suis venu chercher du travail in *Anthologie africaine II : Poésie de Jacques Chevrier*, Coll. Monde Noir Poche © HATIER, 1988 © EDITIONS HATIER INTERNATIONAL - Paris 2002

COMPRENEZ-VOUS?

1. Après avoir lu ce texte, que savez-vous sur le pays d'où vient le narrateur?
2. Comment sa famille a-t-elle réagi quand il a décidé de partir?
3. Est-ce que le narrateur a l'intention de rester en France? Justifiez votre réponse.
4. Décrivez l'apparence et les émotions du narrateur.
5. Comment les gens qui le voient ou à qui il parle réagissent-ils? Justifiez votre réponse.
6. Comment la structure du poème (répétition de la première strophe en fin de texte) souligne-t-elle le message de l'auteur?

ET LE TITRE?

Puisque le poète n'a pas donné de titre à son poème, trouvez-lui-en un. Ne citez pas un des vers du poème.

CHERCHEZ LA FORME

Faites une liste de tous les verbes conjugués du poème. Identifiez le temps de chaque verbe et expliquez pourquoi le poète a utilisé ce temps.

> **RAPPEL** There are two major tenses for talking about the past in French. The **passé composé** tells *what happened* in the past, the imperfect (**l'imparfait**) describes *how things were*, i.e., the conditions in the past. For more details, see pages 165–169.

Applications

A **Une histoire d'immigration réussie.** Nadia, une jeune femme d'origine algérienne, raconte l'histoire de ses parents. Mettez son récit au passé composé en faisant tous les changements nécessaires.

En 1952, mon père, à dix-sept ans, traverse la Méditerranée et trouve immédiatement un travail comme poseur de rails (*laying railroad tracks*). Dans les années qui suivent, il fait venir ses frères et ses neveux. Au bout d'une quinzaine d'années il réussit à acheter une petite maison et il décide de repartir repartir en Algérie pour se marier. Peu après, il revient avec sa femme. Ses frères laissent leurs épouses au village et vivent dans des foyers de travailleurs. Ma mère se voit donc brutalement transplantée dans un monde étranger. Mais elle s'adapte bien parce qu'elle peut suivre des cours de français et d'alphabétisation (*literacy*).

B **Autrefois.** Marianne Mathéus, artiste guadeloupéenne, parle du tabou de ses origines, du fait d'être descendante d'esclave. Mettez la description à l'imparfait.

Dans mon enfance, on ne parle pas de l'esclavage, on l'évoque de manière allusive, comme s'il y a un malaise à en parler. Pourtant ce n'est pas si vieux: c'est du temps de nos arrière-grands-parents. Dans les familles antillaises, l'éducation est très sévère, les enfants sont très tenus (*children are kept on a tight leash*). On nous demande beaucoup, nous avons moins le droit à l'erreur que les autres, nous devons travailler plus que les autres. On nous transmet une sorte de complexe. Je ne sais pas que nous sommes descendants d'esclaves, cela ne se dit pas.

Adapté de: *Le français dans le monde*, N° 352

C **Un ancien soldat.** Guy Etienne Ahizi Elliam, originaire de Côte d'Ivoire, raconte pourquoi et comment il s'est engagé dans l'armée française pendant la Deuxième Guerre mondiale. Mettez tous les verbes en caractère gras au temps du passé approprié. Notez que le passé composé devient ici le plus-que-parfait.

Quand la Deuxième Guerre mondiale **éclate** j'**ai** 16 ans. Je **veux** m'engager dans l'armée, mais on me **dit** : « Non, vous êtes trop petit, revenez quand vous serez majeur ». A l'époque, la Côte d'Ivoire est une colonie française. Je **nais** le 21 juillet 1924 à Grand-Bassam, à côté d'Abidjan, la première capitale de la Côte d'Ivoire, où les Français **débarquent** pour la première fois. Moi je me **sens** Français. Quand la France est envahie, je **dis**: « Les pauvres, il faut aller à leur secours ». Alors à 19 ans, je **viens** de finir mes études d'instituteur à l'Ecole normale et je **pars** à la guerre. Il y **a** d'autres volontaires, mais ils **sont** peu nombreux. Certains même **ont fui** le pays parce que parfois, on **prend** les gens sans leur demander, s'ils **sont** costauds et **ont** l'âge qu'il faut. C'**est** un idéal d'aller en France. Ceux d'avant, qui **ont fait** 14–18, **racontent** le soir et nous **sommes** émerveillés. Nous aussi, on voulait voir comment c'était, là-bas. Je voulais m'engager pour la vie, jusqu'à ma mort, mais le règlement, c'était seulement cinq ans renouvelables ».

Adapté de: Histoires singulières, http://www.histoire-immigration.fr/

D **Un sans-papiers.** Sema, un jeune Malien, est revenu dans son village au Mali et il parle de son séjour difficile en France. Mettez les infinitifs au **passé composé** ou à l'**imparfait,** selon le cas.

Quand je (arriver) en France, je (vivre) dans un foyer à Paris où je (connaître) beaucoup d'autres jeunes immigrés. La plupart d'entre eux (envoyer) au pays la plus grande partie de leurs revenus pour aider leurs familles et leur village. Moi aussi, je (vouloir) le faire mais je (ne pas pouvoir) parce que je (avoir) beaucoup de mal à trouver un boulot. Les autres sans-papiers et moi, nous (se cacher) de la police. Nous (passer) notre temps à chercher de petits boulots et évidemment, nous (ne pas gagner) beaucoup d'argent. Un jour, je (décider) de participer à une manifestation contre les lois sur l'immigration. Malheureusement, des policiers (me demander) mes papiers. Puisque je n'en avais pas, ils (m'expulser) de France. Je (devoir) rentrer chez moi. Il n'y a pas de travail ici, alors je ne sais pas ce que je vais faire.

E **Une famille curieuse.** Imaginez que vous êtes un des membres de la famille de Sema (voir exercice **D**). Il est rentré au Mali après avoir été expulsé de France. Vous ne l'avez pas vu depuis deux ans. Posez-lui des questions (à l'**imparfait** et au **passé composé**) sur ce qu'il a fait en France pour trouver du travail et un logement.

Modèle: Qu'est-ce que tu as fait quand tu es arrivé à Paris? Pourquoi? Pourquoi voulais-tu aller en France?

F **Ce n'est pas facile quand on est jeune.** On parle de la vie de Kim N'Guyen, jeune infirmière d'origine vietnamienne. Récrivez les phrases ci-dessous en utilisant **après + l'infinitif passé.** Faites tous les changements nécessaires.

Modèle: Elle a fini ses études avant de partir en France.
Après avoir fini ses études, elle est partie en France.

1. Elle a obtenu son diplôme avant de travailler comme bénévole en Afrique.
2. Elle est rentrée en France avant de chercher un stage.
3. Elle a fait un stage avant de faire de l'intérim.
4. Elle a fait de l'intérim avant de trouver un poste permanent.
5. Elle a travaillé pendant deux ans avant de gagner assez pour pouvoir quitter la maison de ses parents.
6. Elle a lu les petites annonces avant de louer un studio.
7. Elle a vécu seule avant de se marier.
8. Elle s'est mariée avant d'avoir des enfants.

RAPPEL To say you miss something or someone, use the verb **manquer** (à). *What* or *whom* you miss is the *subject*, and *you* are the *indirect object*. To say that something makes you feel a certain way, use the verb **rendre** + an *adjective*. For more details, see page 172.

G **De retour.** Vous rentrez chez vous après avoir travaillé à l'étranger pendant un an. Vous racontez à votre famille ce qui vous a manqué, ce qui vous a rendu(e) heureux(-euse), etc. pendant votre séjour à l'étranger.

Modèle: la bonne cuisine de maman / le froid, malade
La bonne cuisine de maman m'a manqué. Le froid m'a rendu(e) malade.

1. mes amis / mon travail, heureux(-euse)
2. mon chat / être seul(e), triste
3. parler anglais / ne pas bien parler la langue du pays, anxieux(-euse)
4. ma maison / voyager, joyeux(-euse)
5. le soleil / la pluie incessante, triste

Continuez avec vos propres idées.

H **Mon tout premier boulot.** Avec deux ou trois partenaires, posez-vous des questions sur votre premier emploi.

1. Pourquoi voulais-tu travailler?
2. Est-ce que tu as eu du mal à trouver un travail?
3. Qu'est-ce que tu as fait pour trouver un boulot?
4. Quelle sorte de travail faisais-tu?
5. Quels étaient tes horaires de travail?
6. Tu étais content(e) de ton salaire?
7. Est-ce que le travail était intéressant? Explique.

Saviez-vous que... ?

Depuis le 1er septembre 1998, tout enfant né en France de parents étrangers acquiert la nationalité française à sa majorité si, à cette date, il réside en France et s'il a résidé en France pendant une période d'au moins cinq ans, depuis l'âge de onze ans. Un étranger majeur, résidant habituellement sur le sol français depuis au moins cinq ans peut demander à être naturalisé. Cette durée de résidence peut être réduite à deux ans si le demandeur a accompli avec succès deux années d'études dans un établissement d'enseignement supérieur français ou s'il a rendu, ou peut rendre, « des services importants à la France ». Un(e) étranger(-ère) marié(e) depuis quatre ans à un(e) citoyen(ne) français(e) peut demander à acquérir la nationalité française par déclaration.

Source: www.vie-publique.fr

Lecture

Printemps (1989) est une nouvelle de J.M.G. Le Clézio, né à Nice en 1940. Il a grandi bilingue, d'un père anglais et d'une mère française, mais a décidé d'écrire en français. Auteur de plus de trente livres, romans, essais, nouvelles, traductions de mythologie indienne, il reçoit le prix Nobel de littérature en 2008. La nouvelle dont vous allez lire quelques extraits est l'histoire d'une jeune Marocaine, Saba, qui a passé les douze premières années de sa vie comme fille adoptive de M. et Mme Herschel, un couple américain installé au Maroc. A l'adolescence, elle est retournée vivre chez sa mère biologique. Dans les passages ci-dessous, elle pense à la jeunesse de sa mère et à des événements qui ont marqué sa vie, tels que sa propre naissance et son adoption.

ENTRONS EN MATIERE

Quelles difficultés rencontre un père (une mère) quand il (elle) doit élever son enfant seul(e)?

POUR MIEUX COMPRENDRE

Il est plus facile de comprendre un texte si on sait qui en est le (la) narrateur(-trice) et de quelles personnes il (elle) parle. Lisez les deux premières phrases du passage qui suit. Qui parle? De qui parle cette personne? Puis, continuez à lire en cherchant le pronom sujet qui apparaît le plus souvent dans les phrases qui suivent. A qui ce pronom personnel se réfère-t-il? Et quel pronom apparaît le plus souvent dans les trois dernières phrases du premier paragraphe? A qui ce pronom personnel se réfère-t-il?

© Geoff Wiggins/Alamy

Printemps

PREMIÈRE PARTIE

C'est la nuit quand Saba commence son récit. Sa mère dort près d'elle pendant qu'elle se souvient de son histoire.

J'entends le bruit de la respiration de ma mère. Elle aussi, elle est partie de chez elle, une nuit, et elle n'est jamais revenue. Peut-être qu'on voulait la marier de force, ou bien elle a suivi un homme de passage°. Elle a quitté le village des Zayane[5], dans la montagne, elle a marché jusqu'à la mer. Son père était un guerrier°, un fils du grand
5 Moha ou Hammou[6] qui avait fait la guerre aux Français, à Khénifra[7]. Quand ma mère a quitté la montagne, elle avait mon âge, et déjà elle me portait dans son ventre°. Elle a voyagé seule dans toutes ces villes qu'elle ne connaissait pas, elle a travaillé dans les fondoucs°, sur les marchés. Celui qui était mon père avait pris le bateau, il est allé travailler de l'autre côté de la mer, en France, en Allemagne peut-être. Mais, il n'est jamais
10 revenu. Il est mort en tombant d'un échafaudage°, ou bien de maladie. Il n'a rien laissé derrière lui, pas même son image°.

de... qui ne reste pas longtemps / **guerrier** homme qui fait la guerre

me... *was pregnant with me*

fondoucs auberge dans les pays arabes

échafaudage *scaffolding*

image ici, photo

---

[5] Le nom de famille du grand-père de Saba. Les Zayane sont aussi une confédération de tribus berbères au Maroc.
[6] Moha ou Hammou est devenu chef de la confédération des Zayane en 1877, à l'âge de 20 ans.
[7] Une ville dans les montagnes du Maroc. En 1914, quand le Maroc était une colonie française, les Zayane ont battu l'armée française à Khénifra.

Ma mère m'a dit un jour qu'elle avait reçu une lettre en français, et le patron du restaurant où elle travaillait l'a lue pour elle. Dans la lettre, on disait que mon père était mort à Marseille. Ensuite, mes oncles et mes tantes Zayane sont venus de la montagne,

15 pour ramener° ma mère, parce qu'ils voulaient lui trouver un autre mari, et me garder avec eux. Ma mère a dit oui, et qu'une nuit elle s'est échappée°, elle s'est cachée dans un fondouc jusqu'à ce que ses frères et ses sœurs se lassent° de la chercher et retournent dans la montagne. Alors, elle a décidé de partir, elle aussi. Elle m'a mise dans une boîte de carton°, et elle a voyagé en camion° et en autocar. Dans les marchés, elle s'asseyait°

20 par terre, avec la boîte à côté d'elle, et elle attendait qu'on lui donne à manger. Et un jour, elle est arrivée à Nightingale[8], et elle a déposé° le carton sur le sol° de la cuisine, elle a pris les billets de banque du Colonel[9], et elle est partie.

ramener retourner avec
s'est... est partie sans être vue
se lassent... se fatiguent

boîte... *cardboard box*
camion *truck*
s'asseyait *would sit*
déposé mis / **sol** *floor*

COMPRENEZ-VOUS?

A. Globalement

1. Où se déroule cette histoire? Comment le savez-vous?
2. Qui sont les personnages? Qu'est-ce que vous apprenez sur eux?
3. A quelles difficultés la mère a-t-elle dû faire face?
4. Qu'est-ce qui s'est passé à Nightingale quand la mère y est allée avec son bébé?

B. Les événements. En vous référant à la première partie, mettez les événements dans la vie de la mère de Saba dans l'ordre correct.

1. Elle a quitté le village dans la montagne.
2. Elle a rencontré un homme.
3. Le père de Saba a pris un bateau pour aller travailler en Europe.
4. Elle a voyagé et elle a travaillé.
5. Elle a laissé son bébé chez les Herschel à Nightingale.
6. Les oncles et les tantes voulaient ramener Saba et sa mère chez eux.
7. Elle est tombée enceinte.
8. Elle s'est cachée de sa famille et a mendié.
9. Elle a reçu une lettre qui annonçait la mort du père de Saba en France.

CHERCHEZ LA FORME

Expliquez l'usage de l'imparfait dans la phrase qui commence par: « Dans les marchés, elle… ».

ALLEZ PLUS LOIN

1. Pourquoi, à votre avis, Saba dit-elle « aussi » dans la deuxième phrase du premier paragraphe?
2. Décrivez le caractère de la mère de Saba. Comment était-elle? (courageuse, timide, jeune, vieille, heureuse…) Justifiez votre description.

---

[8] la plantation des Herschel où Saba a passé son enfance
[9] Saba appelle M. Herschel « le Colonel ».

Printemps

Deuxième partie

Dans cette partie, Saba ajoute des détails à son histoire. En lisant, pensez à ce que vous apprenez de nouveau.

Tout ça, c'est mon histoire, mais je peux y penser maintenant comme si c'était vraiment arrivé à quelqu'un d'autre. Je peux penser à mon père inconnu, qui est mort à
25 Marseille au moment où je commençais à vivre à Khénifra. Je peux imaginer ma mère, elle n'avait que seize ans, elle était si fragile, avec ses yeux de biche°, ses cheveux coiffés en nattes°, et pourtant elle était si audacieuse, si forte. Un jour le Colonel m'a parlé d'elle, quand il l'a rencontrée pour la première fois, elle portait ce tout petit enfant sur la hanche°. Il y avait quelque chose qui troublait son regard°, comme des larmes. Il la
30 revoyait toujours, cette jeune femme au visage d'enfant, l'allure° sauvage et décidée, et le bébé qu'elle tenait contre elle et qui suçait° son lait. Lui qui était si riche, si puissant, qui avait commandé aux hommes pendant la guerre[10], le malheur et la jeunesse de ma mère le subjuguaient°, le rendaient timide et dérisoire°. Ce qui l'émouvait lui, le soldat de l'armée américaine, c'était le secret sombre et âpre° dans les yeux de cette femme,
35 un secret semblable au pays des Zayane, les montagnes et les forêts de rouvres°, la lumière dure dans ses yeux, la méchanceté° de l'enfance interrompue.

Elle respire lentement, à côté de moi, dans l'alcôve. Je pense à ce qu'elle m'a fait. Je pense qu'elle errait° sur les routes blanches de poussière°, devant son ombre°, et j'étais serrée° contre sa hanche dans les plis° de sa robe, je suçais le lait de sa poitrine. Je pense
40 qu'elle m'a laissée dans la maison des Herschel, endormie dans le carton, et Amie[11] m'a prise et m'a posée doucement dans le lit blanc qu'elle avait préparé à côté du sien, dans sa chambre. Je pense aux billets de banque roulés et liés par un élastique, qu'elle avait cachés dans les pans° de sa robe serrée par une ceinture, entre ses seins°. Je pense à la route vide devant elle, personne ne l'attendait, personne ne l'aimait. Le bateau qu'elle a
45 pris pour Marseille, le pont inférieur° chargé d'émigrants, et le voyage à travers ce pays inconnu, où personne ne parlait sa langue, où personne ne lui ressemblait. Je pense aux endroits où elle a vécu, à Marseille, en Allemagne, à Hambourg, le travail, l'eau qui fait gercer° les mains, les ateliers où on se brûle les yeux. Peut-être qu'elle roulait déjà les billets de banque avec un élastique et qu'elle les cachait dans sa chambre, dans
50 un carton à chaussures, comme elle fait encore maintenant?

COMPRENEZ-VOUS?

Faites une liste de ce que vous avez appris dans cette partie sur:
1. la mère: son âge, son apparence, son caractère
2. le Colonel: sa profession, son caractère, sa réaction face à la mère
3. la vie de Saba à Nightingale: Quel détail dans le deuxième paragraphe symbolise la meilleure vie qu'aura le bébé?
4. la décision de la mère: Quels mots dans le deuxième paragraphe soulignent sa solitude? Où va-t-elle? Comment voyage-t-elle? Ensuite, comparez votre liste à celles de vos camarades de classe pour vous aider à comprendre cette partie de l'histoire.

[10]M. Herschel, ancien colonel dans l'armée américaine, est probablement venu au Maroc avec les forces alliées pendant la seconde guerre mondiale.
[11]Saba appelle Mme Herschel « Amie ». Son vrai nom était Aimée.

Glossary (margin)

yeux... *doe-like eyes*
coiffés... *braided*

hanche *hip* / regard *expression* / allure apparence générale
suçait buvait
subjuguaient captivaient
dérisoire *insignifiant*
âpre dur, pénible
rouvres sorte d'arbres
méchanceté ici, misère

errait marchait sans but
poussière *dust* / ombre *shadow* / serrée *held tightly* / plis *folds*

pans... *loose parts*
seins *breasts*

pont... *lower deck*

gercer *to chap*

CHERCHEZ LA FORME

Choisissez un paragraphe dans une des deux parties du texte. Faites une liste de tous les verbes au passé, classez-les par temps et expliquez ensuite pourquoi Le Clézio a utilisé ces temps.

ALLEZ PLUS LOIN

1. A quel moment dans la vie de Saba recommence-t-elle à raconter l'histoire de sa mère et de ce que celle-ci a fait avant d'aller en France?
2. Dans le deuxième paragraphe de la deuxième partie, quelle expression Saba utilise-t-elle à six reprises? Pourquoi, selon vous, utilise-t-elle cette répétition?

Activites d'expansion

Rendez-vous sur le site web de **Sur le vif** pour regardez la vidéo du Chapitre 3, puis complétez les activités à la page 49 du **Student Activities Manual**.

A Votre réaction

Que pensez-vous de ce qu'a fait la mère de Saba? Imaginez une autre fin pour cette histoire.

B La lettre

Ecrivez la lettre que la mère a reçue à la mort du père de Saba.

Commencez par: **Madame,**
J'ai le regret de vous annoncer…

A la fin, mettez: **Veuillez recevoir, Madame, mes sincères condoléances.**

C Mère et fille se retrouvent

Quand Saba a douze ans, sa mère vient la rechercher chez M. et Mme Herschel. Avec un(e) partenaire, jouez les rôles de la mère et de la fille et posez-vous des questions sur les douze années passées.

D Ouvriers immigrés dans votre pays

Dans la région où vous avez grandi, est-ce qu'il y a aussi des ouvriers immigrés? Qu'est-ce que vous savez d'eux?

1. D'où viennent les ouvriers immigrés?
2. Quelle(s) langue(s) parlent-ils?
3. Où habitent-ils?
4. Pourquoi veulent-ils travailler dans notre pays?
5. Quelles sortes de travail font-ils? Dans quels secteurs économiques les retrouve-t-on?
6. Quels avantages notre pays tire-t-il de leur travail?
7. Est-ce qu'ils sont bien intégrés dans la société? Expliquez votre réponse.
8. Connaissez-vous ou avez-vous déjà fait la connaissance d'ouvriers immigrés? Racontez ce qu'ils vous ont appris.

Saviez-vous que… ?

La « Cité nationale de l'histoire de l'immigration » a ouvert ses portes à Paris en 2007. Le rôle de ce musée est de rassembler, sauvegarder, mettre en valeur et rendre accessible les éléments relatifs à l'histoire de l'immigration en France, notamment depuis le XIXe siècle. Les expositions veulent faire connaître au grand public les développements de l'immigration, aussi bien que les difficultés auxquelles les immigrés ont dû faire face et leurs contributions au cours de l'histoire.

Source: www.histoire-immigration.fr

Interlude I

Loukoum et Camembert

© Clare Tufts

Lecture

Voici les paroles d'une chanson tirée du premier album des Escrocs[1], *Faites-vous des amis,* sorti en 1994. Originaires de Paris, les trois membres du groupe sont tous nés dans les années 60. Ils ont grandi avec le son des Beatles et des Rolling Stones mais leurs chemins musicaux ont subi de multiples influences, telles la soul, le jazz, le reggae, la salsa et la chanson française. Percussions, accordéons, synthé et guitare sont les principaux instruments utilisés par le combo. Leurs concerts et leurs tournées s'enchaînent dans les petites salles comme dans les grandes devant des publics enthousiastes.

[1] En anglais: *swindlers or con men*

© Clare Tufts

© Clare Tufts

Groupe impertinent et drôle, mais très concerné par les grands sujets de société, les Escrocs apportent une touche swing à la chanson française à travers des titres bien ancrés dans la vie quotidienne. Dans *Loukoum et Camembert* ils utilisent la cuisine pour lutter contre le racisme.

ENTRONS EN MATIERE

Qu'est-ce qui distingue un groupe ethnique d'un autre? Donnez quelques exemples précis. D'après son titre, à quels groupes ethniques la chanson fait-elle allusion? Le titre représente-t-il un stéréotype? Dans quels sens? Dans le refrain (« Donnez-vous la main… »), trouvez des noms de famille. Qu'est-ce que vous pouvez en déduire? Lisez ensuite la première strophe. Qui est le « tu » du premier vers? Cette personne a-t-elle une réaction positive ou négative envers celui qui est « différent » d'elle? Ecoutez maintenant la chanson et dites ce que vous pensez de la musique. La chanson traite d'un sujet très sérieux. A-t-on cette impression en l'écoutant?

Loukoum² et Camembert

 CD 1, track 4

Tu les aimes pas,
Les autres marionnettes,
Celles en djellaba°
Et turban sur la tête.
5   Elles font des prières,

Toi, t'en as pas besoin,
T'as du bon camembert
Et t'as du bon vin.
Pendant que tu cavales°,
10 Amassant de l'oseille°,

djellaba longue robe à capuchon portée par hommes et femmes en Afrique du Nord

cavales *run around*
oseille (*argot*) argent

² Confiserie orientale associée aux Maghrébins (*Turkish Delight*)

Elles n'ont pour capital
Qu'un rayon de soleil.
Elles grillent des merguez°
Le soir sur le balcon.
15 Toi, t'astiques° ta « R16 »°
Et tu planques tes « ronds »°.

Donnez-vous la main,
Loukoum et Camembert,
Car vous êtes en chemin
20 Vers le même cimetière.
Ben Saïd et Durand
Sont à la même école,
Des petits figurants
Dans un grand guignol°.

merguez saucisses épicées

astiques *wax* / **R16** voiture de la marque Renault construite entre 1965 et 1979 / **planques…** (*argot*) caches ton argent

guignol théâtre de marionnettes, farce

COMPRENEZ-VOUS?

1. **Vers 1 à 16:** Faites une liste des caractéristiques de ces deux groupes, les Français et les Maghrébins.
2. **Vers 2:** Le chanteur dit « les autres marionnettes », ce qui suggère que les deux groupes dans la chanson sont des marionnettes. En général, comment sont les marionnettes?
3. **Le refrain:** En quoi ces deux groupes se ressemblent-ils?
4. **Pourquoi le groupe les Escrocs a-t-il choisi Ben Saïd et Durand pour représenter les deux groupes? Que signifient les deux noms mentionnés?

25 Mais toi le Gaulois,
Le Ducon Lajoie,
Tu les aimes pas
Ces gens-là!
Ils ont d'autres coutumes
30 Que celles des gens du nord
Qui font dans le costume
Et la côte de porc.
Dans tes vilaines entrailles°,
Tu sens monter la haine.
35 Tu voudrais qu'elles s'en aillent
Et tu cries vive Le Pen³

entrailles ici, cœur ou âme

³ (1928–) homme politique français d'extrême droite, fondateur du Front national en 1972, qui s'oppose à l'immigration. Actuellement c'est sa fille, Marine, qui dirige ce parti politique.

Qu'ils rentrent chez eux,
Ces fumeurs de haschisch,
On reste entre petits vieux,
40 Au pays des caniches.

Elles font pleins de rejetons°,   **rejetons** ici, enfants
Toi, tu préfères les chiens.
Tu te dis à quoi bon
S'encombrer de gamins.
45 Et pendant que tu t'angoisses,
Sous tranquillisants,
La marionnette d'en face,
Elle fait des enfants.
Elle fait de beaux gamins[4]
50 Avec les yeux brillants,
Plus brillants que les tiens
Qui crient au droit du sang,[5]
Car sais-tu, pauvre con°,   **con** *(vulg.)* personne stupide
Que le mariage consanguin°,   **consanguin** entre parents
55 Ça fait pas des canons°,   proches / **canons** personnes
Ça fait des crétins°.   idéales / **crétins** idiots

COMPRENEZ-VOUS?

1. Vers 25–40: Pourquoi « le Gaulois » n'aime-t-il pas « ces gens-là » ? Qu'est-ce qu'ils doivent faire, selon lui ? Et quel parti politique soutient-il ? Pourquoi?

2. Vers 41–56 Selon le chanteur, les Français ne veulent pas avoir d'enfants. Qu'est-ce qu'ils préfèrent ? Et les Maghrébins?

3. Quelles sont les implications de la critique du « mariage consanguin » (entre parents proches)?

[4] Bien que la chanson suggère que les Français n'ont pas beaucoup d'enfants, le taux de natalité (*birth rate*) en France est le plus élevé de l'Union européenne après l'Irlande.

[5] Selon le droit du sang, la pratique suivie en Allemagne, les enfants ont la nationalité de leurs parents. Selon le droit du sol comme aux Etats-Unis et en France (avec quelques restrictions), les enfants prennent la nationalité du pays où ils sont nés.

© STOCKFOLIO® / Alamy

ALLEZ PLUS LOIN

Selon vous, quelle est la position du groupe Les Escrocs dans ce débat? Recherchez les pronoms utilisés dans la chanson. Qu'est-ce qu'ils nous disent sur le point de vue des musiciens? Citez des exemples qui illustrent leurs opinions. Selon vous, pourquoi la chanson finit-elle avec le mot « crétins »?

ET VOUS?

Selon vous, pourquoi a-t-on parfois tant de mal à accepter les gens qui ne nous ressemblent pas? Qu'est-ce qu'on peut faire pour faciliter l'entente entre des groupes d'origines différentes?

QUELQUES STATISTIQUES: LE MARIAGE ET LA NATALITE

© Daly & Newton/Getty Images

En France un mariage sur sept est mixte:[6] En 2009, on a compté respectivement 16 525 mariages où l'époux est étranger et l'épouse française et 15 081 avec un époux français et une épouse étrangère, sur un total de 245 151 mariages célébrés en France. Dans la majorité de ces unions, le (la) conjoint(e) étranger(-ère) a la nationalité d'un pays d'Afrique du Nord. Suivent les Européens autres que Français, les ressortissants d'un pays d'Afrique sub-saharienne et les Asiatiques (notamment les Turcs et les Chinois).

Au cours de la dernière décennie, la part des enfants nés d'une mère étrangère a progressé: 13% en 2010, contre 10,1% en 2000. En 2010, les mères étrangères ont donné naissance à 108 000 bébés en France (sur 832 799): 57% de ces mères sont de nationalité africaine, dont 35% ressortissantes des pays du Maghreb, et 17% sont de nationalité européenne hors l'ex-URSS.

Source: Insee (Institut national de la statistique et des études économiques) 2011.

Naissances vivantes selon la nationalité des parents en %

Année	Deux parents français	Couples mixtes	Deux parents étrangers
2002	83,1	9,8	7,1
2003	82,6	10,3	7,1
2004	81,8	10,9	7,3
2005	81,4	11,5	7,1
2006	81,1	11,9	7,0
2007	80,8	12,3	6,9
2008	80,5	12,6	6,9
2009	79,9	13,1	7,0
2010	80,1	13,3	6,6

Source: Insee, Statistiques d'état civil sur les naissances.
http://www.ined.fr/fr/france/naissances_fecondite/naissances_nationalite_parents/ 5/2012

[6] Le recensement (*census*) français n'a pas de catégorie pour l'origine ethnique, comme aux Etats-Unis.

En route!

A LES MOYENS DE TRANSPORT

Mots apparentés: l'automobile *f.* (l'auto), la motocy-clette (la moto), le taxi, le train, le tramway (le tram)

la voiture...	... *car*
neuve	*new*
d'occasion	*used*
électrique	*electric*
hybride	*hybrid*
propre	*"green"*
le camion	*truck*
le monospace	*minivan*
le break	*station wagon*
le 4X4 (le quatre-quatre)	*four-wheel drive*
le pick-up	*pickup truck*
la décapotable, le cabriolet	*convertible*
l'autobus *m.* (le bus)	*city bus*
l'autocar *m.* (le car)	*commercial bus line*
le métro	*subway*
le scooter	*motorscooter, moped*
...à trois roues	*three-wheeled scooter*
la trottinette	*push scooter*
le vélo	*bicycle*
le VTT (vélo tout-terrain)	*mountain bike*
les rollers *m.*	*inline skates*
le skateboard, le skate	*skateboard*
les transports en commun *m.*	*public transportation*
la marche	*walking*

B LES GENS QUI SE DEPLACENT

l'automobiliste *m./f.*	*car driver*
le (la) conducteur (-trice)	*driver*
le chauffeur	*driver (taxi, bus)*
le (la) covoitureur (-euse)	*person who carpools*
le (la) cycliste	*bicycle rider*
le (la) motocycliste	*motocycle rider*

© Clare Tufts

le (la) piéton(ne)	*pedestrian*
le (la) passager (-ère)	*passenger (car, city bus, plane)*
le (la) rolleur (-euse)	*in-line skater*
le (la) skateur (-euse)	*skateboarder*
le (la) voyageur (-euse)	*passenger (train, commercial bus)*

C LE DEPLACEMENT

le permis de conduire	*driver's license*
le code de la route	*traffic laws*
la vitesse maximum	*speed limit*
la circulation	*traffic*
l'essence *f.*	*gas*
la station-service	*service station*
la borne de recharge	*recharging station (for electric car)*
le parking	*parking lot*
le stationnement	*parking*
... sur la chaussée	*(on the) street parking*

 Pour obtenir des exercices et activités supplémentaires sur le contenu de ce chapitre, rendez-vous sur le site www.cengagebrain.com

l'assurance automobile f.	car insurance
le covoiturage	carpool
le casque	helmet
l'antivol m.	anti-theft device
la voie cyclable	bike lane (part of the street)
la piste cyclable	bike path (off the street)
le trottoir	sidewalk

D LES ACTIVITES

monter dans... la voiture, l'autobus	to get into . . . a car, (on) a bus
descendre de... la voiture, l'autobus	to get out of . . . the car, (off) the bus
démarrer	to start off
conduire	to drive
se promener en voiture	to go for a car ride
emmener quelqu'un en voiture	to give someone a ride
accélérer	to accelerate
ralentir	to slow down
rouler	to go (a car, a bike, etc.)
doubler, dépasser	to pass
freiner	to brake
garer la voiture	to park the car
se garer	to park
faire du vélo	to bike
faire du roller	to rollerblade
faire du skate	to skateboard
prendre... le bus, le train, le métro	to take . . . the bus, the train, the subway

E LES PROBLEMES ET LES SOLUTIONS

le bouchon, l'embouteillage m.	traffic jam
l'heure f. de pointe	rush hour

tomber en panne...	to break down
d'essence	to run out of gas
de courant	to run out of battery power (for electric car)
faire le plein	to fill up with gas
brancher la voiture sur une prise	to plug the car into an outlet
marcher (machine/appareil électrique)	to work, function
le pneu crevé	flat tire
la roue de secours	spare tire
la batterie à plat	dead battery
rentrer dans	to run into
écraser	to run over
déraper	to skid
le garage	garage
le (la) garagiste	car mechanic
dépanner, réparer	to repair
la dépanneuse	tow truck
remorquer	to tow
l'excès m. de vitesse	speeding
la contravention, le PV (procès-verbal)	traffic ticket
prendre une contravention, un PV	to get a ticket
la fourrière	the car pound
emmener une voiture à la fourrière	to impound a car
le feu (de signalisation) (rouge, orange[1], vert)	traffic light
la police	the police
le poste, le commissariat de police	police station
le policier, l'agent de police, le flic (argot)	policeman

[1] En France, on utilise un **feu orange** au lieu d'un **feu jaune** (entre le rouge et le vert).

© Clare Tufts

Vocabulaire

A **Comment se déplacer?** A votre avis, quel moyen de transport chacun des Français suivants va-t-il choisir? Justifiez votre réponse.

1. une mère qui emmène ses quatre enfants chez leurs grands-parents
2. un retraité *(retired man)* qui veut traverser Paris et qui a beaucoup de temps
3. un homme d'affaires qui doit traverser Paris aux heures de pointe
4. un adolescent qui va chez un copain le samedi après-midi
5. un couple qui veut profiter du beau temps le dimanche
6. une femme qui habite en banlieue et qui emmène son fils malade chez le médecin
7. une étudiante qui descend sur la Côte d'Azur au mois d'août avec des copines
8. des touristes à Paris qui veulent voir les monuments de la capitale
9. une femme qui est à l'aéroport et qui veut se rendre au centre-ville
10. un enfant qui habite en banlieue et joue dans son jardin

B **Les associations.** Quels mots (noms, adjectifs, verbes) associez-vous à chacun de ces moyens de transport?

1. le monospace
2. le vélo
3. la décapotable
4. les rollers
5. le train
6. le 4×4
7. la voiture propre
8. la marche

C **Comment conduire?** D'abord, mettez les verbes suivants dans l'ordre logique pour expliquer les actions d'un automobiliste.

1. se garer
2. monter dans
3. accélérer
4. descendre de
5. démarrer
6. freiner
7. doubler
8. rouler

Ensuite, expliquez ce qu'Alain a fait quand il a pris la voiture hier après-midi. Faites des phrases complètes et ajoutez des détails pour rendre le récit plus intéressant.

D'abord, Alain est monté dans la voiture…

PRÉPARATION GRAMMATICALE

Avant de continuer, révisez les articles, pages 173–176.

D **Finissez la phrase.** Cherchez dans la liste E du vocabulaire un mot ou une expression qui vous aide à terminer les phrases suivantes de façon logique.

1. Il y a des embouteillages parce que c'est…
2. Si je ne trouve pas de station-service, je vais…
3. La voiture dérape et…
4. Elle attend la dépanneuse parce que (qu')…
5. Quand on ne s'arrête pas au feu rouge, on risque de (d')…
6. Je demande au garagiste de (d')…
7. Si la voiture ne marche pas, il faut…
8. Une roue de secours est très utile quand on…

PREPARATION GRAMMATICALE

Avant de continuer, révisez les pronoms d'object direct et indirect, **y** et **en**, pages 176–180.

© Clare Tufts

Saviez-vous que… ?

Il y a deux associations pour la randonnée en rollers officiellement reconnues à Paris: « Pari-Roller » et « Rollers & Coquillages ». Les randonnées organisées par Pari-Roller, qui ont lieu le vendredi soir avec un parcours dans la ville de Paris de 26,9 kms. Les randonnées organisées par Rollers & Coquillages ont lieu le dimanche après-midi et ont un parcours de 20,4 kms. Pari-Roller propose des parcours qui comportent des difficultés techniques, comme des pavés (*cobblestones*) et des descentes assez raides, aussi bien qu'un rythme assez soutenu, ou rapide. En revanche, le nom même « Rollers & Coquillages » révèle une philosophie très différente: « coquillage » fait penser à la plage, et la plage fait penser aux vacances ou à la détente. Cette association veut que ses randonnées soient conviviales et relaxantes. La Préfecture de Police de la ville de Paris met à disposition des deux associations une trentaine de policiers en rollers et quelques motocyclettes chargées de sécuriser certains carrefours sensibles.

Source: www.paris-roller.com and www.rollers-coquillages.org

Lecture

En juillet 2007, la ville de Paris a lancé « Vélib' », le service de vélos en libre-service sur les voies parisiennes. Quatre ans plus tard, en juillet 2011, on comptait plus de 20 000 vélos disponibles dans 1 800 stations, et plus de 75 000 trajets quotidiens. Les vélos Vélib' sont accessibles 7 jours sur 7, 24 heures sur 24, dans tout Paris, et il y a une station Vélib' tous les 300 mètres environ. Mais quatre ans après sa naissance euphorique, Vélib' doit faire face à quelques difficultés dans son développement.

ENTRONS EN MATIERE

Le service de vélos en libre-service (Vélib') de Paris a fêté ses cinq ans en 2012. A votre avis, quels problèmes et/ou dangers les Parisiens et les touristes ont-ils dû affronter pendant ces cinq ans? Qu'est-ce que la ville de Paris a pu faire pour faciliter la location d'un Vélib' et pour réduire les inconvenients et les dangers pour le public en général?

Le service de vélos en libre-service affiche un bilan° mitigé° en 2011

bilan *assessment* / **mitigé** *mixed*

En 2011, il y avait 180 186 abonnés au Vélib, ce qui représente une augmentation par rapport à 2010 (161 887), mais une diminution depuis sa première année (200 100). Afin d'inciter plus d'usagers à s'abonner, le prix d'un abonnement « classique » Velib' d'un an (29€) n'a pas bougé depuis sa mise en service, et on a ajouté un tarif préférentiel pour les jeunes de 14–26 ans (19€). En revanche, le prix pour une journée
5   est monté de 1 à 1,70€, et pour un ticket de sept jours de 5 à 8 €. Un deuxième point négatif: selon JCDecaux, la société qui gère le service Vélib', 16 000 vélos ont été vandalisés dans les trois premières années. Troisième bilan décourageant: 700 accidents par an à Paris en vélo, et 7 personnes sont mortes sur un Vélib' depuis 2007. La dernière

verbalisé *subject to a fine*   mode chez les jeunes Parisiens, c'est de prendre un Vélib' pour rentrer d'une soirée en
10   état d'ébriété, ce qui est évidemment dangereux mais aussi verbalisable°: comme pour la conduite en voiture, la limite est fixée à 0,5 gramme d'alcool par litre de sang, et la

garde à vue *placed in custody*   sanction peut aller d'une garde à vue° à six mois de suspension du permis de conduire.

Du côté positif, la Mairie de Paris ne cesse de promouvoir l'utilisation du Vélib'. En
15   mai 2010, le maire Bertrand Delanoë a annoncé un plan de densification du réseau parisien cyclable de 30%, et en 2011 la mairie a créé l'application officielle Vélib' qui permet de connaître en temps réel les vélos et points d'attache° disponibles en stations

points d'attache *bike posts*   sur l'iPhone ou le smartphone Nokia. La fonction « Chrono » de cette App donne en temps réel le coût du trajet, le CO^2 économisé et le nombre de calories dépensées.
20   Le site web officiel Vélib' (www.velib.paris.fr) offre toute les informations nécessaires sur la location et les tarifs. On y trouve aussi des liens multiples avec d'autres sources d'informations: « Newsletter iVelib' », « Blog Vélib' et moi », « Vélib' sur Facebook », « Vélib' sur Twitter », et « Vélib' sur iPhone ». On peut même accéder à la boutique Vélib' pour s'acheter des objets réfléchissants et un casque pour la sécurité; un panier et
25   un shopping bag Vélib'; et des gants, un couvre-selle, un protège panier et un poncho pour se protéger contre la pluie et le froid.

Source: www.lefigaro.fr and www.blog.velib.paris.fr

COMPRENEZ-VOUS?

1. Pourquoi, à votre avis, y avait-il le plus d'abonnements Vélib' la première année de ce service de location de vélos à Paris?
2. Après avoir bu de l'alcool, est-ce qu'on court moins de risques en rentrant chez soi à vélo ou en voiture? Expliquez.
3. En quoi l'App Vélib' facilite-t-elle l'utilisation du Vélib'?
4. En quoi les articles offerts en boutique Vélib' peuvent-ils encourager plus de gens à se servir plus souvent du Vélib' pour leurs déplacements en ville?

CHERCHEZ LA FORME

1. Expliquez l'usage de « d' » dans « d'autres » (ligne 21).
2. Expliquez l'usage de « des » dans « des objets réfléchissants » (lignes 23–24).
3. Expliquez l'usage de « un » dans « un casque » (ligne 24).

ALLEZ PLUS LOIN

Le service Vélib' est bon pour l'environnement, mais est-ce qu'il offre d'autres avantages à la ville de Paris et/ou à ceux qui s'en servent?

© Clare Tufts

RAPPEL   The *definite article* in French (**le, la, l', les**) is the equivalent of *the* in English. The *indefinite article* (**un, une**) is the equivalent of *a* or *an*. The *partitive article* (**du, de la, de l', des**) is the equivalent of *some*. There are several differences in the use of these articles in the two languages. For more details, see pages 173–176.

Applications

A Le code de conduite à VTT.

En quoi consiste la bonne conduite d'un cycliste en VTT? Voici quelques règles qu'il vaut mieux connaître avant de faire du vélo tout-terrain. Pour chacune d'elles, relevez les articles définis (ou contractés avec les prépositions *à* ou *de*) et les articles indéfinis.

1. Accorder la priorité aux marcheurs et aux cavaliers (*horseback riders*), ne pas les gêner ni les effrayer.
2. Ne pas effrayer les animaux sauvages ou domestiques.
3. Refermer les portails et les barrières; tenir compte des interdictions et de la signalisation routière et forestière.
4. Respecter la faune, la flore, les cultures et les pâturages.
5. Ne pas s'écarter, dans la forêt, des chemins et des sentiers.
6. Participer à la sauvegarde de l'environnement.
7. Pour la sécurité de chacun, veiller au bon fonctionnement de votre vélo.
8. Porter le casque en toutes circonstances.

© Geoff Waugh/Alamy

B Se déplacer.

Formez des phrases complètes en ajoutant des articles et des prépositions aux endroits appropriés. Faites les changements nécessaires. Attention! Les mots sont dans l'ordre correct.

1. Français / font / moins / covoiturage / que / Américains
2. prendre / bus / à Paris / offre / possibilité / de / voir / monuments
3. métro / est / plus / pratique / pour / gens / qui / n'ont pas / beaucoup / temps
4. cycliste / en ville / doit / avoir / courage / et / patience
5. rollers / sont / moyen de transport / que / jeunes / préfèrent
6. essence / coûte / plus / cher / en / France / qu'à / Etats-Unis
7. pour / éviter / problèmes / de / stationnement à Paris/ on / peut / prendre / Vélib'
8. il y a / moins / bouchons / tôt / matin
9. si / on / a / panne / de / essence / il / faut / trouver / station-service
10. vous / risquez / de / prendre / PV / si / vous / brûlez / feu rouge *(run a red light)*

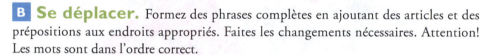

RAPPEL *Direct object pronouns* replace nouns that are acted on directly by the verb; *indirect object pronouns* replace the preposition **à** + *a person*; **y** replaces the preposition **à** + *a thing, an idea* or *a place*; **en** replaces **de** + *a thing* or *a place*. For more details, see pages 176–180.

C **Assez de questions!** M. et Mme Dupont et leur fille Alice sont en route pour la mer. Alice, qui n'a que 4 ans, est très curieuse. Elle pose des questions sur tout! Pour aider ses pauvres parents, trouvez une réponse logique à chacune de ses questions. Dans votre réponse, remplacez les mots soulignés dans la question par le(s) pronom(s) approprié(s).

PRÉPARATION GRAMMATICALE

Avant de continuer, révisez l'ordre des pronoms, page 181.

1. ALICE: Papa, pourquoi as-tu besoin <u>d'un permis de conduire?</u>
   M. DUPONT: _____.

2. ALICE: Maman, pourquoi faut-il respecter <u>la vitesse maximum?</u>
   MME DUPONT: _____.

3. ALICE: Qu'est-ce qu'on achète <u>dans une station-service?</u>
   MME DUPONT: _____.

4. ALICE: Quand est-ce qu'on téléphone <u>au garagiste?</u>
   M. DUPONT: _____.

5. ALICE: Pourquoi faut-il s'arrêter <u>au feu rouge?</u>
   MME DUPONT: _____.

6. ALICE: Pourquoi voulons-nous éviter <u>les heures de pointe?</u>
   MME DUPONT: _____.

7. ALICE: Pourquoi est-ce que nous n'avons pas <u>de décapotable?</u>
   MME DUPONT: _____.

8. ALICE: Quand est-ce que je peux descendre <u>de la voiture?</u>
   M. DUPONT: _____.

D **Jouez le prof!** Mettez-vous à deux ou trois pour jouer le rôle d'un prof d'un cours intermédiaire de français. Ensemble, corrigez le devoir d'un de vos étudiants. Pour cela, éliminez les répétitions de noms en insérant les pronoms nécessaires (d'objet direct, d'objet indirect, *y* et *en*). Après avoir corrigé le texte, comparez-le à ceux des autres groupes de votre classe.

Un soir, je devais emmener mon amie au cinéma dans la voiture de mon père. D'abord, je n'arrivais pas à retrouver les clés. Enfin, j'ai retrouvé les clés sous le siège de la voiture. J'ai aussi trouvé sous le siège de la voiture un billet de vingt dollars. J'ai demandé à mon père s'il avait perdu ce billet de vingt dollars. Il a dit non et il a donné ce billet de vingt dollars à moi. Puis, j'ai remarqué qu'il n'y avait pas assez d'essence. Quel dommage! J'allais être obligé de dépenser cet argent pour acheter de l'essence. Je me suis tout de suite rendu à la station-service. Quand je suis arrivé à la station-service, j'ai découvert que j'avais aussi un pneu crevé! Après avoir payé l'essence et la réparation du pneu, je n'avais plus d'argent. Alors, j'ai téléphoné à mon amie pour dire à mon amie que je ne pouvais plus emmener mon amie au cinéma. Quand j'ai raconté à mon amie cette histoire de panne d'essence et de pneu crevé, elle a dit à moi que j'avais inventé cette histoire!

RAPPEL   The word order for pronouns in affirmative commands is different from the regular word order. To review this imperative pronoun word order, see the chart on page 181.

E Avant le départ. Les Martin préparent leur départ en vacances. Mme Martin donne des ordres à tout le monde. Sa mère de 85 ans, qui veut l'aider, répète tout ce que dit Mme Martin! Imaginez les ordres de la grand-mère en remplaçant tous les mots soulignés par des pronoms.

Modèle: Mme Martin: Robert, mets tes rollers dans ton sac.
Grand-Mère: **Oui, mets-les-y!**

1. Mme Martin: Cécile, demande à ton père s'il a les billets.
Grand-mère: Oui, _____!

2. Mme Martin: Max, n'oublie pas ton casque!
Grand-mère: Non, _____!

3. Mme Martin: Roger, va acheter de l'essence.
Grand-mère: Oui, _____!

4. Mme Martin: Mettons les valises dans la voiture!
Grand-mère: Oui, _____!

5. Mme Martin: Dites aux voisins que nous partons.
Grand-mère: Oui, _____!

Continuez cet exercice avec un(e) partenaire.

© Cengage Learning

PREPARATION GRAMMATICALE

Avant de continuer, révisez les pronoms disjoints, pages 182–183.

F Des incidents de route de plus en plus graves! Avec un(e) partenaire, créez un dialogue entre deux ami(e)s qui se revoient après des vacances. Vous avez tous (toutes) les deux un « incident de route » à raconter, et chacun(e) de vous pense que ce qui lui est arrivé est plus grave et plus intéressant que l'incident de l'autre. Utilisez la liste E du vocabulaire (au début du chapitre) et autant de pronoms disjoints que possible.

Modèle: Moi, j'ai un incident de route incroyable à te raconter…

Mes parents, eux, n'étaient pas du tout contents…

Lecture

Fernand Raynaud (1926–1973) a longtemps été l'un des comiques français les plus connus. Apprécié aussi des étrangers, Raynaud a reçu un télégramme de Charlie Chaplin en 1960 annonçant son intention de venir assister à son premier grand spectacle. Ses sketchs, improvisés et présentés sur scène au fil des ans, ont été mis par écrit beaucoup plus tard quand Raynaud les a dictés à sa secrétaire. Le public français d'aujourd'hui continue à rire en lisant les histoires drôles de ce comique, et plusieurs fois par an ses sketches sont diffusés à la télévision.

ENTRONS EN MATIERE

On dit souvent que les femmes au volant sont plus prudentes que les hommes et qu'elles ont moins d'accidents graves de voiture. Pensez-vous que ce soit vrai? Donnez des exemples personnels pour justifier votre réponse.

POUR MIEUX COMPRENDRE

Souvent les histoires comiques nous semblent encore plus comiques si nous comprenons le caractère du protagoniste (ou de la « victime »). Un bon comique sait donc bien décrire ses personnages. Parcourez le deuxième paragraphe de ce sketch de Fernand Raynaud où le narrateur décrit sa sœur. Qu'est-ce que nous y apprenons sur cette femme? Quelle est l'attitude du narrateur envers son personnage?

© Jakob Kamender/istockphoto.com

La 2 CV[2] de ma sœur

PREMIÈRE PARTIE

Si un jour une de vos amies vous dit: « Veux-tu que je te parle franchement »? répondez-lui: « Non! Non! Non! Continue à me parler comme avant ». Donc, avec ma sœur… Ne soyez pas sincère, c'est-à-dire, soyez diplomate, ne lui demandez pas pour quoi sa 2 CV n'est plus peinte en rouge!

5 Ah! Oui, il lui est arrivé un incident—j'ai pas dit accident mais incident. Parce que ma sœur est très prudente. Elle ne dépasse jamais le vingt-cinq à l'heure° et elle roule toujours au milieu de la route, et elle dit: « Si tout le monde était comme moi, y'aurait pas souvent d'accident »! Elle en est à son seizième mort, parce que, y'a des gens qui veulent doubler, des imbéciles, des artistes! C'est nuisible° à la société!

10 L'autre jour, ma sœur roulait avec sa 2 CV et il y avait un convoi° du cirque Tantini. Comme le convoi roulait à vingt-cinq à l'heure, ma sœur dit: « J'y va-t-y, j'y va-t-y pas°? Allez, je me paye le culot°, je double le convoi »! Elle l'a fait, et v'là qu'après avoir doublé trois roulottes°, cinq camions, deux caravanes, un gros camion s'était arrêté pour laisser prendre aux éléphants leurs ébats°—parce que tous les quarante kilomètres

15 il faut s'arrêter pour laisser descendre les éléphants, afin qu'ils puissent se détendre, s'ébrouer°, enfin, tout ce que les éléphants ont besoin de faire lorsqu'ils sortent d'un camion… Ma sœur a donc été obligée de stopper avec sa 2 CV rouge, et quelle n'a pas été sa stupeur de voir arriver lentement vers elle, alors qu'elle était assise dans sa 2 CV, un gros pachyderme, qui se tourne vers elle, lui fait voir son arrière-train, lève la queue

20 et crac! Il s'assoit sur le devant de la 2 CV!

Ma sœur, ça lui a fait comme un coup. Elle se croyait en pleine nuit, elle s'est trouvée mal°. Le cornac° est arrivé précipitamment, a fait lever l'éléphant, a ranimé ma sœur à grands coups de gifles. Le directeur est arrivé en courant: « Rassurez-vous, nous sommes assurés°, on vous paiera les réparations! Je vais vous expliquer pourquoi

25 l'éléphant s'est assis sur la 2 CV. C'est parce que, chaque soir, au cours de son numéro, au milieu de la piste°, il s'assoit sur un tonneau° qui est rouge comme votre voiture »! Ma sœur était tellement suffoquée que le directeur du cirque Tantini l'a emmenée dans un petit café, lui a fait prendre un cognac, puis un deuxième, puis un troisième. Le cornac a payé sa tournée, ma sœur n'a pas voulu être en reste°, elle a payé la sienne…

30 Et elle est repartie en fredonnant° « Cerisiers roses et pommiers blancs ».

le… 25 kilomètres à l'heure (approx. 16 mph)

nuisible qui fait du mal
convoi… groupe de véhicules qui roulent ensemble
J'y… (fam.) j'y vais, je n'y vais pas / me… (fam.) me permets de faire une chose inhabituelle
roulottes maisons roulantes/

laisser… let the elephants move about / s'ébrouer s'agiter vivement

s'est… s'est évanouie (fainted) / cornac trainer

assurés insured

piste circus ring / tonneau barrel

être… to be indebted to
en… humming

---

[2] The **2 CV** (**deux chevaux-vapeur**) is often referred to in France as the **deuch.**

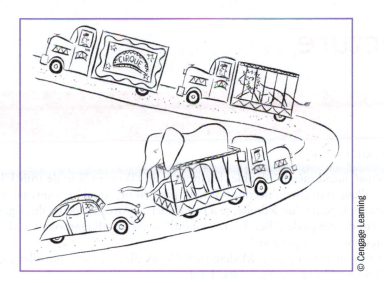

© Cengage Learning

COMPRENEZ-VOUS?

1. Qu'est-ce qu'on apprend au sujet de la voiture de la sœur du narrateur dans le premier paragraphe?
2. Comment conduit la sœur, et quel est le résultat de sa façon de conduire?
3. Pourquoi la sœur a-t-elle été obligée d'arrêter sa voiture sur la route?
4. Pourquoi la sœur s'est-elle trouvée mal?
5. Pourquoi l'éléphant a-t-il agi ainsi?
6. Combien de verres de cognac la sœur a-t-elle bu au café?

CHERCHEZ LA FORME

Cherchez tous les pronoms compléments d'objet indirects dans le premier paragraphe de la lecture.

POUR MIEUX COMPRENDRE

La première partie de ce texte de Fernand Raynaud est une narration. Dans la deuxième partie, que vous allez lire, il s'agit plutôt d'un dialogue. Parcourez le texte pour découvrir qui parle.

Lecture

La 2 CV de ma sœur

 CD 1, track 6

direction *steering*
talus *embankment*
motards motocyclistes de la gendarmerie / **Rangez-vous** Arrêtez-vous

DEUXIÈME PARTIE

Elle a réussi quand même à doubler le cirque mais v'là qu'au bout de trois kilomètres, elle dit: « Pourvu que ma direction° n'en ait pas pris un coup! Vérifions s'il n'y a rien. Montons sur le petit talus° à droite, ça a l'air d'aller… Voyons le petit talus à gauche… » On entend des coups de sifflet. Deux motards° arrivent: « Rangez-vous° à droite, non
35 mais dites donc, ça va pas vous?

Vous êtes un danger public, Mademoiselle! Vous allez à droite, vous allez à gauche… Mais dites donc! Vous avez eu un accident?

—Non, non! C'est un éléphant qui s'est assis sur ma voiture!

—Ah… Oui, oui, je vois très bien ce que c'est! Marcel! Viens voir! Y'a un éléphant
40 qui s'est assis sur le devant de la voiture de Madame!

—Mademoiselle s'il vous plaît!

—J'vais vous en donner moi, du Mademoiselle!

—Oui! Je vous assure Monsieur l'agent! C'est un éléphant qui s'est assis sur le devant de ma voiture!

puez *reek*

45 —Mais vous puez° le cognac, vous?

—Mais, Monsieur…

—Y'a pas de « Mais, Monsieur ». Vous allez à droite, vous allez à gauche, vous sentez le cognac et vous nous dites qu'un éléphant s'est assis sur votre voiture? Vous nous prenez pour des enfants de chœur°? Suivez-nous au poste »!

enfants… garçons qui aident le prêtre à l'église (ici, personnes très naïves)

50 Ils ont fait une prise de sang à ma sœur et, comme il y avait évidemment de l'alcool, ils l'ont gardée quarante-huit heures. Elle hurlait: « Oui, oui, oui! C'est vrai! Un éléphant s'est assis sur mon auto! Je le vois arriver, je vois un éléphant… Ouh! Le gros n'éléphant »!³ Ils voulaient l'interner°, il a fallu que le directeur du cirque vienne témoigner que les faits étaient exacts. Ils l'ont relâchée°.

interner mettre à l'hôpital psychiatrique / **relâchée** remise en liberté

55 Elle a fait repeindre sa voiture en vert et, si vous la rencontrez, surtout ne lui dites pas: « Pourquoi votre 2 CV est-elle verte maintenant, expliquez-moi ça »? Surtout ne lui dites pas, car elle verrait rouge.

---

1 sketch in *"Heureux! - L'intégrale des sketchs"* de Fernand Raynaud © Flammarion, 2000 Fernand Raynaud, La 2 CV de ma soeur in *"Heureux!"*. Avec l'aimable autorisation de Pascal Raynaud.

³ The use of **n'** before a noun beginning with a vowel comes from child's speech; since French children must learn to make the liaison between the final consonant **n** of **un** and the initial vowel of the following noun (**un éléphant**) they often assume that the noun actually begins with the consonant **n.**

COMPRENEZ-VOUS?

1. Pourquoi la sœur a-t-elle commencé à zigzaguer d'un côté à l'autre de la route?
2. Pourquoi les gendarmes ne croyaient-ils pas l'explication de la sœur?
3. Quelle raison la police avait-elle de garder la sœur pendant quarante-huit heures?
4. Qui a convaincu la police de relâcher cette femme?
5. Pourquoi ne faut-il pas poser de questions à la sœur sur le changement de couleur de sa voiture?

CHERCHEZ LA FORME

Identifiez et analysez les éléments soulignés dans la phrase suivante (lignes 50–51): « Ils ont fait une prise de sang à ma sœur et, comme il y avait évidemment de l'alcool, ils l'ont gardée quarante-huit heures ».

ALLEZ PLUS LOIN

1. Quelles sont les raisons possibles pour lesquelles Fernand Raynaud a décidé de faire parler les personnages dans la deuxième partie de son histoire (sous forme de dialogue) au lieu de raconter (sous forme de narration) leurs actions?
2. Quelle(s) technique(s) le comique utilise-t-il dans son sketch pour attirer l'attention du public qui l'écoute? Trouvez-en des exemples dans *La 2 CV de ma sœur*.

© Cengage Learning

Rendez-vous sur le site web de **Sur le vif** pour regardez la vidéo du Chapitre 4, puis complétez les activités à la page 65 du **Student Activities Manual.**

Activités d'expansion

A **Faites du théâtre!** A trois, mettez-vous à la place de la sœur et des gendarmes (lignes 34–49) et jouez la scène où elle essaie de leur expliquer ce qui est arrivé à sa voiture.

B **La voiture la plus économique.** Avec trois ou quatre camarades de classe, essayez de vous mettre d'accord sur la voiture la plus économique du monde. Il faut trouver une voiture qui est économique du point de vue du prix et de l'usage. Quels sont les avantages et les inconvénients de cette voiture?

Mots et expressions utiles:
confortable, maniable *(easy to handle)*, puissante *(powerful)*, sûre *(reliable)*
consomme peu d'essence *(uses little gas)*
ne coûte pas cher, est bon marché *(cheap)*
a une bonne tenue de route *(holds the road well)*
à deux (quatre) portes, à traction avant *(front-wheel drive),* à boîte automatique *(automatic transmission),* à boîte manuelle

Pour exprimer votre opinion:

Moi, je pense que…	Il me semble que…
A mon avis…	Je trouve que…
Pour ma part…	Je crois que…

Pour exprimer votre accord:

Je suis (tout à fait) d'accord.	Bien sûr!
Je suis de ton (votre) avis.	Absolument!
C'est vrai.	Sans aucun doute!
Tu as (Vous avez) raison.	

Pour exprimer votre désaccord:

Je ne suis pas d'accord.	Absolument pas!
Au contraire!	Tu as (Vous avez) tort.
Par contre…	Pourtant
Cependant…	Pas du tout!

C **Qui sont les conducteurs les plus dangereux?** Il y a des gens qui pensent que les conducteurs les plus dangereux sur la route sont ceux qui conduisent trop vite; d'autres, en revanche, pensent que ce sont ceux qui conduisent trop lentement. Qu'en pensez-vous et pourquoi? Si possible, donnez des exemples pour justifier votre opinion.

D **La voiture: malheur du monde?** La plupart des gens en Amérique du Nord et en Europe considèrent la voiture comme un objet absolument indispensable, mais on ne nie pas que sa prolifération dans le monde entraîne des conséquences très graves comme la pollution, les embouteillages et le gaspillage d'énergie. Qu'est-ce que vous en pensez? La voiture est-elle vraiment essentielle à la vie? Quelle(s) solution(s) voyez-vous à ce problème?

© Clare Tufts

Les voyages

© Clare Tufts

 ## A POURQUOI?

s'amuser (à)	*to enjoy oneself, to have fun*
se cultiver	*to improve one's mind*
découvrir	*to discover*
se détendre	*to relax, to unwind*

B COMMENT?

faire du stop	*to hitchhike*
prendre le car, le train, etc.	*to take the bus, the train, etc.*
voyager en avion, en car, en train, en voiture, à pied	*to travel by plane, bus, train, car, on foot*

C OU?

l'auberge *f.* de jeunesse	*youth hostel*
la caravane	*camping trailer*
le chalet	*small vacation house (in the mountains)*
la colonie de vacances	*summer camp (for children)*
coucher...	*to sleep . . .*
sous la tente	*in a tent*
à la belle étoile	*out in the open*
en plein air	*outdoors*
le terrain de camping	*campground*
la chambre d'hôtes	*bed and breakfast*

Pour obtenir des exercices et activités supplémentaires sur le contenu de ce chapitre, rendez-vous sur le site www.cengagebrain.com.

© AVAVA/Shutterstock.com

faire du bateau	to go boating
du canoë	canoeing
de la planche à voile	windsurfing
de la voile	sailing
du rafting	white-water rafting
du scooter des mers	jet-skiing
du ski nautique	waterskiing
du surf	surfing
de la plongée	diving, scuba diving
se baigner	to go swimming
aller à la pêche, pêcher	to go fishing
aller à la chasse, chasser	to go hunting
faire de l'alpinisme *m.*	to go mountain climbing
de l'escalade	rock climbing
du parapente	hang-gliding
de la randonnée	hiking, backpacking
faire du ski alpin	to go downhill skiing
du ski de fond	cross-country skiing
du snowboard	snowboarding
de la motoneige, du scooter des neiges	snowmobiling
de la raquette	snowshoeing
faire de l'équitation	to go horseback riding
une promenade à cheval	for a horseback ride
faire une promenade/une balade...	to go for a walk; ride
en bateau	boat
à vélo	bike
en voiture	car
le décalage horaire mal supporter le décalage horaire	time difference; jet lag to suffer from . . .

le sac de couchage	sleeping bag
la maison de campagne	country house
la résidence secondaire	second home
la mer	sea
la montagne	mountain
la plage	beach
la station balnéaire	seaside resort
la station de sports d'hiver	winter (sports) resort

D QUOI?

descendre, loger à (un hôtel, un condo, etc.)	to stay (in a hotel, condo, etc.)
faire la grasse matinée	to sleep in, to sleep late
faire une croisière	to go on a cruise
bronzer	to tan, to get a tan
le coup de soleil	sunburn
attraper, prendre un coup de soleil	to get a sunburn

PREPARATION GRAMMATICALE

Avant de commencer ce chapitre, révisez l'usage des prépositions avec les noms géographiques, pages 185–186.

"Souris" Les Vacances, Michel Serre (auteur) © Glénat, 1984www.glenat.com

Qui sont les personnes sur ce dessin? Où sont-elles? Qu'est-ce qui est arrivé? Que font-elles?

Saviez-vous que... ?

Plus de 40% des Français ne partent jamais en vacances - un pourcentage énorme, qui a tendance à croître. Ensuite, ceux qui font leurs valises restent à plus de 80% sur le territoire national. En majorité, ils vont à la mer et logent dans la famille ou chez des amis. Depuis une vingtaine d'années, ces grandes masses ne bougent guère. Quatre Français sur dix ne partent jamais en vacances pour des questions économiques. S'il faut payer un logement, se nourrir tous les jours, et aussi faire des activités, cela peut coûter cher. Surtout si on part en famille. Mais une autre raison, plus méconnue, est un frein: partir veut dire devoir apprendre quelque chose de nouveau, s'adapter à de nouvelles situations. Notamment pour les classes populaires. Beaucoup préfèrent s'attacher à ce qu'ils connaissent, garder leurs habitudes. N'oublions pas que partir en vacances peut être perçu comme un risque ou une aventure. Et l'aventure peut faire peur à beaucoup.

Source: http://www.sudouest.fr

Vocabulaire

A **Devinettes.** Choisissez un mot (ou une expression) des listes C et D du vocabulaire. Expliquez-le (la) en français pour que vos camarades de classe devinent ce que vous avez choisi.

B **Qui ferait cela?** Quelle sorte de personne aimerait pratiquer les activités suivantes? Indiquez leur sexe et leur âge, puis décrivez leur caractère. Si possible, inventez-leur aussi une profession.

> **Modèle:** faire du rafting
>
> **Je pense qu'un garçon de 16 ans aimerait faire du rafting. J'imagine qu'il s'agit d'un lycéen qui recherche l'aventure, qui est courageux et qui, bien sûr, nage bien!**

1. faire une croisière
2. faire du stop
3. faire de la randonnée
4. aller à la chasse
5. faire de l'équitation
6. faire de l'alpinisme
7. coucher à la belle étoile
8. passer la nuit dans une auberge de jeunesse

C **Les vacances idéales.** Imaginez des vacances idéales pour chacune des personnes suivantes. Où iront-elles? (Donnez une destination précise.) Comment voyageront-elles? Où logeront-elles? Que feront-elles? Mentionnez aussi au moins trois activités.

1. un étudiant sportif qui adore l'eau mais qui n'a pas beaucoup d'argent (en juin)
2. votre professeur de français (en mai)
3. le président des Etats-Unis (en juillet)
4. une mère de famille nombreuse (après Noël)
5. deux Françaises de 19 ans qui viennent de réussir leur bac (en août)
6. un homme d'affaires de 60 ans qui vient de divorcer (en décembre)
7. l'ex-femme de cet homme d'affaires (en décembre)
8. trois étudiantes américaines à qui leurs grands-parents offrent des vacances (en été)
9. un adolescent de 16 ans qui est obligé de partir avec sa famille (en février)

D **Mais qu'est-ce qu'on y fait?** Vos amis et vous voulez passer vos vacances dans une région ou un pays francophone. Mettez-vous d'accord sur la destination en vous posant des questions sur les endroits proposés. Précisez aussi à quelle saison aura lieu votre voyage. Une fois que vous aurez choisi votre destination, expliquez vos raisons à la classe.

Modèle: la Guyane

VOUS: **Où se trouve la Guyane?**
Qu'est-ce qu'on peut y faire en été (en hiver)?

VOS CAMARADES: **La Guyane se trouve en Amérique du Sud, près du Vénézuela.**
En Guyane, on va à la plage, on fait des randonnées en forêt, on va à la pêche. L'hiver, c'est la saison du carnaval.

1. la Martinique
2. le Sénégal
3. le Viêt Nam
4. le Québec
5. la Louisiane
6. Tahiti
7. la Suisse
8. le Maroc

E **Ennuyeuses ou amusantes?** Mettez-vous par groupes de trois ou quatre. A tour de rôle, décrivez les vacances les plus ennuyeuses ou les plus amusantes que vous ayez jamais passées. Donnez beaucoup de détails et exagérez autant que vous le pouvez. Choisissez les meilleurs récits de votre groupe pour les présenter à la classe.

PREPARATION GRAMMATICALE

Avant de continuer, révisez la formation du futur, pages 186–188.

Saviez-vous que... ?

Lorsqu'on demande aux jeunes (de 15 à 30 ans) ce qu'ils aimeraient faire de leur été s'ils avaient le choix, ils citent majoritairement partir en vacances (62%), mener un projet personnel (26%) et travailler (24%). Pour ces derniers, il apparaît clairement que bosser pendant l'été relève plutôt de la nécessité que d'un choix librement consenti. Parmi les jeunes travaillant pendant l'été, seuls 28% affirment l'avoir choisi. Il est également intéressant de constater qu'un jeune sur cinq souhaiterait s'engager dans un projet de solidarité (20%). En 2010, 28% des jeunes ne sont pas partis en vacances. Parmi les raisons invoquées, les deux principales sont le manque de moyens financiers (39%) et le manque de temps (38%).

Source: http://www.joc.asso.fr 2011

© Clare Tufts

Lecture

D'abord professeur d'anglais, Marcel Pagnol (1895–1974) s'est mis à écrire très jeune. Ses pièces, *Marius*, *Fanny*, etc., dépeignent avec tendresse et humour l'âme méridionale et l'atmosphère de Marseille. Ses souvenirs d'enfance, *La Gloire de mon père* et *Le Château de ma mère* (tous les deux publiés en 1957) se situent en Provence (Marseille et ses environs) et constituent un réel hommage à sa famille. Marcel Pagnol a lui-même adapté un grand nombre de ses œuvres au cinéma. Plus tard, d'autres réalisateurs ont continué à tourner des films basés sur ses romans, par exemple *Manon des sources* (1986), *Le Château de ma mère* et *La Gloire de mon père* (1990).

ENTRONS EN MATIERE

Quand vous étiez à l'école primaire, comment étaient vos grandes vacances (les vacances d'été)? Combien de temps duraient-elles? Etiez-vous conscient(e) du passage du temps? Etiez-vous content(e) de retourner à l'école?

POUR MIEUX COMPRENDRE

Le passage que vous allez lire est au passé simple, un temps littéraire (voir pages 194–195). La plupart du temps, il n'est pas difficile d'identifier les verbes au passé simple: **il se versa (il s'est versé), je demandai (j'ai demandé),** etc. Trois verbes ont des formes qui ne ressemblent pas beaucoup à leur infinitif: **être: ce fut/ cela a été, faire: il fit/ il a fait et avoir: j'eus/ j'ai eu.** Parcourez maintenant le texte ci-dessous et identifiez quatre autres verbes au passé simple.

Le Château de ma mère

Le narrateur, qui a à peu près onze ans, raconte ses vacances à la campagne avec sa famille.

« Qu'est-ce qu'elle dit?

—Elle dit, répondit l'oncle, que les vacances sont finies »!

Et il se versa° paisiblement un verre de vin.

Je demandai, d'une voix étranglée°:

5 « C'est fini quand?

—Il faut partir après-demain matin, dit mon père. Aujourd'hui, c'est vendredi.

—Ce *fut* vendredi, dit l'oncle. Et nous partons dimanche matin.

—Tu sais bien que lundi, c'est la rentrée des classes »! dit la tante.

Je fus un instant sans comprendre, et je les regardai avec stupeur°.

10 « Voyons, dit ma mère, ce n'est pas une surprise! On en parle depuis huit jours ».

C'est vrai qu'ils en avaient parlé, mais je n'avais pas voulu entendre. Je savais que cette catastrophe arriverait finalement, comme les gens savent qu'ils mourront un jour mais ils se disent: « Ce n'est pas encore le moment d'examiner à fond° ce problème. Nous y penserons en temps et lieu ».

15 Le temps était venu: le choc me coupait la parole, et presque la respiration. Mon père le vit, et me parla gentiment.

« Voyons, mon garçon, voyons! Tu as eu deux grands mois de vacances[1]…

—Ce qui est déjà abusif! interrompit l'oncle. Si tu étais président de la République, tu n'en aurais pas eu autant »!

20 Cet ingénieux argument ne me toucha guère°, car j'avais décidé de n'aspirer à ces hautes fonctions qu'après mon service militaire.

« Tu as devant toi, reprit mon père, une année qui comptera dans ta vie: n'oublie pas qu'en juillet prochain, tu vas te présenter à l'examen des Bourses, pour entrer au lycée au mois d'octobre suivant!

25 —Tu sais que c'est très important! dit ma mère. Tu dis toujours que tu veux être millionnaire. Si tu n'entres pas au lycée, tu ne le seras jamais ».

se versa	*poured himself*
étranglée	*strangled*
stupeur	étonnement
à fond	*thoroughly*
guère	*hardly*

© Marcel Pagnol, *"Le Château de ma mère"* - Éditions de Fallois, 2004.

COMPRENEZ-VOUS?

1. Qu'est-ce que le narrateur apprend au début du passage?
2. Pourquoi cette nouvelle ne devrait-elle pas le surprendre?
3. Comment réagit-il? Quel mot utilise-t-il pour décrire la nouvelle? A quoi la compare-t-il?
4. Que pense l'oncle de la durée des vacances scolaires?
5. Pourquoi l'année scolaire qui vient sera-t-elle importante pour le narrateur?

[1] A l'époque de ce récit, les grandes vacances avaient lieu entre la mi-juillet et septembre.

CHERCHEZ LA FORME

1. Trouvez les pronoms objets dans le passage et indiquez leurs antécécents.
2. Trouvez les verbes au futur et au conditionnel dans le passage et mettez-les à l'infinitif.

ALLEZ PLUS LOIN

Imaginez, au présent, les vacances d'un garçon de 10 ans qui passe deux mois à la campagne.

RAPPEL The *future tense*, whose stem is based on the infinitive, is used to talk about what will happen in the future. When one event is expected to happen before another in the future, the earlier one is expressed in the *future perfect* (**futur antérieur**). For more details, see pages 189–190.

Applications

A **Les vacances et les voyages changeront-ils?** Dans l'avenir, est-ce que tout changera ou nos habitudes de vacances resteront-elles les mêmes? Finissez les phrases selon votre propre vision de l'avenir.

> **Modèle:** Aujourd'hui, je voyage en voiture. Dans l'avenir, …
> **Je ne voyagerai plus en voiture. Je prendrai l'avion ou peut-être un vaisseau spacial** *(space ship)*.

1. Aujourd'hui, nous allons à la plage. Dans l'avenir, …
2. Ces jours-ci, je fais du camping. Quand j'aurai des enfants, …
3. A l'heure actuelle, la plupart des Américains n'ont que quinze jours de congé. Dans vingt ans, …
4. Aujourd'hui, ma famille se détend à la mer. Quand mes parents seront à la retraite, …
5. D'habitude, mes amis s'amusent à la montagne. Lorsqu'ils auront 50 ans, …
6. Mon prof passe toujours ses vacances en Tunisie. A partir de l'année prochaine, …
7. Actuellement, je prends souvent le car. Dès que j'aurai gagné assez d'argent, …
8. De temps en temps, ma mère et moi, nous visitons des musées. Aussitôt que nous ne voyagerons plus ensemble, …

B **Des interviews imaginaires.** Mettez-vous à deux. L'un(e) d'entre vous est journaliste et l'autre est un personnage célèbre: une vedette de cinéma, un(e) chanteur/chanteuse, un personnage d'une série télévisée, le président des Etats-Unis, etc. Le (La) journaliste pose des questions à la célébrité sur ses projets de vacances et celle-ci répond au futur.

Notez bien: Il y a dans ce genre de situation un certain protocole. Faites attention aux formes interrogatives et utilisez « **vous** » dans les questions.

> **Modèle:** Où irez-vous en vacances?
> **J'irai à la Martinique.**

C Une chaîne d'événements. Avec vos camarades, faites des projets d'avenir d'après le modèle. Une personne complète la phrase donnée. Les autres enchaînent en formant des phrases contenant les mêmes conjonctions et les mêmes temps que dans le modèle.

> **Modèle:** Après avoir reçu mon diplôme, je…
>
> **Après avoir reçu mon diplôme, j'ai l'intention de trouver un poste.**
> **Dès que j'aurai trouvé un poste, je gagnerai beaucoup d'argent.**
> **Lorsque j'aurai gagné beaucoup d'argent, je me marierai.**
> **Aussitôt que je me serai marié(e), ma femme (mon mari) et moi achèterons une belle maison.**
> **Et finalement, nous aurons beaucoup d'enfants et nous serons très heureux.**

1. Après avoir gagné le gros lot *(jackpot)* à la loterie, je…
2. Après avoir pris leur retraite, mes parents…
3. Après avoir fini nos examens à la fin du semestre, mes amis et moi, nous…
4. Après être allé(e) au Sénégal, mon (ma) prof de français…
5. Et moi, après…

RAPPEL The *conditional form* uses the same stem as the future tense, but it has different endings. It is used to express hypotheses (what would or could happen if certain conditions occurred). For more details, see pages 186–190.

D Un rêve. Aimeriez-vous habiter un endroit ou un pays tout à fait différent de celui où vous vous trouvez actuellement? Où iriez-vous? Imaginez votre vie dans cette nouvelle région ou dans cet autre pays: votre logement, votre travail, vos amis, vos distractions, etc. Utilisez le conditionnel pour parler de votre rêve et ensuite, comparez-le à celui d'un(e) ou deux camarades de classe.

E Les parents se font du souci. Quand leurs enfants partent en voyage, les parents veulent savoir s'ils sauront se débrouiller en cas de besoin. Un(e) étudiant(e) joue le rôle du parent inquiet et pose la question. L'autre trouve une réponse rassurante, au conditionnel.

> **Modèle:** perdre ton passeport
> PARENT: Qu'est-ce que tu ferais si tu perdais ton passeport?
> ENFANT: J'irais au consulat américain.

1. rater l'avion
2. tes valises / ne pas arriver
3. ne pas trouver de chambre d'hôtel
4. on / voler ton portefeuille
5. ne plus avoir d'argent
6. les copains avec qui tu voyages / se faire arrêter par la police
7. tomber malade
8. nous / ne pas pouvoir venir te chercher à l'aéroport à ton retour

Continuez le dialogue.

PREPARATION GRAMMATICALE

Avant de continuer, révisez les phrases avec **si**, pages 192-194.

F **Des vacances: réalité, rêve et regrets.** Créez de petits récits en utilisant les débuts de phrases donnés. Attention au temps et à la forme des verbes.

1. **La réalité:**
   a. Si je pars en vacances l'été prochain, je…
   b. S'il fait beau quand j'arrive, …
   c. Mes amis m'accompagneront si…
   d. Nous nous amuserons si…
   e. Mais nous rentrerons tôt si…

2. **Un rêve:**
   a. Si j'avais un mois de vacances et beaucoup d'argent, je…
   b. Mes amis m'accompagneraient si…
   c. Ces vacances nous plairaient si…
   d. Si je louais une voiture, …
   e. Je ne coucherais pas sous la tente si…

3. **Des regrets.** Vous êtes rentré(e) tôt, il a plu la plupart du temps, vous n'avez pas bien mangé, vous avez eu un accident de voiture, vous vous êtes disputé(e) avec vos amis, et quoi d'autre? Exprimez vos regrets et expliquez ce que vous auriez pu ou auriez dû faire autrement.
   a. Si je n'étais pas allé(e) à / en / au / aux…
   b. S'il avait fait beau, nous…
   c. Si je n'avais pas invité mes amis, …
   d. Je n'aurais pas eu d'accident si…
   e. Je me serais reposé(e) si…

G **Tout serait différent.** Décrivez les conséquences possibles ou probables dans chaque cas suivant. Comparez vos idées à celles de vos camarades de classe. Attention à la forme et au temps des verbes!

1. Si tous les Américains avaient cinq semaines de congés payés, …
2. Si mes copains avaient appris à faire de l'escalade, …
3. Si nous pouvions partir pour Tahiti, …
4. Si mon professeur de français voulait se cultiver en vacances, …
5. S'il n'y avait pas de tunnel sous la Manche, …
6. Si ma mère me payait mon billet d'avion, …
7. Si j'avais passé l'été à faire du stop, …

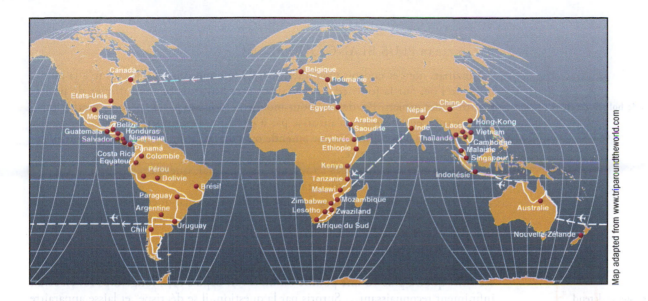

Lecture

En 2007, le Belge Didier Tilman crée un site web pour documenter les trois années de son voyage autour du monde, partager quelques-unes de ses aventures, « faire rêver » et donner envie de partir aux autres, dit-il.

ENTRONS EN MATIERE

Si vous décidiez de partir, de faire le tour du monde, où iriez-vous? Comment voyageriez-vous? Qu'est-ce que vous emporteriez?

Voyage autour du monde: trois ans de vagabondage

PREMIÈRE PARTIE

Préparatifs: Je suis parti avec la certitude de voyager pour une année; l'aventure a duré trois fois plus longtemps.

Je n'ai jamais respecté le moindre itinéraire que je m'étais fixé; celui-ci a toujours été déterminé et a évolué en fonction des rencontres, par définition aléatoires° et
5 imprévisibles.

aléatoires par hasard

Je me suis acheté un billet tour du monde valable un an, je n'ai pu utiliser que le premier trajet (Bruxelles-New York) et je me suis fait rembourser le second tronçon° (Buenos Aires-Auckland).

tronçon partie

J'ai acheté le plus grand sac à dos (que je considérais être mon fil de vie) et l'ai
10 bourré° de tout ce qu'il était recommandé d'emmener (pompe à eau, réchaud°, trousse de pharmacie° préparée par une amie médecin, vêtements de rechange en quantité pour affronter toutes les conditions météorologiques, etc.). Peu à peu je l'ai vidé de son contenu; après plusieurs mois, je l'ai vendu et me suis satisfait d'un plus petit.

bourré *stuffed* / **réchaud** *camping stove* **trousse...** *first aid kit*

La plus belle des surprises enfin: Plus longtemps on voyage, moins on dépense.

A Zanzibar PLUS BLANC QUE BLANC

pas de bol pas de chance

15   Zanzibar: nom et endroit magiques. Je loue une moto pour aller jusqu'à la pointe nord de l'île. Sur la journée, je me fais arrêter huit fois par un officier de police. Contrôle des papiers. Pas de bol° pour moi: je ne possède pas de permis international; mon permis européen ne m'autorise pas à conduire l'engin sur lequel je me trouve assis. Si je dois payer huit fois une amende ou « une contribution », j'aurais mieux fait
20   de louer une voiture de luxe.

Les sept premiers passages sont franchis sans mal: quelques palabres et excuses confondues suffisent à m'ouvrir (gratuitement) la porte.

Le huitième policier a lui tout de suite repéré « mon manquement grave aux lois du pays »… il le sait… et va vouloir en abuser. Début des discussions; c'est mal parti, il a
25   tout son temps et est décidé à le prendre.

Je suis tout à coup ébloui par la blancheur de son uniforme… Admiratif, je le lui dis et demande comment lui ou son épouse font pour obtenir une telle couleur. Mon tee-shirt qui n'a plus vu une poudre ou un savon depuis bien longtemps lui en serait infiniment reconnaissant… Surpris par la question, il se décrispe° et laisse apparaître

décrispe se détend

30   un sourire assorti à l'uniforme. On enchaîne sur tout et rien et échangeons finalement nos adresses!

Au moment de le saluer, impossible de faire repartir la moto.

Pas de problème, c'est maintenant mon meilleur copain: il appelle un ami garagiste et me pousse pour redémarrer…

envoûté enchanté

35   L'Afrique m'a emballé; les Africains m'ont envoûté°.

Pour toujours.

COMPRENEZ-VOUS?

1. Comparez ses préparatifs et la réalité de son voyage.
2. Quels mots du texte caractérisent sa façon de voyager?
3. Quel moyen de transport choisit-il à Zanzibar?
4. Pourquoi a-t-il des ennuis avec la police?
5. Comment se lie-t-il d'amitié avec le huitième policier?
6. Comment trouve-t-il l'Afrique? Quels mots vous le disent?

CHERCHEZ LA FORME

Expliquez l'usage du conditionnel dans la phrase: « Si je dois payer… » (lignes 19–20) Est-ce que l'auteur du passage suit les règles que vous apprenez dans ce chapitre? Pourquoi?

Voyage autour du monde: trois ans de vagabondage

DEUXIÈME PARTIE

Notre voyageur se trouve en Amérique du Sud.

EVITA, L'AMOUR EN VOYAGE

Pour traverser la région des lacs et aller de Puerto Montt[2] (Chili) à Bariloche (Argentine), pas d'autres choix que de passer par une agence de tourisme-Cruce de
40 Lagos-qui offre, sur une journée, de combiner bus, ferries, snow car° pour traverser la frontière.

Pour limiter les frais, je fais le premier tronçon en auto-stop et rejoins Petrohue où une famille m'accueille pour la nuit. Après un solide petit déjeuner j'attends les touristes arrivés en bus et me mêle à eux pour prendre le premier ferry de la journée. Une jolie
45 coordinatrice me demande mon billet et m'accueille à bord. Le temps est exécrable: une enveloppe épaisse de nuage empêche de voir le paysage qui, en principe, doit être la seule raison d'être là… J'entame donc la rédaction de mon journal de bord… avant d'être rejoint par la charmante coordinatrice… Eva–c'est son nom–prend grand soin de moi (sauf à l'heure du repas: je me contente de mon sandwich alors que les autres
50 profitent d'un bon restaurant). Le temps ne s'améliore pas. Nous passons donc une grande partie de la journée à parler ensemble.

Arrivés au soir à Bariloche, le bus dépose un à un les touristes dans leur hôtel respectif. Je reste le dernier à bord… et invite Eva à continuer notre conversation autour d'un bon steak au soir. Elle accepte.
55 Avant de retourner sur Puerto Montt, Eva a trois jours libres que nous passons ensemble. Je promets de venir la revoir après avoir été jusque tout en bas du continent.

Un mois plus tard je la retrouve… et reste dans sa famille un mois supplémentaire.

Mon tour du monde a failli° s'arrêter là–ce qui aurait sans doute été une frustration éternelle–et un beau matin je décide de continuer ma route, le plus loin
60 possible: 48 heures de bus non stop et second avion de mon tour du monde pour la Nouvelle-Zélande… Eva est toujours restée dans mes esprits et souvent mentionnée dans mon journal intime. On a gardé pendant deux ans contact de manière régulière par courrier, téléphone et fax. Elle a accepté ma seconde invitation de venir visiter l'Europe à mon retour de voyage. Elle est venue, a vu et a vaincu.
65 C'était sans doute un signe indéfectible° de notre légende personnelle (dixit Paulho Coelho[3]): notre mini-trip nous amène au musée océanographique Jacques Cousteau à Monaco. Sur le haut des façades du bâtiment, une dizaine de noms gravés. Notre regard tombe sur ceux de la façade principale: Belgica–Talisman–Valdivia. La Belgique et Valdivia (ville d'où est originaire Eva) déjà protégés et réunis par la magie (de l'amour)…
70 Nous nous sommes depuis lors mariés et avons aujourd'hui deux charmants bambins, Océane et Amadéo.

snow car *snow cat*

a failli s'est presque

indéfectible sûr

---

www.triparoundtheworld.com © Didier Tilman

---

[2] Ville du sud du Chili, sur le Pacifique
[3] Ecrivain brésilien

Eva et Didier au Chili

COMPRENEZ-VOUS?

1. Quels sont les moyens de transport qu'il doit utiliser pour traverser la frontière entre le Chili et l'Argentine?
2. Quels détails indiquent que le narrateur a moins d'argent que les touristes avec qui il fait le voyage?
3. Quel temps fait-il pendant le trajet? Quel rôle joue la météo dans le rapport qui se développe entre le narrateur et Eva?
4. Que font le narrateur et Eva pour permettre à leur relation d'évoluer?
5. A quel moment décident-ils de rester ensemble?

CHERCHEZ LA FORME

1. Du présent au passé: Dans le paragraphe qui commence par « Pour limiter les frais… », mettez tous les verbes conjugués au passé composé.
2. Le passé et les infinitifs: Dans le paragraphe qui commence par « Eva est toujours restée… », identifiez les verbes au passé composé et donnez leur infinitif.

ALLEZ PLUS LOIN

Avec un(e) camarade de classe, créez des dialogues entre Didier et Eva: (1) sur le ferry quand ils viennent de se rencontrer; (2) dans sa famille après un mois, juste avant le départ de Didier pour la Nouvelle-Zélande; (3) quand ils se retrouvent en Europe.

Activites d'expansion

A En famille. Il n'est pas toujours facile de se mettre d'accord sur la destination des vacances. La situation se complique s'il y a plusieurs enfants ou même des grands-parents qui partent ensemble. Formez un groupe de quatre ou cinq et jouez la scène où une famille essaie de se mettre d'accord.

Rendez-vous sur le site web de *Sur le vif* pour regardez la vidéo du Chapitre 5, puis complétez les activités à la page 81 du **Student Activities Manual**.

1. D'abord, choisissez votre rôle: mère, père, grand-parent ou enfant (de quel âge?).
2. Ensuite, pendant quelques minutes, travaillez seul(e) et pensez à ce que votre personnage voudrait faire en vacances. Où désire-t-il aller? Avec qui?, etc.
3. Enfin, discutez de vos idées en groupe. Il faut trouver une solution qui convient à tout le monde et que vous expliquerez plus tard à la classe.

Si vous voulez interrompre:

Patiemment	*Impatiemment*
Une minute…	Attends! / Attendez!
Pardon…	Mais enfin…
Excuse-moi… / Excusez-moi…	Non, mais écoute!…
J'aimerais dire une chose…	Alors là…
	Mais attention…

B Débat: L'importance des voyages

Formez deux groupes. Un groupe va expliquer la validité de la première phrase. L'autre groupe va soutenir l'opinion exprimée dans la deuxième phrase. Les membres des deux groupes préparent individuellement des arguments pour justifier leur point de vue et choisissent ensuite en groupe les meilleurs d'entre eux. Ils les présentent ensuite à l'autre groupe qui donne ses réactions. Pour conclure, votez pour voir ce que pensent la plupart des étudiants.

1. Les voyages ne nous apprennent plus rien puisqu'avec Internet, on a accès au monde entier sans sortir de chez soi.
2. Voyager joue un rôle essentiel dans l'éducation de chaque individu.

Si vous êtes d'accord, vous pouvez dire:

Oui, c'est vrai…

Moi aussi, je pense que…
C'est une bonne idée de…
Tu as raison de dire que…
C'est génial ce que tu dis, parce que…
Je suis entièrement d'accord avec toi car…

Si vous n'êtes pas d'accord, vous pouvez répondre:

Non, je ne crois pas que…
Je crois que tu te trompes…
Je regrette, mais tu as tort de dire que…
A mon avis…
Moi, je ne suis pas d'accord parce que…
Au contraire, je pense que…
Je ne partage pas ton point de vue à ce sujet car…

© Clare Tufts

C Paris Plages.
Lisez le texte suivant sur Paris Plages. Si vous deviez passer une semaine à Paris en août, participeriez-vous aux activités de Paris Plages? Auxquelles et pourquoi? Faites des recherches sur Internet pour voir ce qu'on peut y faire.

Paris Plages est une opération estivale menée par la mairie de Paris depuis 2002. Chaque année, entre juillet et août, pendant environ 4 à 5 semaines, sur 3,5 km, la voie sur berge rive droite de la Seine et la place de l'Hôtel-de-Ville ainsi que des sites annexes—comme le bassin de la Villette—accueillent des activités ludiques et sportives (pétanque, mini-golf, taï-chi, fitness, baignade, bateau, etc.), des plages de sable et d'herbe, des palmiers… L'objectif principal est de donner l'occasion aux habitants de la région ne partant pas en vacances de profiter d'activités qui sont habituellement pratiquées sur les plages du littoral. En 2011, avec plus de 3 millions de personnes et presque 200 000 entrées aux nombreuses activités proposées, Paris Plages a séduit les Parisiens comme les touristes de tous les âges!

Source: www.parisplages.fr

Ciné et télé

© Clare Tufts

A LE CINEMA

Mots apparentés: le cinéma; la salle de cinéma; le film: comique, musical, d'animation, d'aventures, de science-fiction, d'horreur, historique, politique, érotique, pornographique; la comédie musicale; le drame (psychologique); le western; le documentaire; le thriller

le film...	... movie
policier	detective
d'espionnage	spy
de guerre	war
fantastique	fantasy

le (grand) classique	classic
le court métrage	short film
le dessin animé	cartoon
la bande annonce	preview, trailer
le film en couleurs	film in color
en noir et blanc	in black and white
en version originale (en VO)	original version
doublé	dubbed
sous-titré	subtitled
muet	silent
l'écran m.	screen

Pour obtenir des exercices et activités supplémentaires sur le contenu de ce chapitre, rendez-vous sur le site
www.cengagebrain.com

© Clare Tufts

le (la) réalisateur (-rice)	director
le (la) scénariste	screenwriter
l'acteur (-trice)	actor (actress)
la vedette, la star	star
le personnage (principal)	(main) character
le (la) cinéphile	movie buff
l'intrigue f.	plot
le dénouement	ending, conclusion
le décor	set
les effets m. spéciaux	special effects
jouer, interpréter un rôle	to play a role
tourner un film	to make a movie
regarder un film	to watch a movie

B LA TELEVISION

le téléviseur	TV set
à la télé	on TV
le (la) téléspectateur (-trice)	television viewer
la chaîne	channel
la télévision par câble	cable television
avoir le câble	to have cable television
la télévision par satellite	satellite television
la télévision par internet	internet television
le home cinéma	home theater entertainment system
la programmation	programming
l'émission f.	program
les informations f. (les infos), le journal (télévisé) (le JT)	the news
le feuilleton	soap opera
la série	television series
le téléfilm	movie made for television
la télé-réalité	reality television
le jeu télévisé	game show
la publicité, la pub	ads, commercials
la télécommande	remote control
zapper	to channel surf
le zapping	channel surfing
le caméscope (numérique)	(digital) video camera
le lecteur DVD	DVD player
graver un DVD	to burn a DVD
télécharger	to download

PRÉPARATION GRAMMATICALE

Avant de commencer ce chapitre, révisez la négation, pages 197–200.

© Clare Tufts

Vocabulaire

A **Les films que je préfère…** Parmi les six catégories suivantes, choisissez-en quatre. Pour chacune d'elles, donnez le titre de votre film préféré.

film de science-fiction   film d'horreur   grand classique

film d'aventures   film français   dessin animé

Ensuite, trouvez une personne dans la classe avec qui vous avez au moins un titre en commun. Discutez des raisons de vos choix.

B **Comment dit-on?** Trouvez le mot de la liste A du vocabulaire qui correspond à chaque explication suivante.

1. ensemble des événements qui forment l'action principale d'un film
2. personne qui dirige toutes les opérations de préparation et de réalisation d'un film
3. artiste dont la profession est de jouer un rôle à l'écran (télé ou cinéma)
4. amateur et connaisseur en matière de cinéma
5. personne qui jouit d'une grande renommée, une célébrité
6. film dont la bande sonore originale a été remplacée par une bande sonore en langue étrangère
7. conclusion de l'intrigue
8. extrait d'un film qu'on projette avant le début du film principal

C **Devinettes.** Choisissez un mot de la liste B du vocabulaire et expliquez-le en français. Vos camarades de classe vont deviner de quel mot il s'agit.

Modèle: Ce qu'on utilise pour changer la chaîne à la télé.
      la télécommande

D **Qu'est-ce qu'on regarde?** Avec trois de vos ami(e)s, vous décidez de regarder la télé ce soir, mais vous n'arrivez pas à vous entendre sur le choix de l'émission: le journal télévisé, un jeu télévisé, un feuilleton ou un téléfilm? Mettez-vous par groupes de quatre. Parmi les quatre émissions proposées, chaque personne choisit « sa préférée ». A tour de rôle, chaque personne essaie de convaincre les trois autres que son émission sera la meilleure.

Lecture

From Albert Robida, *Le Vingtième Siècle*, 1883

Auteur, dessinateur, graveur, Albert Robida (1848–1926) était un visionnaire du XX\u1d49 siècle beaucoup moins connu que son contemporain Jules Verne. Dans ses trois romans (*Le Vingtième Siècle*, 1883, *La Guerre au vingtième siècle*, 1887 et *La Vie électrique*, 1890), Robida imagine le siècle à venir: le métro, le train à grande vitesse, l'avion à réaction (le jet), les infos à la radio 24/7, les bombardements, les rayons X, mais aussi les technologies de communication et en particulier le téléphonoscope, véritable préfiguration de la télévision[1]. Dans le texte qui suit, vous lirez la description de cette invention, extraite du *Vingtième Siècle*. Notez que l'histoire se passe au début des années 1950.

[1] Le 7 septembre 1927 est la date de la première transmission électronique de vidéo, inventée par l'Américain Philo T. Farnsworth; en revanche, la télévision pour le grand public ne s'est répandue ni aux Etats-Unis ni à l'étranger avant la fin des années 1940.

ENTRONS EN MATIERE

L'image à la page 87 est une des illustrations faites par Robida pour la première édition du *Vingtième Siècle*. Qu'est-ce que vous y voyez? Comment sont les gens? Que font-ils?

La télévision—un rêve du XIXᵉ siècle

Parmi les sublimes inventions dont le XXᵉ siècle s'honore, parmi les mille et une merveilles d'un siècle si fécond en magnifiques découvertes, le téléphonoscope peut compter pour une des plus merveilleuses, pour une de celles qui porteront le plus haut la gloire de nos savants. L'ancien télégraphe électrique[2], cette enfantine application de l'électricité,
5 a été détrôné par le téléphone[3] et ensuite par le téléphonoscope, qui est le perfectionnement suprême du téléphone. L'ancien télégraphe permettait de comprendre à distance un correspondant ou un interlocuteur, le téléphone permettait de l'entendre, le téléphonoscope permet en même temps de le voir. Que désirer de plus? […]

Les théâtres eurent ainsi, outre° leur nombre ordinaire de spectateurs dans la salle,
10 une certaine quantité de spectateurs à domicile, reliés au théâtre par le fil° du téléphonoscope. Nouvelle et importante source de revenus. Plus de limites maintenant aux bénéfices, plus de maximum de recettes°! Quand une pièce° avait du succès, outre les trois ou quatre mille spectateurs de la salle, cinquante mille abonnés°, parfois, suivaient les acteurs à distance; cinquante mille spectateurs non seulement de Paris,
15 mais encore de tous les pays du monde.

Auteurs dramatiques, musiciens des siècles écoulés! ô Molière, ô Corneille, ô Hugo, ô Rossini![4] qu'auriez-vous dit au rêveur qui vous eût annoncé qu'un jour cinquante mille personnes, éparpillées° sur toute la surface du globe, pourraient de Paris, de Pékin ou de Tombouctou, suivre une de vos œuvres jouée sur un théâtre parisien,
20 entendre vos vers, écouter votre musique, palpiter aux péripéties violentes° et voir en même temps vos personnages marcher et agir?

Voilà pourtant la merveille réalisée par l'invention du téléphonoscope. La Compagnie universelle du téléphonoscope théâtral, fondée en 1945, compte maintenant plus de six cent mille abonnés répartis dans toutes les parties du monde;
25 c'est cette Compagnie qui centralise les fils et paye les subventions° aux directeurs de théâtres.

L'appareil consiste en une simple plaque de cristal, encastrée dans une cloison d'appartement°, ou posée comme une glace au-dessus d'une cheminée quelconque. L'amateur de spectacle, sans se déranger, s'assied devant cette plaque, choisit son
30 théâtre, établit sa communication et tout aussitôt la représentation° commence.

Avec le téléphonoscope, le mot le dit, on voit et l'on entend. Le dialogue et la musique sont transmis comme par le simple téléphone ordinaire; mais en même temps, la scène elle-même avec son éclairage°, ses décors et ses acteurs, apparaît sur la grande plaque de cristal avec la netteté de la vision directe; on assiste donc réellement à
35 la représentation par les yeux et par l'oreille. L'illusion est complète, absolue; il semble que l'on écoute la pièce du fond d'une loge de premier rang°.

outre en plus de

fil *wire*

recettes l'argent reçu (pour les billets d'entrée) / **pièce** *play* / **abonnés** ici, ceux qui ont un téléphonoscope chez eux

éparpillées dispersées

palpiter… *tremble through the violent episodes*

subventions *subsidies*

encastrée… *recessed in the wall*

représentation *performance*

éclairage *lighting*

loge… *front row seat*

From Albert Robida, *Le Vingtième Siècle*, 1883

---

[2] inventé par Samuel Morse; premier message envoyé en 1844
[3] inventé en 1876 par Alexander Graham Bell
[4] Molière (1622–1673), Corneille (1606–1684), Hugo (1802–1885): auteurs dramatiques français; Rossini (1792–1868): compositeur italien, notamment d'opéras

COMPRENEZ-VOUS?

1. Pourquoi le téléphonoscope est-il considéré comme « le perfectionnement suprême du téléphone » ?
2. Quelle programmation Robida imagine-t-il pour ses téléspectateurs des années 1950 ?
3. Qu'est-ce que la Compagnie universelle du téléphonoscope théâtral ?
4. En quoi l'installation du téléphonoscope décrite dans ce roman ressemble-t-elle à l'installation sophistiquée du home cinéma d'aujourd'hui ?
5. Quels sont les avantages d'avoir un téléphonoscope chez soi selon ce roman ?

CHERCHEZ LA FORME

1. Identifiez le temps et l'infinitif de **eurent** (ligne 9) et de **auriez-vous** dit (ligne 17).
2. **Eût annoncé** (ligne 17) est la forme alternative (2ᵉ forme) du conditionnel passé. Mettez-la à la forme que vous avez apprise dans le chapitre 5.
3. Plusieurs infinitifs sont liés au verbe **pourraient** (ligne 18). Identifiez le temps et le mode de **pourraient** et énumérez les infinitifs.

ALLEZ PLUS LOIN

Pourquoi, à votre avis, Robida ne parle-t-il pas d'une programmation plus variée ? En plus des pièces de théâtre et des opéras, quelles autres possibilités pouvez-vous imaginer pour les années 1950 ?

> **RAPPEL** The *negative construction* in French consists of two parts: **ne + pas** (or **jamais, personne, rien,** etc.). The first part of the negative (**ne**) directly precedes the verb; the second part generally follows the verb, but certain expressions require a different placement within the sentence. For more details, see pages 197–200.

Applications

A **A la recherche de l'argent.** Vous rêvez de devenir scénariste et vous avez choisi le dessin animé comme point de départ pour cette nouvelle carrière. Imaginez que vous vous trouvez en réunion avec un directeur de production *(producer)* chez Walt Disney Studios qui vient de rejeter votre premier scénario. Complétez le dialogue en utilisant des expressions négatives variées.

Modèle: VOUS: Mais monsieur, tout le monde aimerait ce dessin animé.
LE DIRECTEUR: **Non. Personne n'aimerait ce dessin animé.**

1. VOUS: Il y a quelque chose de nouveau dans mon film.
   LE DIRECTEUR:
2. VOUS: L'intrigue est très intéressante.
   LE DIRECTEUR:
3. VOUS: Tous les personnages sont fascinants.
   LE DIRECTEUR:

4. Vous: Le dénouement est heureux et romantique.
   Le directeur:
5. Vous: Les critiques aiment toujours ce genre de dénouement.
   Le directeur:
6. Vous: Avez-vous déjà lu tout le manuscrit?
   Le directeur:

Continuez ce dialogue avec un(e) partenaire...

B **Vive la télé!** Vous aimez regarder la télévision et vous trouvez qu'elle a une influence très positive sur les adultes aussi bien que sur les enfants. Défendez les avantages de la télévision en mettant les phrases suivantes à la forme affirmative.

1. Aucune émission n'est bonne.
2. La pub n'est jamais captivante.
3. Personne ne regarde les émissions de télé-réalité.
4. Le journal télévisé n'est pas encore aussi bon que la presse.
5. Les enfants ne trouvent rien qu'ils aiment à la télé.
6. Ni les téléfilms ni les feuilletons ne sont meilleurs que les films qui passent au cinéma.
7. La télévision n'aide pas du tout les enfants à développer leur imagination.
8. Je ne connais personne qui aime les séries.
9. Rien n'est logique dans la programmation.
10. La plupart des téléspectateurs ne sont jamais contents.

C **Le positif et le négatif.** Pierre et Norbert sont frères, mais ils n'ont pas du tout le même caractère ni les mêmes intérêts. Pierre est toujours positif et Norbert est toujours négatif! Voici une petite histoire au sujet de Pierre. Transformez cette histoire pour qu'elle s'applique à Norbert en mettant les phrases à la forme négative.

1. Pierre était très content d'aller au cinéma.
2. Il a beaucoup aimé le film qu'il a vu.
3. Il avait déjà vu d'autres films du même réalisateur.
4. Tout était intéressant dans l'intrigue.
5. Tous les acteurs étaient très bons.
6. Il a été impressionné par les décors et les effets spéciaux.
7. Il a parlé avec beaucoup de gens qui ont aimé ce film.
8. Il est rentré très satisfait de sa soirée.
9. Ses amis lui ont demandé comment il avait trouvé ce film.
10. Pierre a toujours préféré le cinéma à la télévision.

RAPPEL   In French, as in English, *relative pronouns* allow you to qualify or expand on something you are saying by attaching a second clause. In this second clause (called a relative or subordinate clause) the relative pronoun can function as the subject, the direct object, or the object of a preposition. For more details, see pages 200–202.

D **Le fabuleux destin d'Amélie Poulain.** Identifiez la fonction de chaque pronom relatif souligné dans les phrases suivantes. Choisissez parmi:

> sujet
> objet direct
> objet de la préposition **de**
> objet d'une préposition autre que **de**
> équivalent d'une préposition + **lequel** (exprime le temps ou le lieu)

1. *Amélie* est le titre <u>qu'</u>on donne à la version anglaise du film français *Le fabuleux destin d'Amélie Poulain.*
2. Amélie est une fille <u>dont</u> la mère est morte écrasée par une personne tombée de Notre-Dame.
3. Elle a un père <u>qui</u> s'intéresse plus à son nain de jardin qu'à elle.
4. Elle quitte la maison de ses parents et s'installe à Paris <u>où</u> elle travaille comme serveuse.
5. Un jour, elle trouve <u>ce qu'</u>elle veut faire dans la vie: améliorer la vie des autres.
6. Elle aide la concierge <u>qui</u> ne s'est jamais remise de la mort de son mari.
7. Elle aide son voisin <u>qu'</u>on appelle « l'homme de verre » parce que ses os se cassent facilement.
8. Elle aide un jeune homme <u>dont</u> le patron se moque de manière assez cruelle.
9. Elle rend visite à son père <u>à qui</u> le nain de jardin disparu envoie des cartes postales de partout dans le monde!
10. Il faut voir le film pour savoir <u>ce qui</u> se passe une fois qu'Amélie a rencontré Nino.

E **Une comédie classique.** Complétez les phrases suivantes avec les pronoms relatifs qui conviennent.

1. *Le Viager* est un film comique français _____ on m'a parlé récemment.
2. Goscinny, _____ on connaît comme scénariste de la bande dessinée *Astérix*, a écrit le scénario de ce film avec Pierre Tchernia.
3. C'est l'histoire d'un célibataire de 59 ans _____ est persuadé par son médecin de lui vendre en viager[5] sa propriété à Saint-Tropez.
4. Mais il ne meurt pas, _____ désespère la famille du médecin.
5. En fait, ce vieil homme semble retrouver une seconde jeunesse dans sa propriété sur la Côte d'Azur _____ il fête son centième anniversaire avant le dénouement de l'histoire!

F **Donnez un coup de main!** Pour son cours de français, un de vos amis doit écrire un court texte sur son film préféré. Afin de rendre le style plus fluide, le professeur a demandé d'utiliser autant de pronoms relatifs que possible. Aidez votre ami à lier les phrases de son texte avec des pronoms relatifs variés. Vous pouvez aussi changer des noms sujets en pronoms sujets, si nécessaire.

Je vais parler de *Titanic*. *Titanic* est un de mes films préférés. Les personnages principaux de cette histoire sont une jeune femme et un jeune homme. La jeune femme voyage avec son fiancé riche. Le jeune homme est très pauvre. Le fiancé n'est pas gentil. La jeune femme a un peu peur de lui. Le jeune homme fait un dessin de la jeune femme nue. Le fiancé découvre le dessin. La jeune femme tombe amoureuse du jeune homme. Le fiancé se méfie de *(distrusts)* la jeune femme. Quand le bateau commence à couler *(sink)*, le fiancé monte dans un

[5] Vendre en viager *to sell a house so as to provide the seller with a life of annuity.*

canot de sauvetage *(lifeboat)*. Cette action réduit le nombre de places disponibles pour les femmes et les enfants. La jeune femme refuse de quitter le bateau sans le jeune homme. Je trouve cela très romantique! Le jeune homme reste trop longtemps dans l'eau. La température de l'eau est très basse. Le jeune homme meurt dans l'eau froide. La jeune femme se rend compte de cela quand elle se réveille. La jeune femme est sauvée par des gens. Ces gens entendent le bruit de son sifflet *(whistle)*. L'acteur Leonardo DiCaprio est devenu le héros de toutes les adolescentes à la sortie du film. Leonardo DiCaprio a interprété le rôle du jeune homme. La chanson thème du film était interprétée par Céline Dion. Beaucoup de gens ont acheté l'enregistrement de cette chanson.

G **Vous et la télé.** Créez des phrases originales en utilisant les éléments donnés.

1. l'émission de télé-réalité / que
2. le journal télévisé / qui
3. un jeu télévisé / dont
4. un feuilleton / dans lequel
5. la pub / où

Lecture

© Clare Tufts

Albert Camus (1913–1960) est né en Algérie mais a passé la plus grande partie de sa vie adulte en France. Ses œuvres les plus connues sont les romans *L'Etranger* (1942) et *La Peste* (1947), les pièces de théâtre *Caligula* (1938) et *Le Malentendu* (1944) et les essais philosophiques *Le Mythe de Sisyphe* (1942) et *L'Homme révolté* (1951). Camus est mort dans un accident de voiture en 1960, trois ans après avoir reçu le Prix Nobel. Au moment de sa mort, il préparait une nouvelle œuvre à laquelle il avait donné le titre provisoire *Le Premier Homme*. Le texte que vous allez lire est tiré de ce manuscrit inachevé, publié chez Gallimard en 1994.

ENTRONS EN MATIERE

Avez-vous déjà vu un film muet? Si oui, lequel? Quel âge aviez-vous quand vous l'avez vu? Quelle a été votre réaction? Si vous n'avez jamais vu de film muet, expliquez pourquoi. Pensez-vous qu'un spectateur regarde un film muet de la même façon qu'il regarde un film parlant? Quelles pourraient être les différences?

POUR MIEUX COMPRENDRE

Aujourd'hui, avant le début d'un film, on projette souvent des annonces publicitaires ou des bandes annonces. Parcourez les premières lignes du texte de Camus pour découvrir ce qu'on projetait au cinéma décrit par le narrateur.

Le Premier Homme

PREMIÈRE PARTIE

Les séances de cinéma réservaient d'autres plaisirs à l'enfant... [...] Jacques escortait sa grand-mère qui, pour l'occasion, avait lissé ses cheveux blancs et fermé son éternelle robe noire d'une broche d'argent. [...] Le cinéma projetait alors des films muets, des actualités° d'abord, un court film comique, le grand film et pour finir un film à
5 épisodes, à raison d'un bref épisode par semaine. La grand-mère aimait particulièrement ces films en tranches dont chaque épisode se terminait en suspens. Par exemple le héros musclé portant dans ses bras la jeune fille blonde et blessée s'engageait sur un pont de lianes° au-dessus d'un cañon° torrentueux. Et la dernière image de l'épisode hebdomadaire° montrait une main tatouée qui, armée d'un couteau primitif, tran-
10 chait les lianes du ponton°. Le héros continuait de cheminer superbement malgré les avertissements vociférés des spectateurs des « bancs »°. La question alors n'était pas de savoir si le couple s'en tirerait°, le doute à cet égard n'étant pas permis, mais seulement de savoir comment il s'en tirerait, ce qui expliquait que tant de spectateurs, arabes et français[6], revinssent° la semaine d'après pour voir les amoureux arrêtés dans leur
15 chute mortelle par un arbre providentiel. Le spectacle était accompagné tout au long au piano par une vieille demoiselle qui opposait aux lazzis° des « bancs » la sérénité immobile d'un maigre dos en bouteille d'eau minérale capsulée d'un col de dentelle°. Jacques considérait alors comme une marque de distinction que l'impressionnante demoiselle gardât des mitaines° par les chaleurs les plus torrides. Son rôle d'ailleurs n'était pas
20 aussi facile qu'on eût pu° le croire. Le commentaire musical des actualités, en particulier, l'obligeait à changer de mélodie selon le caractère de l'événement projeté. Elle passait ainsi sans transition d'un gai quadrille° destiné à accompagner la présentation des modes de printemps à la marche funèbre de Chopin à l'occasion d'une inondation° en Chine ou des funérailles d'un personnage important dans la vie nationale ou inter-
25 nationale. Quel que soit le morceau, en tout cas, l'exécution était imperturbable [...]. C'était elle en tout cas qui arrêtait d'un coup le vacarme° assourdissant en attaquant à pleines pédales le prélude qui était censé créer l'atmosphère de la matinée. Un énorme vrombissement° annonçait que l'appareil de projection se mettait en marche, le calvaire° de Jacques commençait alors.

actualités informations

lianes *vines* / **cañon** canyon
hebdomadaire qui passe toutes les semaines / **ponton** *floating bridge* / **bancs** les places bon marché / **s'en...** échapperait à cette situation

revinssent (imparfait du subjonctif) sont revenus
lazzis *jeers, hooting*
col... *lace collar*

mitaines gants dont les doigts sont coupés / **eût...** (plus-que-parfait du subjonctif) aurait pu
quadrille air de danse
inondation *flood*

vacarme grand bruit fait par les spectateurs
vrombissement *humming* /
calvaire *suffering*

---

[6] Cette histoire se passe en Afrique du Nord.

COMPRENEZ-VOUS?

1. Qu'est-ce qui assurait le retour des spectateurs chaque semaine?
2. Est-ce que la salle était silencieuse pendant la projection du film muet? Expliquez.
3. Que pensait Jacques de la femme qui jouait du piano? Comment est-ce que l'apparence physique de cette femme aide à créer cette impression?
4. Selon Jacques, pourquoi le travail de cette femme n'était-il pas facile?
5. Comment se comportaient les autres spectateurs dans la salle?
6. Dites quel temps verbal prédomine dans cette description. Qu'est-ce que ce temps suggère au sujet de l'importance du cinéma dans la vie de Jacques et de sa grand-mère?

CHERCHEZ LA FORME

Trouvez tous les pronoms relatifs dans ce passage, puis identifiez leur fonction (sujet, objet direct, etc.).

Le Premier Homme

DEUXIÈME PARTIE

30 Les films, étant muets, comportaient en effet de nombreuses projections de texte écrit qui visaient° à éclairer l'action. Comme la grand-mère ne savait pas lire, le rôle de Jacques consistait à les lui lire. Malgré son âge, la grand-mère n'était nullement sourde°. Mais il fallait d'abord dominer le bruit du piano et celui de la salle, dont les réactions étaient généreuses. De plus, malgré l'extrême simplicité de ces textes, beaucoup des
35 mots qu'ils comportaient n'étaient pas familiers à la grand-mère et certains même lui étaient étrangers. Jacques, de son côté, désireux d'une part de ne pas gêner les voisins et soucieux surtout de ne pas annoncer à la salle entière que la grand-mère ne savait pas lire (elle-même parfois, prise de pudeur, lui disait à haute voix, au début de la séance: « tu me liras, j'ai oublié mes lunettes »), Jacques donc ne lisait pas les textes aussi fort
40 qu'il eût pu le faire. Le résultat était que la grand-mère ne comprenait qu'à moitié, exigeait qu'il répète le texte et qu'il le répète plus fort. Jacques tentait de parler plus fort, des « chut »° le jetaient alors dans une vilaine honte, il bafouillait°, la grand-mère le grondait° et bientôt le texte suivant arrivait, plus obscur encore pour la pauvre vieille qui n'avait pas compris le précédent. La confusion augmentait alors jusqu'à ce que
45 Jacques retrouve assez de présence d'esprit pour résumer en deux mots un moment crucial du *Signe de Zorro* par exemple, avec Douglas Fairbanks père. « Le vilain veut lui enlever la jeune fille », articulait fermement Jacques en profitant d'une pause du piano ou de la salle.

Tout s'éclairait, le film continuait et l'enfant respirait. En général, les ennuis
50 s'arrêtaient là. Mais certains films du genre *Les Deux Orphelines* étaient vraiment trop compliqués, et, coincé° entre les exigences de la grand-mère et les remontrances de plus en plus irritées de ses voisins, Jacques finissait par rester coi°. Il gardait encore le souvenir d'une de ces séances où la grand-mère, hors d'elle, avait fini par sortir, pendant qu'il la suivait en pleurant, bouleversé à l'idée qu'il avait gâché° l'un des rares
55 plaisirs de la malheureuse et le pauvre argent dont il avait fallu le payer.

visaient *aimed*
sourde *deaf*

« chut » *"hush"* / **bafouillait**
parlait de façon incohérente /
grondait *scolded*

coincé *pris*
coi *silencieux*

gâché *spoiled*

COMPRENEZ-VOUS?

1. Qu'est-ce qui, dans les films muets, aidait les spectateurs à comprendre l'action?
2. Qu'est-ce que Jacques et sa grand-mère voulaient cacher aux autres spectateurs?
3. Que faisait Jacques pour aider sa grand-mère à comprendre?
4. Pourquoi est-ce que Jacques ne réussissait pas toujours à aider sa grand-mère?
5. Expliquez le comportement de Jacques à la fin de ce passage.

CHERCHEZ LA FORME

Il y a six pronoms relatifs dans ce passage. Trouvez-en cinq, puis transformez les propositions relatives en phrases complètes logiques.

Notez que le sixième et dernier pronom relatif du texte (**dont,** ligne 55) remplace **de** dans l'expression **payer de,** synonyme de **payer avec***: « … il la suivait en pleurant, bouleversé à l'idée qu'il avait gâché… le pauvre argent dont (avec lequel) il avait fallu payer (l'un des rares plaisirs de la malheureuse) ».

ALLEZ PLUS LOIN

En quoi la situation des spectateurs de films muets décrits par Jacques ressemble-t-elle à celle des spectateurs d'un film sous-titré?

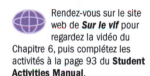

Rendez-vous sur le site web de **Sur le vif** pour regardez la vidéo du Chapitre 6, puis complétez les activités à la page 93 du **Student Activities Manual**.

Activités d'expansion

A **Les films étrangers.** Que pensez-vous des films étrangers? Les préférez-vous aux films américains? Préférez-vous les films étrangers sous-titrés ou doublés? Pourquoi? Quel est votre film étranger favori? Quel est le film étranger le plus mauvais que vous ayez jamais vu?

B **Chez soi?** Préférez-vous regarder un film au cinéma, à la télévision, en DVD ou sur l'ordinateur? Quels sont les avantages et les inconvénients de chaque méthode de diffusion?

C **Débat: La technologie exerce-t-elle une bonne ou une mauvaise influence sur les enfants?** La classe est divisée en trois pour débattre de l'influence (1) de la télévision, (2) des jeux vidéo et (3) d'Internet sur les enfants. Les membres de chaque groupe préparent individuellement une liste des raisons pour lesquelles « leur » technologie exerce la meilleure influence sur les enfants. Ensuite, ils comparent leurs listes à celles des autres membres de leur groupe et choisissent les cinq meilleurs arguments. Enfin, les groupes présentent leurs arguments au cours d'un débat.

T'étais pas né

Lecture

Voici les paroles d'une chanson tirée de l'album *Parlons-nous*, d'Eric Frasiak, sorti en 2009. Bien que son site Internet indique huit CDs dans sa discographie, Frasiak lui-même a précisé dans une interview qu'il y en a trois qui comptent dans son évolution comme chanteur: *Repartir à zéro* (2003), un album « d'introspection »; *Itinéraires* (2006), « des chansons de route » écrites à l'époque où il voyageait beaucoup; et *Parlons-nous*, « celui qui me ressemble le plus, un mélange de passion, de révolte et d'humour ». Influencé dans sa jeunesse par la musique de plusieurs musiciens/chanteurs français (Léo Ferré, Bernard Lavilliers, François Béranger), mais également de Dylan, de Bruce Springsteen et de Pink Floyd, Frasiak révèle dans ses compositions un goût pour l'éclectisme. Né dans les Ardennes (nord-est de la France), Frasiak a passé quelques années à Paris au milieu des années 1980, mais quand les deux albums produits pendant ce séjour ne lui ont pas apporté de succès, il a quitté la capitale et a créé un studio de production puis une radio locale à Bar-le-Duc. En 1996 il est revenu à la composition et à la production de ses propres chansons, mais pour pouvoir vivre « normalement » aujourd'hui il continue son travail à la radio et dans le studio d'enregistrement. L'inspiration pour les chansons de Frasiak vient de tout: « Mon inspiration c'est la vie, les rencontres, l'amour, la connerie humaine, la politique, les bons moments, enfin tout ce qui fait qu'on existe ».

ENTRONS EN MATIERE

Comment la technologie a-t-elle rendu votre vie très différente de celle que menaient vos parents quand ils avaient votre âge? Et vos grands-parents? Est-ce que ces deux autres générations comprenaient le mot « ami » de la même façon que vous le faites aujourd'hui? Pourquoi?

UNE PREMIERE ECOUTE

Ecoutez maintenant la chanson et notez tous les mots et expressions qui sont les mêmes que ceux que vous utilisez en anglais. Pour quelle raison Frasiak les met-il dans cette chanson, selon vous?

T'étais pas né

 CD 1, Track 7

Tout c' qu'on avait, c'était nos potes°	**potes** amis
Un vieux pat' d'eph'°, une paire de bottes	**pat' d'eph' (pattes d'éléphant)** *bell-bottoms* /
Avec nos guitares à deux balles°	**à deux balles** à deux francs
Les new Rimbaud[1] d' la Place Ducale[2]	(ou deux euros)
5 On avait des rêves plein la tête	
Y avait pas encore internet	
C'était des zozos° un peu space	**zozos** ici, garçons naïfs et un
Mes vrais amis, pas ceux d' Myspace	peu stupides
Z'étaient pas sur Wikipédia	
10 Nos mots d'amour, nos gueules de bois°	**gueule de bois** bouche sèche,
Et nos p'tits matins qui titubent°	causée par l'abus d'alcool /
Personne les mataït° sur Youtube	**tituber** *stagger* / **mater** *here, to peep or spy on*
Nos vies, c'était un p'tit peu l' souk°	**l'souk (le souk)** ici, tout en
On les mettait pas sur Facebook	désordre
15 Ça craquait sur nos trente-trois tours°	**trente-trois tours** disques
Pendant qu'on attendait l'amour	vinyles
On la cherchait pas sur Google	
Celle qu'en pincerait pour nos p'tites gueules°	**en pincerait...** *to have a crush on them*
Mais tu t'en fous bien de tout ça	
20 Parce que t'étais pas encore là	
J' t'avais même pas imaginé	
T'étais pas né	

[1] Rimbaud (1854–1891): poète français qui a écrit toute son œuvre avant l'âge de vingt ans, puis a laissé tomber la poésie pour une vie d'aventure et de voyages loin de la France.

[2] La Place Ducale, construite en 1606, est la place principale de la ville Charleville-Mézières, dans le département des Ardennes.

potable ici, très attrayante

Quand on trouvait une fille potable°
Pas d' SMS sur son portable
25 Pas d' longues soirées sur MSN
Pour dire qu'elle en valait la peine
Qu'on l'aimerait pour la vie qui vient
Au moins celle qui va jusqu'à demain

On n' chattait pas sur les forums
à la gomme sans valeur,
sans intérêt
30 Avec des pseudos à la gomme°
Des filles plus belles que des mannequins
Y en avait au café du coin
Et on comptait pas sur Meetic[3]
Pour nous trouver la plus magique

35 J'y avais même jamais pensé,
T'étais pas né
Quand y'a une coupure internet
C'est le monde entier qui s'arrête
Les mots d'amour dans les modems
40 Ça remplace pas les vrais « Je t'aime »

J't'avais même pas imaginé,
T'étais pas né

ordi ordinateur
Eteins un p'tit peu ton ordi°
Vas voir dehors c'est la vraie vie
45 J'sais bien qu'elle te fait un peu peur
Mais faut pas tout croire au 20H[4]
T'as pas besoin d'ADSL
ailes *wings*
Pour que la vie te donne des ailes°

J't'avais même pas imaginé
50 J'savais même pas que tu viendrais,
T'étais pas né

T'étais pas né
Paroles et musique: Eric Frasiak / Crocodile Productions 2009

[3] Un site de rencontres sur Internet, plus ou moins l'équivalent de « Match.com » aux Etats-Unis.
[4] Les journaux télévisés du soir commencent à 20h en France.

COMPRENEZ-VOUS?

1. Le chanteur identifie sa propre génération dans la première strophe. Il était adolescent/jeune adulte en quelle décennie? Quel(s) mot(s) vous donne(nt) cette idée?

2. Selon la deuxième strophe (vers 7–12), comment le chanteur et ses amis passaient-ils leurs soirées? Justifiez votre réponse.

3. Quel rôle la musique jouait-elle dans la vie du chanteur et de ses amis quand ils étaient adolescents? Comment le savez-vous?

4. Dans les strophes 2 et 3 le chanteur parle de plusieurs réseaux sociaux, d'un moteur de recherche, et d'une encyclopédie en ligne. Lesquels? Est-ce que vous les utilisez vous-même? Pour chacun, indiquez la fréquence de votre utilisation en précisant: *tous les jours / de temps en temps / rarement / jamais*.

5. Le refrain reprend le titre de cette chanson: « Tu n'étais pas né ». En écoutant cette chanson (sans lire les paroles), peut-on savoir si « tu » est un homme ou une femme? Peut-on le savoir en lisant les paroles? Comment? Qui est cette personne, à votre avis?

6. Où et comment le chanteur et ses amis parlaient-ils aux filles quand ils étaient jeunes?

7. Est-ce que « tu » se comporte de la même façon envers les filles de son âge? Expliquez.

8. Dans la dernière strophe (vers 45–46), le chanteur associe les mots « peur » et « 20h ». Pourquoi?

9. Dans sa chanson, Frasiak montre une attitude plutôt négative envers cette technologie qui n'existait pas quand il était jeune. Pourquoi la vie était-elle meilleure pour lui et ses amis?

LA CHANSON EN VIDEO

En 2010 Frasiak a produit un clip vidéo de cette chanson. On peut le visionner sur son site personnel (www.frasiak.com) et sur YouTube. Sur son site personnel le chanteur dit qu'il avait « envie de mettre des images sur **T'étais pas né**, cette chanson dédiée à mon fils et ses 26H/jour sur internet. Une chanson qui parle des réseaux pas si sociaux que ça ». Il précise que celui qui joue son fils est un jeune homme qui s'appelle Faustin Tirelli, et que son fils joue le rôle du bassiste vers la fin du clip. C'est Frasiak lui-même qui joue le père.

Regardez ce clip, puis mettez-vous par groupes de trois ou quatre pour analyser vos réactions. Est-ce que vos idées sur la chanson ont changé après avoir vu les images? Comment?

L'HOMME DE VOTRE VIE VOUS ATTEND PEUT-ÊTRE SUR UNE PLAGE. RESTE À TROUVER LAQUELLE.

© Clare Tufts

ALLEZ PLUS LOIN

Dans l'interview publiée sur Internet mentionnée dans l'introduction (http://3-2-1-chansons.wifeo.com/rencontre-avec-eric-frasiak.php), Frasiak parle de la difficulté de gagner sa vie parce qu'il n'est pas un chanteur « connu ». Il dit: « Il est aussi difficile de se produire sur scène quand on n'est pas trop médiatisé mais des circuits de concerts 'à la maison' existent. Et puis il y a internet et son ouverture incroyable sur le monde. Que de belles rencontres j'ai pu faire grâce au Web… » Maintenant que vous connaissez bien sa chanson « T'étais pas né » et que vous avez regardé le clip, trouvez-vous de l'ironie dans sa remarque et dans la production de ce clip? Pourquoi?

Traditions

© Clare Tufts

 A **LES PERSONNAGES**

Mots apparentés: le héros, l'héroïne, le prince, la princesse, le (la) magicien(ne), le dragon, le monstre, le vampire

le roi (la reine)	*king (queen)*
le chevalier	*knight*
la dame	*lady*
la demoiselle	*young lady*
la fée, la bonne fée	*fairy, fairy godmother*
la marâtre	*wicked stepmother*

le diable	*devil*
le (la) sorcier (-ière)	*wizard, sorcerer, witch*
le spectre, le fantôme, le (la) revenant(e)	*ghost*
le (la) nain(e)	*dwarf*
le lutin	*elf*
le (la) géant(e)	*giant*
l'ogre (l'ogresse)	*ogre*
le loup-garou (les loups-garous)	*werewolf (werewolves)*
la licorne	*unicorn*

Pour obtenir des exercices et activités supplémentaires sur le contenu de ce chapitre, rendez-vous sur le site www.cengagebrain.com

© Famille Thibault

B LES CONTES

Mots apparentés: imaginer, s'imaginer, enchanter

Il était une fois...	*Once upon a time there was/were . . .*
Ils vécurent heureux et eurent beaucoup d'enfants.[1]	*They lived happily ever after . . .*
raconter	*to tell (a story, a tale)*
le conte de fées	*fairy tale*
le bien	*good*
le mal	*evil*
une histoire à dormir debout	*tall tale (hard to believe)*
rêver (à, de)	*to dream (about)*
le rêve	*dream*
le cauchemar	*nightmare*
rêvasser, être dans la lune	*to daydream*

bâtir des châteaux en Espagne	*to build castles in the air*
le merveilleux	*the supernatural*
ensorceler, jeter un sort (à)	*to cast a spell (on)*
hanter	*to haunt*
le charme, le sortilège	*magic spell*
rompre le charme	*to break the spell*
la magie (noire)	*(black) magic*
la malédiction	*curse*
maudire	*to curse (someone or something)*
craindre	*to fear, to be afraid of*
faire...	
la cour (à)	*to court, to woo*
peur (à)	*to frighten*
semblant (de)	*to pretend*

[1] la fin traditionnelle des contes de fées français

Gustave Doré, Les Contes de Charles Perrault, "La Barbe bleue/Bluebeard"

PREPARATION GRAMMATICALE

Avant de commencer ce chapitre, révisez la formation du subjonctif, pages 204–207.

Saviez-vous que... ?

En 1697, Charles Perrault publie les *Contes de ma mère l'Oye* ou *Histoires et contes du temps passé,* un recueil de huit contes merveilleux. Parmi ces contes se trouvent *Cendrillon, Le Petit Chaperon Rouge* et *La Belle au bois dormant.* Avec ce recueil, Perrault inaugure le genre littéraire des contes de fées. Il transforme le conte oral traditionnellement destiné aux adultes des communautés villageoises en un texte littéraire destiné aux enfants (et aux lecteurs adultes).

Source: adapté de www. ricochet-jeunes.org. 2009

Vocabulaire

A **Devinettes.** Choisissez un mot ou une expression de la liste du vocabulaire. Donnez-en une définition en français pour que vos camarades de classe devinent ce que vous avez choisi.

Modèle: Vous: **Ce sont de grands bâtiments élégants, souvent avec des tours, où habitent les rois et les reines. On en trouve beaucoup dans la vallée de la Loire en France.**

Vos camarades: **Ce sont des châteaux.**

B **Transformations.** Si vous pouviez vous transformer en l'un des personnages de la liste A du vocabulaire, lequel choisiriez-vous? Faites votre choix, puis circulez dans la classe pour trouver d'autres étudiants qui ont choisi le même personnage. Ensemble, discutez des raisons de votre choix pour pouvoir les présenter à la classe.

C **Associations.** Choisissez deux mots de la liste B et associez-les à quatre personnages de la liste A. Expliquez vos associations à la classe.

Modèle: le bien: le héros, la princesse, le chevalier, le prince
Ces personnages sont souvent des héros de contes. Ils représentent le bien.

D **Vos réactions.** Quand vous étiez petit(e) et qu'on vous lisait ou qu'on vous racontait des contes de fées (ou quand vous regardiez des dessins animés ou des films pour enfants), quelle était votre réaction face aux personnages de la liste suivante? Expliquez vos réactions.

Vocabulaire utile: effrayer, amuser, intéresser, ennuyer, faire peur, faire rire, rendre heureux(-euse) / triste, etc.

Modèles: les loups-garous
Ils me faisaient rire parce que je les trouvais ridicules.

le chevalier
Il m'intéressait parce qu'il avait toujours un cheval et que j'adorais les chevaux.

1. les vampires
2. la licorne
3. la sorcière
4. la bonne fée
5. le géant

6. la marâtre
7. les nains
8. le dragon
9. les fantômes
10. les monstres

Lecture

ENTRONS EN MATIERE

Vous connaissez certainement quelques fables (d'Esope, par exemple). Quelles en sont les caractéristiques? Qui sont les personnages des fables? Quels adjectifs associez-vous aux différents personnages? A qui s'adressent les fables? Quel est le but *(purpose)* de la fable?

AVANT DE LIRE

Une image ou une illustration peut vous donner une idée du sujet, du thème, des personnages et même de l'intrigue d'un texte. Avant de lire la fable, regardez bien l'illustration à la page suivante. Qu'est-ce que vous voyez? Comment sont ces deux animaux? Comparez-les.

La Grenouille qui veut se faire aussi grosse que le bœuf

Les fables françaises les plus connues sont celles de Jean de La Fontaine (1621–1695). Bien qu'il imite les fables de l'Antiquité (d'Esope, par exemple), il les adapte aussi pour plaire à ses contemporains. Très appréciées de Louis XIV, de l'aristocratie et de la bourgeoisie du XVIIe siècle, ses fables ne s'adressent pas seulement aux enfants, bien que les enfants aiment les lire encore aujourd'hui. On continue à les apprendre par cœur à l'école en France.

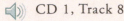

CD 1, Track 8

Une grenouille vit un bœuf
Qui lui sembla de belle taille.
Elle, qui n'était pas grosse en tout
comme un œuf,
5   Envieuse, s'étend°, et s'enfle°
et se travaille,
Pour égaler l'animal en grosseur,
Disant: « Regardez bien, ma sœur;
Est-ce assez? dites-moi: n'y suis-je
10   point encore?
—Nenni°—M'y voici donc?
—Point du tout. —M'y voilà?
—Vous n'en approchez point ».
La chétive pécore°
15   S'enfla si bien qu'elle creva°
Le monde est plein de gens qui ne
sont pas plus sages.
Tout bourgeois veut bâtir comme les
grands seigneurs,
20   Tout petit prince a des ambassadeurs,
Tout marquis veut avoir des pages.

s'étend *expands itself*
s'enfle *inflates itself*

Nenni Non, pas du tout

chétive pécore *petit animal faible* / **creva** *burst, died*

La grenouille qui voulait se faire aussi grande que le boeuf, Willy Aractingi, 1930–2003, Huile sur toile 100x100cm, Février 1994. Copyright famille Aractingi.

« La Grenouille qui veut se faire aussi grosse que le bœuf » par Jean de la Fontaine, *Fables*
Recording: © Cengage Learning

COMPRENEZ-VOUS?

1. Pourquoi la grenouille admire-t-elle le bœuf?
2. Quel adjectif montre sa réaction face au bœuf?
3. Qu'est-ce qu'elle fait pour « égaler » le bœuf?
4. Est-ce facile ou difficile pour la grenouille? Comment le savez-vous?
5. Qu'est-ce qui arrive à la grenouille?
6. Utilisez vos propres mots pour résumer la morale ou la leçon de cette fable en une ou deux phrases.

CHERCHEZ LA FORME

1. Trouvez les verbes au passé simple dans la fable et donnez leur infinitif.
2. Trouvez les pronoms relatifs dans la fable, donnez leur antécédent et expliquez leur fonction grammaticale.

ALLEZ PLUS LOIN

1. Comment La Fontaine caractérise-t-il la grenouille dans cette fable? Quel est le rapport entre la manière dont il la présente et les caractéristiques de cet animal dans la nature? (Vocabulaire utile: coasser (*to croak*).)
2. Dans le vers 5 quel son est répété plusieurs fois? Comment s'appelle cette technique poétique?

Applications

RAPPEL   The *subjunctive* is a verb form that appears in a subordinate clause connected to the main clause by the conjunction **que** and used when the verb in the main clause expresses *emotion, opinion, desire,* or *will.* The subjunctive suggests *subjectivity* or *possibility* rather than fact. When the subject of both clauses is the same, an infinitive replaces the subjunctive. For more details, see pages 204–211.

A **Des ambitions.** La grenouille explique ce qu'elle pense au bœuf. Donnez la réaction du bœuf en complétant ses réponses.

1. LA GRENOUILLE: Nous sommes sœurs.
   LE BŒUF: Je ne crois pas que…
2. LA GRENOUILLE: Je suis toute petite.
   LE BŒUF: Il est évident que tu…
3. LA GRENOUILLE: Etre grand est admirable.
   LE BŒUF: Il n'est pas vrai que…
4. LA GRENOUILLE: Je peux t'égaler en grosseur.
   LE BŒUF: Je doute que tu…
5. LA GRENOUILLE: Je fais un gros effort.
   LE BŒUF: Il est ridicule de…
6. LA GRENOUILLE: Regarde! Je réussis.
   LE BŒUF: Il n'est pas possible que tu…

B **Vos réactions.** Faites quelques remarques sur les fables et les contes de fées. Complétez les phrases en choisissant entre l'infinitif, l'indicatif et le subjonctif.

1. Dans une fable, il est important que les animaux…
2. Il faut que la morale…
3. Il est probable que les enfants d'aujourd'hui…
4. Et moi, j'espère que…
5. Dans des contes, les enfants veulent…
6. Il est important que les petites filles…
7. Parfois, les enfants ont peur…
8. Je crois que…

C **Les contes de fées et les enfants: un débat.** Certaines personnes pensent que les contes de fées sont trop violents pour être lus aux enfants, tandis que d'autres les trouvent importants pour leur éducation. Choisissez votre point de vue et, avec des camarades de classe qui pensent comme vous, complétez les phrases. Puis présentez-les sous forme de débat.

CONTRE: Il vaut mieux que…   POUR: Il est important…
CONTRE: Je regrette que…   POUR: Il faut que les parents…
CONTRE: Je doute que…   POUR: Je préfère que…
CONTRE: Il est essentiel de…   POUR: Mes enfants veulent…

Continuez avec vos propres expressions.

RAPPEL   Verbs or expressions that indicate certainty are followed by the indicative rather than the subjunctive. For more details, see pages 209–210.

D **La reine et le marchand de potions magiques.** Lisez le texte ci-dessous, puis complétez les phrases selon ce qui est demandé.

Il était une fois une reine veuve, mère de trois enfants, un fils de 17 ans et deux filles de 15 et 20 ans. Elle s'entendait bien avec sa famille, son peuple l'aimait, mais pendant les longues soirées d'hiver, elle s'ennuyait et se sentait seule. Un soir de janvier, pendant une tempête de neige, quelqu'un frappa à la porte de son palais. Puisque ses demoiselles d'honneur *(ladies in waiting)* s'étaient déjà couchées, elle ouvrit la porte elle-même. Devant elle se trouvait un jeune homme d'une vingtaine d'années qui voulait lui vendre des potions magiques. Elle le pria d'entrer, ils se parlèrent toute la nuit, et le lendemain matin, la reine se dit « Je suis amoureuse de lui et je vais l'épouser ».

Comment vont réagir ses demoiselles d'honneur et ses enfants? Imaginez leurs réactions lorsque la reine leur fait part de sa décision.

Modèle: LA REINE: Je peux me marier avec lui.
LES DEMOISELLES: **Il n'est pas évident que vous puissiez vous marier avec lui.**

LA REINE:	C'est le plus bel homme du monde.
LES DEMOISELLES:	Nous doutons que…
LA REINE:	Il m'aime à la folie.
LES DEMOISELLES:	Il est possible que…
LA REINE:	Nous voulons nous marier immédiatement.
LES DEMOISELLES:	Il est ridicule de…
LA REINE:	Il ne connaît pas mes enfants.
LES DEMOISELLES:	Mais il faut que…
LA REINE:	Nous leur en parlerons demain.
LES DEMOISELLES:	Nous espérons que…

L'histoire continue. Le couple se retrouve avec les enfants de la reine. Comment réagissent les enfants? Complétez leurs phrases.

LA FILLE DE 15 ANS:	Je veux…
LE FILS:	J'insiste pour que…
LA FILLE DE 20 ANS:	Il est probable…
TOUS LES ENFANTS:	Il est évident…

Maintenant, travaillez à trois pour trouver une fin à cette histoire. Quel groupe a la fin la plus amusante, réaliste, romantique ou tragique?

Gustave Doré, Les Contes de Charles Perrault, "Petit Chaperon Rouge/Little Red Riding Hood"

E **Une question de points de vue.** Vous connaissez certainement le conte du *Petit Chaperon rouge*, qui apporte une galette à sa grand-mère et se fait manger par le loup. Dans la version des frères Grimm—celle connue par les anglophones—il y a un bûcheron *(woodcutter)* qui sauve le Petit Chaperon rouge à la fin. (Vous travaillez avec cette version-ci.) Dans la version française, la petite fille meurt. Mettez-vous à la place des personnages (colonne A) et donnez votre réaction (colonne B) face aux événements (colonne C). Faites les changements nécessaires selon le personnage qui parle. N'hésitez pas à ajouter des expressions.

Modèle: Le petit chaperon rouge: **Je regrette que ma grand-mère soit malade.**

Le loup: **Je suis content qu'elle soit malade.**

A. Personnages	B. Réactions	C. Événements
La mère	être content	La grand-mère est malade.
Le petit chaperon rouge	avoir peur	La mère envoie sa fille chez la grand-mère.
La grand-mère	regretter	Le Petit Chaperon rouge rend visite à sa grand-mère.
Le loup	vouloir	Le loup a faim.
Le bûcheron	être vrai	Il va vite chez la grand-mère.
	être dommage	Il la dévore.
	croire	Il met ses vêtements.
	Il faut	Le Petit Chaperon rouge ne comprend pas.
	??	Elle s'approche du lit.
		Le bûcheron peut la sauver.

F **Que de complications!** Voici des extraits de l'histoire d'une belle princesse et d'un beau chevalier qui s'aiment. Lisez-les, puis, avec un(e) partenaire, finissez les phrases pour créer un conte amusant, tragique ou heureux, au choix!

1. Une jeune et jolie princesse aime un beau chevalier quoique…
2. Son père, le roi, leur permet de se marier à condition que…
3. Le triste chevalier part pour…
4. Il voyage pendant un an avant de…
5. Il demande à un nain de l'aider afin de…
6. Mais le nain refuse, jusqu'à ce que…
7. Heureusement, le chevalier réussit, sans…
8. (Inventez la fin vous-même.)

G **Réactions et expériences personnelles.** Travaillez en groupes de trois et à tour de rôle, posez-vous les questions suivantes sur les contes de fées, le merveilleux, les films d'horreur, etc.

1. Quel est le pire cauchemar que vous puissiez imaginer?
2. Quel est le plus beau rêve que vous puissiez faire?
3. Croyez-vous au merveilleux? Expliquez votre opinion.
4. Croyez-vous à la magie noire? Dans quel(s) pays est-ce qu'on y croit?
5. Quel est votre conte de fées favori? Pourquoi?
6. Connaissez-vous des histoires à dormir debout? Lesquelles?
7. Aimez-vous les films d'horreur? Pourquoi ou pourquoi pas?

Saviez-vous que… ?

Pendant longtemps, certains folkloristes pensaient que la pantoufle qui joue un rôle si important dans *Cendrillon* n'était pas en « verre » mais en « vair », une fourrure grise venant d'un animal qui ressemble à un écureuil. Mais aujourd'hui, on croit que Perrault voulait vraiment dire « verre ». Le verre était, à l'époque de Perrault, un matériau rare et précieux, symbolique donc d'une personnalité exceptionnelle, particulièrement fine et légère, au point de pouvoir porter de telles chaussures sans les briser ni en être incommodée. On pourrait conclure en plus, « au nom de la raison », qu'il serait bien difficile de chausser une pantoufle de verre si elle ne s'ajustait pas exactement à la forme et à la taille du pied, ce qui se produit dans l'histoire.

Source: adapté de www.snopes.com

Lecture

L'histoire que vous allez lire a ses origines en Corse, une île située à moins de 200 km au sud-est de Nice, dans la mer Méditerranée. Cette « île de beauté », où est né Napoléon, est française depuis 1768 mais ses habitants se sont toujours sentis différents du reste des Français. La moitié d'entre eux continuent à parler corse (parallèlement au français), une langue qui ressemble beaucoup à l'italien. C'est pourtant en français qu'un vieux berger° de 90 ans raconte cette histoire qu'il a entendue au cours d'une veillée° quand il avait 20 ans.

berger la personne qui s'occupe des moutons
veillée réunion le soir

© Cengage Learning

ENTRONS EN MATIERE

Si vous vouliez trouver quelqu'un avec qui vous passeriez le reste de votre vie, quelles qualités devrait posséder cette personne?

POUR MIEUX COMPRENDRE

Vous allez lire un conte. Qu'attendez-vous de ce genre littéraire? Quelles en sont les caractéristiques? Après avoir lu tout le conte, dites si ses caractéristiques correspondent à celles que vous aviez indiquées avant de l'avoir lu.

La fleur, le miroir et le cheval

PREMIÈRE PARTIE

fréquentaient voyaient souvent

Una volta era[2]… une fois il y avait trois jeunes gens. Ils fréquentaient° tous les trois la même jeune fille dans l'espoir de l'avoir en mariage. Depuis longtemps ils lui faisaient la cour de la sorte; alors, le plus jeune des trois garçons a dit:

—Mes camarades, il faut le dire! Nous ne pouvons pas continuer cette vie. Il faut
5 qu'elle nous dise celui qu'elle veut, de nous trois.

Alors, les voilà qui vont trouver la jeune fille, et lui demandent lequel d'entre eux elle souhaiterait avoir pour mari.

Elle a répondu:

—Partez tous les trois pendant un an; au bout de l'an, vous reviendrez me voir:
10 celui qui m'apportera le plus joli cadeau sera mon mari.

Un beau matin, ils sont donc partis tous les trois. Le soir, ils arrivent devant une maison, où ils restent pour coucher, la nuit. Le lendemain, de bonne heure, ils se sont quittés, après s'être dit:

—Au bout de l'an, nous nous retrouverons ici. Le premier arrivé attendra les autres.
15 Et puis, là-dessus, ils sont partis, chacun suivant son chemin.

Le premier est arrivé dans un endroit où on ne voyait que des fleurs. Il voit une

proposait offrait

femme qui proposait° une boîte bien fermée, à vendre. C'était une boîte contenant des fleurs. Il lui demande:

—Madame, combien cette boîte?
20 —Mille francs.

[2] *Una volta era…* (langue corse) Une fois il y avait: Il était une fois…

Alors le jeune homme lui dit:

—Mais pourquoi est-ce si cher?

Elle lui répond:

—Vous ouvrirez la boîte. Il y a dedans une fleur: si vous vous trouvez en face d'un
25 mort, en lui frottant° la fleur sur le visage, vous verrez qu'il vivra, et il ne mourra plus.

en... *by rubbing*

Le jeune homme a donné mille francs à la femme, et il a emporté la boîte avec lui.
Puis il a repris le chemin de la maison où ils devaient se retrouver tous les trois.

Quant au° second des jeunes gens, il est arrivé dans un pays où il voit un homme
tenant par la bride° un beau cheval. Tout de suite, il lui demande:

Quant... *En ce qui concerne*
la bride *bridle*

30 —Combien en voulez-vous?

—Trois mille francs.

—C'est cher!

—Mais c'est un cheval qui fait en une heure le chemin qu'on fait en un an!

Alors, le jeune homme lui achète le cheval, et l'emmène avec lui jusqu'au lieu fixé
35 pour le rendez-vous.

Le troisième, lui, arrive dans un endroit où il y avait des miroirs à vendre.
Il demande à un monsieur, qui en avait un dans une boîte:

—Bonjour, Monsieur! Vous vendez des miroirs?

—Oui.

40 —Combien celui-là?

—Quatre mille francs!

—C'est joliment cher! Pourquoi le faites-vous ce prix-là?

—Parce que, dans ce miroir, vous voyez la personne que vous demandez à voir, au
moment où vous le désirez.

45 Le jeune homme achète le miroir, et s'en retourne à la maison, où il devait retrouver
les deux autres. Et là, dans la maison où ils s'étaient quittés tous les trois, ils se retrouvent tous les trois, avec chacun un cadeau pour la jeune fille qu'ils aimaient.

Mais ils n'étaient pas encore arrivés au village de leur fiancée! Ah, il leur faudrait
bien un an pour y aller![3]

COMPRENEZ-VOUS?

1. Pourquoi les trois jeunes gens ne sont-ils pas contents?
2. Comment la jeune fille va-t-elle décider qui épouser?
3. Qu'est-ce que les trois jeunes hommes achètent?
4. Pourquoi les objets achetés sont-ils si chers? Selon vous, l'objet le plus cher est-il
   aussi le meilleur cadeau? Pourquoi ou pourquoi pas?
5. Quand les trois hommes se retrouvent, sont-ils près ou loin de leur bien-aimée?
   Comment le savez-vous?

CHERCHEZ LA FORME

Le futur: identifiez les verbes au futur dans les paragraphes qui commencent par les
phrases suivantes: 1. « Partez tous les trois ». 2. « Vous ouvrirez la boîte ». Donnez
l'infinitif de ces verbes.

A DISCUTER

Avec un(e) ou deux camarade(s) de classe, imaginez maintenant avec quel jeune
homme la jeune fille se mariera. Justifiez votre choix.

[3] Le temps écoulé dans cette première partie est un peu ambigu. Il faut un jour aux jeunes gens pour aller
de chez eux à la maison d'où ils partent. La durée de leurs voyages pour chercher des cadeaux n'est pas
précisée. A la fin, on dit qu'il leur faudra un an pour retourner chez leur fiancée.

La fleur, le miroir et le cheval

de... encore

50 Enfin, ils font de nouveau° route ensemble. Le troisième, qui avait le miroir, le regardait sans cesse, pour y voir les traits de la jeune fille. Un beau jour, en le regardant, il se met à pleurer. Les deux autres lui demandent ce qu'il a, mais il ne voulait pas le dire.

—Mais pourquoi pleures-tu?

—Notre fiancée est morte! dit-il.

55 Alors, le premier, qui avait la boîte avec la fleur, dit aux autres:

—Si seulement nous pouvions y arriver avant son enterrement!

Son camarade voyait la jeune fille dans son miroir, mais lui pouvait la faire revivre avec sa fleur.

—Oh! dit celui qui avait le miroir, comment ferions-nous? Il y a un an à marcher

60 avant d'arriver chez elle!

—On peut y arriver quand même, dit le second, qui avait le cheval.

—Comment? dirent les autres.

Lui, il avait un cheval qui faisait en une heure le chemin qu'on fait en un an!

Alors, comme le cheval était prêt à partir, tous les trois montent dessus, et les voilà

65 en route. Il y avait un an à marcher, mais au bout d'une heure les voilà arrivés!

Tous les trois, ils montent dans la maison de leur fiancée. Les parents et toute la famille de la jeune fille étaient réunis là, en train de pleurer.

Alors, le premier, qui avait la fleur, leur a dit:

—Retirez-vous tous, et laissez-moi seul avec la jeune fille.

70 Tous se retirent de la chambre où elle reposait.

Lui, prend la fleur dans sa boîte, et la passe sur la figure de sa fiancée. Et voilà qu'elle vit!

Alors, les gens rentrent dans la chambre, et la voient debout!

Maintenant, quant à savoir lequel des trois jeunes gens sera son mari, cherchez

75 donc! L'un avait la fleur, qui l'a fait vivre, mais l'autre avait le cheval, qui les a fait

auprès près

arriver auprès° d'elle, et le troisième, le miroir, où il l'avait vue!

Source: La fleur, le miroir et le cheval

COMPRENEZ-VOUS?

1. Pourquoi le jeune homme au miroir se met-il à pleurer?
2. Qu'est-ce qu'ils font pour arriver vite chez « leur fiancée »?
3. Combien de temps dure leur voyage?
4. Que fait le jeune homme avec la fleur?
5. Quel est le résultat de cette action?
6. Quel est le dilemme à la fin du conte? Comparez la situation à la fin de l'histoire à celle qui existait au début. Y a-t-il maintenant un favori parmi les jeunes hommes?

CHERCHEZ LA FORME

Que de pronoms! Relisez les paragraphes qui commencent par les phrases suivantes. Faites la liste des pronoms (personnels et relatifs) qui s'y trouvent, et donnez la fonction et l'antécédent de chacun d'entre eux. **1.** (lignes 6–7): « Alors, les voilà... avoir pour mari ». **2.** (lignes 50–52) « Enfin, ils font de nouveau... il ne voulait pas le dire ».

A DISCUTER

Avec qui la jeune fille devrait-elle se marier à la fin? Donnez votre opinion et justifiez-la.

ALLEZ PLUS LOIN

1. **La répétition.** Cette histoire, racontée par un vieux berger, fait partie de la tradition orale. La répétition est une caractéristique typique de la littérature orale. Soulignez les répétitions que vous avez remarquées en lisant. Selon vous, pourquoi y a-t-il des répétitions dans un texte oral? Y voyez-vous aussi des détails qui changent au cours du conte? Y a-t-il une fleur ou plusieurs fleurs?

2. **Le merveilleux.** Vous avez certainement remarqué que ce qui se passe dans ce conte ne correspond pas à la réalité. Soulignez les éléments du merveilleux que vous avez remarqués. Pourquoi veut-on s'échapper de la réalité?

Activites d'expansion

A **Les conseils de la famille.** Mettez-vous à cinq et jouez les rôles de la jeune fille et de quatre membres de sa famille (la mère, le père, le frère, la sœur, la grand-mère). Ceux-ci essaient de la conseiller après le retour des jeunes hommes et elle réagit à leurs suggestions. Attention à l'usage de l'infinitif, du subjonctif et de l'indicatif.

 Rendez-vous sur le site web de ***Sur le vif*** pour regardez la vidéo du Chapitre 7, puis complétez les activités à la page 106 du **Student Activities Manual**.

> **Pour exprimer votre opinion:**
>
> | | | |
> |---|---|---|
> | Je crois... | Je ne crois pas... | Je voudrais ... |
> | Il faut... | Il est nécessaire... | Je veux... |
> | Il vaut mieux... | Il est préférable... | Je refuse de... |

B **Le courrier du cœur.** Mettez-vous à la place d'un des trois jeunes hommes. D'abord, écrivez à un site Internet ou une lettre au courrier du cœur (il en existe où on peut demander des conseils pour les affaires du cœur) dans laquelle vous expliquez votre dilemme: ce que vous avez fait et ce qui est arrivé. Demandez des conseils. Ensuite, répondez à une des lettres de vos camarades de classe.

C **Mon conte favori.** Voici les noms français de quelques contes célèbres: *Blanche-Neige, Cendrillon, Le Petit Chaperon rouge, La Belle au bois dormant, Barbe-Bleue, Le Chat botté, La Belle et la Bête.* Les connaissez-vous? Résumez brièvement un de ces contes (ou un autre conte très connu de votre choix) à deux camarades qui vont deviner de quel conte il s'agit. Puis celui qui a deviné résume un autre conte, et ainsi de suite.

En famille

© Famille Planchot

A LA FAMILLE MODERNE

le beau-père	father-in-law, step-father
la belle-mère	mother-in-law, step-mother
le père (la mère) célibataire	single father (mother)
le demi-frère	step-brother, half-brother
la demi-sœur	step-sister, half-sister
aîné(e) *adj./n.*	older, oldest (brother/sister/child)
cadet(-te) *adj./n.*	younger, youngest (brother/sister/child)
l'enfant unique *m./f.*	only child
la famille...	
éclatée	broken family
homoparentale	homoparental
monoparentale	single-parent family
nombreuse[1]	family with many children
recomposée	blended family
la femme au foyer	housewife, woman who does not work outside the home

le foyer, le ménage	household
l'union libre *f.*	living together without being married
vivre ensemble	to live together

B LES AMIS

le copain (la copine)	friend, buddy, chum
mon copain, ma copine	my boyfriend, my girlfriend

C LES RAPPORTS

s'entendre (bien/mal)	to get along (well/badly)
se comprendre	to understand each other
se disputer (avec)	to argue, to disagree, to fight (with)
se fâcher (contre)	to get angry (with)
en vouloir à	to be mad at
Ma sœur m'en veut.	My sister is mad at me.
gronder	to scold (parent/child)
(s')engueuler *(fam.)*	to yell at (each other)
s'inquiéter (de), se faire du souci (pour quelqu'un)	to worry (about)
se calmer	to calm down
(s')embrasser	to kiss (each other)
faire confiance à (quelqu'un)	to trust (someone)
se marier (avec)	to get married (to)
divorcer (de, d'avec)	to divorce (someone)

[1] En 2011 toutes les familles de deux enfants de moins de 20 ans ont droit à des allocations familiales: 2 enfants = 125,18 €, 3 enfants = 286,95€, et 161,17 par enfant de plus par mois. Les familles nombreuses (une famille d'au moins trois enfants) qui ont des revenus modestes reçoivent des allocations de rentrée scolaire (de 284,97 € pour un enfant âgé de 6 à 10 ans jusqu'à 311,11 € pour un enfant âgé de 15 à 18 ans), une réduction d'impôts, des tarifs réduits pour les transports, etc.

Pour obtenir des exercices et activités supplémentaires sur le contenu de ce chapitre, rendez-vous sur le site www.cengagebrain.com/login

© Clare Tufts

super	*neat, great, terrific*
génial(e)	*fantastic, great*
sympathique (sympa)	*nice*

E AU FOYER

l'intimité *f.*	*privacy*
le (la) colocataire	*housemate*
coloc *(fam.)*	
déménager	*to move (out)*
emménager	*to move in*
louer	*to rent*
le loyer	*(the) rent*
les charges *f.*	*utilities, maintenance or service costs*
la facture	*bill (phone, electric, etc.)*
les frais *m.*	*expenses*
s'occuper de	*to take care of*
faire...	
les tâches ménagères	*to do housework*
les courses	*to go grocery shopping, to run errands*
la cuisine	*to cook*
la lessive	*to do (the) laundry*
le ménage	*to do (the) housework, to clean*
la vaisselle	*to do (the) dishes*
passer l'aspirateur	*to vacuum*
ranger	*to pick up, to straighten up (house, room)*
repasser	*to iron*
sortir la poubelle	*to take out the trash*
tondre le gazon/la pelouse	*to mow the lawn*

verser une pension alimentaire	*to pay alimony*
se sentir à l'aise/mal à l'aise	*to feel (be) comfortable / uncomfortable*
soutenir	*to support, to stand by*
Mes parents me soutiennent (moralement / financièrement).	*My parents support me (emotionally / financially).*
supporter	*to put up with, to stand*
Je ne le supporte pas.	*I can't stand him (it).*

D DES TRAITS DE CARACTERE

autoritaire	*authoritarian*
juste	*fair*
impartial(e)	*impartial, unbiased*
être de bonne / mauvaise humeur	*to be in a good / bad mood*
être facile / difficile à vivre	*to be easy / hard to get along with*

Vocabulaire

PREPARATION GRAMMATICALE

Avant de commencer ce chapitre, révisez la formation et l'usage des adverbes, pages 213–215.

A **Devinettes.** Choisissez un des mots de la liste de vocabulaire. Donnez-en une définition pour que vos camarades de classe puissent deviner quel mot vous avez choisi.

> **Modèle:** Vous: **C'est une famille où les parents ne vivent plus ensemble et ne se parlent plus.**
>
> Camarade: **C'est une famille éclatée.**

B **C'est tout le contraire.** Une copine idéaliste voit la vie familiale en rose, mais vous, vous croyez qu'elle rêve. Répondez à ce qu'elle vous dit en la contredisant. Utilisez le vocabulaire du chapitre autant que possible.

> **Modèle:** Elle: Dans ma famille, tout le monde s'entend toujours bien.
>
> Vous: Tu exagères! **Tout le monde se dispute de temps en temps.**

1. Elle: Je me marierai pour la vie.
   Vous: Tu rêves!…
2. Elle: Les femmes au foyer sont toujours de bonne humeur.
   Vous: Tu plaisantes!…
3. Elle: Un père doit être un peu autoritaire pour que ses enfants lui obéissent.
   Vous: Quelle horreur!…
4. Elle: Une famille nombreuse, c'est l'idéal.
   Vous: Mais non!…
5. Elle: Les grands-parents ne grondent jamais leurs petits-enfants.
   Vous: Ce n'est pas réaliste!…
6. Elle: Les parents sont toujours contents quand leur enfant adulte choisit de vivre chez eux
   Vous: Tu exagères! ….

C **Positive ou négative?** Il y a des personnes pour qui le mot « famille » évoque le bonheur, pour d'autres, l'horreur. Mettez-vous par groupes de trois ou quatre. Chaque personne fait deux listes d'au moins cinq mots tirés du vocabulaire du chapitre: (1) des mots ou expressions à connotation positive et (2) des mots ou expressions à connotation négative. Comparez vos listes à celles des membres de votre groupe. Si vous n'avez pas les mêmes mots, échangez vos points de vue.

D **Des portraits.** A trois ou à quatre, faites un portrait détaillé (positif ou négatif) d'un des foyers de la liste suivante. N'hésitez pas à exagérer. Inventez les membres de chaque famille (âge, sexe, profession, etc.). Que fait chaque personne? Comment sont les rapports entre ces personnes?

© Stanislas LIBAN

1. une famille monoparentale
2. une famille nombreuse
3. deux jeunes gens vivant ensemble
4. une famille recomposée
5. une famille éclatée

E **Avec mon (ma) coloc.** Les jeunes vivent souvent avec des colocataires. Quels sont les avantages et les inconvénients de la colocation? Comment est le (la) colocataire idéal(e)? Comparez vos idées sur ce sujet à celles de deux autres camarades de classe. Est-ce que la colocation marcherait bien pour vous trois?

PRÉPARATION GRAMMATICALE

Avant de continuer, révisez la comparaison des adverbes et des noms, pages 215–216.

Lecture

« Génération Tanguy » doit son nom à un film, *Tanguy*, sorti en 2001. Cette comédie noire montre un jeune homme de 28 ans qui habite encore chez ses parents et n'a pas hâte de les quitter. Ce phénomène de société est de plus en plus d'actualité. En 2008, dans l'Union européenne, un homme sur trois et une femme sur cinq, âgés de 18 à 34 ans, habitaient toujours chez leurs parents. En dehors de l'Europe la situation n'est pas bien différente comme vous le constaterez dans les extraits d'un article paru dans *Femme Magazine* du *Journal de l'Île de la Réunion*[2].

ENTRONS EN MATIÈRE

Pour quelles raisons, selon vous, un jeune adulte (entre l'âge de 18 et 30 ans) vivrait-il chez ses parents? Quels sont les avantages et les inconvénients pour l'enfant? Et pour les parents?

Génération « Tanguy » ou l'indépendance tardive°

tardive *delayed*

Pas de loyer à débourser°, pas de linge à laver, pas de dîner à préparer... Le « Tanguy » mène la belle vie chez ses parents. Pas vraiment pressés de quitter le nid°, ces « vingtenaires », plus connus sous le nom de génération « Tanguy »! Ils squattent le domicile de papa-maman, jusqu'à ce que toutes les conditions soient réunies pour
5 voler de leurs propres ailes°. Et cela peut prendre du temps...

débourser *payer*

nid *nest*

ailes *wings*

Je suis une « Tanguy »

« Je suis une « Tanguy ». Je vis toujours chez papa-maman. Et ça m'arrange bien parfois », avoue Mickaëlle. À 20 ans, cette étudiante en première année d'espagnol profite pleinement des avantages qu'offre la vie chez ses parents. Peu ou pas de tâches ménagères, adieu les factures et les fourneaux°. La belle vie quoi!

fourneaux *ovens*

Précarité économique

10 Phénomène de société, la génération Tanguy touche aussi bien les filles que les garçons. « Je reste chez mes parents pour le confort. J'ai 29 ans et concernant l'avenir, il est encore incertain. Pourtant, j'ai un emploi stable, un CDI[3], mais je ne peux pas prendre un appartement. Je n'aurais plus assez d'argent pour le reste. Alors à quoi bon partir? Chez mes parents, j'ai moins de contraintes. Je participe au loyer, mais je ne m'occupe

[2] L'Île de la Réunion est un département français d'outre-mer (DOM) qui se trouve dans l'Océan indien, à l'est de Madagascar.
[3] Contrat à durée indéterminée, c'est-à-dire, un poste permanent.

15 pas des tâches ménagères », avoue Frédéric, graphiste à Sainte-Marie. Sympa, la vie chez les parents! Nourri, logé, blanchi° et en prime, grandes économies. Et dire qu'il y a quarante ou cinquante ans, les jeunes ne cherchaient qu'à quitter au plus vite leur famille. À devenir indépendants. À l'heure actuelle, c'est plutôt l'inverse que l'on observe. L'entrée dans l'âge adulte ne coïncide plus forcément avec l'accès à un premier emploi
20 ou l'installation en couple. « La fin des études ne correspond plus systématiquement à l'obtention d'un poste stable, mais à une période plus ou moins longue de recherche d'emploi, de petits boulots, de stages, de formations… L'insertion professionnelle est plus tardive, plus difficile. C'est pourquoi ils restent confortablement chez papa-maman et font quelques économies », analyse Thierry Malbert, anthropologue et
25 spécialiste de la parenté. Outre cette précarité économique, les jeunes sortent de plus en plus diplômés du système éducatif français. Des études plus longues retardent aussi, mais dans de moindres proportions, l'âge de la décohabitation avec les parents. Et l'intimité dans tout cela?

Vous avez dit intime?

Ramener son petit ami *at home*, impensable pour Aline. « Je ne dis pas aux hommes
30 que je vis encore chez mes parents, c'est trop la honte! (Rires) Et quand je me décide à l'avouer… Ils ont peur car pour eux ça signifie « présentation des parents ». C'est très frustrant comme situation ». Même discours chez Geneviève, 31 ans, assistante d'éducation dans une école primaire à Saint-André. « L'intimité? ça n'existe pas lorsqu'on vit chez ses parents. Alors on s'arrange comme on peut, on va chez lui ou à
35 l'hôtel. Honnêtement, je ne pense pas tenir longtemps »! Et vos parents, ils en pensent quoi du fait que vous squattez (encore!) leur domicile? « Ma mère est contente, elle est très protectrice alors… Elle n'est pas prête de me jeter dehors. Au contraire, quand je parle de déménager, elle flippe », confie Geneviève en rigolant. En revanche, Eric, le père d'Adrien, 26 ans, ne partage pas le même enthousiasme. « Il se lève à 14h, ne fait
40 pas de lessive, mange n'importe quoi à n'importe quelle heure, et bien sûr, la vaisselle il connaît pas! C'est vrai qu'on en a un peu marre°, mais on ne peut pas le foutre° à la porte ». Certains parents sont déçus. Ils se sont tellement investis dans l'avenir de leur(s) enfant(s) qu'ils attendent un retour sur efforts fournis. Et puis, ils souhaiteraient passer à autre chose... leur rôle de parents assumé, ils estiment pouvoir vivre
45 leur vie conjugale. Mais comment profiter pleinement avec un Tanguy dans les pattes?

Le Journal de l'île de la Réunion, Femme Magazine par Audrey Hoarau

COMPRENEZ-VOUS?

1. Faites une liste des raisons principales pour lesquelles les jeunes dans l'article continuent à vivre chez leurs parents.
2. En quoi la situation était-elle différente il y a cinquante ans?
3. Quels sont les inconvénients mentionnés?
4. Qu'en pensent les parents? Ont-ils tous les mêmes réactions?

CHERCHEZ LA FORME

La comparaison. Trouvez trois exemples de formes comparatives dans le paragraphe « Précarité économique ». Qu'est-ce qu'on compare, des adjectifs, des adverbes ou des noms?

ALLEZ PLUS LOIN

Le phénomène Tanguy est accentué dans les pays du Sud et de l'Est de l'Europe. Dans les pays du Nord de l'Europe, les jeunes adultes ont tendance à quitter plus tôt le domicile familial.[4] Selon vous, s'agit-il plutôt de la situation économique ou est-ce une question de culture?

Applications

RAPPEL Many adverbs are made by adding **-ment** to a form of the adjective (usually feminine). Most adverbs *immediately follow the verb* they modify. Certain adverbs (for instance, adverbs of time and place) can take other positions in the sentence. For more details, see pages 213–215.

A **Les tâches ménagères.** En utilisant des adverbes variés, créez des phrases qui expliquent comment ou quand les personnes indiquées font les activités suivantes.

Modèle: (repasser) votre mère / votre frère / vous
Ma mère repasse constamment.
Mon frère repasse mal.
Moi, je repasse rarement.

1. (tondre le gazon) vous / votre mère / votre grand-père
2. (passer l'aspirateur) vos colocataires / votre petit(e) frère (sœur) / vous
3. (faire la lessive) votre professeur / un étudiant de première année / vous
4. (sortir la poubelle) vous / votre père / vos colocataires
5. (faire la vaisselle) vos parents / le président des Etats-Unis / vous
6. (payer les factures) votre mère / votre colocataire / vous

B **Les rapports.** Trouvez trois adverbes pour modifier chacun des verbes, puis faites trois phrases—la première au présent, la deuxième au passé et la troisième au futur—en utilisant le verbe donné et vos adverbes. Variez les sujets et ajoutez des détails pour rendre les phrases plus intéressantes.

Modèle: (crier) fort, tout le temps, jamais
Mon petit frère crie très fort quand on lui refuse quelque chose. Quand j'étais petit(e), je criais tout le temps quand je me mettais en colère. Nous ne crierons jamais quand nous aurons des enfants.

1. se fâcher contre quelqu'un
2. soutenir
3. être de bonne humeur
4. faire confiance (à)
5. s'habituer (à)
6. s'embrasser
7. divorcer

Saviez-vous que... ?

Les Français expriment aujourd'hui un très fort attachement à la famille. La majorité considère que pour être le plus heureux possible, il faut d'abord réussir sa vie familiale (54%), loin devant sa vie amoureuse (24%), sa vie intérieure (10%) ou encore sa vie professionnelle (8%) et sa vie sociale (4%). La famille arrive en tête de classement chez les plus jeunes (citée par 34% des 16–24 ans, devant la vie amoureuse: 28%) comme chez les plus âgés (40% chez les 55 ans et plus). La quasi-totalité des Français considère d'ailleurs que la famille reste la valeur centrale de leur société (90% dont 53% pensent même que c'est « tout à fait » le cas). Les plus jeunes croient que la famille est le principal élément structurant de la société française (79% des 15–24 ans).

Source: www.ipsos.fr 2011

[4] "Un trentenaire sur trois vit chez papa et maman" http://lci.fr 2011

C Qui le fait le mieux? Présentez votre famille (parents, frères, sœurs, oncles, tantes, cousins, grands-parents, etc.) en les comparant. Suivez les indications données. Exagérez, si vous voulez. Si personne de votre famille ne fait l'activité mentionnée, remplacez-la par une autre activité qui vous semble plus appropriée. Variez les adverbes!

> **Modèle:** chanter
>
> **Dans ma famille, mon père chante mieux que ma mère, mais c'est ma cousine qui chante le mieux.**

1. faire du vélo
2. regarder la télé
3. jouer de la guitare
4. parler français
5. faire du ski
6. travailler
7. dormir
8. *au choix*

D Ce n'est pas pareil. En utilisant les éléments donnés, comparez la vie d'une jeune personne qui habite chez ses parents à celle d'une personne qui vit seule dans son propre appartement. Utilisez le verbe indiqué.

> **Modèle:** le loyer
>
> **On paie moins de loyer quand on vit chez ses parents que lorsqu'on vit seul.**

1. les tâches ménagères (faire)
2. les factures (payer)
3. la liberté (avoir)
4. les fêtes (organiser)
5. l'argent (dépenser)
6. le temps libre (avoir)
7. les repas (préparer)
8. les courses (faire)

PREPARATION GRAMMATICALE

Avant de continuer, révisez les pronoms démonstratifs, pages 216–217.

E **Qui est-ce?** Voici deux listes: une liste de personnes et une liste de définitions ou d'explications. Créez des phrases logiques en associant chaque personne avec la définition ou l'explication qui convient. Employez un pronom démonstratif et le pronom relatif qui convient pour relier les deux parties. Commencez chaque phrase par: **Dans une famille…**

> **Modèle:** le fils aîné / se quereller parfois avec ses sœurs
> **Dans une famille, le fils aîné est celui qui se querelle parfois avec ses sœurs.**

Personnes	Définitions ou explications
1. une belle-mère	savoir s'amuser seul
2. un père célibataire	les enfants ont peur (de)
3. de bons parents	être décrit(e) de manière stéréotypée
4. une mère compréhensive	soutenir leurs enfants
5. un enfant unique	écouter ses enfants
6. un grand-père autoritaire	élever son enfant seul

F **Leurs rôles.** Comparez de deux façons différentes les membres de chaque type de famille, en utilisant des adverbes et des pronoms démonstratifs.

> **Modèle:** (la mère) une famille nombreuse / une famille avec un seul enfant
> **La mère d'une famille nombreuse dort moins que celle d'une famille avec un seul enfant.**
> **La mère d'une famille nombreuse s'énerve plus souvent que celle d'une famille avec un seul enfant.**

1. (le père) une famille traditionnelle / une famille moderne
2. (les frères et les sœurs) une famille recomposée / une famille nombreuse
3. (la grand-mère) une famille monoparentale / une famille traditionnelle
4. (l'homme) une union libre / une famille monoparentale
5. (l'enfant unique) une famille monoparentale / une famille traditionnelle
6. (les filles) une famille traditionnelle / une famille moderne

Design: gregoire@bureaugraphique.com
Photo: Gilles Dacquin - proimages@free.fr

G **Parlons de nos familles et de nos amis.** Avec un(e) camarade de classe, posez-vous des questions sur vos rapports avec vos amis et votre famille.

1. Est-ce que tu t'entends bien avec tous les membres de ta famille? Est-ce qu'il y a quelqu'un avec qui tu te disputes de temps en temps? Explique.
2. Qu'est-ce qui provoque des disputes chez toi?
3. De quoi est-ce que tu parles avec tes parents? De quoi est-ce que tu ne leur parles pas?
4. Est-ce que tu demandes des conseils à tes parents? Si oui, à propos de quoi? Est-ce que tu consultes tes amis quand tu as besoin de conseils? Est-ce que tu suis leurs conseils?
5. Est-ce que tes parents connaissent tes amis? Comment les trouvent-ils? Et que pensent tes amis de tes parents?

Lecture

Les passages suivants sont extraits d'une œuvre autobiographique de Simone de Beauvoir (1908–1986). Romancière et philosophe, ses œuvres les plus connues sont *Le Deuxième Sexe* (1949), devenu l'ouvrage de référence du mouvement féministe, son roman *Les Mandarins* (1954), qui a gagné le Prix Goncourt et sa série autobiographique: *Mémoires d'une jeune fille rangée, La Force de l'âge* et *La Force des choses*. Elle rencontre Jean-Paul Sartre (1905–1980) à la Sorbonne en 1929 et lui reste unie jusqu'à sa mort. La première partie de la lecture vous présente le début de ses mémoires. Dans la deuxième partie, elle parle de son adolescence.

ENTRONS EN MATIERE

Qu'est-ce que vous voyez sur cette photo? Décrivez les personnes et imaginez leurs rapports. Selon vous, de quand date cette photo?

POUR MIEUX COMPRENDRE

Faites des prédictions avant de lire les passages qui suivent. Vous savez que vous allez lire le début des mémoires de Simone de Beauvoir. D'habitude, par quoi commence-t-on une autobiographie? A quel moment de sa vie commence-t-on? De qui parle-t-on? Maintenant, lisez les premières phrases de chaque paragraphe. Vos prédictions sont-elles correctes?

© Brand X Pictures/Getty Images

Mémoires d'une jeune fille rangée°

rangée sérieuse, sage

Première partie

Je suis née à quatre heures du matin, le 9 janvier 1908, dans une chambre aux meubles laqués° de blanc qui donnait sur le boulevard Raspail[5]. Sur les photos de famille prises l'été suivant, on voit de jeunes dames en robes longues, aux chapeaux empanachés de plumes d'autruche°, des messieurs coiffés de canotiers° et de panamas qui sourient à un
5 bébé: ce sont mes parents, mon grand-père, des oncles, des tantes, et c'est moi. Mon père avait trente ans, ma mère vingt-et-un, et j'étais leur premier enfant. Je tourne une page de l'album; maman tient dans ses bras un bébé qui n'est pas moi; je porte une jupe plissée°, un béret, j'ai deux ans et demi, et ma sœur vient de naître. Je fus, paraît-il, jalouse, mais pendant peu de temps.

10 Aussi loin que je me souvienne, j'étais fière d'être l'aînée: la première. Déguisée en chaperon rouge, portant dans mon panier galette et pot de beurre, je me sentais plus intéressante qu'un nourrisson° cloué dans son berceau°. J'avais une petite sœur: ce poupon° ne m'avait pas…

Ma mère m'inspirait des sentiments amoureux; je m'installais sur ses genoux, dans
15 la douceur parfumée de ses bras, je couvrais de baisers sa peau de jeune femme; elle apparaissait parfois la nuit, près de mon lit, belle comme une image, dans sa robe de verdure mousseuse° ornée° d'une fleur mauve, dans sa scintillante robe de jais° noir. Quand elle était fâchée, elle me « faisait les gros yeux »; je redoutais° cet éclair orageux° qui enlaidissait son visage; j'avais besoin de son sourire.

20 Quant à mon père, je le voyais peu. Il partait chaque matin pour « le Palais »[6] portant sous son bras une serviette° pleine de choses intouchables qu'on appelait des dossiers°. Il n'avait ni barbe ni moustache, ses yeux étaient bleus et gais. Quand il rentrait le soir, il apportait à maman des violettes de Parme. Papa riait aussi avec moi; il me faisait chanter; il m'ébahissait° en cueillant au bout de mon nez des pièces de cent
25 sous[7]. Il m'amusait et j'étais contente quand il s'occupait de moi, mais il n'avait pas dans ma vie de rôle bien défini.

laqués *laquered*

plumes… *ostrich feathers*
canotiers *boaters (hats)*

plissée *pleated*

nourrisson tout petit bébé
cloué… *stuck in her crib*
poupon petit bébé

mousseuse *soft* / **ornée** décorée
jais noir profond / **redoutais** craignais / **éclair…** *stormy flash*

serviette *briefcase*
dossiers *files*

m'ébahissait m'étonnait

COMPRENEZ-VOUS?

1. Que voit l'auteur sur la première photo? Qu'est-ce qui a changé sur la deuxième photo?
2. Quelle a été la réaction de Simone à la naissance de sa petite sœur? Pourquoi ce sentiment n'a-t-il pas duré longtemps?
3. Décrivez ses rapports avec sa mère et comparez-les à ceux qu'elle avait avec son père.

CHERCHEZ LA FORME

Dans le deuxième paragraphe ci-dessus, Simone de Beauvoir décrit sa mère. Trouvez cinq adjectifs à la forme féminine et donnez-en la forme masculine.

[5] nom d'une rue à Paris
[6] Palais de Justice
[7] *magic trick, when coins, here franc pieces, appear at the tip of the nose*

ALLEZ PLUS LOIN

D'après les trois paragraphes de la première partie de la lecture, avez-vous l'impression que Simone de Beauvoir a eu une enfance heureuse? Justifiez votre réponse avec des exemples tirés du texte.

POUR MIEUX COMPRENDRE

Comment l'attitude d'un enfant envers ses parents change-t-elle à l'adolescence? Pourquoi y a-t-il un tel changement?

Dans l'extrait qui suit, Simone de Beauvoir décrit ses rapports avec ses parents, surtout avec sa mère, à l'âge de 13 ans.

Simone de Beauvoir

Mémoires d'une jeune fille rangée

DEUXIÈME PARTIE

fléchi *weakened*
s'éveillait *was awakening*
corvées tâches pénibles

pesait *weighed me down*

missel livre de prières de la messe / **cuir...** *fawn-colored leather* / **toile** *canvas*

tirelire *piggy bank*

je... *I stood up to her*
céder *to give in*

qu'elle... *she would have made me rebel*

menus petits / **moudre** *grind*
caisse... poubelle

J'avais perdu la sécurité de l'enfance; en échange je n'avais rien gagné. L'autorité de mes parents n'avait pas fléchi° et comme mon esprit critique s'éveillait°, je la supportais de plus en plus impatiemment. Visites, déjeuners de famille, toutes ces corvées° que
30   mes parents tenaient pour obligatoires, je n'en voyais pas l'utilité. Les réponses: « Ça se doit. Ça ne se fait pas » ne me satisfaisaient plus du tout. La sollicitude de ma mère me pesait°. Elle avait « ses idées » qu'elle ne se souciait pas de justifier, aussi ses décisions me paraissaient-elles souvent arbitraires. Nous nous disputâmes violemment à propos d'un missel° que j'offris à ma sœur pour sa communion solennelle: je le voulais relié de
35   cuir fauve° comme celui que possédait la plupart de mes camarades; maman estimait qu'une couverture de toile° bleue serait bien assez belle; je protestai que l'argent de ma tirelire° m'appartenait; elle répondit qu'on ne doit pas dépenser vingt francs pour un objet qui peut n'en coûter que quatorze. Pendant que nous achetions du pain chez le boulanger, tout au long de l'escalier et de retour à la maison, je lui tins tête°. Je dus
40   céder°, la rage au cœur, me promettant de ne jamais lui pardonner ce que je considérais comme un abus de pouvoir. Si elle m'avait souvent contrariée, je crois qu'elle m'eût précipitée dans la révolte°. Mais dans les choses importantes—mes études, le choix de mes amies—elle intervenait peu; elle respectait mon travail et même mes loisirs, ne me demandant que de menus° services: moudre° le café, descendre la caisse à ordures°.
45   J'avais l'habitude de la docilité, et je croyais que, en gros, Dieu l'exigeait de moi; le conflit qui m'opposait à ma mère n'éclata pas; mais j'en avais sûrement conscience.

Son éducation, son milieu l'avaient convaincue que pour une femme la maternité est le plus beau des rôles: elle ne pouvait le jouer que si je tenais le mien°, mais je refusais d'entrer dans la comédie des adultes. [...] Ma mère devinait en moi des réticences qui

50 lui donnaient de l'humeur°, et elle me grondait souvent. Je lui en voulais de me maintenir dans la dépendance et d'affirmer sur moi des droits. En outre, j'étais jalouse de la place qu'elle occupait dans le cœur de mon père car ma passion pour lui n'avait fait que grandir.

si.... *if I played my role*

lui... *put her in a bad mood*

Simone de Beauvoir, *Mémoires d'une jeune fille rangée* © Editions Gallimard; Tous les droits d'auteur de ce texte sont réservés. Sauf autorisation, toute utilisation de celui-ci autre que la consultation individuelle et privée est interdite. www.gallimard.fr

COMPRENEZ-VOUS?

1. Qu'est-ce que l'auteur a du mal à accepter quand elle arrive à l'adolescence?
2. Que pense-t-elle maintenant des « obligations » de famille?
3. Pourquoi se dispute-t-elle avec sa mère à propos d'un cadeau pour sa sœur?
4. Diriez-vous que Simone de Beauvoir est têtue *(stubborn)*? Pourquoi?
5. Quelles tâches ménagères doit-elle faire à l'époque?
6. Pourquoi ne se révolte-t-elle pas ouvertement contre sa mère?
7. Quel est le rôle le plus important pour une femme, selon la mère? Qu'en pense la fille?
8. Qu'est-ce qui suggère que la mère se rend compte des opinions de sa fille?

CHERCHEZ LA FORME

1. **Le passé**. Relisez le deuxième paragraphe et le troisième paragraphe (de la première partie). Identifiez et justifiez le temps de tous les verbes. Pourquoi est-ce que l'auteur utilise ce temps?
2. **Des adverbes**. Dans la deuxième partie, on trouve trois adverbes formés à partir d'adjectifs: **impatiemment** (ligne 29), **violemment** (ligne 33) et **sûrement** (ligne 46). Quel est l'adjectif qui correspond à chaque adverbe et quel verbe ou quelle expression verbale cet adverbe modifie-t-il?

ALLEZ PLUS LOIN

Qu'est-ce que nous apprenons dans la dernière phrase de cet extrait (lignes 51–53)? Est-ce une réaction assez typique pour une jeune fille de cet âge? Expliquez votre réponse.

Rendez-vous sur le site web de **Sur le vif** pour regardez la vidéo du Chapitre 8, puis complétez les activités à la page 119 du **Student Activities Manual**.

Activites d'expansion

A **Qu'est-ce qui caractérise les parents d'aujourd'hui?** Selon vous, comment sont les parents actuels? Travaillez en groupes et trouvez ensemble cinq mots qui caractérisent la situation des parents. Comparez vos idées aux résultats d'un sondage d'IPSOS pour *Enfant Magazine & Femme Actuelle,* juillet 2011. Discutez des différences.

	Ensemble	Parents	Non parents
Manque d'autorité	71	67	73
Stress	40	44	37
Difficulté	38	37	38
Fatigue	34	38	32
Conflit	28	29	28
Besoin d'aide	27	24	28
Responsabilité	25	28	23
Incompréhension	24	25	24
Tendresse	24	27	23
Manque de connaissance	23	20	24

Source: adapté d'*Ipsos.fr* 2011

B **L'indépendance.** La majorité des Français entre 15 et 29 ans vivent encore chez leurs parents. A votre avis, que se passe-t-il quand l'enfant annonce son départ à ses parents ou bien son retour au foyer? Mettez-vous par groupes de trois (le père, la mère et le jeune) et jouez les scènes suivantes.

1. Une jeune personne de 18 ans veut quitter le foyer familial. Ses parents ne sont pas d'accord, alors leur enfant essaie de les convaincre. Quels sont les arguments des parents et ceux de l'adolescent(e)?
2. La situation a maintenant changé. Après avoir fini ses études, l'enfant décide de revenir habiter chez ses parents. Mais cette fois-ci, les parents préfèreraient qu'il/elle cherche son propre appartement. Expliquez les raisons de chacun.

C **On cherche un(e) coloc.** Toute la classe participe au jeu de rôle suivant. On désigne trois ou quatre étudiants qui cherchent un appartement. Ceux-ci doivent faire une liste de questions à poser aux groupes de colocataires éventuels. Les autres membres de la classe se mettent par groupes de deux ou trois: ils vivent déjà ensemble en colocation. Pour choisir un nouveau (une nouvelle) coloc, ils discutent d'abord des qualités « essentielles » recherchées, puis ils font une liste de questions à poser aux « candidats ». Faites preuve de créativité et d'imagination. Il se peut que les « candidats » doivent passer plusieurs entretiens avant de trouver un appart.

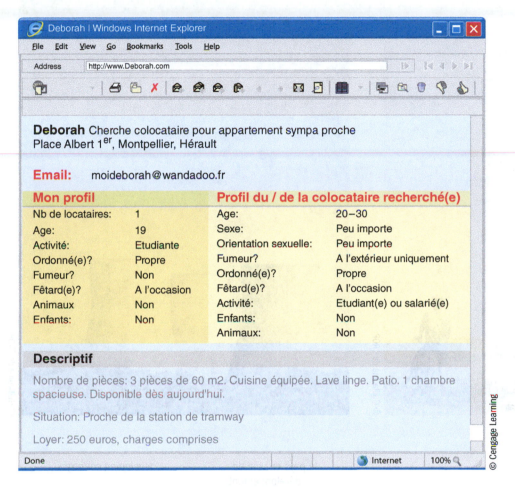

Deborah | Windows Internet Explorer

File   Edit   View   Go   Bookmarks   Tools   Help

Address   http://www.Deborah.com

Deborah Cherche colocataire pour appartement sympa proche
Place Albert 1er, Montpellier, Hérault

Email: moideborah@wandadoo.fr

Mon profil		Profil du / de la colocataire recherché(e)	
Nb de locataires:	1	Age:	20–30
Age:	19	Sexe:	Peu importe
Activité:	Etudiante	Orientation sexuelle:	Peu importe
Ordonné(e)?	Propre	Fumeur?	A l'extérieur uniquement
Fumeur?	Non	Ordonné(e)?	Propre
Fêtard(e)?	A l'occasion	Fêtard(e)?	A l'occasion
Animaux	Non	Activité:	Etudiant(e) ou salarié(e)
Enfants:	Non	Enfants:	Non
		Animaux:	Non

Descriptif

Nombre de pièces: 3 pièces de 60 m2. Cuisine équipée. Lave linge. Patio. 1 chambre spacieuse. Disponible dès aujourd'hui.

Situation: Proche de la station de tramway

Loyer: 250 euros, charges comprises

Done   Internet   100%

Sans frontières

© Guillaume de CROP

© Guillaume de CROP

🔊 A LE MONDE

Mots apparentés: le climat, l'économie (*f.*), le gouvernement, négocier, le (la) réfugié(e)

le (la) citoyen(ne)	*citizen*
le traité	*treaty*
l'accord (*m.*)	*agreement*
le commerce équitable	*fair trade*
délocaliser	*to outsource*
l'ONG (l'organisation (*f.*) non gouvernementale)	*NGO (non-governmental organization)*
l'ONU (Organisation (*f.*) des Nations-Unies)	*UN (United Nations)*

le pays en voie de développement	*developing country*
le tiers monde	*third world*
le marché	*market*
le (la) bénévole, volontaire	*volunteer*
se porter volontaire	*to volunteer*
la guerre	*war*
l'asile (*m.*) (politique)	*(political) asylum*
la catastrophe (naturelle)	*(natural) disaster*
la région sinistrée	*disaster area*
le patrimoine	*heritage*

Pour obtenir des exercices et activités supplémentaires sur le contenu de ce chapitre, rendez-vous sur le site www.cengagebrain.com

Clare Tufts

B L'ENVIRONNEMENT

Mots apparentés: consommer, la pollution, polluer, l'émission (*f.*), la surpopulation

gaspiller	*to waste*
le combustible fossile	*fossil fuel*
le pétrole	*oil*
le charbon	*coal*
la centrale nucléaire	*nuclear power plant*
l'effet (*m.*) de serre	*greenhouse effect*
le gaz à effet de serre	*greenhouse gas*
la tempête, l'orage (*m.*)	*storm*
le trou d'ozone	*hole in the ozone*
le réchauffement climatique	*global warming*
l'empreinte (*f.*) carbone	*carbon footprint*
le glacier	*glacier*
la calotte polaire	*polar ice cap*
fondre	*to melt*
l'ours (*m.*) polaire	*polar bear*
les déchets (*m.*)	*trash, refuse, waste*
la déchetterie (déchèterie) (France)	*recycling center*
l'écocentre (*m.* Québec)	*recycling center*

C DÉMARCHES[1]

Mots apparentés: la biodiversité, conserver, l'écotourisme (*m.*), recycler, le recyclage

trier	*to sort*
le tri	*sorting*
la propreté	*cleanliness*
bio (biologique)	*organic*
les produits bio	*organic food*
le potager	*vegetable garden*
le biocarburant	*biofuel*
le développement durable	*sustainable development*
renouvelable *adj.*	*renewable*
l'énergie	
solaire	*solar*
éolienne	*wind*
nucléaire	*nuclear*
le (la) militant(e)	*activist*
la campagne	*countryside*
.... politique, environnementale	*political, environmental campaign*
à la campagne	*in the country*

[1] *Steps, approaches (f.)*

Saviez-vous que... ?

Le 1er juin 2007 la France a créé le Ministère de l'Écologie, de l'Énergie, du Développement durable et de l'Aménagement du Territoire. Récemment, le nom a été changé en Ministère de l'Écologie, du Développement durable, des Transports et du Logement. Il est chargé de mener la « métamorphose » de la société afin de pouvoir gérer la raréfaction des ressources naturelles et les changements climatiques. Cette métamorphose doit constituer un nouveau moteur pour l'économie. Son but est de démontrer, concrètement dans les faits, que la protection de l'environnement ne coûte pas plus cher et qu'elle se traduit souvent par plus de bien-être et de pouvoir d'achat.

Source: http://www. developpement-durable.gouv.fr

Vocabulaire

A **Devinettes.** Choisissez un des mots de la liste A du vocabulaire. Donnez-en une définition ou expliquez le mot sans le révéler, afin que vos camarades de classe puissent le deviner.

> **Modèle:** Vous: **ne pas tout jeter, trouver une autre façon d'utiliser un objet**
> Vos camarades: **recycler**

B **Des familles de mots.** Voici quelques mots apparentés au vocabulaire de ce chapitre. Trouvez les mots correspondants dans les listes A, B, et C. Donnez la partie du discours (nom, verbe, adjectif, etc.) de tous les mots.

1. réchauffer
2. le gaspillage
3. le soleil
4. la consommation
5. la délocalisation
6. émettre
7. le bénévolat
8. renouveler
9. militer
10. pétrolier

C **Qu'est-ce qu'on fait?** Avec un(e) partenaire, finissez les phrases suivantes de façon logique. Faites autant de phrases que possible en utilisant le vocabulaire du chapitre ou votre propre vocabulaire. Comparez vos phrases à celles d'autres groupes.

> **Modèle:** Quelqu'un qui est persécuté pour ses opinions politiques…
> **peut demander l'asile politique dans un autre pays.**

1. Un militant qui organise une campagne pour le recyclage…
2. Une personne qui ne veut pas utiliser un combustible fossile pour se déplacer doit…
3. Quelqu'un qui veut changer le monde mais qui n'aime pas la politique…
4. Après une catastrophe naturelle, des gens qui se portent volontaires…
5. Ceux qui font très attention à ce qu'ils mangent…
6. Une famille qui ne veut pas jeter trop de choses…
7. Le chef d'un restaurant qui cherche des produits frais…
8. Un citoyen responsable…

D **Trouvez le mot.** Voici dix définitions qui correspondent à dix mots tirés des listes de vocabulaire. Quel est le mot défini?

1. combustible solide, de couleur noire
2. endroit où on met des déchets
3. acheter des produits dont on n'a pas vraiment besoin, consommer avec excès
4. un aliment produit sans pesticide, sans herbicide chimique, sans fertilisant artificiel
5. l'énergie qui vient du vent
6. ce que cherche une personne en danger pour des raisons politiques
7. conflit armé entre groupes sociaux ou entre pays
8. usine qui produit du courant électrique en utilisant de l'uranium
9. grand mammifère carnivore blanc
10. une personne qui apporte son aide volontaire sans être rémunérée

RAPPEL Interrogative forms allow you to *request information.*
To review question formation, see **Structures,** Chapter 2, pages 160–163.

E **Le ministre.** Vous avez l'occasion d'interviewer le nouveau ministre de l'Écologie, du Développement durable, des Transports et du Logement (voir **Saviez-vous que…?** page 128). Avec un(e) ou deux camarade(s) de classe, préparez des questions à lui poser sur son ministère ou sur les problèmes de l'environnement en France. Commencez par l'expression interrogative donnée et utilisez le pronom **vous.**

1. combien
2. depuis quand
3. que
4. avec qui
5. pourquoi
6. de quoi
7. qui
8. quel(le)(s)
9. où

F **Une table ronde d'experts.** Avec un(e) partenaire, préparez cinq questions que vous pourriez poser à une des personnes suivantes sur le sujet indiqué.

1. une infirmière: son séjour en Somalie avec Médecins sans frontières (au passé)
2. une femme politique membre des Verts (parti écologiste): la politique environnementale (au futur)
3. un ingénieur: l'énergie nucléaire dans le monde (temps au choix)
4. un employé de la Banque de France: l'euro (au futur)
5. un ancien volontaire du *Peace Corps:* le travail des associations humanitaires (au passé)

Lecture

Actuellement, l'écologie, une question qui préoccupe le monde entier, est aussi un thème d'excellence pour les poètes et artistes de la chanson française. Pierre Perret est l'un de ces chanteurs engagés. Né en 1934, il est considéré comme une légende de la chanson française. Il maîtrise les subtilités de la langue française et de l'argot (il a réécrit les fables de La Fontaine), et interprète avec un sourire malicieux des thèmes sérieux et pertinents sur un ton enfantin qui peut sembler naïf. Ses plus grands succès datent des années 1960 et 1970, mais il continue d'écrire et d'interpréter aujourd'hui. La chanson que vous allez lire et écouter est sortie en 1998 mais reste très actuelle.

AVANT DE LIRE

Les couleurs s'associent souvent aux émotions. On peut être rouge de honte, ou voir tout en rose, si on est trop optimiste. Une peur bleue est une peur violente, par exemple. Quand on est très fâché, on peut dire qu'on est vert de rage. Mais le vert fait aussi allusion à la protection de l'environnement ou au parti écologiste, les Verts. En tout cas, si quelqu'un vous dit qu'il est vert, cela veut probablement dire qu'il soutient le mouvement écologiste. Lisez la première strophe de la chanson qui est aussi le refrain. Comment le chanteur associe-t-il les différents sens du mot **vert?**

www.ecolabel.eu

POUR MIEUX COMPRENDRE

Parcourez le texte de la chanson qui est présenté comme le chanteur l'a écrit. Vous verrez qu'il y a des apostrophes qui remplacent certaines lettres pour reproduire la façon dont le chanteur les prononce. De quelle lettre s'agit-il la plupart du temps?

Je suis vert de colère

 CD 1, Track 9

bousillent *wreck*

Refrain
Je suis vert, vert, vert,
Je suis vert de colère
Contre ces pauv'typ's
Qui bousillent° la terre,

5 Cette jolie terre
Que nos pères, nos
grands-pères
Avaient su préserver
Durant des millénaires.

10 Les rivières écument°.
Les usines fument.
Les moutons mang'leurs papas
Changés en granulés[2]
Les déchets ultimes,
15 La vach'folle° en prime,
Sont un p'tit cadeau du ciel
De nos industriels.

Refrain

De Brest aux Maldives[3],
Vont à la dérive°
20 Des poubell's radio-activ's
Jusqu'au fond des lagunes
Et, mêm'sans tapage°,
Des maires de village
En enterr'dans leur commun'
25 Pour faire entrer des thunes°.

Refrain

Les blés, les patates°
Sont bourrés d'nitrates.
On shoote° aussi bien les veaux°
Qu'les champions haut-niveau[4].
30 On s'fait des tartines
Au beurr'de dioxine.
En voiture, on a l'point vert
Pour doser nos cancers.

Refrain

Sous la couch'd'ozone,
35 L'oxyd'de carbone°
Tue nos forêts si précieus's
Autant qu'les tronçonneus's°.

L'air pur s'amenuise°.
Nos sources s'épuisent°
40 Mais colorants, salmonelloses
Nous font la vie en rose.

Refrain

Pour qu'y ait pas d'panique,
Leurs poisons transgéniques,
Ils les nomment « sciences de la vie »
45 Ou « biotechnologies ».
Leur's gènes font la nique°
Aux antibiotiques.
Pour guérir nos infections,
Faudra d'l'inspiration.

Refrain

50 Tous les ans, bonhomme,
Sept milliards de tonnes
De gaz mortel CO_2
S'envolent dans les cieux.
L'effet d'serr'menace.
55 Ça fait fond'les glaces.
La mer mont': c'est sans danger,
Y aura qu'à éponger°.

Je suis vert, vert, vert,
Je suis vert de colère
60 Contre ces pauv'typ's
Qui bousillent la terre.
Il y a ceux qui chantent
La chanson du profit
Contre tous ceux qui aiment
65 La chanson de la vie.

écument *foam*

s'amenuise *devient plus petit*

sources... *springs are drying up*

vach'folle *mad cow (disease)*

font la nique *thumb their nose at*
à la dérive *adrift*

tapage *bruit*

thunes *argent*

patates *pommes de terre*

shoote *injecte de la drogue*
veaux *petits de la vache*
éponger *mop up*

l'oxyd'de carbone *carbon monoxide*
tronçonneus' *chain saw*

Je suis vert de colère, Pierre Perret © Editions Adèle

COMPRENEZ-VOUS?

1. Dans chaque strophe le chanteur mentionne plusieurs problèmes de l'environnement. Identifiez-en autant que possible.
2. Qui sont les responsables ou les coupables mentionnés dans la chanson?
3. Quels sont les résultats de ces formes de pollution?

[2] La maladie de la vache folle est une infection dégénérative du système nerveux central des vaches, des moutons, etc. Elle était très répandue entre 1986 et les années 2000, touchant plus de 190 000 animaux. Cette épidémie trouve son origine dans les farines animales incorporées à l'alimentation des bovins. Ces farines animales étaient obtenues à partir de parties non consommées de carcasses bovines et de cadavres d'animaux.

[3] Les Maldives, officiellement la République des Maldives, sont un pays d'Asie du Sud-Ouest, constitué de 1 199 îles, dont 202 habitées, situées à environ 451 km au sud de l'Inde.

[4] On injecte des hormones de croissance aux veaux pour qu'ils grandissent plus vite, comme le font certains sportifs pour se donner plus de force ou de muscles.

CHERCHEZ LA FORME

1. Trouvez les verbes pronominaux dans la chanson et mettez-les au passé composé.
2. Relisez les quatre derniers vers de la chanson. Qui sont « ceux » dont le chanteur parle?

ALLEZ PLUS LOIN

Trouvez des exemples d'humour noir, de cynisme ou d'ironie dans cette chanson.

RAPPEL To make *hypotheses,* that is, to suggest what might happen or how things would be or how they could have been, use the *conditional* mood in French. See **Structures,** Chapter 5, page 190.

Applications

A Si elle/il pouvait tout changer. Si les personnes suivantes avaient le pouvoir de résoudre les problèmes du monde que feraient-elles? Quels seraient les résultats? Comment serait le monde? Utilisez le conditionnel dans vos réponses.

1. un ingénieur
2. une agricultrice
3. une maîtresse d'école
4. un infirmier
5. une star du cinéma
6. un éboueur (*trash collector*)

Saviez-vous que... ?

Tous écolos, les Européens? Les résultats d'un sondage publié en octobre 2009 par la Commission européenne montrent l'attachement fort de l'opinion publique européenne à la protection de l'environnement: le changement climatique est considéré comme la préoccupation planétaire la plus urgente pour 47% des Européens interrogés. La plupart d'entre eux pensent également que les solutions à ce problème global doivent être trouvées à une échelle globale: deux tiers (67%) des Européens préfèrent que les décisions destinées à protéger l'environnement soient prises en commun au sein de l'UE. Les dirigeants de l'Union européenne ont bien conscience du défi environnemental et des attentes qu'il suscite. C'est pourquoi ils ont adopté en décembre 2008 un premier engagement qu'est le Paquet Energie-Climat.

Source: www.touteleurope.eu

B Un tout autre monde. Décrivez les résultats probables ou possibles dans chaque cas suggéré. Comparez vos idées à celles de vos camarades de classe.

1. S'il n'y avait plus de pétrole dans le monde,...
2. Si l'UE n'existait plus,...
3. Si tous les glaciers fondent,...
4. Si le mur de Berlin n'était pas tombé en 1989,...
5. Si on n'arrive pas à arrêter le réchauffement climatique,...
6. Si la frontière entre le Mexique et les Etats-Unis n'existait plus,...
7. Si le Canada envahissait les Etats-Unis,...
8. Si les Etats-Unis avaient un président « vert »....

RAPPEL To *describe* people, places, and events, review *adjectives* and *comparisons* (**Structures,** Chapter 2, pages 158–159), *adverbs* (**Structures,** Chapter 8, pages 213–215), and *relative pronouns* (**Structures,** Chapter 6, pages 200–202).

C **Optimiste ou pessimiste?** Décrivez, au futur, comment vous imaginez l'avenir dans vingt ans. Utilisez les thèmes indiqués ou d'autres de votre choix. Comparez vos réponses à celles de vos camarades.

Modèle: la guerre

PESSIMISTE: **La guerre sera encore plus atroce parce qu'on utilisera des armes biologiques qui tueront encore plus de personnes et qui détruiront l'environnement pour ceux qui survivront. Les hommes seront encore plus méchants.**

OPTIMISTE: **Il n'y aura plus de guerre parce que nous nous comprendrons mieux. Les hommes seront plus pacifiques et ils ne voudront plus se battre. Il y aura un seul gouvernement mondial, et on sera tous des citoyens du monde.**

1. l'environnement
2. le statut de la femme
3. le statut des groupes minoritaires
4. la technologie
5. l'économie
6. les médias
7. l'énergie

D **La France et votre pays.** Décrivez et comparez les deux pays et leurs habitants en utilisant ce que vous avez appris sur les catégories indiquées dans les chapitres précédents de *Sur le vif.*

Modèle: l'immigration

L'immigration est un aussi gros problème en France qu'aux Etats-Unis. Pendant longtemps en Amérique, les immigrés trouvaient assez facilement du travail mais depuis quelques années, c'est devenu plus difficile. Aujourd'hui, il y a moins d'immigrés d'Amérique centrale, et certains des autres immigrés, comme les informaticiens indiens, rentrent dans leur pays d'origine pour y travailler. En France, où le taux de chômage est plus élevé, c'est encore plus compliqué. La plupart des immigrés qui sont francophones viennent d'Afrique. Il n'y a pas de travail chez eux. Dans les deux pays, on n'accepte pas toujours très bien les immigrés, surtout ceux qui ne parlent pas la langue, et ils ont parfois du mal à s'intégrer.

1. les langues étrangères
2. les écoles et les universités
3. les jeunes
4. les voitures
5. les vacances
6. le cinéma et la télévision
7. la famille

RAPPEL To express *opinions*, certain verbs or expressions followed by the **subjunctive**, *indicative,* or *infinitive* can be used (review **Structures,** Chapter 7, pages 204–211), as well as *negative constructions* when you disagree (review **Structures,** Chapter 6, pages 197–200).

Saviez-vous que... ?

Voulez-vous découvrir la France d'une autre manière? L'écologie et le bio vous tiennent à cœur? N'hésitez plus! Le WWOOFing est fait pour vous. WWOOF vous offre la possibilité de découvrir les différentes techniques de l'agriculture biologique en partageant le quotidien de fermiers bio ou de personnes ayant un rapport privilégié avec la nature. Quel meilleur moyen pour découvrir la France, pays si fier de sa culture gastronomique et de son terroir, que de séjourner avec ses habitants en partageant leur vie quotidienne? Du petit déjeuner au dîner en passant par les soins aux animaux d'élevage et/ou « l'aide aux champs », découvrez une façon de vivre saine, alternative, simplement naturelle.

Source: www.wwoof.fr

E C'est vrai? Votre sœur, qui a 12 ans, commence à s'intéresser à ce qui se passe dans le monde; donc elle est toujours en train de poser des questions. En jouant le rôle du membre de la famille indiqué, utilisez les expressions données pour lui répondre et des pronoms pour éviter la répétition.

1. VOTRE SŒUR: Est-il vrai que la France et l'Allemagne sont les deux pays les plus forts dans l'UE?
   VOUS: Oui, il est vrai que…

2. VOTRE SŒUR: Si on est français, est-ce qu'on a besoin d'un passeport pour aller en Italie?
   PAPA: Si on est français, il n'est pas nécessaire de…

3. VOTRE SŒUR: Est-ce que les Européens veulent tous parler anglais?
   MAMAN: Je doute que…

4. Votre sœur: Les Européens savent beaucoup de choses sur l'Amérique?
   VOUS: Il est possible que…

5. VOTRE SŒUR: Et nous, est-ce que nous nous intéressons au tiers monde?
   PAPA: Pas beaucoup. C'est dommage que…

6. VOTRE SŒUR: Est-ce que la prospérité s'établit rapidement en Russie?
   MAMAN: Il est peu probable que…

7. VOTRE SŒUR: Avons-nous encore besoin d'une armée?
   VOUS: Oui, je crois que…

8. VOTRE SŒUR: Est-ce que les Américains parlent beaucoup de langues?
   MAMAN: Je ne pense pas que…

9. VOTRE SŒUR: Penses-tu que je devrais apprendre à parler plusieurs langues?
   MAMAN: Oui, il faut que…

10. VOTRE SŒUR: Vous aimez répondre à mes questions?
    TOUS: Bien sûr, nous sommes contents de…

F Des images stéréotypées? Préparez une description détaillée des groupes ou des concepts de la liste, en tenant compte du point de vue indiqué entre parenthèses. Votre partenaire trouve que vous exagérez et vous contredit en faisant le portrait opposé.

Modèle: les hommes politiques (portrait négatif)

VOUS: **Moi, je crois que tous les hommes politiques sont corrompus. Ils veulent tous avoir du pouvoir et de l'argent. Ils mentent pour être élus et ne pensent jamais au bien-être des citoyens.**

VOTRE PARTENAIRE: **Je ne suis pas d'accord. Il est vrai que certains hommes politiques sont corrompus, mais je ne crois pas qu'ils soient tous corrompus. Ils ne cherchent qu'à aider les citoyens, ce qui n'est pas toujours facile.**

1. les réfugiés politiques (portrait positif)
2. les écolos (portrait négatif)
3. les partis politiques (portrait positif)
4. l'Union européenne (portrait négatif)
5. l'aide humanitaire (portrait positif)

© Falconia/istockphoto.com

G **Tout le monde exagère!** Avec un(e) partenaire, imaginez que vous vous êtes trouvé(e) dans une des situations de la liste suivante. Racontez en trois ou quatre phrases ce qui s'est passé en exagérant beaucoup. Comparez votre récit à ceux de vos camarades de classe.

1. A Paris: Vous avez dîné au Palais de l'Elysée avec le président de la République française.
2. A Moscou: Vous avez servi d'interprète au président des Etats-Unis.
3. En Turquie: Vous visitiez le pays quand il y a eu un tremblement de terre.
4. Au Brésil: Vous avez participé aux préparations pour la Coupe du monde de football en 2014.
5. A Washington: Le vice-président des Etats-Unis vous a invité(e) à visiter la ville.
6. A Londres: Vous êtes allé(e) au théâtre et un des membres de la famille royale était assis à côté de vous.
7. En France: Vous avez participé au Tour de France.
8. En Chine: Vous avez participé à une manifestation et on n'a pas voulu vous laisser quitter le pays.

H **Leurs rêves de jeunesse.** Imaginez les rêves et les activités des personnes de la liste quand elles avaient l'âge indiqué.

Modèle: Napoléon, à 7 ans
Il voulait être officier et commander beaucoup d'hommes.
Il n'obéissait plus à ses parents mais il voulait que ses amis le suivent.
Il montait souvent à cheval et jouait avec des petits soldats de plomb.

1. Nelson Mandela, à 14 ans
2. Einstein, à 12 ans
3. le pape, à 15 ans
4. Jeanne d'Arc, à 10 ans
5. Gustave Eiffel[5], à 7 ans
6. Martin Luther King Jr., à 9 ans
7. Fidel Castro, à 10 ans
8. vous, à 13 ans
9. votre professeur de français, à 15 ans

[5] L'ingénieur qui a fait construire la Tour Eiffel en 1889.

Lecture

patrimoine *héritage*

Fondée en 2003 pour préserver l'agriculture locale et aider les agriculteurs à transmettre leur patrimoine°, l'association Terre de Liens a commencé à acquérir des terres afin de permettre aux fermes de continuer à vivre. En 10 ans, les prix de la terre ont augmenté de 40% à cause de l'urbanisation et chaque semaine, près de 200 fermes disparaissent. Depuis 2009, l'association a établi un fonds de dotation° afin de faciliter les dons et la transmission d'exploitations.°

fonds de dotation *endowment*
exploitations *fermes*

ENTRONS EN MATIERE

Selon vous, pourquoi les fermes disparaissent-elles? Quel rôle joue l'agriculture locale dans la protection de l'environnement?

POUR MIEUX COMPRENDRE

Lisez la première phrase. Pourquoi est-il difficile de s'établir comme agriculteur? Continuez à lire jusqu'à la fin du paragraphe. Olivier et Julie achètent-ils une ferme ou en louent-ils une?

© Terre de Liens

UNE RICHESSE À CULTIVER

© Terre de liens

Terre de Liens pour la préservation du patrimoine rural

PREMIÈRE PARTIE

parcours du combattant *obstacle course*

exploitation *ici* ferme

bail *lease*

vignes *vines* / chèvres *goats*
ruches *beehives*

gîte *logement* / couvert *repas*

Pour de nombreux jeunes agriculteurs, s'installer relève du parcours du combattant°: prix des terrains trop chers, investissements de départ trop importants, difficultés à trouver une exploitation°. Olivier, 29 ans, et sa femme Julie en ont fait l'expérience puisqu'ils ont mis plus d'un an avant de trouver une exploitation. Grâce au fonds Terre
5 de Liens qui leur a proposé un bail° rural environnemental—c'est-à-dire la location de terre en échange de sa préservation—ils ont pu reprendre une installation, *la Ferme des Vignes*°, pour y élever des chèvres° et installer des ruches°. Ce bail rural environnemental signifie qu'ils s'engagent à respecter l'environnement, la biodiversité, les paysages et la qualité de l'eau ou des produits.
10   Originaire d'Alsace et fils de paysan, le jeune homme réalise après des études dans l'agroalimentaire que reprendre une ferme l'intéresse plus. Il se forme alors aux pratiques agricoles en faisant du *wwoofing*[6] (il s'agit d'aider sur une exploitation en échange du gîte° et du couvert°, idéal pour apprendre de nouvelles pratiques agricoles) en France et en Roumanie.

[6] Wwoofing: voir www.wwoofinternational.org. On fait du travail bénévole sur des fermes biologiques.

COMPRENEZ-VOUS?

1. A quelles difficultés un jeune agriculteur qui veut acheter une ferme doit-il faire face?
2. Qu'est-ce qu'Olivier et sa femme ont l'intention de faire sur leur ferme?
3. Qu'est-ce qu'un bail rural environnemental? Quelles sont les obligations de celui qui tient un bail?
4. Comment Olivier s'est-il préparé pour devenir agriculteur?

CHERCHEZ LA FORME

L'infinitif. Dans le paragraphe d'introduction, trouvez tous les exemples d'un infinitif après une préposition.

Terre de Liens

DEUXIÈME PARTIE

15 Fin 2010, après l'échec de la négociation pour reprendre une ferme, le couple apprend qu'une exploitation de 35 hectares[7] va se libérer en Saône et Loire[8]. Abandonnée au milieu des années 1970, des exploitants ont remis en état cette ferme et y ont développé l'agriculture en biodynamie (forme d'agriculture biologique basée sur les cycles lunaires et des préparations spécifiques). Puis, pour en assurer la pérennité°, le

20 terrain a été confié à une association qui le louait. Apprenant le départ des précédents exploitants, Olivier et Julie sont allés à la rencontre de Terre de Liens avec leur projet d'apiculture° et d'élevage avec transformation fromagère°. Après avoir effectué une étude économique prévisionnelle et l'acceptation de leur dossier par le fonds Terre de Liens, l'association gestionnaire° de la *Ferme des Vignes* a accepté d'en faire don

25 au fonds Terre de Liens. Ce dernier accorde alors à Julie et Olivier un bail rural environnemental qui durera tant qu'ils seront en activité. « Cette formule a changé mon regard. Pour tout vous dire, à la base, nous voulions devenir propriétaires, mais nous nous sommes rendus compte que le bail rural environnemental offre au final beaucoup d'avantages. Nous avons gagné en sécurité, nous nous sommes moins endettés° et

30 cela nous a permis d'investir ailleurs que dans le foncier° ».

En contrepartie, Olivier et Julie s'engagent à pratiquer l'agriculture biologique et à préserver la biodiversité.: « Par exemple, nous respectons les haies°, nous nous efforçons de les garder hautes afin qu'elles puissent continuer d'abriter de nombreuses espèces alors que dans la région certains exploitants les coupent à 1 mètre 20 de hauteur »,

35 explique le jeune exploitant, avant d'ajouter qu'il laisse fleurir ses pâturages avant d'y laisser paître° ses 35 chèvres. Les ruches sont installées à proximité des bois présents sur le terrain. La majeure partie de la production de la ferme est vendue localement. « Nous sommes très contents d'avoir pu conduire ce projet avec l'aide de Terre de Liens. Ils nous ont offert un véritable confort dans nos démarches », conclut Olivier. Fort de

40 son expérience, l'association a déjà soutenu plus de 80 exploitations en France, le fonds de dotation a pour le moment étudié et validé sept projets et 12 autres sont en cours d'étude et devraient bientôt se concrétiser.

pérennité durée

projet d'apiculture apiary
d'élevage... cheese making
gestionnaire managing

endettés fait des dettes
foncier propriété, terre

haies hedges

paître graze

Terre de Liens © (www.terredeliens.org)

[7] 35 hectares est l'équivalent d'à peu près 86.5 acres.
[8] Département de la Bourgogne, au centre de la France.

COMPRENEZ-VOUS?

1. Combien de temps durera le bail d'Olivier et de Julie?
2. Olivier aurait préféré être propriétaire d'une ferme mais il voit des avantages à avoir signé un bail. Résumez-les.
3. Que font Olivier et Julie pour conserver la biodiversité?
4. Qu'est-ce qu'ils produisent? Où vendent-ils leurs produits?

CHERCHEZ LA FORME

Des pronoms. Dans cette deuxième partie, trouvez l'antécédent des pronoms objets suivants: **y** ont développé (l.17), pour **en** assurer (l.19), qui **le** louait (l.20), d'**en** faire don (l.24), nous nous efforçons de **les** garder hautes (l.33), avant d'**y** laisser paître (l.35)

ALLEZ PLUS LOIN

Selon vous, doit-on protéger l'agriculture locale? Pourquoi et comment?

Guillaume de CROP

Activités d'expansion

Rendez-vous sur le site web de *Sur le vif* pour regardez la vidéo du Chapitre 9, puis complétez les activités à la page 133 du **Student Activities Manual**.

A **Des entretiens d'embauche.** Avec un(e) partenaire, choisissez une des situations suivantes et jouez la scène de l'entretien d'embauche. Un(e) étudiant(e) est le (la) candidat(e) et l'autre fait passer l'entretien.

1. un poste avec l'ONG l'Homme et l'Environnement à Madagascar
2. un stage à Genève avec la Croix-Rouge
3. un poste avec Médecins sans frontières
4. une mission (*assignment*) avec le *Peace Corps*

B **Je veux changer de vie.** On vous a offert un poste que vous êtes prêt/e à accepter mais certaines personnes ne comprennent pas votre décision. En groupe de deux ou trois, jouez les rôles.

1. Vous occuper d'une ferme et faire du fromage. Vos parents vous croient fou (folle).
2. Travailler deux ans à Bruxelles avec l'UE: Vous manquerez à votre copain (copine).
3. Enseigner pendant deux ans dans une école primaire sur l'Ile de la Réunion: Vos amis ne comprennent pas pourquoi.
4. Vous porter volontaire au Guatemala avec *Habitat for Humanity:* Vos grands-parents ne savent pas ce que c'est.
5. Partir au Togo avec le *Peace Corps:* Votre employeur n'est pas content.

C **Un monde sans frontières.** Quels sont les avantages et les inconvénients d'un monde sans frontières? Mettez-vous par groupes de deux ou trois et décidez si vous êtes oui ou non en faveur d'un monde sans frontières. Justifiez votre opinion en énumérant les avantages ou les inconvénients. Quelle est l'opinion de la majorité des étudiants de la classe?

© Clare Tufts

Les Cajuns

De la musique Cajun: Bruce Daigrepont à l'accordéon avec sa femme Sue au frottoir.

© David Redfern/Redferns/Getty Images

© Getty Images

Lecture

AVANT DE LIRE ET D'ECOUTER

Dans quelles régions de l'Amérique essaie-t-on de conserver l'héritage français? Quels aspects de cet héritage veut-on garder?

QUE VEUT DIRE «CAJUN» ET QUI SONT LES CAJUNS?

Le mot « cajun » est une altération du mot anglais *acadian*. C'est en 1755 que les autorités britanniques entreprennent la déportation des Acadiens (habitants de langue française de la Nouvelle-Ecosse et du Nouveau-Brunswick au Canada). Pendant les huit années suivantes, plus de 10 000 Acadiens seront déportés en France, sur l'Ile-du-Prince-Edouard, sur la côte est des Etats-Unis et vers la Louisiane où il y avait aussi des Français (qui s'appelaient « créoles ») depuis le début du XVIIIᵉ siècle.

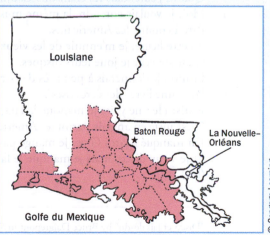

Louisiane

Baton Rouge ★

La Nouvelle– Orléans

Golfe du Mexique

© Cengage Learning

Au vingtième siècle, en 1968, la Louisiane s'est déclarée officiellement bilingue et a créé un ensemble de lois destinées à promouvoir le français comme seconde langue de tout l'Etat. De nos jours, les Cajuns sont toujours fiers de leurs origines françaises et essaient de préserver leur héritage linguistique, gastronomique et musical. La musique cajun, comme la langue cajun, est un mélange de traditions variées. A la base, il y a surtout l'influence de la France (en particulier des régions comme la Normandie, la Bretagne, le Poitou et la Picardie), du Québec et du Nouveau-Brunswick (influences anglaises, écossaises et irlandaises). Les Noirs et les Espagnols des Antilles ont apporté leur propre accent et ont créé la variation qui s'appelle le zydeco. Les instruments typiques de la musique cajun sont l'harmonica, le violon, la guitare, l'accordéon, le triangle et les cuillères. Dans la musique zydeco on trouve aussi le frottoir *(washboard)*.

Voici les paroles d'une chanson cajun, écrite et chantée par Bruce Daigrepont, un musicien de La Nouvelle-Orléans. Cette chanson exprime la nostalgie que ressent le chanteur pour son « pays ». En lisant, essayez d'imaginer la musique qui accompagne les paroles.

Disco et fais-do-do[1]

je... j'étais impatient	A peu près cinq ans passés, je pouvais pas espérer°
	Pour quitter la belle Louisiane; 🔊 CD 1, Track 10
	Quitter ma famille, quitter mon village,
	Sortir de la belle Louisiane.
	5 J'aimais pas l'accordéon, j'aimais pas le violon.
	Je voulais pas parler le français.
	A cette heure, je suis ici dans la Californie.
	J'ai changé mon idée.
	Je dis: Hé yaie yaie. Je manque la langue Cadjin.
	10 C'est juste en anglais parmi les Américains.
	J'ai manqué Mardi Gras. Je mange pas du gombo.
fais... soirées pour danser et faire la fête	Et je va au disco, mais je manque le fais do-do°.
	J'avais l'habitude de changer la station
	Quand j'entendais les chansons Cadjins.
	15 Moi, je voulais entendre la même musique
	Pareil comme les Américains.
	A cette heure, je m'ennuie de les vieux Cadjins.
	C'est souvent je joue leurs disques.
	Et moi, je donnerais à peu près deux cents piastres
livre *pound* / **écrevisses** *crayfish*	20 Pour une livre° des écrevisses°.
	Je dis: Hé yaie yaie. Je manque la langue Cadjin.
	C'est juste en anglais parmi les Américains.
	J'ai manqué Mardi Gras. Je mange pas du gombo.
	Et je va au disco, mais je manque le fais do-do.
	(bis)

"Disco et fais do-do" by Bruce Daigrepont in *Stir up the Roux,* 1987.

[1] En français de France, *faire do-do* est une expression enfantine qui veut dire *dormir* ou *se coucher.* [En anglais: *nighty-night* ou *beddy-by*] En cajun, un « fais-do-do » est une fête où on danse !

COMPRENEZ-VOUS?

1. Depuis combien de temps le chanteur n'habite-t-il plus en Louisiane?
2. Pourquoi a-t-il quitté son « pays »?
3. Qu'est-ce qui lui manque?
4. Quelle sorte de musique aimait-il écouter quand il était encore en Louisiane?
5. Quelle sorte de musique aime-t-il écouter en Californie?
6. Pour quel plat paierait-il 200 dollars?
7. Dans la chanson, qu'est-ce qui montre qu'il ne se sent pas tout à fait « américain »?

QUESTIONS DE LANGUE

Vous avez certainement remarqué que le français de cette chanson ne ressemble pas tout à fait au français standard. Réécrivez les phrases ou propositions suivantes comme si vous étiez professeur de français.

© Cengage Learning

1. A peu près cinq ans passés…
2. Je manque la langue Cadjin.
3. Je mange pas du gombo.
4. Je va au disco…
5. Pour une livre des écrevisses…
6. … dans la Californie

ET LA MUSIQUE?

Selon vous, comment est la musique de cette chanson? Maintenant, écoutez-la. Comment réagissez-vous à cette musique?

© Clare Tufts

Structures

I. Verb Review

A. Payer and other verbs that end in **-ayer** can be conjugated two ways: they can retain the **y** throughout, or the **y** can change to **i** before the unpronounced verb endings **-e, -es, -ent** and in all forms of the future and conditional.

Present		Subjunctive	
je pa**ie** (paye)	nous pa**y**ons	je pa**ie** (paye)	nous pa**y**ons
tu pa**ie**s (payes)	vous pa**y**ez	tu pa**ie**s (payes)	vous pa**y**iez
il/elle/on pa**ie** (paye)	ils/elles pa**ie**nt (payent)	il/elle/on pa**ie** (paye)	ils/elles pa**ie**nt (payent)

Future		Conditional	
je pa**ie**rai (payerai)	nous pa**ie**rons (payerons)	je pa**ie**rais (payerais)	nous pa**ie**rions (payerions)
tu pa**ie**ras (payeras)	vous pa**ie**rez (payerez)	tu pa**ie**rais (payerais)	vous pa**ie**riez (payeriez)
il/elle/on pa**ie**ra (payera)	ils/elles pa**ie**ront (payeront)	il/elle/on pa**ie**rait (payerait)	ils/elles pa**ie**raient (payeraient)

B. S'ennuyer and other verbs that end in **-uyer** always change the **y** to **i** before the unpronounced verb endings **-e, -es, -ent** and in all forms of the future and conditional.

Present		Subjunctive	
je m'ennu**ie**	nous nous ennu**y**ons	je m'ennu**ie**	nous nous ennu**y**ions
tu t'ennu**ie**s	vous vous ennu**y**ez	tu t'ennu**ie**s	vous vous ennu**y**iez
il/elle/on s'ennu**ie**	ils/elles s'ennu**ie**nt	il/elle/on s'ennu**ie**	ils/elles s'ennu**ie**nt

 SELF-CHECK Student Activities Manual, *Exercise I, A, p. 7.*

II. Present Indicative

Grammar Video Tutorials

A USAGE

The *present tense* of the indicative is used to:

- tell about what is happening now;

    Nous **écrivons** sur nos copies.
    La maîtresse **choisit** les mots.
    Je **cherche** le sujet de la phrase.
    Chaque étudiant **prend** son livre et **lit.**

- make generalizations or speak about habitual actions;

    Les cours **sont** interactifs.
    Ils **ont** toujours beaucoup de devoirs.
    Il y **a** beaucoup de lectures à faire chez soi.
    Les élèves **aiment** les vacances.

- indicate what is going to happen in the near future;

    Ce soir, nous **allons** à une fête chez le professeur.
    Demain, il y **a** un contrôle de vocabulaire.
    J'**obtiens** mon diplôme à la fin de l'année.

- indicate what is going to happen in the near future using **aller** + *infinitive;*

    Je **vais étudier** au Canada l'année prochaine.
    Nous **allons rendre** nos devoirs à la fin de l'heure.
    La maîtresse **va indiquer** les fautes.
    Les professeurs **vont demander** de meilleures conditions de travail.

- indicate what has just happened using **venir de** + *infinitive;*

    Ses parents **viennent de recevoir** son relevé de notes.
    Ce nul **vient de se réveiller** après une petite sieste.
    Vous **venez de voir** votre prof de chimie dans la rue.

- indicate that an action which started in the past is continuing into the present, when used with the preposition **depuis.**

    Depuis cinq ans, je **rêve** de parler russe sans accent.
    Cette jeune Française **fait** ses études à Vancouver **depuis** six mois.

B FORMATION

General observations: While reviewing, it is important to pay attention to the present indicative forms for the 1st and 3rd person plural forms **(nous, ils)** and to the spelling of the infinitive, because other tenses use these forms as their base.

1. The three major groups of regular verbs

a. Verbs with infinitive ending in **-er:**
  aimer, assister, discuter, étudier, passer, etc.

To conjugate these verbs, drop the **-er** of the infinitive and add **-e, -es, -e, -ons, -ez, -ent.**

j'étudi**e**	nous étudi**ons**
tu étudi**es**	vous étudi**ez**
il/elle/on étudi**e**	ils/elles étudi**ent**

A large group of **-er** verbs undergo spelling changes for pronunciation consistency.

- Verbs whose stem ends in **-g** (parta**ger**) add an **e** before the **-ons** ending in the **nous** form: parta**geons.**
- Verbs whose stem ends in **-c** (commen**cer**) change the **c** to **ç** in the **nous** form: commen**çons.**

Some verbs have two different stems, one for the **je, tu, il** and **ils** forms and another for the **nous** and **vous** forms.

- Verbs like **appeler** and **jeter** double the **l** or the **t** in the stem for all but the **nous** and **vous** forms.

j'appe**lle**	nous appelons
tu appe**lles**	vous appelez
il/elle/on appe**lle**	ils/elles appe**llent**

- Verbs like **acheter** and **modeler** change the **e** to **è** in the stem for all but the **nous** and **vous** forms.

j'ach**è**te	nous achetons
tu ach**è**tes	vous achetez
il/elle/on ach**è**te	ils/elles ach**è**tent

- Verbs like **préférer** and **sécher** change the **é** to **è** in the stem for all but the **nous** and **vous** forms.

je préf**è**re	nous préférons
tu préf**è**res	vous préférez
il/elle/on préf**è**re	ils/elles préf**è**rent

b. Regular verbs with infinitives ending in **-ir:**
        agir, choisir, finir, réussir, etc.

These verbs are conjugated by dropping the **-r** from the infinitive and adding **-s, -s, -t, -ssons, -ssez, -ssent.**

je réussi**s**	nous réussi**ssons**
tu réussi**s**	vous réussi**ssez**
il/elle/on réussi**t**	ils/elles réussi**ssent**

The verbs **dormir, partir, sentir,** and **sortir** have some irregularities in their formation. To find the stem for their singular forms, *drop the last three letters of the infinitive* and add the regular ending for **-ir** verbs **(-s, -s, -t).** For the plural forms, drop only the ending **-ir** from the infinitive and add **-ons, -ez, -ent.**

je dor**s**	nous dorm**ons**
tu dor**s**	vous dorm**ez**
il/elle/on dor**t**	ils/elles dorm**ent**

The verbs **couvrir, offrir, ouvrir,** and **souffrir** are conjugated like **-er** verbs.

j'offr**e**	nous offr**ons**
tu offr**es**	vous offr**ez**
il/elle/on offr**e**	ils/elles offr**ent**

See Appendix C for more examples of irregular verb conjugations.

c. Regular verbs with infinitives ending in **-re:**
     entendre, rendre, répondre, etc.

To conjugate these verbs, drop the **-re** and add **-s, -s, –, -ons, -ez, -ent.**

je rend**s**	nous rend**ons**
tu rend**s**	vous rend**ez**
il/elle/on rend	ils/elles rend**ent**

2. Pronominal verbs

Pronominal or reflexive verbs are conjugated like nonreflexive verbs, but are accompanied by reflexive pronouns **(me, te, se, nous, vous, se),** which refer back to the subject.

> Je **m'inscris** dans ce cours.
> Vous **vous envoyez** des e-mails.
> La maîtresse **se promène** entre les pupitres.

There are four categories of pronominal verbs.

a. Pronominal verbs that express the idea that the *subject* and the *object* are doing something to each other are called *reciprocal verbs.*

> Les étudiants **se** parlent.
> *The students are talking to **each other**.*

> Nous **nous** aidons dans ce cours.
> *We help **each other** in this course.*

Many verbs that take direct or indirect objects can be turned into reciprocal verbs by adding a reflexive pronoun.

> Je vois mon prof dans la rue. → Nous **nous** voyons dans la rue.
> Il téléphone à son copain. → Ils **se** téléphonent.

b. Pronominal verbs that express the idea that the subject is doing something to himself or herself are called *reflexive verbs.*

> Les élèves **se** calment.
> *The students calm (**themselves**) down.*
>
> L'étudiant **se** réveille.
> *The student wakes (**himself**) up.*
>
> Ma mère **se** demande si je travaille bien à l'école.
> *My mother is wondering if I am working well at school.*

c. Some verbs are used only reflexively, and with these the reflexive pronoun is often untranslatable.

> Ils **se souviennent** bien de leur premier professeur de français.
> *They **remember** well their first French professor.*
>
> Nous **ne nous moquons pas** de ceux qui ratent l'examen.
> *We **don't make fun** of those who fail the exam.*
>
> L'université **s'occupe** de tout.
> *The university **takes care** of everything.*

d. A reflexive construction is frequently used in French to avoid having a passive construction.

> Comment est-ce que cela **se fait?**
> *How is that **done?***

III. Infinitives

 USAGE

Infinitives are used in a variety of ways.

- When one verb follows another, with no conjunction (like **que**) between them, the first verb is conjugated and the second verb remains an infinitive.

> Je **veux suivre** ce cours.
> Il **espère réussir** à cet examen.
> Nous **n'aimons pas faire** les devoirs.
> On se prépare pour **pouvoir participer.**

NOTE: Pay attention to the difference between the construction above (a conjugated verb + an infinitive) and the construction of the **passé composé** (a conjugated auxiliary verb + a past participle).

> Il **a séché** son cours de maths hier.
> Elle **est arrivée** en retard à l'examen.

- When pronominal (reflexive) verbs are used as infinitives following a conjugated verb, the reflexive pronoun agrees with the subject of the main verb.

  Nous espérons **nous** inscrire sans problèmes.
  We hope to register without problems.

  Est-ce que **tu** peux **te** débrouiller en français?
  *Can **you** get along in French?*

- A verb appears in its infinitive form following a preposition (except **en;** see Appendix B).

  Il travaille dur **afin d'avoir** de bonnes notes à la fin de l'année.
  *He's working hard **in order to have** good grades at the end of the year.*

  On n'obtient pas un diplôme **sans avoir** assez d'UE.
  *One doesn't graduate **without having** enough credits.*

  Dans une dictée, il faut faire attention **de bien accorder** les verbes avec les sujets.
  *In a dictation, you have to be careful **to make** subjects and verbs **agree.***

- After the preposition **après,** the past infinitive must be used. (For formation of the past infinitive, see the following section B).

  Après avoir fini ses études, elle est retournée chez ses parents.
  ***After having finished** her studies, she went back to her parents' (house).*

  Après avoir travaillé avec Nabil, j'ai enfin compris les devoirs.
  ***After I worked with Nabil,** I finally understood my homework.*

- An infinitive can be the subject of a sentence.

  Bosser à la dernière minute, ce n'est pas une bonne idée.
  ***Cramming** at the last minute is not a good idea.*

  Choisir une université canadienne, c'est faire l'expérience de la vie nord-américaine.
  ***Choosing** a Canadian university means experiencing life in North America.*

B FORMATION

There are two tenses for the infinitive: the present and the past. The past infinitive is formed with the infinitive **avoir** or **être** + *the past participle of the main verb.*

Present Infinitive	Past Infinitive
étudier	**avoir** étudié
rendre	**avoir** rendu
rentrer	**être** rentré(e)(s)
s'inscrire	**s'être** inscrit(e)(s)

Après avoir étudié tout l'après-midi, il est sorti avec ses copains.
***After having studied** all afternoon, he went out with his friends.*

NOTE: The agreement rules that apply to the **passé composé** also apply to the past infinitive. In verbs conjugated with the auxiliary **être,** the past participle agrees with the subject of the sentence.

> **Après être rentrée** de vacances, **elle** a recommencé à travailler sur sa thèse.
> *After having returned from vacation, she started working again on her dissertation.*

To negate an infinitive, both **ne** and **pas** (or other negative form) are placed in front of the infinitive.

> Je bosse toute la nuit pour **ne pas échouer** à l'examen.
> *I am cramming all night so I won't fail the exam.*

> Il est préférable de **ne jamais redoubler** une année.
> *It is best never to repeat a year.*

✔ **SELF-CHECK** Student Activities Manual, *Exercises II–III, B-G, pages 8–10.*

IV. Imperatives

Grammar Video Tutorials

A USAGE

The imperative forms are used to give *commands, orders,* or even to extend *invitations*.

> **Choisis** les cours qui t'intéressent.
> **Rendez** vos devoirs à la fin du cours.
> **Etudions** à la bibliothèque ce soir.
> **Souviens-toi** de la règle.

You can soften the command by using **s'il te plaît** (with familiar commands) or **s'il vous plaît** (with formal or plural commands).

> **Explique**-moi les devoirs, s'il te plaît.
> **Répétez** la question, s'il vous plaît.

If you wish to be less direct or abrupt in expressing a command, you can phrase your request as a question.

> Tu peux m'expliquer les devoirs?
> Pourriez-vous répéter la question?

B FORMATION

There are three different imperative forms you can use, depending on whom you are addressing.

1. The second person singular form, based on the **tu** form of the present: for commands given to someone you know well.

> **Réponds!**
> **Finis** tes études!
> **Fais** tes devoirs!

a. -**er** verbs (and those verbs conjugated like -**er** verbs) drop the -**s** of the **tu** form.

> Ne **parle** pas!
> **Ecoute** bien!

NOTE: When the second person singular (**tu** form) is followed immediately by **y** or **en,** the ending **-s** is retained to make it easy to pronounce.

> **Vas-y!**
> **Manges-en!**

b. Pronominal verbs keep the reflexive pronoun. **Te** changes to **toi** when it follows the affirmative imperative.

> **Débrouille-toi!** (se débrouiller)
> **Rappelle-toi** qu'il y a un contrôle demain! (se rappeler)

2. The first person plural form, based on the **nous** form of the present: for commands in which the speaker is including himself or herself.

> **Assistons** à cette conférence!
> **Remercions** le prof!

3. The second person plural form, based on the **vous** form of the present: for commands to more than one person or to someone you do not know well.

> **Écoutez!**
> **Taisez-vous!** (se taire)

Three verbs frequently used in the imperative are irregular: their forms are based on the subjunctive.

avoir:	Aie! Ayons! Ayez!	**Ayez** confiance!
être:	Sois! Soyons! Soyez!	**Soyons** attentifs!
savoir:	Sache! Sachons! Sachez!	**Sache** que le prof est fâché!

When the imperative is negative, the **ne** precedes the verb, and the **pas** (or other negative form) follows. If there is a reflexive pronoun it will appear after the **ne,** in front of the verb.

> Ne **vous disputez** pas!
> Ne **sèche** jamais ce cours!
> N'**oublions** pas la date de l'examen!

 SELF-CHECK Student Activities Manual, *Exercises IV, L–M, pages 12–13.*

V. *Faire causatif*

To indicate that the subject is having something done (and not doing it himself or herself) use the verb **faire** + *infinitive*.

> Quand je m'endors en classe, le prof me **fait écrire** des phrases au tableau.
> *When I fall asleep in class, the professor **makes** me **write** sentences on the board.*

> Parfois un élève **fait rire** toute la classe.
> *Sometimes a student **makes** the whole class **laugh**.*

Quand nous sommes insolents en cours, le prof nous **fait** nous **excuser** par écrit.
*When we talk back to the teacher, he **makes** us **excuse** ourselves in writing.*

Le prof **fait signer** le bulletin par les parents.
*The teacher **has** the parents **sign** the report card.*

Mon père me **fait venir** dans son bureau quand j'ai une mauvaise note.
*My father **makes** me **come** into his study when I have a bad grade.*

Ce prof est très exigeant. Il nous **fait** beaucoup **travailler.**
*This professor is very demanding. He **makes** us **work** a lot.*

NOTE: The pronouns that accompany the infinitives in the last two examples are direct object pronouns. The infinitive in the **faire causatif** construction can also take an indirect object, an indirect object pronoun, or **y.**

Elle **a fait envoyer** son dossier à l'université.
*She **had** her record **sent** to the university.*

Elle l'y **a fait envoyer.**
*She **had** it **sent** there.*

Elle **a fait envoyer** son dossier (dir. obj.)
à M. Dupont (ind. obj.).
*She **had** her record **sent** to Mr. Dupont.*

Elle le lui **a fait envoyer.**
*She **had** it **sent** to him.*

 SELF-CHECK Student Activities Manual, *Exercises V, O, page 14.*

Structures

I. Verb Review

A. Décrire (**écrire, inscrire,** etc.) is irregular in the **present indicative tense** and **past participle.**

je décris	nous décrivons
tu décris	vous décrivez
il/elle/on décrit	ils/elles décrivent
Past participle: décrit	

Formation of other tenses and modes is standard.

Imperfect stem:	(Stem of present indicative **nous** form)	décriv-
Future/Conditional stem:	(Drop the final **e** of the infinitive)	décrir-
Subjunctive stem:	(Stem of present indicative **ils/elles** form)	décriv-

B. S'asseoir is unusual in that it has two stems for the conjugation of the present indicative, the present subjunctive, the imperfect, the future, and the conditional. The one below is the most commonly used.

Present		**Future**	
je m'assieds	nous nous asseyons	je m'assiérai	nous nous assiérons
tu t'assieds	vous vous asseyez	tu t'assiéras	vous vous assiérez
il/elle/on s'assied	ils/elles s'asseyent	il/elle/on s'assiéra	ils/elles s'assiéront

Past participle:	assis
Imperfect stem:	nous nous assey-
Conditional stem:	je m'assiér-
Subjunctive stem:	ils/elles s'assey-

NOTE: Do not confuse:
	Je m'assieds.	*I'm sitting down [action].*
	Je me suis assis(e).	*I sat down [action].*
	Je suis assis(e).	*I'm seated [state].*

 SELF-CHECK Student Activities Manual, *Exercises I, A, page 23.*

II. Descriptive Adjectives

Adjectives are used to modify (qualify or describe) nouns or pronouns.

 A FORMATION

In French, adjectives agree in gender (masculine / feminine) and in number (singular / plural) with the nouns or pronouns they modify. For example:

> Elle a les **cheveux longs** et **ondulés.**

General rules for formation of descriptive adjectives:

- The majority of adjectives follow a standard pattern of formation.

  masculine singular form + **s** *= masculine plural form*
  impoli impoli**s**

  masculine singular form + **e** *= feminine singular form*
  impoli impoli**e**

  masculine singular form + **es** *= feminine plural form*
  impoli impoli**es**

- If the masculine singular form already ends in **-e,** the feminine singular form is the same.

  un **jeune** homme **mince**   une **jeune** femme **mince**

- If the masculine singular form already ends in **-s,** the masculine plural form is the same.

  un jeune étudiant **français**   de jeunes étudiants **français**

Masculine Singular	Feminine Singular	Masculine Plural	Feminine Plural
• ends in a consonant or a vowel other than **-e** **content**	+ **e** contente	+ **s** contents	+ **es** content**es**
• ends in **-e** **mince**	no additional ending mince	+ **s** mince**s**	+ **s** mince**s**
• ends in **-s** **français**	+ **e** français**e**	no additional ending français	+ **es** français**es**

1. Variation of feminine forms

There are many adjectives that do not follow the regular pattern for the formation of the feminine in the preceding chart. These are difficult to group, as there are many variations, but some of the broader categories are explained below.

a. Adjectives that end in **-er** and **-f** form the feminine using these patterns:

Endings		Examples	
Masculine	**Feminine**	**Masculine**	**Feminine**
-er	**-ère**	premi**er**	premi**ère**
-f	**-ve**	acti**f**	acti**ve**

b. Adjectives that end in **-x** form the feminine several different ways. Since there is no pattern, the masculine and feminine forms should be learned together.

Frequently used adjectives of this type:

Masculine	Feminine
heur**eux**	heur**euse**
f**aux**	f**ausse**
d**oux**	d**ouce**
r**oux**	r**ousse**
vi**eux**	vi**eille**

c. Adjectives that end in **-eur** have several different feminine endings.

• Most adjectives with the masculine singular ending **-eur** change to the feminine singular ending **-euse.**

flatt**eur**	flatt**euse**
moqu**eur**	moqu**euse**
travaill**eur**	travaill**euse**
tromp**eur**	tromp**euse**

However, some frequently used exceptions to this pattern are:

extéri**eur** / intéri**eur**	extéri**eure** / intéri**eure**
supéri**eur** / inféri**eur**	supéri**eure** / inféri**eure**
maj**eur** / min**eur**	maj**eure** / min**eure**
meill**eur**	meill**eure**

- Some adjectives with the masculine singular ending **-teur** change to the feminine singular ending **-trice.** These cases have to be learned.

créa**teur**	créa**trice**
conserva**teur**	conserva**trice**

However, there are exceptions to this pattern, including:

men**teur**	men**teuse**

d. Many adjectives that have a masculine singular form ending in a *vowel + a consonant* form the feminine by doubling the consonant before adding an **e.**

bo**n**	bo**nne**
genti**l**	genti**lle**
gra**s**	gra**sse**
gro**s**	gro**sse**
italie**n**	italie**nne**
nature**l**	nature**lle**
ne**t**	ne**tte**
parei**l**	parei**lle**

However, some adjectives that have a masculine singular form ending in **-et** add an accent and an **-e** instead of doubling the consonant.

compl**et**	compl**ète**
discr**et**	discr**ète**
inqui**et**	inqui**ète**
secr**et**	secr**ète**

e. Finally, there are some frequently used descriptive adjectives that do not follow a regular pattern for formation of the feminine.

blan**c**	blan**che**
favor**i**	favor**ite**
lon**g**	lon**gue**
publi**c**	publi**que**
se**c**	sè**che**

2. Variation of plural forms

The majority of descriptive adjectives, including all of the irregular forms explained above, form the plural by adding **-s** to both the masculine and feminine singular forms. However, there are a few exceptions to this pattern.

a. Adjectives that have the masculine singular ending **-al** form the masculine plural ending two different ways, while the feminine singular has only one pattern for plural formation.

Masculine singular	Feminine singular	Masculine plural	Feminine plural
norm**al**	norm**ale**	norm**aux**	norm**ales**
fin**al**	fin**ale**	fin**als**	fin**ales**

NOTE: The pattern of **final** is only used for a few additional adjectives: **banal, fatal, glacial, natal, naval.**

b. There are five adjectives in French that use alternate masculine singular forms when they precede nouns that begin with a vowel or a mute **h.** The feminine forms of these adjectives are derived from the alternate masculine singular forms.

The masculine and feminine plural forms are not based on the alternate singular forms.

Masculine singular	Feminine singular	Masculine plural	Feminine plural
beau (bel)	belle	beaux	belles
fou (fol)	folle	fous	folles
mou (mol)	molle	mous	molles
nouveau (nouvel)	nouvelle	nouveaux	nouvelles
vieux (vieil)	vieille	vieux	vieilles

3. Invariable adjective forms

Some descriptive adjectives are invariable. This means that the same form of the word is used to modify all nouns, whether they are masculine, feminine, singular, or plural.

a. Some frequently used adjectives of color that are actually formed from nouns fall into this category: **bordeaux, cerise, marron, orange.**

b. A frequently used adjective that has a plural form but no feminine form is: **snob (snobs).** As explained on page 23, it is becoming more common to see the invariable adjective **chic** written **chics** in the plural.

c. The adjectival expression **bon marché** is invariable.

B POSITION

Descriptive adjectives *generally follow* the nouns they modify.

> C'est un garçon **heureux.**
> Il porte un pantalon **gris.**

There are, however, some adjectives that normally precede the nouns they modify, and others that change meaning depending on whether they precede or follow the noun.

1. Adjectives that normally precede the noun include:

beau, joli, jeune, vieux, bon, mauvais, gentil, petit, nouveau, autre[1]

> Je porte souvent cette **vieille** jupe.
> Sa sœur est une très **jolie** femme.

2. Some frequently used adjectives that change meaning depending on whether they precede or follow the noun are:

ancien	mon **ancienne** maison	my *former* house
	une maison **ancienne**	an *old* house
cher	mon **cher** ami	my *dear* friend
	un blouson **cher**	an *expensive* jacket
dernier	le **dernier** train	the *last* train (in a series)
	la semaine **dernière**	*last* week (= preceding)

---

[1] English-speaking students learning French often use the acronym "**BAGS**" to help them remember this group of adjectives: **B**eauty / **A**ge / **G**oodness / **S**ize.

grand	un **grand** homme	a **great** man
	un homme **grand**[2]	a **tall** man
même	le **même** jour	the **same** day
	le jour **même**	the **very** day
pauvre	le **pauvre** homme	the **poor** man (= deserving to be pitied)
	l'homme **pauvre**	the **poor** man (= not rich)
propre	sa **propre** chambre	his **own** room
	des draps **propres**	**clean** sheets

 SELF-CHECK Student Activities Manual, *Exercises II, B and C, pages 23–24.*

III. Comparative and Superlative of Adjectives

When comparing people or things, you will want to say that one is *equal to, superior to,* or *inferior to* the other, just as in English.

Equality	Superiority	Inferiority
aussi + adjective + **que**	**plus** + adjective + **que**	**moins** + adjective + **que**

Ton tee-shirt est **aussi** sale **que** ton jean!
*Your T-shirt is **as** dirty **as** your jeans!*

Mon père est **plus** conservateur **que** ma mère.
*My father is **more** conservative **than** my mother.*

Je suis **moins** chic **que** ma sœur.
*I'm **less** chic **than** my sister.*

NOTE: The adjective **bon(ne)** becomes **meilleur(e)** in comparisons of superiority.

Est-ce que son deuxième album est **meilleur que** le premier?
*Is his second album **better than** the first one?*

Be careful not to confuse **meilleur,** the comparative form of the adjective **bon,** with **mieux,** the comparative form of the adverb **bien.** The adjective is used to modify or qualify a noun, whereas the adverb is used to modify a verb/an action.

Adjective meilleur(e)(s):	**Adverb** mieux:
C'est une **bonne** chanson.	Elle chante **bien**.
*It is a **good** song.*	*She **sings** well.*
Elle est **meilleure** que les autres.	Elle chante **mieux** que les autres.
*It is **better** than the others.*	*She sings **better** than the others.*

For more examples of the use of the adverb **mieux,** see **Structures,** Chapter 8, page 215.

---

[2] Normally one would say: **Cet homme est grand** or **Il est grand.**

To describe someone or something as being better or worse than all others, use a superlative construction.

Most	Least
le/la/les plus + adjective (+ **de**)	**le/la/les moins** + adjective (+ **de**)

Victor est **le plus** sympathique
   (**des** enfants).
*Victor is **the nicest***
   *(**of** the children).*

Sophie est **la moins** paresseuse
   (**des** filles).
*Sophie is the **least lazy***
   *(**of** the girls).*

NOTE: The adjective **bon(ne)** becomes **le/la/les meilleur(e)(s)** in superlative statements.

C'est **la meilleure** description de la mode punk.
*It's the **best description** of punk fashion.*

 SELF-CHECK Student Activities Manual, *Exercises III, F and G, pages 25–26.*

IV. *Tout*

The word **tout** can function in several different ways.

A THE ADJECTIVE *TOUT*

As an adjective, **tout** has four forms:

Masculine singular	Feminine singular	Masculine plural	Feminine plural
tou**t**	tou**te**	tou**s**[3]	tou**tes**

The adjective **tout** means *the entire, the whole, all, every.*

Toute la famille est désagréable.
*The **whole** family is unpleasant.*

Elle m'envoie un texto **tous** les jours.
*She sends me a text message **every** day.*

B THE PRONOUN *TOUT*

The pronoun **tout** has three forms. There is only one singular form, which means *everything*. There are two plural forms, but they both mean *everyone* or *all of them*.

Tes robes? Elles sont **toutes** dans la valise.
*Your dresses? **All of them** are in the suitcase.*

---

[3] The **-s** of **tous** is not pronounced when used as an adjective: **Tous mes amis aiment ce musicien.**

Masculine singular	Feminine singular		Masculine plural	Feminine plural
tout	—		tous[4]	toutes

Tout est moche dans cette boutique.
Everything is tacky in this shop.

Toutes s'habillent de la même façon.
All of them (= all the girls / women) dress the same way.

 SELF-CHECK Student Activities Manual, *Exercise VI, J, pages 27–28.*

V. Interrogatives

Grammar Video Tutorials

There are two general kinds of questions, those that ask for an affirmative or negative response (**oui, si**[5]**, non**), and those that ask for specific information.

A QUESTIONS THAT REQUIRE A SIMPLE AFFIRMATIVE OR NEGATIVE ANSWER

There are four ways to ask this type of question:

1. *Est-ce que*

> **Est-ce que** tu aimes cette robe?
> *Do you like this dress?*

2. Inversion (of subject pronoun and verb). This is the most formal way to ask a question.

> **Aimes-tu** cette robe?
> *Do you like this dress?*

a. If the verb is negative, **ne** precedes the verb as usual, and **pas** follows the verb-pronoun group.

> **N'**aimes-tu **pas** mes tatouages?
> *Don't you like my tattoos?*

b. If the verb is in a compound tense, the auxiliary verb and the subject pronoun are inverted.

> **As-tu** acheté son nouveau CD?
> *Did you buy her new CD?*

---

[4] The -s of **tous** is pronounced when used as a pronoun: **Ils sont tous allés au concert.**
[5] **Si** is used to give an affirmative answer to a negative question: **–Tu n'aimes pas la musique de Diam's? –Si! Je l'aime beaucoup.**

c. If the subject is a noun, the noun remains in its normal place in the sentence, and a corresponding pronoun is inverted with the verb.

Monique aime tes dreads. → Monique aime-t-**elle** tes dreads?
Monique likes your dreadlocks. *Does Monique like your dreadlocks?*

Note that for ease of pronounciation, a **-t-** is inserted between two vowels that come together during inversion.

3. Addition of *n'est-ce pas*

Tu aimes jouer de la guitare, **n'est-ce pas**?
*You like playing the guitar, **don't you**?*

4. Intonation

The use of interrogative tone of voice (rising intonation) is the most informal way to ask a question, and also perhaps the most frequently used in conversation.

Tu aimes faire des courses?
You like going shopping?

B QUESTIONS THAT ASK FOR SPECIFIC INFORMATION

This type of question begins with an interrogative word. This interrogative word can be an adverb, an adjective, or a pronoun.

1. Interrogative adverbs: *combien, comment, où, pourquoi, quand*

Following an interrogative adverb, use either **est-ce que** or inversion to form your question.

Combien *avez-vous payé* ce collier?
OR
Combien *est-ce que* vous avez payé ce collier?
} *How much did you pay for this necklace?*

Quand *vous êtes-vous fait teindre* les cheveux?
OR
Quand *est-ce que* vous vous êtes fait teindre les cheveux?
} *When did you have your hair dyed?*

With any interrogative adverb *except* **pourquoi,** when asking a question made up of only a verb in a simple tense (present, future, conditional, imperfect) and a noun subject, invert the verb and the subject.

Où est mon chapeau? **Comment** va ta sœur?
***Where** is my hat?* ***How** is your sister (doing)?*

With **pourquoi,** however, the noun subject remains in its normal position, and the verb is inverted with the corresponding subject pronoun.

Pourquoi Sophie veut-elle un piercing au nombril?
***Why** does Sophie want a navel ring?*

2. Interrogative adjectives: *quel, quelle, quels, quelles*

The interrogative adjective **quel (quelle, quels, quelles)** is the equivalent of *which* or *what*. It can *only* be followed by a noun or by a conjugated form of the verb **être**.

Quel maillot préfères-tu?
***Which** swimsuit do you prefer?*

Quelle est la différence entre un manteau et un blouson?
What is the difference between a coat and a jacket?

3. Interrogative pronouns

There are two types of interrogative pronouns: invariable (no change of form for gender or number) and variable (agrees in gender and number with the noun it modifies or replaces).

a. Invariable interrogative pronouns

Qui is always used to ask a question about a person. To ask a question about a thing, use **qu'est-ce qui** as a subject, **que / qu'est-ce que** as a direct object, and **quoi** as an object of a preposition.

People		
Subject	qui	**Qui** aime Diam's? ***Who** likes Diam's?*
Direct object	qui (+ inversion)	**Qui** as-tu vu au concert? ***Who (Whom)** did you see at the concert?*
Object of preposition	qui (+ inversion)	Avec **qui** sors-tu ce soir? *With **whom** are you going out tonight?*

Things		
Subject	qu'est-ce qui	**Qu'est-ce qui** t'intéresse? ***What** interests you?*
Direct object	que / qu' (+ inversion) OR qu'est-ce que	**Que** fais-tu? ***What** are you doing?* **Qu'est-ce que** tu as acheté? ***What** did you buy?*
Object of preposition	quoi (+ inversion) OR quoi est-ce que	De **quoi** parles-tu? ***What** are you talking about?* Avec **quoi** est-ce qu'elle se teint les cheveux? ***What** is she dying her hair with?*

NOTE: To ask for a definition, use **qu'est-ce que c'est que** or **qu'est-ce que.**

> **Qu'est-ce que c'est que** la Fête de la Musique? (**Qu'est-ce que** la Fête de la Musique?)
> ***What** is the Fête de la Musique?*

b. Variable interrogative pronouns

The variable interrogative pronoun **lequel (laquelle, lesquels, lesquelles)** is always placed at the beginning of a question, and indicates a choice. This pronoun contracts with the prepositions **à** and **de** in the same way that the definite articles **le** and **les** do.

Lequel de ces jeunes hommes joue de la guitare?
Which one of these young men plays the guitar?

Il y a deux concerts de rock ce soir. **Auquel** veux-tu aller?
There are two rock concerts tonight. Which one do you want to go to?

 SELF-CHECK Student Activities Manual, *Exercises V, L and M, pages 28–29.*

VI. *Il (Elle) est vs. C'est*

Il (Elle) est is generally followed by an *adjective*.

> **Il est** sympathique.
> *He is nice.*

> **Il est** regrettable qu'elle soit toujours au régime.
> *It is too bad that she's always on a diet.*

C'est is generally followed by a *noun*.

> **C'est** le copain de Vincent au téléphone.
> *It's Vincent's friend on the phone.*

C'est is also used to refer to a previously mentioned idea or situation.

> Tu n'as pas aimé le concert? **C'est** vraiment dommage!
> *You didn't like the concert? That's really too bad!*

 SELF-CHECK Student Activities Manual, *Exercises VI, P, page 30.*

Structures

I. Verb Review

A. The verb **accueillir** *(to welcome, to greet)* is conjugated like an **-er** verb in the present tense.

j'accueille	nous accueillons
tu accueilles	vous accueillez
il/elle/on accueille	ils/elles accueillent

Imperfect:	j'accueillais
Past participle:	accueilli
Future:	j'accueillerai

B. **Mort** is the past participle of the verb **mourir** *(to die)*.

> Il **est mort** à Marseille.   *He **died** in Marseilles.*

It can also be an adjective meaning *dead.* This creates some ambiguity in the following sentence:

> Mes grands-parents **sont morts.**
> *My grandparents **are dead.***   OR   *My grandparents **have died.***

Only the context will tell you which of these is meant.

 SELF-CHECK Student Activities Manual, *Exercise I, A, page 38.*

II. Passé Composé

Grammar Video Tutorials

The **passé composé** is a tense used in French to tell what happened in the past. It is often referred to as the tense for *narration* of past time.

The **passé composé** is made up of two parts:

the present indicative form of
*the auxiliary verb (**avoir** or **être**)* + *the past participle of the main verb*

> J'**ai commencé** à marcher dans la vieille ville.
> Je **suis allée** jusqu'à la maison de M. Herschel.

A THE AUXILIARY

There are seventeen verbs that normally use the auxiliary **être** in their **passé composé** formation. These verbs are: **aller, arriver, entrer, descendre*, devenir, monter*, mourir, naître, partir, passer*, rentrer*, rester, retourner*, revenir, sortir*, tomber, venir.** Normally these verbs do not take direct objects.

The six verbs marked with an asterisk (*) can also be conjugated in the **passé composé** using the auxiliary **avoir.** This enables them to take a direct object.

> Je **suis sorti** de la maison.
> *I **went out** of the house.*
>
> (*direct object*)
>
> J'**ai sorti** mon **stylo** de mon sac.
> *I **took** my **pen out** of my bag.*

> Il **est descendu** du sixième étage.
> *He **came down** from the sixth floor.*
>
> (*direct object*)
>
> Il **a descendu** l'**escalier** en courant.
> *He **ran down** the staircase.*

Reflexive verbs also use the auxiliary verb **être** in the **passé composé.**

> Ma mère a dit oui, et une nuit, elle **s'est échappée** et elle **s'est cachée.**
> *My mother said yes, and one night she **ran away** and she **hid.***

B THE PAST PARTICIPLE

Regular verbs follow this pattern in the formation of their past participle.

> parl**er** → parl**é**   fin**ir** → fin**i**   vend**re** → vend**u**

To review the past participle forms of other verbs, see Appendix C.

Past participle agreement is determined by the auxiliary verb. The past participle of a verb conjugated with the auxiliary **être** agrees in gender and number with the *subject* of that verb.

> Une nuit, **ma mère** est **partie** de chez elle.

The past participle of a verb conjugated with the auxiliary **avoir** agrees with the *preceding direct object*. To find the direct object, one uses the question **qui?** or **quoi?** after the main verb. If the direct object follows the verb, the past participle remains invariable (no agreement is made).

> Mon père a quitté **ma mère.**
> Mon père l'**a quittée.** (**la [l']** = direct object)

J'ai vu **les Herschel** à Marseille.
Je **les** ai vus à Marseille. (**les** = direct object)

NOTE: For more details about object pronouns, see Chapter 4, **Structures,** pages 176–180. To review past participle agreement in past infinitive constructions, see Chapter 1, **Structures,** pages 149–150.

NEGATION

In a negative sentence, it is the auxiliary verb, not the past participle, that is negated.

> Mon père est allé travailler en France, mais il **n'**est **jamais** revenu.

✔ **SELF-CHECK** Student Activities Manual, *Exercises II, B and C, pages 38–39.*

Grammar Video Tutorials

III. Imperfect (*Imparfait*)

The imperfect tense is used to describe *conditions* that *were taking place* when another action occurred. It is also used to talk about habitual actions or occurrences. It is referred to as the tense for *describing the past.*

A FORMATION

The imperfect is formed as follows:

Stem of first person plural | + | -ais -ions
of the present indicative | | -ais -iez
(the **nous** stem) | | -ait -aient

Les gens **venaient** me voir. Il y **avait** des gens que je ne **connaissais** pas.

Stem: **-er**	je rest**ais**	nous rest**ions**
nous rest**ons**	tu rest**ais**	vous rest**iez**
	il/elle/on rest**ait**	ils/elles rest**aient**
Stem: **-ir**	je finiss**ais**	nous finiss**ions**
nous finiss**ons**	tu finiss**ais**	vous finiss**iez**
	il/elle/on finiss**ait**	ils/elles finiss**aient**
Stem: **-re**	j'entend**ais**	nous entend**ions**
nous entend**ons**	tu entend**ais**	vous entend**iez**
	il/elle/on entend**ait**	ils/elles entend**aient**

B EXCEPTION: *ETRE*

Être is the exception; the stem used is **ét-**.

> Je lui disais qu'elle n'**était** rien du tout, qu'elle n'**était** pas ma mère, que c'**était** Amie qui **était** ma mère.

j'étais	nous étions
tu étais	vous étiez
il/elle/on était	ils/elles étaient

 SELF-CHECK Student Activities Manual, *Exercises III, E and F, pages 40–41.*

IV. *Passe Compose* vs. Imperfect

When you are telling a story in the past, you should have no trouble deciding when to use the **passé composé** and when to use the imperfect if you keep in mind the following three questions:

1. What happened? What happened once? What happened next? Then what happened? (Use the **passé composé.**)

2. What were the conditions at the time? (Use the imperfect.)

3. Was the action expressed by the verb a habitual action? Did it occur repeatedly? (Use the imperfect.)

Study the following passages carefully:

> C'**était** le plein hiver, il **pleuvait**, la nuit **tombait** tôt. Quand je **suis partie**, Amie m'**a embrassée**. Je n'**ai** pas **pris** grand-chose, juste deux ou trois livres que j'**aimais,** ma pendulette *(travel clock),* une brosse à dents, un peu de linge *(underwear).* Je n'**avais** plus de jouets *(toys)* ni de poupées *(dolls).* Ça n'**avait** pas d'importance. Je **partais** pour ne jamais revenir. Ils **sont restés** sur le seuil *(doorstep)* de la maison, pour me regarder partir.

1. What actions happened (once; next)? *(passé composé)*

  a. je suis partie *(I left)*

  b. Amie m'a embrassée *(Amie kissed me)*

  c. Je n'ai pas pris grand-chose *(I didn't take much)*

  d. Ils sont restés sur le seuil *(They stayed on the doorstep)*

2. What were the conditions at the time? *(imperfect)*

  a. C'était le plein hiver *(It was the middle of winter)*

  b. il pleuvait *(it was raining)*

  c. la nuit tombait *(night was falling)*

  d. juste deux ou trois livres que j'aimais *(just two or three books that I liked)*

  e. je n'avais plus de jouets *(I no longer had any toys)*

  f. Ça n'avait pas d'importance *(That didn't matter)*

  g. Je partais pour ne jamais revenir *(I was leaving for good)*

> À Nightingale, quand le jour **se levait**, j'**étais** dehors avant tout le monde. Lassie **était** avec moi. Lassie, elle **est arrivée** chez nous un jour, sans qu'on sache d'où *(without anyone knowing from where)*. Au début, elle ne **se laiss**ait pas approcher, et quand on lui **donnait** à manger, elle **attendait** qu'on se soit éloignés *(everyone to move away)* pour venir jusqu'au plat *(dish)*. Elle **mangeait** avec les oreilles rabattues en arrière, sans cesser de nous observer. Et un jour, sans que je comprenne pourquoi, elle **est restée** quand je **me suis approchée** d'elle. Je l'ai **caressée** doucement, sur la tête, le long du nez. Elle s'**est laissé** faire. Je l'**ai embrassée.**

1. What actions were habitual in this story? *(imperfect)*

   a. quand le jour se levait *(when the sun came up [at daybreak])*

   b. j'étais dehors *(I would be outside)*

   c. Lassie était avec moi *(Lassie would be with me)*

   d. elle ne se laissait pas approcher *(she would not let anyone approach her)*

   e. quand on lui donnait à manger *(when someone gave her something to eat)*

   f. elle attendait *(she would wait)*

   g. Elle mangeait *(She would eat)*

2. What actions happened (once; next)? *(passé composé)*

   a. elle est arrivée *(she arrived)*

   b. elle est restée *(she stayed)*

   c. je me suis approchée d'elle *(I approached her)*

   d. Je l'ai caressée *(I patted her)*

   e. Elle s'est laissé faire *(She let herself be touched)*

   f. Je l'ai embrassée *(I kissed her)*

Helpful hints for use of the *passé composé* and imperfect

1. When used in a past context, the verb **venir** + **de** is always in the imperfect.

> Elle **venait de** s'installer chez sa mère quand elle est tombée gravement malade.
> She **had just** moved in with her mother when she got very sick.

2. Certain verbs usually appear in the imperfect when used in a past context. They are: **avoir, être, savoir, connaître, pouvoir,** and **vouloir.** These verbs change meaning when they are used in the **passé composé.**

> *avoir*

> Quand le bateau est arrivé à Marseille, il y **avait** beaucoup de monde sur le quai.
> *When the boat arrived at Marseilles, there **were** a lot of people on the dock.*
>   (= conditions upon arrival)

> Quand Saba a vu tous les gens sur le quai, elle **a eu** peur.
> *When Saba saw all the people on the dock, she **became** afraid.*
>   (= what happened when she saw the people)

être

La mère de Saba **était** très jeune quand elle a laissé son enfant chez les Herschel.
*Saba's mother **was** very young when she left her child at the Herschels'.*
   (= conditions upon leaving)

Saba **a été** malade quand elle a appris la vérité.
*Saba **got** sick when she learned the truth.*
   (= what happened when she learned the truth)

savoir

La mère ne **savait** pas parler français.
*The mother **did** not **know** how to speak French.*
   (= general condition)

Saba **a su** plus tard que son père était mort en France.
*Saba **discovered** later that her father had died in France.*
   (= what happened)

connaître

Saba ne **connaissait** personne dans sa nouvelle école.
*Saba **did** not **know** anyone (**knew** no one) at her new school.*
   (= general condition)

La mère de Saba **a connu** M. Herschel à Mehdia.
*Saba's mother **met** Mr. Herschel in Mehdia.*
   (= what happened)

pouvoir

Saba ne **pouvait** pas oublier son enfance heureuse à Nightingale.
*Saba **could** not (**was** not **able to**) forget her happy childhood at Nightingale.*
   (= general condition)

Les Herschel n'**ont** pas **pu** garder leur fille adoptive.
*The Herschels **were** not **able to** keep (**did** not **succeed in** keeping) their adopted daughter.*
   (= what happened)

vouloir

Saba ne **voulait** pas partir avec sa mère.
*Saba **did** not **want** to leave with her mother.*
   (= general condition)

Saba **a voulu** échapper à sa nouvelle vie chez sa mère.
*Saba **tried (decided)** to escape from her new life with her mother.*
   (= what happened)

3. Certain words and expressions can help you decide whether to use the **passé composé** or the imperfect.

For the **passé composé** these words pinpoint a definite time of occurrence: **hier, une fois, tout à coup,** etc.

For the imperfect the words suggest repeated occurrences: **souvent, tous les jours, toutes les semaines, chaque année, en général,** etc.

 SELF-CHECK Student Activities Manual, *Exercises IV, I and J, page 42.*

V. Pluperfect *(Plus-que-parfait)*

The pluperfect tense is used in French as the past perfect is used in English. When one action precedes another in the past, the verb describing the first action will be in the pluperfect; the tense of the second verb will be the **passé composé** or the imperfect.

A FORMATION

The pluperfect is made up of two parts: the imperfect of the auxiliary verb (**être** or **avoir**) + the past participle of the main verb.

> Ma mère m'a dit un jour qu'elle **avait reçu** une lettre en français.
> *My mother told me one day that she **had received** a letter in French.*

> Je n'ai plus jamais parlé de Lassie. Elle **était sortie** de ma vie pour toujours.
> *I no longer ever spoke of Lassie. She **had gone out** of my life for good.*

1. The auxiliary

The use of auxiliary verbs follows the same rules in the pluperfect as in the **passé composé**:

- The same seventeen verbs use the auxiliary verb **être** in the formation of the pluperfect (see page 165).
- Reflexive verbs use the auxiliary verb **être** in the pluperfect.
- All other verbs use **avoir** as the auxiliary verb in the pluperfect.
- In a negative sentence, the auxiliary verb, not the past participle, is negated.

2. The past participle

- The past participle of a verb conjugated with the auxiliary **être** agrees in gender and number with the subject of that verb.
- The past participle of a verb conjugated with **avoir** agrees in gender and number with the preceding direct object, if there is one.

B USAGE

Study the following passage carefully:

> Je me rappelle le mariage de Jamila. Ma mère m'**avait préparée**, elle m'**avait habillée** et **coiffée**, pour aller au mariage de sa cousine Jamila… Ma mère m'**avait fait** des tresses, en mêlant de la laine aux cheveux, et elle m'**avait mis** du rouge sur les joues… Ensuite elle m'a **emmenée**, nous **avons marché** sur la route jusqu'à Mehdia, et nous **avons pris** le car pour Kenitra. J'**étais** dans une grande ville que je ne **connaissais** pas, avec des avenues plantées d'arbres, des grands immeubles *(buildings)*, et toutes ces petites maisons blanches et pauvres chacune avec sa cour intérieure. Il y **avait** des chèvres, des poulets. Partout il y **avait** des enfants,…

1. What actions in this story preceded other past actions? *(pluperfect)*

   a. Ma mère m'avait préparée *(My mother had prepared me)*

   b. m'avait habillée et coiffée *(had dressed me and fixed my hair)*

   c. m'avait fait des tresses *(had braided my hair)*

   d. m'avait mis du rouge sur les joues *(had put blush on my cheeks)*

2. What actions happened (once; next)? *(passé composé)*

   a. elle m'a emmenée *(she took me)*

   b. nous avons marché *(we walked)*

   c. nous avons pris *(we took)*

3. What were the conditions surrounding this trip? *(imperfect)*

   a. J'étais dans une grande ville *(I was in a large city)*

   b. que je ne connaissais pas *(that I didn't know [was not familiar with])*

   c. Il y avait des chèvres *(There were goats)*

   d. il y avait des enfants *(there were children)*

 SELF-CHECK Student Activities Manual, *Exercises V, M and N, pages 43–44.*

VI. Past Infinitives

Compare the structures:

    avant de + present infinitive   →   **avant de partir**

    après + past infinitive   →   **après être parti(e)**

                                             (avoir / être + past participle)

Infinitives are used after prepositions, with the exception of **en** (see *Appendix B,* pages 228–229). Following the preposition **après,** a *past infinitive* must be used, as in the example above. In English, a subject-verb construction or the *-ing* form of a verb (gerund) is the most common equivalent.

   Après être allés en France, ses parents ont ouvert un restaurant.
   After they went to France, her parents opened a restaurant.

   Après avoir retrouvé Saba, sa mère l'a emmenée en France.
   After finding Saba **again**, her mother took her to France.

 SELF-CHECK Student Activities Manual, *Exercises VI, O–Q, pages 44–46.*

VII. *Le mot juste*

A MANQUER (À)

Manquer (à) *(to miss)* follows the same pattern in French as in English if you want to say *miss the bus*, for example.

> J'ai manqué le bus.
> *I missed the bus.*

However, if you want to say that you *miss someone or something,* i.e., that you are sad because a person or thing is not with you, the structure of the sentence in French is different from that in English.

> Les Herschel **manquent à Saba.**   Mes parents **me manquent.**
> *Saba misses the Herschels.*   *I miss my parents.*

B RENDRE

To express the idea that *something or someone makes you feel a certain way,* the verb **rendre** is used (not the verb **faire**).

> Cette nouvelle me **rend** triste.   Son retour **a rendu** ses parents heureux.
> *This news **makes** me sad.*   *His return **made** his parents happy.*

C PARTIR, SORTIR, QUITTER

These three verbs have generally the same meaning *(to leave)* but are used differently. Both **sortir** *(to leave, to go out)* and **partir** *(to leave)* are conjugated with **être;** when used with a location, the preposition **de** follows the verb.

> Nous **sommes sortis.**   Elle **est partie.**
> *We **went out.***   *She **left.***

> Elle **sort de** sa chambre.   Ils **sont partis du** Maroc.
> *She **leaves (goes out of)** her room.*   *They **left** Morocco.*

Quitter *(to leave)* is conjugated with **avoir**. This verb *must always* be followed by a direct object, i.e., what or whom is being left *must* be stated.

> Elle **a quitté sa famille.**
> *She **left her family.***

> Mes ancêtres **ont quitté l'Angleterre** il y a deux cents ans.
> *My ancestors **left England** two hundred years ago.*

NOTE: **Quitter** is a false cognate and does not mean *to quit.* Use the verbs **cesser (de)** or **arrêter (de)** to say that you have stopped or quit doing something.

> J'ai arrêté de fumer.
> *I quit smoking.*

Structures

I. Verb Review

The verbs **conduire** and **mettre** are irregular in the **present indicative** tense.

je conduis	nous conduisons	je mets	nous mettons
tu conduis	vous conduisez	tu mets	vous mettez
il/elle/on conduit	ils/elles conduisent	il/elle/on met	ils/elles mettent
Imperfect stem:	conduis-	mett-	
Future/Conditional stem:	conduir-	mettr-	
Past participle:	conduit	mis	

 SELF-CHECK Student Activities Manual, *Exercise I, A, pages 55–56.*

II. Articles

Grammar Video Tutorials

There are three types of articles in French: definite, indefinite, and partitive. These have the equivalent meaning in English of *the, a / an,* and *some.*

	Singular		Plural
	Masculine	**Feminine**	**Masculine and Feminine**
Definite article	le (l')	la (l')	les
Indefinite article	un	une	des
Partitive article	du (de l')	de la (de l')	

A DEFINITE ARTICLE

1. Definite articles precede nouns that are used in a very specific sense. This is similar to English usage.

> **La** voiture qu'elle achète est neuve.
> *The car she is buying is new.*
> (Here a specific car is being talked about.)

2. Definite articles also precede nouns used in a general sense. Often in English the definite article is omitted in this case.

> **L'**essence coûte trop cher en France.
> *Gas costs too much in France.*

Remember that there are four frequently used verbs in French that express this generality: **aimer, adorer, préférer, détester.** These verbs require the use of a definite article when they are followed by a direct object.

> J'aime **le** bus mais je déteste **le** métro.
> *I like **the** bus but I hate **the** subway.*

3. Definite articles are used before abstract nouns.

> **La** patience est très utile pendant **les** heures de pointe.
> *Patience is very useful during rush hour.*

4. Definite articles are used before the names of the seasons.

> **Le** printemps est la meilleure saison pour faire du vélo.
> *Spring is the best season to go biking.*

5. Definite articles are used before the days of the week to indicate habitual action.

> Elle prend le métro **le** mardi matin et **le** jeudi après-midi.
> *She takes the subway Tuesday mornings and Thursday afternoons.*

6. Definite articles are used before names that denote nationality, before the names of countries and geographic regions, and before the names of famous buildings or monuments.

> **Les** Français font rarement du covoiturage.
> *The French rarely carpool.*

> **La** tour Eiffel est le monument le plus visité de Paris.
> *The Eiffel Tower is the most visited monument in Paris.*

7. Definite articles are used before names of disciplines and languages, except when the language follows the verb **parler.**

> Ce chauffeur de taxi étudie **l'**informatique le soir après son travail.
> *This taxi driver studies computer science at night after work.*

> Il parle couramment anglais, et il comprend **le** français.
> *He speaks English fluently, and he understands French.*

B INDEFINITE ARTICLE

1. Indefinite articles are used before the names of indeterminate people and things, much the same way as in English.

Il y a **un** feu rouge au prochain carrefour.
*There is **a** red light at the next intersection.*

Il y a **une** station Vélib' dans la prochaine rue.
*There is **a** Vélib' station on the next street.*

Il y a **des** gens qui se garent sur les voies cyclables.
There are people who park in bike lanes.

NOTE: The plural indefinite article in French (**des**) is often not required in English.

2. When the verb is negative, the indefinite article is replaced by **de.**

Vous avez **une** voiture.   Vous n'avez pas **de** voiture.
*You have **a** car.*   *You don't have **a** car.*

However, if the negative verb is **être,** the indefinite article does not change to **de.**

C'est **une** voiture d'occasion.   Ce n'est pas **une** voiture d'occasion.
*It's **a** used car.*   *It isn't **a** used car.*

3. The plural indefinite article **des** has almost the same meaning as the plural partitive article **des;** they both can be translated as *some.*

Il y a **des** casques dans le placard.
*There are **some** helmets in the closet.*

NOTE: Before the adjective **autres,** the plural indefinite (or partitive) article **des** changes to **d'.**

J'ai **d'autres** voisins qui font toujours du covoiturage.
*I have **other** neighbors who always carpool.*

C PARTITIVE ARTICLE

1. Partitive articles indicate a part of something, an unspecified amount or quantity. They are usually used with nouns referring to things that cannot be counted.

Il me faut **de l'**argent pour acheter un VTT.
*I need (**some**) money to buy a mountain bike.*

Ne te mets pas au volant si tu bois **du** vin au dîner!
Don't get behind the wheel if you drink wine at dinner!

2. When the verb is negative, the partitive articles **du, de la, de l',** and **des** change to **de.**

Il y a **de l'**essence dans la voiture.   Il **n'y a pas d'**essence dans la voiture.
There is gas in the car.   *There is no gas in the car.*

Tu as **des** rollers?   Tu **n'as pas de** rollers?
Do you have inline skates?   *You don't have inline skates?*

3. When a plural adjective precedes the noun, the partitive article **des** changes to **de.**

Les agents d'entretien du service Vélib' se déplacent dans **de** petits
  véhicules électriques.
The maintenance crews for Vélib' get around in small electric vehicles.

D ARTICLES WITH EXPRESSIONS OF QUANTITY

I. Following expressions of quantity (**beaucoup, trop, peu, assez, autant, plus, moins, un verre, une bouteille, un litre, un kilo,** etc.), **du, de la, de l',** and **des** change to **de.**

> Il y a beaucoup **de** taxis à l'aéroport.
> *There are **a lot of** taxis at the airport.*

> Elle achète cinq litres **d'**essence.
> *She is buying **five liters of** gas.*

> Il y aura plus **de** bouchons ce soir que demain matin.
> *There will be **more** traffic jams tonight than tomorrow morning.*

> **Trop de** cyclistes ne portent pas de casque.
> *Too **many** cyclists don't wear helmets.*

EXCEPTION: This change does not occur following **la plupart, bien,** and **encore.**

> **La plupart des** automobilistes respectent les droits des cyclistes.
> ***Most*** *motorists respect the rights of bikers.*

> **Bien des** jeunes conduisent trop vite.
> *A **lot** of young people drive too fast.*

2. When the expression **avoir besoin de** is followed by a noun used in a general sense, the definite articles **le, la, l',** and **les** are not used.

> J'ai besoin **d'**argent pour payer l'essence.
> *I need money to pay for the gas.*

The definite article is added, however, if the noun is specific.

> J'ai besoin **de l'**argent que mon père m'a promis pour acheter de l'essence.
> *I need **the money** my father promised me in order to buy gas.*

 SELF-CHECK Student Activities Manual, *Exercises II, B and C pages 56–57.*

III. Object Pronouns, *y* and *en*

Grammar Video Tutorials

A DIRECT AND INDIRECT OBJECT PRONOUNS

A direct object receives the direct action of the verb in a sentence without an intervening preposition.

> Je vois **l'éléphant**.
> *I see **the elephant**.*

Direct object nouns can be replaced by direct object pronouns.

> Je **le** vois.
> I see *it/him.*

The direct object pronouns in French are:

	Singular	Plural
1st person	me (m')	nous
2nd person	te (t')	vous
3rd person	le/la (l')	les

The indirect object, which is also acted upon by the verb, is preceded by the preposition **à.**

> Il offre un cognac **à ma sœur.**
> *He offers a cognac **to my sister.***

When the indirect object is a person, it can be replaced by an indirect object pronoun.

> Il **lui** offre un cognac.
> *He offers **her** a cognac.*

The indirect object pronouns in French are:

	Singular	Plural
1st person	me (m')	nous
2nd person	te (t')	vous
3rd person	lui	leur

There are three main rules that govern the use of the direct and indirect object pronouns in French.

1. The pronoun *precedes the verb* of which it is the object, *unless* the verb is an affirmative imperative.

> Ma sœur suit **les policiers** au poste.
> *My sister follows **the police officers** to the station.*

> Ma sœur **les** suit au poste.
> *My sister follows **them** to the station.*

> Elle explique **aux policiers** ce qui est arrivé.
> *She explains **to the police officers** what happened.*

> Elle **leur** explique ce qui est arrivé.
> *She explains **to them** what happened.*

2. If the verb is an affirmative imperative, the object pronoun follows the verb and is connected to it by a hyphen.

> Suivez **les policiers** au poste!
> *Follow **the police officers** to the station!*

> Suivez-**les** au poste!
> *Follow **them** to the station!*

Demandez **à ma sœur** pourquoi elle conduit mal.
*Ask **my sister** why she drives poorly.*

Demandez-**lui** pourquoi elle conduit mal.
*Ask **her** why she drives poorly.*

NOTE: With an affirmative imperative verb, the pronouns **me** and **te** are replaced by **moi** and **toi**.

Suivez-**moi**!   Calme-**toi**!
*Follow **me**!*   *Calm down!*

3. If the verb is a compound tense (**passé composé,** past conditional, pluperfect, etc.), the pronoun *precedes* the auxiliary verb. The past participle agrees with the *direct object pronoun* in gender and in number.

On a gardé **ma sœur** au poste de police pendant dix heures.
*They kept **my sister** at the police station for ten hours.*

On **l**'a gardé**e** au poste de police pendant dix heures.
*They kept **her** at the police station for ten hours.*

There is *no agreement* with a preceding *indirect object pronoun.*

Un incident bizarre est arrivé **à ma sœur.**
*A strange incident happened **to my sister**.*

Un incident bizarre **lui** est arrivé.
*A strange incident happened **to her**.*

NOTE: Direct object pronouns are used for people and things. The pronoun **le** can also be used to express an idea.

Elle pense **qu'ils ont tort.**   Elle **le** pense.
*She thinks **they are wrong**.*   *She thinks **it**.*

 SELF-CHECK Student Activities Manual, *Exercises III–IV, F–I, pages 58–59.*

 Y

The pronoun **y** can be used to replace the preposition **à** + *a noun* when referring to a thing or an idea, but not when referring to a person.

A-t-elle répondu **à la question des policiers**?
*Did she respond **to the police officers' question**?*

Y a-t-elle répondu?
*Did she respond **to it**?*

The pronoun **y** is also used to replace expressions of location starting with **à** or other prepositions, *except* **de.**

Elle va **au café** avec le directeur du cirque.
*She is going **to the café** with the circus director.*

Elle **y** va avec le directeur du cirque.
*She is going **there** with the circus director.*

On remet l'éléphant **dans le camion.**
*They put the elephant back **in the truck**.*

On **y** remet l'éléphant.
*They put the elephant back **there**.*

As with the object pronouns, the pronoun **y** precedes the verb with which it is associated.

Elle est obligée d'aller **au poste de police.**
*She has to go **to the police station**.*

Elle est obligée d'**y** aller.
*She has to go **there**.*

NOTE: **Y** is not used with the verb **aller** in the future or conditional tenses for reasons of pronunciation.

Elle a dit qu'elle n'irait pas **en prison.**
*She said she wouldn't go **to prison**.*

Elle a dit qu'elle n'irait pas.
She said she wouldn't go.

 SELF-CHECK Student Activities Manual, *Exercise III, J, page 60.*

EN

The pronoun **en** is used in French to express the idea of *some, any,* or *none.* It can replace:

1. the partitive article + *the noun that follows*;

Elle boit **du** cognac.
*She drinks **some** cognac.*

Elle **en** boit.
*She drinks **some**.*

Ils ont pris **du sang** à ma sœur.
*They took **some blood** from my sister.*

Ils **en** ont pris à ma sœur.
*They took **some** from my sister.*

2. a noun preceded by a number or an expression of quantity, but the *number* or the *expression of quantity* must be repeated;

Elle voit **un éléphant** devant sa voiture.
*She sees **an elephant** in front of her car.*

Elle **en** voit **un** devant sa voiture.
*She sees **one** in front of her car.*

Elle voit **deux policiers** derrière sa voiture.
*She sees **two police officers** behind her car.*

Elle **en** voit **deux** derrière sa voiture.
*She sees **two (of them)** behind her car.*

3. the preposition **de** in expressions with **avoir** + *the verb or noun clause that follows* (as in **avoir besoin de, avoir envie de, avoir peur de,** etc.) ;

> Elle avait peur **de l'éléphant.**
> *She was afraid **of the elephant.***

> Elle **en** avait peur.
> *She was afraid **of it.***

> Elle avait envie **de rentrer chez elle.**
> *She wanted **to go home**.*

> Elle **en** avait envie.
> *She wanted **to**.*

4. the preposition **de** + a *place*;

> Les motards arrivent **du village.**
> *The motorcycle police arrive **from the village**.*

> Les motards **en** arrivent.
> *The motorcycle police arrive **(from there)**.*

> Elle sort **de sa voiture.**
> *She gets out **of her car.***

> Elle **en** sort.
> *She gets out **(of it)**.*

5. the preposition **de** + a *clause*.

> Elle est contente **de ne plus avoir de voiture rouge.**
> *She is happy **to no longer have a red car**.*

> Elle **en** est contente.
> *She is happy **(about it)**.*

NOTE: **En** cannot be used to replace the preposition **de** + *a person*. In this case, use a disjunctive pronoun (see **Part V, Structures,** pages 182–183). However, **en** can be used to replace the preposition **de** + *groups of people.*

> Combien de policiers avez-vous vus? J'**en** ai vu cinq.
> *How many **police officers** did you see? I saw five **(of them)**.*

 **SELF-CHECK** Student Activities Manual, *Exercise III, K, page 60.*

IV. Order of Pronouns

Grammar Video Tutorials

A REGULAR PATTERN

The following chart shows the word order used for multiple pronouns that appear with regular affirmative and negative verb constructions and with negative imperative constructions.

	me (m')									
	te (t')		le							
(ne +)	se (s')	+	la	+	lui	+	y	+	en	+	verb (+ pas)
	nous		les		leur					
	vous									
	se (s')									

Ils emmènent **ma sœur au poste de police.**
*They are taking **my sister to the police station.***

Ils **l'y** emmènent.
*They are taking **her there.***

Elle n'a pas très bien expliqué **l'incident aux policiers.**
*She didn't explain **the incident** very well **to the police officers.***

Elle ne **le leur** a pas très bien expliqué.
*She didn't explain **it** very well **to them.***

Ne demande pas **d'explication à ma sœur!**
*Don't ask **my sister for an explanation!***

Ne **lui en** demande pas (une)!
*Don't ask **her for one!***

B AFFIRMATIVE IMPERATIVE CONSTRUCTION

			moi (m')				
	le		toi (t')				
verb	+	la	+	lui	+	y	+	en
	les		nous				
			vous				
			leur				

Explique **cet incident aux policiers!**   Explique-**le-leur!**
*Explain **this incident to the police!***   *Explain **it to them!***

NOTE: Double object pronouns are used less frequently in spoken than in written French.

 SELF-CHECK Student Activities Manual, *Exercise IV, L, pages 60–61.*

V. Disjunctive Pronouns

Disjunctive pronouns (**pronoms accentués**) are another type of personal pronoun used in French. Unlike subject and object pronouns, the disjunctive pronouns can function independently from a verb.

The disjunctive pronoun forms are the following:

Singular	Plural
moi	nous
toi	vous
lui/elle/soi	eux/elles

NOTE: The disjunctive pronoun **soi** is used with the indefinite pronoun **on** or with impersonal expressions such as **chacun, tout le monde,** etc.

Disjunctive pronouns are used:

1. to emphasize the subject(s) or object(s) in a sentence. Their position is variable.

> **Moi**, j'adore conduire.   J'adore conduire, **moi.**
> **Toi**, on t'écoute.   On t'écoute, **toi.**

2. as the object of the preposition **à,** for certain verbs and verbal phrases, when referring to a person or persons. Some of the more common of these verbs and verbal phrases are: **être (à), faire attention (à), penser (à).**

Remember that with other verbs the indirect object pronouns are used.

> C'est la voiture de ton père?
> Oui, elle **est à lui.**
>
> A qui penses-tu?
> A mon ami Paul. Je **pense à lui** depuis ce matin.

> BUT: Qu'est-ce que tu **dis à Paul**? Je **lui dis** de revenir bientôt.

3. as the object of all prepositions other than **à,** when referring to a person or persons.

> Nous sommes revenus **chez eux** à neuf heures.
> Toi, tu n'as pas d'argent **sur toi**?

4. after **c'est/ce sont.** All of the disjunctive pronouns can be used with **c'est** except **eux/elles.** With **eux/elles,** the plural form **ce sont** must be used.

> **C'est elle** qui conduit le mieux.
> **C'est nous** qui vendons cette voiture.

> BUT: **Ce sont eux** qui préfèrent le vélo à l'auto.

5. as a one-word answer to a question.

> Qui a les clés de la voiture?   **Moi.**
> *Who has the car keys?*   *I do.*

6. in comparative constructions.

> J'ai eu **moins d'**accidents **que toi.**
> *I have had **fewer** accidents **than you**.*

7. after **ne… que.**

> L'agent de police **ne** mentionne **que lui** dans son rapport.
> *The police officer **only** mentions **him** in his report.*

8. as part of a compound subject.

> **Lui et moi,** nous avons des idées différentes au sujet de cet accident.
> ***He and I** have different ideas about this accident.*

9. combined with **-même.**

> Tu dois payer la contravention **toi-même.**
> *You must pay the fine **yourself**.*

 SELF-CHECK Student Activities Manual, *Exercise V, M, pages 61–62.*

VI. Le mot juste: *se moquer de*

This reflexive construction is the equivalent of the English expression *to make fun of.* The person or thing being made fun of is the object of the preposition **de.** When the noun refers to a person, the disjunctive pronoun is used. When it refers to a thing or an idea, the pronoun **en** replaces the noun.

> Personne ne **se moque de** moi.
> *No one **makes fun of** me.*

> Mes amis **se moquent de** ma vieille voiture. Ils s'**en** moquent.
> *My friends **make fun of** my old car. They make fun of **it**.*

Structures

I. Verb Review

A. Verbs that end in **-ger** (**voyager, nager, plonger, manger,** etc.) undergo a spelling change to keep the pronunciation of a soft **g** in all forms. An **e** is placed after the **g** as needed for pronunciation regularity.

Compare: je m'amuse   nous nous amus**ons**
           je voyag**e**   nous voyag**eons** (The **e** is needed to keep the pronunciation of the **g** the same in both forms.)

This spelling change occurs in the **nous** form of the present tense and in all forms of the imperfect except that of **nous** and **vous** in verbs whose infinitive ends in **-ger**.

   Je nag**eais** mais vous ne nag**iez** pas.
   Il plong**eait** mais nous ne plong**ions** pas.

B. The verb **prendre** and verbs built on this same stem (**apprendre, comprendre, surprendre**) are irregular in the present tense.

je prends	nous prenons
tu prends	vous prenez
il/elle/on prend	ils/elles prennent

Past participles: **pris, appris, compris, surpris**

C. The verb **découvrir** and verbs like it (**couvrir, offrir, ouvrir, souffrir**) are conjugated like **-er** verbs in the present.

> Je **découvre** Paris.
> Nous **découvrons** le plaisir de voyager.

Past participles: **découvert, couvert, offert, ouvert, souffert**

 SELF-CHECK Student Activities Manual, *Exercise I, A, pages 69–70.*

II. Prepositions with Geographical Names

A. For cities, islands, or groups of islands that are not countries or provinces:

- use the preposition **à** to express *to* or *in*.

  J'habite **à** Dakar. *(city)*
  Ils iront **à** Tahiti l'été prochain. *(island)*

- use the preposition **de** or **d'** (in front of a vowel sound) to express *from*.

  Elle part **de** Guadeloupe. *(island)*
  Nous sommes **de** Montpellier. *(city)*
  Ils viennent **d'**Antibes. *(city)*

NOTE: Cities that have definite articles as part of their name (for example, **La Nouvelle-Orléans, Le Caire, Le Havre**), always keep the article.

> Vous allez **à La** Nouvelle-Orléans.
> Mon père rentre **du** Caire.

B. For singular feminine names of countries and French and Canadian provinces (names ending in **-e**) as well as for the names of all continents (names ending in **-e**), feminine names of states (la Carolin**e** du Nord, la Virgini**e**) and masculine singular names of states and countries beginning with a vowel sound:

- use the preposition **en** to express *to* or *in*.

  Ma famille voyage **en** Afrique. *(continent)*
  Le professeur passe ses vacances **en** Louisiane. *(feminine state)*
  Ma sœur fait du vélo **en** Bretagne. *(feminine French province)*
  Les enfants ont passé une semaine **en** Colombie-Britannique. *(feminine Canadian province)*
  Nous irons **en** Israël l'année prochaine *(masculine country beginning with a vowel)*

- use the preposition **de** or **d'** to express *from*.

  Nous sommes partis **d'**Israël. *(masculine country beginning with a vowel)*
  Jeanne est originaire **de** Normandie. *(feminine name of a French province)*
  Mes voisins viennent **de** Bosnie. *(feminine country)*

C. For singular masculine names of countries, provinces, and states, (NOTE: four countries whose names end in -e are masculine and therefore exceptions to B, above. These countries are **le Mexique, le Zimbabwe, le Mozambique,** and **le Cambodge**) use the preposition **à** + *definite article* (**au**) to express *to* or *in*.

> Ils vivront **au** Sénégal l'année prochaine. *(masculine singular country)*

Nous passerons nos vacances **au** Cambodge en juin.
*We will spend our vacation **in** Cambodia in June.*

- use the preposition **de** + *definite article* (**du**) to express *from*.

Mes ancêtres viennent **du** Danemark. *(masculine singular country)*

D. For all plural names of geographical areas:

- use the preposition **à** + definite article (**aux**) to express *to* or *in*.

Tu verras des tulipes **aux** Pays-Bas. *(masculine plural country)*
Elle part **aux** Philippines. *(feminine plural country)*

- use the preposition **de** + definite article (**des**) to express *from*.

Elles reviendront **des** Etats-Unis au printemps. *(masculine plural country)*
Nous sommes originaires **des** Antilles. *(plural island group)*

E. When talking about states you can also use the following constructions:

- to express *to* or *in*, use **dans l'Etat de/d'** for feminine states and masculine states beginning with a vowel sound, and **dans l'Etat du** for other masculine states.

Nous ferons du cheval **dans l'Etat de** Californie. *(feminine state)*
J'habite **dans l'Etat du** Texas. *(masculine state)*

- to express *from*, use **de l'Etat de/d'** for feminine states and masculine states beginning with a vowel sound, and **de l'Etat du** for other masculine states.

John est **de l'Etat de** Virginie. *(feminine state)*
Je suis rentré **de l'Etat d'**Utah hier. *(masculine state beginning with a vowel sound)*

	in/to	from
Cities	à	de/d'
Continents/fem. countries and provinces/fem. states/masc. states and countries beginning with a vowel sound	en	de/d'
Masc. countries, states, and provinces	au	du
Plural names of geographical areas	aux	des

 SELF-CHECK Student Activities Manual, *Exercise II, B, page 70.*

III. Future Tense and Conditional Forms

Grammar Video Tutorials

The use of the future and the conditional in French is very similar to English. The future tense allows you to talk about what *will happen* at some future time. Note that unlike English, this verb tense has only one word, not two.

Ma famille **partira** en Argentine demain.
*My family **will leave** for Argentina tomorrow.*

Les vacances **finiront** dimanche.
*Vacation **will be** over on Sunday.*

The conditional expresses what *could, might,* or *would happen* if a certain condition existed. This tense also has only one word in French, whereas in English it has two.

> Si je gagnais assez d'argent, j'**achèterais** un chalet à Chamonix.
> *If I earned enough money, I **would buy** a chalet in Chamonix.*

Ⓐ FORMATION OF THE SIMPLE FUTURE (*FUTUR SIMPLE*) AND PRESENT CONDITIONAL (*CONDITIONNEL PRESENT*)

The simple future and the present conditional are formed by adding the following endings to the stem of the verb. This stem is the *infinitive* or a *modified form of the infinitive.*

Future					Conditional				
je	**-ai**	nous	**-ons**		je	**-ais**	nous	**-ions**	
tu	**-as**	vous	**-ez**		tu	**-ais**	vous	**-iez**	
il/elle/on	**-a**	ils/elles	**-ont**		il/elle/on	**-ait**	ils/elles	**-aient**	

Notice that the endings for the future and the conditional are different. The stem remains the same for both.

F. Verbs whose infinitive ends in **-er:** the infinitive is used in most cases.

> Nous **nous amuserons** sur la Côte d'Azur. *(future)*
> *We **will have** a good time on the Riviera.*

> Nous **voyagerions** à pied si nous n'avions pas de vélo. *(conditional)*
> *We **would travel** on foot if we did not have a bike.*

EXCEPTIONS:

aller: stem **ir-**

> Tu **iras** au Maroc avec moi. *(future)*   J'**irais** en Tunisie. *(conditional)*
> *You **will go** to Morocco with me.*   *I **would go** to Tunisia.*

envoyer: stem **enverr-**

> Nous t'**enverrons** des cartes postales. *(future)*
> *We **will send** you postcards.*

> Ses parents l'**enverraient** en colonie. *(conditional)*
> *His parents **would send** him to camp.*

NOTE: **acheter** in the future and conditional has the **accent grave** found in the present. For other stem-change verbs, see Structures, Chapter 1, page 146.

G. Verbs whose infinitive ends in **-ir:** the infinitive is used in most cases.

> Elles **partiront** ce soir. *(future)*   Tu te **divertirais** en Suisse. *(conditional)*
> *They **will leave** tonight.*   *You **would have fun** in Switzerland.*

EXCEPTIONS:

devenir / tenir / venir: stems **deviendr- / tiendr- / viendr-**

Vous **viendrez** avec nous au Chili? *(future)*
Will you come with us to Chile?

Il **deviendrait** moniteur de ski s'il avait le temps. *(conditional)*
*He **would become** a ski instructor if he had the time.*

courir / mourir: stem **courr- / mourr-**

Nous **courrons** le long de la plage. *(future)*
*We **will run** along the beach.*

Vous **mourriez** de peur si vous faisiez du parapente. *(conditional)*
*You **would die** of fear if you went hang-gliding.*

H. Verbs whose infinitive ends in **-re:** the future and conditional stems are formed by dropping the **e** from the infinitive.

Je **prendrai** le train pour Lyon. *(future)*
*I **will take** the train for Lyon.*

Ils **se détendraient** à la montagne s'ils y avaient un chalet. *(conditional)*
*They **would relax** in the mountains if they had a chalet there.*

EXCEPTIONS:

être: stem **ser-**

Nous **serons** à Paris le 15. *(future)*
*We **will be** in Paris on the 15th.*

Vous **seriez** champion de ski nautique si vous vous entraîniez. *(conditional)*
*You **would be** a champion water-skier if you trained.*

faire: stem **fer-**

Tu **feras** du stop cet été. *(future)*
*You **will hitch-hike** this summer.*

Il **ferait** de la randonnée en Espagne. *(conditional)*
*He **would go hiking** in Spain.*

I. Verbs whose infinitives end in **-oir** change in a variety of ways. Some of the most common of these verbs and their stems are:

avoir: **aur-**	devoir: **devr-**	falloir: **faudr-**	pouvoir: **pourr-**
savoir: **saur-**	valoir: **vaudr-**	voir: **verr-**	vouloir: **voudr-**

J'**aurai** assez de temps pour lire en vacances. *(future)*
Tu **pourrais** visiter le Québec. *(conditional)*
Il **devra** prendre le train. *(future)*
Il **faudrait** acheter des souvenirs. *(conditional)*
Nous **saurons** faire du surf après ce stage. *(future)*
Vous **voudriez** bronzer. *(conditional)*
Ils **verront** leurs grands-parents. *(future)*
Il **vaudrait** mieux arriver un peu en avance. *(conditional)*

 SELF-CHECK Student Activities Manual, *Exercises III, D, E, H, and I, pages 71–73.*

B USAGE OF THE FUTURE AND CONDITIONAL

a. Simple future

- The future tense is used to speak about events that are *expected to happen* in the future, in the same way that the future tense is used in English.

  Quand **serons**-nous de retour?
  *When **will** we **be** back?*

  L'avion **atterrira** à 17 heures.
  *The plane **will land** at 5 p.m.*

  Je **coucherai** à la belle étoile ce soir.
  *I **will sleep** out in the open tonight.*

- Unlike English (where the present tense is used), French requires the future tense after certain conjunctions when you are talking about the future. These conjunctions are:

quand, lorsque	*when*
dès que, aussitôt que	*as soon as*
tant que	*as long as*

  Quand nous **irons** à Bruxelles, nous **ferons** un tour en ballon montgolfière.
  *When we **go** to Brussels, we **will go** for a hot-air balloon ride.*

  Tant que tu **feras du stop,** ta mère **s'inquiètera.**
  *As long as you **hitch-hike**, your mother **will worry**.*

  Dès qu'il y **aura** une monnaie unique, on n'aura plus besoin de changer d'argent.
  *As soon as there **is** a common currency, one **will** no longer **need to** change money.*

- In French, as in English, the verb **aller** + *infinitive* means *what is going to happen* (see **Structures,** Chapter 1, page 145). In spoken French, this construction is used much more frequently than the simple future.

  Vous **allez voir** le monde entier.
  *You **are going to see** the whole world.*

Using **aller** + *infinitive* suggests that the future event is more likely to happen or will happen sooner. The simple future suggests a more distant time in the future and somewhat more uncertainty about the events.

  Un jour, des touristes **visiteront** la lune.
  *Some day, tourists **will visit** the moon.*

b. Present conditional

- The conditional can be used to express *politeness* by softening or attenuating a request, a command, or a suggestion. The verbs **vouloir, pouvoir, savoir,** and **devoir** are often used in the conditional in this context.

  Je **voudrais** connaître vos projets.
  *I **would like** to know your plans.*

  Pourrais-tu m'aider à porter ma valise?
  ***Could** you help me carry my suitcase?*

- The conditional is also used in a conjecture or a hypothesis in the future or present, to express a possibility, something that *might* or *could* happen. Often it is accompanied by a subordinate clause (either before or after) in which a condition is stated.

A ta place, je **prendrais** mon sac de couchage.
*If I were you, I **would take** my sleeping bag.*

Nous **ferions la grasse matinée** si nous ne devions pas travailler.
*We **would sleep late** if we didn't have to work.*

S'il faisait plus chaud, ils se **baigneraient.**
*If it were warmer, they **would go swimming.***

When you are reporting what someone else has said (indirect speech) about a future event, and the statement was made in the past, the conditional replaces the future in the part you are indirectly quoting.

DIRECT SPEECH:

Philippe a dit: « Nous **verrons** le Tour de France cet été ».
*Philippe said, "We **will see** the Tour de France this summer."*

INDIRECT SPEECH:

Philippe a dit que nous **verrions** le Tour de France cet été.
*Philippe said that we **would see** the Tour de France this summer.*

DIRECT SPEECH:

Le guide a annoncé: « Le car **partira** dans 30 minutes ».
*The guide announced, "The bus **will leave** in 30 minutes."*

INDIRECT SPEECH:

Le guide a annoncé que le car **partirait** dans 30 minutes.
*The guide announced that the bus **would leave** in thirty minutes.*

NOTE: You may need to change the subject in the quoted sentence when you use indirect speech.

Il a dit: « **Je** ne ferai pas de snowboard ».
He said, "I will not go snowboarding."

Il a dit qu'**il** ne ferait pas de snowboard.
He said he would not go snowboarding.

 SELF-CHECK Student Activities Manual, *Exercise III, J, page 73.*

IV. Future Perfect and Past Conditional

Grammar Video Tutorials

A FORMATION

1. Future perfect *(Futur antérieur)*

The future perfect *(will have + past participle)* is composed of the future tense of the auxiliary (**avoir** or **être**) and the past participle.

> C'est moi qui **aurai fait** le tour du monde.
> *I am the one who **will have travelled** around the world.*

> Quand nous **serons arrivés** à Québec, tu verras le Château Frontenac.
> *When we **arrive** in Quebec City, you will see the Château Frontenac.*

(NOTE: In English we use the present: *When we arrive;* in French you must say the equivalent of: *When we will have arrived . . . .* or *When we have arrived . . .)*

> Dès que je **serai rentré** en Belgique, j'inviterai Eva.
> *As soon as I **get home** to Belgium, I will invite Eva.*

For more examples of usage, see page 192.

 SELF-CHECK Student Activities Manual, *Exercise V, M, page 75.*

2. Past conditional *(Conditionnel passé)*

The past conditional *(would have + past participle)* is composed of the present conditional tense of the auxiliary (**avoir** or **être**) and the past participle.

> Nous **serions allés** en Tunisie si tu nous avais invités.
> *We **would have gone** to Tunisia if you had invited us.*

> Il **aurait** toujours **regretté** de ne pas avoir continué son voyage.
> *He **would have** always **regretted** not continuing his trip.*

> Tu **aurais pu** nous accompagner.
> *You **could have** (**would have been able to**) come with us.*

 SELF-CHECK Student Activities Manual, *Exercise V, O, page 76.*

 USAGE

1. Future perfect

The future perfect is used to talk about events in the future that will have happened *prior to* or *before* another event in the future. It often occurs together with conjunctions that refer to certain points in time. In English, we do not have to use the future or the future perfect with these conjunctions; normally we use the present tense. These conjunctions are:

> **aussitôt que/dès que**   **après que**   **quand/lorsque**   **tant que**

> Quand nous **serons arrivés** à Montpellier, nous te téléphonerons.
> *When we **arrive** in Montpellier, we will call you. (literally: When **we will have arrived**)* [Our arrival will happen before we call.]

> Dès que tu **auras appris** à faire du ski, tu pourras passer tes vacances en Suisse avec nous.
> *As soon as **you have learned** to ski, you will be able to spend your vacation with us in Switzerland. (literally: As soon as you **will have learned**)* [Learning to ski will happen before you go to Switzerland.]

2. Past conditional

The past conditional is used largely in *connection with if-clause constructions.* See the following section.

V. If-clauses *(le **si** de condition)*

Grammar Video Tutorials

When you want to express what *will* or *would* happen *if* something else occurs or occurred, your sentence will have two parts:

a. The *condition,* expressed by **si** plus a verb in the present, imperfect, or pluperfect (*never* the conditional).
b. The result will be stated in the present, future, present conditional, or past conditional.

The sequence of the two clauses is not important. You can begin your sentence with **si** to state the condition first, or start with the main clause to state the result first. Within this pattern, the time frame and the meaning determine the choice of tenses. The usage in French is the same as that in carefully-spoken, grammatically precise English.

- • (a) **si** + *present* + (b) *present* or *future*

When the condition expressed in the *if-clause* (a) is considered as really existing or likely to be true, the present tense is used and the *result* (b) is expressed in the present or future.

> (a) Si tu **refuses** de voyager, (b) tu ne **connaîtras** jamais le monde.
> *If you **refuse** to travel, you will never **get to know** the world.*

> (b) Il nous **prêtera** sa motoneige (a) si nous **rentrons** avant la nuit.
> *He **will lend** us his snowmobile if we **are back** before nightfall.*

(a) Si j'**ai** du courage, (b) je **ferai** du parapente.
*If I **am** brave enough, I **will go** hang-gliding.*

(b) Nous **faisons** du ski de fond le week-end (a) s'il y **a** de la neige.
*We **go** cross-country skiing on the weekends if there **is** snow.*

- (a) **si** + *imperfect* + (b) *present conditional*
  (a) **si** + *pluperfect* + (b) *past conditional*

When the condition expressed in the *if-clause* is considered unlikely to become true, or is hypothetical or contrary to fact, the pattern is also similar to English.

1. **si** + *imperfect* + (b) *present conditional*—The result is still possible.

(a) Si tu **étais** président de la République (b) tu **n'aurais** pas tant de vacances.
*If you **were** president of the French Republic, you **would** not **have** so much vacation.*

2. Vous ne **feriez** pas de bateau (a) si vous **aviez** le mal de mer.
*You **would** not **go** boating if you **suffered** from seasickness.*

(a) **si** + *pluperfect* + (b) *past conditional* —The time frame is the past; the result cannot be changed.

(a) S'il n'**avait** pas **fait** si mauvais, (b) Didier n'**aurait** pas **fait la connaissance** d'Eva.
*If the weather **had** not **been** so bad, Didier **would** not **have gotten to know** Eva.*

(b) Nous **n'aurions** pas eu d'amende (a) si nous **avions eu** le bon permis.
*We **would** not **have gotten** a fine if we **had had** the right license.*

It is also possible to use the *pluperfect* followed or preceded by the *present conditional* if you want to say (a) *if this had happened* (i.e., in the past) (b) *something would happen . . .* (i.e., in the present).

(a) Si j'**avais appris** le chinois, (b) j'**irais** souvent en Chine.
*If I **had learned** Chinese, I **would travel** to China often.*

(b) Nous **serions** plus satisfaits (a) si nous **avions logé** dans des hôtels de luxe.
*We **would be** happier if we **had stayed** in luxury hotels.*

(a) Si tu **avais fait** de la planche à voile, (b) tu **serais** fatigué comme nous.
*If you **had gone** windsurfing, you **would be** tired like we are.*

Summary

If-clause (a)	Result clause (b)
A. Present	**+ Present or Future**
Si nous **faisons de la randonnée,** *If we **go hiking,***	nous ne **dépensons** pas trop d'argent. *we **do** not **spend** too much money.*
Si tu **prends** le train, *If you **take** the train,*	tu **arriveras** à l'heure. *you **will arrive** on time.*
B. Imperfect	**+ Present conditional**
S'il **allait** à la pêche, *If he **went** fishing,*	nous **mangerions** du poisson. *we **would eat** fish.*

If-clause (a)	Result clause (b)
C. Pluperfect	**+ Present conditional**
Si vous **aviez voyagé** en avion, *If you **had traveled** by plane,*	vous **seriez** moins fatigué. *you **would be** less tired.*
D. Pluperfect	**+ Past conditional**
Si elle **avait passé** moins de temps à la plage, *If she **had spent** less time at the beach,*	elle n'**aurait** pas **pris** de coup de soleil. *she **would** not **have gotten** a sunburn.*

 SELF-CHECK Student Activities Manual, *Exercises VII, Q and R, pages 77–78.*

VI. *Passé simple*

 USAGE

The **passé simple** is a past tense used only in writing, usually in literary texts, fairy tales and, less frequently today, in journalism. It indicates that an action has been completed in the past and has no relation to the present.

> Je **fus** un instant sans répondre.
> *For a moment, I **did** not answer.*

> Mon père le **vit** et me **parla** gentiment.
> *My father **noticed** it and **spoke** to me kindly.*

This tense can be considered the literary equivalent of the **passé composé,** although this latter tense suggests more of a connection to the present than the **passé simple.** For stylistic effects, an author may use both the **passé simple** and the **passé composé** in the same passage. The imperfect is used in both written and spoken French to indicate a state of being, a condition, or how things were in the past, and is found in both literary and nonliterary styles.

B FORMATION

For reading, it is helpful to *recognize* the forms of the **passé simple.**

Regular verbs whose infinitive ends in **-er** drop the **-er** and add the endings: **-ai, -as, -a, -âmes, -âtes, -èrent.**

je regard**ai**	nous regard**âmes**
tu regard**as**	vous regard**âtes**
il/elle/on regard**a**	ils/elles regard**èrent**

Regular verbs whose infinitives end in **-ir** or **-re,** drop the **-ir** or **-re** and add the endings:
-is, -is, -it, -îmes, -îtes, -irent.

je répond**is**	nous répond**îmes**
tu répond**is**	vous répond**îtes**
il/elle/on répond**it**	ils/elles répond**irent**

The **passé simple** forms of some frequently used irregular verbs are:

avoir		**être**		**faire**	
j'eus	nous eûmes	je fus	nous fûmes	je fis	nous fîmes
tu eus	vous eûtes	tu fus	vous fûtes	tu fis	vous fîtes
il/elle/on eut	ils/elles eurent	il/elle/on fut	ils/elles furent	il/elle/on fit	ils/elles firent

The **passé simple** of many irregular verbs is built on their past participle. Those with a past participle ending in **-is** (mettre / **mis;** prendre / **pris**) have an **i** in their **passé simple** stem: je m**i**s, nous m**î**mes, tu pr**i**s, vous pr**î**tes. Those whose past participle ends in **-u** (croire / **cru;** savoir / **su**) have a **u** in their **passé simple** stem: tu cr**u**s, vous cr**û**tes, il s**u**t, ils s**u**rent.

Infinitive	Past participle	**Passé simple**
apercevoir	aperçu	nous aperçumes
paraître	paru	elles parurent
remettre	remis	il remit

NOTE: The **passé simple** is a tense you should recognize in order to understand the meaning of what you are reading, but you will not need to produce it.

 SELF-CHECK Student Activities Manual, *Exercises VIII, U and V, pages 79–80.*

Structures

I. Verb Review

A. The verb **préférer** is an **-er** verb that has a stem spelling change in some forms. As you learned in Chapter 1 (p. 146), **préférer** and verbs like it (**accélérer, sécher,** etc.) change the **é** to **è** in the stem for all but the **nous** and **vous** forms in the conjugation of the present indicative. In the imperfect, future, and conditional, these verbs retain the **é** in all forms:

Present		Future (Conditional)	
je préf**è**re	nous préf**é**rons	je préf**é**rerai (-ais)	nous préf**é**rerons (-ions)
tu préf**è**res	vous préf**é**rez	tu préf**é**reras (-ais)	vous préf**é**rerez (-iez)
il/elle/on préf**è**re	ils/elles préf**è**rent	il/elle/on préf**é**rera(-ait)	ils/elles préf**é**reront(-aient)

Imperfect		Past participle	
je préf**é**rais	nous préf**é**rions	préf**é**ré	
tu préf**é**rais	vous préf**é**riez		
il/elle/on préf**é**rait	ils/elles préf**é**raient		

B. The verb **projeter** is another stem-change regular **-er** verb. In the present indicative, the future, and the conditional, **projeter** and verbs like it (**appeler, jeter,** etc.) double the consonant (**l, t**) in all but the **nous** and **vous** forms. The forms of the imperfect do not have a double consonant.

Present		Future (Conditional)	
je proje**tte**	nous proje**tons**	je proje**tterai** (-ais)	nous proje**tterons** (-ions)
tu proje**ttes**	vous proje**tez**	tu proje**tteras** (-ais)	vous proje**tterez** (-iez)
il/elle/on proje**tte**	ils/elles/ proje**ttent**	il/elle/on proje**ttera**(-ait)	ils/elles proje**tteront** (-aient)

Imperfect		Past participle
je proje**tais**	nous proje**tions**	proje**té**
tu proje**tais**	vous proje**tiez**	
il/elle/on proje**tait**	ils/elles proje**taient**	

 SELF-CHECK Student Activities Manual, *Exercise I, A, p. 85.*

II. Negative Expressions

 A NE... PAS

To make a simple negative statement, question, or command in French, **ne... pas** is placed around the verb.

> J'aime beaucoup ce film français.
> Je **n'**aime **pas** beaucoup ce film français.

REMEMBER:

- In simple tenses, **ne** precedes the verb and **pas** follows it.

  Je **n'**aime **pas** ce film.

- In compound tenses, **ne** precedes the auxiliary verb and **pas** follows it.

  Elle **n'**a **pas** vu le film.

- When using inversion, **ne** precedes the inverted subject-verb construction and **pas** follows it.

  Ne vas-tu **pas** au cinéma?
  N'es-tu **pas** allé au cinéma?

- In a command (imperative form), **ne** precedes the verb and **pas** follows it.

  N'allez **pas** au cinéma!

- With a negative infinitive, **ne pas** is placed between the main verb and the infinitive.

  Il préfère **ne pas** aller au cinéma.

- A negative statement, question, etc. can be reinforced, or made stronger, by adding **du tout** to the **ne... pas** expression.

  Je **n'**ai **pas du tout** envie de regarder ce jeu télévisé.
  *I have **no** desire **whatsoever** to watch this game show.*

Pas du tout can also be used alone as a negative answer to a question.

Aimez-vous les films doublés?   —**Pas du tout!**
Do you like dubbed movies?   —**Not at all!**

- A negative statement, question, etc. can be qualified or made more precise, by adding **encore** to **ne... pas.**

Je **n'**ai **pas** vu ce film.
*I have **not** seen this film.*

Je **n'**ai **pas encore** vu ce film.
*I have **not yet** seen this film.*

NOTE: Indefinite articles (**un/une/des**) that follow negative expressions are replaced by **de.** For an explanation of this construction, see **Structures,** Chapter 4, p. 175.

Ma famille **a** une télévision.
Ma famille **n'a pas de** télévision.

Il y **a des** cinémas dans ce petit village.
Il **n'**y **a pas de** cinémas dans ce petit village.

B OTHER NEGATIVE EXPRESSIONS

ne... jamais	*never*
ne... plus	*no longer, not . . . anymore*
ne... personne	*no one*
ne... rien	*nothing*
ne... ni... ni	*neither . . . nor*
ne... aucun(e)	*not any*

NOTE: The expression **ne... que,** which means *only,* is often included with negative expressions, although technically it only limits the verb, rather than negates it. The second part of this expression (**que**) always directly precedes the word it modifies.

Dans ma famille, il **n'**y a **que** ma sœur qui aime regarder les feuilletons.
*In my family, **only** my sister likes to watch the soaps.*

Il **n'**a vu **que** deux films français dans sa vie.
*He has seen **only** two French films in his life.*

1. Ne... jamais

Ne... jamais negates the adverbs **souvent** *(often),* **quelquefois** *(sometimes),* **parfois** *(occasionally),* **toujours** *(always),* and **de temps en temps** *(from time to time).* It functions the same way as **ne... pas.**

Elle **ne** regarde **jamais** les informations.

Jamais can be used alone to answer a question.

Regardez-vous parfois des films de science-fiction?   —**Jamais!**
Do you occasionally watch science fiction movies?   —**Never!**

Jamais can also be used alone in a positive context to mean *ever.*

Avez-vous **jamais** rencontré une vedette de cinéma?
*Have you **ever** met a movie star?*

2. Ne... plus

Ne... plus is used to indicate a negative change in a situation, and it is sometimes used to negate the adverbs **encore** and **toujours** when they mean *still*.

> Je **ne** regarde **plus** la télé.
> I **no longer** watch television.

> —Aimes-tu **toujours** ce feuilleton? —Non, je **ne** l'aime **plus.**
> —Do you **still** like this soap? —No, I **no longer** like it.

3. Ne... personne / ne... rien

Ne... personne and **ne... rien** function in similar ways as negative constructions.

- When used as a subject, both parts of the negative expression precede the verb, and the verb is always in the singular.

  > **Personne n'**aime la télé-réalité.
  > **No one** likes reality television.

  > **Rien n'**est crédible dans ce film.
  > **Nothing** is believable in this movie.

- When used as a direct object, **ne** precedes the verb and **personne / rien** follows it.

  > Je **ne** connais **personne** qui aime ce film.
  > I know **no one** who likes this movie.

  > Il **n'**y a **rien** à la télé ce soir.
  > There is **nothing** on TV tonight.

If the verb is in a compound tense *(auxiliary + past participle of main verb)*, the placement of **personne** and **rien** used as direct objects is not the same. **Rien** precedes the past participle, whereas **personne** follows it.

> Elle **n'**a **rien vu.**   Elle **n'**a vu **personne.**
> She saw **nothing.**   She saw **no one.**

- When used as the object of a preposition, both **personne** and **rien** follow the preposition.

  > Elle **n'**est allée au cinéma avec **personne.**
  > She **didn't** go to the movies with **anyone**. (She went to the movies with **no one.**)

  > Cet acteur **ne** parle de **rien** d'intéressant dans son interview.
  > This actor **doesn't** talk about **anything** interesting in his interview.

NOTE: As in the above example, if **personne** or **rien** is modified by an adjective, the adjective is always masculine and must be preceded by **de (d').**

- Both **personne** and **rien** can be used alone as negative answers.

  > Qui avez-vous vu?   —**Personne.**
  > Who (whom) did you see?   —**No one.**

  > Qu'est-ce qu'il y a à la télé?   —**Rien.**
  > What is on TV?   —**Nothing.**

4. Ne... ni... ni

Ne... ni... ni is used to oppose two people, things, or ideas. **Ne** precedes the verb, as usual, but **ni... ni** directly precede the words they modify. Partitive and indefinite articles are dropped in this construction, but definite articles remain.

> Elle **n'**aime regarder **ni** la télé **ni** les films.
> *She **doesn't** like to watch TV **or** movies. (She likes to watch **neither** TV **nor** movies.)*

> Nous **n'**avons **ni** télévision **ni** lecteur DVD à la maison.
> *We have **neither** a TV **nor** a DVD player at home.*

NOTE: When **ne... ni... ni** is negating the subject rather than the object in a sentence, the verb is generally plural.

> **Ni** ma mère **ni** mon père **n'aiment** les films d'horreur.
> ***Neither** my mother **nor** my father like horror movies.*

5. Ne... aucun(e)

This negative expression can function in various ways in a sentence.

- As a subject pronoun, **aucun** takes the gender of the noun it replaces and is followed by a singular verb.

  > **Aucune** de ces trois séries **n'**est bonne.
  > ***None** of these three television series is good.*

- As an adjective, **aucun** agrees in gender with the noun it modifies. The adjective and noun are always singular.

  > Cet acteur **n'**a **aucun** talent.
  > *This actor **doesn't** have **any** talent. (This actor has **no** talent.)*

 SI

The affirmative response to a negative question or statement is **si,** not **oui.**

> N'avez-vous pas aimé ce film?   —**Si!**
> *Did you not like this film?*   —***Yes (I did)!***

> Avez-vous aimé ce film?   —**Oui.**
> *Did you like this film?*   —***Yes.***

 SELF-CHECK Student Activities Manual, *Exercises II, B–D, pp. 86–87.*

III. Relative Pronouns

Grammar Video Tutorials

Learning to use relative pronouns in French will allow you to speak and write in a more sophisticated manner. Instead of using simple sentences and repetition, you will be able to qualify or expand on your main clause by attaching to it a second (relative, or subordinate) clause.

Simple sentence and repetition:

> J'aime ce film. Ce film vient de sortir.
> *I like this movie. This movie just came out.*

Main clause + relative clause:

> J'aime ce film **qui** vient de sortir.
> *I like this movie **that** just came out.*

NOTE: In the example above, **qui** is the relative pronoun that links the main clause to the relative clause. It functions as the *subject* of the verb in the relative clause (**vient**), and its antecedent (the word in the main clause that it represents) is **film.** There are several relative pronouns to choose from in French, depending on how the pronoun functions in the relative clause.

A. Qui and **que** are the most commonly used relative pronouns in French.

- **Qui** functions as a subject. Its antecedent can be either a person or a thing. The verb in the relative clause agrees in number (singular/plural) with that of the antecedent.

  L'actrice **qui** joue le rôle principal du film n'est pas très bonne.
  [The antecedent **actrice** and verb **joue** are 3rd person singular.]
  *The actress **who** plays the leading role in the film isn't very good.*

  On critique les pubs **qui** montrent trop de nudité.
  [The antecedent **pubs** and verb **montrent** are 3rd person plural.]
  *People are critical of ads **that** show too much nudity.*

  When **qui** is followed by a vowel, there is no elision (combining the **i** of **qui** with the vowel that follows).

  Quel est le nom de l'acteur **qui** a joué le rôle principal dans le film *Titanic*?

- **Que** functions as a direct object. Its antecedent can be either a person or a thing.

  Que takes the gender (masculine/feminine) and number (singular/plural) of its antecedent, so a past participle in the relative clause must agree with the gender and number of the antecedent.

  Le film **que** nous avons vu est très bon.
  (*antecedent* = **film** → *past participle* **vu**)

  L'actrice **que** nous avons vu**e** est très connue.
  (*antecedent* = **actrice** → *past participle* **vue**)

  When the relative pronoun **que** is followed by a vowel, the **e** of **que** is elided with that vowel.

  L'actrice française **qu'**elle aime s'appelle Marion Cotillard.

NOTE: The relative pronoun **que** cannot be omitted in French, as it can in English.

  Quel est le nom du film **que** tu as vu?
  *What is the name of the movie **(that)** you saw?*

B. Ce qui or **ce que** is used instead of **qui** or **que** when the antecedent is not clearly stated. Both of these pronouns are translated as *what.*

  Je ne comprends pas **ce qui** se passe dans ce film.
  (**ce qui** = *subject of relative clause*)
  *I don't understand **what** is happening in this movie.*

  Dites-moi **ce que** vous voulez regarder à la télé.
  (**ce que** = *direct object of relative clause*)
  *Tell me **what** you want to watch on TV.*

C. Dont is the relative pronoun used to replace **de** + its object in a relative clause. The object of the preposition can be either a person or a thing.

- **Dont** is the relative pronoun to use with the following common expressions:

avoir besoin de	être satisfait(e) de	se moquer de
avoir envie de	être fier(-ère) de	parler de
avoir peur de	se souvenir de	
être content(e) de	se servir de	

Le grand classique **dont** il se souvient le mieux est *Casablanca*.
The classic film he remembers best is Casablanca.

La vedette française **dont** nous parlons est Daniel Auteuil.
The star we are talking about is Daniel Auteuil.

NOTE: In the examples above, the relative pronoun cannot be omitted in French, as it can in English.

- **Dont** is the relative pronoun that sometimes translates into English as *whose*.

    Dans le film *Titanic*, le héros tombe amoureux d'une jeune femme **dont** le fiancé est très riche.
    *In the movie **Titanic,** the hero falls in love with a young woman **whose** fiancé is very rich.*

- **Ce dont** is used instead of **dont** when the antecedent is not clearly stated.

    Je ne comprends pas **ce dont** vous avez peur dans ce film d'horreur.
    *I don't understand **what** you are afraid of in this horror film.*

D. If the relative clause has a preposition other than **de,** use the pronoun **qui** when referring to people, and a form of **lequel (laquelle, lesquels, lesquelles)** when referring to things.

Je ne sais plus **à qui** j'ai prêté le DVD.
*I no longer know **to whom** I lent the DVD.*
(In colloquial English: *I don't know anymore **who** I lent the DVD **to**.*)

Explique-moi les raisons **pour lesquelles** tu préfères cette chaîne.
*Explain to me (the reasons) **why** you prefer this channel.*

E. Où is the relative pronoun to use to express time or place.

Jacques n'a jamais oublié le jour **où** sa grand-mère a quitté le cinéma avant la fin du film.
*Jacques never forgot the day **(when)** his grandmother left the cinema before the end of the movie.*

Quel est le nom du restaurant **où** tu as vu Brad Pitt?
*What is the name of the restaurant **where** you saw Brad Pitt?*

 SELF-CHECK Student Activities Manual, *Exercises III, G–I, pp. 88–90.*

IV. *Le mot juste: il s'agit de*

The expression **il s'agit de** can be very useful when talking *about* the content of a work (a book, a play, a movie, etc.) or when talking *about* an event.

NOTE: The subject of this expression is *always* the impersonal **il.**

Dans ce film, **il s'agit d'**un homme qui veut être président des Etats-Unis.
*This movie **is about** a man who wants to be president of the United States.*

De quoi **s'agit-il** dans cette nouvelle émission?
***What is** this new TV program **about**?*

Structures

I. Verb Review

The verb **croire** is irregular in the present tense.

je crois	nous croyons
tu crois	vous croyez
il/elle/on croit	ils/elles croient
Future/Conditional stem: croir-	
Past participle: cru	

A USAGE

croire + direct object = *to believe someone or something*

> Je **crois** mon père.
> I **believe** my father.

croire à = *to believe something is possible, probable, real; to believe in the value of something*

> Il **croit aux** fantômes.   Je ne **crois** pas **à** la magie noire.
> He **believes in** ghosts.   I don't **believe in** black magic.

croire en = *to believe in, to have confidence in*

> Ses parents **croient en** lui.
> His parents **believe in (have confidence in)** him.

> **Croyez**-vous **en** Dieu?
> Do you **believe in** God?

 SELF-CHECK Student Activities Manual, *Exercise I, A, page 99.*

II. What is the Subjunctive?

The *subjunctive* suggests a way of looking at things rather than talking about a moment in time. The *indicative* (present, imperfect, future, **passé composé,** etc.) refers to actions or events in the realm of certainty in varying time frames. But in the example below, the emphasis is not on a real event in time:

> Ses parents veulent qu'elle **soit** heureuse.
> *Her parents want her* ***to be*** *happy.*

Being happy is not a fact in this sentence but a subjective condition that may or may not happen. The parents wish it, but this does not make it reality.

> Il est possible que les trois chevaliers **puissent** sauver la vie de la demoiselle.
> *It is possible that the three knights* ***can (could)*** *save the life of the damsel.*

This sentence stresses the uncertainty of the result. We do not know if they will succeed.

The subjunctive is rare in English and you will see in the translations of the two examples above that it can be translated in different ways. Something close to the subjunctive is expressed in a sentence like:

> *I wish she* ***were*** *a princess.*

Unlike English, the subjunctive occurs fairly frequently in French. When a main verb expresses a feeling or an emotion (happiness, fear, surprise, etc.) or a desire (I want, I demand, etc.) and the verb that follows it has a different subject, this second verb is in the subjunctive mood.

> Ils veulent qu'elle **choisisse** un mari.
> *They want her* ***to choose*** *a husband.*

In this example, she has not chosen a husband, nor do we know whether she will do so, or is doing so; what we know is that they *want* her to do it.

> Je suis étonné qu'une grenouille **veuille** être aussi grosse qu'un bœuf.
> *I am surprised that a frog* ***wants*** *to be as large as an ox.*

We do not know if this frog can or cannot be as large as an ox; we know that the speaker is surprised that it wants to be.

> Je regrette que la licorne **disparaisse.**
> *I am sorry that the unicorn* ***may disappear***.

Since the main verbal expression (**regrette**) states regret, the dependent or subordinate verb (**disparaisse),** which has a different subject, is in the subjunctive.

III. Formation of the Subjunctive

Two tenses of the subjunctive are commonly used in modern French: the present (to express present *or* future) and the past. The imperfect and the pluperfect subjunctive are usually found only in literary texts.

A PRESENT SUBJUNCTIVE

The present tense of the subjunctive for most verbs is formed by taking the third person plural form of the present indicative (**ils/elles choisissent**), dropping the **-ent**, and adding the following endings:

-e	-ions
-es	-iez
-e	-ent

Il est important qu'elle **choisisse** le meilleur cadeau.
*It is important that she **choose** the best gift.*

1. Regular verbs

Regular **-er** verbs

raconter (ils racont*ent*)	
que je racont**e**	que nous racont**ions**
que tu racont**es**	que vous racont**iez**
qu'il/elle/on racont**e**	qu'ils/elles racont**ent**

Regular **-ir** verbs

choisir (ils choisiss*ent*)	
que je chois**isse**	que nous chois**issions**
que tu chois**isses**	que vous chois**issiez**
qu'il/elle/on chois**isse**	qu'ils/elles chois**issent**

Regular **-re** verbs

attendre (ils attend*ent*)	
que j'attend**e**	que nous attend**ions**
que tu attend**es**	que vous attend**iez**
qu'il/elle/on attend**e**	qu'ils/elles attend**ent**

NOTE: The subjunctive is often shown in verb charts preceded by the conjunction **que** to emphasize that these verb forms are used only in *dependent clauses,* i.e., they always follow another conjugated verb. However, just because there is a "**que**" the verb will not necessarily be in the subjunctive. You will often see a dependent clause that begins with a "**que**" where a subjunctive is not needed. See the explanation in section IV below.

2. Verbs with double stems

There are many verbs that have double stems in the subjunctive; one stem is based on the third person plural (ils **vienn**ent: **vienn-**) and is used for **je, tu, il/elle/on, ils/elles;** the other is based on the first person plural (nous **ven**ons: **ven-**) and is used for **nous** and **vous.**

venir	
que je **vienn**e	que nous **ven**ions
que tu **vienn**es	que vous **ven**iez
qu'il/elle/on **vienn**e	qu'ils/elles **vienn**ent

Some of the most common verbs that follow this pattern are: **boire, croire, devoir, mourir, prendre, recevoir,** and **voir.** If you check the conjugation of these verbs in the present indicative, you will see that they follow a similar pattern there since they also have two stems.

Il faut que la sorcière **prenne** le poison.
*The witch must **take** the poison.*

Le magicien veut que nous **prenions** la potion magique.
*The magician wants us **to take** the magic potion.*

Il est important que la princesse **reçoive** la fleur.
*It is important that the princess **get** the flower.*

Je doute que vous **receviez** ce miroir.
*I doubt that you **will receive** this mirror.*

Some other frequently used verbs have two stems in the subjunctive that are not based on the present indicative, but they follow this same pattern (one stem for **je, tu, il/elle/on, ils/elles;** another stem for **nous, vous**).

aller: **aill- / all-**

Il faut que j'**aille** chez ma fiancée.
*I have **to go** to my fiancée's house.*

Il est important que nous y **allions** ensemble.
*It is important for us **to go** there together.*

vouloir: **veuill- / voul-**

Bien qu'elle **veuille** se marier, elle renvoie les trois jeunes hommes.
*Although she **wants** to marry, she sends the three young men away.*

Elle est étonnée que nous **voulions** tous faire ce qu'elle demande.
*She is surprised that we all **want** to do what she asks.*

3. Irregular verbs

These commonly used irregular verbs have only one stem in the subjunctive:

savoir: **sach-**   pouvoir: **puiss-**   faire: **fass-**

The present subjunctive forms of **avoir** and **être** are irregular.

avoir		être	
que j'**aie**	que nous **ayons**	que je **sois**	que nous **soyons**
que tu **aies**	que vous **ayez**	que tu **sois**	que vous **soyez**
qu'il/elle/on **ait**	qu'ils/elles **aient**	qu'il/elle/on **soit**	qu'ils/elles **soient**

The *past tense of the subjunctive* is a compound past tense (like the **passé composé**) and is composed of the present subjunctive of **avoir** or **être** and the past participle of the verb.

> Elle est contente qu'ils **soient arrivés** avant son enterrement.
> *She is happy that they **arrived** before her burial.*

> Ses parents sont étonnés que le jeune homme **ait acheté** une fleur.
> *Her parents are surprised that the young man **bought** a flower.*

The *past subjunctive* is used when the action or condition in the subjunctive clause has taken place before the action or state of the main (indicative) clause. For example, in the second sentence, the parents *are* surprised *now*, in the present, because at some time in the past, the young man *bought* a flower.

> Je suis désolé que vous n'**ayez** pas **trouvé** le sorcier.
> *I am sorry that you **did** not **find** the sorcerer.*

The speaker is sorry *now* that you did not find the magician *in the past.*

 SELF-CHECK Student Activities Manual, *Exercises II/III, B, C, and D, pages 99–100.*

IV. Usage of the Subjunctive

In modern French, the subjunctive is almost always used in a *dependent* or *subordinate clause* introduced by the conjunction **que.**

NOTE: Not all clauses following **que** will require the subjunctive. In the following sentence, for example, **que** is a *relative pronoun* that refers back to the noun, **garçon.**

> Le garçon **que** la jeune fille aime lui a apporté une fleur.
> *The boy **whom** the girl loves brought her a flower.*

A THE SUBJUNCTIVE IS USED...

- following expressions of *volition* (will, intent, desire, wish) or *sentiment* (emotion, judgment, appreciation).

> Il **faut qu**'elle nous **dise** qui elle aime.
> *She **must tell** us whom she loves.*

> Ils **ont peur qu**'elle **soit** morte.
> *They **are afraid** she **may be** dead.*

> Ton père **préfère que** tu ne **lises** pas d'histoires de vampires.
> *Your father **prefers that** you not **read** vampire stories.*

Some verbs in this category are: **admirer, aimer mieux, défendre, demander, désirer, insister, ordonner, permettre, préférer, regretter, vouloir.**

> Les enfants **regrettent que** la grenouille **crève.**
> *The children **are sorry that** the frog **bursts.***

> Le bœuf **aimerait mieux que** la grenouille **soit** contente de sa taille.
> *The ox **would prefer that** the frog **be** happy with its size.*

NOTE: The subjunctive is *not* used after the verb **espérer,** which is often followed by the future.

> Il **espère qu**'elle le **prendra** pour mari.
> *He **hopes** she **will take** him as her husband.*

Some expressions of volition and emotion that are followed by the subjunctive are: **avoir peur que, être heureux (-euse) que** (also: **être triste / content(e) / désolé(e) / étonné(e) / surpris(e) que,** etc.), **il est bon que** (also: **il est utile / important / nécessaire / dommage / temps que,** etc.), **il vaut mieux que, il faut que.**

> Je **suis étonné que** tu **croies** à l'existence des loups-garous.
> *I **am surprised that** you **believe** in werewolves.*

> Il **vaut mieux que** le bœuf **ait** pitié de la grenouille.
> *It **is better** that the ox feels **sorry** for the frog.*

- following verbs and expressions that indicate *doubt* or *possibility* (**il est possible que, il est impossible que, il se peut que, il est peu probable que**).

> Il **se peut que** nous **trouvions** une fleur magique.
> *It **is possible that** we **may find** a magic flower.*

> Je **doute que** le géant **veuille** épouser une naine.
> *I **doubt that** the giant **wants** to marry a dwarf.*

> Il **est peu probable que** la grenouille **se fasse** aussi grosse que le bœuf.
> *It **is unlikely that** the frog **will make** itself as large as the ox.*

EXCEPTION: The expression **il est probable que** suggests greater certainty and is therefore not followed by the subjunctive.

> Il **est probable que** le bœuf **se moque de** la grenouille.
> *It **is likely that** the ox **makes fun of** the frog.*

> Il **est probable que** la grenouille **mourra.**
> *It **is likely that** the frog **will die**.*

- with certain conjunctions. Some of the most common are:

à condition que *provided that*	**jusqu'à ce que** *until*
à moins que *unless*	**pour que, afin que** *in order to*
avant que *before*	**pourvu que** *provided that, so long as*
bien que, quoique *although*	**sans que** *without*

> **Bien qu**'il en **ait** peur, il s'intéresse aux fantômes.
> ***Although** he **is** afraid of them, he is interested in ghosts.*

> La grenouille s'enfle **jusqu'à ce qu**'elle **crève.**
> *The frog inflates itself **until** it **bursts**.*

> Le chevalier part **sans que** la princesse le **voie.**
> *The knight leaves **without** the princess **seeing** him.*

> **Avant que** nous **arrivions,** le loup aura dévoré le Petit Chaperon rouge.
> ***Before** we **arrive,** the wolf will have eaten Little Red Riding Hood.*

NOTE: Traditional grammar books state that the conjunction **après que** is not followed by a verb or a verbal expression in the subjunctive. However, many native speakers of French now use the subjunctive after **après que.**

Some of these conjunctions have equivalent prepositions (with the same meaning) that are used when the subjects of both parts of the sentence are the same. These prepositions are then followed by an infinitive.

Conjunctions (+ Subjunctive)	Prepositions (+ Infinitive)
à condition que	à condition de
à moins que	à moins de
afin que	afin de
avant que	avant de
pour que	pour
sans que	sans

Avant de partir, ils embrassent leur fiancée.
Before leaving, they kiss their fiancée.

Afin d'arriver vite, ils montent tous sur le même cheval.
In order to arrive quickly, they all get on the same horse.

Sans attendre, il entre dans sa chambre.
Without waiting, he goes into her bedroom.

Il pourra se marier avec la belle demoiselle **à condition de trouver** le plus beau cadeau.
*He will be able to marry the lovely damsel **on the condition that** he **find** the most beautiful gift.*

NOTE: The preposition **jusqu'à** is followed by a noun.

Jusqu'à leur retour, on la croyait morte.
Until their return, they thought she was dead.

Bien que, pourvu que, and **quoique** have no preposition equivalents, which means that they are always followed by the subjunctive even when the subjects of both main and dependent clauses are the same.

Bien qu'elle **aime** le garçon à la fleur, elle ne l'épousera pas.
*Although she **loves** the boy with the flower, she will not marry him.*

Quoique la reine **soit** très riche, elle habite un modeste château.
*Although the queen **is** very rich, she lives in a modest castle.*

Pourvu que tu **suives** la fée, tu trouveras le trésor.
*As long as you **follow** the fairy, you will find the treasure.*

- with superlative statements, since these are judgments and not facts. The opinion could easily change.

C'est **le plus beau prince** qu'elle **connaisse.**
*He is the **handsomest prince** she **knows.***

Use of the subjunctive is not mandatory in this case.

B THE SUBJUNCTIVE IS NOT USED...

- with expressions that indicate certainty (**il est clair que, il est évident que, il est vrai que, il est sûr que,** etc.).

Il est vrai que la grenouille **est** plus petite que le bœuf.
It is true that the frog is smaller than the ox.

NOTE: If expressions of this type are used in the negative, they no longer indicate certainty and therefore require the subjunctive.

> **Il n'est pas sûr que** les histoires de fantômes **fassent** peur à tous les enfants.
> *It is not certain that ghost stories frighten all children.*

- with the verbs **croire** and **penser** when they are *affirmative*.

> Je **crois** que la grenouille ne **devrait** pas envier le bœuf.
> *I believe that the frog should not be envious of the ox.*

> Nous **pensons que** le prince **peut** trouver une belle princesse.
> *We think that the prince can find a beautiful princess.*

NOTE: Either indicative or subjunctive can be used to express doubt when **croire** and **penser** are used in negative or interrogative constructions. Use the subjunctive to place emphasis on doubt or uncertainty.

> Il **ne croit pas qu'**elle **aille** au bal avec lui.
> *He does not believe that she will go to the ball with him.*

C INFINITIVE VS. SUBJUNCTIVE

If the subject of the main clause and the subordinate clause is the same, the infinitive should be used instead of the subjunctive.

The following sentences marked (a) all have one subject for several actions:

> subject + conjugated verb + infinitive

The following sentences marked (b) all have two subjects:

> subject + conjugated verb + **que** + different subject + conjugated verb (indicative or subjunctive, depending on the meaning of the first verb)

(1 subject: **il**)
> **a. Il** veut **acheter** un beau cadeau pour sa fiancée.
> *He wants to buy a beautiful gift for his fiancée.*
> *(He wants and he is buying.)*

> vs.

(2 subjects: **elle/il**)
> **b. Elle** veut qu'**il** lui **achète** un beau cadeau.
> *She wants him to buy her a beautiful gift.*
> *(She wants and he is buying.)*

(1 subject: **je**)
> **a. Je** préfère **lire** des romans historiques.
> *I prefer to read historical novels.*
> *(I prefer and I read.)*

> vs.

(2 subjects: **je/tu**)
> **b. Je** préfère que **tu lises** des contes de fées.
> *I prefer that you read fairy tales.*
> *(I prefer and you read.)*

(1 subject: **elle**)
> **a. Elle** est contente de **revoir** sa famille.
> *She is happy to see her family again.*
> *(She is happy and she sees.)*

> vs.

(2 subjects: **ils/elle**)
> **b. Les parents** sont contents que **leur fille soit** de nouveau en vie.
> *The parents are happy that their daughter is alive again.*
> *(The parents are happy, the daughter is alive.)*

NOTE: With expressions such as **être** + *adjective* (Elle **est contente / triste…**, etc.), the preposition **de** must be used in front of the infinitive.

> Il est **important de** raconter des contes de fées à vos enfants.
> *It is **important** to tell fairy tales to your children.*

> Nous sommes **tristes de** devoir partir.
> *We are **sad** to have to leave.*

However, with many other verbs commonly used with infinitives to replace the subjunctive, there is no preposition needed.

> Il **faut** trouver un cadeau.
> Je **préfère** être plus intelligent que la grenouille.
> Nous **voulons** raconter une histoire.

 **SELF-CHECK** Student Activities Manual, *Exercises IV, G, H, and I, pages 101–103.*

Summary: subjunctive vs. indicative or infinitive

- If a sentence has two different subjects: one in the main clause, another in the dependent clause…

1. use the indicative in the dependent clause when the main verb expresses:

	Example:
certainty	**Il est certain que…**
declaring	**Je dis que…**
hoping	**J'espère que…**
probability	**Il est probable que…**
thinking	**Je crois que…**

2. use the subjunctive in the dependent clause when the main verb expresses:

command	**Elle exige que…**
doubt	**Je doute que…**
emotion	**Je regrette que…**
fear	**Elle craint que…**
possibility	**Il est possible que…**
will	**Je veux que…**

- If a sentence has one subject for two verbs, use an *infinitive* after the main verb:

> Il **veut se marier.**
> *He **wants to get married.***

> La grenouille **espère atteindre** la taille du bœuf.
> *The frog **hopes to reach** the size of the ox.*

> Il **est** important de ne pas **faire peur** aux enfants.
> *It **is** important not **to frighten** children.*

Structures

I. Verb Review

A. The verb **vivre** is irregular in the present tense. It has one stem in the singular: **vi-** and another in the plural: **viv-**.

je vis	nous vivons
tu vis	vous vivez
il/elle/on vit	ils/elles vivent
Past participle: vécu	

B. The verb **venir** and verbs built on the same root (**devenir, obtenir, revenir, soute-nir, se souvenir [de], tenir**) are irregular in the present tense. All these verbs have one stem for **je, tu, il/elle, ils/elles,** and another for **nous** and **vous.**

je **vien**s	nous **ven**ons
tu **vien**s	vous **ven**ez
il/elle/on **vien**t	ils/elles **vien**nent
Past participles: venu (devenu, obtenu, revenu, soutenu, souvenu, tenu)	

NOTE: Verbs built on **venir (devenir, revenir, se souvenir)** are conjugated with **être** in the **passé composé** (Elle **est venue** chez nous pour le mariage.) and those built on **tenir (obtenir, soutenir)** are conjugated with **avoir** (Mes parents m'**ont** toujours **soutenu[e].**).

 SELF-CHECK Student Activities Manual, *Exercise I, A, page 111.*

II. Adverbs

Grammar Video Tutorials

An adverb is an invariable word that modifies an adjective, a verb, or another adverb.

A ADVERB TYPE

There are several categories of adverbs:

Manner:	**bien, mal, poliment...**
Quantity:	**beaucoup, énormément, peu, très, trop...**
Time:	**aujourd'hui, demain, hier, souvent, tôt...**
Place:	**ici, là-bas, partout...**

Some adverbs do not fit into a particular category. **Aussi, non, oui,** and **peut-être** are examples of adverbs of this type.

B ADVERB FORMATION

Many (but not all) adjectives can be transformed into adverbs by adding certain endings, as described below.

- Most adjectives ending in a *vowel* form their adverb by adding **-ment** to their *masculine* form.

  poli + **ment** = **poliment**
  vrai + **ment** = **vraiment**

- Many adjectives ending in a *consonant* form their adverb by adding **-ment** to their *feminine* form:

  heureux   **heureuse + ment = heureusement**
  sûr   **sûre + ment = sûrement**

  Some exceptions:

  bref   **briève + ment = brièvement**
  dur   **dur** *(no change)*[1]
  gentil   **genti + ment = gentiment**

- Other adjectives ending in a consonant change the **e** of the feminine form into an **é** before adding **-ment.**

  confuse = **confusément**
  précise = **précisément**
  profonde = **profondément**

- Adjectives ending in **-ent** change **-ent** to **-emment.**

  recent   **réc + emment = récemment**
  impatient **impati + emment = impatiemment**

  An exception:

  lent   **lente + ment = lentement**

---

[1] L'adverbe « **dur** » veut dire « *énergiquement, intensément* », comme dans la phrase: « Il travaille **dur** ». Il y a aussi un adverbe « **durement** » qui veut dire « d'une manière dure »: « Il me répond **durement** ». (*He answers me **harshly***).

- Adjectives ending in **-ant** change **-ant** to **-amment.**

constant	**const** + **amment**	= **constamment**
méchant	**méch** + **amment**	= **méchamment**

Some combinations of words (nouns, adjectives, prepositions, adverbs, etc.) can be used as adverbial expressions:

avec joie
sans doute
petit à petit

NOTE: The adjective **possible** cannot be transformed into an adverb. To say *possibly*, use **probablement** or **peut-être.**

C ADVERB POSITION

When an adverb modifies a verb, its position in the sentence is somewhat variable for stylistic effect, for instance to emphasize something. The following rules present the most common placement.

- Usually an adverb immediately follows the verb it modifies in simple verb tenses (present, imperfect, future, conditional).

  Nous restons **confortablement** chez nos parents.
  Je supporte **mal** les opinions de mon père.
  Les jeunes d'aujourd'hui ne veulent pas **toujours** quitter leur famille.

- With compound tenses (**passé composé,** pluperfect, future past, past conditional), shorter adverbs generally are placed between the auxiliary and the past participle.

  Nous avons **bien** expliqué pourquoi nous voulions déménager.
  Tu t'es **vite** habitué à vivre seul.

- Longer adverbs of *manner* (how something is done) often ending in **-ment** can be placed after the past participle.

  Elle a protesté **énergiquement** quand sa mère lui a dit d'acheter l'autre missel.

- Adverbs of *time* and *place* are usually put at the beginning or at the end of a sentence, but can also be placed after the past participle, depending on what is emphasized.

  Aujourd'hui je m'entends bien avec ma sœur.
  Cela m'arrange bien **parfois.**
  Elle s'est habituée **tôt** à ses nouvelles responsabilités.

NOTE: In French, unlike English, an adverb is NEVER placed between a subject and a verb. Compare:

*I **always** obey my mother.*
J'obéis **toujours** à ma mère.

Adverb Placement		
Simple verb tenses:	subject + verb + **adverb**	Je chante **souvent.**
		Je ne chante pas **souvent.**
Compound verb tenses:	subject + auxiliary + **short adverb** + past participle	J'ai **souvent** chanté.
		Je n'ai pas **souvent** chanté.
	subject + auxiliary + past participle + **long adverb**	J'ai chanté **bruyamment.**
		Je n'ai pas chanté **bruyamment.**

 SELF-CHECK Student Activities Manual, *Exercises II, B, C, and D, pages 111–112.*

III. Comparison of Adverbs

- To compare how something is done, use the same construction you use to compare adjectives (see **Structures,** Chapter 2, pages 158–159).

equality	superiority	inferiority
aussi + adverb + **que**	**plus** + adverb + **que**	**moins** + adverb + **que**

Cette situation touche **aussi bien** les filles **que** les garçons.
Elle s'est mariée **plus** tôt **que** moi.
Mes grands-parents me grondent **moins** souvent **que** mes parents.

NOTE: The adverb **bien** becomes **mieux** in comparisons of superiority.

Elle s'entend **mieux** avec ses parents **que** son frère.
*She gets along **better** with her parents **than** her brother (does).*

- To state that something is done in the best, the worst, the fastest way, the most often, etc., in other words, to state a superlative, use:

le plus + adverb + **(de)**	**le moins** + adverb + **(de)**

C'est l'oncle Albert qui conduit **le moins prudemment de** tous mes oncles.
*It is Uncle Albert who drives **the least carefully of** all my uncles.*

De nous tous, c'est mon petit frère qui crie **le plus fort** quand il se fâche.
*My little brother yells **the loudest of** us all when he gets mad.*

Dans ma famille, c'est ma tante qui me comprend **le mieux.**
*In my family, my aunt understands me **the best.***

 SELF-CHECK Student Activities Manual, *Exercises III, G and H, pages 113–114.*

IV. Comparison of Nouns

- To compare nouns, use:

equality	superiority	inferiority
autant de + noun + **que**	**plus de** + noun + **que**	**moins de** + noun + **que**

Il a **autant de** cousins **que** moi.
*He has **as many** cousins **as** I (do).*

Dans une famille recomposée, il y a souvent **plus d'**enfants **que** dans une famille monoparentale.
*In a blended family, there are often **more** children **than** in a single-parent family.*

Chez mes parents, j'ai **moins de** contraintes **que** dans mon propre appartement.
*At my parents' I have **fewer** restrictions **than** in my own apartment.*

- To talk about something or someone that has the most or the least (superlative), use:

superiority	inferiority
le plus de + noun + **(de)**	**le moins de** + noun + **(de)**

De tous les membres de ma famille, c'est ma belle-mère qui a **le plus d'**énergie.
*My step-mother has **the most** energy **in** the family.*

Mon beau-père a **le moins de** temps.
*My father-in-law has **the least** (amount of) time.*

Cette mère célibataire a **le moins d'**argent.
*This single mother has **the least** (amount of) money.*

 SELF-CHECK Student Activities Manual, *Exercises IV, K and L, page 115.*

Grammar Video Tutorials

V. Demonstrative Pronouns

 **FORMS**

By this point in your study of French, you are adept at using demonstrative adjectives (**ce, cet, cette, ces**) to modify nouns.

Cet enfant est plus sympathique que sa sœur.
Cette famille nombreuse se débrouille bien.
J'admire **ces** femmes au foyer.

In order to avoid unnecessary repetition, these adjectives and the nouns they modify can be replaced by demonstrative pronouns. The demonstrative pronouns in French are:

	Masculine	Feminine
Singular	**celui**	**celle**
Plural	**ceux**	**celles**

B USAGE

Demonstrative pronouns can be used in three ways:

- followed by **-ci** or **-là** to make a distinction between two people or things, or two groups:

  > Regardez ces deux enfants. **Celui-ci** est plus sage que **celui-là.**
  > *Look at these two children. **This one** is better behaved than **that one.***

  > Je connais ses sœurs et je trouve **celle-ci** plus sympa que **celle-là.**
  > *I know her sisters and find **this one** nicer than **that one.***

- followed by **de:**

  > Les jeunes d'aujourd'hui quittent la maison plus tard que **ceux d'**il y a trente ans.
  > *Young people today leave home later than **those of** thirty years ago.*

  > La copine de ton frère cadet est plus amusante que **celle de** ton frère aîné.
  > *Your younger brother's girlfriend is more fun than your older brother's.*

- followed by a *relative pronoun* (**qui, que, dont:** see **Structures,** Chapter 6, pages 200–202):

  > Mon nouveau colocataire paie le loyer plus régulièrement que **celui qui** a déménagé.
  > *My new housemate pays the rent more regularly than **the one who** moved.*

  > Mes cousins de Montpellier sont **ceux que** j'ai vus à Noël.
  > *My cousins from Montpellier are **the ones (that)** I saw at Christmas.*

  > Un père autoritaire typique est **celui auquel** les enfants obéissent.
  > *A typical authoritarian father is **the one whom** the children obey.*

 SELF-CHECK Student Activities Manual, *Exercises V, N and O, page 116.*

VI. *Le mot juste: plaire à*

In English, we say that something or someone *pleases us*; the French say that something or someone is *pleasing to them*. Therefore the verb *to please* (**plaire**) requires the use of the preposition **à**, or an indirect object pronoun, to say who is pleased.

> Est-ce que leur nouvel appart' **leur plaît**?
> *Does their new apartment **please them**?*

> Mes copains ne **plaisent** pas toujours **à mes parents.**
> *My friends do not always **please my parents.***

NOTE: The verb **plaire** is usually used to mean *to be happy with*. The above examples could be translated as:

> Are they **happy with** / **Do** they **like** their new apartment?
> *My parents **are** not always **happy with** / do not always **like** my friends.*

The usage of this verb is like that of **manquer à** (**Structures,** Chapter 3, page 172): the word that is an indirect object in French is the subject of the equivalent sentence in English.

Structures

I. Verb Review

In the context of talking and writing about issues that go beyond the borders of France, such as the environment or international relations, the verb **atteindre** may frequently be found. There is often mention of trying to reach a goal (*atteindre* **un but**). This verb and others like it (see below) have one stem in the singular (-**n**-) and another in the plural (-**gn**-) but are otherwise conjugated like regular -**re** verbs.

Present tense:	j'att**ein**s	nous att**eign**ons
	tu att**ein**s	vous att**eign**ez
	il/elle/on att**ein**t	ils/elles att**eign**ent
Past participle:	att**ein**t	

The other indicative tenses, as well as the subjunctive, are regular in their formation.

imperfect:	ils **atteignaient**
future:	ils **atteindront**
subjunctive:	que j'**atteigne**

The verbs **craindre (craint), joindre (joint), rejoindre (rejoint), peindre (peint), teindre (teint),** etc. follow the same pattern but the first vowel will vary according to their infinitive: je cr**ain**s, nous j**oign**ons, il t**ein**t, etc.

 **SELF-CHECK** Student Activities Manual, *Exercise I, A, p. 123.*

II. What is a Function?

This final chapter of **Sur le vif** is designed to help you review many of the structures of earlier chapters. Instead of presenting additional forms, this **Structures** section is organized around the concept of functions or communicative acts, to encourage you to reflect on the "why" (the function of the forms you have been studying) more than on the "what" (tenses, adjectives, adverbs, pronouns, etc.) or the "how" (conjugations, agreements, formation, etc.).

For example:

Structures	Functions
Adjectives, adverbs, relative clauses	describing something or someone, actions
Subjunctive	expressing opinions, reacting to a statement or event
Conditional	hypothesizing, saying how things could be or could have been
Imperative	telling someone to do something
Negative forms	disagreeing, contradicting

Instead of studying language in terms of its structures or grammatical forms, it is important to consider how or for what purpose language is used. When we speak we always do so for a reason (a purpose or a goal). These purposes are called *functions*.

In order to achieve our goals in speaking, we must use correct grammar; otherwise our message might be lost or misunderstood. You have now studied most of the important grammar structures in French. We will look at them once more with their functions in mind.

Functions are broad categories, and many different forms can be used to carry them out. Just because the subjunctive is listed with one function (*persuading,* for instance), does not mean it cannot be used for another (*expressing emotion,* or *giving commands*). As you read through these pages, refer back, as needed, to the chapters in which the structures mentioned are reviewed. The cross-references are there to help you. You are the best judge of which of these forms you need to study more. The Student Activities Manual provides an opportunity to check your mastery of the grammar structures and their uses, just as it did in the earlier chapters.

III. Requesting Information

Grammar Video Tutorials

We often need to ask for information: directions to a place, how to do things, details about a present, past or future event, clarification of something we have not understood, etc. Interrogative forms allow us to carry out this very frequent communicative act.

To get confirmation or contradiction, *yes* or *no* questions are all you need:

> **Est-ce que** vous pensez que le réchauffement climatique est un vrai problème?
> **A-t-on** encore besoin de combustibles fossiles?

To get an answer that provides more information, an *interrogative adverb* (**comment, où, pourquoi, quand,** etc.), an *interrogative pronoun* (**qui, que, lequel,** etc.), or an *interrogative adjective* (**quel,** etc.) can be used.

> **Quand** va-t-on se mettre d'accord sur une définition du commerce équitable?
> **Pourquoi** ne veux-tu pas prendre ton vélo au lieu de ta voiture?
> **Combien de** pays sont maintenant membres de l'UE?
> **Qui** s'installera sur une ferme?
> **Que** veut dire ONG?
> **Quelle** est la date de ton départ?

(For a complete presentation of interrogative forms, see **Structures,** Chapter 2, pages 160–163.)

 SELF-CHECK Student Activities Manual, *Exercise III, B, pages 123–124.*

IV. Hypothesizing

When we think how things might be, or how they might have been, how we would do something, how something should be, we make *hypotheses* or suppositions. We may be asked, "If you had this problem, what would you do?" or, "If you had to do this over, what would you do differently?" To suggest *how things could be* if certain conditions were fulfilled, the *conditional* mood is used. This is helpful when you *speculate* about the future rather than when you present a more certain view of how things will be (for that, you need the future tense).

> Si la France n'avait pas tant de centrales nucléaires, elle **produirait** plus de CO$_2$.
> *If France did not have as many nuclear power plants, it **would produce** more carbon dioxide.*
>
> Si on n'avait plus de frontières, on n'**aurait** pas besoin de passeports.
> *If there were no longer any borders, one **would** not need passports.*
>
> Les pays du tiers-monde **pourraient** nourrir leurs populations s'ils n'achetaient plus d'armes.
> *Third World countries **could** feed their populations if they no longer bought weapons.*

To suggest how things *would have been* in the past, had the situation been different, use the *past conditional.*

> Si les Français et les Allemands n'avaient pas voulu empêcher d'autres guerres, ils ne se **seraient** pas **mis** d'accord pour créer ce qui est devenu l'Union européenne.
> *If the French and the Germans had not wanted to prevent other wars, they **would** not **have** agreed to create what has become the European Union.*
>
> Elle n'**aurait** pas **loué** une ferme si elle n'avait pas été fille d'agriculteur.
> *She **would** not **have leased** a farm if she had not been the daughter of a farmer.*

(For a complete presentation of the conditional, see **Structures,** Chapter 5, pages 186–194.)

 SELF-CHECK Student Activities Manual, *Exercise IV, D, pages 124–125.*

V. Describing

When we want to describe places, people, and events, we can use many different grammar structures to make our speech more precise and to add details that could interest our listeners.

- *Adjectives* typically modify nouns, that is, people or things. In French, adjectives must agree in gender (masculine or feminine) and number (singular or plural) with the nouns they modify.

> L'Europe est une **grande** puissance économique.
> *Europe is a **major** economic power.*

> Les affaires **étrangères** ne m'intéressent pas.
> ***Foreign** affairs don't interest me.*

> Avec le wwoofing, il apprend de **nouvelles** pratiques agricoles.
> *Through volunteering on an organic farm (le wwoofing) he learns **new** agricultural techniques.*

(For a more complete presentation of adjectives, see **Structures,** Chapter 2, pages 158–159.)

- Another structure that allows you to add details or precision to a description is the relative clause.

> Les gens **qui bousillent la terre** me mettent en colère.
> *The people **who are wrecking the earth** make me angry.*

> L'effet de serre fait fondre les calottes polaires **où vivent les ours polaires.**
> *The greenhouse effect melts the polar ice cap **where the polar bears live.***

> Il y a des centrales nucléaires en France **dont les pays voisins ont peur.**
> *There are nuclear power plants in France **of which neighboring countries are afraid.***

> Ils vendent au marché le fromage et le miel **qu'ils produisent,**
> *They sell the cheese and honey (**which**) **they produce** in the market.*

(For a more complete presentation of relative clauses, see **Structures,** Chapter 6, pages 200–202.)

- A third way to produce a more detailed description is to use an adverb. *Adverbs* tell *how* something is done or give more information about an action.

> Jean-François a **beaucoup** voyagé et il est **déjà** parti en Iran.
> *Jean-François has traveled **a lot** and he has **already** left for Iran.*

> Les citoyens européens se connaissent **mieux** aujourd'hui.
> *The citizens of Europe know each other **better** today.*

> L'euro s'utilise **seulement** dans certains pays membres de l'UE.
> *The euro is used **only** in some of the EU member states.*

> Certains pays sont **cruellement** déchirés par la guerre.
> *Certain countries are **cruelly** torn apart by war.*

(For a more complete presentation of adverbs, see **Structures,** Chapter 8, pages 213–215.)

- When you compare two or more things, people, or actions, you are also describing.

> L'Europe est **aussi grande que** l'Inde mais **plus riche.**
> *Europe is* ***as large as*** *India but* ***richer****.*

> Son père avait **autant de** chèvres **que** lui.
> *His father had* ***as many*** *goats* ***as*** *he does.*

(For a more complete presentation of comparisons, see **Structures,** Chapter 2, pages 158–159 and **Structures,** Chapter 8, pages 215–216.)

DESCRIPTIONS AND TENSES

- Descriptions are not limited to the present tense. When you describe something that happened in the past, you use a past tense, usually the *imperfect.*

> Nous **voulions** devenir propriétaires.
> *We* ***wanted*** *to become owners.*

> Ils ne **coupaient** pas les haies.
> *They* ***did*** *not* ***cut*** *the hedges.*

(For a more complete presentation of the imperfect tense, see **Structures,** Chapter 3, pages 166–169.)

- Of course you can also describe in the future, using the *future* tense.

> La guerre **paraîtra** absurde et **sera** impossible.
> *War* ***will seem*** *absurd and* ***will be*** *impossible.*

> Un jour, il y **aura** des fermes voltaïques dans toutes les régions de France.
> *One day there* ***will be*** *solar energy farms in every region of France.*

(For a more complete presentation of the future, see **Structures,** Chapter 5, pages 186–191.)

 SELF-CHECK Student Activities Manual, *Exercises V, F–I, pages 125–127.*

VI. Expressing Opinions or Reactions

When we want to say how an action or a statement makes us feel or give our point of view about something we have seen or heard, we often use the *subjunctive.*

> Nous **sommes heureux** que tant de jeunes **veuillent** manger bio.
> *We* ***are happy*** *that so many young people* ***want*** *to eat organic food.*

> Il **est important** que nos villes **soient** propres.
> *It is* ***important*** *that our cities* ***be*** *clean.*

> Je **crains** que nos efforts pour recycler ne **soient** pas suffisants.
> *I* ***am afraid*** *that our efforts to recycle* ***are*** *not enough.*

However, it is important to remember that an *infinitive* is used after these expressions instead of a conjugated verb in the subjunctive if the subject of the main verb and the second verb is the same.

> Il **faut préserver** la biodiversité.
> *It **is necessary to protect** biodiversity.*

> Elle **regrette** de ne pas **avoir étudié** la médecine.
> *She **regrets** not **having studied** medicine.*

(For a more complete presentation of the subjunctive, see **Structures,** Chapter 7, pages 204–211.)

 SELF-CHECK Student Activities Manual, *Exercise VI, M, page 128.*

VII. Negating

A *negative construction* can be used to disagree, contradict or state the opposite of something else.

> Nous **ne** jetterons **plus rien.**
> *We will **no longer** throw **anything** away.*

> Moi, je pense qu'on signera bientôt un traité entre Israël et la Palestine. Et vous?
> Nous pensons que la paix **ne** s'établira **jamais** tout à fait au Moyen-Orient.
>
> *I think a treaty will soon be signed between Israel and Palestine. What do you think?*
> *We think that peace will **never** completely come to the Middle East.*

> **Ni** l'énergie solaire **ni** l'énergie éolienne **ne** remplaceront les centrales nucléaires en France.
> ***Neither** solar power **nor** wind energy will replace nuclear power plants in France.*

(For a more complete presentation of the negative, see **Structures,** Chapter 6, pages 197–200.)

VIII. Narrating

We spend a great deal of time telling others about something that will happen or is happening in our lives, or recounting an episode from our past. This narration is done in a variety of tenses, depending on the time frame of the events.

Present tense narration is what we do when we tell someone about what is going on right now.

> Ils **trient** leurs déchets.
> *They **sort** their trash.*

> Un des diplomates **pose** une question.
> *One of the diplomats **is asking** a question.*

> Ils s'**engagent** à pratiquer l'agriculture biologique.
> *They **commit** themselves to practicing organic agriculture.*

(For a more complete presentation of the present tense, see **Structures,** Chapter 1, pages 145–148.)

Past tense narration uses a variety of tenses (imperfect, **passé composé,** pluperfect, and **passé simple**) to locate events in the past and relate them to each other.

> Nous nous **sommes** moins **endettés**.
> *We **took out** fewer loans.*

> Des volontaires **racontaient** leur travail sur le terrain.
> *The volunteers **were talking about** their work in the field.*

> L'association **a** déjà **soutenu** plus d'une quarantaine d'exploitations.
> *The association **has** already **supported** more than forty farms.*

(For a more complete presentation of the imperfect, **passé composé,** and pluperfect, see **Structures,** Chapter 3, pages 165–171.)

The **passé simple** is often found in historic, literary, and expository narrative texts when the author uses a more careful, formal style.

> L'énergie solaire photovoltaïque **fut découverte** en 1839 par Antoine César
> Becquerel, physicien français, né à Châtillon-Coligny (Loiret) le 7 mars 1788
> et mort à Paris le 18 janvier 1878.
> *Solar energy **was discovered** in 1839 by Antoine César Becquerel, French physicist,*
> *born in Châtillon-Coligny (Loire) on March 7, 1788 and died in Paris on*
> *January 18, 1878.*

> C'est seulement au dix-neuvième siècle que l'utilisation des énergies fossiles
> **se développa**, d'abord avec le charbon, puis avec le pétrole au début
> du vingtième siècle et enfin le gaz et le nucléaire dans la seconde moitié
> du vingtième siècle.
> *It was only in the 19th century that the usage of fossil sources of energy **developed**, first*
> *with coal, then with oil at the beginning of the 20th century, and finally with gas and*
> *nuclear in the second half of the 20th century.*

(For a more complete presentation of the **passé simple,** see **Structures,** Chapter 5, pages 194–195.)

Future tense narration uses either the simple future (more frequent in written narration), the future perfect, the **futur proche** (**aller** + *infinitive*), or a verb that suggests future time.

> Nous **verrons** les résultats dans cinq ans.
> *We **will see** the results in five years.*

> Je **vais passer** un an avec Greenpeace.
> *I **am going to spend** a year with Greenpeace.*

> Vous **projetez** de travailler en Afrique.
> *You **are planning** to work in Africa.*

(For a more complete presentation of the future, see **Structures,** Chapter 5, pages 186–192.)

 SELF-CHECK Student Activities Manual, *Exercises VIII, O–P, pages 129–131.*

CONCLUSION

By now you are aware that language does not come in discrete "chunks." It is hard to isolate one grammar point from all the others since several are often needed together to express your meaning. To communicate, you call upon the various forms you have learned. As you continue your study of French, you will find that using increasingly complex language both orally and in writing will become more and more natural.

Bonne route!

Appendix A

Prepositions

I VERBS THAT TAKE PREPOSITIONS IN *ONE* LANGUAGE ONLY

A. In English, there are many verbs that are followed by a preposition, whereas in French the preposition is included in the meaning of the verb itself.

Here are the most common examples:

attendre	*to wait **for***
chercher	*to look **for***
demander	*to ask **for***
descendre	*to go **down***
écouter	*to listen **to***
monter	*to go **up***
payer	*to pay **for***
regarder	*to look **at**; to watch*

B. Many French verbs require prepositions before their objects, when the English equivalent does not.

Here are some examples of these verbs:

assister **à**	*to attend*
changer **de**	*to change (+ object)*
commencer **à** (+ *infinitive*)	*to start*
entrer **dans**	*to enter*
finir **par** (+ *infinitive*)	*to end up*
jouer **à**	*to play (a sport)*
jouer **de**	*to play (a musical instrument)*
obéir **à**	*to obey*
rendre service **à**	*to help*
rendre visite **à**	*to visit (someone)*
répondre **à**	*to answer*
téléphoner **à**	*to call someone (on the phone)*

II VERBS REQUIRING PREPOSITION + *INFINITIVE*

Many verbs in French require a preposition between the verb and a following infinitive. No general rule exists to determine which preposition goes with which verb, so it is a good idea to learn the ones you use most frequently and to check a dictionary in case of doubt.

A. Some verbs require the preposition **à** if they are followed by an infinitive.

aider qqn à	s'habituer à
s'amuser à	hésiter à
apprendre à	s'intéresser à
arriver à	inviter à
s'attendre à	se mettre à
encourager à	réussir à
enseigner à	tenir à

Je n'**arrive** pas **à comprendre** les mathématiques.

B. Other verbs require the preposition **de** if they are followed by an infinitive.

accepter de	essayer de
s'arrêter de	finir de
cesser de	oublier de
craindre de	regretter de
se dépêcher de	rêver de
empêcher qqn de	venir de

J'ai **essayé d'aller** à Paris.

C. A few verbs allow a choice of **à** or **de** if followed by an infinitive.

continuer à/de
se décider à / décider de

D. Some verbs require two prepositions, one in front of the *following noun* and the other in front of the *following infinitive*. This forms a double construction:

verb + **à** + *noun (usually a person)* + **de** + *infinitive*

conseiller à... de...	ordonner à... de...
défendre à... de...	permettre à... de...
demander à... de...	promettre à... de...
dire à... de...	refuser à... de...
écrire à... de...	reprocher à... de...
interdire à... de...	suggérer à... de...

La mère défend **à** ses enfants **de** manger du chocolat.
Les profs ne permettent pas **à** leurs élèves **d'**utiliser leur portable pendant un contrôle.

Appendix B

Present Participles

❶ WHAT IS A PRESENT PARTICIPLE?

The *present participle* is a verbal form (also called a *gerund*), similar to the *-ing* form in English with no stated subject.

> Je mange toujours **en regardant** la télé.
> *I always eat **while watching** TV.*

> **En répondant** immédiatement, j'ai évité une amende.
> **By answering** *immediately, I avoided a fine.*

NOTE: This is *not* the same as the present or the imperfect verb tenses, which can also be translated with an *-ing* verb form:

> Elle **chante** toujours.
> *She is always **singing**.*

> Il m'a téléphoné pendant que je **prenais** une douche.
> *He called me while I **was taking** a shower.*

❷ HOW IS A PRESENT PARTICIPLE FORMED?

The present participle form is based on the **nous** form of the present tense. The **-ons** ending is dropped, and **-ant** is added.

> Il a gagné une médaille **en courant** plus vite que les autres.
> *He won a medal by running faster than the others.*

nous *form*	*present participle*
nous parl~~ons~~ ⟶	parl**ant**
nous finiss~~ons~~ ⟶	finiss**ant**
nous entend~~ons~~ ⟶	entend**ant**

There are three irregular present participles:

être:	**étant**
avoir:	**ayant**
savoir:	**sachant**

HOW IS A PRESENT PARTICIPLE USED?

In French, the present participle is not used as often as in English. Two of the most common uses are:

A. as an adjective, which means it agrees with the noun it modifies.

>Ces enfants sont **agaçants.**
>C'est une personne **charmante.**

B. as a gerund (like the English present participle), usually preceded by the preposition **en.** In this case, the present participle is invariable. Note the English translations.

>Je prends toujours mon dîner **en écoutant** de la musique.
>*I always have dinner **while listening** to music.*

>**En travaillant** tout l'été, j'ai gagné assez d'argent pour payer mon voyage.
>***By working** all summer, I earned enough money to pay for my trip.*

>L'appétit vient **en mangeant.** *(French proverb)*
>***Eating** stimulates the appetite.*

Verb Conjugations

Note that regular **-er, -re** and **-ir** verbs are the most frequent conjugations. Verbs marked with an asterisk (*) are conjugated with **être** in compound past tenses; all others are conjugated with **avoir.** If the verb you are looking for is not listed below, look for one with a similar ending.

---

accueillir *to welcome, to greet*
past participle: **accueilli** / present participle: **accueillant**

Like **accueillir** is **cueillir** *(to pick, to gather)*

Present indicative
j'accueille
tu accueilles
il/elle/on accueille
nous accueillons
vous accueillez
ils/elles accueillent

Passé simple
j'accueillis
tu accueillis
il/elle/on accueillit
nous accueillîmes
vous accueillîtes
ils/elles accueillirent

Present subjunctive
que j'accueille
que tu accueilles
qu'il/elle/on accueille
que nous accueillions
que vous accueilliez
qu'ils/elles accueillent

Imperfect
j'accueillais
tu accueillais
il/elle/on accueillait
nous accueillions
vous accueilliez
ils/elles accueillaient

Future
j'accueillerai
tu accueilleras
il/elle/on accueillera
nous accueillerons
vous accueillerez
ils/elles accueilleront

Imperative
accueille
accueillons
accueillez

Passé composé
j'ai accueilli
tu as accueilli
il/elle/on a accueilli
nous avons accueilli
vous avez accueilli
ils/elles ont accueilli

Conditional
j'accueillerais
tu accueillerais
il/elle/on accueillerait
nous accueillerions
vous accueilleriez
ils/elles accueilleraient

acheter *to buy*

past participle: **acheté** / present participle: **achetant**

Like **acheter** is **racheter** (*to buy back, make up for*)

Present indicative
j'achète
tu achètes
il/elle/on achète
nous achetons
vous achetez
ils/elles achètent

Future
j'achèterai
tu achèteras
il/elle/on achètera
nous achèterons
vous achèterez
ils/elles achèteront

Imperfect
j'achetais
tu achetais
il/elle/on achetait
nous achetions
vous achetiez
ils/elles achetaient

Conditional
j'achèterais
tu achèterais
il/elle/on achèterait
nous achèterions
vous achèteriez
ils/elles achètraient

Passé composé
j'ai acheté
tu as acheté
il/elle/on a acheté
nous avons acheté
vous avez acheté
ils/elles ont acheté

Present subjunctive
que j'achète
que tu achètes
qu'il/elle/on achète
que nous achetions
que vous achetiez
qu'ils/elles achètent

Passé simple
j'achetai
tu achetas
il/elle/on acheta
nous achetâmes
vous achetâtes
ils/elles achetèrent

Imperative
achète
achetons
achetez

agir *to act*
past participle: **agi** / present participle: **agissant**

Like **agir** are **finir** *(to finish)* and about 300 other verbs

---

Present indicative
j'agis
tu agis
il/elle/on agit
nous agissons
vous agissez
ils/elles agissent

Future
j'agirai
tu agiras
il/elle/on agira
nous agirons
vous agirez
ils/elles agiront

Imperfect
j'agissais
tu agissais
il/elle/on agissait
nous agissions
vous agissiez
ils/elles agissaient

Conditional
j'agirais
tu agirais
il/elle/on agirait
nous agirions
vous agiriez
ils/elles agiraient

Passé composé
j'ai agi
tu as agi
il/elle/on a agi
nous avons agi
vous avez agi
ils/elles ont agi

Present subjunctive
que j'agisse
que tu agisses
qu'il/elle/on agisse
que nous agissions
que vous agissiez
qu'ils/elles agissent

Passé simple
j'agis
tu agis
il/elle/on agit
nous agîmes
vous agîtes
ils/elles agirent

Imperative
agis
agissons
agissez

aller* *to go*

past participle: **allé(e)(s)** / present participle: **allant**

Like **aller** is **s'en aller*** *(to go away)*

Present indicative
je vais
tu vas
il/elle/on va
nous allons
vous allez
ils/elles vont

Future
j'irai
tu iras
il/elle/on ira
nous irons
vous irez
ils/elles iront

Imperfect
j'allais
tu allais
il/elle/on allait
nous allions
vous alliez
ils/elles allaient

Conditional
j'irais
tu irais
il/elle/on irait
nous irions
vous iriez
ils/elles iraient

Passé composé
je suis allé(e)
tu es allé(e)
il/elle/on est allé(e)
nous sommes allé(e)s
vous êtes allé(e)(s)
ils/elles sont allé(e)s

Present subjunctive
que j'aille
que tu ailles
qu'il/elle/on aille
que nous allions
que vous alliez
qu'ils/elles aillent

Passé simple
j'allai
tu allas
il/elle/on alla
nous allâmes
vous allâtes
ils/elles allèrent

Imperative
va
allons
allez

s'appeler* *to be called, named*

past participle: **appelé** / present participle: **appelant**

Like **s'appeler** are **appeler** *(to call)*, **se rappeler*** *(to recall, to remember)*

Present indicative
je m'appelle
tu t'appelles
il/elle/on s'appelle
nous nous appelons
vous vous appelez
ils/elles s'appellent

Future
je m'appellerai
tu t'appelleras
il/elle/on s'appellera
nous nous appellerons
vous vous appellerez
ils/elles s'appelleront

Imperfect
je m'appelais
tu t'appelais
il/elle/on s'appelait
nous nous appelions
vous vous appeliez
ils/elles s'appelaient

Conditional
je m'appellerais
tu t'appellerais
il/elle/on s'appellerait
nous nous appellerions
vous vous appelleriez
ils/elles s'appelleraient

Passé composé
je me suis appelé(e)
tu t'es appelé(e)
il/elle/on s'est appelé(e)
nous nous sommes appelé(e)s
vous vous êtes appelé(e)(s)
ils/elles se sont appelé(e)s

Present subjunctive
que je m'appelle
que tu t'appelles
qu'il/elle/on s'appelle
que nous nous appelions
que vous vous appeliez
qu'ils/elles s'appellent

Passé simple
je m'appelai
tu t'appelas
il/elle/on s'appela
nous nous appelâmes
vous vous appelâtes
ils/elles s'appelèrent

Imperative
appelle-toi
appelons-nous
appelez-vous

apprendre (see prendre)

s'asseoir* *to sit down*

past participle: **assis** / present participle: **asseyant**

Present indicative
je m'assieds
tu t'assieds
il/elle/on s'assied
nous nous asseyons
vous vous asseyez
ils/elles s'asseyent

Future
je m'assiérai
tu t'assiéras
il/elle/on s'assiéra
nous nous assiérons
vous vous assiérez
ils/elles s'assiéront

Imperfect
je m'asseyais
tu t'asseyais
il/elle/on s'asseyait
nous nous asseyions
vous vous asseyiez
ils/elles s'asseyaient

Conditional
je m'assiérais
tu t'assiérais
il/elle/on s'assiérait
nous nous assiérions
vous vous assiériez
ils/elles s'assiéraient

Passé composé
je me suis assis(e)
tu t'es assis(e)
il/elle/on s'est assis(e)
nous nous sommes assis(e)s
vous vous êtes assis(e)(s)
ils/elles se sont assis(e)s

Present subjunctive
que je m'asseye
que tu t'asseyes
qu'il/elle/on s'asseye
que nous nous asseyions
que vous vous asseyiez
qu'ils/elles s'asseyent

Passé simple
je m'assis
tu t'assis
il/elle/on s'assit
nous nous assîmes
vous vous assîtes
ils/elles s'assirent

Imperative
assieds-toi
asseyons-nous
asseyez-vous

avoir *to have*

past participle: **eu** / present participle: **ayant**

Present indicative
j'ai
tu as
il/elle/on a
nous avons
vous avez
ils/elles ont

Future
j'aurai
tu auras
il/elle/on aura
nous aurons
vous aurez
ils/elles auront

Imperfect
j'avais
tu avais
il/elle/on avait
nous avions
vous aviez
ils/elles avaient

Conditional
j'aurais
tu aurais
il/elle/on aurait
nous aurions
vous auriez
ils/elles auraient

Passé composé
j'ai eu
tu as eu
il/elle/on a eu
nous avons eu
vous avez eu
ils/elles ont eu

Present subjunctive
que j'aie
que tu aies
qu'il/elle/on ait
que nous ayons
que vous ayez
qu'ils/elles aient

Passé simple
j'eus
tu eus
il/elle/on eut
nous eûmes
vous eûtes
ils/elles eurent

Imperative
aie
ayons
ayez

commencer *to begin*
past participle: **commencé** / present participle: **commençant**

Like **commencer** is **recommencer** *(to begin again, to start over)*

Present indicative
je commence
tu commences
il/elle/on commence
nous commençons
vous commencez
ils/elles commencent

Future
je commencerai
tu commenceras
il/elle/on commencera
nous commencerons
vous commencerez
ils/elles commenceront

Imperfect
je commençais
tu commençais
il/elle/on commençait
nous commencions
vous commenciez
ils/elles commençaient

Conditional
je commencerais
tu commencerais
il/elle/on commencerait
nous commencerions
vous commenceriez
ils/elles commenceraient

Passé composé
j'ai commencé
tu as commencé
il/elle/on a commencé
nous avons commencé
vous avez commencé
ils/elles ont commencé

Present subjunctive
que je commence
que tu commences
qu'il/elle/on commence
que nous commencions
que vous commenciez
qu'ils/elles commencent

Passé simple
je commençai
tu commenças
il/elle/on commença
nous commençâmes
vous commençâtes
ils/elles commencèrent

Imperative
commence
commençons
commencez

comprendre (see prendre)

conduire *to drive*

past participle: **conduit** / present participle: **conduisant**

Like **conduire** are **construire** *(to build, to construct)*, **cuire** *(to cook)*, **réduire** *(to reduce)*, **séduire** *(to seduce)*

Present indicative
je conduis
tu conduis
il/elle/on conduit
nous conduisons
vous conduisez
ils/elles conduisent

Future
je conduirai
tu conduiras
il/elle/on conduira
nous conduirons
vous conduirez
ils/elles conduiront

Imperfect
je conduisais
tu conduisais
il/elle/on conduisait
nous conduisions
vous conduisiez
ils/elles conduisaient

Conditional
je conduirais
tu conduirais
il/elle/on conduirait
nous conduirions
vous conduiriez
ils/elles conduiraient

Passé composé
j'ai conduit
tu as conduit
il/elle/on a conduit
nous avons conduit
vous avez conduit
ils/elles ont conduit

Present subjunctive
que je conduise
que tu conduises
qu'il/elle/on conduise
que nous conduisions
que vous conduisiez
qu'ils/elles conduisent

Passé simple
je conduisis
tu conduisis
il/elle/on conduisit
nous conduisîmes
vous conduisîtes
ils/elles conduisirent

Imperative
conduis
conduisons
conduisez

connaître *to know*

past participle: **connu** / present participle: **connaissant**

Like **connaître** are **apparaître** *(to appear)*, **disparaître** *(to disappear)*, **paraître** *(to seem)*, **reconnaître** *(to recognize)*

Present indicative
je connais
tu connais
il/elle/on connaît
nous connaissons
vous connaissez
ils/elles connaissent

Future
je connaîtrai
tu connaîtras
il/elle/on connaîtra
nous connaîtrons
vous connaîtrez
ils/elles connaîtront

Imperfect
je connaissais
tu connaissais
il/elle/on connaissait
nous connaissions
vous connaissiez
ils/elles connaissaient

Conditional
je connaîtrais
tu connaîtrais
il/elle/on connaîtrait
nous connaîtrions
vous connaîtriez
ils/elles connaîtraient

Passé composé
j'ai connu
tu as connu
il/elle/on a connu
nous avons connu
vous avez connu
ils/elles ont connu

Present subjunctive
que je connaisse
que tu connaisses
qu'il/elle/on connaisse
que nous connaissions
que vous connaissiez
qu'ils/elles connaissent

Passé simple
je connus
tu connus
il/elle/on connut
nous connûmes
vous connûtes
ils/elles connurent

Imperative
connais
connaissons
connaissez

convaincre *to convince*
past participle: **convaincu** / present participle: **convainquant**

Like **convaincre** is **vaincre** *(to defeat, to conquer)*

Present indicative
je convaincs
tu convaincs
il/elle/on convainc
nous convainquons
vous convainquez
ils/elles convainquent

Future
je convaincrai
tu convaincras
il/elle/on convaincra
nous convaincrons
vous convaincrez
ils/elles convaincront

Imperfect
je convainquais
tu convainquais
il/elle/on convainquait
nous convainquions
vous convainquiez
ils/elles convainquaient

Conditional
je convaincrais
tu convaincrais
il/elle/on convaincrait
nous convaincrions
vous convaincriez
ils/elles convaincraient

Passé composé
j'ai convaincu
tu as convaincu
il/elle/on a convaincu
nous avons convaincu
vous avez convaincu
ils/elles ont convaincu

Present subjunctive
que je convainque
que tu convainques
qu'il/elle/on convainque
que nous convainquions
que vous convainquiez
qu'ils/elles convainquent

Passé simple
je convainquis
tu convainquis
il/elle/on convainquit
nous convainquîmes
vous convainquîtes
ils/elles convainquirent

Imperative
convaincs
convainquons
convainquez

courir *to run*

past participle: **couru** / present participle: **courant**

Like **courir** is **parcourir** *(to skim, go over)*

Present indicative
je cours
tu cours
il/elle/on court
nous courons
vous courez
ils/elles courent

Future
je courrai
tu courras
il/elle/on courra
nous courrons
vous courrez
ils/elles courront

Imperfect
je courais
tu courais
il/elle/on courait
nous courions
vous couriez
ils/elles couraient

Conditional
je courrais
tu courrais
il/elle/on courrait
nous courrions
vous courriez
ils/elles courraient

Passé composé
j'ai couru
tu as couru
il/elle/on a couru
nous avons couru
vous avez couru
ils/elles ont couru

Present subjunctive
que je coure
que tu coures
qu'il/elle/on coure
que nous courions
que vous couriez
qu'ils/elles courent

Passé simple
je courus
tu courus
il/elle/on courut
nous courûmes
vous courûtes
ils/elles coururent

Imperative
cours
courons
courez

craindre (see teindre)

croire *to believe*

past participle: **cru** / present participle: **croyant**

Present indicative
je crois
tu crois
il/elle/on croit
nous croyons
vous croyez
ils/elles croient

Future
je croirai
tu croiras
il/elle/on croira
nous croirons
vous croirez
ils/elles croiront

Imperfect
je croyais
tu croyais
il/elle/on croyait
nous croyions
vous croyiez
ils/elles croyaient

Conditional
je croirais
tu croirais
il/elle/on croirait
nous croirions
vous croiriez
ils/elles croiraient

Passé composé
j'ai cru
tu as cru
il/elle/on a cru
nous avons cru
vous avez cru
ils/elles ont cru

Present subjective
que je croie
que tu croies
qu'il/elle/on croie
que nous croyions
que vous croyiez
qu'ils/elles croient

Passé simple
je crus
tu crus
il/elle/on crut
nous crûmes
vous crûtes
ils/elles crurent

Imperative
crois
croyons
croyez

découvrir (see **ouvrir**)

décrire *to describe*
past participle: **décrit** / present participle: **décrivant**

Like **décrire** are **écrire** *(to write)* and **s'inscrire*** *(to register, enroll)*

Present indicative
je décris
tu décris
il/elle/on décrit
nous décrivons
vous décrivez
ils/elles décrivent

Future
je décrirai
tu décriras
il/elle/on décrira
nous décrirons
vous décrirez
ils/elles décriront

Imperfect
je décrivais
tu décrivais
il/elle/on décrivait
nous décrivions
vous décriviez
ils/elles décrivaient

Conditional
je décrirais
tu décrirais
il/elle/on décrirait
nous décririons
vous décririez
ils/elles décriraient

Passé composé
j'ai décrit
tu as décrit
il/elle/on a décrit
nous avons décrit
vous avez décrit
ils/elles ont décrit

Present subjunctive
que je décrive
que tu décrives
qu'il/elle/on décrive
que nous décrivions
que vous décriviez
qu'ils/elles décrivent

Passé simple
je décrivis
tu décrivis
il/elle/on décrivit
nous décrivîmes
vous décrivîtes
ils/elles décrivirent

Imperative
décris
décrivons
décrivez

descendre* (see rendre)

devoir *to owe; to have to*

past participle: **dû** / present participle: **devant**

Present indicative
je dois
tu dois
il/elle/on doit
nous devons
vous devez
ils/elles doivent

Future
je devrai
tu devras
il/elle/on devra
nous devrons
vous devrez
ils/elles devront

Imperfect
je devais
tu devais
il/elle/on devait
nous devions
vous deviez
ils/elles devaient

Conditional
je devrais
tu devrais
il/elle/on devrait
nous devrions
vous devriez
ils/elles devraient

Passé composé
j'ai dû
tu as dû
il/elle/on a dû
nous avons dû
vous avez dû
ils/elles ont dû

Present subjunctive
que je doive
que tu doives
qu'il/elle/on doive
que nous devions
que vous deviez
qu'ils/elles doivent

Passé simple
je dus
tu dus
il/elle/on dut
nous dûmes
vous dûtes
ils/elles durent

Imperative
dois
devons
devez

dire *to say*
past participle: **dit** / present participle: **disant**

Like **dire**, except in the *vous* form of the present, are **contredire** (contredisez) *(to contradict)*, **maudire** (maudissez) *(to curse)*, and **prédire** (prédisez) *(to predict)*

Present indicative
je dis
tu dis
il/elle/on dit
nous disons
vous dites
ils/elles disent

Future
je dirai
tu diras
il/elle/on dira
nous dirons
vous direz
ils/elles diront

Imperfect
je disais
tu disais
il/elle/on disait
nous disions
vous disiez
ils/elles disaient

Conditional
je dirais
tu dirais
il/elle/on dirait
nous dirions
vous diriez
ils/elles diraient

Passé composé
j'ai dit
tu as dit
il/elle/on a dit
nous avons dit
vous avez dit
ils/elles ont dit

Present subjunctive
que je dise
que tu dises
qu'il/elle/on dise
que nous disions
que vous disiez
qu'ils/elles disent

Passé simple
je dis
tu dis
il/elle/on dit
nous dîmes
vous dîtes
ils/elles dirent

Imperative
dis
disons
dites

dormir *to sleep*

past participle: **dormi** / present participle: **dormant**

Like **dormir** are **s'endormir*** *(to fall asleep)* and **se rendormir*** *(to fall asleep again)*

Present indicative
je dors
tu dors
il/elle/on dort
nous dormons
vous dormez
ils/elles dorment

Future
je dormirai
tu dormiras
il/elle/on dormira
nous dormirons
vous dormirez
ils/elles dormiront

Imperfect
je dormais
tu dormais
il/elle/on dormait
nous dormions
vous dormiez
ils/elles dormaient

Conditional
je dormirais
tu dormirais
il/elle/on dormirait
nous dormirions
vous dormiriez
ils/elles dormiraient

Passé composé
j'ai dormi
tu as dormi
il/elle/on a dormi
nous avons dormi
vous avez dormi
ils/elles ont dormi

Present subjunctive
que je dorme
que tu dormes
qu'il/elle/on dorme
que nous dormions
que vous dormiez
qu'ils/elles dorment

Passé simple
je dormis
tu dormis
il/elle/on dormit
nous dormîmes
vous dormîtes
ils/elles dormirent

Imperative
dors
dormons
dormez

écrire (see décrire)

s'ennuyer* _to be bored_

past participle: **ennuyé** / present participle: **ennuyant**

Like **s'ennuyer** is **ennuyer** _(to annoy, bother)_

Present indicative

je m'ennuie
tu t'ennuies
il/elle/on s'ennuie
nous nous ennuyons
vous vous ennuyez
ils/elles s'ennuient

Future

je m'ennuierai
tu t'ennuieras
il/elle/on s'ennuiera
nous nous ennuierons
vous vous ennuierez
ils/elles s'ennuieront

Imperfect

je m'ennuyais
tu t'ennuyais
il/elle/on s'ennuyait
nous nous ennuyions
vous vous ennuyiez
ils/elles s'ennuyaient

Conditional

je m'ennuierais
tu t'ennuierais
il/elle/on s'ennuierait
nous nous ennuierions
vous vous ennuieriez
ils/elles s'ennuieraient

Passé composé

je me suis ennuyé(e)
tu t'es ennuyé(e)
il/elle/on s'est ennuyé(e)
nous nous sommes ennuyé(e)s
vous vous êtes ennuyé(e)(s)
ils/elles se sont ennuyé(e)s

Present subjunctive

que je m'ennuie
que tu t'ennuies
qu'il/elle/on s'ennuie
que nous nous ennuyions
que vous vous ennuyiez
qu'ils/elles s'ennuient

Passé simple

je m'ennuyai
tu t'ennuyas
il/elle/on s'ennuya
nous nous ennuyâmes
vous vous ennuyâtes
ils/elles s'ennuyèrent

Imperative

ennuie-toi
ennuyons-nous
ennuyez-vous

envoyer *to send*

past participle: **envoyé** / present participle: **envoyant**

Like **envoyer** is **renvoyer** *(to send away, dismiss)*

Present indicative
j'envoie
tu envoies
il/elle/on envoie
nous envoyons
vous envoyez
ils/elles envoient

Future
j'enverrai
tu enverras
il/elle/on enverra
nous enverrons
vous enverrez
ils/elles enverront

Imperfect
j'envoyais
tu envoyais
il/elle/on envoyait
nous envoyions
vous envoyiez
ils/elles envoyaient

Conditional
j'enverrais
tu enverrais
il/elle/on enverrait
nous enverrions
vous enverriez
ils/elles enverraient

Passé composé
j'ai envoyé
tu as envoyé
il/elle/on a envoyé
nous avons envoyé
vous avez envoyé
ils/elles ont envoyé

Present subjunctive
que j'envoie
que tu envoies
qu'il/elle/on envoie
que nous envoyions
que vous envoyiez
qu'ils/elles envoient

Passé simple
j'envoyai
tu envoyas
il/elle/on envoya
nous envoyâmes
vous envoyâtes
ils/elles envoyèrent

Imperative
envoie
envoyons
envoyez

essayer *to try*
past participle: **essayé** / present participle: **essayant**

Like **essayer** is **payer** *(to pay)*

Present indicative
j'essaie
tu essaies
il/elle/on essaie
nous essayons
vous essayez
ils/elles essaient

Future
j'essaierai
tu essaieras
il/elle/on essaiera
nous essaierons
vous essaierez
ils/elles essaieront

Imperfect
j'essayais
tu essayais
il/elle/on essayait
nous essayions
vous essayiez
ils/elles essayaient

Conditional
j'essierais
tu essaierais
il/elle/on essaierait
nous essaierions
vous essaieriez
ils/elles essaieraient

Passé composé
j'ai essayé
tu as essayé
il/elle/on a essayé
nous avons essayé
vous avez essayé
ils/elles ont essayé

Present subjunctive
que j'essaie
que tu essaies
qu'il/elle/on essaie
que nous essayions
que vous essayiez
qu'ils/elles essaient

Passé simple
j'essayai
tu essayas
il/elle/on essaya
nous essayâmes
vous essayâtes
ils/elles essayèrent

Imperative
essaie
essayons
essayez

être *to be*

past participle: **été** / present participle: **étant**

Present indicative
je suis
tu es
il/elle/on est
nous sommes
vous êtes
ils/elles sont

Future
je serai
tu seras
il/elle/on sera
nous serons
vous serez
ils/elles seront

Imperfect
j'étais
tu étais
il/elle/on était
nous étions
vous étiez
ils/elles étaient

Conditional
je serais
tu serais
il/elle/on serait
nous serions
vous seriez
ils/elles seraient

Passé composé
j'ai été
tu as été
il/elle/on a été
nous avons été
vous avez été
ils/elles ont été

Present subjunctive
que je sois
que tu sois
qu'il/elle/on soit
que nous soyons
que vous soyez
qu'ils/elles soient

Passé simple
je fus
tu fus
il/elle/on fut
nous fûmes
vous fûtes
ils/elles furent

Imperative
sois
soyons
soyez

faire *to make, to do*

past participle: **fait** / present participle: **faisant**

Present indicative
je fais
tu fais
il/elle/on fait
nous faisons
vous faites
ils/elles font

Future
je ferai
tu feras
il/elle/on fera
nous ferons
vous ferez
ils/elles feront

Imperfect
je faisais
tu faisais
il/elle/on faisait
nous faisions
vous faisiez
ils/elles faisaient

Conditional
je ferais
tu ferais
il/elle/on ferait
nous ferions
vous feriez
ils/elles feraient

Passé composé
j'ai fait
tu as fait
il/elle/on a fait
nous avons fait
vous avez fait
ils/elles ont fait

Present subjunctive
que je fasse
que tu fasses
qu'il/elle/on fasse
que nous fassions
que vous fassiez
qu'ils/elles fassent

Passé simple
je fis
tu fis
il/elle/on fit
nous fîmes
vous fîtes
ils/elles firent

Imperative
fais
faisons
faites

falloir *must, have to, should*

past participle: **fallu**

Present indicative
il faut

Future
il faudra

Imperfect
il fallait

Conditional
il faudrait

Passé composé
il a fallu

Present subjunctive
qu'il faille

Passé simple
il fallut

s'inscrire* (see décrire)

jeter *to throw, to throw away, throw out*
past participle: **jeté** / present participle: **jetant**

Like **jeter** is **projeter** *(to plan)*

Present indicative
je jette
tu jettes
il/elle/on jette
nous jetons
vous jetez
ils/elles jettent

Imperfect
je jetais
tu jetais
il/elle/on jetait
nous jetions
vous jetiez
ils/elles jetaient

Passé composé
j'ai jeté
tu as jeté
il/elle/on a jeté
nous avons jeté
vous avez jeté
ils/elles ont jeté

Passé simple
je jetai
tu jetas
il/elle/on jeta
nous jetâmes
vous jetâtes
ils/elles jetèrent

Future
je jetterai
tu jetteras
il/elle/on jettera
nous jetterons
vous jetterez
ils/elles jetteront

Conditional
je jetterais
tu jetterais
il/elle/on jetterait
nous jetterions
vous jetteriez
ils/ells jetteraient

Present subjunctive
que je jette
que tu jettes
qu'il/elle/on jette
que nous jetions
que vous jetiez
qu'ils/elles jettent

Imperative
jette
jetons
jetez

lire *to read*

past participle: **lu** / present participle: **lisant**

Like **lire** is **relire** *(to re-read)*

Present indicative
je lis
tu lis
il/elle/on lit
nous lisons
vous lisez
ils/elles lisent

Imperfect
je lisais
tu lisais
il/elle/on lisait
nous lisions
vous lisiez
ils/elles lisaient

Passé composé
j'ai lu
tu as lu
il/elle/on a lu
nous avons lu
vous avez lu
ils/elles ont lu

Passé simple
je lus
tu lus
il/elle/on lut
nous lûmes
vous lûtes
ils/elles lurent

Future
je lirai
tu liras
il/elle/on lira
nous lirons
vous lirez
ils/elles liront

Conditional
je lirais
tu lirais
il/elle/on lirait
nous lirions
vous liriez
ils/elles liraient

Present subjunctive
que je lise
que tu lises
qu'il/elle/on lise
que nous lisions
que vous lisiez
qu'ils/elles lisent

Imperative
lis
lisons
lisez

manger *to eat*

past participle: **mangé** / present participle: **mangeant**

Like **manger** are **nager** *(to swim)*, **plonger** *(to dive)*, and **voyager** *(to travel)*

Present indicative
je mange
tu manges
il/elle/on mange
nous mangeons
vous mangez
ils/elles mangent

Future
je mangerai
tu mangeras
il/elle/on mangera
nous mangerons
vous mangerez
ils/elles mangeront

Imperfect
je mangeais
tu mangeais
il/elle/on mangeait
nous mangions
vous mangiez
ils/elles mangeaient

Conditional
je mangerais
tu mangerais
il/elle/on mangerait
nous mangerions
vous mangeriez
ils/elles mangeraient

Passé composé
j'ai mangé
tu as mangé
il/elle/on a mangé
nous avons mangé
vous avez mangé
ils/elles ont mangé

Present subjunctive
que je mange
que tu manges
qu'il/elle/on mange
que nous mangions
que vous mangiez
qu'ils/elles mangent

Passé simple
je mangeai
tu mangeas
il/elle/on mangea
nous mangeâmes
vous mangeâtes
ils/elles mangèrent

Imperative
mange
mangeons
mangez

mettre *to put; to put on*
past participle: **mis** / present participle: **mettant**

Like **mettre** are **admettre** *(to admit)*, **omettre** *(to omit)*, **permettre** *(to allow)*, and **promettre** *(to promise)*

Present indicative
je mets
tu mets
il/elle/on met
nous mettons
vous mettez
ils/elles mettent

Future
je mettrai
tu mettras
il/elle/on mettra
nous mettrons
vous mettrez
ils/elles mettront

Imperfect
je mettais
tu mettais
il/elle/on mettait
nous mettions
vous mettiez
ils/elles mettaient

Conditional
je mettrais
tu mettrais
il/elle/on mettrait
nous mettrions
vous mettriez
ils/elles mettraient

Passé composé
j'ai mis
tu as mis
il/elle/on a mis
nous avons mis
vous avez mis
ils/elles ont mis

Present subjunctive
que je mette
que tu mettes
qu'il/elle/on mette
que nous mettions
que vous mettiez
qu'ils/elles mettent

Passé simple
je mis
tu mis
il/elle/on mit
nous mîmes
vous mîtes
ils/elles mirent

Imperative
mets
mettons
mettez

mourir* *to die*

past participle: **mort** / present participle: **mourant**

Present indicative
je meurs
tu meurs
il/elle/on meurt
nous mourons
vous mourez
ils/elles meurent

Future
je mourrai
tu mourras
il/elle/on mourra
nous mourrons
vous mourrez
ils/elles mourront

Imperfect
je mourais
tu mourais
il/elle/on mourait
nous mourions
vous mouriez
ils/elles mouraient

Conditional
je mourrais
tu mourrais
il/elle/on mourrait
nous mourrions
vous mourriez
ils/elles mourraient

Passé composé
je suis mort(e)
tu es mort(e)
il/elle/on est mort(e)
nous sommes mort(e)s
vous êtes mort(e)(s)
ils/elles sont mort(e)s

Present subjunctive
que je meure
que tu meures
qu'il/elle/on meure
que nous mourions
que vous mouriez
qu'ils/elles meurent

Passé simple
je mourus
tu mourus
il/elle/on mourut
nous mourûmes
vous mourûtes
ils/elles moururent

Imperative
meurs
mourons
mourez

naître* *to be born*
past participle: **né(e)(s)** / present participle: **naissant**

Like **naître** is **renaître*** *(to be born again)*

Present indicative
je nais
tu nais
il/elle/on naît
nous naissons
vous naissez
ils/elles naissent

Future
je naîtrai
tu naîtras
il/elle/on naîtra
nous naîtrons
vous naîtrez
ils/elles naîtront

Imperfect
je naissais
tu naissais
il/elle/on naissait
nous naissions
vous naissiez
ils/elles naissaient

Conditional
je naîtrais
tu naîtrais
il/elle/on naîtrait
nous naîtrions
vous naîtriez
ils/elles naîtraient

Passé composé
je suis né(e)
tu es né(e)
il/elle/on est né(e)
nous sommes né(e)s
vous êtes né(e)(s)
ils/elles sont né(e)s

Present subjunctive
que je naisse
que tu naisses
qu'il/elle/on naisse
que nous naissions
que vous naissiez
qu'ils/elles naissent

Passé simple
je naquis
tu naquis
il/elle/on naquit
nous naquîmes
vous naquîtes
ils/elles naquirent

Imperative
nais
naissons
naissez

ouvrir *to open*
past participle: **ouvert** / present participle: **ouvrant**

Like **ouvrir** are **couvrir** (*to cover*), **découvrir** (*to discover*), **offrir** (*to offer, to give*), **souffrir** (*to suffer, to be ill*)

Present indicative
j'ouvre
tu ouvres
il/elle/on ouvre
nous ouvrons
vous ouvrez
ils/elles ouvrent

Imperfect
j'ouvrais
tu ouvrais
il/elle/on ouvrait
nous ouvrions
vous ouvriez
ils/elles ouvraient

Passé composé
j'ai ouvert
tu as ouvert
il/elle/on a ouvert
nous avons ouvert
vous avez ouvert
ils/elles ont ouvert

Passé simple
j'ouvris
tu ouvris
il/elle/on ouvrit
nous ouvrîmes
vous ouvrîtes
ils/elles ouvrirent

Future
j'ouvrirai
tu ouvriras
il/elle/on ouvrira
nous ouvrirons
vous ouvrirez
ils/elles ouvriront

Conditional
j'ouvrirais
tu ouvrirais
il/elle/on ouvrirait
nous ouvririons
vous ouvririez
ils/elles ouvriraient

Present subjunctive
que j'ouvre
que tu ouvres
qu'il/elle/on ouvre
que nous ouvrions
que vous ouvriez
qu'ils/elles ouvrent

Imperative
ouvre
ouvrons
ouvrez

partir* _to leave_
past participle: **parti(e)(s)** / present participle: **partant**

Like **partir** are **mentir** _(to tell a lie)_, **sentir** _(to feel, to smell)_, **se sentir*** _(to feel)_, **sortir*** _(to go out)._

Present indicative
je pars
tu pars
il/elle/on part
nous partons
vous partez
ils/elles partent

Imperfect
je partais
tu partais
il/elle/on partait
nous partions
vous partiez
ils/elles partaient

Passé composé
je suis parti(e)
tu es parti(e)
il/elle/on est parti(e)
nous sommes parti(e)s
vous êtes parti(e)(s)
ils/elles sont parti(e)s

Passé simple
je partis
tu partis
il/elle/on partit
nous partîmes
vous partîtes
ils/elles partirent

Future
je partirai
tu partiras
il/elle/on partira
nous partirons
vous partirez
ils/elles partiront

Conditional
je partirais
tu partirais
il/elle/on partirait
nous partirions
vous partiriez
ils/elles partiraient

Present subjunctive
que je parte
que tu partes
qu'il/elle/on parte
que nous partions
que vous partiez
qu'ils/elles partent

Imperative
pars
partons
partez

payer (see **essayer**)
peindre (see **teindre**)

plaire *to please, to be pleasing to*
past participle: **plu** / present participle: **plaisant**

Like **plaire** are **déplaire** *(to displease)*, **se taire*** *(to keep silent)*

Present indicative
je plais
tu plais
il/elle/on plaît
nous plaisons
vous plaisez
ils/elles plaisent

Future
je plairai
tu plairas
il/elle/on plaira
nous plairons
vous plairez
ils/elles plairont

Imperfect
je plaisais
tu plaisais
il/elle/on plaisait
nous plaisions
vous plaisiez
ils/elles plaisaient

Conditional
je plairais
tu plairais
il/elle/on plairait
nous plairions
vous plairiez
ils/elles plairaient

Passé composé
j'ai plu
tu as plu
il/elle/on a plu
nous avons plu
vous avez plu
ils/elles ont plu

Present subjunctive
que je plaise
que tu plaises
qu'il/elle/on plaise
que nous plaisions
que vous plaisiez
qu'ils/elles plaisent

Passé simple
je plus
tu plus
il/elle/on plut
nous plûmes
vous plûtes
ils/elles plurent

Imperative
plais
plaisons
plaisez

pleuvoir *to rain*

past participle: **plu** / present participle: **pleuvant**

Present indicative
il pleut

Future
il pleuvra

Imperfect
il pleuvait

Conditional
il pleuvrait

Passé composé
il a plu

Present subjunctive
qu'il pleuve

Passé simple
il plut

pouvoir *to be able to*

past participle: **pu** / present participle: **pouvant**

Present indicative
je peux
tu peux
il/elle/on peut
nous pouvons
vous pouvez
ils/elles peuvent

Imperfect
je pouvais
tu pouvais
il/elle/on pouvait
nous pouvions
vous pouviez
ils/elles pouvaient

Passé composé
j'ai pu
tu as pu
il/elle/on a pu
nous avons pu
vous avez pu
ils/elles ont pu

Passé simple
je pus
tu pus
il/elle/on put
nous pûmes
vous pûtes
ils/elles purent

Future
je pourrai
tu pourras
il/elle/on pourra
nous pourrons
vous pourrez
ils/elles pourront

Conditional
je pourrais
tu pourrais
il/elle/on pourrait
nous pourrions
vous pourriez
ils/elles pourraient

Present subjunctive
que je puisse
que tu puisses
qu'il/elle/on puisse
que nous puissions
que vous puissiez
qu'ils/elles puissent

préférer *to prefer*

past participle: **préféré** / present participle: **préférant**

Present indicative
je préfère
tu préfères
il/elle/on préfère
nous préférons
vous préférez
ils/elles préfèrent

Imperfect
je préférais
tu préférais
il/elle/on préférait
nous préférions
vous préfériez
ils/elles préféraient

Passé composé
j'ai préféré
tu as préféré
il/elle/on a préféré
nous avons préféré
vous avez préféré
ils/elles ont préféré

Passé simple
je préférai
tu préféras
il/elle/on préféra
nous préférâmes
vous préférâtes
ils/elles préférèrent

Future
je préférerai
tu préféreras
ils/elle/on préférera
nous préférerons
vous préférerez
ils/elles préféreront

Conditional
je préférerais
tu préférerais
il/elle/on préférerait
nous préférerions
vous préféreriez
ils/elles préféreraient

Present subjunctive
que je préfère
que tu préfères
qu'il/elle/on préfère
que nous préférions
que vous préfériez
qu'ils/elles préfèrent

Imperative
préfère
préférons
préférez

prendre *to take*

past participle: **pris** / present participle: **prenant**

Like **prendre** are **apprendre** *(to learn)*, **comprendre** *(to understand)*, and **surprendre** *(to surprise)*

Present indicative
je prends
tu prends
il/elle/on prend
nous prenons
vous prenez
ils/elles prennent

Future
je prendrai
tu prendras
il/elle/on prendra
nous prendrons
vous prendrez
ils/elles prendront

Imperfect
je prenais
tu prenais
il/elle/on prenait
nous prenions
vous preniez
ils/elles prenaient

Conditional
je prendrais
tu prendrais
il/elle/on prendrait
nous prendrions
vous prendriez
ils/elles prendraient

Passé composé
j'ai pris
tu as pris
il/elle/on a pris
nous avons pris
vous avez pris
ils/elles ont pris

Present subjunctive
que je prenne
que tu prennes
qu'il/elle/on prenne
que nous prenions
que vous preniez
qu'ils/elles prennent

Passé simple
je pris
tu pris
il/elle/on prit
nous prîmes
vous prîtes
ils/elles prirent

Imperative
prends
prenons
prenez

rendre *to give back, to make*
past participle: **rendu** / present participle: **rendant**

Like **rendre** are **défendre** *(to forbid)*, **descendre*** *(to go down, to get off)*, **perdre** *(to lose)*, **tondre** *(to mow)*, **vendre** *(to sell)*, and most verbs ending in **-re** except for **prendre** and its compounds.

Present indicative
je rends
tu rends
il/elle/on rend
nous rendons
vous rendez
ils/elles rendent

Future
je rendrai
tu rendras
il/elle/on rendra
nous rendrons
vous rendrez
ils/elles rendront

Imperfect
je rendais
tu rendais
il/elle/on rendait
nous rendions
vous rendiez
ils/elles rendaient

Conditional
je rendrais
tu rendrais
il/elle/on rendrait
nous rendrions
vous rendriez
ils/elles rendraient

Passé composé
j'ai rendu
tu as rendu
il/elle/on a rendu
nous avons rendu
vous avez rendu
ils/elles ont rendu

Present subjunctive
que je rende
que tu rendes
qu'il/elle/on rende
que nous rendions
que vous rendiez
qu'ils/elles rendent

Passé simple
je rendis
tu rendis
il/elle/on rendit
nous rendîmes
vous rendîtes
ils/elles rendirent

Imperative
rends
rendons
rendez

savoir *to know*

past participle: **su** / present participle: **sachant**

Present indicative
je sais
tu sais
il/elle/on sait
nous savons
vous savez
ils/elles savent

Future
je saurai
tu sauras
il/elle/on saura
nous saurons
vous saurez
ils/elles sauront

Imperfect
je savais
tu savais
il/elle/on savait
nous savions
vous saviez
ils/elles savaient

Conditional
je saurais
tu saurais
il/elle/on saurait
nous saurions
vous sauriez
ils/elles sauraient

Passé composé
j'ai su
tu as su
il/elle/on a su
nous avons su
vous avez su
ils/elles ont su

Present subjunctive
que je sache
que tu saches
qu'il/elle/on sache
que nous sachions
que vous sachiez
qu'ils/elles sachent

Passé simple
je sus
tu sus
il/elle/on sut
nous sûmes
vous sûtes
ils/elles surent

Imperative
sache
sachons
sachez

soutenir (see venir)

suivre *to follow; to take (a course)*
past participle: **suivi** / present participle: **suivant**

Like **suivre** is **poursuivre** *(to pursue)*

Present indicative
je suis
tu suis
il/elle/on suit
nous suivons
vous suivez
ils/elles suivent

Future
je suivrai
tu suivras
il/elle/on suivra
nous suivrons
vous suivrez
ils/elles suivront

Imperfect
je suivais
tu suivais
il/elle/on suivait
nous suivions
vous suiviez
ils/elles suivaient

Conditional
je suivrais
tu suivrais
il/elle/on suivrait
nous suivrions
vous suivriez
ils/elles suivraient

Passé composé
j'ai suivi
tu as suivi
il/elle/on a suivi
nous avons suivi
vous avez suivi
ils/elles ont suivi

Present subjunctive
que je suive
que tu suives
qu'il/elle/on suive
que nous suivions
que vous suiviez
qu'ils/elles suivent

Passé simple
je suivis
tu suivis
il/elle/on suivit
nous suivîmes
vous suivîtes
ils/elles suivirent

Imperative
suis
suivons
suivez

teindre *to dye*

past participle: **teint** / present participle: **teignant**

Like **teindre** are **atteindre** *(to reach)*, **craindre** *(to fear)*, **peindre** *(to paint)*, **plaindre** *(to feel sorry for)*

Present indicative
je teins
tu teins
il/elle/on teint
nous teignons
vous teignez
ils/elles teignent

Future
je teindrai
tu teindras
il/elle/on teindra
nous teindrons
vous teindrez
ils/elles teindront

Imperfect
je teignais
tu teignais
il/elle/on teignait
nous teignions
vous teigniez
ils/elles teignaient

Conditional
je teindrais
tu teindrais
il/elle/on teindrait
nous teindrions
vous teindriez
ils/elles teindraient

Passé composé
j'ai teint
tu as teint
il/elle/on a teint
nous avons teint
vous avez teint
ils/elles ont teint

Present subjunctive
que je teigne
que tu teignes
qu'il/elle/on teigne
que nous teignions
que vous teigniez
qu'ils/elles teignent

Passé simple
je teignis
tu teignis
il/elle/on teignit
nous teignîmes
vous teignîtes
ils/elles teignirent

Imperative
teins
teignons
teignez

venir* *to come*
past participle: **venu(e)(s)** / present participle: **venant**

Like **venir** are **devenir***(to become)*, **revenir*** *(to come back),* **se souvenir (de)***
(to remember), **soutenir** *(to support),* and **tenir** *(to hold).*

Present indicative
je viens
tu viens
il/elle/on vient
nous venons
vous venez
ils/elles viennent

Future
je viendrai
tu viendras
il/elle/on viendra
nous viendrons
vous viendrez
ils/elles viendront

Imperfect
je venais
tu venais
il/elle/on venait
nous venions
vous veniez
ils/elles venaient

Conditional
je viendrais
tu viendrais
il/elle/on viendrait
nous viendrions
vous viendriez
ils/elles viendraient

Passé composé
je suis venu(e)
tu es venu(e)
il/elle/on est venu(e)
nous sommes venu(e)s
vous êtes venu(e)(s)
ils/elles sont venu(e)s

Present subjunctive
que je vienne
que tu viennes
qu'il/elle/on vienne
que nous venions
que vous veniez
qu'ils/elles viennent

Passé simple
je vins
tu vins
il/elle/on vint
nous vînmes
vous vîntes
ils/elles vinrent

Imperative
viens
venons
venez

vivre *to live*

past participle: **vécu** / present participle: **vivant**

Like **vivre** is **revivre** *(to live again, revive)*

Present indicative
je vis
tu vis
il/elle/on vit
nous vivons
vous vivez
ils/elles vivent

Future
je vivrai
tu vivras
il/elle/on vivra
nous vivrons
vous vivrez
ils/elles vivront

Imperfect
je vivais
tu vivais
il/elle/on vivait
nous vivions
vous viviez
ils/elles vivaient

Conditional
je vivrais
tu vivrais
il/elle/on vivrait
nous vivrions
vous vivriez
ils/elles vivraient

Passé composé
j'ai vécu
tu as vécu
il/elle/on a vécu
nous avons vécu
vous avez vécu
ils/elles ont vécu

Present subjunctive
que je vive
que tu vives
qu'il/elle/on vive
que nous vivions
que vous viviez
qu'ils/elles vivent

Passé simple
je vécus
tu vécus
il/elle/on vécut
nous vécûmes
vous vécûtes
ils/elles vécurent

Imperative
vis
vivons
vivez

voir *to see*
past participle: **vu** / present participle: **voyant**

Like **voir** are **prévoir** (*to foresee*) and **revoir** (*to see again*)

Present indicative
je vois
tu vois
il/elle/on voit
nous voyons
vous voyez
ils/elles voient

Future
je verrai
tu verras
il/elle/on verra
nous verrons
vous verrez
ils/elles verront

Imperfect
je voyais
tu voyais
il/elle/on voyait
nous voyions
vous voyiez
ils/elles voyaient

Conditional
je verrais
tu verrais
il/elle/on verrait
nous verrions
vous verriez
ils/elles verraient

Passé composé
j'ai vu
tu as vu
il/elle/on a vu
nous avons vu
vous avez vu
ils/elles ont vu

Present subjunctive
que je voie
que tu voies
qu'il/elle/on voie
que nous voyions
que vous voyiez
qu'ils/elles voient

Passé simple
je vis
tu vis
il/elle/on vit
nous vîmes
vous vîtes
ils/elles virent

Imperative
vois
voyons
voyez

vouloir *to want, to wish*

past participle: **voulu** / present participle: **voulant**

Present indicative

je veux
tu veux
il/elle/on veut
nous voulons
vous voulez
ils/elles veulent

Imperfect

je voulais
tu voulais
il/elle/on voulait
nous voulions
vous vouliez
ils/elles voulaient

Passé composé

j'ai voulu
tu as voulu
il/elle/on a voulu
nous avons voulu
vous avez voulu
ils/elles ont voulu

Passé simple

je voulus
tu voulus
il/elle/on voulut
nous voulûmes
vous voulûtes
ils/elles voulurent

Future

je voudrai
tu voudras
il/elle/on voudra
nous voudrons
vous voudrez
ils/elles voudront

Conditional

je voudrais
tu voudrais
il/elle/on voudrait
nous voudrions
vous voudriez
ils/elles voudraient

Present subjunctive

que je veuille
que tu veuilles
qu'il/elle veuille
que nous voulions
que vous vouliez
qu'ils/elles veuillent

Imperative

veux (veuille)
voulons
voulez (veuillez)

Lexique français–anglais

This glossary contains French words and expressions, defined as they are used in the context of this book. Easily recognizable words are not included. The number in parentheses indicates the chapter or the part of the program in which the word appears: **pré** = **prélude; int** = **interlude; post** = **postlude; C** = *Cahier.*

The masculine form is given for all adjectives. When a masculine adjective ends in **-e,** the feminine form is the same. To form the feminine of regular adjectives, add an **-e** to the masculine. Irregular feminine endings or forms are given in parentheses.

The gender (*m.* or *f.*) is indicated for most nouns. Nouns that can be either masculine or feminine are indicated with *n.* If the masculine form ends in **-e,** the feminine form is the same. To form the feminine for those ending in a consonant, add an **-e** to the masculine. Other feminine endings or forms are given in parentheses.

The asterisk that precedes some nouns beginning with "h" indicates that articles are not elided with these words (*le héros,* not *l'héros,* for example); when an asterisk precedes an infinitive, there is no elision with the preceding vowel of the subject pronoun (je hante, par exemple).

Abbreviations

adj.	adjective	*fam.*	familiar	*n.*	noun
adv.	adverb	*inv.*	invariable	*prep.*	preposition
conj.	conjunction	*m.*	masculine	*pron.*	pronoun
f.	feminine	*pl.*	plural	*	aspirate h

A

abîmer to damage, spoil (1)

abonné *n.* subscriber (6)**; abonnement** *m.* subscription (2)

abord *m.* approach, access; **au premier abord** initially (2); **d'abord** *adv.* at first (3)

aboutir to end up (at) (in) (1)

abri *m.* shelter (6); **sans-abri** *n.* homeless person

abuser to exploit, take advantage of (6)

accéder (à) to reach (1)

accélérateur *m.* accelerator (4)

accès *m.* access, entry (1)

accessoire *m.* accessory (2)

s'accommoder to accept **(pré)**

accord *m.* agreement (9); **d'accord** okay; **être d'accord** to agree, be in agreement (1)

s'accorder to agree (9)

s'accoutumer to get used to (C8)

s'accrocher (à) to hang (on to); to be very determined (1)

accroissement *m.* increase (6)

accroître to increase (8)

accueil *m.* reception, welcome (3); **accueillant** *adj.* welcoming (3); **accueillir** to welcome, greet (3)

acharnement *m.* determination (1)

achat *m.* purchase (C2); **acheter** to buy

s'achever to finish, accomplish (1)

acquérir to acquire (2)

acteur (-trice) *n.* actor (actress) (5)

actif (-ive) *adj.* active (2); working; *n.* person in the workforce; **activement** *adv.* actively (9)

actualité *f.* current event (2); newsreel (6); **actuel (le)** *adj.* current (3)

acquérir acquire (9)

adhérer (à) to join (C9)

adjoint *n. & adj.* assistant, deputy (3)

admettre to admit, allow

adoptif (-ive) *adj.* adoptive, adopted (8)

s'adresser (à) to address; turn to (C9)

aérobic *m.* aerobics (2)

affaiblir to weaken (C2)

affaires *f. pl.* business (6); things, belongings (C5)

affectif (-ive) *adj.* emotional (8)

affectueux (-euse) *adj.* affectionate, loving (5)

afficher to display, advertise, post (2)

affligeant *adj.* pathetic (1)

affreux (-euse) *adj.* frightful, horrible (C5)

affronter to face, to confront (6)

afin de *prep.* in order to, so as to (1); **afin que** *conj.* in order that, so that (7)

agacer to annoy (C4)

agence *f.* agency (C2); **agence de voyages** travel agency (5)

agent de police *m.* policeman (4)

agir to act, behave (1); **s'agir de** to be about, be a question of (pré)

agneau *m.* lamb (C6)

aguets *m. pl.* **aux aguets** watchful (6)

aïeul *n.* **aïeux** *pl.* ancestor (C3)

aile *f.* wing (2)

ailleurs *adv.* elsewhere (1); **d'ailleurs** besides, moreover

aîné *adj.* older, oldest (C3)

air *m.* tune, air; **avoir l'air (de)** to look (like) (2); **en plein air** outdoors, in the open (5)

aisance *f.* ease (1)

aise *n. f. & adj.* ease, comfort; delighted, pleased (7), **se sentir à l'aise** to feel comfortable, at ease; **se sentir mal à l'aise** to feel uncomfortable

ajouter to add (9)

alcool *m.* alcohol (C2)

alcoolémie *f.* acohol level in the blood (4)

aléatoire *adj.* by chance, random (5)

alentours *m. pl.* the surrounding area (2)

allemand *adj., n..* German, German language (pré); **Allemand** *n.* German person (pré)

allonger to stretch out, lengthen (4)

allumer to turn on (2)

allure *f.* behavior, manner (3); looks, appearance

alors *adv.* then, so (C1)

alphabétisation *f.* literacy (3)

alpinisme *m.* mountaineering; **faire de l'alpinisme** to go mountain climbing (5)

amateur *inv.n. adj.* lover of (6); amateur

ambassade *f.* embassy (2)

âme *f.* soul (8)

améliorer to improve (C2)

aménagement *m.* planning, laying out (9)

amende *f.* ticket, fine; **amende pour excès de vitesse** speeding ticket (4)

s'amenuiser to diminish (9)

amer (amère) *adj.* bitter (9)

amérindien *adj.* native American (3); **Amérindien** *n.* native American person (3)

ami *n.* friend; **petit (e) ami (e)** boyfriend (girlfriend) (8)

amorcer to begin, undertake (9)

amour *m.* love (5)

amphithéâtre *m.* lecture hall (1)

amusant *adj.* funny (2); **s'amuser** to have fun, have a good time (3)

an *m.* year (1)

ancêtre *n.* ancestor (pré)

ancien (ne) *adj.* old, former (2)

âne *m.* donkey (4)

ange *m.* angel (C1)

angoissant *adj.* distressing, alarming (C7); **angoisse** *f.* anxiety, anguish (1); **s'angoisser** to become anxious (int. 1)

animer to liven up, rouse (1)

année *f.* year (pré)

annonce *f.* **publicitaire** advertisement (6)

antenne *f.* antenna (4); **antenne satellite** satellite dish (6)

antiquité *f.* antiquity (7)

antivol *m.* anti-theft device, lock (4)

antonyme *m.* antonym; word with opposite meaning

anxieux (-euse) *adj.* worried, anxious

apaiser to calm (2)

apercevoir to perceive, notice (5)

appartenir (à) to belong (to) (7)

appeler to call; **s'appeler** to be called, named (pré)

s'appliquer to apply oneself (5)

apporter to bring (9)

apprécier to appreciate (3)

apprendre to learn (pré)

apprentissage *m.* learning; **apprentissage précoce** learning in elementary school (pré)

s'apprêter (à) to get ready (to) (1)

approche *f.* approach (1); **approcher** to approach, draw near (3)

s'approprier to take over (C3)

appui *m.* support (1); **appuyer** to press (4); to support (1)

âpre *adj.* harsh (3)

après *prep.* after (1); **d'après** *prep.* according to (2)

arbre *m.* tree (3)

argent *m.* money (pré); silver (6); **argent de poche** pocket money, allowance (1)

argot *m.* slang (2)

armature *f.* framework (4)

arpenter to criss-cross (5)

arrêt *m.* stop (bus, trolley) (2); **s'arrêter (de)** to stop (from)

arrière *adv.* back (4); **à l'arrière** in the back (4)

arriéré *adj.* backwards (2)

arrière-train *m.* hindquarters (4)

arriver to arrive (3); to happen (5)

arrondir to round off, make round (4)

asile *m.* refuge, asylum (9)

aspirateur *m.* vacuum cleaner; **passer l'aspirateur** to vacuum (8)

aspirer to drink, suck up (C7)

s'asseoir to sit (2)

assez *adv.* enough; **en avoir assez de** to be fed up with

assimilé *adj.* assimilated (2)

assister (à) to be present, attend (1)

associer to associate (3)

assorti *adj.* matching (2); **bien (mal) assorti** to go well (badly) with (2)

assourdissant *adj.* deafening (6)

assurance *f.* insurance (4); **assurer** to assure, guarantee (3)

astiquer to polish (**int. 1**)

atelier *m.* textile mill; workshop; artist's studio (3)

atout *m.* advantage, trump card (2)

s'attarder to linger (8)

atteindre to reach, attain (5)

attendre to wait (for); **s'attendre (à)** to expect (7)

attente *f.* wait; expectation (6)

attention *f.* attention; **faire attention (à)** to pay attention (to) (C1)

atterrer to dismay, appall (4)

atterrir to land (airplane, ship) (5)

attester to prove, demonstrate (9)

attirer to attract, draw (1)

attrayant *adj.* attractive, pleasant (6)

attribuer to assign (1)

aube *f.* dawn, daybreak (1)

auberge *f.* inn; **auberge de jeunesse** youth hostel (5)

aucun *adj. & pron.* no one, none (6)

audacieux (-euse) *adj.* bold, daring (3)

augmentation *f.* increase (C9); **augmenter** to increase (C9)

aujourd'hui *adv.* today, nowadays (**pré**)

auparavant *prep.* formerly (C3)

auprès de *prep.* close to, near (C5)

aussi *adv.* also (**pré**); **aussi (bien) que** as (well) as (C1)

aussitôt que *conj.* as soon as (9)

autant *adv.* as much (2); **d'autant que** all the more so since (9)

autocar *m.* bus (3)

automatisme *m.* reflex (9)

autonomie *f.* autonomy, self-sufficiency (2)

autoritaire *adj.* authoritarian (8)

autoroute *f.* interstate (C9)

auto-stop *m.* hitchhiking (5)

autour *adv.* around (8)

autre *adj. & pron.* other (1); **autrement** *adv.* otherwise, differently (5)

autrefois *adv.* in the past, formerly (3)

autruche *f.* ostrich (8)

avaler to swallow (**pré**)

avancement *m.* promotion (C2)

avant (de) *prep.* before (**pré**)

avantageux (-euse) *adj.* advantageous (9)

avec *prep.* with (**pré**)

avenir *m.* future (1)

s'aventurer to venture (C3)

avertissement *m.* warning (6)

aveu *m.* confession (6)

s'avilir to lower oneself, debase oneself (6)

avion *m.* airplane (2)

avis *m.* opinion; **à mon avis** in my opinion (1)

avocat (e) *n.* lawyer (5)

avoir to have; **avoir besoin (de)** to need (3); **avoir mal (à)** to hurt (C1); **avoir peur (de)** to be afraid (of) (7)

avouer to admit

B

bachelier (-ère) *n.* person who has passed the baccalauréat (1)

bachoter *fam.* to cram; **faire du bachotage** *fam.* to cram (1)

bafouiller to stammer, mumble (6)

bagarrer to argue, fight (1)

bagnole *f. fam.* car (4)

baie *f.* bay (5)

baignade *f.* swimming, bathing (5); **se baigner** to swim, bathe (5)

bail *m.* lease (9)

baiser *m.* kiss (C1)

baisse *f.* decrease (C9); **baisser** to decrease, lower (6)

bal *m.* ball, dance (C6)

balade *f.* stroll, short walk (5)

balancer to swing, go back and forth (C2); to send (away) (9)

ballerine *f.* ballet slipper (2)

balnéaire *adj.* seaside (5)

banc *m.* bench (6)

bande *f.* gang (2); tape; **bande annonce** *f.* preview, trailer (6); **bande dessinée** comic strip (1); **bande sonore** sound track (6)

banderole *f.* banner, advertising streamer (1)

banlieue *f.* public housing area (2); suburb (4); **banlieusard** *n.* person who lives in public housing project (2); suburbanite

banque *f.* bank; **banque de données** data bank (2)

barbe *f.* beard (2)

barème *m.* scale (4)

barge *adj. fam.* crazy, wacky (2)

barre de torsion *f.* torsion bar (4)

barrière *f.* fence, barrier (4)

bas *m.* stocking; **bas résille** fishnet stocking (2)

basket *f.* basketball shoe (2)

bataille *f.* battle (5)

bâtard *adj.* weak, adulterated (**pré**)

bateau *m.* boat (3); **faire du bateau** to go boating (5)

bâtir to build (7)

batterie *f.* battery; drums; **batterie à plat** dead battery (4)

(se) battre to fight, beat up (9); **battu** *adj.* beaten, well-used (5)

bavard *adj. & n.* talkative (C2); talkative person (8)

bavure *f.* smudge, smear (1)

beau (bel, beaux, belle, belles) *adj.* handsome, beautiful (2); **beauté** *f.* beauty (2)

beau-père *m.* stepfather; father-in-law (8)

bec *m.* kiss (Québec) (**pré**)

belle-mère *f.* stepmother; mother-in-law (8)

bénévolat *m.* volunteer work (9); **bénévole** *n.* volunteer (3); **bénévolement** *adv.* without being paid (2)

berceau *m.* cradle (8)

berger (-ère) *n.* shepherd (shepherdess) (6); **berger allemand** German shepherd (**pré**)

besoin *m.* need (9); **avoir besoin (de)** to need (3)

bête *adj.* silly, stupid (2)

beur *adj. fam.* born in France of North African parents (2); **Beur** *n. m.*, **Beurette** *n. f.* person born in France of North African parents

biche *f.* doe (3)

bien *adv.* well; **bien sûr** of course (C1); **bien** *m.* good (7); **biens** *pl.* goods, property (2) **bien que** *conj.* although (7)

bien-être *m.* well-being (4)

bienvenue *f.* welcome; **souhaiter la bienvenue** to welcome (C3)

bijou *m.* piece of jewelry; **bijoux de fantaisie** costume jewelry (2)

bilan *m.* balance sheet (4); **bilan carbone** carbon footprint (4)

billet *m.* ticket; paper money (3)

bio *adj.* organic (9); **biocarburant** *m.* biofuel (9)

bise *f. fam.* kiss (**pré**)

blague *f.* joke (4)

blâmer to blame (2)

blanc (blanche) *adj.* white (2); **blanc** *m.* blank (C1); **examen blanc** practice test (1)

blanchir to wash (laundry) (8)

blé *f.* wheat (9)

blême *adj.* pale, sick-looking (2)

blesser to wound (6)

blocage *m.* mental block (1); **faire un blocage** to freeze up (1)

bloqué *adj.* blocked, obstructed (4)

blouson *m.* jacket (2); **blouson en cuir** leather jacket (2)

bobine *f.* reel (of film) (C6)

bœuf *m.* ox (7)

boire to drink (7)

bois *m.* wood (6)

boîte *f.* box (7); **boîte automatique** automatic transmission (4)

bol *m. fam. argot* luck (5)

bombarder to bombard (1)

bon(ne) *adj.* good

bondé *adj.* crowded, crammed (4)

bonheur *m.* happiness (C1)

bonnet *m.* cap, hat (C5)

bordeaux *adj. inv.* wine-colored (2)

border to border, run alongside (1)

borne *f.* terminal, marker; **borne de recharge** electric terminal (for recharging car batteries) (4)

bosser *fam.* to study hard (1); to work (3); **bosseur (-euse)** *n.* hard-working student (1)

botte *f.* boot (2)

bouchon *m.* traffic jam (4)

boucle *f.* ring; **boucle d'oreille** earring (2)

boue *f.* mud (C4)

bouffe *f. fam.* food (2); **bouffer** *fam.* to eat (5)

bouger to move, to be lively (2)

bouleverser to upset, distress (6)

boulot *m. fam.* work, job, task (1)

bouquin *m. fam.* book

bourgeois *n. & adj.* upper middle class; middle class person (C3)

bourlinguer *fam.* to travel around (1)

bourrer to stuff (1); **se bourrer le crâne** *fam.* to stuff your head (1)

bourse *f.* scholarship (1); **boursier (-ière)** *n.* person with a scholarship

bousiller *fam.* to wreck, to ruin (9)

bout *m.* bit, piece; **à tout bout de champ** all the time (**pré**); **au bout de** at the end of (7); **venir à bout de** to overcome (7)

bouteille *f.* bottle (C3)

boutique *f.* shop, boutique (2)

boutonner to button (up) (1)

bracelet *m.* bracelet (2)

branché *adj.* in the know, up-to-date (2); **brancher** to plug in, connect (4)

break *m.* station wagon (4)

bref (brève) *adj.* brief, short (2)

breveter to patent (6)

bricolage *m.* do-it-yourself project; **bricoler** to do odd jobs, tinker (5)

bride *f.* bridle (7)

brièvement *adv.* briefly (2)

brigand *m.* robber (C5)

brillant *adj.* brilliant (C2); shiny

broche *f.* brooch (6)

bronzage *m.* tanning (5); **bronzer** to tan (5)

brosse à dents *f.* toothbrush (3)

brouillon *m.* rough draft

broyer to grind, crush (5)

bruit *m.* noise (3); **bruyant** *adj.* noisy (1)

brûler to burn (3); **brûler un feu rouge** to run a red light (4)

brumisateur *m.* spray (5)

brut *adj.* uncut, rough, natural (2)

bûcher *fam.* to study hard (1)

bûcheron *m.* woodcutter (7)

bulletin *m.* report card (1)

bureau *m.* desk (**pré**); office (3)

busqué *adj.* hooked (2)

but *m.* goal, purpose (3)

C

cabane *f.* cabin; **cabane à sucre** maple sugaring cabin (**pré**)

câble *m.* cable; **télévision par câble** cable TV (6)

cabriolet *m.* convertible (4)

(se)cacher to hide (oneself) (3)

cadeau *m.* gift

cadet(te) *adj.* younger, youngest (8)

caisse *f.* chest, box (4); checkout (store) (C7)

caleçon *m.* boxer shorts (8) **calmer** to calm (someone) down; **se calmer** to calm down (8)

calotte polaire *f* polar ice cap (9)

calvaire *m.* suffering (6)

camarade *n.* friend; **camarade de chambre** roommate (8)

caméra *f.* movie camera (2)

caméscope *m.* video camera (6)

camion *m.* truck (3)

campagne *f.* country(side); open country (5); campaign (C-int. 2)

camping *m.* campground; **faire du camping** to go camping (5)

canard *m.* duck (**pré**)

cancre *m.* bad student, dunce (1)

candidature *f.* application; **poser sa candidature** to apply for a position (3)

caniche *m.* poodle (**pré**)

canicule *f.* heatwave, dog days of summer (5)

canne *f.* cane, walking stick (6)

canoë *m.* canoe; **faire du canoë** to go canoeing (5)

canon *m.* model, perfect example (**int. 1**)

canot *m.* dinghy; **canot de sauvetage** lifeboat (6)

canotier *m.* boater (hat) (8)

capot *m.* car hood (4)

capsuler to put a top on (a bottle) (6)

car *m.* bus (3)

car *conj.* because (1); for

caractère *m.* nature, character; **caractère gras** boldface

caravane *f.* travel trailer (5)

caresser to pet, caress (3)

carré *adj.* square (2)

carrefour *m.* intersection (4)

carrière *f.* career, profession

carrosse *m.* coach, carriage (C7)

carton *m.* cardboard (box) (3)

cas *m.* case

casque *m.* helmet (4); **Casques bleus** UN Peacekeeping Troops (C9)

casquette *f.* cap (2)

casser to break (5)

caste *f.* group (2)

cauchemar *m.* nightmare (7)

cavaler to be on the go (**int. 1**)

cavalier (-ière) *n.* horseback rider (4)

céder to give up, give in, give way to (8)

ceinture *f.* belt (3); **ceinture de sécurité** seat belt (4)

célèbre *adj.* famous (2)

célibataire *adj.* unwed (8)

celui (ceux, celle, celles) *pron.* the one(s), this one, that one, these, those (8)

cendre *f.* ash (8); **cendrier** *m.* ashtray (**pré**)

censé *adj.* supposed to (5)

centrale nucléaire *f.* nuclear power plant (9)

cercle *m.* circle; group (8)

cerise *f.* cherry (1); **cerisier** *m.* cherry tree (4)

cesser (de) to stop (5); **sans cesse** continually, constantly, relentlessly (2)

chacun(e) *pron.* each, each one, everyone (9)

chaîne *f.* chain; channel (6)

chair *f.* flesh (7)

chaise *f.* chair (C1)

chalet *m.* small wooden vacation house (mountains) (5)

chaleur *f.* heat (C4); **chaleureux (-euse)** *adj.* cordial, friendly (C2)

chambre *f.* bedroom (C1)

chameau *m.* camel (5)

champ *m.* field (3)

chance *f.* luck, possibility, opportunity (C2)

chanceler to stagger, totter (6)

changement *m.* change (1)

chanson *f.* song **(pré)**

chant *m.* singing (C2); song; **chanter** to sing (2); **chanteur (-euse)** *n.* singer (2)

chantier *m.* construction site (1)

chapeau *m.* hat (2)

chaque *adj.* each, every **(pré)**

charbon *m.* coal (9)

charge *f.* cost (for utilities, etc.) (8); **prendre en charge** to take care of (1)

charger to fill, load (3)

charme *m.* magic spell (7)

charte *f.* charter (4)

chasse *f.* hunting; **aller à la chasse** to go hunting (5); **chasser** to hunt, chase away **(post)**

chauffeur *m.* driver (4)

chaussée *f.* pavement, street (4)

chaussette *f.* sock

chaussure *f.* shoe, footwear (2)

chauve *adj.* bald (2)

chef *m.* leader, head (2); **chef d'Etat** head of state (C3)

chemin *m.* road, path (3); **cheminer** to go one's way (6)

chemise *f.* shirt (2); **chemisier** *m.* blouse (2)

cher (chère) *adj.* expensive, dear (1)

chercher to look for **(pré)**

chétif (-ive) *adj.* puny, scrawny (7)

cheval *m.* horse (4)

chevalerie *f.* knighthood (7); **chevalier** *m.* knight (7)

chevelu *adj.* long-haired, hairy (2)

cheveux *m. pl.* hair (2)

chèvre *f.* goat (3)

chez *prep.* at, to (the house, family, business, etc.) **(pré)**

chiant *adj. fam.* extremely annoying (2)

chic *adj.* stylish (2)

chiffre *m.* number (1)

chinois *adj.* Chinese (C8); **Chinois** *n.* Chinese (C8)

chirurgien(ne) surgeon (C3)

choisir to choose **(pré)**; **choix** *m.* choice (1)

chômage *m.* unemployment (2); **taux de chômage** unemployment rate (3); **chômeur (-euse)** *n.* unemployed person (3)

choquant *adj.* shocking, offensive (2)

choucroute *f.* sauerkraut **(pré)**

chute *f.* fall (6); **chuter** to fall down

cibler to target, aim for **(pré)**

ci-dessous *adv.* below (2)

ci-dessus *adv.* above (2)

ciel *m.* sky (6)

cigale *f.* cricket, cicada (7)

cinéma *m.* movies, movie theatre **(pré)**

cinéphile *n.* movie buff (6)

circulation *f.* traffic (4)

cité *f.* dormitory (1); urban neigborhood (2)

citoyen (-nne) *n.* citizen (9)

citrouille *f.* pumpkin (C6)

civil *n. & adj.* civil; civilian (9); **état civil** *m.* marital status (C5)

clair *adj.* light (2); clear, obvious (7)

classe *f.* **d'âge** age group, age cohort (1)

clé, clef *f.* key (2)

clignotant *m.* turn signal, car blinker (4)

cloison *f.* partition (6)

clouer to nail, attach (8)

cochon *m.* pig **(pré)**

cocotier *m.* coconut palm (C5)

code *m.* rule, code; **code de la route** rules of the road (4)

cœur *m.* heart; **par cœur** by heart, memorized (1)

coffre *m.* car trunk (4)

coffret *m.* small chest, box (C5)

coi (coite) *adj.:* **rester coi** to remain silent (6)

coiffé *adj.* (hair) styled (2); **(se) coiffer** to style (one's) hair (2); wear on one's head (8)

coin *m.* corner **(pré)**

coincé *adj. fam.* uptight (2); **coincer** to wedge, catch (6)

colère *f.* anger **(pré)**

collège *m.* middle school (1)

coller to stick to, glue **(pré)**; **coller au...** *fam.* to shove up your ... (8)

collier *m.* necklace (2)

collision *f.* collision; **entrer en collision avec** to run into, collide (4)

colocataire *n.* person with whom a house or apartment is shared (8)

colonie *f.* colony (6); **colonie de vacances** camp (for children) (5)

combat *m.* fighting, hostilities (C3)

combien (de) *adv.* how many, how much (1)

combustible *m.* fuel (9)

commander to command, give orders (3)

comme *adv.* like, as, how (3)

commencer to start (1)

comment *adv.* how (3)

commerce *m.* trade, business (C9); **commerce equitable** fair trade (9)

commercial *adj.* business (3)

commissariat *m.* **de police** police station (in town) (4)

communauté *f.* community (9)
comparable (à) comparable (to) (C8)
complément *m.* object (grammar) (1)
complet (-ète) *adj.* complete, entire, full (2)
complicité *f.* bond, closeness, emotional tie (8)
comportement *m.* behavior; **comporter** to include (6), **se comporter** to behave
composer to compose, make up; dial (phone); **se composer de** to consist of, be composed of
compréhensif (-ive) *adj.* understanding, kind (4); **comprendre** to understand; to include; **se comprendre** to understand one another (8)
compte *m.* account (8); **prendre en compte** to take into account (2); **compter** to count (1); **compter** + *infinitif* to plan, mean (to do)
con(ne) *n. fam.* stupid person (1) **(int. 1)**; **connerie** *f. fam.* stupidity **(int.2)**
concevoir to conceive, create (9)
concours *m.* competitive exam (1)
concret (-ète) *adj.* concrete (2)
concubinage *m.* unmarried people living together (8)
concurrence *f.* competition (6); **concurrent** *n.* competitor (9)
se consacrer (à) to devote oneself (to) (2)
à condition de (que) *prep. (conj.)* provided that (7)
condoléances *f. pl.* condolences (3)
conducteur (-rice) *n.* driver (4); **conduire** to drive (4); **se conduire** to behave, to conduct oneself (2); **examen de conduite** *f.* driving test (4)
conférence *f.* lecture (1)
confiance *f.* trust; **faire confiance (à)** to trust in (8); **confier** to confide, trust (C5)
confirmer to confirm (C4)
confondre to confuse (1)
confort *m.* comfort (4); **confortable** *adj.* comfortable (clothing, furniture, house) (2)
confus *adj.* confused, embarrassed, muddled (2); **confusément** *adv.* confusedly (2)
congé *m.* leave, vacation (5)
congénère *n.* peer, someone alike (2)
conjoint *n.* spouse **(int. 1)**; **conjointement** *adv.* jointly (9)
connaître to know; **faire la connaissance (de)** to meet **(pré)**; **connu** *adj.* known (7)
conquête *f.* conquest (5)
consacrer to devote (6)
consanguin *adj.* related by blood **(int. 1)**
consciencieux (-euse) *adj.* conscientious (C2)
conseil *m.* advice (1); **conseiller (-ère)** *n.* advisor, counselor (9)
consentir to consent (7)

consommer to use, consume (4)
constamment *adv.* constantly (2)
construire to build (C9)
contact *m.* starter (car) (4); **mettre le contact** to switch on the ignition (4)
conte *m.* story, tale; **conte de fées** fairy tale (7)
contemporain *n. & adj.* contemporary (1)
contenir to contain (5)
content *adj.* happy (3); **contenter** to make happy, to satisfy (C7)
contenu *m.* content (C1)
continu *adj.* continuous (4)
contrainte *f.* restriction (8)
contraire *m.* opposite; **au contraire** on the contrary (1)
contrat *m.* contract; **contrat à durée déterminée (CDD)** fixed term employment contract (3); **contrat à durée indéterminée (CDI)** permanent position (3)
contravention *f.* traffic ticket, fine (mostly for parking) (4)
contre *prep.* against (3)
contredire to contradict (C4)
contrevenant *m.* person receiving a traffic ticket (4)
contrôle *m.* test (1); traffic stop by the police (4); **contrôler** to check, inspect (9)
convaincre to convince (4)
convenable *adj.* appropriate (C1); **convenir** to fit, be suitable (C1)
convenu *adj.* conventional, agreed upon (9)
convoi *m.* convoy, procession; **convoi de cirque** circus convoy (4)
copain (copine) *n.* friend; boyfriend (girlfriend) (8)
copie *f.* sheet of paper, exercise (1); copy
coq *m.* rooster **(pré)**; **passer/sauter du coq-à-l'âne** change the subject abruptly **(pré)**
coquillage *m.* shell (4)
cornac *m.* elephant trainer (4)
corne *f.* horn (animal) (C7)
correspondre to tally, agree, correspond (7)
corrompre to corrupt (9)
corvée *f.* onerous task, burden, chore (8)
costaud *adj.* robust, sturdy (2)
costume *m.* man's suit (2)
côte *f.* coast (1)
côté *m.* side; **à côté de** *prep.* next to (5)
couche *f.* layer; **couche d'ozone** ozone layer (9)
se coucher to go to bed, sleep (C1); **coucher à la belle étoile** sleep out in the open; **coucher sous la tente** to sleep in a tent (5)
coude *m.* elbow (9)
couler to sink (6); to flow (4)

couleur *f.* color (C2)

couloir *m.* hallway (2)

coup *m.* hit, blow; **coup de sifflet** whistle blast (4); **coup de soleil** sunburn (5); **coup de veine** stroke of luck (1); **tout à coup** all of a sudden (3)

couplet *m.* verse

cour *f.* yard, courtyard (3); **faire la cour (à)** to court, woo (7)

couramment *adv.* fluently (C3)

courant *adj.* everyday, standard (2); *m.* electricity (4); **courant** *m.* **d'air** draft (4)

courriel *m.* e-mail (C-**int. 2**)

courrier *m.* mail (7)

courir to run (3)

cours *m.* course; **au cours de** during (4); **cours magistral** lecture course (1)

course *f.* race; shopping errand; **course aux armements** arms race (9); **faire les courses** to run errands; go shopping (8)

court *adj.* short (2)

couscous *m.* North African dish, made with semolina, vegetables, etc.

coût *m.* cost (4); **coût de la vie** cost of living

couteau *m.* knife (6)

coûter to cost (4); **coûteux (-euse)** *adj.* costly

couvert *m.* place, place setting (8); *adj.* covered

couvrir to cover (1)

covoiturage *m.* carpooling (4); **covoiturer** to carpool (4); **covoitureur (-euse)** *n.* person who carpools

craindre to fear (7); **crainte** *f.* fear

crâne *m.* skull (2); **crâne d'œuf** egghead, brainy (1)

cravate *f.* necktie (2)

crédit *m.* funding (1)

crête *f.* comb (of rooster); crest; spiked hair (2)

crétin *m.* imbecile (**int. 1**)

crever to burst, die *fam.* (7); **pneu crevé** flat tire (4)

crier to shout, yell (8)

croire to believe (7)

croiser to cruise, cross (5); **croisière** *f.* cruise (5)

croissance *f.* growth (9); **croissant** *adj.* increasing, growing (4)

croyant *n. & adj.* believer in God, person who practices their religion (2)

cruauté *f.* cruelty (6)

crudité *f.* coarseness, crudeness (6)

cueillette *f.* picking (**pré**); **cueillir** to gather, pick (C7)

cuillère *f.* spoon (**post**)

cuir *m.* leather (2)

cuisine *f.* kitchen; cooking; **faire la cuisine** to cook (8)

cul *m. fam.* backside, rear end (**pré**)

culot *m.* daring, nerve (4)

cultiver to cultivate, farm (3); **se cultiver** to improve one's mind (5)

culture *f.* land under cultivation (4); culture

curé *m.* priest, curate (C9)

cursus *m.* curriculum (1)

cycle *m.* cycle, years for a degree (1)

cypriote *adj.* from the island of Cyprus (2)

D

d'abord *adv.* at first (3)

d'accord okay; **être d'accord** to agree, be in agreement (1)

dame *f.* lady (7)

davantage *adv.* more (**pré**)

se débarrasser (de) to get rid of (4)

déborder to overflow (8)

débourser to pay out (8)

debout *adj.* upright, standing (1)

débrancher to unplug, disconnect

débrayer to let out the clutch (4)

débrouillard *adj.* able, resourceful (2); **se débrouiller** to manage, get along (1)

début *m.* beginning; **au début** in the beginning (3); **débutant** *n. adj.* beginner, novice (4)

décalage *m.* gap, interval; **décalage horaire** jet lag (5)

décapotable *f.* convertible (4)

décennie *f.* decade (9)

déchet *m.* trash, refuse (9); **déchetterie déchèterie** *f.* recycling center (9)

(se) déchirer to tear (up) (apart) (3)

décider to decide, determine (3)

décliner to enumerate (9)

déconcertant *adj.* disconcerting (C4)

décontracté *adj.* relaxed, laid-back (2); **décontraction** *f.* laid-back attitude (1)

décor *m.* set (6)

décousu *adj.* disjointed, disconnected (8)

découvrir to discover (4)

décret *m.* decree, ruling (4)

décrire to describe (**pré**); **(se) décrisper** to relax (5); defuse

décrocher to take down (2); to unhook, pick up (telephone) (1); to land, get (job, prize) *fam.*

dedans *adv.* inside (7)

défaite *f.* defeat (9)

défavorisé *adj.* underprivileged (C9)

défendre to forbid, prohibit (7)

défi *m.* challenge (C9)

dégager to bring out, extract (1)
dégoûter to disgust (6)
dégueulasse *adj. fam.* disgusting (2)
déguiser to disguise (6)
dehors *adv.* out, outside **(pré)**
déjà *adv.* already **(pré)**
délavé *adj.* faded (2)
délivrer to set free; to rescue (C7)
délocaliser to outsource (9)
demander to ask; **se demander** to wonder (C2)
démarche *f.* step (9)
démarrer to start off (4)
déménager to move, move out (8)
demi-frère *m.* stepbrother; half-brother (8)
demi-sœur *f.* stepsister; half-sister (8)
démission *f.* resignation (from a job) (1)
démodé *adj.* out-of-style (2)
demoiselle *f.* young lady (7); **demoiselle d'honneur** lady in waiting (7)
dénouement *m.* ending, conclusion (6)
dent *f.* tooth (C4)
dépanner to repair (4); **dépanneuse** *f.* tow truck (4)
départ *m.* departure (3)
dépasser to go past, pass (4)
se dépayser to get a change of scenery (5)
dépeindre to depict (5)
dépendre (de) to depend (on) (9)
dépens *m. pl.* (legal) costs; **aux dépens de** at the expense of (C2)
dépenser to spend
déplacé *n. & adj.* displaced (person) (9); **déplacement** *m.* travel (C5)
déplaire to displease, offend **(pré)**
dépliant *m.* leaflet, brochure (5); **déplier** to unfold (C6)
déposer to put down, place, drop off (3)
dépourvu (de) *adj.* deprived, lacking (7)
déprimant *adj.* depressing (C6)
depuis *prep.* since, for (1)
déraper to skid (4)
dérisoire *adj.* pathetic; laughable; insignificant (3)
dérive *f.* drift (9)
se dérober to run away from (7)
déroulement *m.* development, unfolding; **se dérouler** to unfold, develop (2)
derrière *adv.* behind (3)
dès *prep.* from; **dès lors** from that time onwards (5); **dès que** as soon as (1)
désastre *m.* disaster (9)
descendre to go down, take down (3)
désespérer to despair, lose hope (6); **désespérément** *adv.* hopelessly (6)

(se) déshabiller to undress (oneself) (C1)
désolé *adj.* distressed; sorry; unhappy (3)
désormais *adv.* from now on (2); from then on
dessin *m.* drawing (1)
dessous *adv.* under (2)
dessus *adv.* above (2); *prep.* above, beyond (1); **par-dessus** *adv.* over, in addition (C3)
se détendre to relax, unwind (5); **détente** *f.* relaxation (5)
détenir to hold, have in one's possession (1)
détester to hate, detest (1)
détourner to divert, twist (4)
détrôner to oust, supplant (6)
deux-chevaux (2 CV) *f.* a car that used to be made by Citroën, originally with a two horsepower engine (4)
devant *prep.* before, in front of (3); *m.* front (4)
devanture *f.* display, store window (1)
développement durable *m.* sustainable development (9)
devenir to become (C2)
deviner to guess; **devinette** *f.* riddle
devoir to have to; to owe (C1); *m.* duty; **devoirs** *pl.* homework (1)
diable *m.* devil (7)
dieu *m.* god; **Dieu** God
difficile *adj.* difficult; **difficile à vivre** hard to get along with (8)
diffuser to broadcast (6); **diffusion** *f.* broadcasting (6)
digne *adj.* worthy (1)
dire to say; **c'est-à-dire** in other words, that is to say
direction *f.* steering (4), management
directives *f. pl.* rules of conduct, directives (4)
dirigeant *n.* person in authority (C9)
discernement *m.* judgement (1)
discutailler *fam.* to discuss, to argue in vain (6)
disparaître to disappear (7); **disparu** *adj.* gone; dead (7)
disponible *adj.* available (4)
disposer (de) to have at one's disposal (5)
dispute *f.* quarrel (1); **se disputer** to argue (8)
disque *m.* record **(post)**; **disque compact** compact disc (C1)
dissertation *f.* essay, paper (for a course) (1)
distinguer to distinguish (C8); **se distinguer** to stand out, be noticeably different (2)
distraire to entertain; **distrait** *adj.* absent-minded (C1)
divergence *f.* divergence, difference (7)
se divertir to amuse oneself, enjoy oneself (5)

divorcer (de/d'avec) to divorce (someone) (8)

djellaba *f.* traditional Moroccan robe with long sleeves and hood (**int. 1**)

dodo *m. fam.* sleep, nap (5); **fais dodo** *m.* (*cajun*) party for dancing

domestique *n.* servant, domestic; *adj.* **les travaux domestiques** domestic, household work (3)

dommage *m.* harm; **c'est dommage** what a shame! (2)

donc *conj.* therefore, so (5)

données *f. pl.* data (2)

donner to give (3); **donner sur** to open onto, look onto, face (5)

dont *pron.* whose; of whom/which; from whom/which; about whom/which

dormir to sleep (1)

dossier *m.* file; student record (1)

doter to endow (**post**)

doubler to double (3); to pass, overtake (car) (4); to dub (film) (6)

doucement *adv.* gently, quietly (3); **douceur** *f.* gentleness, softness (4); **doux (douce)** *adj.* sweet, soft, gentle (2)

douer to endow (C7)

douleur *f.* pain, suffering, grief (7)

douter to doubt (7); **douteux (-euse)** *adj.* doubtful, dubious, uncertain (7)

dresser to draw up (4)

droit *m.* right, *as in:* I have the right to …; law (2); **droits d'inscription** tuition, registration fees (1); *adj.* straight (2)

droite *f.* right *direction* (5)

drôle *adj.* funny

dur *adj.* hard (2)

durée *f.* length of time (6); **durer** to last, continue (6)

dynamique *adj.* dynamic (2)

E

eau *f.* water (3)

ébahir to amaze, dazzle (8)

ébats *m. pl.* frolics, movements; **prendre ses ébats** to frolic (4)

éblouir to dazzle (5)

éboueur *m.* trash collector (9)

ébouriffé *adj.* uncombed (2)

s'écarter to go away from, deviate from (4)

échafaudage *m.* scaffolding (3)

échantillon *m.* sample (2)

s'échapper to escape (3)

écharpe *f.* scarf (C2)

échec *m.* failure (2)

échouer (à) to fail (1)

éclair *m.* flash of light (8); **éclairage** *m.* lighting (6); **éclairer** to light up (6)

éclat *m.* burst, excitement (9)

éclatant *adj.* dazzling (6)

éclater to burst out, explode (4); **une famille éclatée** a broken family (8)

école *f.* school (**pré**); **école maternelle** pre-school; **école primaire** elementary school (1)

écolier (-ère) *n.* elementary school pupil (1)

écoute *f.* listening time, viewing time (6); **écouter** to listen to; **écouteurs** *m. pl.* earphones

écran *m.* screen (6)

écraser to run over, crush (2)

écrevisse *f.* crayfish (**post**)

écrire to write

écureuil *m.* squirrel (7)

effacer to erase (**pré**)

effectivement *adv.* effectively, in actuality (5)

effectuer to carry out (2)

effet *m.* effect; **effets spéciaux** special effects (6); **effet de serre** greenhouse effect (9)

efficacité *f.* efficiency (2)

effort *m.* effort, endeavor (5)

effrayant *adj.* terrifying (C7); **effrayer** to frighten (4)

égal *adj.* equal; **également** *adv.* equally; as well (7)

égard *m.* regard (6)

église *f.* church

élastique *m.* rubber band (3)

élégamment *adv.* elegantly (2)

élève *n.* elementary or secondary school student (1)

s'éloigner to distance, move away (3)

s'embarquer to embark upon; get on board (5)

embauche *f.* hiring (8); **embaucher** to hire (3)

embellir to embellish, make prettier (C2)

embêter to annoy (8)

embouteillage *m.* traffic jam (4)

embrasser to embrace, kiss, hug; **s'embrasser** to embrace (kiss) each other (8)

émettre to send, put out (6); **émission** *f.* television (radio) program (6)

emménager to move in (house, apartment, room) (8)

emmener to take someone, lead (someone) (4)

émouvoir to touch emotionally; affect (3)

empanaché *adj.* plumed (8)

empêcher to prevent

emplacement *m.* site, placement (C2)

emploi *m.* job (3)

empoisonné *adj.* poisoned (C7)

emporter to take, win over, conquer (4)

emprunter to borrow (2)

en *prep.* in; to; of

encastrer to embed, fit flush, recess (6)

enchaînement *m.* series, sequence (C6);
enchaîner to move on (5)

enchanter to enchant (7)

encore again; still; **pas encore** not yet (pré)

encombrant *n. & adj.* unwieldy, bulky (object) (9)

(s')encombrer to burden (oneself) with (int. 1)

endormi *adj.* asleep (2); **s'endormir** to fall
asleep (1)

endroit *m.* place (3)

énerver to irritate; **s'énerver** to get excited, get
worked up (C-pré)

enfance *f.* childhood (2); **enfant** *m./f.* child;
enfant adopté adopted child (8); **enfant
unique** only child

enfer *m.* hell (8)

enfin *adv.* finally

s'enfler to swell (7)

engagement *m.* dedication (2); agreement,
enlistment, commitment (9); **engager** to
hire (3); **s'engager** to commit oneself to;
engagé *adj.* (politically) committed (2)

engrais *m.* fertilizer (9)

(s') engueuler *fam.* to yell at (each other) (8)

enlaidir to make ugly (8)

enlever to take off (5)

ennemi *n. & adj.* enemy (9)

ennui *m.* boredom; anxiety (2); **ennuyer** to bore,
annoy; **s'ennuyer** to be bored (1); **ennuyeux
(-euse)** *adj.* boring

énormément *adv.* tremendously (2)

enregistrement *m.* recording (pré); **enregistrer** to
record (C2)

enseignant *n.* teacher (1);
enseignement *m.* education (pré)

ensemble *adv.* together; **ensemble** *m.* set;
development (housing); whole (1)

ensorceler to cast a spell, bewitch (7)

ensuite *adv.* next, then (3)

entamer to start, begin (5)

entendre to hear (1); **entendre par** to mean,
intend; **s'entendre (avec)** to get along (with) (8);
entente *f.* understanding, harmony (8)

enterrer to bury (9)

en-tête *m.* heading (6)

entourer to surround, care for (8)

entraide *f.* mutual help (8)

entrailles *f.* guts (int. 1)

entre *prep.* between (1)

entreprendre to undertake (C3);
entreprise *f.* business, company (pré)

entretenir to chat with, converse (C3); to
maintain, keep up; **entretien** *m.* interview (3);
maintenance, upkeep (4)

envahir to invade (9)

envers *prep.* toward

envie *f.* desire; **avoir envie (de)** to want; **envieux
(-euse)** *adj.* envious (7)

environ *adv.* around, about (1)

envisager to envisage, imagine (C3)

envol *m.* flight, take off (8)

envoyer to send (3)

éolien(ne) *adj.* referring to the wind; *n. f.*
(electric) windmill (9)

épais(se) *adj.* thick (2)

épave *f.* wreck (ship) (C5)

épine *f.* spine, thorn (C7)

éponger to wipe up, mop up (9)

époque *f.* age, time (3)

épouser to wed, marry (7)

épouvantable *adj.* dreadful, horrible (9);
épouvante *f.* terror (6); **film
d'épouvante** horror movie (6)

épreuve *f.* test, examination (1); challenge (7);
éprouver to experience (5)

équipe *f.* team; **équiper** to outfit (5)

équitable *adj.* fair (8)

équitation *f.* horseback riding (5)

érable *m.* maple (pré)

errer to wander (3)

escalader to climb, scale (5)

escale *f.* stop (for boat) (5)

escalier *m.* staircase, stairs (3)

escargot *m.* snail (pré)

esclavage *m.* slavery (3)

escroc *m.* crook, swindler (int. 1)

espace *m.* space

espérer to hope (2); **espoir** *m.* hope (5)

espionnage *m.* spying, espionage (6)

esprit *m.* spirit (C2); **état d'esprit** state of
mind (6)

esquisser to sketch (2)

essayer to try

essence *f.* gasoline (4)

essuie-glace *m.* windshield wiper (4)

estimer to consider, esteem

s'établir to establish oneself, settle, take hold (9);
établissement *m.* establishment, institution (1)

état *m.* state (post); **état civil** *m.* civil (marital)
status (C5)

Etats-Unis *m. pl.* United States

été *m.* summer (pré)

éteindre to turn off (TV, lights) (2)

s'étendre to stretch oneself out, expand (7)

ethnie *f.* ethnic group (3)

étoile *f.* star (C3)

étonner to surprise, astonish (3)

étouffer to stifle, suffocate (8)

étranger (-ère) *n. & adj.* foreigner; foreign (3)

étroit *adj.* narrow

étude *f.* study (1); **étudiant (e)** *n.* university student (1)

s'évader to escape (C4)

évaluer to evaluate (1)

éveil *m.* alertness (6); **éveiller** to awaken; **s'éveiller** to wake up (9); **éveillé** *adj.* awake, alert (2)

événement *m.* event (6)

éventuellement *adv.* possibly (1)

évident *adj.* obvious (7)

éviter to avoid (2)

évoluer to evolve, change (2)

examen *m.* exam; **examen blanc** practice test (1)

exécrable *adj.* horrendous (5)

exécuter to carry out (an order) (5)

exercer to exert (5); to pursue, practice (a profession) (6)

exigeant *adj.* demanding (1); **exigence** *f.* demand, requirement (6); **exiger** to demand, require (8)

exotique *adj.* exotic, foreign (2)

expérience *f.* experiment (C6); experience

s'exprimer to express oneself (C2)

s'extasier sur to go into ecstasies **(pré)**

F

fabricant *n.* manufacturer (4)

fabuleux (-euse) *adj.* from a fable, imaginary (C7)

face à *prep.* facing, in light of (5)

fâcher to anger; **se fâcher (avec)** to get angry (at) (1)

facile *adj.* easy; **facile à vivre** easy to get along with (8)

facilité *f.* ease (1); **faciliter** to facilitate (1)

façon *f.* way, manner (1)

facture *f.* bill (C1)

fac(ulté) *f.* faculty, college, school within a university (1); **faculté de droit** law school (1); **faculté de lettres** college, school of humanities (1); **faculté de médecine** medical school (1)

faible *adj.* weak (C2)

faillir + *infinitif* to almost …

faillite *f.* bankruptcy; **faire faillite** to go bankrupt (3)

faim *f.* hunger; **avoir faim** to be hungry (3)

faire to do, make **(pré)**; **faire (la) grève** to go on strike; **faire la cour (à)** to court, woo (7); **faire la grasse matinée** to sleep in, sleep late (5) **faire le plein** to fill up the gas tank (4); **faire peur (à)** to frighten (7); **faire semblant (de)** to pretend (7); **faire une demande** to apply (3) **se faire du souci** to worry (about) (8)

fait *m.* fact; **en fait** in fact (1)

falloir to be necessary; **il faut** it is necessary

familial (familiaux, familiale, familiales) *adj.* family (life, ties, etc.) (2)

famille *f.* family; **famille monoparentale** single parent family (8); **famille recomposée** blended family (8)

(se) familiariser (avec) to become familiar (with) (1)

fan(atique) *n.* fan; fanatic (5)

fantastique *adj.* fantastic, uncanny (rare); *n.* fantasy; **film fantastique** science fiction movie (6)

fantôme *m.* ghost (7)

farine *f.* flour; **farines animales** bone meal (9)

fatal *adj.* fatal; fated (2)

fatiguer to tire (8)

se faufiler to dodge in and out of (C4)

faute *f.* mistake, error **(pré)**

fauteuil *m.* armchair (2); **fauteuil roulant** wheelchair (2)

fauve *adj.* fawn-colored; wild (8)

faux (fausse) *adj.* false, wrong (2)

favori (-te) *adj.* favorite, preferred (2)

fécondité *f.* fertility **(int. 1)**

fée *f.* fairy; **bonne fée** fairy godmother (7); **conte de fées** fairy tale (7)

félicitations *f. pl.* congratulations (1)

femme au foyer *f.* housewife (8) ; **femme d'affaires** *f.* businesswoman

fenêtre *f.* window (5)

fermer to close, shut **(pré)**

fête *f.* party, holiday, festival, celebration (5); **fêter** to celebrate (C2)

feu *m.* traffic light (4); fire

feuille *f.* sheet of paper (1); leaf

feuilleton *m.* TV series; soap opera (6)

fève *f.* bean (C7)

fiche *f.* note card, file card; **fiche de lecture** notes on a reading (1)

fidèle *adj.* faithful (C7); **fidélité** *f.* faithfulness (2)

fier (fière) *adj.* proud (5); **fierté** *f.* pride (C2)

figer to set; to stiffen, congeal (6)

figurant *n.* extra, walk-on **(int. 1)**

fil *m.* thread (5); wire (6)

filiation *f.* descent (8)

filière *f.* area of concentration (1)

film *m.* **d'actualité** newsreel (6)

fin *adj.* fine, subtle (2)

fin *f.* end (C1); **mettre fin à** to end (C1)

final *adj.* final (2); **finalement** *adv.* finally (9)

financier (-ère) *adj.* financial (8); **financièrement** *adv.* financially (8)

finir to finish (1)

flacon *m.* bottle (4)

flanc *m.* side (6)

fléchir to weaken, give way (8)

fleur *f.* flower (C5); **fleurir** to bloom (9)

flic *m. fam.* cop (4)

flipper *fam.* to freak out (8)

flux *m.* flood, flow (6)

fois *f.* time, instance; **il était une fois** once upon a time (7); **à la fois** at the same time (8)

follement *adv.* madly, wildly (2)

foncé *adj.* dark (color) (C5)

foncer to go for, charge (1)

foncier *m.* land (9)

fonctionnaire *n.* government employee (C9)

fond *m.* bottom; essence (1); **fonds** *m.* fund (9)

fonder to start, set up (business, family) (C2)

fondouc *m.* warehouse, market; inn (in Arab countries) (3)

fondre to melt (9)

force *f.* strength; **force est de** + *infinitif* to have no choice (4)

forêt *f.* forest (3)

formation *f.* training, education (1)

formulaire *m.* form, application (3)

formule *f.* formula (C8)

fort *adj.* strong (1)

fou (fol, fous, folle, folles) *adj.* crazy, insane (2)

foulard *m.* headscarf (**int. 1**)

foule *f.* crowd (5)

fourneau *m.* stove, oven (8)

fournir to supply, furnish (C9)

fourrière *f.* car pound (4)

fourrure *f.* fur (7)

foyer *m.* hearth; home; residence, hostel (3); household (5)

frais (fraîche) *adj.* cool; fresh (2)

frais *m. pl.* expenses (1)

franc (franche) *adj.* honest, open (2); **franchement** *adv.* openly, honestly (4)

franchir to cross (4)

francophone *n. & adj.* native French, native French speaker (3)

frange *f.* fringe (2)

frapper to knock (8)

fredonner to hum (4)

frein *m.* brake (4); **freiner** to brake (4)

fréquenter to frequent, go around with, spend time with (1)

fret *m.* freight (4)

friperie *f.* second-hand clothing store

frisé *adj.* frizzy, curly (2); **friser** to curl (C2)

froid *m.* cold (3)

fromage *m.* cheese (**pré**)

frontière *f.* border (9)

frotter to rub (7); **frottoir** *m.* washboard (**post**)

fruit *m.* fruit; **fruits de mer** seafood (C5)

fuir to flee, run away from (1)

funèbre *adj.* funeral (6)

funérailles *f. pl.* funeral service (6)

fuser to burst forth (6)

G

gâcher to spoil (6)

gagner to earn; to win (1); **gagner sa vie** to earn a living (3)

gai *adj.* happy (5)

galette *f.* round flat cake (8)

gamin *n.* child (**int. 1**)

gant *m.* glove (C4)

garagiste *m.* garage mechanic (C2)

garantir to guarantee (1)

garder to keep, protect (3); **garder la ligne** to stay thin (5); **en garde à vue** in police custody (4)

gare *f.* train station (5)

(se) garer to park (4)

garniture *f.* fittings, trimmings (C4)

gaspillage *m.* waste (4); **gaspiller** to waste (9); **gaspilleur** (**-euse**) *adj.* wasteful (4)

gâteau *m.* cake (1)

gauche *f.* left (5)

gazon *m.* lawn; **tondre le gazon** to mow the lawn (8)

géant *n. & adj.* giant (7)

geler to freeze (5)

gencive *f.* gum (mouth) (**pré**)

gendarme *m.* policeman (state patrol) (4); **gendarmerie** *f.* police station, police (in the country) (4)

gêne *f.* discomfort, embarrassment; **gêner** to bother, annoy, embarrass (1)

génial *adj.* great, terrific, awesome (1)

génie *m.* genius

genre *m.* style, manner (5)

gens *m. pl.* people (3)

gentil(le) *adj.* nice (2); **gentiment** *adv.* nicely, kindly (2)

gercer to chap, crack (3)

gestion *f.* management (2); **gestionnaire** *adj.* managing (9)

geste *m.* gesture, motion (6)

gifle *f.* slap (in the face) (4)

gîte *f.* lodging, shelter (9)

gomme *f.* **à la ...** pathetic; worthless *fam.* (**int. 2**)

gorgée *f.* sip, swallow (**pré**)

gosse *n.* kid (2)

goût *m.* taste; **goûter** to taste (1)

grâce à thanks to (1)

grain *m.* seed, grain (7)

grandir to grow up (1); to get bigger/taller

graphique *m.* graph, chart

gras(se) *adj.* fat (2); **faire la grasse matinée** to sleep in, sleep late (5)

gratuitement *adv.* without pay, free of charge (3)

grave *adj.* serious; **gravement** *adv.* seriously (3)

grec (grecque) *adj.* Greek (2); **Grec (Grecque)** *n.* Greek (2)

grenouille *f.* frog (7)

grève *f.* strike (2); **faire (la) grève** to go on strike (3)

griffe *f.* claw (C7)

grincheux (-euse) *adj.* grumpy (2)

gronder to scold (6)

gros(se) *adj.* big, fat (2)

groupe *m.* group; band (musical) (2)

gueuler to yell at, shout (2); **gueule de bois** hangover (int. 2)

guère *adv.* not much, a little (7); **ne... guère** scarcely

guérir to heal (7)

guerre *f.* war (9); **guerre civile** civil war; **guerre froide** Cold War (9); **guerrier (-ère)** *n.* soldier, warrior (3)

guichet *m.* ticket window (6)

guignol *m.* puppet show (int. 1)

H

habillement *m.* dress, clothing (C2)

habit *m.* outfit, clothes (2)

habitant *n.* resident; local person (5); inhabitant; **habiter** to live (8)

habitude *f.* habit, custom (C9); **s'habituer à** to get used to (1)

*haie *f.* hedge (9)

*haine *f.* hate, hatred (int. 1)

*hanche *f.* hip (3)

*hanter to haunt (7)

*hasard *m.* chance; **par hasard** by chance (C4); ***hasardeux (-euse)** *adj.* risky, dangerous (9)

*hausse *f.* increase (C9)

*haut *adj.* high, tall (5); ***hauteur** *f.* height (C5)

hebdomadaire *adj.* weekly (6)

*héros (héroïne) *n.* hero (heroine) (7)

heure *f.* hour; **heures de permanence** office hours (1); **à l'heure** on time; **heure de pointe** rush hour (4)

heureux (-euse) *adj.* happy (2); **heureusement** *adv.* fortunately (2)

hier *adv.* yesterday (3)

hiver *m.* winter (3)

HLM *m.* (**habitation** *f.* **à loyer modéré**) low income housing (2)

homme *m.* man; **homme d'affaires** businessman; **homme de passage** drifter (3)

*honte *f.* shame (4)

horaire *m.* schedule (1)

*hors *adv.* except, beyond, outside of; **hors de soi** beside oneself (with anger, emotion, etc.) (6)

hôtesse *f.* hostess (C5)

*houspiller to argue, fight (6)

huile *f.* oil (C4)

humeur *f.* temperament; mood; **de bonne (mauvaise) humeur** in a good (bad) mood (8); **donner de l'humeur (à)** put in a bad mood (8)

*hurler to scream, shriek (4)

I

ignorer to not know (2)

île *f.* island (5)

illettré *adj./n.* illiterate (person) (1)

illusoire *adj.* illusory (C8)

illustre *adj.* famous, illustrious (C4)

il n'y a pas de quoi you're welcome (C4)

image *f.* image, likeness, picture (3); **imaginer** to imagine; **s'imaginer** to imagine oneself (being, doing) (7)

immeuble *m.* building (3)

immigré *n. & adj.* immigrant (3)

impatient *adj.* impatient; **être impatient de** to be eager to, looking forward to (1)

imperméable *m.* raincoat (2); *adj.* waterproof

imperturbable *adj.* unshakeable, unmoved (6)

impliquer to imply

impoli *adj.* impolite, rude (2)

importer to matter; **n'importe qui** anybody; **n'importe quel(le)** any (C3)

impressionner to impress (C5)

imprévu *adj.* unexpected

inachevé *adj.* incomplete, unfinished (6)

inattendu *adj.* unexpected (7)

inciter to encourage (1)

inconnu *adj.* unknown (1)

inconvénient *m.* disadvantage, drawback (1)

incrédule *adj.* incredulous (1)

incroyable *adj.* unbelievable (4)

indéfectible *adj.* indestructible (5)

indiquer to indicate (1)

individu *m.* individual (person) (8)

inégal *adj.* unequal, unfair (C3)

inexplicable *adj.* unexplainable, inexplicable (C7)

inférieur *adj.* lower; inferior (3)

informations *f. pl.* news (6)

informatique *f.* computer science (4)

ingénieur *m.* engineer (int. 2)

inhospitalier (-ère) *adj.* inhospitable (C5)
s'initier to start to learn (5)
inondation *f.* flood (6)
inquiet (-ète) *adj.* worried (2); **s'inquiéter** to worry (1)
s'inscrire to register (1)
insensible *adj.* insensitive (2)
insister to insist (7)
inspirer to inspire; **s'inspirer (de)** to be inspired by (2)
s'installer to move in, set up (9); to settle
instituteur (-trice) *n.* elementary school teacher (1)
instruire to educate (1)
intégration *f.* integration (3); **intégrer** to integrate (3); **s'intégrer** to integrate oneself (C2)
intention *f.* intention; **avoir l'intention de** to intend to (1)
interdiction *f.* ban (what is forbidden) (4); **interdire** to forbid
intéresser to interest; **s'intéresser à** to be interested in (C-pré)
intérim *m.* temporary work (3), **faire de l'intérim** to temp (3)
intérieur *m. & adj.* inside (2)
interne *n.* (medical) residency, intern (medical); (C9); **interner** to put in a psychiatric hospital (4)
interro(gation) *f. (fam.)* test, quiz (1); **interroger** to question
interrompre to interrupt (1)
intervenir to participate (in class) (1)
intimité *f.* intimacy, privacy (8)
intrigue *f.* plot (6)
intrus *m.* intruder (2)
inverse *m.* opposite (9); **inversion** *f.* reversal, inversion (2)
investir to invest (C9); **investissement** *m.* investment (C4)
irrespectueux (-euse) *adj.* disrespectful (1)
isolant *adj.* isolating (C5)
issu *adj.* stemming from (7)

J

jais noir *adj.* jet-black (8)
jaloux (-ouse) *adj.* jealous (C7)
jamais *adv.* ever, never; **ne... jamais** never (6)
japonais *adj.* person Japanese (pré); **Japonais** *n.* Japanese (pré)
jardin *m.* garden (C1)
jaune *adj.* yellow (2); **jauni** *adj.* yellowed (1)
jean *m.* jeans; **jean délavé** faded jeans (2)
jeter to throw (1); to throw out; **jeter un sort (à)** to cast a spell (on) (7)
jeu *m.* set (of keys) (C4); game; **jeu d'acteur** acting (C6); **jeu télévisé** game show (6); **jeu vidéo** computer game, video game (1)

jeune *adj.* young (2); **jeunesse** *f.* youth (3)
je vous en prie you're welcome (C4)
joli *adj.* pretty (2)
joue *f.* cheek (C2)
jouer to play (1); **jouet** *m.* toy (3)
joufflu *adj.* fat-cheeked (2), jowly
jumeau (jumelle) *n.* twin (C1)
journal *m.* newspaper, diary (pré); **journal télévisé** news on TV (6)
jupe *f.* skirt (2)
jusqu'à *prep.* up to, until (C1); **jusqu'à ce que** *conj.* until (7)
juste *adv.* only, just (3); fair (8)

K

khâgne *f.* post-high school preparatory course for the **Grandes Écoles**
kif-kif *fam.* makes no difference (1); **kiffer** to love; to enjoy
klaxon *m.* horn (vehicle) (C4); **klaxonner** to honk (4)

L

là-bas over there (2)
laid *adj.* ugly (2)
laine *f.* wool (3)
laisser to leave; to let, allow
lait *m.* milk (pré)
lancer to launch, put out (pré); to throw
langue *f.* language; **langue maternelle** first language (pré)
laqué *adj.* lacquered (8)
large *adj.* wide
larme *f.* tear (3)
se lasser to become tired (3)
lave-linge *m.* washing machine (C8); **lave-vaisselle** *m.* dishwasher
lazzi *m.* jeer, gibe, taunt (6)
lèche-vitrine *m.* window-shopping; **faire du lèche-vitrine** to go window-shopping (2)
lecteur (-trice) *n.* reader; **lecteur DVD** DVD player (6); **lecture** *f.* reading (1)
léger (-ère) *adj.* light (4)
lendemain *m.* next day, following day (9)
lent *adj.* slow (2); **lentement** *adv.* slowly (2)
lessive *f.* laundry (8); **faire la lessive** to do the laundry (8)
lettre *f.* letter (3) **lettre de candidature** application letter; **lettres** *f. pl.* humanities (1)
se lever to get up
levier *m.* **de changement de vitesse** gearshift (4)
lèvre *f.* lip (2)

libre *adj.*   free (3); **union libre**   cohabitation (8)

licencier   to lay off, dismiss (3)

licorne *f.*   unicorn (7)

lien *m.*   tie, bond (**pré**); **lier**   to bind, tie, fasten (3)

lieu *m.*   place; **au lieu de**   instead of (1)

lieue *f.*   (= 4 kilomètres)   league (C6)

limite *f.*   edge, limit (1)

linge *m.*   underwear (3); linen, washing (8)

lire   to read

lisser   to smooth (6)

lit *m.*   bed (3)

livrer   to deliver, send (7)

location *f.*   rental (5)

loger   to live (in a house, hotel, etc.) (5); put up, house (9)

loi *f.*   law (**post**)

loin (de) *prep.*   far (from) (C1); **lointain** *adj.*   far away (3)

long (longue) *adj.*   long (2); **à la longue**   in the long run (6); **longueur** *f.*   length

longtemps *adv.*   a long time (3)

lors de *adv.*   at the time of, during (1)

lorsque *conj.*   (at the moment) when (5)

lot *m.*   prize, lot (2); **gros lot**   jackpot (lottery) (5)

louer   to rent (8)

loukoum *m.*   Turkish delight (candy) (**int. 1**)

loup *m.*   wolf (7); **loup-garou** *m.*   werewolf (7)

loupe *f.*   magnifying glass

lourd *adj.*   heavy (1)

loyal *adj.*   loyal, faithful (2)

loyer *m.*   rent (8); **loyer modéré**   low income (rent)

lueur *f.*   light (6)

luge *f.*   sled, toboggan (5)

lumière *f.*   light (3)

lune *f.*   moon; **être dans la lune**   to daydream (C7); **lune de miel**   honeymoon (2); **pleine lune**   full moon (C7)

lunettes *f. pl.*   glasses, spectacles

lutin *m.*   elf (7)

lutte *f.*   fight, struggle (C3); **lutter**   to fight (4)

lycée *m.*   high school (1)

M

machine à écrire *f.*   typewriter (C3)

maçon *m.*   stone mason (C3)

maghrébin *n. & adj.*   North African (3)

magie *f.*   magic; **magie noire**   black magic (7)

magret *m.*   **de canard**   fillet of duck (**pré**)

maigre *adj.*   skinny (2)

maillot de bain *m.*   swimsuit (2)

maintenant *adv.*   now

maintenir   to maintain, keep (6); **les forces de maintien de la paix**   peacekeeping forces (9)

maire *m.*   mayor; **mairie** *f.*   city hall (9)

mais *conj.*   but (**pré**)

maison *f.*   house (3); **maison de campagne**   country house (5)

maître (maîtresse) *n.*   elementary school teacher (1); virtuoso (6); master (7); mistress

maîtrise *f.*   mastery; MA degree (1); **maîtrise de soi**   self-control

majeur *adj.*   of legal age (2)

mal *adv.*   badly (3); **mal** *m.*   evil (7); **avoir le mal de mer**   to be seasick (5); **avoir le mal du pays**   to be homesick (3); **avoir mal**   to hurt (C1)

malade *adj.*   sick, ill; *n.*   sick person (3); **maladie** *f.*   sickness, illness (3)

maladroit *adj.*   clumsy (2)

malédiction *f.*   curse (7)

malgré *prep.*   in spite of (4)

malheur *m.*   misfortune (5); **malheureux (-euse)** *adj.*   unhappy; unfortunate (C2)

malicieux (-euse) *adj.*   mischievous (2)

malin (maligne) *adj.*   smart, shrewd, clever (2)

maltraiter   to mistreat (C3)

manche *f.*   sleeve; **la Manche**   the English Channel (5)

manger   to eat (3)

maniable *adj.*   easy to handle (4)

manif(estation) *f.* (*fam.*)   demonstration, protest march (**pré**); **manifester**   to protest (2); **se manifester**   to make oneself noticed (1)

manque *m.*   lack, shortage of (4)

manquer   to miss (3)

manteau *m.*   coat, cloak (2)

maquillage *m.*   make-up (2); **se maquiller**   to put on make-up (2)

marâtre *f.*   wicked stepmother (7)

marchand *n.*   storekeeper, merchant (6); **marchandise** *f.*   merchandise (4)

marche *f.*   walking (4); **marcher**   to walk; to function, work (4); **marcheur (-euse)** *n.*   person who walks (4)

marché *m.*   market (3); **bon marché**   inexpensive (1); **marché aux puces**   flea market

marge *f.*   margin, border (6)

mari *m.*   husband (3)

marier   to marry; **se marier (avec)**   to get married (to) (1)

marquant *adj.*   striking, outstanding (6)

marque *f.*   brand name (**pré**); **marquer**   to record, mark (8)

marre *adv.:* **en avoir marre**   to be fed up with (**int. 2**)

marron *m.*   chestnut; *adj. inv.*   brown (2)

maternel(le) *adj.*   maternal; **langue maternelle**   first language (**pré**)

mater *fam.* to ogle (**int. 2**)

matière *f.* subject matter (1); (school) course (1); material

maudire to curse (**pré**)

mauvais *adj.* bad, poor

mec *m. fam.* guy (2)

méchanceté *f.* wickedness, hardness (3); **méchant** *adj.* spiteful, wicked

méconnaître to underrate; ignore; not recognize (1)

mécontent *adj.* dissatisfied (C8); **mécontentement** *m.* displeasure (2)

médecin *m.* doctor (5); **médicament** *m.* medication, medicine (C5); **faculté de médecine** medical school (1)

se méfier de to be suspicious, distrust (9)

meilleur *adj.* better (1)

mêler to mix

mélo(drame) *m.* soap opera (6)

même *adj.* same (1); even (2)

ménage *m.* household; **faire le ménage** to do housework (8)

mendier to beg (3)

mener to lead, take (C3)

mensonge *m.* lie, untruth (C6)

mensuel *adj.* monthly

menteur (-euse) *adj.* lying (2); *n.* liar; **mentir** to lie (9)

menu *adj.* small, minor (8)

mépriser to scorn, look down on (C4)

mer *f.* sea, ocean (3)

merguez *f.* a North African lamb sausage (**int. 1**)

méridional *adj.* southern, from the Midi (5)

merveilleux (-euse) *adj.* wonderful; *m.* supernatural (7)

messagerie *f.* voice mail

métier *m.* trade, job (3)

mettre to put (on); **mettre le contact** to switch on the ignition (4); **mettre fin à** to end (C1); **mettre en relief** to call attention to (C8); **se mettre d'accord** to come to an agreement (1)

meuble *m.* (piece of) furniture (C4)

Midi *m.* South of France (C3)

mieux *adv.* better (1)

milieu *m.* surroundings (1), middle; **au milieu (de)** in the center of (4)

militant(e) *n.* activist (9)

mimique *f.* gesticulations (6)

mince *adj.* slender (2)

mine *f.* appearance; **faire mine** to pretend

minet *m.* pretty boy (2)

minoritaire *adj.* of a minority (5)

missel *m.* missal, book for Mass (8)

mitaine *f.* mitten, glove (6)

mitigé *adj.* mixed, moderate (4)

mixte *adj.* co-ed (for schools) (1)

mobylette *f.* moped

mode *f.* fashion; **à la mode** in fashion (**pré**)

moindre *adj.* least (2)

moins *adv.* less (2); **à moins de** *prep.*, **à moins que** *conj.* unless (7)

moitié *f.* half (1)

moment *m.* moment, a while; **au moment où** at the moment when (7)

monde *m.* world (3); **tout le monde** everybody (2)

moniteur (-trice) *n.* instructor (sports); counselor; supervisor (5)

monnaie *f.* currency, change (C9)

monoparental *adj.* single-parent (8)

monospace *m.* minivan (4)

montagne *f.* mountain (C1)

montant *m.* sum, amount

monter to go up (C9)

montrer to show (3)

se moquer (de) to make fun (of); **moqueur (-euse)** *adj.* mocking, making fun of (2)

morale *f.* moral

morceau *m.* piece, part (6)

mortel *adj.* extraordinary *fam.* (2); fatal

mot *m.* word; **mot apparenté** cognate (2)

motard *m.* motorcyclist; motorcycle policeman (4)

moteur *m.* engine, motor (4)

motoneige *f.* snowmobile (5)

mou (mol, mous, molle, molles) *adj.* soft, limp (2)

mouche *f.* fly (7)

mouchoir *m.* handkerchief (1)

moudre to grind (8)

moule *f.* mussel (C5)

mourir to die (3)

mousseux (-euse) *adj.* sparkling (8)

moustache *f.* mustache (2)

moyen(ne) *adj.* average (2); **moyenne** *f.* average (1); **moyens** *m. pl.* financial means

Moyen-Orient *m.* Middle East (C9)

muet(te) *adj.* silent, mute (6)

munir to equip, furnish (9)

mur *m.* wall (1)

museau *m.* snout, muzzle (**pré**)

N

nager to swim (5)

naïf (naïve) *adj.* naive (6)

nain *n. & adj.* dwarf (7); **nain de jardin** garden gnome (6)

naissance *f.* birth (8)

naître to be born (2)

narrateur (-rice) n. narrator (3)

natal adj. native (2)

natalité: taux (m.) de natalité birth rate (8)

natation f. swimming; faire de la natation to go swimming (5)

natte f. braid (2); nattes africaines cornrows (2)

naval adj. naval, nautical (2)

néanmoins adv. nevertheless (1)

neige f. snow (7)

net(te) adj. clean (2)

neuf (neuve) adj. brand-new (4)

nez m. nose (2)

ni... ni... neither ... nor (6)

nid m. nest (8)

nier to deny

n'importe quel(le) any, any ... whatever (C3); n'importe qui anybody

niveau m. level (1); niveau de vie standard of living

nœud m. crux (of the plot) (6); knot

noir adj. black (5)

nombreux (-euse) adj. numerous; famille nombreuse large family (8)

nombril m. navel, belly-button (2)

note f. grade; note (1)

noter to give a grade (1)

nourrir to feed; se nourrir to eat (1)

nourrisson m. infant (8)

nourriture f. nourishment; food (C2)

nouveau (nouvel, nouveaux, nouvelle, nouvelles) adj. new (2); de nouveau again, anew (7); nouveau-né m. nouveau-née f. newborn (baby boy, baby girl) (8)

nouvelle f. news (3)

nuancer to shade, qualify (an opinion)

nuisible adj. harmful, detrimental (4)

nuit f. night (3)

nul(le) n. & adj. useless, hopeless; hopeless student (1); nullement adv. not at all, not in the least (6)

numéro m. number (4)

nuque f. nape of the neck

O

obéir to obey (7); obéissant adj. obedient (C2)

objectif m. goal, objective (8)

obliger to oblige, compel; être obligé de to have to, be obliged, compelled, forced to (1)

observer to look at (3); to watch

obtenir to get, obtain (1)

occasion f. occasion; bargain; d'occasion used (4)

occupé adj. busy (1); s'occuper (de) to take care (of) (1)

œil m. (pl. yeux) eye (5)

œuf m. egg (5)

offrir to offer; give (as a gift) (1)

ombre f. shadow (3)

oncle m. uncle (8)

ondulé adj. wavy (2)

ONG (organisation non gouvernementale) f. NGO (non-governmental organization) (9)

ongle m. fingernail (2)

ONU (Organisation des Nations Unies) f. U.N. (9)

orage m. storm

ordinateur m. computer

ordonnance f. prescription (5)

ordonner to organize; to order (7)

ordre m. order, command (C3)

ordure f. rubbish, garbage (8)

oreille f. ear (pré); boucle d'oreille f. earring (2)

organisme m. organization (3)

orner to decorate (8)

os m. bone (6)

oser to dare

OTAN (Organisation du traité de l'Atlantique Nord) f. NATO (9)

où adv. where

oublier to forget

ours m. bear (C7); ours polaire polar bear (9)

outre prep. as well as; en outre besides, furthermore (1) outre-mer m. overseas (3)

ouvert adj. open (C2); ouvertement adv. openly (2); ouverture f. opening (5)

ouvrier (-ère) n. worker (3); ouvrier saisonnier migrant worker (C9)

ouvrir to open (1)

P

pachyderme m. elephant (4)

page m. page boy (7)

paisible adj. peaceful, calm, quiet (9); paisiblement adv. calmly (5) paix f. peace (9)

paître to graze (9)

palabres f. pl. endless discussions (5)

pâle adj. pale (2); pâlir to turn pale (C2)

palmier m. palm tree

pan m. piece; side; pan d'une robe side, fold, top of a dress (3)

panier m. basket (8)

panne f. breakdown; tomber en panne to break down (4)

panneau m. panel panneau solaire solar panel (4)

pantalon m. pants, trousers (2)

pantoufle f. slipper (7)

papier m. paper (1); papiers m. pl. identity papers (3)

papille *f.* **gustative** taste bud **(pré)**

paquet *m.* package, bundle (5)

par *prep.* by (3)

paraître to seem (1)

parapente *m.* hand-glider (5)

parc *m.* park

parce que *conj.* because (3)

parcelle *f.* parcel, piece (3)

parcourir to skim (1); to travel through, go through

parcours *m.* route, journey (2); **... du combattant** obstacle course (9)

par-dessus *prep.* above, beyond (1); **par-dessus** *adv.* over, in addition (C3)

pareil(le) *adj.* same, similar (2)

parent *m.* parent; relative (1)

paresseux (-euse) *adj.* lazy (2)

parfaitement perfectly

parfois *adv.* sometimes (1)

parier to bet

parking *m.* parking lot (4)

parmi *prep.* among

parole *f.* word; speech (1)

partager to share (1)

partie *f.* part, portion **(pré)**

partiel *m.* mid-course exam (1)

partir to leave

partout *adv.* everywhere (3)

pas encore not yet **(pré)**

passable *adj.* passable, passing (grade) (1)

passage *m.* passage; crossing; **homme de passage** drifter (3); **passager (-ère)** *n.* passenger (5)

passer to pass, show (a film) (6); **passer un examen** to take a test (1); **se passer** to take place (1); **se passer de** to do without

passe-temps *m.* pastime (2)

passible *adj.* liable to (a fine) (9)

patinage *m.* skating; **faire du patinage** to go ice skating (5); **patiner** to skate (5)

patois *m.* dialect **(pré)**

patrie *f.* native land, homeland (9)

patrimoine *m.* heritage, tradition (9)

patron(ne) *n.* boss, owner (3)

patte *f.* paw, foot (animal) **(pré)**; **...d'éf** bell-bottom trousers **(int. 2)**

paupière *f.* eyelid **(pré)**

pauvre *adj.* poor (2); **pauvreté** *f.* poverty (3)

pavé *m.* paving stone **(pré)**

payer after (for) (1); **se payer** to treat oneself, afford (8)

pays *m.* country; **pays d'origine** homeland, native country (C3); **pays en voie de développement** developing country (9)

paysan(ne) *n. & adj.* peasant

peau *f.* skin (2)

pêche *f.* fishing; **aller à la pêche** to go fishing (5); **pêcher** to fish (5)

pécore *f.* country bumpkin (7)

peindre to paint (4); **peintre** *n.* painter (C1)

peine *f.* pain; punishment; **à peine** scarcely, hardly (1)

pelouse *f.* lawn (C1)

(se) pencher to bend, lean (over) (1)

pendant *prep.* during, while

pendre to hang (C6)

pendule *f.* clock (C6); **pendulette** *f.* travel clock (C3)

pénible *adj.* tiresome, difficult (C7)

pension *f.* small hotel; meals; **pension alimentaire** alimony (8)

perdre to lose (C3); **perdre la tête** to lose one's head

pérennité *f.* continuity, perpetuity (9)

période *f.* period of time (C8)

péripétie *f.* event, episode (6)

périr to perish; to die (7)

permanence *f.* **heures de...** (1) office hours

permis de conduire *m.* driver's license (4)

perquisition *f.* search (8)

personnage *m.* character, person (in literature) (1)

personne *f.* person, someone (3); **ne... personne** no one (6); **personnellement** *adv.* personally (1)

perte *f.* loss (9)

perturbateur (-trice) *n. & adj.* troublemaker; disruptive

peser to weigh (2); to burden (8)

petit *adj.* small, little **(pré)**; **petit à petit** little by little (C3)

pétrole *m.* crude oil (C4); **pétrolier (-ère)** *adj.* oil-producing (C5)

peu *adv.* little (1); **à peu près** about, approximately **(post)**

peur *f.* fear, dread (7); **avoir peur (de)** to be afraid (of) (7); **faire peur** to frighten (7)

peut-être *adv.* maybe, perhaps **(pré)**

phrase *f.* sentence **(pré)**

piastre *f. (canadien, cajun)* piastre; dollar **(post)**

pièce *f.* room; coin (9); play

pied *m.* foot (C3); **pieds nus** *adj.* barefoot (C3)

piercing *m.* body piercing (2)

piéton(ne) *n.* pedestrian (4); **rue piétonne** *f.* pedestrian street (4)

pinceau *m.* brush (C1)

pincée *f.* pinch (5); **pincer** to pinch (C2)

pique-nique *m.* picnic; **faire un pique-nique** to have a picnic (5)

pire *adj.* worse, worst (1)

pis *adv.* worst (2)

piste *f.* track; circus ring (4); ski slope (5); **piste cyclable** bike path (4)

placard *m.* closet (1)

plage *f.* beach (C2)

se plaindre to complain (**pré**)

plaire to please (7); **plaisir** *m.* pleasure (6)

planche *f.* board; **planche à voile** sailboard (5)

plancher *m.* floor (**pré**)

planifier to plan out (1)

planquer *fam.* to hide, stash away (**int. 1**)

planter to plant; to put, put up (9)

plaque d'immatriculation *f.* license plate (4)

plat *m.* dish (3)

plébisciter to choose by an overwhelming majority

plein *adj.* full (3); **faire le plein** to fill the gas tank (4); **en plein air** outdoors (C5)

pleurer to cry (3)

pli *m.* fold (3)

plissé *adj.* pleated (8)

plongée *f.* diving; **faire de la plongée** to dive (scuba) (5); **plongeon** *m.* dive (5); **plonger** to dive (5)

pluie *f.* rain (C4)

plume *f.* feather (8)

plupart *f.* most (1)

plus *adv.* more (**pré.**); **plus que** more than (3); **ne... plus** no longer, not anymore (6)

plusieurs *adj. & pron.* several (1)

plus-que-parfait *m.* pluperfect tense (3)

plutôt *adv.* (**que**) rather (than)

pneu *m.* tire (C-**pré**); **pneu crevé** flat tire (4)

poche *f.* pocket (8)

poids *m.* weight (2); **poids lourd** big truck

point point; **mettre au point mort** to put in neutral (4); **point de vue** *m.* point of view (**pré**)

pointu *adj.* pointed (2)

poisson *m.* fish; **poisson rouge** goldfish (C4)

poitrine *f.* chest (3)

poli *adj.* polite (C2); **poliment** *adv.* politely (2)

polluer to pollute (4)

pomme *f.* apple (C7); **pommier** *m.* apple tree (4)

pomper to copy, cheat *fam.* (1)

ponctuel (-le) *adj.* localized (4)

ponctuer to punctuate, interrupt (1)

pont *m.* bridge, deck (3); **ponton** *m.* pontoon, floating bridge (6)

portable *m.* cell phone (2)

portail *m.* gate (4)

portefeuille *m.* wallet (3)

porter to wear (2); to carry (3); **porter sur** to rest on, have to do with (8); **se porter volontaire** to volunteer (9)

portugais *adj.* Portuguese; **Portugais** *n.* Portuguese person (3)

poser to place, put; **poser une question** to ask a question (3)

poste *f.* post office (9)

poste *m.* position, job (3); police station (4)

postuler to apply (for a position) (9)

potable *adj. fam.* acceptable, decent (**int. 2**)

potager *m.* vegetable garden (9)

pote *m. fam.* buddy, pal (2)

poubelle *f.* trash can; **sortir la poubelle** to take out the trash (8)

poudre *f.* powder, dust (5)

poulet *m.* chicken (3)

poupée *f.* doll (3)

poupon *m.* little baby (8)

pour *prep.* for, in order to (**pré**); **pour que** *conj.* in order to (7)

pourcentage *m.* percentage (3)

pourquoi *adv. & conj.* why (**pré**)

poursuivre to pursue (1)

pourtant *adv.* yet, nevertheless (3)

pourtour *m.* region (5)

pourvu que *conj.* provided that, so long as (7)

pousser to push

poussière *f.* dust (3)

pouvoir to be able to (**pré**); **il se peut que** it's possible that (7); *m.* power (9)

préalablement *adv.* first, beforehand, prior to (8)

précisément *adv.* precisely, exactly (2); **préciser** to specify; to go into detail (C6)

précoce *adj.* early (**pré**)

prédire to predict (5)

prédominer to predominate; prevail (3)

préfecture *f.* central government office of a French **département** (C9)

préférer to prefer, like better (6)

préjugé *m.* prejudice (3)

premièrement *adv.* first (of all)

prendre to take (**pré**); **prendre en charge** to take care of; **prendre en compte** to take into account; **prendre sa retraite** to retire; **prendre un verre** to have a drink

préoccupé *adj.* preoccupied (C2)

président *m* president; **président-directeur général** (**PDG**) CEO (3)

presque *adv.* almost (5)

prêt *adj.* ready (7)

prétendre to claim, maintain, say (5)

prêter to loan (5); **prêter main-forte** to lend a hand (C9)

prévenir to warn, alert to (C3)

prévoir to plan for, anticipate (8)

prier to pray, beg, invite; **je vous en prie** you're welcome (C4)

prime *f.* free gift (8)

principal *adj.* principal, primary, main (3)

printemps *m.* spring(time) (3)

priorité *f.* right-of-way (4)

prise *f.* sample, small amount; plug, outlet (4); **prise de sang** blood test (4)

priser to value, prize (5)

priver to deprive; **se priver (de)** to do without (1)

privilégier to favor (4)

prix *m.* price; prize (1)

probable *adj.* probable (7); **probablement** *adv.* probably (2)

procès-verbal (pv) *m.* traffic ticket (4)

prochain *adj.* next; following (2); *n.* fellow man, neighbor (9)

proche *m.* close relation (1); *adj.* near (5)

(se) procurer to obtain, procure (4)

produire to produce, make (C7); **produit** *m.* product (3)

profiter (de) to profit (from) (1); take advantage of (6)

profond *adj.* deep (2); **profondément** *adv.* profoundly, deeply (2); **profondeur** *f.* depth (2)

programmation *f.* programming (TV) (6); **programme** *m.* program; **programme du jour** day's programming (TV) (6)

progrès *m.* progress (9)

projeter (de) to project (6); to plan

promenade *f.* walk; **promenade à cheval** horseback ride (5); **promenade à vélo** bike ride (5); **promenade en voiture** car ride (5); **faire une promenade (à pied)** to take a walk; **se promener** to take (go for) a walk (5)

promouvoir to promote (9)

propos *m. pl.* remarks; **à propos de** about (1)

proposer to suggest, offer (7); **se proposer (de)** to plan (to) (9)

proposition *f.* clause (in a sentence) (1); proposal, proposition (C3)

propre *adj.* clean (2); non-polluting (4); own (C3); **propreté** *f.* cleanliness (9)

provincial *n.* someone who does not live in or very close to Paris (C2)

provoquer to provoke, instigate (1)

prudemment *adv.* cautiously (2)

publicité *f.* advertising (1)

pudeur *f.* modesty, sense of propriety (6)

puer to stink **(pré)**

puis *adv.* then (C3)

puisque *conj.* since, because (3)

puissance *f.* power (4); **puissant** *adj.* powerful (3)

pull *m.* pullover, sweater (C3)

pulsion *f.* urge (8)

pupitre *m.* school desk

putain *(exclamation) vulgar* damn **(pré)**

Q

quadrille *m.* style of dance (6)

quai *m.* wharf (3)

quand *adv.* when **(pré); quand même** even though, nevertheless (C3)

quant à *prep.* as for, regarding (7)

quart *m.* one-quarter (1)

quartier *m.* neighborhood (C3)

quatrième fourth; **en quatrième** in eighth grade in French schools **(pré)**

que *rel. & interrog. pron.* that, which, whom; **ne... que** only (6); **qu'est-ce que** *int. pron.* what **(pré)**

quel (le) *adj.* what, which **(pré)**

quelconque *adj.* some sort; any (6)

quelque *adj.* some; several **(pré); quelqu'un** *pron.* someone **(pré)**

quelquefois *adv.* sometimes (1)

se quereller to quarrel (8)

quête *f.* search

queue *f.* line (1); tail (4); **faire la queue** to stand in line (1)

qui *rel. & interrog. pron.* who, what, which, that (6)

quitter to leave (1)

quoi *pron.* what **(pré); il n'y a pas de quoi** you're welcome (C4)

quoique *conj.* although (7)

quotidien(ne) *adj.* daily (1)

R

rabais *m.* discount (9)

rabattre to pull down, pull back (3)

raccompagner to take back, accompany someone home (3)

racine *f.* root **(pré)**

raconter to tell **(pré); se raconter** to tell each other (7)

raffinage *m.* refining (oil) C4

rafting *m.* white-water rafting (5)

ragoût *m.* stew **(pré)**

raide *adj.* stiff, straight (2)

railleur (-euse) *adj.* mocking, teasing (2)

raison *f.* reason; **avoir raison** to be right

rajouter to add again (1)

rajuster to readjust (6)

ralentir to slow down (4)

ralliement *m.* gathering (1)

ramasser to gather, collect (C7)

ramener to bring back (3)

randonnée *f.* hike; hiking; **faire de la randonnée** to go hiking (5); **randonneur (-euse)** *n.* hiker (C5)

rang *m.* row (1)

rangée *f.* row, tier (6)

ranger to put away, straighten up; **rangé** *adj.* well-behaved, serious (8)

ranimer to revive, restore (4)

rappeler to remind; **se rappeler** to remember, recall (5)

rapport *m.* relationship (1); report (4)

raquette *f.* snow shoe (5)

rasé *adj.* shaved (2)

rassembler to gather, assemble (9)

rater to fail (1); to miss (5)

rattraper to make up (1); to catch (9)

ravir to ravish, delight (6)

réagir to react (2)

réalisateur (-rice) *n.* director (6)

réaliser to realize, achieve (9)

récapitulation *f.* summing up (3)

récemment *adj.* recently (2)

recensement *m.* census (3)

recette *f.* receipt, yield (6); recipe

recevoir to receive **(pré)**

recharger to charge again, load (battery) (4)

réchaud *m.* camping stove (5)

recherche *f.* research; search (3); **rechercher** to research (5)

réclamer to claim, demand (C3)

récolte *f.* harvest (C3)

recommander to recommend

récompense *f.* reward (C5)

recomposé *adj.* blended, as in "blended family" (8)

reconnaissable *adj.* recognizable (2); **reconnaître** to recognize (1)

recours *m.* resort, recourse

recouvrer to recover (9)

recouvrir to cover (again) (C3)

récrire to rewrite

rectifier to straighten, correct (C2)

recueil *m.* collection (5)

récupérer to retrieve, get (4)

rédaction *f.* composition (1)

rédiger to write, compose (4)

redoubler to repeat; **redoubler une classe** to repeat a grade (1)

redouter to fear (1)

se référer (à) to refer (to something) (6)

réfléchir to think, reflect **(pré)**

reflet *m.* reflection (C7)

refrain *m.* refrain (song, poem) **(pré)**

refroidir to cool off, discourage (8)

se réfugier to take refuge (C9)

regard *m.* look, glance, gaze (3); **regarder** to look (at) **(pré)**

région sinistrée *f.* disaster area (9)

règle *f.* ruler (1), rule; **régler** to regulate, determine (2)

regretter to regret, be sorry (7)

régulier (-ère) *adj.* regular, steady (2)

reine *f.* queen (7)

rejeter to reject (6)

rejeton *m. fam.* kid (**int. 1**)

rejoindre to rejoin (C3)

relâcher to let go, free (4)

relatif (-ive) *adj.* relative (C2)

relevé *m.* statement, summary; **relevé de notes** report card (1)

relever to lift, point out (1)

relier to bind (book) (8)

relief *m.:* **mettre en relief** to call attention to (C8)

remarquer to observe, notice

remettre to put again; **se remettre** to start again **(pré)**, recover (from) (6)

remontrance *f.* reproof, reprimand (6)

remorquer to tow (4)

remplir to fill (3)

remporter to win **(pré)**

se remuer to move, move about, get a move on (1)

rencontre *f.* meeting, encounter (C2)

rendre to give back; + *adj.* to make (2); **rendre visite (à)** to visit (people); **se rendre (à)** to go (to)

renommée *f.* fame, renown (6)

renseignement *m.* piece of information (5)

(se) renseigner to inquire, to get information (1)

rentrée *f.* return to school in the fall (1)

rentrer to return (1); **rentrer dans** to run into (car) (4)

renvoyer to dismiss, fire (3)

répandre to spread **(pré)**; **répandu** *adj.* widespread

réparer to fix, repair (4)

repartir to leave again

répartir to spread out **(pré)**; to distribute **(pré)**

repas *m.* meal (7)

repasser to iron (8)

se répéter to repeat oneself

répondre to answer, respond

report *m.* delay, postponement (8)

reportage *m.* report

reporter to postpone (1)

reposer to ask again (a question) (1); to lay, lie (7); **se reposer** to rest (5)

repousser to push back, hold up (8)

reprendre to take back (up) (1)

reproche *m.* reproach (1)

réseau *m.* network (4)

résidence *f.* dorm (1); **résidence secondaire** second home, vacation home (5); **résidentiel (le)** *adj.* residential (C8)

résoudre to solve (C9)

respectueux (-ueuse) *adj.* respectful (C2)

respirer to breathe (3); **respiration** *f.* breathing (3)

ressentir to feel, experience (1)

ressortir to stand out (6)

reste *m.* remainder; **en reste** indebted to (4)

rester to stay, remain

restituer to restore; present

résultat *m.* result (1)

résumé *m.* summary (3)

retard *m.* delay; **en retard** late; **retarder** to slow down, hold up (4)

retenir to hold back; remember (4); **retenue** *f.* restraint (8)

retirer to withdraw (7)

retour *m.* return (3); turn, reversal (C3)

retournement *m.* reversal (6)

retourner to return (3); **se retourner** to turn around, go back (8)

retracer to retrace, recall

retraite *f.* retirement

rétrécir to shrink (C6)

retrouvailles *f. pl.* rediscovery (5); **retrouver** to find again (3); **se retrouver** to meet (by arrangement) (7)

réussir to succeed (5); **réussir (à) un examen** to pass a test (1)

revanche *f.* revenge; **en revanche** on the other hand (4)

rêvasser to daydream (7)

rêve *m.* dream (7); **rêver** to dream (7); **rêveur (rêveuse)** *n. & adj.* dreamer (2)

révéler to reveal (4)

revenant *n.* ghost (7); **revenir** to come back

revenir to come back; **revenir de** to get over (a surprise) (4)

réviser to review (1)

revoir to see again (1)

rien *pron.* nothing (3); **ne... rien** nothing (6); **de rien** it's nothing (C4)

rigoler to laugh (1)

rire to laugh (1)

risquer to risk, venture (7)

rite *m.* rite

rivière *f.* river (C3)

robe *f.* dress (3)

robuste *adj.* robust, sturdy (C2)

rocher *m.* rock (5)

roi *m.* king (7)

rôle *m.* role

rollers *m. pl.* roller blades (4)

rolleur (-euse) *n.* skater (4)

roman *m.* novel (6)

rond *adj.* round (2); cent (**int. 1**)

roue *f.* wheel (4); **roue de secours** spare tire (4)

rouge *m. & adj.* red; blush (3); **rouge à lèvres** lipstick (2)

roulement *m.* rotation (8)

rouler to roll; to go (car) (4)

roulotte *f.* house on wheels, trailer (4)

rouspéter *fam.* to grumble (2); **rouspéteur (-euse)** *n. & adj.* grouchy; grouchy person (2)

route *f.* road; **faire la route** to commute

routier (-ère) *n. & adj.* of the road (4); truck driver; **vieux routier** *m.* experienced person (C9)

rouvre *m.* type of small oak tree (3)

roux (rousse) *n. & adj.* redheaded (person) (2)

royaume *m.* kingdom (7)

rubrique *f.* column, heading, category (4)

ruche *f.* beehive (9)

russe *adj.* Russian (**pré**); **Russe** *n.* Russian person (**pré**)

S

sable *m.* sand (C4)

sac *m.* bag (3); **sac de couchage** sleeping bag (5); **sac à dos** backpack (C5)

sage *adj.* well-behaved

saisir to grasp, seize

saison *f.* season (C-**pré**)

salaire *m.* salary (2); **salarié** *n.* wage earner (3)

sale *adj.* dirty (2); **salir** to make dirty

salon *m.* living room (C3)

sang *m.* blood; **prise de sang** *f.* blood test (4)

sans *prep.* without (**pré**); **sans que** *conj.* without (7); **sans-abri** *m.* homeless person (3); **sans-papiers** *m.* illegal immigrant (3)

santé *f.* health (C4)

(se) saouler *fam.* to get drunk (**pré**)

sauf *prep.* except (8)

sauter to jump (C5)

sauvage *adj.* wild (3)

sauvegarde *f.* protection (4); **sauvegarder** protect, keep (3)

sauver to save (C4)

scandaleux (scandaleuse) *adj.* scandalous (C2)

scène *f.* stage (6), scene; **scénariste** *n.* scriptwriter (6)

sciences politiques *f. pl.* political science (1)

scolaire *adj.* academic (1); **scolarité** *f.* schooling (1)

scooter des mers *m.* jet ski (5)

scrupule *m.* scruple (C8)

SDF *n.* (sans domicile fixe) homeless person (3)

séance *m.* showing (movie) (6)

sec (sèche) *adj.* dry (2); **sécher** *fam.* to skip (a class) (1); to dry (5)

secours *m.* help; **Au secours!** Help! (4)

séduire to seduce (2); **séduisant** *adj.* seductive (2)

seigneur *m.* lord, nobleman (7)

sein *m.* breast (3)

séjour *m.* stay (**pré**); **salle de séjour** *f.* living room

séjourner to stay, remain (C3)

sélectionner to select, choose (1)

selle *f.* saddle, seat (bike) (4)

selon *prep.* according to (**pré**)

semblable *adj.* similar, like (3)

semblant: faire semblant (de) to pretend (7)

sens *m.* meaning; direction (4); **double sens** double meaning (6)

sensible *adj.* sensitive (2); **sensiblement** *adv.* noticeably (8); **sensibiliser** to sensitize (9)

sentier *m.* path, way (4)

sentir to feel; **se sentir à l'aise (mal à l'aise)** feel comfortable (uncomfortable, ill at ease)

série *f.* serial (6)

serre *f.* greenhouse **effet de serre** greenhouse effect (9)

serrer to hold tight, grip (3)

serviette *f.* towel, napkin; briefcase (2)

servile *adj.* servile, cringing (2)

servir to serve; **servir à (rien)** to be good for (nothing) (1); to be used for (7); **se servir de** to use

seuil *m.* threshold, doorstep (3)

seul *adj.* only; alone (1)

sévère *adj.* strict (8)

SIDA *m.* AIDS

siècle *m.* century (9)

siège *m.* seat (4)

sien(ne) *pron.* his/hers; **le (la) sien(ne)** his/hers (4)

sieste *f.* siesta, nap (1)

siffler to whistle (1); **sifflet** *m.* whistle (4)

signification *f.* significance, meaning

situer to locate (6)

sixième *adj.* sixth; **en sixième** in sixth grade in French schools (**pré**)

sketch *m.* skit, short play (4)

skateboard (skate) *m.* skateboard (4)

ski *m.* ski; **faire du ski (alpin) (de fond)** to go (downhill) (cross country) skiing (5); **ski nautique** water-skiing (5); **skier** to ski (5)

société *f.* society (3); company (**pré**)

soi *pron.* oneself, himself, herself (4)

soin *m.* care, attention; **prendre soin de** to take care of (C4)

soir *m.* evening (1); **soirée** *f.* evening (6)

soit… soit *conj.* either … or, whether … or (6)

sol *m.* floor (3)

soldat *m.* soldier (9)

solde *m.* sale; **en solde** on sale, reduced price (C2)

solidarité *f.* solidarity, interdependence (9)

sondage *m.* opinion poll (2); **sonder** to survey (2)

songer to muse, reflect (7)

sorcier (-ère) *n.* wizard (witch) (7)

sordide *adj.* squalid, filthy (C2)

sort *m.* spell (7)

sortie *f.* excursion; exit (6); **sortir** to go out; **sortir avec** to go out with, date (2); **s'en sortir** to pull through, get to the end of (1)

sortilège *m.* magic spell (7)

sou *m.* money; small coin

souche *f.* stock, origin (**int. 1**)

souci *m.* worry, care; **se faire du souci** to worry (8); **soucieux (soucieuse)** *adj.* worried, anxious (6)

souffrir to suffer (1)

souhait *m.* wish (2); **souhaiter** to wish (4)

souk *m.* Arab market, mess (*fam.*) (**int. 2**)

soulager to relieve (1)

souligner to underline, emphasize (9)

soupe *f.* **populaire** soup kitchen (C3)

source *f.* spring (water) (9); source

sourd *adj.* deaf (6)

sourire to smile (C4)

sous *prep.* under (C3); **sous-titré** *adj.* subtitled (6)

soutenir to support; **soutien** *m.* support (8)

souvenir *m.* memory, recollection; **se souvenir (de)** to remember

souvent *adv.* often (**pré**)

se spécialiser (en) to major in (1)

spectre *m.* ghost (7)

sportif (-ive) *adj.* athletic (2)

stage *m.* internship, training period (1); **faire un stage** to have an internship (3); stagiaire *n.* intern

star *f.* celebrity, movie star (2)

station *f.* station (**post**); **station balnéaire (de sports d'hiver)** seaside (winter sports) resort (5); **station-service** service station (4);

stop *m.* stop sign; hitchhiking; **faire du stop** to hitchhike (5)

strophe *f.* stanza (poem or song) (**pré**)

stupeur *f.* dazed state, stupor (4)

subir to subject to (8)

subjuguer to charm; to dominate (3)

subordonné *adj.* subordinate, dependent (1)

subvention *f.* subsidy (6)

succéder to follow (C8)

sucer to suck, suckle (3)

sucre *m.* sugar; **sucrerie** *f.* candy, sweet (C4)

sud *m.* south (7); **sud-est** *m.* southeast (7)

suffire to suffice, be enough (9)

suggérer to suggest

suite *f.* continuation (5)

suivant *adj.* next, following (pré); **suivre** to follow (pré); **suivre un cours** to take a course (1)

supérieur *adj.* higher

supplémentaire *adj.* additional (C4)

supporter to put up with, endure (8)

sûr *adj.* sure, certain (3)

surcharge *f.* overwhelming amount (1)

surmonter to overcome, conquer

surprendre to surprise (5); **surprenant** *adj.* surprising

surtout *adv.* especially (1)

surveiller to look after (C5); to watch over, supervise

sympathique *adj.* nice (1)

T

tableau *m.* board; picture (6)

tache *f.* spot (5); **taches de rousseur** freckles (2)

tâche *f.* task (5); **tâches ménagères** household chores (8)

taille *f.* size (7) waist

tailleur *m.* woman's suit (2)

se taire to be quiet (6)

talus *m.* embankment (4)

tandis que *conj.* whereas, while (C2)

tant *adv.* so much, so many (3); **tant que** as long as (5)

tante *f.* aunt (3)

tapage *m.* noise

tard *adv.* late (1)

tas *m. fam.* (a) lot (5); pile

tatouage *m.* tattoo (2)

taux *m.* rate (1); **taux de chômage** unemployment rate (3); **taux de natalité** birth rate (8)

teindre to dye (2); **teint** *m.* coloring (2); complexion, skin color (C5)

tel(le) *adj.* such (1)

télécommande *f.* remote control (6)

téléfilm *m.* movie made for TV (6)

téléspectateur (-rice) *n.* television viewer (6)

téléviser téléviseur *m.* TV set to televise (6)

tellement *adv.* so many; so much (6)

témoignage *m.* testimony (2); **témoigner** to testify, witness (4); **témoin** *m.* witness

tempête *f.* storm

temps *m.* time (2); **de temps en temps** from time to time (6)

tendance *f.* tendency (1)

tendu *adj.* tense (C2)

tenir to control (3), hold; **tenir tête (à)** to stand up to (8)

tennis *m. pl.* tennis shoes (2)

tente *f.* tent (5)

tenue *f.* manner of dress (2); **tenue de route** holding of the road (car) (4)

terminale *f.* last year of French high school (C2)

terminer to finish (3)

terrain *m.* field; piece of land; **terrain de camping** campground (5)

terre *f.* earth; **par terre** on the ground (floor) (3)

tête *f.* head (3); very smart student *fam.* (1); **tenir tête (à)** to stand up to

têtu *adj.* stubborn (8)

thème *m.* subject, theme

thèse *f.* thesis (1)

thunes *fam. f. pl.* money (9)

tiers *m.* one-third (6); **deux tiers** two-thirds (6); **tiers-monde** third world (9)

timide *adj.* shy (3)

tirelire *f.* piggy-bank (8)

tirer to pull (C5); **tirer à sa fin** to come to an end (pré); **se tirer (de)** to get out of (2) extricate, escape; take from (9)

titre *m.* title (2); **à titre de** by virtue of, by right of (C8)

tituber to stagger (int. 2)

toile *f.* canvas; screen (6)

tollé *m.* outcry (int. 1)

tombeau *m.* tomb (C7)

tomber to fall (3); **tomber en panne** to break down (4)

tondre to mow, trim (8)

tonneau *m.* barrel (4)

tort *m.* wrong; **avoir tort** to be wrong

tôt *adv.* early (1)

totalement *adv.* completely (C2)

toujours *adv.* always; still (3)

tour *m.* walk; turn

tournage *m.* filming, production (film) (C6); **tourner** to make (a film) (6)

tournée *f.* round, circuit (4)

tournure *f.* turn of phrase (pré)

tout (tous, toute, toutes) *n., adj., & adv.* all (2); **tout le monde** everyone (3)

traction *f.* drive (car); **traction avant** front wheel drive (4)

train *m.* train; **en train de** in the process of; **train-train** *m.* routine (1)

traîneau *m.* sleigh (**pré**)

traîner to hang around, loiter; **laisser traîner** to leave lying around (8)

trait *m.* stroke, line (1); feature, trait (7)

traité *m.* treaty, compact (9)

traiter to deal with (C8)

tranche *f.* slice; **tranche d'âge** age cohort (2); **film à épisodes** serialized film of which episodes are shown each week (6); **trancher** to cut, slice (6)

transmettre to transmit, pass on (1)

transport *m.* transportation; **transports en commun** public transportation (4)

travail *m.* work (3); **travaux dirigés** discussion section, lab (1); **travaux domestiques** housework (3); **petits travaux** odd jobs (3)

travailleur (-euse) *adj.* hardworking (C2)

travers *prep.* across; **à travers** across, through (3); **traverser** to cross (5)

trek *m.* hiking (5)

tremper to make wet (**pré**)

trentaine *f.* around thirty (4)

trésor *m.* treasure (7)

tresse *f.* cornrow (2), braid (3)

tri *m.* sorting (9); **trier** to sort (9)

tribu *f.* tribe (2)

tricher to cheat (1); to cheat on (2)

trimestre *m.* quarter (school year) (1)

triste *adj.* sad (3)

tromper to deceive, trick; **se tromper** to be wrong; **trompeur (-euse)** *adj.* deceptive (2)

tronçon *m.* section, stretch (5)

tronçonneuse *f.* chainsaw (9)

trop *adv.* too much, too many

trottinette *f.* push scooter (4)

trottoir *m.* sidewalk

trou *m.* hole (**pré**)

troubler to bother (3)

trousse *f.* case, kit; **trousse de pharmacie** first aid kit (5)

trouver to find; **se trouver** to be located (5)

truc *m. fam.* thing (1)

tumultueux (-euse) *adj.* tumultuous (6)

tuque *f. québec* wool cap (**pré**)

type *m. fam.* guy (1)

U

UE (Union européenne) *f.* EU, European Union (9)

une *f.* **la une** front page of a newspaper

uni *adj.* unified (1)

union *f.* union; **union libre** cohabitation (8)

unique *adj.* only, *as in:* **enfant unique** only child (8); **uniquement** *adv.* only, solely (2)

unité *f.* unit; **unité de valeur** course credit (1)

universitaire *adj. (of a)* university; **bibliothèque universitaire** university library (1)

usage *m.* use (4); **usager (-ère)** *n.* user (4); **user** to wear out (1)

usine *f.* factory (3)

utile *adj.* useful (**pré**); **utiliser** to use (3)

V

vacances *f. pl* vacation (5); **vacancier (-ère)** *n.* vacationer (5)

vacarme *m.* racket, noise (6)

vache *f.* cow (C7); **maladie de la vache folle** *f.* mad cow disease (9)

vain *adj.* vain, useless (C2)

vaincre to conquer, defeat (5); **vainqueur** *m.* conqueror (9)

vair *m.* type of squirrel with gray-white fur (7)

valorisant *adj.* fulfilling (2)

vaisselle *f.* dishes; **faire la vaisselle** to do the dishes (8)

valable *adj.* valid (5)

valeur *f.* value (9); **valoir** to be worth (3); **il vaut mieux** it is better (7)

valise *f.* suitcase (5)

se vanter to boast (1)

veau *m.* veal (**pré**); calf (9)

vedette *f.* movie star (6)

veille *f.* day before, night before (1)

veillée *f.* evening spent with friends or family (7); **veiller sur/à ce que** to look after, see to (4)

veine *f. fam.* luck; **coup de veine** stroke of luck (1)

vélo *m.* bicycle (4)

vendange *f.* harvest (**pré**)

vendre to sell (3)

venir to come; **venir de** to have just; **venir à bout de** to overcome (7)

vent *m.* wind (C6)

ventre *m.* belly (3)

verdure *f.* greenery (8)

vérifier to check (C4)

vérité *f.* truth (3)

vernis *m.* polish; **vernis à ongles** nail polish (2)

verre *m.* glass (4); **prendre un verre** to have a drink

vers *m.* verse, line of poetry

verser to pour (5); to pay; **verser une pension alimentaire** to pay alimony (8)

vertige *m.* fear of heights (C5)

veste *f.* suit jacket (2)

vêtement *m.* garment, article of clothing (2)

veuf (veuve) *adj. & n.* widower, widow (7)

vexer to annoy (8)

viager *m.* property mortgaged for a life annuity (6)

vide *adj.* empty; **vider** to empty

vie *f.* life; **vie privée** private life (8)

vieillir to grow old (2); **vieux (vieil, vieux, vieille, vieilles)** *adj.* old (2)

vignette *f.* illustration, single frame of cartoon

vilain *adj.* nasty, mean (C7)

ville *f.* city, town (C-pré)

violemment *adv.* violently (2)

violet(te) *adj.* violet (C2)

virage *m.* curve, sharp turn (4)

virer *fam.* to kick out, expel

vis-à-vis de *prep.* opposite; with regards to

visage *m.* face (2)

vite *adv.* fast; **vitesse** *f.* speed (4); **à toute vitesse** at full speed (C4)

vivant *adj.* alive; **langue vivante** modern language (pré)

vivre to live; **facile à vivre** easy to get along with (8)

vociférer to shout (6)

voie *f.* way; **voie cyclable** bike lane (4); **pays en voie de développement** developing country (9)

voile *f.* sail; **faire de la voile** to go sailing (5)

voir to see; **voyons** let's see; **se voir** to see each other (C-pré)

voisin *n.* neighbor

voiture *f.* car (4)

voix *f.* voice (C3)

volant *m.* steering wheel (4)

volet *m.* window shutter (C3)

volontaire *n.* volunteer (2)

volonté *f.* will, willingness (9)

vouloir to want; **vouloir dire** to mean (1); **en vouloir à** to be mad at (8)

voyage *m.* trip, travel (3); **voyager** to travel

vrai *adj.* true; **vraiment** *adv.* really

VTT (vélo tout-terrain) mountain bike (4)

vue *f.* sight; **en vue de** in order to

Y

yaourt *m.* yogurt (pré)

yeux *m. pl.* eyes (3)

Z

zapper to zap, change channels (with remote control) (6); **zappeur (-euse)** *n.* person who zaps (TV) (6); **zapping** *m.* zapping (TV) (6)

zéro *m.* extremely poor student (1)

zigzaguer to swerve, zigzag (4)

zozo *m.* nitwit (int. 2)

Indices